Microeconomics – II

Microeconomics – II

For University of Delhi
As per the syllabus of B.Com. (Hons) course

D. N. Dwivedi

Professor of Economics
Maharaja Agrasen Institute of Management Studies
New Delhi

Pearson

ISBN 978-81-317-6449-7

First Impression

Published by Pearson India Education Services Pvt. Ltd, CIN: U72200TN2005PTC057128.

Head Office: 15th Floor, Tower-B, World Trade Tower, Plot No. 1, Block-C, Sector 16, Noida 201 301, Uttar Pradesh, India.
Registered Office: The HIVE, 3rd Floor, Metro zone, No 44, Pilliayar Koil Street, Jawaharlal Nehru Road, Anna Nagar, Chennai, Tamil Nadu 600040, Fax: 080-30461003, Phone: 080-30461060
Website: in.pearson.com, Email: companysecretary.india@pearson.com

Digitally printed in India by Saurabh Printers Pvt. Ltd. in the year of 2020.

Syllabus

B.Com. (Hons)

Paper – CH 2.3: Semester – II

Microeconomics – II

Duration: 3 Hours | **Max. Marks: 100**

Lectures: 75

Objective: The objective of the course is to acquaint the students with various market structures within which a firm operates. The course also deals with long-term decision making and market efficiency.

Learning Outcome: It is expected that students will be able to apply this knowledge to business firms' decision-making process in the framework of markets.

Course Contents

Unit – I

Monopoly market structure: Kinds of monopoly, Monopolist's decision and equilibrium, Shifts in demand curve and the absence of the supply curve. Measurement of monopoly power and the rule of thumb for pricing. Horizontal and vertical integration of firms. Comparison of pure competition and monopoly. The social costs of monopoly power. Price discrimination, Peak-load pricing.

15 lectures

Unit – II

Monopolistic competition and oligopoly: Monopolistic competition price and output decision-equilibrium. Monopolistic competition and economic efficiency, Oligopoly and interdependence—Cournot's duopoly model, Stackelberg model, Kinked demand model. Prisoner's dilemma, collusive oligopoly—price-leadership model—dominant firm, cartels, sales maximization. Contestable markets theory. Pricing public utilities.

15 lectures

Unit – III

Market for factor inputs: Determination of factor rewards in perfect input markets in the short and long runs under conditions of perfect and imperfect commodity markets. Determination of factor rewards under conditions of monopsony, monopolistic and monopsonistic exploitation. Role of trade unions. Rental element in factor remuneration. Government intervention in factor market. Direct or through regulatory agency. **15 lectures**

Unit – IV

Inter-temporal analysis and choice under uncertainty: Intertemporal choice—stocks versus flows, present discounted values, capital investment decisions, investment decisions by consumers, determination of interest rates. Risk, preferences towards risk, reducing risk. **15 lectures**

Unit – V

General equilibrium and market failure: General equilibrium and efficiency (in Pareto optimal terms). Market failure and the sources of market failure. Market power and inefficiency, asymmetric information—quality uncertainty, market signalling, moral hazard, principal-agent problem, public goods and externalities. **15 lectures**

Contents

Preface

The purpose of this book is to present a comprehensive and authentic text for the undergraduate students of Microeconomics. It is based on the latest B.Com.(H) Microeconomics – II syllabus of the University of Delhi.

An attempt has been made throughout the book to simplify the analytical treatment of the microeconomic theories wherever necessary, without sacrificing the standard of the book. Besides this, several examples and illustrations have been added to different chapters.

I am sure that this book would prove easily comprehensible to the undergraduate students. The technical treatments of some modern microeconomic theories have been shifted to the appendix of the relevant chapter to complete the elaboration of the theories. Advanced topics falling outside the syllabus have been excluded. Review questions and numerical problems have been added to each chapter.

I am confident that this book would fully meet the study requirements of the B.Com.(H) students of Microeconomics – II of the University of Delhi. I express my gratitude to the teachers and my students for their comments and suggestions. Last but not the least, I express my gratefulness to the editorial team of Pearson Education, especially Dhiraj Pandey, for their suggestions and tremendous help in revising the book.

Comments and suggestions from the teachers and students of the subject are most welcome.

D. N. Dwivedi

About the Author

Dr Dwivedi retired as Reader in Economics from Ramjas College, University of Delhi, in 2004. Since his retirement, he has been working as Professor of Economics at Maharaja Agrasen Institute of Management Studies, Delhi. He has taught undergraduate and postgraduate students of Economics over the past four decades. He has been on the visiting faculty of several management institutes of Delhi. Dr Dwivedi has also worked as Economic Consultant in the Center of Investment in Finance, Riyadh, Saudi Arabia, for about a decade. He was also awarded Senior Fellowship by the Indian Council of Social Science Research (ICSSR), New Delhi. He has published more than fifty research papers and articles on different economic issues of the country in national and international journals, periodicals and books. His research publications include *Problems and Prospects of Agricultural Taxations in Uttar Pradesh* and *Economic Concentration and Poverty in India.* Dr Dwivedi has also authored some popular textbooks like *Managerial Economics, Macroeconomics* and *Principles of Economic*s and also edited the book *Readings in Indian Public Finance.*

Part I

Theory of Firm: Determination of Price and Output

Chapter 1

The Objectives of Business Firms and Their Market Powers

CHAPTER OBJECTIVES

In this and the subsequent four chapters, we shall discuss the theories that deal with price and output determination by the firms. There are two most important factors that play the major role in a firm's decision on price and output determination: (i) firm's own objectives, i.e., what the firm wants to achieve and (ii) its market power to decide on the price and output that meet its objectives. The objectives of this chapter are to explain the following aspects:

- What are the various objectives of business firms under different kinds of market conditions;
- Why profit maximization is assumed, at least theoretically, to be the basic objective of business firms;
- What are and what can be the alternative objectives of business firms, i.e., the objectives other than profit maximization; and
- What are the different kinds of markets—the play ground of firms—and how the nature of the market determines firm's power to make a decision on price and output for its profit maximization.

THE OBJECTIVES OF BUSINESS FIRMS

The economists of different ages have perceived different objectives of business firms. The economics literature reveals that business objectives are various and vary from firm to firm. The various objectives of business firm that appear in economics literature are as follows:

1. Maximization of profit
2. Maximization of sales revenue
3. Maximization of firm's growth rate
4. Maximization of managerial utility function

5. Maximization of firm's net worth
6. Satisfactory or standard profit
7. Long-run survival and market share.

Of these objectives, profit maximization forms the basis of the traditional theory of firm. This objective has, however, been a matter of controversy. Profit maximization is, therefore, discussed in detail. Other objectives are briefly described under *Alternative Objectives of Business Firms.*

Profit Maximization as Business Objective

The traditional economic theory assumes profit maximization as the sole objective of business firms. This assumption has a long history in economic literature and, as mentioned above, conventional theory of price determination is based on this very assumption. The profit-maximization assumption is regarded as the most realistic and analytically most 'productive' assumption. The strength of this assumption lies in the fact that it has never been unambiguously disproved.

Another argument in support of the profit-maximization objective is that the theory of firm based on *this objective has a great predictive power.* It helps in predicting the behaviour of business firms in the real world. The profit-maximization objective helps also to predict the price and output determination under changing market conditions. It is generally accepted that no other business objective explains and predicts behaviour of the business firms better than profit-maximization objective.

When Is the Profit Maximum? Total profit (Π) is defined as the excess of total revenue (TR) over the total cost (TC), i.e.,

$$\Pi = TR - TC.$$

Profit, defined as above, is maximum when $TR - TC$ is maximum. A profit-maximizing firm seeks to maximize $TR - TC$. To achieve this goal, the firm chooses a price and an output which maximizes $TR - TC$. Let us now discuss the technical conditions of profit maximization.

Profit-Maximization Conditions

There are *two conditions* that must be satisfied for the profit to be maximum. These conditions are known as:

1. necessary or first-order conditions and
2. supplementary or second-order condition.

The technical meaning of these conditions and their application are explained below:

The Necessary or First-Order Condition The first-order condition for profit maximization requires that marginal cost (MC) must be equal to marginal revenue (MR), i.e., profit is maximum at the level of output (Q) at which

$$MC = MR \tag{1.1}$$

This is a *necessary condition* in the sense that it *must* satisfy for profit to be maximum: profit is not maximized if this condition is not fulfilled.

Marginal cost (*MC*) equals the first derivative of the total cost (*TC*) function. That is,

$$MC = \frac{\partial TC}{\partial Q} \tag{1.2}$$

Similarly, given the *TR* function, marginal revenue (*MR*) can be obtained as the first derivative of the *TR* function, i.e.,

$$MR = \frac{\partial TR}{\partial Q} \tag{1.3}$$

Having defined *MC* and *MR*, as given in Eqs. (1.2) and (1.3), respectively, the first-order condition of profit maximization may now be stated as follows:

Profit is maximum where

$$\frac{\partial TC}{\partial Q} = \frac{\partial TR}{\partial Q}$$

or

$$\frac{\partial TC}{\partial Q} - \frac{\partial TR}{\partial Q} = 0 \tag{1.4}$$

This point can be proved by using *TC* and *TR* functions. Suppose *TC* and *TR* function are given as follows:

$$TC = 100 + 60Q - 12Q^2 + Q^3 \tag{1.5}$$

and

$$TR = 60Q \tag{1.6}$$

(where Q = quantity produced and sold).

Given the total cost (*TC*) function as in Eq. (1.5), we get

$$MC = \frac{\partial TC}{\partial Q} = 60 - 24Q + 3Q^2 \tag{1.7}$$

And, by differentiating the *TR* function as given in Eq. (1.6), we get

$$MR = \frac{\partial TR}{\partial Q} = 60 \tag{1.8}$$

Going by the necessary condition, we need to find profit-maximizing output. The *profit-maximization output* (*Q*) is obtained by equating *MC* and *MR* functions as given in Eqs. (1.7) and (1.8), respectively, and finding the value for *Q*.

$$\begin{aligned} &MC = MR \\ &60 - 24Q + 3Q^2 = 60 \\ &Q = 8 \end{aligned}$$

In accordance with the first-order condition, given the *TC* function (Eq. (1.5)) and *TR* function (Eq. (1.6)), profit is maximum at output Q = 8. Given the *first-order condition*, profit is maximized at Q = 8 and at no other output.

The Second-Order Condition The *second-order condition normal* of profit maximization requires that the first-order condition must be fulfilled under the condition of *rising marginal cost*.

In technical terms, the second-order condition of profit maximization requires that the second derivative of *TR* function is *less* than that of *TC* function. Or, in other words, the first derivative of *MR* function is *less* than that of *MC* function. The second-order condition may be expressed as

$$\frac{\partial^2 TR}{\partial^2 Q} < \frac{\partial^2 TC}{\partial^2 Q}$$

or

$$\frac{\partial MR}{\partial Q} < \frac{\partial MC}{\partial Q} \tag{1.9}$$

In the example above, $MR = 60$ and $MC = 60 - 24Q + 3Q^2$. So the second-order condition (Eq. (1.9)) can be written as

$$\frac{\partial MR}{\partial Q} - \frac{\partial MC}{\partial Q} < 0 \tag{1.10}$$

By substituting *MR* and *MC* function, in Eq. (1.10), we express the second-order condition as

$$\frac{\partial(60)}{\partial Q} - \frac{\partial(60 - 24Q + 3Q^2)}{\partial Q} < 0$$

or

$$0 - (-24 + 6Q) < 0 \tag{1.11}$$

This point can be proved as follows. In our example, profit-maximization output is 8. By substituting 8 for Q in Eq. (1.11), we get

$$24 - 48 < 0.$$

Thus, the second-order condition is also fulfilled at Q = 8.

Numerical Illustration

We have illustrated above the application of necessary and supplementary conditions of profit maximization by using the *TC* and *TR* functions. Now, we illustrate the application of profit-maximization conditions numerically by using the same *TC* and *TR* functions.

For the purpose, let us recall the *TC* and *TR* functions in Eqs. (1.5) and (1.6), given respectively as

$$TC = 100 + 60Q - 12Q^2 + Q^3$$

and

$$TR = 60Q$$

Table 1.1 *Cost and Revenue Functions*

Q	$TC = 100 + 60Q - 12Q^2 + Q^3$	$TR = 60Q$	$\Pi = TR - TC$	$MC^* = \partial TC/\partial Q = 60 - 24Q + 3Q^2$	$MR = \partial TR/\partial Q$
(1)	(2)	(3)	(4)	(5)	(6)
0	100	0	–100	100	60
1	149	60	–89	39	60
2	180	120	–60	24	60
3	199	180	–19	15	60
4	212	240	28	12	60
5	225	300	75	15	60
6	244	360	116	24	60
7	275	420	145	39	60
8	**324**	**480**	**156**	**60**	**60**
9	397	540	143	87	60
10	500	600	100	120	60
11	639	660	21	159	60
12	820	720	–100	204	60

*Except for zero output.

The cost and revenue data generated for output from 0 to 12 are presented in Table 1.1. Columns (2) and (3) show the *TC* and *TR*, respectively, for output from 0 to 12. Column (4) shows the total profit, $TR - TC = \Pi$. As the table shows, the total profit (Π) is maximized at Rs 156 and the profit-maximizing output is 8 units. Note that, at output of 8 units, $MC = MR =$ Rs 60. This satisfies the *necessary condition* of profit maximization.

A look at the *MC* figures in column (5) reveals that the profit-maximizing output ($Q = 8$) satisfies also the *supplementary conditions*. That is, the necessary condition ($MC = MR$) of profit maximization is satisfied under rising *MC*. As column (5) shows, *MC* begins to rise at output 5 units and continues to rise as output increases. The rising *MC* equals *MR* at output 8 units.

This description provides a numerical proof of the profit-maximization conditions presented algebraically in Eqs. (1.1)–(1.11).

Graphical Instruction

The firm's cost and revenue functions are presented graphically in Figure 1.1. Since price is assumed to be constant (at Rs 60), *TR* curve, as shown in Figure 1.1(a), is a straight line with a slope equal to $\partial TR/\partial Q = 60$. It shows that *TR* increases at a constant rate of Rs 60 with each unit produced and sold. The cost function, which is of *cubic form*, gives a *TC* curve that shows increase in total cost at varying rates, it increases first at increasing rates and then at decreasing rates, as shown in Figure 1.1(a).

As panel (a) of Figure 1.1 shows, up to three units of output, *TC* curve lies above the *TR* curve. It means $TC > TR$ till three units of output. The firm is, therefore, incurring loss to the extent of $TC - TR$. At $Q = 4$, its *TR* exceeds *TC* and the firm begins to earn profits from output four units onwards. Beyond

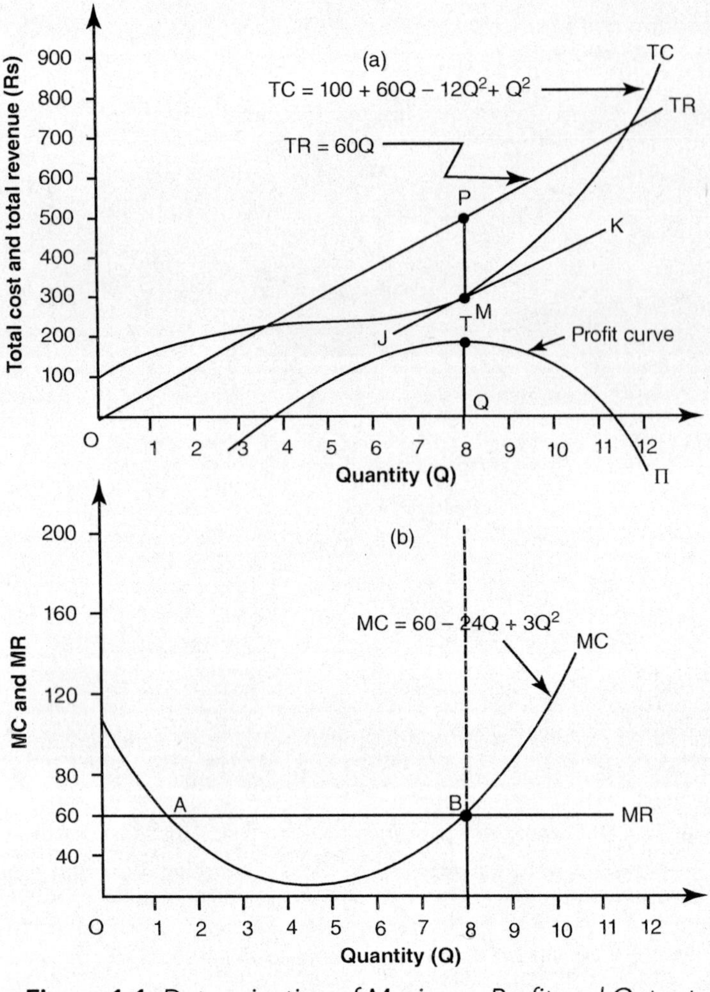

Figure 1.1 *Determination of Maximum Profit and Output*

11 units, however, *TC* overtakes *TR*. It means that the firm's profitable range of output lies between 4 and 11 units. But the total profit (Π) varies from output to output. Note that the distance between *TR* and *TC* first increases and then decreases. It implies that profit first increases with the increase in output, but beyond a certain level of output, it begins to decrease. In simple words, profitable range of output lies between 4 and 11 units of output and the maximum profit lies in between.

Given the *TC* and *TR* functions, graphical method requires drawing a tangent to *TC* in the range output at which *TR* > *TC* and parallel to *TR*, as shown by the line *JK* in panel (a) of Figure 1.1. The line *JK* is tangent to *TC* at point *M*. As Figure 1.1(a) shows, the gap between *TR* and *TC* is maximum at point *M*. A perpendicular drawn from point *M* to *TR* gives the maximum difference, *PM*, between *TR* and *TC*. Thus, *PM* is the maximum possible profit. The *profit-maximizing output* can, now, be obtained by extending the line *PM* to the output axis. Going by this process as shown in Figure 1.1(a), eight units of output maximize the profit. This is, incidentally, also the optimum level of output for the firm.

The maximum of profit at output eight units can also be shown by plotting the profit data, as shown by the curve marked Π. The profit curve shows the rise and fall in the total profit with the increase in output. It can be seen that profit reaches its maximum level (TQ) when output reaches eight units. Note also the PM and TQ fall on the same line and $PM = TQ$, at $Q = 8$.

Controversy on Profit-Maximization Objective

Although profit-maximization assumption continues to form the basis of the price theory, there has been a good deal of controversy on this assumption. The profit-maximization objective has been criticized on the following grounds:

First, Hall and Hitch[1] have made the most damaging criticism of profit-maximization objective. In their empirical study 'Price Theory and Business Behaviour', they produced a startling result that firms do not attempt to maximize their profit.

Secondly, profit-maximization approach is too simple to explain the real world business phenomenon. According to Baumol, even business executives are not fully aware of objectives which they really pursue in their business decisions. In his own words, 'It is most frequently assumed in economic analysis that the firm is trying to maximize its total profit. However, there is no reason to believe that all businessmen pursue the same objective.' He adds,

In fact, it is common experience when interviewing executives to find that they will agree to every plausible goal about which they are asked. They say they want to maximize sales and also to maximize profits; that they wish, in the bargain, to minimize costs; and so on. Often most of these objectives conflict with one another and it is normally impossible to serve such a multiplicity of goals at a time.[2]

Thirdly, there exist alternative and equally plausible hypotheses that can better explain the reality in the business world. It is likely that a small, owner-managed firm seeks to maximize its profit. In large business organizations, however, management is separated from ownership and managers use their discretion in setting the goal(s) for the firm they manage. A variety of alternative hypotheses have therefore been put forward, particularly in respect of objectives of the business firms, such as sales maximization, a target rate of return on investment, a target market share, 'preventing price competition' and so on.

Fourthly, a very important controversy surrounds the idea of marginalism. It is argued that real world firms do not have the necessary knowledge and *a priori* data to equalize their MR and MC. Hence, they cannot maximize their profits in terms of profit-maximization conditions. Even if they do possess the necessary information, they may not maximize their profits. Most economists agree that real world firms do not have necessary information to maximize their profits in as exact a manner as proclaimed under profit-maximization hypothesis. Most firms actually have only a vague idea about the demand curve for their product and also about their MR and MC curve. It is, also, argued that empirical evidence on whether firms maximize profits is not unambiguous.

Defence of Profit-Maximization Objective The arguments against profit-maximization hypothesis should not mean that pricing theory has no relevance to the actual pricing policy of the business firms. A section of economists, popularly known as 'marginalists', have successfully defended the 'marginal principle' of pricing and output decisions. The empirical and theoretical support put forward by them in defence of the marginal rule of pricing may be summed up as follows.

In two empirical studies of 110 'excellently managed companies', Early[3] has concluded that firms do apply the marginal rules in their pricing and output decisions. Fritz Machlup[4] has argued in abstract theoretical terms that empirical studies by Hall and Hitch, and Lester do not provide conclusive evidence against the marginal rule and these studies have their own weaknesses. He argues that there has been a misunderstanding regarding the purpose of the traditional theory of value. According to him, the traditional theory seeks to explain market mechanism, resource allocation through price mechanism and has a predictive value, rather than deal with specific pricing practices of the firms. He has further argued that the relevance of marginal rules in actual pricing system of firms could not be established because of lack of communication between the businessmen and the researchers as they use different terminology. Businessmen are not quite familiar with economic terminology like *MR*, *MC* and elasticities. Besides, businessmen, even if they do understand economic concepts, would not admit that they are making abnormal profits on the basis of marginal rules of pricing. They would instead talk of a 'fair profit'. Also, Machlup is of the opinion that the practice of setting price equal to average variable cost plus a profit margin is not incompatible with the marginal rule,[5] and that the assumptions of traditional theory are plausible.

It is however difficult to give judgement on the controversy between the economists supporting marginalism in profit maximization and the empirical researchers. The controversy remains unresolved. The proponents of profit-maximization hypothesis have, however, put forward the following arguments in defence of the profit-maximization objective.

First, it is argued that only those firms will survive in a competitive market which is able to make reasonable profits. That is, for their survival, the firms will have to make profits and maintain their total earnings above their total costs. Since they are in business, they would always try to maximize their profits. *All other objectives are secondary to this primary objective.* In their effort to maximize their profits, firms would eventually tend to behave in accordance with the marginal rules of profit maximization, at least approximately.

Secondly, the strength of profit-maximization hypothesis lies in the fact that economists have found this hypothesis extremely accurate in predicting certain aspects of a firm's behaviour. Milton Friedman argues that one cannot judge the validity of profit-maximization hypothesis either by *a priori* logic or by asking business executives. The ultimate test is predictive ability of the hypothesis. And, predictive ability of profit-maximization hypothesis is greater than any alternative hypothesis.[6]

Thirdly, profit maximization is a time-honoured hypothesis and the evidence against this hypothesis is not unambiguous. 'Most economists today ... believe that the assumption of profit maximization provides a close enough approximation for the analysis of many problems, and it has become the standard assumption regarding the behaviour of the firm.'[7]

For the sake of completeness, however, we have briefly discussed below some major alternative hypotheses which have been suggested by different economists to analyse firm's behaviour.

Alternative Objectives of Business Firms

Although, profit-maximization assumption continues to remain the most popular hypothesis in economic analysis, as Baumol has argued 'there is no reason to believe that all businessmen pursue that same objective'.[8] The observed facts reveal that business firms, in fact, pursue multiple objectives, often conflicting with each other. Some major alternative objectives of firms, suggested by different economists, may be grouped as follows:

1. Maximization of the managerial utility function
2. Satisfying goals of the firms
3. Long-run survival and market-share goals
4. Entry prevention and risk avoidance.

These business objectives are briefly discussed herein.

Maximization of Managerial Utility Function Managerial theories of firms postulate that owners and managers are separate entities in large corporations. The dichotomy between the ownership and the management allows managers to use their discretion in setting the goals for the organization they manage. The managers of such corporations, instead of maximization profits, set such goals that can keep the owners satisfied, on the one hand, and secure and promote their own interest in the firm, on the other. *The managers have, in fact, their own utility function to maximize* and, at the same time, keeping owners of the firm satisfied. Although there is no unanimity on the variable that are included in the utility functions of the managers, the most common ones are *manager's salary, job security, managers' perks, a reasonable profit, market share, prestige of the firm* and *trouble-free management*.

The main theories under maximization of managerial utility functions are:

1. Baumol's sales revenue maximization hypothesis;
2. Marris's theory of growth rate maximization; and
3. Williamson's theory of managerial discretion.

Managerial objectives of this category are briefly discussed herein.

Baumol's Theory of Sales Revenue Maximization Baumol[9] has postulated maximization of sales revenue as an alternative objective to profit maximization. The reason behind this objective is dichotomy of ownership and management. This dichotomy gives managers an opportunity to set their own goals, other than profit maximization which most owner businessmen pursue. Given the opportunity, managers choose to maximize their own utility function. According to Baumol, the most plausible factor in manager's utility function is *maximization of sales revenue*.

The factors which explain the pursuance of this goal by the managers are as follows:

First, salary and other earnings of managers are more closely related to sales revenue than the profits.

Secondly, banks and financial corporations look at sales revenue while financing the corporation. The reason is while sales data are available periodically whereas the final profit data are available only annually.

Thirdly, trend in sales revenue is the readily available indicator of performance of the firm. It also helps in handling the personnel problems.

Fourthly, increasing sales revenue enhances the prestige of managers while profits go to the owners.

Fifthly, managers find profit maximization a difficult objective to fulfil consistently over time and at the same level. Profits may fluctuate with changing conditions.

Finally, growing sales strengthen competitive spirit of the firm in the market.

So far as empirical validity of sales maximization hypothesis is concerned, empirical evidences are inconclusive.[10] Most empirical works are based on inadequate data since requisite data are mostly not available. Besides, it is also argued that, in the long run, sales- and profit-maximization hypotheses converge into one. For, in the long run, the sales maximization objective tends to yield only normal level of profit and normal profit turns out to be the maximum profit under competitive conditions. Thus, sales maximization is not incompatible with profit maximization.

Marris's Hypothesis of Growth Rate Maximization Marris has suggested[11] another alternative objective to profit maximization, i.e., *maximization of balanced growth rate of the firm*. It means 'maximization of demand of firm's product and growth of capital supply'. According to Marris, by maximizing these variables, managers maximize both their own utility function and that of the owners.

The managers can do so because most of the managerial variables (salaries, status, job security, power and so on) appearing in their utility function and those appearing in the utility function of the owners (e.g. profits, capital, market share and so on) are positively and strongly correlated with a single variable, i.e., size of the firm. Maximization of these variables depends on the maximization of the growth rates of the firm. The managers, therefore, seek to maximize the steady growth rate.

Although Marris's theory is more rigorous and sophisticated than Baumol's sales maximization, it has its own weaknesses. It fails to deal satisfactorily with oligopolistic interdependence. A serious shortcoming of his model is that it ignores the price determination which is the main concern of profit-maximization hypothesis.

Williamson's Maximization of Managerial Utility Function Like Baumol and Marris, Williamson[12] argues that managers have discretion to pursue objectives other than profit maximization. That is, managers seek to maximize their own *utility function* subject to a minimum level of profit. A minimum profit is necessary to satisfy the shareholders or else security of the manager's job is endangered.

The *utility function*, which managers see to maximize, include a *quantifiable variable*, e.g., *salary, sales and so on*, and *such non-quantifiable variables* as prestige, power, status, job security, professional excellence and so on. The non-quantifiable variables are expressed quantitatively so as to make them operational, in terms of expense preference which is defined as 'satisfaction derived out of certain types of expenditures' (such as slack payments), and ready availability of funds for discretionary investment.

Like other alternative hypotheses, Williamson's theory too suffers from certain weaknesses. His model fails to deal with the problem of oligopolistic interdependence. This hypothesis is said to hold only where rivalry is not strong. Where rivalry is strong, profit maximization is claimed to be a more appropriate hypothesis. Thus, Williamson's *managerial utility function* too does not offer a hypothesis more satisfactory than profit maximization.

It may be explained, at the end, that the hypotheses suggested by Baumol, Marris and Williamson are similar in nature. They differ in respect of the variables to be maximized.

Satisfying Goals of the Firms Some economists[13] argue that the real business world is full of uncertainty; accurate and adequate data are not readily available; where data are available, managers have little time and ability to process them; and managers work under a number of constraints. Under such conditions, it is not possible for the firms to act in terms of postulated profit-maximization hypothesis. Nor do the firms seek to maximize sales, growth or anything else. Instead they seek to achieve a *satisfactory profit* or *satisfactory growth*, and so on. This behaviour of firms, he terms, as 'satisfying behaviour'. The underlying assumption of satisfying behaviour of firms is that a firm is a coalition of different groups connected with various activities of the firm, e.g., shareholders, managers, workers, input suppliers, customers, bankers, tax authorities and so on. All of these groups have expectations—often conflicting—from the firm, and the firm seeks to satisfy all of them in one way or another by sacrificing their own profit to some extent.

The behavioural theory has, however, been criticized on the following grounds: *First*, though behavioural theory deals realistically with the firm's activity, it cannot explain the firm's behaviour under dynamic conditions in the long run. *Secondly*, it cannot be used to predict exactly the future course of firm's activities. *Thirdly*, this theory does not deal with equilibrium of the industry. *Fourthly*, like other alternative hypotheses, this theory too, fails to deal with interdependence and interaction of the firms under oligopolistic conditions.

Long-run Survival and Market-share Goals Another alternative objective to profit-maximization hypothesis, suggested by Rothschild[14] is that the primary goal of the firm is to survive in the long run. Some others have suggested that *attainment and retention of a constant market share*, is the objective of the firms. The managers, therefore, seek to secure their market share and long-run survival, the firms may seek to maximize their profit in the long run, though it is not certain.

Entry Prevention and Risk Avoidance Another objective of the firms suggested by some authors is to *prevent entry of new firms* into the industry. The motive behind entry prevention may be (a) profit maximization in the long run, (b) securing a constant market share and (c) avoidance of risk caused by the unpredictable behaviour of the new entrants. They argue that the evidence on whether firms maximize profits in the long run is not conclusive. Some economists argue also that where management is divorced from the ownership, the possibility of profit maximization is reduced. Some also argue that only profit-making firms can survive in the long run. They can achieve all other subsidiary goals easily if they maximize their profits.

No doubt, preventing entry may be the major objective in the pricing policy of the firm, particularly in case of limit pricing but then the motive behind entry prevention is to secure a constant share in the market. Securing constant market share is thus compatible with profit maximization.

Conclusion

Although profit maximization continues to remain the most popular hypothesis in economic analysis, there is no reason to believe that this is the only objective that firms pursue. Modern corporations, in fact, pursue multiple objectives. The economists have suggested a number of alternative objectives that firms pursue. The main factor behind the multiplicity of the objective, particularly in case of large corporations, is the dichotomy of management and the ownership. Besides, objectives of business firms keep changing under the changing market conditions. For example, the objective of Air India in 2009–2010 was not to make profit—let alone the profit maximization. Its main objective was to cut cost with the purpose of reducing its losses over the past four years.

However, profit-maximization hypothesis is a time-honoured one. It is easier to handle. The empirical evidence against this hypothesis is not unambiguous or conclusive. The alternative hypotheses are not strong enough to replace the profit-maximization hypothesis. What is more important, *profit-maximization hypothesis has a greater explanatory and predictive power than the alternative hypotheses.* Therefore, profit-maximization hypothesis still forms the basis of price theory.

THE MARKET STRUCTURE AND POWER OF FIRMS

Apart from firm's objective, another factor that plays an important role in firm's choice of price and output is the nature of market structure. The term *market structure* refers to the organizational features of an industry that influence the firm's behaviour in its choice of price and output. The difference in the market structure is an economically significant feature of the market. It determines the powers and the behaviour of firms in respect of their production and pricing decisions. Market structure is classified on the basis of the nature of competition in the industry, more specifically, on the basis of degree of competition among the firms. In general, the organizational features include the number of firms, distinctiveness of their products, elasticity of demand and the degree of firm's control over the price of the product.

In this section, we present a brief description of the market structure, i.e., the playing field of the firms. This will give us an idea of the coverage and subject matter of this part of the book. The nature and the characteristics of different kinds of market will be discussed in detail in the subsequent chapters along with price and output determination in each kind of market. Here, we present only an overview of the market structure.

The market structure is generally classified on the basis of the nature of competition as follows:

1. Perfect competition
2. Imperfect competition
3. Monopoly.

The basic features of these kinds of markets are summarized in Table 1.2 and below are the brief description of each market.

Table 1.2 *Kinds of Market Structure*

Types of Market	Number of Firms	Nature of Product	Firm's Control over Price
1. Perfect competition	Very large	Homogeneous (wheat, sugar, vegetables and so on)	None
2. Imperfect competition			
(a) Monopolistic competition	Many	Real or perceived difference in product (most retail trade)	Some
(b) Oligopoly	Few	1. Product without differentiation (e.g. bread, steel, and chemical, sugar and so on) 2. Differentiated products (e.g. tea, toothpastes, soaps, detergents, automobiles and so on)	Some
3. Monopoly	Single	Products without close substitutes, like gas, electricity and telephones	Full but generally regulated

Perfect Competition

Perfect competition is a market situation in which a large number of producers offer a homogenous product to a very large number of buyers of the product. The number of sellers is so large that each seller offers a very small fraction of the total supply, and therefore, has no power to control the market price. Likewise, the number of buyers is so large that each buyer buys an insignificant part of the total supply and has no power to control the market price. Both buyers and sellers are *price takers*, not *price makers*. The price of a commodity is determined in this kind of markets by the market demand and market supply. Each seller faces a horizontal demand curve (with $e = \infty$), which implies that a seller can sell any quantity at the market determined price. *Each firm is in competition with so large number of firms that there is virtually no competition*. This kind of market is, however, more of a hypothetical nature rather than being a common or realistic one. Some examples of a perfectly competitive market include share markets, vegetable markets, wheat and rice *mandis* where goods are sold by auction.

Imperfect Competition

Perfect competition, in strict sense of the term, is a rare phenomenon. In reality, markets for most goods and services have imperfect competition. Imperfect competition is said to exist when a number of firms sell homogeneous or differentiated products with some control over the price of their product. Barring a few goods such as shares and vegetable (daily) markets, you name any commodity, its market is imperfect. In spite of a large number of dealers (*arhatias*) in wheat market, the Food Corporation of India is the biggest buyer and seller of wheat in India, with a great degree of control over wheat prices.

Sources of Imperfect Competition Imperfect competition arises mainly from the barriers to entry. Barriers to entry of new firms are generally created by the following factors:

First, large-size firms which enjoy economies of scale can cut down their prices to the extent that can eliminate new firms or prevent their entry to the industry, if they so decide.

Secondly, in some countries, like India, industrial licencing policy of the government creates barrier for the new firms to enter an industry.

Thirdly, patenting of rights to produce a well-established product or a new brand of a commodity prevents new firms from producing that commodity.

Fourthly, sometimes entry of new firms to an industry is prevented by law, with a view to enabling the existing ones to have economies of scale so that prices are low.

Imperfect competition creates two different forms of markets, with different number of producers, with different degrees of competition, classified as (a) monopolistic competition and (b) oligopoly.

1. ***Monopolistic Competition***. Monopolistic competition is a kind of market where a large number of firms supply differentiated products. The number of sellers is so large that each firm can act independently of others, without its activities being watched and countervailed by others. Besides, it is not only extremely difficult to keep track of competitors' strategy, but also it is not of any avail. In this respect, it is similar to perfect competition. It differs from perfect competition in that the products under monopolistic competition are somewhat differentiated whereas they are homogeneous under perfect competition. In perfect competition, there is free entry and free exit of firms.
2. ***Oligopoly***. Oligopoly is an organizational structure of an industry in which a small number of firms supply the entire market, each seller having a considerable market share and control over the price. Most industries in our country are oligopolistic. A small number of companies supply the entire range of products such as sugar, tea, soaps, medicines, cosmetics, refrigerators, TV sets and VCRs, cars, trucks, jeeps, salt, vegetable oils (vanaspati), and so on. The producers of all these goods have some control over the price of their products. Their products are somewhat differentiated, at least made to look different in the consumers' perception. Products of different firms in the industry are treated as close substitutes for one another, for example, Britannia and Modern breads. Therefore, demand curve for their product has high cross-elasticity, but less than infinity, unlike under perfect competition.

Monopoly

Monopoly is the kind of market in which there is a single seller with control over of a product price and output. Monopoly is the antithesis of perfect competition. Absolute monopolies are rare these days.

They are found mostly in the form of government monopolies in public utility goods, e.g., electricity, telephone, water, gas, petrol and petroleum products, rail and postal services and so on.

A PRELUDE TO THE THEORY OF FIRM

The theory of firm came into existence during the 1930s with Joan Robinson's *The Economics of Imperfect Competition* and Edwin H. Chamberlin's *The Theory of Monopolistic Competition*, both written independently in 1933. Earlier, the theory related to price determination was known as the *Theory of Value* attributed mainly to Alfred Marshall formulated in his *Principles of Economics*. The theory of value founded by Marshall on the assumptions of perfect competition and in static equilibrium system was taken to provide answer to all questions regarding price, output and income. The existence of perfect competition was, however, challenged by Sraffa. He showed that perfect competition was not logically consistent with partial equilibrium analysis. This led to the abandonment of the assumption of the perfect competition and Robinson and Chamberlin developed independently their own theories of imperfect competition and theory of monopolistic competition, respectively. Joan Robinson and Chamberlin have demonstrated that price and output are determined by firm's individual decisions under the conditions of imperfect competition. They had, however, retained the earlier assumption of profit maximization. Later this assumption was challenged, as we explained in profit-maximization conditions, and many new theories of firms were suggested. None of the theories has, however, received a universal acceptance.

In the forthcoming chapters, we will discuss in detail the various theories of firm dealing with price and output determination.

REVIEW QUESTIONS AND EXERCISES

1. Write a note on the objectives of business firms and their acceptability in the theory of firms.
2. Profit is maximum when the difference between the total revenue and the total cost is the largest. How is this equivalent to saying that the profit is maximized when marginal revenue equals marginal cost?
3. Show graphically that profit is maximum where marginal cost equals marginal revenue. Is there any exception to this rule?
4. Suppose revenue and cost function of a firm are given, respectively, as follows:

$$C = 100 + 60Q - 12Q^2 + Q^3$$
$$R = 60$$

   Find (i) MC and MR (ii) profit-maximization output.
5. Given the cost function as $C = 128 + 169Q - 14Q^2 + Q^3$ and $P = 60$, find MC, MR at output that maximizes profit.

   (**Ans.** $MC = 60$, $MR = 60$, $Q = 9$)
6. Find maximum-profit output and maximum profit from cost function, $C = 50 - 6Q^2$, and price function $P = 100 - 4Q$. Also derive MC and MR.

   (**Ans.** $Q = 5$, Maximum profit = 200)
7. What are the arguments against profit maximization as the objective of business firm? Is there conclusive evidence against profit-maximization hypothesis?

8. What are the alternative objectives to profit maximization by the firms? On what grounds are based the alternative hypothesis?
9. Compare and contrast Baumol's sales revenue maximization hypothesis and Williamson's hypothesis of maximization of managerial utility function.
10. What is meant by market structure? What are the main kinds of market structure? How does organizational set-up of an industry influence the firm's behaviour in its choice of price and output?

ENDNOTES

1. Hall, R.L. and Hitch, C.J. (1952), 'Price Theory and Business Behaviour', *Oxford Econ. Pap.*, 1939, reprinted in *Studies in Price Mechanism*, T. Wilson and P.W.S. Andrews (ed), (Oxford: Oxford University Press).
2. Baumol, W.J. '*Economic Theory and Operations Analysis*', (New Delhi: Prentice-Hall), pp. 377 and 3780.
3. Early, J.S. (1956), 'Recent Developments in Cost Accounting and the Marginal Policies of Excellently Managed Companies', *American Economic Review*.
4. Machlup, F. (1946), 'Marginal Analysis and Empirical Research', *Am. Eco. Rev.*, and 'Theories of the Firm: Marginalist, "Managerialist, Behavioural"', *American Economic Review*, 1967.
5. This point has been discussed in detail in Chapter 5.
6. Friedman, M. 'The Methodology of Positive Economics', *op. cit.*
7. Browning, E.K. and Browning, J.M. *Microeconomic Theory and Application*, (*op. cit.*), p. 231.
8. Baumol, W.J. 'Economic Theory and Operations Analysis', (op. cit.), p. 378.
9. ——— W.J. (1959), *Business Behaviour, Value and Growth* (New York: Macmillan), and rev. edn (Harcourt Brace and World Inc., 1967).
10. For more details, see Koutsoyiannis, *op. cit.*, pp. 346–351.
11. Marris, R.L. (1963), 'A Model of the Managerial Enterprise', *Q.J.E.* See also his *Theory of Managerial Capitalism* (New York: Macmillan, 1963).
12. Williamson, O.E. (1963), 'Managerial Discretion and Business Behaviour', *American Economic Review.*
13. Cyert, R.M. and March, J.G. (1963), *A Behavioural Theory of Firm* (Englewood Cliffs, NJ: Prentice Hall). Earlier this theme was developed by H.A. Simon in his 'A Behavioural Model of Rational Choice', *Q.J.E.*, 1995, pp. 99–118.
14. Rothschild, K.W. (1947), 'Price Theory and Oligopoly', *Economic Journal*, 57: 297–320.

FURTHER READINGS

Baumol, W.J. (1980), *Economic Theory and Operations Analysis* (New Delhi: Prentice Hall of India), 4th Edn., pp. 377–380.

Browning, E.K., Browning, J.M. (1986), *Microeconomic Theory and Application* (New Delhi: Kalyani Publications), p. 231.

Early, J.S. (1956), 'Recent Developments in Cost Accounting and the Marginal Policies of Excellently Managed Companies', *American Economic Review.*

Friedman, M. (1953), *The Methodology of Positive Economics*, in his *Essays in Positive Economics* (Chicago: University of Chicago Press).

Hall, R.L., Hitch, C.J. (1952), 'Price Theory and Business Behaviour', *Oxford Economic Paper*, 1939, reprinted in *Studies in Price Mechanism*, T. Wilson and P.W.S. Andrews (eds), (Oxford University Press).

Machlup, F. (1946), 'Marginal Analysis and Empirical Research', *American Economic Review*, 1946, and 'Theories of the Firm: Marginalise "Managerialist, Behavioural"', *American Economic Review* (1967).

Rothschild, K.W. (1947), 'Price Theory and Oligopoly', *Economic Journal*, 57: 297–320.

Chapter 2

Price and Output Determination Under Perfect Competition

CHAPTER OBJECTIVES

The objective of this chapter is to explain the theory of price and output determination by a firm under perfect competition. This chapter helps you learn:

- What is the meaning of and what are the characteristics of a perfectly competitive market;
- How firms under perfect competition achieve their equilibrium—the point where they maximize their profit;
- How short-run supply curve of a firm and of an industry is derived;
- How equilibrium of the firms and of the industry as a whole are determined in the long run; and
- How long-run supply curve of the industry is derived under constant, increasing and decreasing cost conditions.

In Chapter 1, we have discussed the objectives of business firms (with emphasis on profit-maximization objective) and have also described briefly the market structure, kinds of markets, their features and powers of firms. Now, we proceed to discuss the theory of price and output determination in different kinds of markets—perfect competition, monopoly, monopolistic competition and oligopoly. In this chapter, we will discuss price and output determination under *perfect competition* and *equilibrium of the firm and industry*. Section 2.1 describes the characteristics of perfect competition. Section 2.2 discusses the relative position of a firm in a perfectly competitive industry. Section 2.3 analyses how a firm reaches its equilibrium. We have shown in Section 2.4 the derivation of short-run supply curves of both the firm and the industry. Section 2.5 provides an analysis of the short-run equilibrium of the industry. Section 2.6 analyses firm's and industry's equilibrium in the long run. Section 2.7 explains the derivation of the long-run industry supply curve under different cost conditions.

CHARACTERISTICS OF PERFECT COMPETITION

A perfectly competitive market is one in which there is large number of buyers and sellers of a homogeneous product and neither a seller nor a buyer has any control on the price of the product. As mentioned earlier, perfect competition as perceived by the economists is a rare phenomenon. Nevertheless, analysis of price and output determination under perfect competition 'lays the foundation' of pricing theory. This kind of a notional market is therefore created by assumption for theoretical purpose. A perfectly competitive market is assumed to have the following characteristics:

1. ***Large Number of Sellers and Buyers.*** Under perfect competition, the number of sellers (the firms) is assumed to be so large that the share of each seller in the total supply of a product is very small. Therefore, no single seller can influence the market price by changing his supply or can charge a higher price. Therefore, firms *are price-takers, not price-makers*. Similarly, the number of buyers is so large that the share of each buyer in the total demand is very small and that no single buyer or a group of buyers can influence the market price by changing their individual or group demand for a product.
2. ***Homogeneous Product.*** The commodities supplied by all the firms of an industry are assumed to be homogeneous or almost identical. Homogeneity of the product implies that buyers do not distinguish between products supplied by the various firms of the industry. Product of each firm is regarded as a perfect substitute for the products of other firms. Therefore, no firm can gain any competitive advantage over the other firms. This assumption eliminates the power of all the firms, the supplier, to charge a price higher than the market price.
3. ***Perfect Mobility of Factors of Production.*** Another important characteristic of perfect competition is that the factors of production are freely mobile between the firms. Labour can freely move from one firm to another or from one occupation to another. There is no barrier to labour mobility—legal, linguistic, climate, skill, distance or otherwise. There is no trade union. Similarly, capital can also move freely from one firm to another. No firm has any kind of monopoly over any industrial input. This assumption implies that factors of production—land, labour, capital and entrepreneurship—can enter or exit a firm or the industry at will.
4. ***Free Entry and Free Exit.*** In a perfectly competitive market, there is no legal or market barrier on the entry of new firms to the industry. Nor is there any restriction on the exit of the firms from the industry. A firm may enter the industry or exit it at its will. Therefore, when firms in the industry make supernormal profit for some reason, new firms enters the industry and supernormal profits are eliminated. Similarly, when profits decrease or more profitable opportunities are available elsewhere, firms exit the industry.
5. ***Perfect Knowledge About the Market Conditions.*** Both buyers and sellers have perfect knowledge about the market conditions. This means that all the buyers and sellers have *full information* regarding the prevailing and future prices and availability of the commodity. As Marshall put it, '... though everyone acts for himself, his knowledge of what others are doing is supposed to be generally sufficient to prevent him from taking a lower or paying a higher price than others are doing.'[1] Information regarding market conditions is available free of cost. There is *no uncertainty in the market*.
6. ***No Government Interference.*** Government does not interfere in anyway with the functioning of the market. There are no discriminatory taxes or subsidies; no licencing system, no

allocation of inputs by the government, or any other kind of direct or indirect control. That is, the government follows the free enterprise policy. Where there is intervention by the government, it is intended to correct the market imperfections if there are any.

7. ***Absence of Collusion and Independent Decision Making by Firms.*** Perfect competition assumes that there is no collusion between the firms, i.e., the firms are not in league with one another in the form of guild or cartel. Nor are the buyers in any kind of collusion between themselves, i.e., there are no consumers' associations. This condition implies that buyers and sellers take their decisions independently and they act independently.

Perfect versus Pure Competition

Sometimes, a distinction is made between *perfect competition* and *pure competition*. The difference between the two kinds of competition is a matter of degree. While 'perfect competition' has all the features mentioned earlier, under 'pure competition', there are no perfect mobility of factors and no perfect knowledge about market conditions. That is, *perfect competition less 'perfect mobility' and 'perfect knowledge' is pure competition*. 'Pure competition' is 'pure' in the sense that it has absolutely no element of monopoly.

The perfect competition, with its all characteristics mentioned earlier is considered as a rare phenomenon in the real business world. The actual markets that approximate to the conditions of a perfectly competitive market include markets for stocks and bonds and agricultural market (*mandis*). Despite its limited scope, perfect competition model has been widely used in economic theories due to its analytical value.

ROLE OF A FIRM IN A PERFECTLY COMPETITIVE MARKET

In a perfectly competitive market, the role of a firm is limited to producing a commodity or service and selling it at the market determined price. In fact, an individual firm is one among a very large number of firms producing an almost identical commodity. The share of a firm in the total supply of the commodity is, therefore, very small. A firm's status in a perfectly competitive market can be described as follows.

1. ***A Firm Has No Control Over Price.*** As mentioned earlier, the market share of an individual firm is so small, rather insignificant, that a firm cannot determine the price of its own product, nor it can influence the prevailing market price by changing its supply. In other words, *an individual firm has no control over the market price.*
2. ***A Firm is a Price-Taker.*** Under perfect competition, an individual firm *does not* determine the price of its own product. Price for its product is determined by the market demand and market supply for the industry as a whole. The determination of market price is reproduced in Figure 2.1(a). The demand curve, *DD′*, represents the market demand for the commodity of an industry as a whole. Likewise, the supply curve, *SS′*, represents the total supply created by all the firms of the industry. As Figure 2.1(a) shows, market price for the industry as a whole is determined at *OP* and equilibrium output for the industry is determined at output *OQ*. Equilibrium price *OP* is given for all the firms of the industry. No firm has power to change this price. At this price, a firm can sell any quantity. It implies that the demand curve for an individual firm is a straight horizontal line, as shown by the line, *pd*, in Figure 2.1(b), with infinite elasticity.

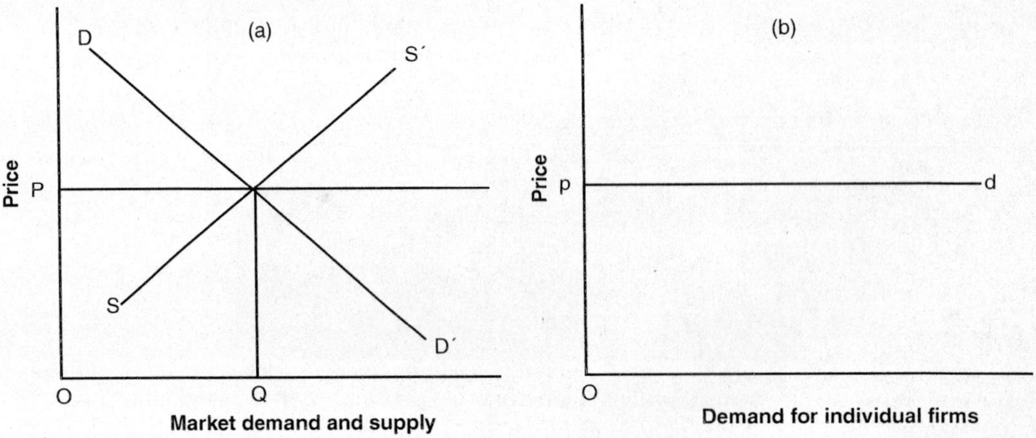

Figure 2.1 *Determination of Market Price and Demand for Individual Firms*

3. ***No Control over Cost.*** Because of its small purchase of inputs (labour and capital), under perfect competition a firm has no control over input prices. Nor can it influence the technology. Therefore, cost function for an individual firm is given. This point is, however, not specific to firms in a perfectly competitive market. This condition applies to all kinds of market except in case of bilateral monopoly.

What Are the Firm's Options

The firm's option and role in a perfectly competitive market are very limited. The firm has *no option* with respect to price and cost. It has to accept the market price and produce with a given cost function. The only option the firm has is to produce a quantity that maximizes its profits given the price and cost. Under profit-maximizing assumption, a firm has to produce a quantity which maximizes its profit and attains its equilibrium. This point is explained further in the following section.

SHORT-RUN EQUILIBRIUM OF THE FIRM

As explained earlier, in the traditional theory of firm, the equilibrium of a firm is determined in the following conditions: (i) *profit maximization* is assumed to the basic objective of a business firm and (ii) *profit is maximized* at the level of output at which $MR = MC$, under rising MC. Given these conditions, profit-maximizing firm attains its equilibrium at the level of output at which its $MC = MR$. This condition applies in both short run and long run, even though MR and MC conditions are somewhat different in the long run. In this section, we discuss *firm's short-run equilibrium*. Long-run equilibrium of the firm will be discussed in the forthcoming section.

Assumptions

The short-run equilibrium of a firm is analysed under the following assumptions:

1. capital cost is fixed but labour cost is variable;
2. prices of inputs are given;

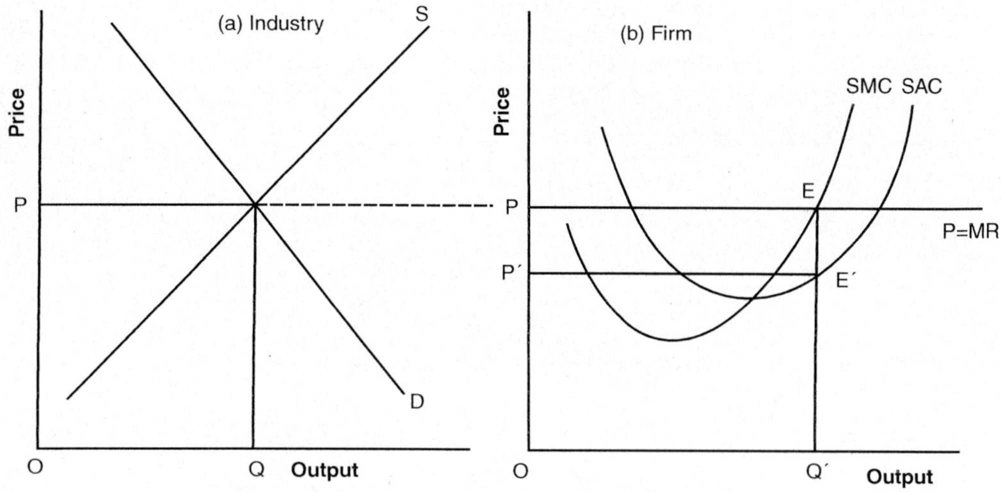

Figure 2.2 *Short-run Equilibrium of the Firm*

3. price of the commodity is fixed; and
4. the firm is faced with short-run U-shaped cost curves.

The firm's equilibrium in the short run is illustrated in Figure 2.2. The determination of market price is shown in panel Figure 2.2(a). As shown in Figure 2.2(a), the market price of a commodity is determined at *OP* by the market forces—demand and supply—in a perfectly competitive market. The price *OP* is fixed for all the firms of the industry. Therefore, a firm faces a straight line or horizontal demand curve, as shown by the line $P = MR$. The straight horizontal demand line implies that price equals marginal revenue, i.e., $AR = MR$. The short-run average and marginal cost curves of the firm are shown by *SAC* and *SMC*, respectively.

Firm's short-run equilibrium is illustrated in panel Figure 2.2(b). As can be seen in panel Figure 2.2(b), *SMC* curve intersects the $P = MR$ line at point *E*, from below. At point *E*, $SMC = MR$. Point *E* determines, therefore, the point of firm's equilibrium. A perpendicular drawn from point *E* to the output axis determines the equilibrium output at *OQ*. It can be seen in the figure that output *OQ* meets both *the first* and the *second order conditions* of profit maximization. At output *OQ*, therefore, profit is maximum. The output *OQ* is, thus, the equilibrium output. At this output, the firm is in equilibrium and is making maximum profit. Firm's maximum pure profit is shown by the area $PEE'P'$ which equals $PP' \times OQ$ (=PE) where PP' is the per unit super normal profit at output *OQ*.

Does a Firm Always Make Profit in the Short-run?

Figure 2.2 shows that a firm makes supernormal profit in the short run. A question arise here: Does a firm make necessarily a supernormal profit in the short run? In the short-run equilibrium, a firm may not always make profits. In the short run, it may make just a normal profit or even make a loss. Whether a firm makes abnormal profits, normal profits or makes losses depends on its cost and revenue conditions. If its short-run average cost (*SAC*) is below the price ($P = MR$) at equilibrium (Figure 2.2), the firm makes abnormal or pure profits. If its *SAC* is tangent to $P = MR$ line, as shown in Figure 2.3(a), the firm makes only a normal profit as it covers only its *SAC* which includes *normal profit*. But, if its *SAC* falls above the price ($P = MR$) line the firm makes losses as shown in Figure 2.3(b), it makes loss. The per unit loss = $SAC - AR$. As Figure 2.3(b) shows, at equilibrium output OQ, per unit loss = $E'Q - EQ = E'E$. The total loss is shown by the area $PEE'P'$ (= $PP' \times OQ'$), while per unit loss $PP' = EE'$.

Shut-down or Close-down Point

In case a firm is making loss in the short run, it must minimize its losses. In order to minimize its losses, it must cover its *short-run average variable cost* (*SAVC*). The behaviour of *short-run average variable cost* is shown by the curve *SAVC* in Figure 2.4. A firm unable to recover its minimum *SAVC* will have

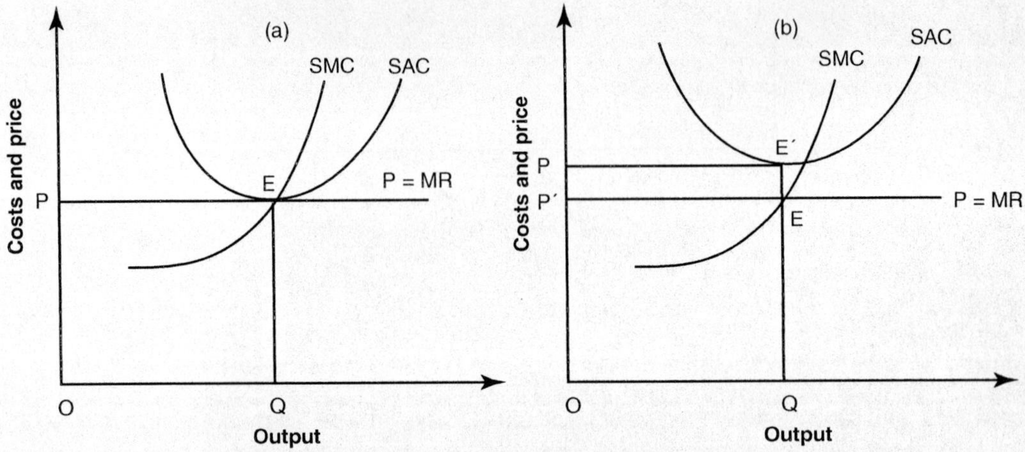

Figure 2.3 *Short-run Equilibrium of Firm with Normal and Losses*

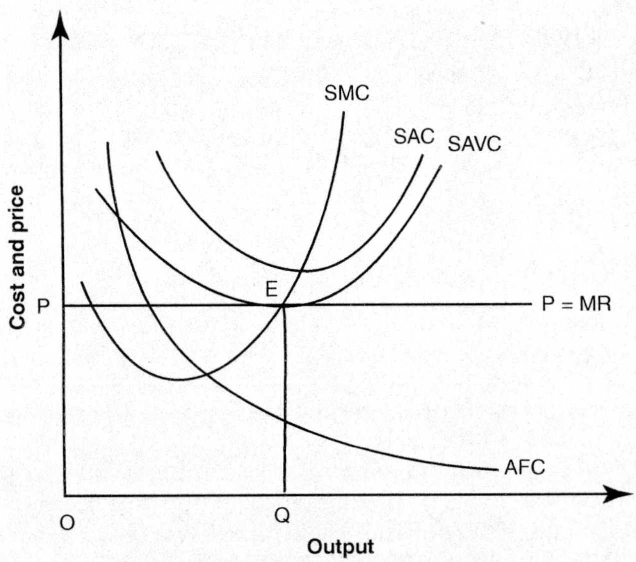

Figure 2.4 *Shut-down Point*

to close down. Its *SAVC* is minimum at point *E* where it equals its *MC*. Note that *SMC* intersects *SAVC* at its minimum level as shown in Figure 2.4. At point *E*, therefore, firm's loss is minimum.

Another condition that must be fulfilled for loss minimization is that $P = MR = SMC$. That is, for loss to be minimum, $P = MR = SMC = SAVC$. This condition is fulfilled at point *E* in Figure 2.4. Point *E* denotes the *shut-down point* or *break-down point* because at any price below *OP*, it pays the firm to close down as it fails to recover even its variable cost.

DERIVATION OF SUPPLY CURVE: A DIGRESSION

We have drawn the supply curve so for—whenever required—on the basis of the *law of supply*, i.e., the supply of a product increases when its price increases, all factors other than cost remaining the same. 'Why does this law come into operation' has not been explained so for. This is the right opportunity to answer this question. That is why we digress from the main topic and explain the factor behind the law of supply.

Derivation of Firm's Supply Curve

The supply curve of an individual firm is derived on the basis of its equilibrium output. The equilibrium output, determined by the intersection of *MR* and *MC* curves, is the optimum supply by a profit maximizing (or cost minimizing) firm. Under increasing *MC*, a firm will increase supply only when price increases. This forms the basis of a firm's supply curve. The derivation of supply curve of a firm is illustrated in Figure 2.5(a) and (b). As Figure 2.5(a) shows the firm's *SMC* passes through point *M* on its *SAVC*. The point *M* marks the minimum of firm's *SAVC* which equals MQ_1. The firm must recover its $SAVC = MQ_1$ to remain in business in the short run. Point *M* is the shut-down point in the sense that if price falls below OP_1, it is advisable for the firm to close down. However, if price increases to OP_2, *MR* increases to OP_2, firm's equilibrium point ($MR = MC$) shifts to *R* and output increases to OQ_2. Let the price increase further to OP_3. Then the equilibrium output rises to OQ_3. When price rises to OP_4, the equilibrium output rises to OQ_4. By plotting this information, we get a *supply curve* (*SS′*) as shown in

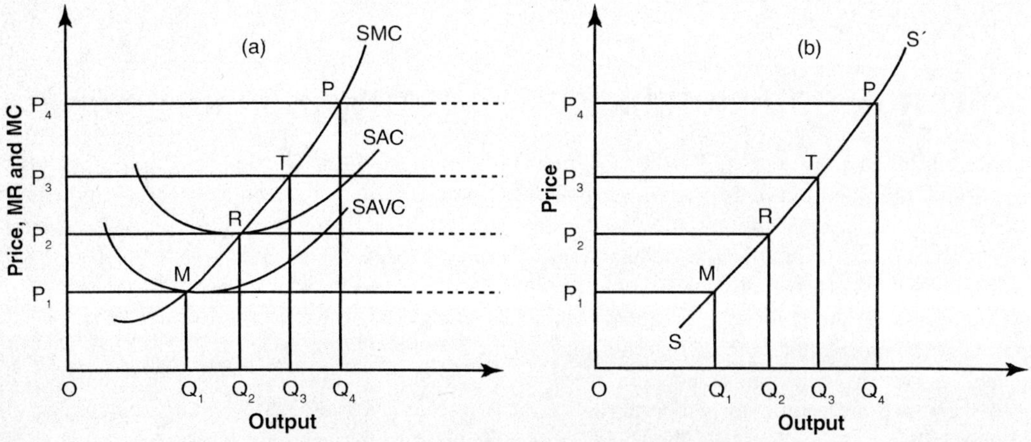

Figure 2.5 *Derivation of Firms Supply Curve*

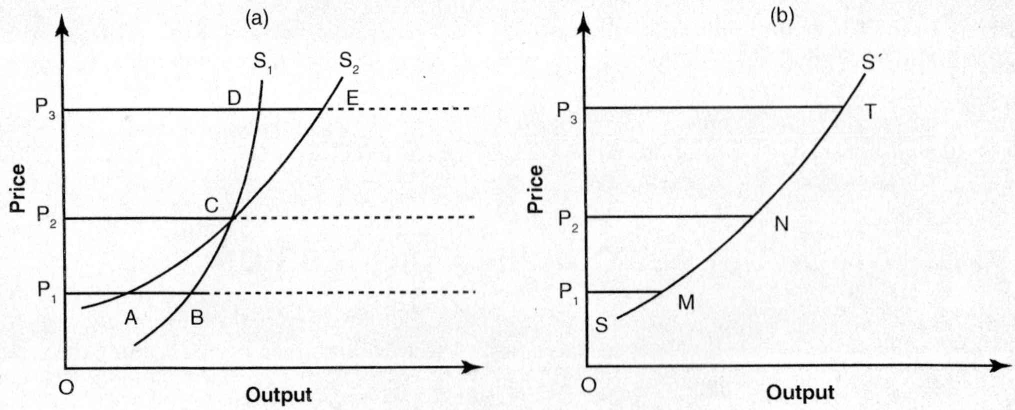

Figure 2.6 *Derivation of Industry Supply Curve*

Figure 2.5(b). In fact, it is the *SMC* curve beyond the point *M* where *SMC* = *SAVC*, which represents the *supply curve.*

Derivation of Industry Supply Curve

The industry supply curve, or what is also called market supply curve, is the horizontal summation of the supply curves of the individual firms. If cost curves of the individual firms of an industry are identical, their individual supply curves are also identical. In that case, industry supply curve can obtain by multiplying the individual supply at different prices by the number of firms. In the short run, however, the individual firm's supply curves may not be identical. If so, the market supply curve can be obtained by summing horizontally the individual supply curves. Let us consider only two firms having their individual supply curves as S_1 and S_2 in Figure 2.6(a). At price OP_1, the market supply equals $P_1A + P_1B$ which equal P_1M in Figure 2.6 (b). (Note that output scale in part (b) is different from that in part (a).) Similarly, at price OP_2, the industry supply equals $2(P_2C) = P_2N$ in Figure 2.6(b). In the same way, point *T* is located, i.e., at point *T*, total supply equals $P_3D + P_3E$. By joining the points *M*, *N* and *T*, we get the market or industry supply curve, *SS′*.

SHORT-RUN EQUILIBRIUM OF INDUSTRY AND FIRM

We have discussed above the equilibrium of the firm in the short run. To complete the discussion on short-run price and output determination, we discuss now the short-run equilibrium of the industry.

An industry is in equilibrium in the short run when market is cleared at a given price, i.e., when the total supply of the industry equals the total demand for its product. The price at which the market is cleared is the equilibrium price. When an industry reaches its equilibrium, there is no tendency to expand or to contract the output. The equilibrium of industry is shown at point *E* in Figure 2.7. The industry demand curve *DD′* and supply curve *SS′* intersect at point *E*, determining equilibrium price *OP*. At price *OP*, *D* = *S*. The industry is supplying as much as consumers demand. In the short-run equilibrium of the industry, some individual firms may make pure profits, some normal profits and some may make even losses, depending on their cost and revenue conditions. As we have explained below, this situation will, however, not continue in the long run.

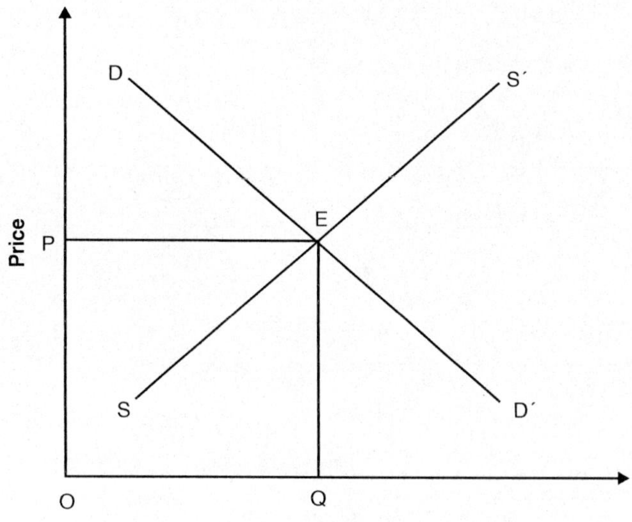

Figure 2.7 *Equilibrium of the Industry*

Link Between Short-run Equilibrium of the Industry and the Firm

The short-run equilibrium of the firm and industry have been analysed separately in the previous sections. There exists, however, a link between a firm's and industry's equilibrium. In a perfectly competitive market, change in the equilibrium of an individual firm does not affect the industry's equilibrium, for the simple reason that the total output of a single firm constitutes a small fraction of the industry's output. But, a change in the industry's equilibrium does alter the equilibrium of an individual firm. In this section, we show how individual firms move from one equilibrium position to another, when there is a change in industry's equilibrium. For the sake of simplicity, we assume that all the firms of an industry have *identical cost conditions* and *cost curves.*

The link between industry's and firm's equilibrium is illustrated in Figure 2.8. Suppose industry's initial demand and supply curves are given as *DD* and *SS*, respectively (Figure 2.8(a)). As shown in Figure 2.8(a), industry's demand and supply curves intersect each other at point *P*, determining the market price at $PQ = OP_1$ and industry's equilibrium output is *OQ*. Thus, the price *PQ* is given to all the firms of the industry. Given the price *PQ* and firm's cost curves, an individual firm finds its equilibrium at point *E* in Figure 2.8(b), where its $MC = MR$. Firm's equilibrium output is *OM* (see Figure 2.8(b)). At price $EM = PQ$, the firm is making an abnormal profit in the short run to the extent of *EN* per unit of output. The firm's total pure profit is shown by the shaded area, P_1ENT.

Let industry demand curve *DD* now shift downward for some reason to *DD′*, supply curve remaining unchanged. As a result, market price falls to *P′Q′* and industry's equilibrium output falls to *QQ′*. With the fall in price, firm's equilibrium shifts from point *E* to *E′* where its $MC = MR$. At this point, the firm is making a loss because its *AR* which equals *E′M′* is lower than its *AC* (see the difference between *AC* curve at point *E′*). Thus, change in industry's equilibrium changes firm's equilibrium. Firms making loss is, however, a short-run situation. Losses will disappear in the long run through a process of market adjustment. The process of market adjustment begins with loss-making firms exiting the industry. When loss-making

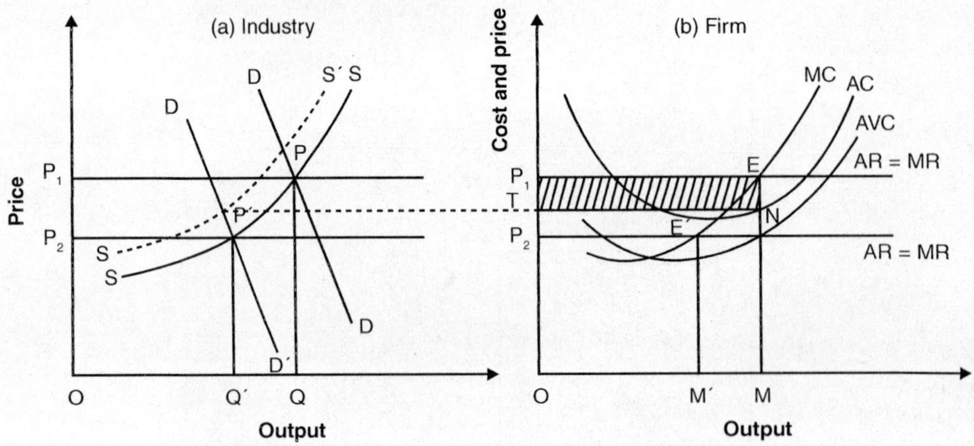

Figure 2.8 *Industry's Vs. Firm's Equilibrium in the Short Run*

firms quit the industry, supply declined and the supply curve shifts left side as shown by the dotted supply curve *SS′*. Price goes up and loss *disappears* and firm reaches another equilibrium point.

LONG-RUN EQUILIBRIUM OF THE FIRM AND INDUSTRY

To begin the discussion on the long-run equilibrium of the firm and industry, let us have comparative look at the short- and long-run market conditions. The short run is, by definition, a period in which (i) firm's cost and revenue curves are given, (ii) firms cannot change their size—their capital is fixed, (iii) existing firms do not have the opportunity to leave the industry and (iv) new firms do not have the opportunity to enter the industry. In contrast, *long run* is a period in which these constraints disappear. Long run permits improvement in production technology and a larger employment of both, labour and capital, i.e., firms can change their size. Some of the existing firms may leave and new firms may enter the industry. In the long run, supply curve not only shifts downward but also becomes more elastic. In this section, we will analyse the equilibrium of the firm and industry in the long run.

Equilibrium of the Firm in the Long-run

To explain how a firm reaches its long-run equilibrium, let us begin with a short-run equilibrium of the firms. Suppose (i) short-run price is given at OP_1 (Figure 2.9(a)) and (ii) that firm's short-run cost curves are given by SAC_1 and SMC_1, as shown Figure 2.9(b). Given the price OP_1, firms are in equilibrium at point E_1. It can be seen in Figure 2.9(b) that the firms are making an abnormal profit of $E_1M = E_1Q_1 - MQ_1$ per unit of output. Abnormal profit brings about two major changes in the industry. *First*, existing firms get incentive to increase the scale of their production. Their average and marginal costs go down caused by the economies of scale. This phenomenon is shown by SAC_2 and SMC_2. When we draw the *LAC* and *LMC* curves, these curves show decreasing costs in the long run. *Secondly*, attracted by the abnormal profit, new firms enter the industry increasing the total supply.

For these reasons, the industry supply curve, SS_1 shifts downward to SS_2 (Figure 2.9(a)). This shift, in the supply curve brings down the market price from OP_1 to OP_2 which is the long-run equilibrium market price. Thus, the equilibrium price is once again determined for the industry though at a lower level.

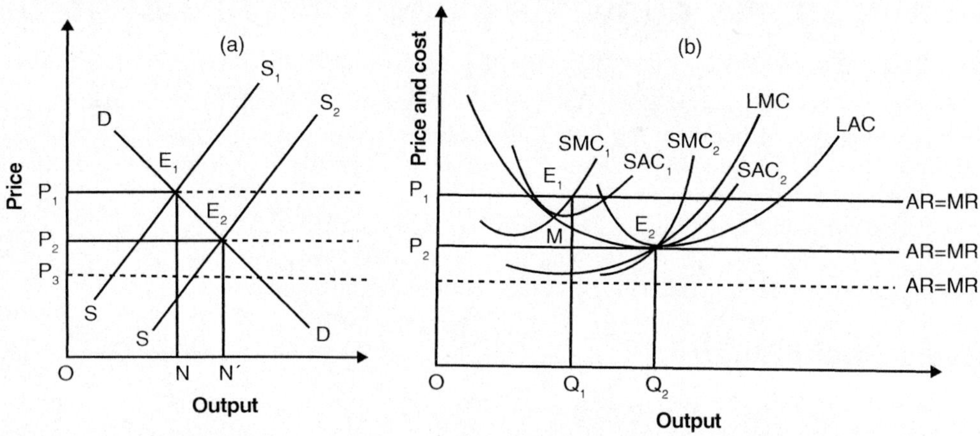

Figure 2.9 *Long-run Equilibrium of the Firm and Industry*

Given the new market price, OP_2, firms attain their equilibrium in the long run at point E_2 where $AR = MR = LMC = LAC = SMC = SAC$ as shown in Figure 2.9(b). As the figure shows, the firms of industry reach their equilibrium in the long run where both short- and long-run equilibrium conditions are satisfied simultaneously. In a perfectly competitive market, the cost and revenue conditions are given for the firms. Therefore, when price goes down to OP_2, what firms are required to do is to adjust their output to the given revenue and cost conditions in order to maximize their profit. Through this process of adjustment for output, the firms reach the equilibrium in the long run at point E_2. Point E_2 is the point of equilibrium for all the firms in the long run.

In case market price falls below OP_2, say, to OP_3, all the firms make losses. This brings in a reverse process of adjustment. While some firms quit the industry, some firms cut down the size of the firm. As a result, total supply decreases, demand remaining the same. Consequently, price tends to rise. This process of output adjustment continues until industry reaches back to its equilibrium at point E_2, where LAC is tangent to $P = AR = MR$ for each firm in the industry. At point E_2, the point of equilibrium, $P = MR = LMC = LAC = SMC = SAC$. Since $P = LAC$, the firms make only normal profits in the long run. If firms deviate from point E_2, due to some short-run disturbances, the market forces will restore the equilibrium.

Equilibrium of Industry

An industry is in equilibrium at a price and output at which its market demand equals its market supply. The equilibrium of the industry is illustrated in Figure 2.9(a). When an industry is in equilibrium, all its firms are supposed to be in equilibrium (as shown in Figure 2.9(b)) and earn only normal profits. This is so because under the conditions of perfect competition, all the firms are assumed to achieve the same level of efficiency in the long run. Since industry yields only normal profits, there is no incentive for new firms to enter the industry. These conditions are fulfilled at price OP_2 in Figure 2.9(a) and (b). At price OP_2, all the firms are in equilibrium, as for each firm, $LMC = LMR = SMC = SAC = P = LAC$.

Since $P = LAC$, all the firms are earning only normal profit. At industry's equilibrium output OM, market demand equals market supply (Figure 2.9(a)). At price OP_2, therefore, market is cleared. The output OM may remain stable in the long run. For, there is no incentive for new firms to enter the industry and no reason for the existing ones to leave the industry. The industry is, therefore, in equilibrium.

LONG-RUN SUPPLY CURVE OF A COMPETITIVE INDUSTRY

We have earlier derived the short-run supply curve of the industry by summing up horizontally the supply curves of the individual firms (see Figure 2.6). The long-run supply curve of a competitive industry, however, has nothing to do with the *LMC* curves. The shape of the long-run supply curve of an industry, under perfect competition, depends on whether factor prices remain constant, decrease or increase in the long run as a result of expansion of the output of the industry. Depending on whether industry's cost is constant, increasing or decreasing, industries are classified as *constant cost industry, increasing cost industry* and *decreasing cost industry.* Let us, now, derive the long-run supply curve of industries conforming to their firms having constant, increasing and decreasing cost.

Constant Cost Industry

An industry with constant cost in the long run is referred to as constant cost industry. In other words, *when the expansion of output in an industry does not entail an increase in factor prices, the industry is said to be a constant cost industry.* The shape of the supply curve of such an industry is illustrated by the line *LRS* in Fig. 2.10(a) and (b). To explain the horizontal shape of the supply curve, let us suppose that the industry is in equilibrium at *P* where demand curve DD_1 and supply curve SS_1 intersect each other. The industry is in equilibrium at price OP_1 and output OQ_1. At price OP_1, all firms are in equilibrium as their $LMC = P = MR = SMC = SAC$.

Now, let the demand curve DD_1 shift to DD_2 due to, say, increase in consumers' income or increase in population or due to both, supply curve remaining the same. As a result market price increases to OP_2. In the short run, this increase in price can induce an increase in supply by the individual firms only by *MN*. Figure 2.10(b) as determined by the point of intersection between firms' *SMC* and new price line through P_2. The firms enjoy abnormal profit to the extent of $AR_2 - LAC$.

In the long run, however, the abnormal profits attract new firms to the industry. The entry of new firms leads to increase in demand for inputs. However, the industry being a constant-cost industry, factor prices do not increase. Cost of production for all the firms remains constant at the previous level. But, due to the entry of new firms, market supply increases and market supply curve shifts from SS_1 to

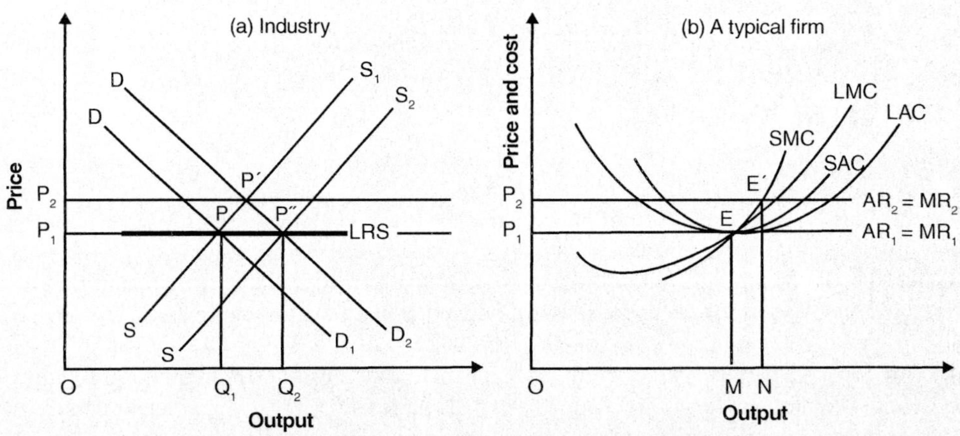

Figure 2.10 *Long-run Supply Curve of the Constant Cost Industry*

SS_2 (Figure 2.10(a)). Consequently, in the long run, market price falls to its previous level, OP_1, and firms return to their previous equilibrium point E. But the industry output increases from OQ_1 to OQ_2 and industry moves from equilibrium point P to P''. By joining the two points of industry equilibrium P and P'', we get long-run supply curve (*LRS*) of the constant cost industry. Obviously, *LRS* of a constant cost industry is a horizontal straight line, as given by the line *LRS*.

Increasing Cost Industry

An increasing cost industry is one which faces increasing input prices. The increase in input prices may be caused by increase in demand for inputs by the firms for increasing their production. The long-run supply curve of an *increasing cost industry* has a positive slope as illustrated in Figure 2.11(a).

The derivation of long-run market supply curve under increasing cost condition is demonstrated in Figure 2.11. Let the original demand and supply curves of the industry be given, respectively, as DD_1 and SS_1 and industry be in equilibrium of point A. Let us also suppose that demand curve DD_1 shifts to DD_2, supply curve remaining the same. As a result, short-run market price increases from OP_l to OP_3 given the supply curve S_1. With this increase in price, the demand curve for the firms shifts upward to $AR_3 = MR_3$ as shown in Figure 2.11(b). The firms, therefore, enjoy a supernormal or economic profit to the extent of P_1P_3.

This supernormal profit attracts new firms to the industry and demand for inputs increases. If supply of inputs is less than infinitely elastic, the entry of new firms causes an increase in demand for inputs and, therefore, an increase in the input prices. Consequently, cost curves, both short and long run, shift upward from LAC_1 to LAC_2. In this process of adjustments, however, industry supply increases and market supply curve SS_1 shifts downward to SS_2. With this shift in the supply curve, the industry reaches another equilibrium position at point C where new demand and supply curves intersect each other. A new market price QP_2 is determined. At price OP_2, (Figure 2.11(b)), the long- and short-run cost curves are tangent to the price line $OP_2 = AR_2 = MR_2$. The individual firms shift to a new long-run equilibrium point E_2, their individual output remaining the same. Whether equilibrium output of the firms remains constant, increases or decreases, depends on whether cost curves shifts upward vertically, upward to the right or upward to the left.

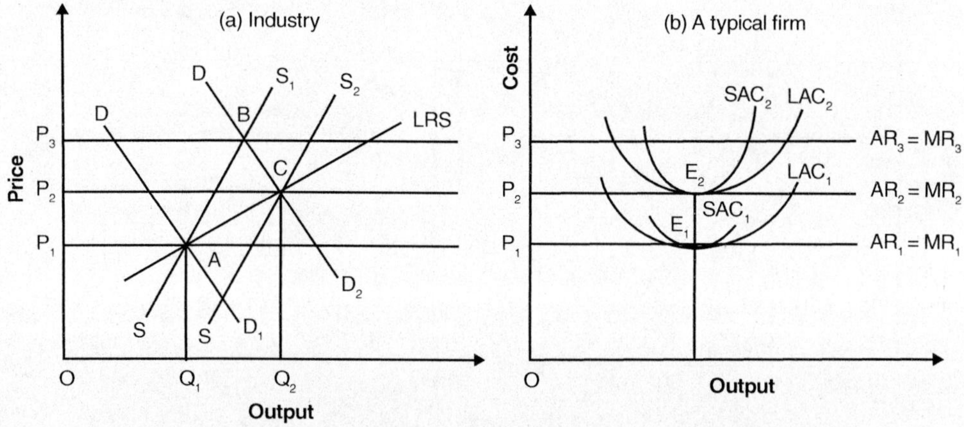

Figure 2.11 *Long-run Supply Curve of an Increasing Cost Industry*

Note that at price OP_2, both industry and individual firms are in equilibrium. In the absence of any further disturbance, the equilibrium of both firms and industry will remain stable. Thus, at the new equilibrium price OP_2, the industry output increases from OQ_1 to OQ_2 and the equilibrium point shifts from point. *A* to point *C*. By joining the long-run equilibrium points *A* and *C*, we get the *long-run supply curve* for the industry, as shown by the curve *LRS*. Obviously, the *LRS* has a positive slope in an increasing cost industry.

Decreasing Cost Industry

If expansion of output of an industry is associated with decrease in the input prices, the industry is referred to as a *decreasing cost industry*. A decreasing cost industry has a long-run supply curve with a negative slope.

The derivation of long-run industry supply curve (*LRS*) under decreasing cost condition is illustrated in Figure 2.12(a) and (b). Let the industry be initially in equilibrium at point *A* in Figure 2.12(a) and firms at point E_2 in Figure 2.12(b). Now suppose that demand curve shifts from DD_1 to DD_2 and, consequently, price rises from OP_2 to OP_3. The short-run equilibrium of firms at price OP_3 in Figure 2.12(b) moves upward on the SMC_2 where the firms make abnormal profits. The abnormal profits attract new firms to the industry causing increase in demand for inputs. If industries are enjoying increasing returns to scale due to economies of scale, the increase in demand for inputs would encourage increased supply of inputs. Increase in the supply of inputs causes input prices to fall. The industry, therefore, enjoys the external economies to scale. As a result, their long- and short-run cost curves shift downward, from LAC_2 to LAC_1 (Figure 2.12(b)).

From the industry's point of view, industry supply increases due to the entry of new firms, even if the existing firms maintain their old level of output. Therefore, as shown in Figure 2.12(a), the industry supply curve shifts from SS_1 to SS_2 which intersects with the new demand curve DD_2 at point *C*. Thus, the equilibrium of the industry shifts from *A* to *C*. Industry output increases from OQ_1 to OQ_2. In the absence of any external disturbance, the industry equilibrium point *C*, would tend to stabilize. By joining the two equilibrium points, *A* and *C*, we get the long-run supply curve (*LRS*) of the decreasing cost industry. The *LRS* has a negative slope.

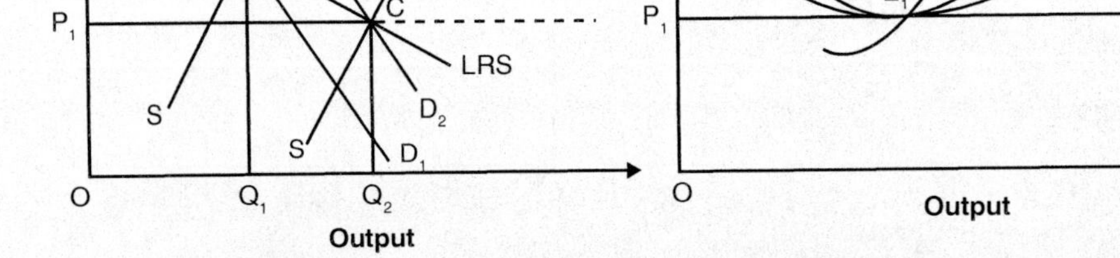

Figure 2.12 *Long-run Supply Curve of a Decreasing Cost Industry*

Whether Decreasing Cost

Some authors argue that the 'phenomenon of decreasing cost ... is not consistent with all the requirements of perfect competition.'[2] However, the possibility of a decreasing cost industry cannot be ruled out in a very long period. One reason for this is the likelihood of the existence of large external economies of scale, particularly in case of young industries in the undeveloped areas.[3] An increase in the number of industries and the consequent growth of transportation, marketing facilities and financial institutions may reduce the industry's cost of production. Nevertheless, it depends on how substantial are the external economies of scale. R.G. Lipsey has cited the car industry of England as an example of decreasing cost industry. In his own word,

As the output of cars increased, the industry's demand for tyres grew greatly. This ... would have increased the demand for rubber and tended to raise its price, but it also provided the opportunity for tyre manufacturers to build large modern plants and reap the benefits of increasing returns in tyre production. At first, these economies were large enough to offset any factor price increases and tyre price charged to car manufacturers fall. Thus car costs fell because of lower prices of an important input.[4]

CONCLUSION

To conclude, whether costs of an industry remain constant or decrease due to increase in the price of some of its inputs, depends also on what proportion of the total input supply is consumed by the industry. For example, output of pencil industry can be increased without substantially affecting the lumber prices as pencil industry uses a small proportion of lumber Output.

But a large increase in the output of furniture industry will not leave lumber prices unaffected. Similarly, output of a pin industry can be substantially increased without affecting the steel price. But a substantial increase in car output cannot leave steel prices unaffected.

Another factor which may cause a rise in input prices is whether or not input industries enjoy economies of scale.

Moreover, the most common cases are of the constant and increasing cost industries. Decreasing cost industries are most unlikely to exist for a long time. The constant and decreasing cost industries tend over time to become increasing cost industries because external economies have a limit.

REVIEW QUESTIONS AND EXERCISES

1. What are the characteristics of perfect competition? Distinguish between perfect and pure competition.
2. What is the relative position of a firm in a perfectly competitive industry? How does a profit-maximizing firm determine the price of its product under perfect competition.
3. Analyse the equilibrium of a firm under the conditions of perfect competition in the short run? Discuss in this regard the importance of *AR*, *AC*, *MR* and *MC* under perfect competition.
4. Explain the short-run equilibrium of a competitive firm. When would a competitive firm close. Do down its business in the short run?
5. You agree that perfect competition leads to optimum size of the firm? Give reasons for your answer.

6. Under perfect competition, average revenue equals average cost in the long-run equilibrium. Yet why do firms produce under such a condition?
7. Show how under the condition of perfect competition in the long run, the price of a commodity equal to its average and marginal cost.
8. Distinguish between short- and long-run equilibrium of a firm under perfect competition. What differences, if any, are there in conditions of equilibrium in the two cases?
9. Bring out the essential difference in the nature of equilibrium of a firm under perfect competition in the short run and in the long run.
10. How is short-run supply curve of a firm derived under perfect competition? Why can't it be downward sloping?
11. Write a short note on the relationship between firm's short-run cost curves and supply curve. Under what conditions is the industry supply curve is a downward sloping one?
12. Show graphically how long-run supply curves of an industry are drawn under perfect competition? Also illustrate graphically the derivation of the long-rum supply curve of a firm under perfect competition.
13. The long-run supply curve of a competitive industry may be upward sloping, downward sloping or a horizontal line. Explain the conditions under which the long-run supply can take these forms.
14. If all the firms in a perfectly competitive industry have U-shaped cost curves, can then supply curve of the industry be downward sloping?
15. Suppose a competitive firm is in long-run equilibrium. What will happen to price in the long run if there is a rise in demand for the product of the industry?
16. Which of the following statements are correct?
    - (a) Perfect competition less perfect knowledge and perfect factor mobility is pure competition,
    - (b) Under perfect competition, a firm fixes its price where its $AR = MR$,
    - (c) A firm is a price-taker under perfect competition,
    - (d) In a perfectly competitive industry, a firm is in equilibrium in the short run only when its $AC = AR = MR = MC$,
    - (e) Firm's short-run supply curve has a negative slope,
    - (f) A firm reaches its shut-down point when price goes below its AC,
    - (g) Industry supply curve is a horizontal summation of its firms' supply curves,
    - (h) An industry is in equilibrium in the short run when market is cleared,
    - (i) Change in the industry equilibrium changes firm's equilibrium,
    - (j) Industry supply curve has a positive slope under decreasing cost conditions,
    - (k) In the long run, a firm is in equilibrium when its $AR = MR = LAC = LMC$.

    [**Ans.** (a), (c), (g), (h), (i) and (k)]
17. Which of the following features are absent in pure competition?
    - (a) Large number of buyers and sellers,
    - (b) Free entry and free exit,
    - (c) Perfect knowledge,
    - (d) Perfect mobility,
    - (e) Absence of collusion.

18. For a firm under perfect competition the 'shut-down' point falls under which of the following conditions?
    (a) any where below *SAC*,
    (b) where $SMC = SAVC = P$,
    (c) where $SMC = SAC$, or
    (d) where $SAC = SAVC$.
19. Which of the following is relevant for a perfectly competitive industry?
    (a) Industry equilibrium is affected by the change in firm's equilibrium,
    (b) Change in industry's equilibrium affects firm's equilibrium,
    (c) Change in industry's equilibrium does not affect firm's equilibrium,
    (d) Change in firm's equilibrium does not affect industry's equilibrium,
20. Under perfect competition, firms are in equilibrium in the long run, where
    (a) $P = SMC = SAC$,
    (b) $SMC = SAC = AR = MR$,
    (c) $LAC = LMC = AR = MR$, or
    (d) $AR = MR$ but $LMC > LAC$?

    Write the correct statement.

[**Ans.** 19: (c) and (d); 20: (b), 21: (b), 22: (c)]

ENDNOTES

1. Marshall, Alfred (1920), *Principles of Economics*, (London: Mamillan) p. 341.
2. See, for example, Ferguson, C.E., *Microeconomic Theory*, 2nd Edn., *op. cit.*, p. 276.
3. Leftwitch, R.H., *The Price System and Resource Allocation*, 5th Edn., *op. cit.*, p. 220.
4. Lipsey, R.G., *An Introduction to Positive Economics*, 5th Edn., *op. cit.*, p. 257.

FURTHER READINGS

Browning, E.K. and Browing, J.M. (1998), *Microeconomic Theory and Applications* (New Delhi Hall): Kalyani Publishers), 2nd Edn., Chapters 8 and 9.

Clark, J.M. (1940), 'Towards a Concept of Workable Competition', *American Economic Review*, 30 (2): 241–256.

Gould, J.P. and Lazear, E.P. (1993), *Microeconomic Theory* (Homewood, IL: Richard D. Irwin), 6th Edn., Chapter 9.

Koutsoyiannis, A. (1978), *Modern Microeconomics* (London: Macmillan), 2nd Edn., Chapter 5.

Maddala, G.S. and Miller, E. (1989), *Microeconomics: Theory and Applications* (New York, NY: McGraw-Hill Book Co.), Chapter 10.

Marshall, A. (1920), *Principles of Economics*, Book VI (London: Macmillan).

Pindyck, R.S. and Rubinfeld, D.L. (2001), *Microeconomics* (New York, NY: Prentice Hall), 5th Edn., Chapters 8 and 9.

Chapter 3

Price and Output Determination Under Monopoly

CHAPTER OBJECTIVES

The objective of this chapter is to explain the theory of price and output determination by a monopoly firm. By going through this chapter, you will learn:

- The definition and factors that create monopoly firms;
- Why and how monopoly demand and revenue curves differ from those under perfect competition;
- How a monopoly firm determines its equilibrium price and output to maximize its profit in the short run and in the long run;
- Why there is no supply curve under monopoly;
- How a multi-plant monopoly firm determines its optimum output for each of its plants;
- Why and how a monopoly charges different prices from different categories of consumers of its product;
- How existence of monopolies creates deadweight loss and it affects the social welfare; and
- How government control and regulation of monopoly price and production affect the monopoly and the society.

INTRODUCTION

In the preceding chapter, we have discussed the theory of price and output determination in a perfectly competitive market—a rare kind of market. In this chapter, we will discuss how price and output are determined in a *monopoly* market—another kind of rare markets. *Monopoly* is an extreme opposite of perfectly competitive market. In a perfectly competitive market, the number of sellers is so large that no single seller can influence the market price all firms are *price takers*. In contrast, in a monopoly market, there is a single seller who has an absolute power to determine the price of its product: a monopoly is a *price maker*. In this chapter, we will discuss

1. Meaning and sources of monopoly power,
2. Price and output determination in the short and long runs,
3. Price discrimination by a monopoly firm,
4. Comparison of price and output under monopoly and perfect competition,
5. Government control of monopolies and
6. Measures of monopoly power.

MONOPOLY AND SOURCES OF MONOPOLY POWER

Definition and Features

The word monopoly has been derived from Greek word *monos*, meaning 'alone' and *polein* meaning 'seller'. By definition, *monopoly is market situation in which there is a single seller of a commodity of 'lasting distinction' without close substitutes.*[1] A monopoly firm enjoys an absolute power to produce and sell a commodity.

In real world today, the existence of a pure monopoly in the private sector is the rarest of the rare market conditions. Most monopolies, wherever there exists, are public sector monopolies. The government has the sole control on price and production. This, however, does not mean that a monopoly firm is absolutely free from any kind of competition. Monopoly firms too, have to face *indirect competition*, especially in regard to setting the price of the product. There are at least *two potential sources of indirect competition*.

One, potential source of indirect competition is the rivalry between monopoly good and other goods produced by other monopolies and competitive firms, for claiming a considerable share in consumers' budget. Therefore, a monopolist cannot charge any price for its product. For example, New Delhi Power Limited (NDPL), a public sector electricity producing and supplying company is at present a monopolist in New Delhi. When it is privatized (which is likely to be), it will have to take into account in its pricing policy, not only its cost of production and distribution, but also what people can afford after meeting such essential needs as food, clothing, shelter, education and medicine.

The second source of potential indirect competition comes from the availability and price of *inferior substitutes*. For example, consider again the case of NDPL. In its pricing policy, NDPL will have to take into account the availability and price of other sources of energy for lighting, cooking and cooling, e.g. diesel operated generator sets, cooking gas, etc. These substitutes are not close substitutes but their availability at a relatively lower price is in all probability likely to influence the pricing strategy of the NDPL. Similarly, the Mahanagar Telephone Nigam Limited (New Delhi), still a monopolist in telecommunications, is facing competition from the cell phone companies: its monopoly power is considerably eroded. So is the case with New Delhi Transport Corporation with increasing number of private operators of charted buses

Given these problems confronting the monopolies, one can hardly find many cases of a *pure* or *absolute monopolies, especially in the private sector*. However, notwithstanding these problems in defining an absolute monopoly firm, the discussion on price and output determination under monopoly confines, in general, to the case of a *pure monopoly*, i.e. a monopoly firm enjoying absolute power in determining the price and output of its product.

Finally, an *important feature* of a pure monopoly is that a monopolized industry is a single-firm industry, i.e., there is no distinction between the firm and the industry. Therefore, there is no distinction between market demand curve and monopoly firm's own demand curve, i.e., the demand curve for the monopoly firm's product is same as the market demand curve.

Sources and Kinds of Monopolies

The emergence and survival of monopoly are attributed to the factors which prevent the entry of other firms into the industry. The barriers to entry are, therefore, the sources of monopoly power. The major sources of barriers to entry are (i) legal restrictions, (ii) sole control over the supply of certain scarce and key raw materials, (iii) efficiency and (iv) patent rights. How these factors prevent the entry of new firms is described below.

1. ***Legal Restrictions.*** Some monopolies are created by law in public interest. Such monopolies may be created in both public and private sectors. Most of the state monopolies in the public utility sector, including postal, telegraph and telephone services, generation and distribution of electricity, railways, airlines and state roadways, etc., are public monopolies. Such monopolies are created by the government in the public sector. The government may create monopolies in the private sector also through licence or patent. Such monopolies are intended to reduce cost of production by the economies of scale and investment in technical innovations. Such monopolies are also known as franchise monopolies.
2. ***Control over Key Raw Materials.*** Some firms acquire monopoly power from their legally granted control over certain scarce and key raw materials that are essential for the production of certain other goods, e.g. bauxite, graphite, diamond, etc. For instance, Aluminum Company of America had monopolized the aluminum industry before the World War II because it had acquired control over almost all sources of bauxite supply.[2] Such monopolies are often called 'raw material monopolies'. The monopolies of this kind emerge also because of monopoly over certain specific technical knowledge or techniques of production.
3. ***Efficiency.*** A primary and technical reason for growth of monopolies is the economies of scale. In some industries, long-run minimum cost of production, i.e., the most efficient scale of production coincides almost with the size of the market. In such industries or products, a large-size firm finds it profitable, in the long run, to eliminate competition by cutting down its price for a short period. Once a monopoly is established, it becomes almost impossible for the new firms to enter the industry and survive. Monopolies born out of efficiency are known as *natural monopolies*. A natural monopoly may emerge out of the technical conditions of efficiency or may be created by the law on efficiency grounds in public interest.
4. ***Patent Rights.*** Another source of monopoly is the patent rights of the firm for a product or for a production process. Patent rights are granted by the government to a firm to produce a commodity of specified quality and character or to use a specified technique of production. Patent rights give firm exclusive rights to produce the specified commodity or to use the specified technique of production. Such monopolies are called *patent monopolies*.

COST AND REVENUE CURVES UNDER MONOPOLY

The cost curves—the *AC* and *MC* curves—faced by the monopoly firm are U-shaped, just as faced by the firms under perfect competition. The monopoly firms face U-shaped *AC* and *MC* cost curves because the laws of production apply to monopoly firms also. However, the demand of *AR* and *MR* curves that a monopoly firm faces are different from those faced by the firms under perfect competition. Therefore, before we discuss price and output determination and firm's equilibrium under monopoly, it will be useful to look into the nature of revenue curves faced by a monopoly firm.

As noted earlier, in a perfectly competitive market, there is dichotomy between the firm and the industry. While firms face a horizontal, straight-line demand curve, industry faces a downward sloping demand curve. Under monopoly, however, there is no distinction between the firm and the industry. The monopoly industry is a single-firm industry and industry demand curve has a negative slope. A monopoly firm faces, therefore, a downward sloping demand curve—it may be a linear or a non-linear demand curve. It is important to note here that, given the demand curve, a monopoly firm has the option to choose between price to be charged or output to be sold. Once it chooses price, the demand for its output if fixed. Similarly, given its demand curve, if the firm decides to sell a certain quantity of output, then its price is fixed—it cannot charge any other price inconsistent with the demand curve.

This price–quantity constraint is demonstrated in Figure 3.1. Suppose that the demand curve for a monopolized industry is given as *DM* in Figure 3.1. Demand curve, *DM*, shows the quantities that can be sold at different prices. For instance, if monopoly firm chooses price *OP*, the quantity that it can sell at this price is fixed at *OQ*—no other quantity can be sold at this price. Similarly, if it decides to sell quantity *ON*, its price is fixed at *OP′*—it cannot sell *ON* output at a higher price. This means that if demand curve is given, the options of monopoly firm become limited—it can choose either price or quantity at a time, not a price and a quantity inconsistent with the demand curve.

AR and *MR* Curves under Monopoly

The *AR* curve for a monopoly firm is the same as its demand curve. Since a monopoly firm faces a downward sloping demand curve, its *AR* also slopes downwards to the right. For example, the demand curve *DM* in Figure 3.1 is the same as the firm's *AR* curve.

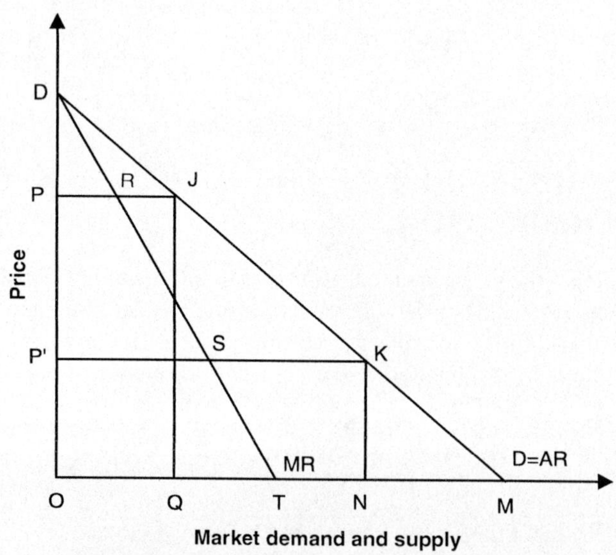

Figure 3.1 *AR and MR Curves for Monopoly*

What is much more *important* in the analysis of equilibrium of a monopoly firm is the *relationship between the AR and MR* curves. When price is fixed, as in case of perfect competition, firm's demand curve takes the form of a horizontal line. In that case, $AR = MR$ and MR is a straight line too. But, in case of a monopoly firm, demand curve has a negative slope. Therefore, its MR curve too has a negative slope. There is, however, a *specific relationship* between AR and MR, i.e., *the slope of MR curve is twice that of that AR curve*. That is, given the linear demand function, marginal revenue curve is twice as steep as the average revenue curve.

This relationship can be proved as follows. Let us assume that a monopoly firm is faced with a price function[3] given as

$$P = a - bQ \tag{3.1}$$

We know that

$$TR = Q \cdot P$$

By substituting Eq. (3.1) for P in TR-*function*, we get

$$\begin{aligned} TR &= Q(a - bQ) \\ &= aQ - bQ^2 \end{aligned} \tag{3.2}$$

Since MR equals the first derivative of the TR-function,

$$\begin{aligned} MR &= \frac{\partial TR}{\partial Q} = \frac{\partial(aQ - bQ^2)}{\partial Q} \\ &= a - 2bQ \end{aligned} \tag{3.3}$$

Note that the slope of the price function (3.1) equals b whereas the slope of the MR-function (3.3) equals $2b$. It means that the slope of the MR-function is *twice* that of the AR function. It implies that MR curve is always to the left of AR curve and MR bisects the demand at all levels of price. For example, in Figure 3.1, if price is OP, demand is PJ, and MR passes through point R which divides PJ in two equal parts. Geometrically, $PR = RJ$. Similarly, at price OM, demand equals $P'K = P'S + SK$ where $P'S = SK$. And, at $P = 0$, demand equals OM and $OT = TM = 1/2\ (OM)$.

SHORT-RUN EQUILIBRIUM OF THE MONOPOLY: PRICE AND OUTPUT DETERMINATION

According to the traditional theory of firm, a firm is said to be in equilibrium where it maximizes its profit. As in case of perfect competition, equilibrium of a monopoly is studied under both *short-run* and *long-run* conditions. In this section, we explain price and output determination under monopoly in the *short run*. The equilibrium of monopoly in the *long run* will be discussed in the next section.

The *short-run equilibrium of monopoly* can be explained by two approaches:

1. Total revenue–total cost (TR–TC) approach and
2. Marginal revenue–marginal cost (MR–MC) approach

The short-run equilibrium of monopoly is explained below by both the approaches—first by TR–TC approach and then by MR–MC approach.

Monopoly Equilibrium by Total Revenue–Total Cost Approach

According to the *total revenue–total cost* (*TR–TC*) approach, a profit maximizing monopoly firm is in equilibrium at the level of output and price at which it's *TR–TC* = *Total Profit* is maximum. The equilibrium of monopoly by *TR–TC* approach is illustrated graphically in Figure 3.2 under the following assumptions:

1. The monopoly firm faces a *cubic TC function* of the form $TC = F + bQ - cQ^2 + dQ^3$ (where $F =$ *fixed cost*) and
2. Its demand curve is given by a demand function of the form $Q = a - bP$.

When *TC function* is graphed, it produces a *TC* curve as shown in Figure 3.2. From the demand function, we can derive a price function as $P = a/b - Q/b$. Using this price function, we can derive monopoly's *TR* function[4] as $TR = (aQ - Q^2)/b$.

The *TR function* when graphed produces a *TR* curve as shown in Figure 3.2. The *TC* curve shows monopoly's *total cost* at different level of output and *TR* curve shows its total revenue at different level of output and price. As Figure 3.2 shows, the monopoly firm faces a loss till output OQ_1 and beyond output OQ_3 That is, monopoly's profitable range of output lies between OQ_1 and OQ_3 because it is only in this range of output that monopoly's $TR > TC$. Now a question arises: how to find the profit maximizing output?

It is obvious that total profit is maximum where the vertical difference between *TR* and *TC* curves is maximum. The maximum difference between the *TR* and *TC* curves can be obtained by a simple technique, i.e., by drawing *parallel tangents* to *TR* and *TC* curves as shown by the tangent *ab* and *cd*. Note that the line *ab* is tangent to the *TR* curve at point *P* and line *cd* is tangent to the *TC* curve at point *M* and line *ab* and *cd* are parallel. As a matter of rule, the vertical gap between tangential points *P* and *M* is maximum. That is, given the revenue and cost conditions, the monopoly firm can make a maximum

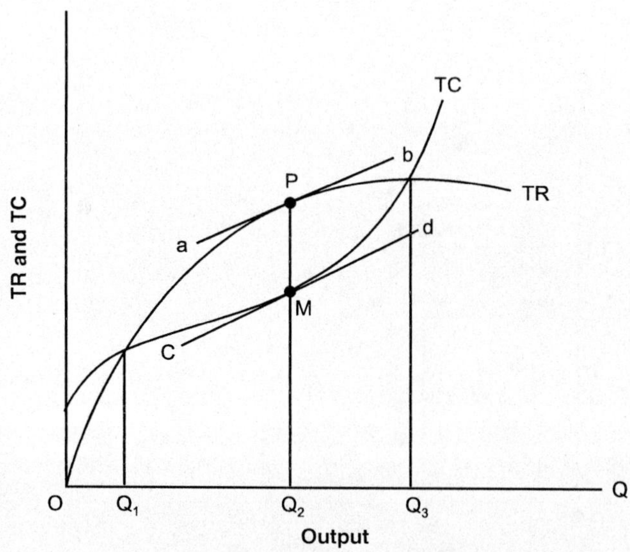

Figure 3.2 *Short-run Equilibrium of Monopoly: TR–TC Approach*

profit of *PM*. A line drawn from point *P*, through point *M* to *X*-axis determines profit maximizing output at OQ_2. It means that a profit maximizing monopoly reaches its equilibrium at output OQ_2.

This equilibrium solution satisfies the necessary condition of profit maximization that profit is maximum where $MR = MC$. Recall that the slope of the *TR* curve gives $\partial TR/\partial Q = MR$ and the slope of the *TC* curve gives $\partial TR/\partial Q = MR$ at their respective points of tangency. Since tangents *ab* and *cd* are parallel, their slopes are equal. It means that at the tangential points, $MR = MC$. This satisfies the necessary condition of profit maximization.

Monopoly Equilibrium by *MR–MC* Approach

The equilibrium of the monopoly firm by *marginal revenue–marginal cost approach* is illustrated in Figure 3.3. The short-run revenue curves of the monopoly firm are shown by the *AR* and *MR* curves and its short-run cost curves are given by the *SAC* and *SMC* curves. The *AR* and *MR* curves, as given in Figure 3.3, can be derived from the *TR* function used in *TR–TC* approach. Similarly, *SAC* and *SMC* curves given in the figure can be derived from the *TC* function.

Given the revenue and cost curves and the profit maximization rule, the equilibrium of the monopoly firm can easily be traced. Recall once again the profit maximization rule, i.e., profit is maximum where $MR = MC$. It can be seen in the figure that *MR* and *MC* curves intersect at point *N*. Note that point *N* satisfies both the conditions of profit maximization: (i) $MR = MC$ and (ii) *MC* curve intersects *MR* curve from below. Point *N*, therefore, determines the equilibrium output and price. An ordinate drawn from point *N* to *X*-axis determines the profit maximizing output at *OQ*. The ordinate *NQ* extended upwards to the *AR* curve gives the price *PQ* at which output *OQ* can be disposed of, given the demand function. Thus, the *MR–MC* approach to monopoly equilibrium determines both equilibrium output and price simultaneously. No other output and price can increase the monopoly's profit.

Once equilibrium price and output are determined, given the revenue and cost curve, the maximum monopoly profit can be easily determined as follows.

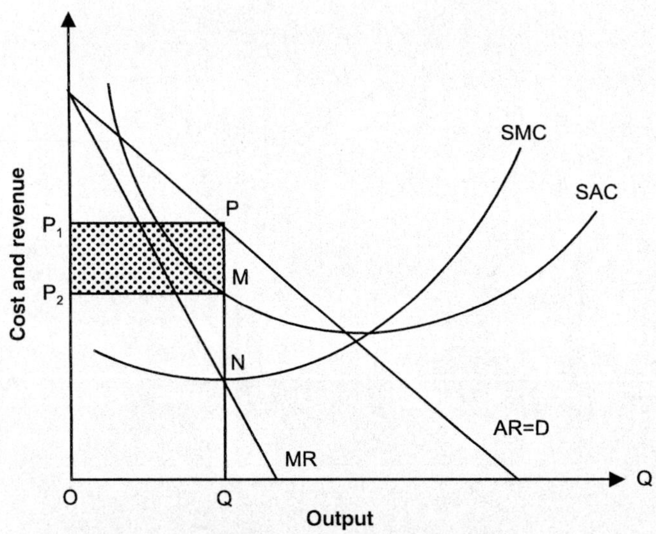

Figure 3.3 *Monopoly Equilibrium: MR–MC Approach*

$$\text{Per unit monopoly profit} = AR - SAC.$$

In Figure 3.3, $AR = PQ$ and $SAC = MQ$. By substitution, we get

$$\text{Per unit monopoly profit} = PQ - MQ = PM$$

Given the equilibrium output OQ,

$$\text{Total monopoly profit} = OQ \cdot PM$$

Since $OQ = P_2M$, total monopoly profit at equilibrium can be worked out as

$$P_2M\ PM = P_1PMP_2$$

The total monopoly profit is shown by the shaded area in the Figure 3.3. Since cost and revenue conditions of the monopoly firm are supposed to be given, the monopoly equilibrium is supposed to be stable.

Algebra of Profit Maximization: A Numerical Illustration

Price and output determination by monopoly in the short run has been discussed earlier theoretically by TR–TC and MR–MC approaches and illustrated graphically. Now we illustrate the determination of equilibrium price and output by a monopoly firm through a numerical example assuming hypothetical demand and cost functions.

Let us suppose that demand and total cost functions of a monopoly firm are given as follows.

Demand function:

$$Q = 100 - 0.2P \tag{3.4}$$

Cost function:

$$TC = 50 + 20Q + Q^2 \tag{3.5}$$

The problem before the monopoly firm is to find the profit maximizing output and price. The problem can be solved as follows.

We know that profit is maximum at an output at which $MR = MC$. So the first step is to find MR and MC functions from the demand and cost functions, respectively. We have noted earlier that MR and MC are the first derivative of TR and TC functions, respectively. TC function is given, but TR function is not. So, let us drive TR function first. By definition,

$$TR = P \cdot Q$$

Since TC function is expressed in terms of Q, the TR function too has to be expressed in terms of Q for the purpose of uniformity in TC and TR functions. This can be done by converting demand function in Eq. (3.4) into a price function as given below. Given the demand function (3.4), price function, also called 'reverse demand function', can be derived[5] and expressed as

$$P = 500 - 5Q \tag{3.6}$$

Since $P = 500 - 5Q$, by substitution, we get

$$TR = (500 - 5Q)Q$$

$$TR = 500Q - 5Q^2 \tag{3.7}$$

Now MR function can be obtained by differentiating the *TR function* given in Eq. (3.7).

$$MR = \frac{\partial TR}{\partial Q} = 500 - 10Q$$

Likewise, MC function can be obtained by differentiating the *TC function* given in Eq. (3.5).

$$MC = \frac{\partial TC}{\partial Q} = 20 + 2Q$$

Now that MR and MC functions are known, profit maximizing output can be easily obtained. The profit maximizing output can be obtained by equating the MR and MC functions given earlier and finding the solution as shown below.

$$\begin{aligned} MR &= MC \\ 500 - 10Q &= 20 + 2Q \\ 480 &= 12Q \\ Q &= 40 \end{aligned}$$

The output $Q = 40$ is the profit maximizing output. Now profit maximizing price can be obtained by substituting 40 for Q in the price function.

Thus,

$$\begin{aligned} P &= 500 - 5(40) \\ &= 300 \end{aligned}$$

Profit maximizing price is Rs 300.

Given the price, total profit (π) can be obtained by using $TR - TC$ approach as follows.

$$\pi = TR - TC$$

By substitution, we get

$$\begin{aligned} \pi &= 500Q - 5Q^2 - (50 + 20Q + Q^2) \\ &= 500Q - 5Q^2 - 50 - 20Q - Q^2 \end{aligned}$$

By substituting profit maximizing output (40) for Q, we get

$$\begin{aligned} \pi &= 500(40) - 5(40)(40) - 50 - 20(40) - (40 \times 40) \\ &= 20{,}000 - 8{,}000 - 50 - 800 - 1600 \\ &= 9{,}550 \end{aligned}$$

Thus, the maximum profit is Rs 9,550. No other output and price can increase firm's profit.

Does a Monopoly Firm always Make Pure Profit?

There is no certainty that a monopoly firm will always earn a pure or supernormal profit. Whether a monopoly firm earns supernormal profit or normal profit or incurs loss depends on (i) its cost and revenue conditions; (ii) threat from potential competitors; (iii) time period—short run or long run and

(iv) government policy in respect of monopoly. If a monopoly firm operates at the level of output where $MR = MC$, its profit depends on the relative levels of AR and AC. Given the level of output, there are three possibilities:

1. If $AR > AC$, there is economic profit for the firms,
2. If $AR = AC$, the firm earns only normal profit and
3. If $AR < AC$, the firm makes losses: a theoretical possibility in the short run.

Two Common Misconceptions There are two common misconceptions about monopolies: (i) monopolies always make profits and (ii) they can charge any price arbitrarily. These misconceptions must be clarified before we proceed to discuss other related issues.

1. ***A Monopoly does not Necessarily Make Profit in the Short run.*** There is no guarantee that a monopoly firm will always make profits in the short run. In fact, as noted earlier, whether a monopoly makes profit or loss in the short run depends on its revenue and cost conditions. It is quite likely that its SAC curve lies above its AR curve as shown in Figure 3.4. At profit maximizing output (OQ), SAC exceed AR by PM. The monopoly firm therefore, makes losses to the extent of $PM \times OQ = P_2MPP_1$ in the short run. The firm may yet survive in the short run, in the hope of making profits in the long run when economics of scale become available to the firm and it does happen. The monopoly firm will however stick to the profit maximization rule (i.e. $MR = MC$) in order to minimize its losses in the short run. Furthermore, if monopoly firm operates in the short run at a level of output where its $MR = SMC$ and $AR = SAC$, it makes just normal profits like a competitive firm in the long run.
2. ***Monopolies cannot Charge an Arbitrary Price.*** Another common misconception about monopoly is that a monopoly firm, by virtue of being a single seller of a commodity, can charge *any* price or an exorbitantly high price for its product. In fact, the demand curve faced by

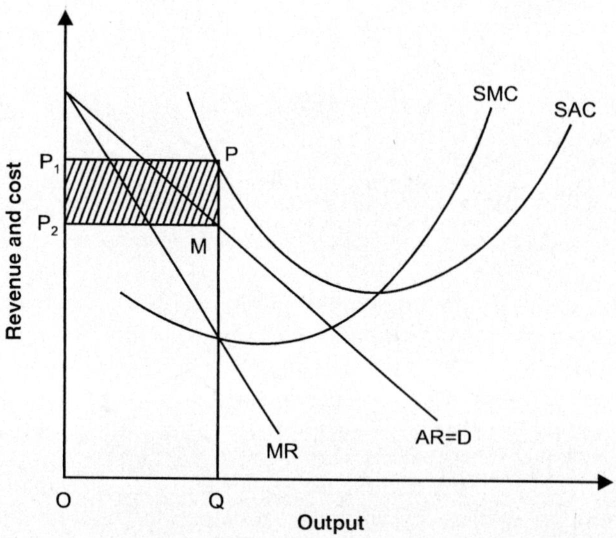

Figure 3.4 *Monopoly Equilibrium in the Short Run: Losses*

a monopolist, is also the industry's demand curve. And, most market demand curves are negatively sloped, being highly elastic in the region of upper half and highly inelastic in the lower half. As proved earlier, at mid-point of the demand curve, $e = 1$. Over the upper half of the demand curve, $e > 1$; and over its lower half, $c < 1$. Therefore, a revenue-maximizing monopoly firm cannot charge any price. If it does so, it will lose it revenue and profit.

Profit Maximization by Using *MC* and Price Elasticity

We have explained earlier the determination of equilibrium price under monopoly by using the profit maximization rule, i.e. $MC = MR$. It may imply that if MR or MC is unknown, equilibrium price cannot be found out. That is not exactly the case. If the monopoly firm is aware of its MC and price elasticity (e) of demand for its product, it can easily find out its profit-maximizing price using the relationship between AR and MR. Suppose firm's $MC = 4$ and elasticity of its demand curve $e = -2$. Given these variables, the profit maximizing price can be obtained as follows.

Profit is maximum where

$$MC = MR$$

Since $MC = 4$, at equilibrium, MR must be equal to 4, i.e.

$$MC = 4 = MR$$

We know that

$$MR = P\left(1 - \frac{1}{e}\right)$$

Since $MC = 4 = MR$, and $e = -2$, by substitution, we get

$$4 = P\left(1 - \frac{1}{2}\right)$$

or

$$P = 4 \Big/ \left(1 - \frac{1}{2}\right)$$

$$P = 8$$

Thus, *under the given conditions*, profit-maximizing price = 8. Note that if MR is known, MC can be found out, and if P and e are known, MC and MR can be worked out for the equilibrium output.

NO SUPPLY CURVE UNDER MONOPOLY: A DIGRESSION

In the preceding section, we have discussed the determination of equilibrium price and output under monopoly. Before we proceed to discuss the determination of price and output by a monopoly in the long run, let us deviate from the main subject to find answer to a question whether supply curve exists

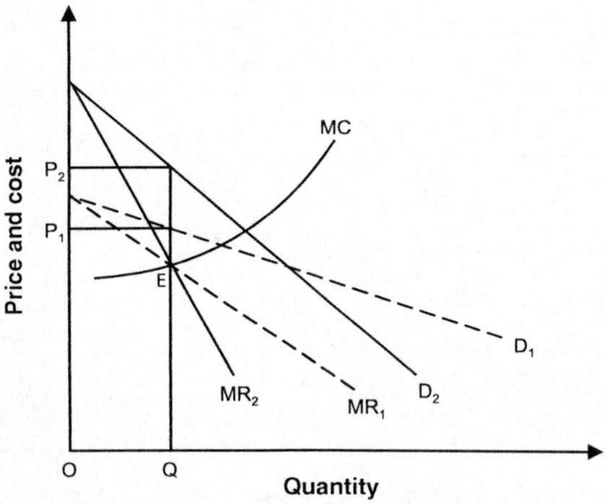

Figure 3.5 *Same Quantity Supplied at Two Different Prices: Case I*

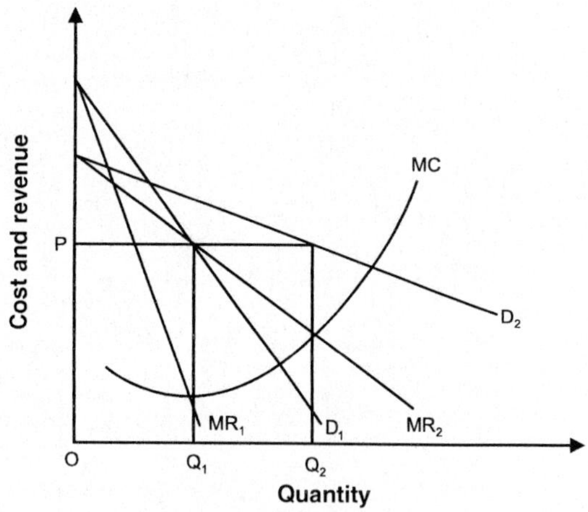

Figure 3.6 *Different Quantities Supplied at the Same Price: Case II*

under monopoly. Economists believe that, *there is no unique or precise supply curve under monopoly.* In order to examine this issue, let us try to trace supply curve under monopoly by using the method and logic of deriving supply curve. (For method used, see Chapter 2, Section 2.4).

We know that a supply curve exhibits a unique relationship between price and quantity supplied. This unique relationship between market price and quantity supplied does not exist under monopoly, at least at the theoretical level. A profit maximizing monopoly firm determines its equilibrium output where $MR = MC$ and $P > MC$. Under these conditions, a *unique* relationship between price ($AR = P$) and quantity supplied cannot be established. The reason is that there are two different possibilities: (i) that given the MC, the same output is supplied at different prices and (ii) that at a given price, different quantities may be supplied if the two downward sloping demand curves have different elasticities. The two cases are illustrated in Figures 3.5 and 3.6, respectively.

Figure 3.5 shows that the same quantity can be supplied at two different prices. Suppose a monopoly firm is faced with two demand curves, D_1 and D_2 with different slopes, and the corresponding MR curves as MR_1 and MR_2. Suppose also that firm's MC curve passes through the point of intersection of the two-demand curves point E—determining equilibrium output at OQ. As Figure 3.5 shows, the same quantity (OQ) can be supplied at two different prices—at price OP_1 when demand curve is D_1 and at price OP_2 when demand curve is D_2. Obviously, there is no unique relationship between price and quantity supplied.

Figure 3.6 presents the case of different quantities supplied at the same price, OP. Given the MC curve, quantity OQ_1 is supplied when demand curve is D_1 and quantity OQ_2 is supplied when demand curve is D_2 at the same price, OP. In this case too, there is no unique relationship between price and quantity supplied. These points lead one to the conclusion that *there is no unique supply curve under monopoly.*

MONOPOLY EQUILIBRIUM IN THE LONG RUN

The long-run equilibrium conditions of a monopolist are different from those faced by the competitive firms in another important respect. The main differentiating factor is the possibility of the entry of new

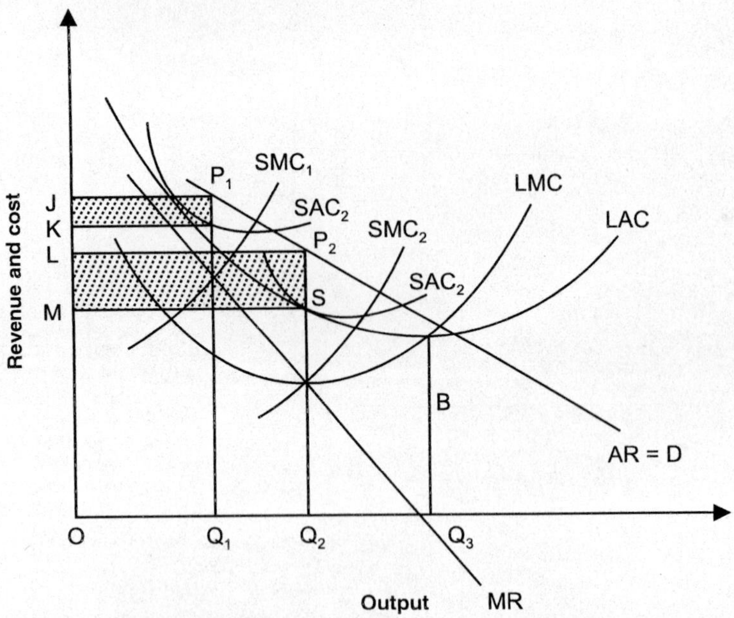

Figure 3.7 *Long-Run Equilibrium of the Monopoly Firm*

firms into the industry. While in a competitive market, there is free entry to the industry, a monopoly firm is protected by the *barriers to entry*. The barriers to entry may be in the form of patent rights, legal protection, economies of scale and the well established long standing of the monopolist and its powers to eliminate the potential competitors by waging a price war.

More importantly, a monopoly firm is free to choose between the alternatives available to it in the long run. The alternatives are whether to close down in case of losses or to continue in the business. If $SAC > AR$, the monopolist incurs losses in the short run. If market size is so small that no plant-size can ensure pure profit in the long run (see Figure 3.4), the monopolist goes out of business. If its $AR > SMC_1$ it earns a short-run profit as shown at output OQ_1 in Figure 3.3. The firm would, therefore, not only continue in the business but would also expand its business to the size that yields maximum profit in the long run.

A monopolist gets an opportunity to expand the size of its plant with a view to maximizing its long-run profits. The expansion of the plant size may, however, be subject to such conditions as: (a) size of the markets; (b) expected economic profits and (c) risk of inviting legal restrictions, like *MRTP* Act in India.

A general case of monopoly equilibrium in the long run is presented in Figure 3.7, assuming none of the above conditions limits the expansion of monopoly firm. The *AR* and *MR* curves show the market demand and marginal revenue conditions faced by the monopoly. The *LAC* and *LMC* curves show the long-term cost conditions. As shown in the figure, the point of intersection between *LMC* and *MR* curves determine the equilibrium output at OQ_2. Given the *AR* curve, price is determined at P_2Q_1 Thus the long-run equilibrium output is OQ_2 and equilibrium price is P_2Q_2 This price–output combination maximizes the monopolist's long-run profits. The total long-run profit has been shown by the area $LMSP_2$. Here the monopoly firm is in the long-run equilibrium. Price P_1Q_1 and output OQ_1 present the short-run equilibrium. Its total short-run profit is shown by the smaller shaded area.

CAPACITY UTILIZATION UNDER MONOPOLY

Monopoly firms are often charged for underutilization of their production capacity. Underutilization of capacity by monopolies, in general, has been an important issue raised in the context of the social cost of monopolies. Utilization of capacity is measured with reference to the optimum production capacity of the firm. The optimum capacity of a firm is given by its minimum *LAC*. A firm producing less than its optimum capacity is underutilizing its capacity and a firm producing more than its optimum capacity is over utilizing its capacity.

The question that we will answer in this section is: *Does a monopoly firm always produce at less than its optimum capacity?* The answer is: not necessarily—it depends on the cost and revenue conditions of the firm and the market size. Let us look at the conditions for under utilization and over utilization of production capacity by monopolies.

1. ***Under Utilization of Capacity.*** The case of capacity under utilization by a monopoly firm is illustrated in Figure 3.8. The optimum size of the monopoly firm is given by point *B* where *LAC* is at its minimum and $LAC = LMC$. At this point. the optimum output is OQ_2. But, a profit maximizing monopoly firm is in equilibrium at point *E* where it produces only OQ_1 which is less than its optimum capacity. There is, thus, underutilization of capacity by the monopoly firm to the extent of Q_1Q_2.
2. ***Over Utilization of Capacity.*** If size of the market and cost conditions permit, the monopoly firm may not only use its capacity to its optimum level, but may even exceed the optimum size of the plant and over utilize its long-run capacity. Figure 3.9 illustrates the case of more-than-optimal utilization of the plant capacity. This is a case of over utilization. The optimum size of the plant is given at point *B*, the point of intersection between *LAC* and *LMC*, whereas the monopoly firm chooses output at *M* where its profit is maximum.

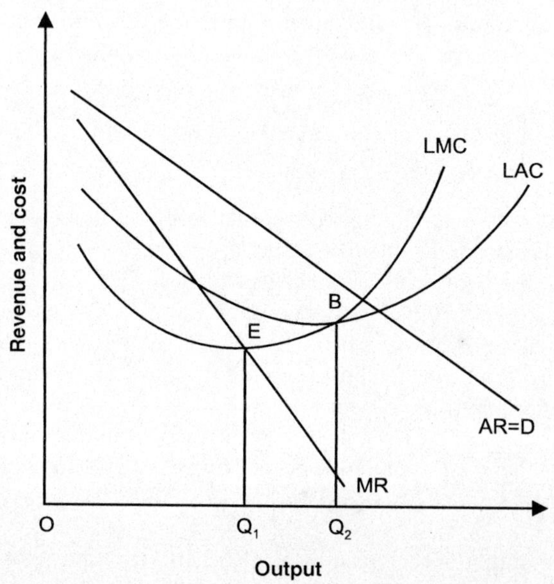

Figure 3.8 *Monopoly Equilibrium: Underutilization of Capacity*

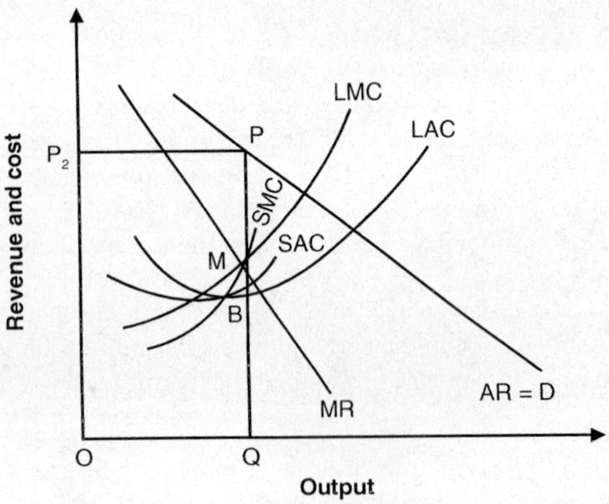

Figure 3.9 *Monopoly Equilibrium: Over Utilization of Capacity*

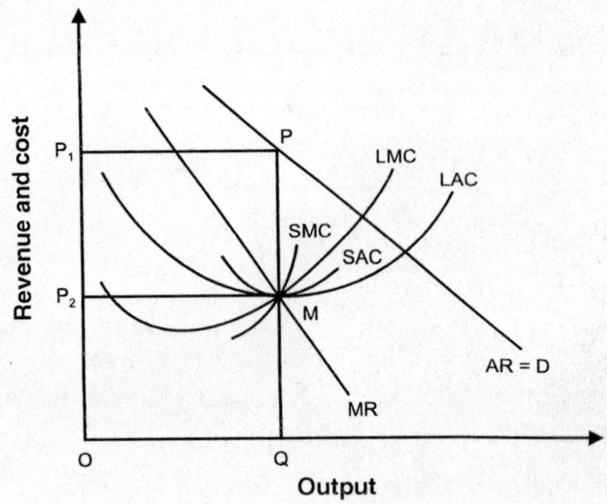

Figure 3.10 *Monopoly Equilibrium at Optimal Size of the Plant*

3. Alternatively, the monopoly firm may find its equilibrium just at the optimum size of the plant. This is possible only when the market-size is just large enough to permit optimum utilization of the firm's capacity. This possibility has been illustrated in Figure 3.10. This may also happen as a matter of coincidence and when production is accurately planned, given the revenue curves.

EQUILIBRIUM OF A MULTI-PLANT MONOPOLY

We have so far analysed the equilibrium of a single-plant monopoly firm. In this section, we will explain the case of a multi-plant monopoly—a monopoly firm producing a homogeneous product in more than one plant. For the sake of simplicity, we make the following assumptions.

1. A monopoly firm has two plants *A* and *B*;
2. Its cost conditions differ from one plant to another and
3. The firm is aware of its *AR* and *MR* curves.

Let us now see, how a profit maximizing monopoly determines its total output and how it allocates the total output between the two plants, so that output of each unit is optimum.

The cost conditions of the two plants are given as shown in Figure 3.11(a) and (b). The combined marginal cost, *MC*, can be obtained by horizontally summing the MC_A and MC_B, so that $MC = MC_A + MC_B$. The combined *MC* curve is shown in panel (c) of Figure 3.11. When *MR* and *MC* are known, the monopolist can easily find the profit maximizing output and price. Going by the profit maximizing rule ($MC = MR$), the total equilibrium output would be *OQ* as shown in panel (c) of Figure 3.11. Now the problem is how to allocate *OQ* between the two plants, so that output of each plant is optimum. The optimum output for each plant can be obtained by applying the profit maximization rule, i.e.

$$MR = MC_A = MC_B$$

The profit maximizing output of each plan that satisfies this rule can be obtained by drawing a horizontal line $MR = MC$ (parallel to X-axis) from point *E* through MC_B and MC_A. As shown in Figure 3.11,

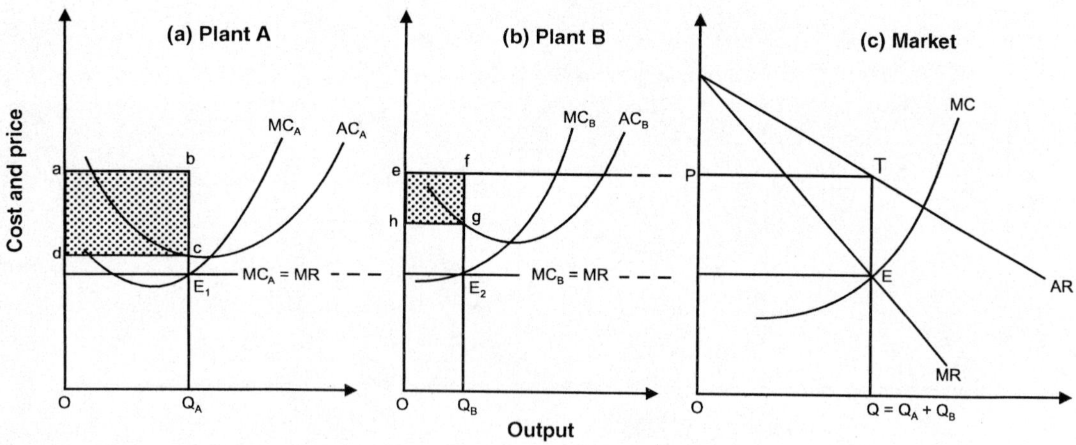

Figure 3.11 *Multi-Plant Monopoly Output Allocation*

the points of intersection E_1 and E_2 determine the optimum output for plants *A* and *B*, respectively. Thus, the optimum output is determined at OQ_A for plant *A* and OQ_B for plant *B*.

Turning to the question of price determination, the profit maximization price is determined at *OP* (=*QT*) in panel (c) of Figure 3.11. Once profit-maximizing price is determined at *OP*, the total maximum profit of each plant can be worked out. For example, total profit from plant *A* can be worked out as follows.

Total profit of Plant $A = (AR - AC)\,Q$

In plant A, $AR = OP = aO$,

$$AC = dO = cQ_A$$

and

$$Q = OQ_A = dc$$

Thus, total profit of plant

$$A = (aO - dO)dc$$
$$= a\ b\ c\ d \text{ at price } OP$$

Thus, at price *OP*, total profit from plant *A* is *abcd* ($= ad \times OQ_A$) and from plant *B*, it is *efgh* ($= eh \times OQ_B$). Although this analysis is based on only two plants, it can be extended to a large number of plants.

The Long-run Adjustments

In the long run, a multi-plant monopoly firm adjusts the size and number of plants so as to maximize its long-run profits. The monopolist makes long-run adjustments when the existing size of the minimum-cost-plant is smaller compared to the size of the market, and there exist economies of scale. If such conditions do exist, the monopolist would adjust the size of each plant in the long run, so that the minimum of *SAC* coincides with the minimum of *MC*, as shown in Figure 3.12(a). If the monopolist

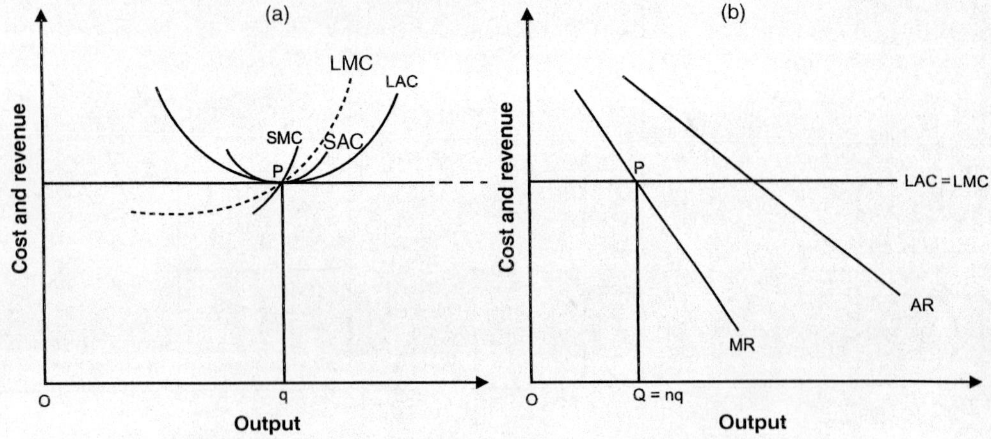

Figure 3.12 *Long-Run Equilibrium of Multiplant Monopoly*

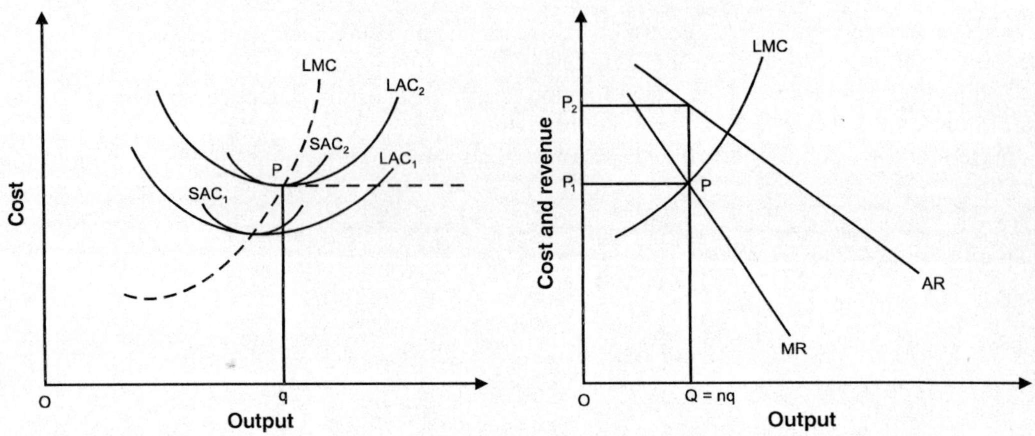

Figure 3.13 *Long-Run Equilibrium of Multi-Plant Firm: Increasing Costs*

does not increase the number of plants or if addition of new plants does not affect the factor prices, it will have a constant minimum cost at *Pq*. In that case, its *LAC* = *LMC*. The long-run cost conditions for a multi-plant monopoly firm can then be represented by the horizontal *LAC* = *LMC* line. The long-run equilibrium of the multi-plant monopoly firm will be determined by the intersection of *LMC* and *MR* curves. The *LMC* and *MR* curves intersect at point *P* in Figure 3.12(b). Thus, the firm will be in the long-run equilibrium at output $OQ = nq$ (where n = number of plants and q = average output of the plants).

However, if addition of new plants causes an increase in the factor prices, the cost curves for each plant would shift upwards, as shown in Figure 3.13. The monopoly firm would then be able to produce more by adding new plants only at an increasing cost. Under this condition, its *LMC* would be positively sloped as shown by *LMC* curve in output of the multi-plant monopolist will be at output *OQ nq* and its equilibrium price will be OP_2.

PRICE DISCRIMINATION UNDER MONOPOLY

Price Discrimination

The theory of pricing under monopoly, as discussed earlier, gives the impression that once a monopolist fixes the price of its product, the same price will be charged from all the consumers. This is, however, not the case generally. A monopolist, simply by virtue of its monopoly power, is capable of charging different prices from different consumers or groups of consumers. When the same (or somewhat differentiated) product is sold at different prices to different consumers, it is called *price discrimination*. When a monopolist sells an identical product at different prices to different buyers, it is called a *discriminatory monopoly*.

Consumers are discriminated in respect of price on the basis of their income or purchasing power, geographical location, age, sex, quantity they purchase, their association with the seller, frequency of purchases, purpose of the use of the commodity or service, and also on other grounds which the monopolist may find suitable.

Some common examples of consumers being discriminated on the basis of their incomes are found in the following cases:

- Consulting physicians charge different fees from different clients on the basis of their paying capacity even if quantity and quality of service rendered is the same.
- Price discrimination on the basis of age is found in railways, roadways and airways: children between 3 and 12 years are charged only half the adult rates.
- Price discrimination on the basis of quantity purchased is very common. It is generally found that private businessmen charge lower price (or give discount) when bulk purchase is made
- In case of public utility services, however, lower rates are charged when commodity or service is consumed in smaller quantity. For example, MNTL (New Delhi) charges lower rates on the night telephone calls, and DESU charges lower tariff rates on lower slabs of electricity consumption.
- The most common practice of price discrimination is found in entertainment business, e.g. cinema shows, musical concerts, game shows, etc. Different rates are charged from different class of audience.

The product or service in question may be identical or slightly modified. For example, services of consulting physicians and lawyers are identical. The services of railways, roadways and entertainment shows may be slightly modified by providing more comfortable seats, sleepers, security and air-conditioning, etc. for the purpose of price discrimination. The modification in service may involve some additional cost. But price differentials are much more than what is justified by cost differentials.

Although price discrimination is a common practice under monopoly, it should not mean that this practice exists only under monopoly. Price discrimination is quite common also in other kinds of market structures, particularly when market imperfection exists. Most business firms discriminate between their customers on the basis of personal relationship, quantity purchased, duration of customer ship and so on.

Necessary Conditions for Price Discrimination

Although price discrimination is a general practice adopted by the monopoly firms, it can be adopted successfully under the following conditions.

- ***First, markets are so separated that resale is not profitable.*** The markets for different classes of consumers are so separated that buyers of low-price market do not find it profitable to resell the commodity in the high-price market. The factors that separate markets include are: (i) geographical distance involving high cost of transportation, e.g. domestic versus foreign markets; (ii) exclusive use of the commodity, e.g. doctor's services, entertainment shows, etc. and (iii) lack of distribution channels, e.g. transfer of electricity and gas.
- ***Secondly, price elasticity of demand is different in different markets.*** If market is divided into sub-market, the elasticity of demand at a given price must be different in each sub-market. It is the difference in price elasticities that provides opportunity for price discrimination. If price elasticities of demand in different markets are the same, price discrimination would not be gainful.
- ***Thirdly, the firm must have some monopoly power to control production and price. This condition applies also to discrimination under imperfect competition in the market.*** The monopoly firm must possess some monopoly power over the supply of the product to be able to distinguish between different classes of consumers and to charge different prices.

Degrees of Price Discrimination

The degree of price discrimination refers to the extent to which a seller can divide the market and can take advantage of market division in extracting the consumer's surplus. According to Pigou,[6] there are three degrees of price discrimination practiced by the monopolists: (i) first-degree price discrimination; (ii) second-degree price discrimination and (iii) third-degree price discrimination.

1. ***First-degree[7] Price Discrimination.*** The discriminatory pricing that attempts to take away the entire consumer surplus is *called first-degree price discrimination.* First-degree discrimination is possible only when a seller is in a position to know the price each buyer is willing to pay. That is, the monopolist knows buyer's demand curve for the product. What the seller does is that he first sets price at the highest possible level at which all those who are willing to buy purchase at least one unit each of the commodity. When the consumer surplus of this section of consumers is exhausted, he gradually lowers down the price, so that the consumer surplus of the lower income groups can be extracted. This procedure is continued until the whole consumer surplus available at the price where $MR = MC$ is extracted. Also, consider the case of services of exclusive use, e.g. medical services. A doctor, who knows or can guess the paying capacity of his patients, can charge the highest possible fee from visibly the richest patient and the lowest fee from the poorest one. The first degree of price discrimination is the limit of discriminatory pricing.
2. ***Second-degree Price Discrimination.*** The second-degree price discrimination is adopted by the monopolist when marked fairly large and divided according to different kinds of buyers but the ability-to-pay of different groups is unknown. Also, the second degree of discriminatory pricing is adopted also to charge different prices for the different quantities of purchase. The second-degree price discrimination is also called 'block pricing system'. A different price is charged from different category of consumers. A monopolist adopting the *second-degree price discrimination* intends to siphon off only the major part of the consumer surplus, rather than the entire of it. The second-degree price discrimination is feasible where
   (a) The number of consumers is large and price rationing can be effective, as in case of utilities like telephones, natural gas and also consumer durables;

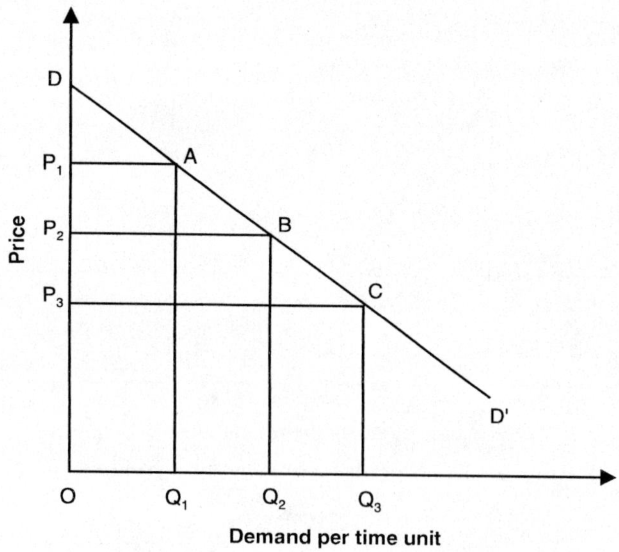

Figure 3.14 *Second-Degree Price Discrimination*

(b) Demand curves of all the consumers are identical and
(c) A single rate is applicable only for a group of large number of buyers.

As shown in Figure 3.14, a monopolist using a second-degree price discrimination sets the price first at OP_1 and sells OQ_1 over a period of time. After this market segment is exhausted, the monopolist sets a lower price, OP_2, and sells Q_1O_2 units over a period of time to the second market segment. After the sale of Q_1Q_2 additional units, the monopolist sets still a lower price, OP_3, for the third lowest segment of the consumer group to sell an additional quantity of Q_2Q_3 units. Thus, by adopting a *block-pricing system*, the monopolist maximizes his total revenues (TR) as

$$TR = (QO_1 \times OP_1) + (Q_1O_2 \times OP_2) + (Q_2O_3 \times OP_3)$$

If monopolist is restrained from price discrimination and is forced to choose any one of the three prices—OP_1, OP_2, or OP_3—his total revenue will be much less.

3. ***Third-degree Price Discrimination.***[8] When a profit maximizing monopoly firm sets different prices in different markets having demand curves with different elasticitiness, it is using third-degree price discrimination. A monopolist is often faced with two or more markets, completely separated from each other—each having a demand curve with different elasticity. Therefore, a uniform price cannot be set for all the markets without loosing the possible profits. The monopolist, therefore, allocates total output between the different markets and fixes different prices, so that profit is maximized in each market. Profit in each market would be maximum only when $MR = MC$ in each market. The monopolist, therefore, allocates its total output between the markets in such proportions that in each market $MR = MC$.

The process of output allocation and determination of price for different markets is illustrated in Figure 3.15. Suppose that a monopolist has to sell its goods in only two markets, A and B. The two

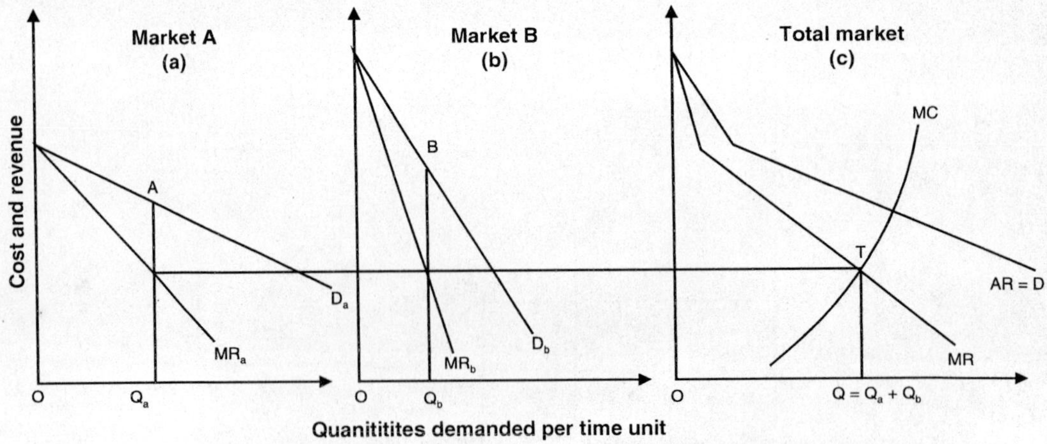

Figure 3.15 *Third-Degree Price Discrimination*

markets are so separated that resale of commodity is not feasible. The demand curve (D_a) and marginal revenue curve (MR_b) given in Figure 3.15(a) represent the *AR* and *MR* curves in market *A* and the curves D_b and MR_b in Figure 3.15(b) represent the *AR* and *MR* curves, respectively, in market *B*. The horizontal summation of demand curves D_a and D_b gives the total demand curve for the two markets, as shown by the curve $AR = D$, and the horizontal summation of MR_d and MR_b as given by the curve *MR* in Figure 3.15(c). Firm's marginal cost is shown by *MC*. Given the *MR* and *MC* curve, the firm's profit maximization output is determined by the intersection of the two curves. Panel (c) of Figure 3.15 shows *MR* and *MC* curves interested at point *T* determining the equilibrium output at *OQ*. Thus, the optimum level of output for the firm is determined at *OQ*. The whole of *OQ* cannot be profitably sold in any one market because of their limited size.

Therefore, the monopolist has to allocate output *OQ* between the two markets in such proportions that the necessary condition of profit maximization is satisfied in both the markets, i.e., on both the markets $MC = MR$. The profit maximizing output for each market can be obtained by drawing a line from point *T*, parallel to *X*-axis, through MR_b and MR_a. The points of intersection on curved MR_a and MR_b determine the optimum share for each market. As shown in Figure 3.15, the monopolist maximizes profit in market *A* by selling OQ_a units at price AQ_a and by selling OQ_b units in market *B* at price BQ_b.

The firm's total equilibrium output is $OQ = OQ_a + OQ_b$. Since at OQ_a, $MR_a = MC$ in market *A*, and at OQ_b, $MR_b = MC$ in market *B*,

$$MC = TQ = MR_a = MR_b$$

Thus, the equilibrium condition is satisfied in both the sub-markets and the monopoly firm adopting the *third degree* method of price discrimination maximizes its profits.

The third degree method of price discrimination is most suitable where the total market is divided between the home and the foreign markets. However, it may be suitably practised between any two or more markets separated from each other by any two or more of such factors as geographical distance, transport barriers, cost of transportation, legal restrictions on the inter-regional or inter-state transfer of commodities by individuals, etc.

Is Price Discrimination Desirable?

Prices discrimination, i.e., charging different prices from different set of consumers for the same commodity is generally not acceptable to the society. In the past, it has been condemned as illegal and immoral. The objection is: why charge a higher price from some consumers and lower price from others while there is no extra advantage to those who pay a higher price, or why benefit some at the cost of some others? In the United Kingdom and the United States, railways were prohibited to charge discriminatory rates.[9] Discriminatory pricing has also been criticized as a destructive tool in the hands of monopoly. For, in the past, large corporations had sought to use price discrimination to prevent the growth of competition. Besides, price discrimination may cause misallocation of resources and, hence, may be deterrent to social welfare.

This is, however, not the case always. In some cases, price discrimination is socially advantageous. In fact, as Lipsey[10] has observed. 'Whether an individual judges price discrimination to be good or bad is likely to depend upon the details of the case as well as upon his own personal value judgements.' He adds, 'Certainly there is nothing in economic theory to suggest that price discrimination is always in some sense worse than non-discrimination under conditions of monopoly or oligopoly.'

However, *price discrimination* is considered to be *desirable* when it adds to total social welfare. Price discrimination is generally justified on the following grounds.

Ensuring Supply of High-cost Essential Service

Price discrimination is socially desirable in case of goods and services which are essential for the society as a whole but their production is unprofitable because long-run average cost curve (LAC) lies much above the aggregated market demand curve. In that case, such goods and services cannot be produced. But, production of such goods and services can be possible provided price discrimination is possible and permitted. Price discrimination, thus, becomes essential for the survival of the industry, on the one hand, and availability of such goods and services, on the other.

The desirability of price discrimination from social welfare point of view was illustrated in Figure 3.16. Suppose (i) there are two markets, I and II, with their individual demand curves given as D_1 and D_2, (ii) market demand curve is given by ABC and (iii) the long-run average cost curve is given by LAC (Figure 3.16). Note that LAC lies throughout above the total demand curve ABC. Therefore, a profitable production is not possible if a price along the market demand curve ABC is to be charged from all its consumers. However, if price discrimination is adopted and prices are so charged in the two markets that the total revenue exceeds LAC at some level of output, then monopoly may profitably survive to the advantage of the society. Let us suppose that the monopoly firm sets price OP_1 in the market I in which demand is inelastic and price OP_2 in market II in which demand is highly elastic. It would sell OQ_1 units at price OP_1 in market I and OQ_2 at price OP_2 in market II. The total output would then be $OQ = OQ_1 + OQ_2$. His total revenue (TR) would be

$$TR = (OP_1 \times OQ_1) + (OP_2 \times OQ_2)$$

and

$$AR = \frac{OP_1 \times OQ_1 + OP_2 \times OQ_2}{OQ}$$

Suppose AR is worked out at OP_a as shown in Figure 3.16 for selling output OQ. At output OQ, the LAC is $OT = QS$. Thus, total cost

$$TC = OQ \times OT = OQST$$

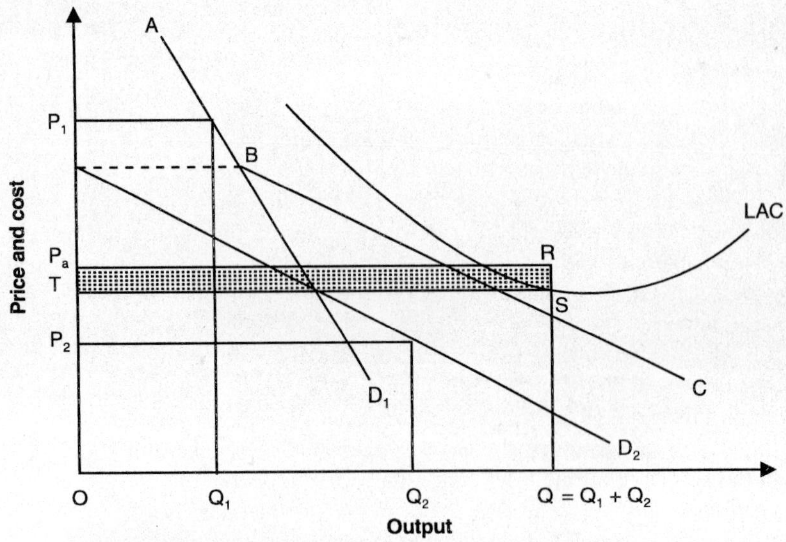

Figure 3.16 *Price Discrimination for Industry's Survival*

and its total revenue

$$TR = OQ \times OP_a = OQRP_a$$

Since $OQRP_a > OQST$, the monopoly firm not only covers its cost but also makes pure profit. Its total profit (Π) can be expressed as

$$\Pi = OQRP_a - OQST = P_a RST$$

This kind of situation arises mostly in public utility services, like railways, roadways, post and telegraph services, etc. in which high-paying sections of the market subsidize the low-paying sections. In other words, rich subsidize the consumption by poor. If low-paying section is not subsidized, no production would be possible.

Making Essential Services Available to Low-income Groups Discriminatory pricing can be adopted with justification where a uniform, single profitable price is likely to restrict the output and deprive many (particularly the people of lower income groups) of the essential good or service. For example, if specialist doctors in private practice, who often charge discriminatory price for their services, are asked to charge a uniform fee from all the patients, they would charge a fee high enough to maintain the level of their income. The high fee may deprive the poor of the doctor's services and may force them to opt for an inferior or inadequate treatment. This leads to a socially undesirable situation: rich patients who can pay a still higher fee gain as they pay a price lower than what they could afford, and on the other hand, poor patients are deprived of proper medical care. What is worse, doctor's services remain underutilized.

Ensuring Cost–benefit Equity in Consumption of Public Goods There may be cases where a section of consumers gain more than the people of other sections from the use of the same product. For example, factory-owners gain more from the use of electricity than the households; irrigation projects benefit big farmers more than the marginal farmers; motorists benefit from roads more than cyclists, and so on. In such cases, uniform price would be unjustified from a normative point of view, provided the objective is not to restrain the household consumption of goods like electricity and spare it for productive purposes. There is, on the other hand, full justification for discriminatory pricing of electricity.

The Gain to Monopolist from Price Discrimination

We have shown earlier why, in some cases, price discrimination is justified from social welfare point of view. There is also a strong justification from monopolist's point of view so long as he gains from price discrimination. We show, in this section, that price discrimination yields a higher total revenue (*TR*) than uniform pricing.

Let us suppose that there are only two markets—market 1 and market 2. The two markets have two different demand curves as shown by AR_1 and AR_2, respectively, in Figure 3.17, and MR_1 and MR_2 are their respective *MR* curves. The aggregate demand (i.e. sum of the two *AR* curves) is shown by the curve labelled $AR = AR_1 + AR_2$, and the sum of their *MR* curves is shown by the curve $MR = MR_1 + MR_2$. The curve *MC* shows marginal cost of the monopoly firm.

Given the cost and revenue conditions, as in Figure 3.17, the monopoly firm has two options: (i) to charge uniform price in both the markets or (ii) to fix two different prices in the two markets, i.e., make price discrimination. The monopoly firm will opt for a pricing strategy that maximizes its profit or revenue. Let us now compare total revenue with and without price discrimination.

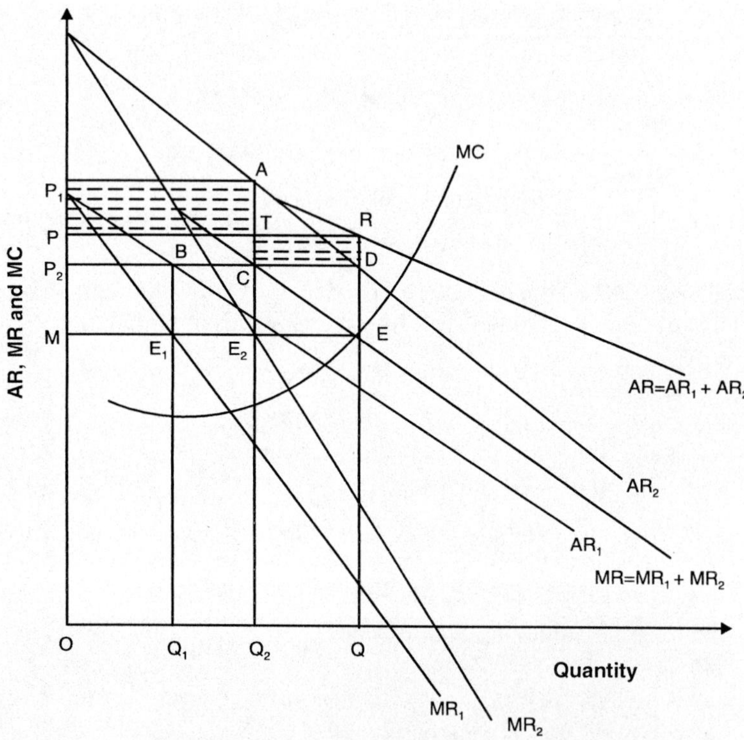

Figure 3.17 *Price and Output Under Simple and Discriminatory Monopoly*

Given the cost and revenue curves, a profit maximizing *simple* monopoly is in equilibrium at point E where its $MC = MR$. At its equilibrium outputs OQ, it will charge a uniform price OP ($= RQ$). Thus, in case of a simple monopoly,

$$\text{Equilibrium output} = OQ$$
$$\text{Price} = OP \ (= RQ)$$
$$\text{Total revenue } (TR) = OQ \times OP = \text{Area } OPRQ$$

where TR is total revenue of simple monopoly.

A discriminating monopoly will fix different prices in the two markets in such a way that it maximizes its profits in both the markets. To this end, the monopoly will allocate its output OQ between the two markets in such a way that its

$$MC = MR_1 = MR_2$$

The division of total output (OQ) which satisfies the above condition can be obtained by drawing a line from point E to the vertical axis, as shown by line ME in Figure 3.17. The line ME can be regarded as $MC = MR$ line. It intersects MR_1 at point E_1 and MR_2 at point E_2. Points E_1 and E_2 determine, respectively, the profit maximizing sales for the two markets—OQ_1 for market 1 and OQ_2 for market 2. Note that at these sales in the two markets, monopoly's $MC = MR_1 = MR_2$. The equilibrium price in market 1 is BQ_1 and in market 2, it is AQ_2. The total revenue of discriminating monopoly (TR) from the two markets is the sum of revenues in markets 1 and 2. It can be worked out as follows.

$$\text{Revenue from market } 1 = OP_2(OQ_1) = \text{area } OP_1BQ_1$$
$$\text{Revenue from market } 2 = OP_1(OQ_2) = \text{area } OP_1AQ_2$$
$$\text{Total revenue } (TR_d) = OP_2BQ_1 + OP_1AQ_2$$

Let us now compare the TR of simple and discriminating monopolies.

$$\text{Simple monopoly } TR_s = OPRQ$$
$$\text{Discriminating monopoly } TR = OP_1AQ_2 + OP_2BQ_1$$

Note that $OP_2BQ_1 = Q_2CDQ$. This is so because $CD = P_2B$. It is simply the addition of AR_1 and AR_2 for measuring the total of discriminatory monopoly. Therefore, by substitution, we get,

$$TR_d = OP_1\,AQ_2 + Q_2CDQ = OP_1CDQ$$

It can be shown that $TR_d > TR_s$ or $OP_1ACDQ > OPRQ$. This can be done by subtracting the common areas from the two sides and comparing the residuals. Note that area OP_2DQ is common to both TR_s and TR_d. By subtracting OP_2DQ from both sides, we get

$$(OP_1ACDQ - OP_2DQ) > (OPRQ - OP_2DQ)$$
$$P_2P_1ATRD > P_2PRD$$

Note also that the $PTCP_2$ is common to both the areas—P_2P_1ATRD and P_2PRD. By subtracting the common area, we get

$$(P_2P_1\,ATRD - PTCP_2) > (P_2PRD - DTCP_2)$$
$$P_1ATP > TRDC$$

This conclusion is obvious in Figure 3.17. It is thus proved that, under certain given revenue and cost conditions, price discrimination yields a higher revenue than the uniform pricing

MONOPOLY VS. PERFECT COMPETITION

This section answers the question whether perfect competition or monopoly is more desirable from society's point of view. This question can be answered (i) by comparing the price and output in the two kinds of markets and (ii) by measuring the deadweight loss under the two kinds of market conditions.

Comparison of Long-run Price and Output

Comparison of long-run price and output under monopoly and perfect competition easier than that of short run because long-run equilibrium is settled and shows the final status of the firms, whereas short-run equilibrium is subject to change over time making comparison uncertain. Therefore, we compare here long-run price and output for an industry under monopoly and under perfect competition.

Figure 3.18 presents a comparative analysis of equilibrium price and output under perfect competition and monopoly in the long run. Let us assume that *LMC* and *LAC* curves are identical for both a competitive industry and a monopoly.

The long-run equilibrium of a competitive industry requires that all its firms are in equilibrium, i.e., all the firms have their $AR = MR = LAC = LMC$. This condition is satisfied at point E_1 in Figure 3.18. Thus, in a competitive industry, equilibrium price is OP_1 and equilibrium output OQ_2. Now if this industry were to be monopolized, the revenue conditions (*AR* and *MR*) will be different. The *AR* and *MR* curves for the monopolized industry are given by the *AR* and *MR* curves, respectively, in Figure 3.18. Given its *AR* and *MR* curves, the monopoly firm will reach its equilibrium and maximize its total profits at the level of output where its $MR = MC$. This level of output is shown by point *B*—the point of intersection of *MR*

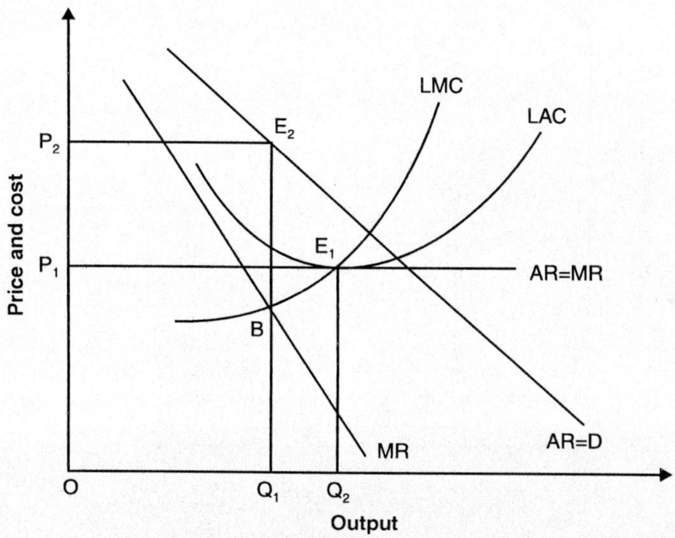

Figure 3.18 *Comparison of Price and Output: Monopoly Vs Competitive Industry*

and *LMC* curves. Thus, the equilibrium output under monopoly will be OQ_1 and the equilibrium price will be OP_2. The following table presents a comparison of the equilibrium price and output under perfect competition and monopoly.

Price/Output	Perfect Competition	Monopoly	Comparison
Price	OP_1	OP_2	$OP_1 < OP_2$
Output	OQ_2	OQ_1	$OQ_2 > OQ_1$

Conclusion If both monopoly and competitive industries are faced with identical cost conditions, the output under perfect competition is higher than that under monopoly (since $OQ_2 > OQ_1$), and price in the competitive industry is lower than in monopoly as $OP_1 < OP_2$. Perfect competition is, therefore, more desirable from social welfare angle, under the given conditions.

The Deadweight Loss under Monopoly

A general complaint against monopolies is that monopoly causes loss of social welfare and distortions in resource allocation. The suboptimal allocation of resources and loss of social welfare are illustrated in Figure 3.19, assuming a constant-cost industry which has $LAC = LMC$. The revenue conditions are shown by the *AR* and *MR* curves. Given the cost and revenue conditions, a perfectly competitive industry will produce OQ_2 at which $LAC = LMC = AR$. Its price will be OP_1.

On the other hand, under the same cost and revenue conditions, a monopoly firm finds its equilibrium at point *K*. Given the equilibrium point, the monopoly firm produces OQ_1 and charges price OP_2. The comparison of prices and outputs under monopoly and perfect competition gives the measure of the loss of social welfare.

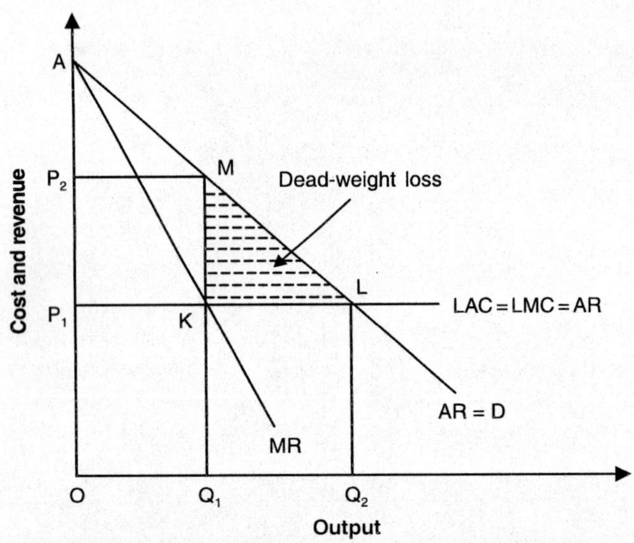

Figure 3.19 *Deadweight Loss Under Monopoly*

Loss of Social Welfare under Monopoly The loss of social welfare is measured in terms of loss of consumer surplus. The total consumer surplus equals the difference between the total price which a society is willing to pay for the consumption of a commodity and the total price that it pays for that commodity. If an industry is perfectly competitive, the total output available to the society will be OQ_2 at price OP_1 (see Figure 3.19). The total price which the society pays for OQ_2 is given by the area $OP_1LQ_2 = OP_1 \times OQ_2$. The total price which it is willing to pay for the output OQ_2 is given by the area $OALQ_2$ which, in Marshallian terminology, is the value which society would be willing to pay for output OQ_2. Thus,

$$\text{Consumer's surplus} = OALQ_2 - OP_1LQ_2 = ALP_1$$

If the industry is monopolized, the equilibrium output is set at OQ_1 and price at OP_2. This leads to a loss of a part of consumer surplus:

$$\text{Loss of consumer surplus under monopoly} = ALP_1 - AMP_2 = P_2MLP_1.$$

Of this total loss of consumer surplus (P_2MLP_1), P_2MKP_1 goes to the monopolist as monopoly profit or pure profit. The remainder $MKL = P_2MLP_1 - P_2MKP_1$ goes to none. Therefore, it is termed as *deadweight loss* to the society caused by monopoly.

Algebraic Solution of Deadweight Loss We have discussed and illustrated earlier graphically the deadweight loss to the society caused by the monopoly firms. Here we present an algebraic measurement of the deadweight loss by comparing the equilibrium price and output under monopoly and perfect competition. As noted earlier, the deadweight loss can be measured by comparing the price and output under perfect competition and monopoly. Therefore, let us proceed with finding the price and output under perfect competition and monopoly by assuming revenue and cost functions.

Let us suppose that the price function (the reverse demand function) for a product is given as $P = 20 - 0.2Q$. Given the price function, firm's TR function can be derived as

$$\begin{aligned} TR &= P \cdot Q \\ &= (20 - 0.2Q)Q \\ &= 20Q - 0.2Q^2 \end{aligned}$$

From this TR-function, the MR-function can be derived as

$$MR = 20 - 0.4Q$$

Let us suppose also that the TC function of the product is given as $TC = 10Q$ and that $MC = AC = 10$.

Given the MR and MC functions, let us now find the equilibrium price and output for the monopoly and for a firm under perfect competition.

Monopoly Equilibrium Output and Price

Monopoly Output: Going by the profit maximization rule, the equilibrium output, i.e. the profit maximizing output is determined where

$$\begin{aligned} MR &= MC \\ 20 - 0.4Q &= 10 \\ Q &= 25 \end{aligned}$$

Thus, monopoly equilibrium output is 25.

Monopoly Price: Given the price function and equilibrium output = 25, monopoly price can be worked out as follows. Given the price function as $P = 20 - 0.2\ Q$, monopoly equilibrium price can be obtained by substituting 25 for Q in the price function. Thus,

$$P = 20 - 0.2\ (25)$$
$$= 15$$

Under monopoly price will be fixed at 15.

Equilibrium Output and Price Under Perfect Competition

Output: Going by the profit maximization rule, the equilibrium output for a firm under perfect competition is determined where

$$AR = AC = MC$$

AR is given by the price function and $AR = MC = 10$. Thus, equilibrium output under perfect competition is determined where

$$AR = AC$$
$$20 - 0.2Q = 10$$
$$Q = 50$$

Thus, equilibrium output under perfect competition is 50.

Price: Given the price function and equilibrium output = 50, price under perfect competition can be worked out as follows. Given the price function as $P = 20 - 0.2Q$, the equilibrium price can be obtained by substituting 50 for Q the price function. Thus,

$$P = 20 - 0.2Q$$
$$= 10$$

The equilibrium price under perfect competition will be 10.

The Deadweight Loss Under Monopoly The deadweight loss under monopoly can be measured by measuring the part of consumer surplus lost which benefits no body. As shown in the graphical analysis, given the demand function and constant MC and AC, the deadweight appears in the form of a triangle. It means that the area of the triangle gives the measure of the deadweight loss. Using the formula for measuring the area of triangle, the deadweight loss with reference to change in price and output can be measured as follows.

$$\text{Deadweight loss} = \frac{1}{2}(\Delta P)(\Delta Q)$$

Recall that when a market changes from perfect competition to monopoly, price changes from Rs 10 to 15, i.e. $\Delta P = 15 - 10 = 5$, and output changes from 50 to 25 units, i.e. $\Delta Q = 50 - 25 = 25$. By substituting these values for ΔP and ΔQ, we get,

$$\text{Deadweight loss} = 0.5\ (5)\ (25) = 62.5$$

Thus, the deadweight loss under monopoly equals the loss of a value of Rs 62.2.

Empirical Evidence of Deadweight Loss Theoretically, there is a strong possibility of a deadweight loss under monopoly in comparison to perfect competition. However, empirical evidence of the deadweight loss attributed to monopoly is inconclusive. Harberger[11] was the first to estimate the loss of welfare—in fact, loss of efficiency—due to monopoly in the United States. To estimate the loss of welfare, he assumed constant cost and unitary elastic demand curve for all industries and used 1924–1928 data of 73 manufacturing industries. He regarded the loss of welfare as the difference between the monopoly price and the competitive price. According to his estimates, the US economy had suffered a loss of social welfare to the extent of 0.1 per cent of its national income, which was obviously negligible. An implication of this finding was that efforts to curb monopolies were a sheer waste of time. Interestingly, 'One economist quipped that economists might make a larger social contribution fighting fires and eradicating termites than attempting to curb monopolies.'[12]

Although many other studies confirmed Harberger's finding, some economists were highly critical of his data and approach. For example, Stigler[13] criticized Harberger's results on the ground of statistics used in his study. Kamerschen[14] used 1956–1961 data in a similar study and produced a considerably different result. According to his findings, the welfare loss due to monopolies in the US was about 6 per cent of national income. Scherer and Ross find welfare loss due to monopolistic mal-allocation of resources somewhere between 0.5 and 2 per cent of the US GDP. Some other critics of Harberger have estimated the social loss to be of the order of 4–8 per cent of national income. However, the methodology and statistics used by Harberger's critics have been criticized by others. In the mean time, some other aspects of monopoly have been added to the debate, e.g. the dynamic efficiency that arises due to technological advanced made by monopolistic competition, the poor quality of goods supplied by them, advantage of the resources unused by the monopolies, and the use and abuse of monopoly profits. Finally, it may be concluded that the issue of deadweight loss attributed to monopolies remains a *controversial issue*. Some even argue that the *MRTP* Acts adopted by many countries is a futile exercise.

SOME OTHER MONOPOLY-RELATED ISSUES

Until Section 3.10, we were concerned with the basic theory of simple, multi-plant and discriminatory monopolies. In this section, we will discuss *two important* issues related to monopoly. The issues that we will discuss here include

1. Incidence of taxes and effect of subsidy under monopoly and
2. Peak load pricing under monopoly.

Incidence of Taxes and Effect of Subsidy Under Monopoly

The question that we will answer theoretically is as follows: Who bears the tax burden when a tax is imposed on monopoly product and on monopoly profit? Let us first answer this question in respect of the *commodity tax*.

Incidence of a Commodity Tax A commodity tax may be in the form of a *sales tax* or *excise duty*. These taxes may be imposed either at a specific rate (a fixed tax per unit of output) or at an *ad valorem rate*, i.e., at some percentage of the value of the commodity. In our analysis, we will assume a *specific* commodity tax.

Let us suppose that cost and revenue conditions of a monopoly firm are given as in Figure 3.20. Prior to the imposition of tax, the firm would be in equilibrium at point E where its $MC = MR$. Its equilibrium output is OQ and equilibrium price PQ.

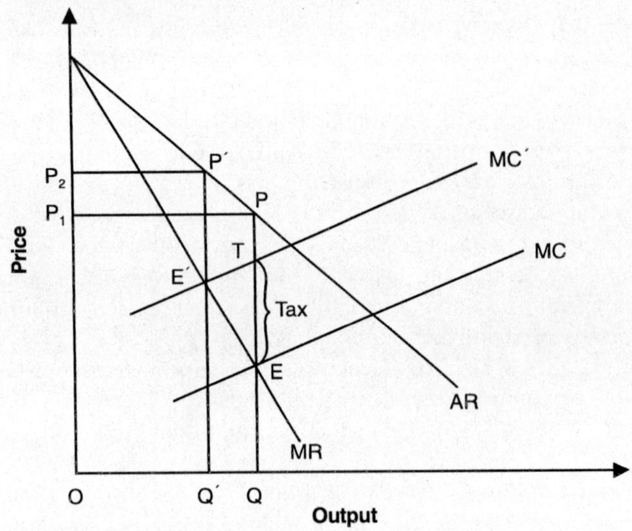

Figure 3.20 *Effects of Specific Sales Tax on Monopoly*

Let the government now impose a specific or unit tax by an amount *ET* per unit on the monopoly product—it may be in the form of specific sales tax or excise duty per unit of output. The imposition of tax increases firm's supply price and will thereby make its *MC* curve shift upwards to the position of *MC′*. As a result, firm's equilibrium shifts to point *E′*. As Figure 3.20 shows, equilibrium output falls to *OQ′* and price rises to *P′Q′*. Note that price increases only by P_1P_2 which is less than the amount of tax *ET*. This conclusion holds even if a monopoly firm is producing at constant *MC*.

This analysis shows that the effect of commodity tax on monopoly is similar to one applicable to a competitive industry. That is, a monopoly firm is able to pass only a part of the tax on to the consumers and bears a part of the tax itself. It can, however, be shown that output under monopoly declines by less than it does under competition.

Can a Monopolist Raise Price More Than the Amount of Tax? Monopoly's power to raise its price after tax imposition depends on the elasticity of demand for its product—the lower the elasticity, the greater the power. A monopolist can pass the entire tax burden on to the consumer when the demand for its product is perfectly inelastic. For example, consider essential goods like life-saving drugs, electricity, telephone, cooking gas, etc. Such goods have nearly zero elasticity ($e_p \cong O$). In case of such goods, a monopoly may raise price by the entire amount of tax—even by more than that. But, in case of products with downwards sloping demand curve with price elasticity greater than zero, monopoly's power to raise price depends on the elasticity of demand as follows:

1. If $e = 1$, monopoly can raise price by half of the tax.
2. If $e < 1$, price can be raised by more than half of the tax.
3. If $e > 1$, price can be raised only by less than half of the tax.

These conditions hold for a profit maximizing monopoly only. It is important to note that in the absence of government control of monopoly prices, however, a monopoly may raise price by the entire amount of tax—even by more than the amount of tax, if $e = 0$.

Effect of Lump-Sum Tax on Monopoly Profit In general, one would expect a monopoly firm to be in a better position to shift a tax on its profit income. 'But closer consideration shows that the monopolist must absorb the tax. The reason is that the pure monopolist will have maximized profits prior to tax and hence can do no better after the tax is imposed.'[15] Looking at the matter theoretically, a lump-sum tax on monopoly does not affect the equilibrium of a monopoly making pure profit either in the short run or in the long run. The reason is that imposition of a lump-sum tax affects monopoly's *fixed cost*, not its *variable cost* and, therefore, its *marginal cost* (*MC*) remains unaffected. Since *MC* is not affected by the lump-sum tax, monopoly's equilibrium remains unaffected. However, imposition of lump-sum tax reduces monopoly's pure profit. Monopoly's equilibrium will not be affected as long as lump-sum tax does not exceed its super normal profit. This implies that the monopolist bears the entire burden of the lump-sum tax.

Who Gains from Subsidy Subsidy is opposite of tax. It is a negative tax. Therefore, the effect of subsidy on monopoly equilibrium is the reverse of the tax effect. The effects of subsidy on monopoly output and price are illustrated in Figure 3.21. The *AR* and *MR* curves show the revenue and *LMC* shows the long-run cost conditions—long run allows the time for output and price adjustment. The analysis of effects of subsidy on monopoly equilibrium is presented below.

Let the monopoly be in equilibrium at point *E* prior to the grant of subsidy. The pre-subsidy equilibrium output is OQ_1 and price is AQ_1 (= OP_4). Now, let the government provide a subsidy of an amount *ES* per unit. As a result, firm's $LAC = LMC$ shifts down to $LAC' = LMC'$ and its equilibrium shifts to point E'. At new equilibrium, monopoly output increases from OQ_1 to OQ_2 and post-subsidy price falls to BQ_2. It is important to note that monopoly price decreases by P_3P_4 which is less than the amount of subsidy, P_1P_2. It means monopolists do not pass the entire benefit of subsidy to the consumers, even if it is so intended—they retain a part to themselves.

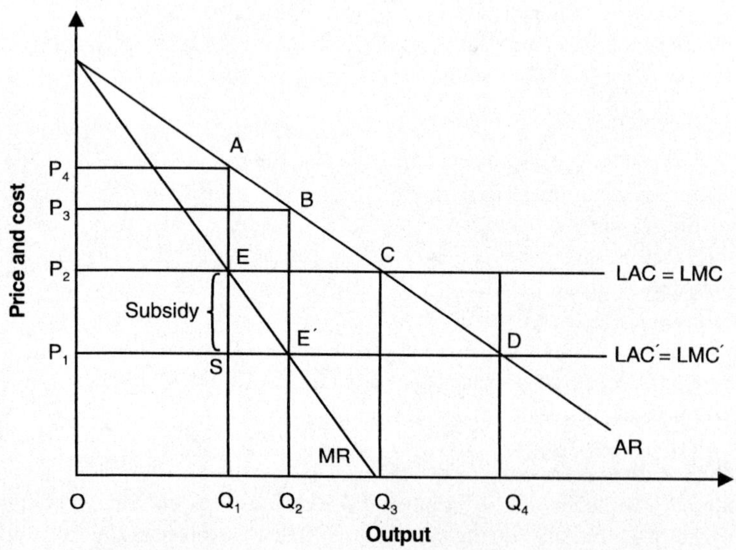

Figure 3.21 *Subsidy and Monopoly Equilibrium*

Comparison of Subsidy under Monopoly and Competitive Industry Figure 3.21 provides also a comparison of subsidy effect on price and output under monopoly and perfect competition with constant cost. Given the revenue and cost conditions, a competitive firm will be in pre-subsidy equilibrium at point *C* where its $AR = LAC$. Its equilibrium output is OQ_3 and price is OP_2 ($= CQ_3$). After the grant of subsidy, its equilibrium shifts to point *D* where its output OQ_4 and price is OP_1 ($= DQ_4$).

The effect of subsidy on the price and output of a monopoly and competitive industry is compared below assuming subsidy is granted under the same cost and revenue conditions.

1. A competitive firm passes the entire benefit of subsidy to the consumers while a monopoly firms retains a part of it.
2. Increase in output is much larger under competitive conditions.
3. Decrease in monopoly price (P_4P_3) is less than (P_2P_1) under perfect competition.

Peak-Load Pricing by a Monopoly

There are certain non-storable goods, e.g., electricity, telephone and transport services, etc., which are demanded in varying quantities in different seasons and in day and night times. Consumption of electricity reaches its peak in day time. It is called 'peak-load' time. It reaches its bottom in the night. This is called 'off–peak' time. Electricity consumption peaks in daytime because all business establishments, offices and factories come into operation. It decreases during nights because most business establishments are closed and household consumption falls to its basic minimum. Also, in India, demand for electricity peaks during summers due to use of AC*s* and coolers, and it declines to minimum level during winters. Similarly, consumption of telephone services is at its peak at daytime and at its bottom at nights. Another example of 'peak' and 'off–peak' demand is of railway services. During festivals and summer holidays, 'Pooja' vacations, the demand for railway services rises to its peak.

A technical feature of such products is that they cannot be stored. Therefore, their production has to be increased in order to meet the 'peak-load' demand and to be reduced to 'off–peak' level when demand decreases. Had these goods been storable, the excess production in 'off–peak' period could be stored and supplied during the 'peak-load' period. But this cannot be done. Besides, given the installed capacity, their production can be increased but at an increasing marginal cost (*MC*).

The Problems in Pricing The monopoly firms producing non-storable goods and services with high seasonal and day–night variations in demand often face the problem of how to price the product, so that profit is maximized. For example, pricing of goods like electricity is problematic. The nature of the problem in a short-run pricing is depicted in Figure 3.22. The 'peak-load' and 'off-load' demand curves are shown by D_H and D_L curves, respectively, showing high and low demand. The short-run supply curve is given by the short-run marginal cost curve, *SMC*. The problem is 'how to price electricity'.

As Figure 3.22 shows, if electricity price is fixed in accordance with peak-load demand, OP_3 will be the price and if it is fixed according to off-load demand, price will be OP_1. The problem is: where to fix the price of electricity? If a 'peak-load' price (OP_3) is charged uniformly in all seasons, it will be unfair because consumers will be charged for what they do not consume. Besides, it will affect business activities adversely as it increase a variable cost of production. If electricity production is a public monopoly, the government will not allow a uniform 'peak-load' price.

On the other hand, if a uniform 'off load' price (OP_1) is charged, production will fall to OQ_2 and there will be acute shortage of electricity during peak hours. It leads to 'breakdowns' and 'load-shedding' during the peak-load period, which disrupts production and makes life miserable. This is a regular

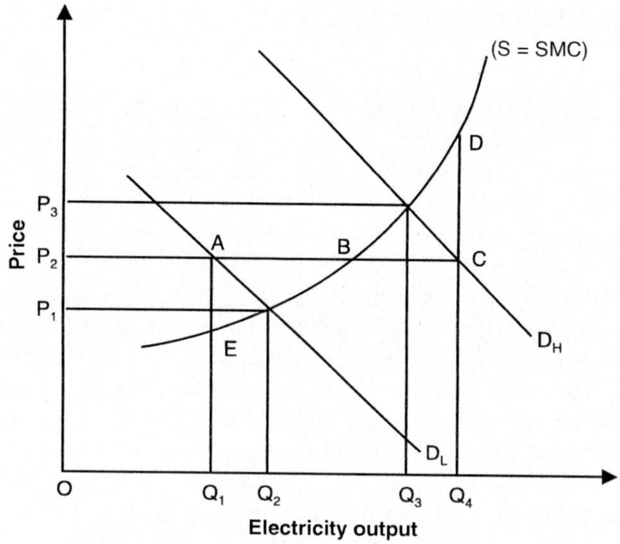

Figure 3.22 *Peak-Load Pricing of Electricity*

feature in New Delhi, the capital city of India. This is because electricity rates in New Delhi are said to be one of the lowest in the country and power theft runs close to 50%.

Alternatively, if an average of the two prices, say P_2 is charged, it will have the demerits of both 'peak-load' and 'off-load' prices. There will be an excess production to the extent of *AB* during the 'off-load' period, which will go waste as it cannot be stored. If production is restricted to OQ_1, price P_2 will be unfair. And, during the 'peak-load' period, there will be a shortage to the extent of *BC*, which can be produced only at an extra marginal cost of *CD*.

Double Pricing System For the above reasons, generally, a double pricing system is adopted. A higher price, called 'peak-load' price (OP_3) is charged for the 'peak-load' period and a lower price (OP_1) is charged for the 'off–peak' period. During the 'peak-load' period, production is increased to OQ_3 at which D_H intersects *SMC*, and production is reduced to OQ_1 during the 'off–peak' period. This system has both its *advantages* and *disadvantages*.

Advantages Peak-load pricing system has two advantages.

1. It results in an efficient distribution of electricity consumption. Housewives run their dish-washers and washing machines during the 'off–peak' period.
2. It helps in preventing a loss to the electricity company and ensures regular supply of electricity in the long run.

Disadvantages The peak load pricing system has two disadvantages too.

1. The businesses which are by nature day-business pay higher rates than those which can be shifted to 'off–peak' period.
2. Billing system is the greatest problem. Each consumer will have to install two metres—one for 'peak-load' and another for 'off-load' period with an automatic switch-over system. This can be done.

Alternatively, the problem can be resolved by adopting a progressive tariff rate for the use of electricity, as is the case in New Delhi.

GOVERNMENT REGULATION OF MONOPOLY PRICES

The monopolies are, in general, alleged to restrict production, consumption and employment to widen income and wealth disparities to exploit consumers and employees, to distort resource allocation and to reduce the social welfare. In most countries, therefore, government intervenes and makes laws to control and regulate monopolies to the advantage of the society. There are various measures—direct, indirect, price, non-price, legal and otherwise, controls—to control and regulate the monopolies. We have discussed below a general method of controlling monopolies, i.e. price regulation of natural monopolies.

Price regulation is a common feature in case of natural monopolies. When the size of the market is small relative to the optimum size of the firm, market size cannot support more than one firm of optimal size. A monopoly in such a market is a natural monopoly, protected by market size itself. The government may either nationalize such monopolies or regulate their prices to eliminate the excess profits. If government intends to regulate the monopoly price, the question arises: what price should be fixed for the monopolist to charge? The two controlled price systems have been suggested: one that allows some *excess profit* to the monopolist, and the second that allows only *normal profit* to the monopolist. Both the systems of controlled prices, along with their repercussion on output, are illustrated in Figure 3.23.

Given its cost and revenue conditions, as shown in Figure 3.23, an unregulated monopoly would produce OQ_1 units, charge price OP_1 and make excess profit of MT per unit. If government intends to regulate monopoly price allowing some super normal profit, then one reasonable price is $OP_2 = PQ_2$, where $LMC = AR$. Alternatively, if government intends to regulate monopoly price with only normal profit, it will fix price at $OP_1 = CQ_3$ at which $AR = LAC$. When OP_2 is the price set for the monopolist, the firm is allowed only normal profit, but the output is maximum possible under the given cost and revenue conditions. On the other hand, if price is fixed at OP_2, then the monopolist gets some abnormal profit,

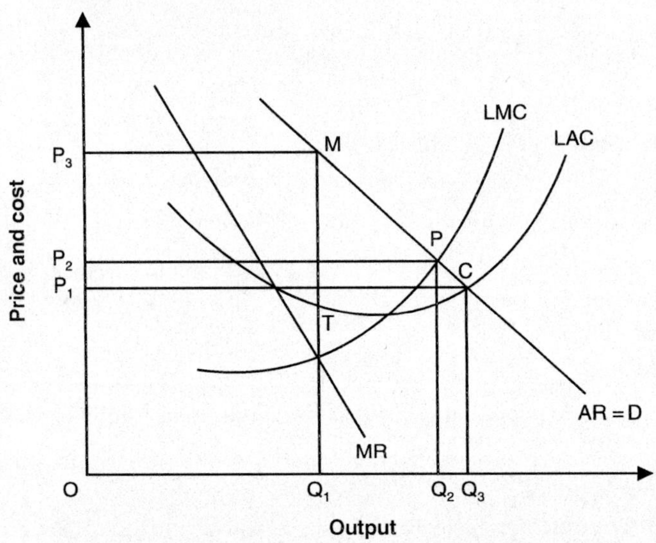

Figure 3.23 *Government Regulated Monopoly*

but the output is less than that at price OP_1. In both the cases, however, the total output under regulated monopoly is much greater than that under unregulated monopoly. Which of the two alternative prices (OP_1 or OP_2) is more appropriate is a matter of debate and policy.

MEASURES OF MONOPOLY POWER

The degree of monopoly power matters a great deal in pricing and output decisions of a monopolist and in respect of control and regulation of monopolies. We discuss here the various measures of monopoly power.

Measuring monopoly power has been a very difficult problem. The efforts to devise a method for measuring monopoly power have not yielded any universal or non-controversial measure. As Hunter has observed, 'The idea of devising a measure of monopoly power, with reference both to its general incidence and to particular situation, has been and probably always will remain an attractive prospect for economists who wish to probe in this field'[16] If not for any other reason, then for 'sheer intellectual curiosity', economic theorists feel compelled to work on this problem, for they could not with good conscience go on talking about 'great' or 'little' monopoly power or about various degrees of monopoly without trying to ascertain the meaning of these words'.[17]

Therefore, to devise at least a 'conceivable measures of monopoly, even if 'practical' measurement is impossible, continues to remain the interest of the economists, for at least *two reasons.*

First, apart from intellectual curiosity, people would like to know about the economy in which they live, its industrial structure, and the industries from which they get their supplies.

Secondly, growth of monopolies have forced governments of many countries to formulate policies and devise legislative measures to control and regulate monopolies. If the government is to succeed in its policy of restraining monopoly, it must have at least some practicable measure of monopoly power and monopolistic trade practices.

Measures of Monopoly Power

The economists have suggested several devices to measure the degree of monopoly power, though none of the measures is free from flaws. Yet, the various measures do provide an insight into the monopoly power and its impact on the market structure. Besides, they also help in formulating an appropriate public policy to control and regulate the existing monopolies. We have briefly discussed here some important measures of monopoly power.

Number of Firms One of the simplest measures of degree of monopoly power is to count the number of firms in the industry. In case there is a single firm in an industry, the firm has the total, the absolute monopoly power. As the number of firms increases, the degree of monopoly decreases, as is the case under monopolistic competition and oligopoly. The smaller the number of firms, the greater the degree of monopoly power of each firm in the industry, and conversely, the larger the number of firms, the greater the possibility of absence of monopoly power. A corollary of this criterion is that if there is a single firm in an industry, the firm has an absolute monopoly power. This criterion seems to have been derived from the characteristics of the perfect competition in which the number of firms is so large that each firm supplies only an insignificant proportion of the market and no firm has any control on the price.

This criterion has, however, a serious *drawback.* The number of firms alone does not reveal much about the relative position of the firms within the industry because (i) 'firms are not of equal size', and

(ii) their number does not indicate the degree of control each firm exercises in the industry, if an industry with a large number of firms is dominated by a large firm or by a few large firms. Therefore, the numerical criterion of measuring monopoly power is of little practical use.

Concentration Ratio The concentration ratio is one of the widely used criteria of monopoly power. The concentration ratio is obtained by calculating the percentage share of the largest group of the firms in the total output of an industry. In the words of Hunter, 'The number of firms chosen for calculating the ratio usually depends on some fortuitous element—normally the census of production arrangements of the country concerned.'[18] In Britain, the share of the largest three firms of a census industry, and in the USA, the share of the largest four firms is the basis of calculating concentration ratio.[19] Apart from the share of the largest firms in the industry output, 'the size of the firms and the concentration of control in the industry may be measured... in terms of production capacity, value of assets, number of employees or some other characteristics.'[20]

These measures too are, however, not free from drawbacks. They have *three major drawbacks*.

First, they involve statistical and conceptual problems. For example, production capacity may not be used straightaway as it may include 'unused obsolete or excess capacity' and the value of assets involves valuation problem as accounting method of valuation and market valuation of assets may differ. Employment figure may not be relevant in case of capital-intensive industries. The use of such figures may be misleading. The two other convenient measures are 'gross output value' or 'net output' (value added). But the former involves the risk of double counting and the latter, the omission of inter-establishment transfers.[21]

Secondly, an important objection to concentration ratio as the measures of degree of monopoly power is that this measure does not take into account the size of the market. Size of the market may be national or local. A large number of firms supplying the national market may be much less competitive than the small number of firms supplying the local market. For, it is quite likely that the national market is divided among thousand sellers, so that each seller has the status of a monopolist in his own area.

Thirdly, the most serious defect of concentration ratio as an index of monopoly power is that it does not reflect the competition from other industries. The degree of competition is measured by the elasticity of substitution between the products of different industries. The elasticity of substitution may be different under different classification of industries. Therefore, an industry with concentration ratio under a classification of industries may have a very low elasticity of substitution and hence a high degree of monopoly. But, if classification of industries is altered, the same industry with a high concentration ratio may have a very low elasticity of substitution, and hence may show a low degree of monopoly.

Excess Profitability Criterion J.S. Bain and, following him, many other economists have used *excess profit* as a measure of monopoly power. If profit rate of a firm continues to remain sufficiently higher than all opportunity costs required to remain in the industry, it implies that neither competition among the sellers nor the entry of new firms prevents the firm from making a pure or monopoly profit. While calculating the excess profit, the opportunity cost of owner's capital and margin for the risk must be deducted from the actual profit made by the firm. Assuming no risk, the degree of monopoly may be obtained by calculating the divergence between the opportunity costs (O) and the actual profit (P) as $(P - O)/P$. If $[(P - O)/P] = O$, there exists no monopoly, and if $[(P - O)/P] > 0$, there is monopoly. The higher the value of $(P - O)/P$, the greater the degree of monopoly.

Lerner's Index of Monopoly Power Another measure of degree of monopoly based on excess profitability has been suggested by A.P. Lerner.[22] According to Lerner, for a competitive firm, equilibrium price equals marginal cost but for a monopoly price exceeds MC. Therefore, a logical measure of monopoly power is ratio of $P - MC$ to P, where P is equilibrium price. Thus, the degree of monopoly power (M^P) may be measured as

$$M^P = \frac{P - MC}{P}$$

where P = price, MC = marginal cost.

Since for a profit maximizing firm, $MR = MC$, Lerner's measure of monopoly power may also be expressed as,

$$M^P = \frac{P - MR}{P}$$

Since $P/(P - MR) = e$ (elasticity), $(P - MR)/P = 1/e$. It means that $M^{P\prime}$ equals the reciprocal of elasticity. Thus, Lerner's measure of monopoly power may also be expressed as $M^P = 1/e$. It may thus be inferred that lower the elasticity, the greater the degree of monopoly, and vice versa. According to Lerner's formula, monopoly power may exist even if firm's $AR = AC$ and it earns only normal profit.

Lerner's formula of measuring the degree of monopoly power is considered to be theoretical most sound. Nevertheless, it has been criticized on the following grounds.

First, it is suggested that any formula devised to measure degree of monopoly power should bring out the difference between the monopoly output and competitive output or the 'ideal' output under the optimum allocation of resources. The divergence between *P and MC used in Lerner's formula does not indicate the divergence between the monopoly and the* 'ideal' output. 'This substitution of a price–cost discrepancy for a difference between actual and 'ideal' output is probably the greatest weakness of formula which is supposed to measure deviation from the optimum allocation of resources.'[23]

Secondly, price–cost discrepancy may arise for reasons other than monopoly, and price and cost may be equal or close to each other in spite of monopoly power. Under those conditions, Lerner's criterion does not give the measure of monopoly power.

Thirdly, since data on MC are hardly available, this formula is of little practical use.

Triffin's Cross-Elasticity Criterion Triffin's criterion seems to have been derived from the definition of monopoly itself—monopolist is a single seller of a product without close substitutes. According to Triffin's criterion, cross-elasticity is taken as the measure of degree of monopoly—the lower the cross-elasticity of the product of a firm, the greater the degree of its monopoly power. But, this criterion is based on the inter-relationships between the individual firms and indicates only the relative power of each firm. It does not furnish a single index of monopoly power.

APPENDIX

The Third-Degree Price Discrimination: An Algebraic Solution

Price and output determination for two different markets under three-degree price discrimination has been explained and illustrated graphically in Section 3.9 of this chapter. Here, we present an algebraic solution to the problem of determination of equilibrium price and output for different markets by a monopoly firm.

Let us suppose that a monopoly firm has to sell its product in two markets, A and B, both having a different demand function as given below.

$$\text{Market A: } Q_a = 16 - 0.5P_a \qquad \text{(A.1)}$$

and

$$\text{Market B: } Q_b = 22 - P_b \tag{A.2}$$

From these demand functions can be derived the price functions for the two markets to be used in their *TR*-function. The derived price factions are given as follows.

$$\text{Market A: } P_a = 32 - 2Q_a \tag{A.3}$$

$$\text{Market A } P_b = 22 - Q_b \tag{A.4}$$

Suppose also that the firm's total cost function (*TC*) is given as

$$TC = 10 + 2Q + Q^2 \tag{A.5}$$

The problem is how to determine the most profitable output and how to allocate the output between the two markets, so that profit in each market is maximized. Profit (π) is maximum where

$$\pi = TR - TC \text{ is maximum} \tag{A.6}$$

In our example, *TC*-function is known, but *TR*-function is not. So we need to first find the *TR*-function. For a price discriminating monopoly, total revenue (*TR*) equals the sum of revenue from the two markets. That is,

$$TR = P_a \cdot Q_a + P_b \cdot Q_b \tag{A.7}$$

By substituting Eqs. (A.3) and (A.4) for P_a and P_b, respectively, in Eq. (A.7), we get

$$\begin{aligned} TR &= (32 - 2Q_a)\, Q_a + (22 - Q_b)Q_b \\ &= 32Q_2 - 2Q_a^2 + 22Q_b - Q_b^2 \end{aligned} \tag{A.8}$$

Now total profit (π) function can be obtained by substituting Eqs. (A.5) and (A.8) for *TC* and *TR*, respectively, in Eq. (A.6). Thus, we get the profit function as

$$\begin{aligned} \pi &= 32Q_a - 2Q_a^2 + 22Q_b - Q_b^2 - (10 + 2Q + Q^2) \\ &= 32Q_a - 2Q_a^2 + 22Q_b - Q_b^2 - 10 - 2Q_a - Q^2 \end{aligned} \tag{A.9}$$

For profit to be maximum, *Q* in Eq. (A.9) must be equal to profit maximizing sales in markets *A* and *B*. That is,

$$Q = Q_a + Q_b$$

By substituting, $Q_a + Q_b$ for Q in Eq. (A3) we get

$$\begin{aligned} \pi &= 32Q_a - 2Q_a^2 + 22Q_b - Q_b^2 - 10 - 2\,(Q_a + Q_b) - (Q_a + Q_b)^2 \\ &= 32Q_a - 2Q_a^2 - 22Q_b - Q^2 - 10 - 2Q_a - 2Q_b - Q_a^2 - 2Q_aQ_b - Q_b^2 \\ &= 30Q_a + 20Q_b - 3Q_b - 2Q_b^2 - 2Q_aQ_b, - 10 \end{aligned} \tag{A.10}$$

Equation (A.10) represents the total profit function. A necessary condition for π to be maximum is that marginal change in profit must be equal to zero. It implies, therefore, that for total profit to be maximum, marginal change in profit in both the markets must equal zero. The marginal change in profits in markets *A* and *B* can be expressed in terms of first derivative of the total profit-function with respect to Q_a and Q_b. Thus, marginal profit in market *A* can be expressed as

$$\frac{\partial \pi}{\partial Q_a} = 30 - 6Q_a - 2Q_b \tag{A.11}$$

and for market *B*, as

$$\frac{\partial \pi}{\partial Q_b} = 20 - 4Q_b - 2Q_a = 0 \tag{A.12}$$

The profit maximizing condition for markets A and B can be restated as follows. For profit to be maximum in market *A*,

$$30 - 6Q_a - 2Q_b = 0 \tag{A.13}$$

and in market *B*,

$$20 - 4Q_b - 2Q_a = 0 \tag{A.14}$$

We have now two simultaneous equations—Eqs (A.13) and (A.14) with two unknowns (Q_a and Q_b)—which can be solved for Q_a and Q_b as follows.

$$30 - 6Q_a - 2Q_b = 0 \ (1)$$

$$20 - 2Q_a - 4Q_b = 0 \ (2)$$

To solve for Q_b, multiply Eq. (2) by 3 and subtract from Eq. (1).

$$\begin{array}{r} 30 - 6Q_a - 2Q_b = 0 \\ 60 - 6Q_a - 12Q_b = 0 \\ - \quad + \quad + \quad \\ \hline -30 \qquad + 10Q_b = 0 \\ \hline 10Q_b = 0 \\ Q_b = 3 \end{array}$$

The value of Q_a can now be obtained by substituting 3 for Q_b in equation (1) or (2). Thus,

$$30 - 6Q_a - 2(3) = 0$$

$$-6Q_a = -24$$

$$Q_a = 4$$

To conclude, the monopoly firm maximizes its total profit by selling 4 units in market *A* and 3 units in market *B*.

Price Determination. The profit maximizing prices can now be obtained by substituting Q_a and Q_b with their estimated values (4 and 3, respectively) in price functions (A.3) and (A.4), respectively. The price for market A can be obtained as

$$\begin{aligned} P_a &= 32 - 2Q_a \\ &= 32 - 2(4) \\ &= 24 \end{aligned}$$

and price for market B as

$$\begin{aligned} P_b &= 22 - Q_b \\ &= 22 - 3 \\ &= 19 \end{aligned}$$

Thus, in market A, price = Rs 24 and in market B, price = Rs 19.

Profit Determination. Now that prices and sales for the two markets arc known, total profit can be obtained by substituting numerical values for Q_a and Q_b in profit function (A.10) reproduced below.

$$\pi = 30Q_a + 20Q_b - 3Q_a^2 - 2Q_b^2 - 2Q_aQ_b - 10$$

By substituting 4 for Q_a and 3 for Q_b, we get

$$\begin{aligned} \pi &= 30(4) + 20(3) - 3(4)(4) - 2(3)(3) - 2(4)(3) - 10 \\ &= 120 + 60 - 48 - 18 - 24 - 10 \\ &= 80 \end{aligned}$$

Given the revenue and cost functions, the total profit is worked out at Rs 80. This profit satisfies the conditions for profit maximization.

REVIEW QUESTIONS AND EXERCISES

1. What is monopoly? How does existence of a close substitute affect the monopoly power? What are the factors that create conditions for the emergence and survival of a monopoly?
2. Are the revenue and cost curves under monopoly different from those under perfect competition? Illustrate and explain the difference between *AR* and *MR* curves faced by monopoly and a competitive firm.
3. Write a note on the relationship between average revenue and marginal revenue under (i) perfect competition and (ii) monopoly.
4. Explain the equilibrium of a monopoly firm in the short run by using short run *AC*, *MC*, *AR* and *MR* curves. Why is monopoly price always higher than the competitive price?
5. A monopoly firm may earn normal or abnormal profits or may even incur losses in the short run. Do you agree with this statement? Give reasons for your answer.
6. Will a monopolist remain in business in the short run if it is just covering its average variable costs? Explain with the help of a diagram.

7. Suppose demand function for a monopoly product is given as $Q = 500 - 0.5P$ and cost function is given as $C = 100 + 40\ Q + Q^2$. Find the equilibrium level of price and output for the monopoly firm.
8. 'There is no supply curve of a monopoly firm'. Do you agree with this statement? Give reasons.
9. Compare monopoly and perfect competition with regard to the following: (i) price, (ii) output, (iii) welfare cost and (iv) relationship between *MC* and price.
10. Show the difference between the long-run equilibrium of a competitive firm and the long-run equilibrium of a monopoly firm with regard to the following: (i) price, (ii) profits and (iii) use of capacity.
11. What is meant by 'deadweight loss'? How is 'deadweight loss' measured? Why does it arise only under monopoly and not under perfect competition?
12. What is price discrimination? Explain and distinguish between the first, second and the third degrees of price discrimination. Which one makes a general case for price discrimination and why?
13. What is a discriminating monopoly? What are the conditions which force the monopolist in practicing price discrimination? State the conditions under which price discrimination is possible and profitable as well.
14. Suppose a monopolist faces two markets, *A* and *B*, with their respective demand functions given as $Q_A = 500 - 0.5P$ and $Q_B = 980 - 2P$. Find the equilibrium price and output sales for each market.
15. What are the necessary conditions of price discrimination under monopoly? Show how a profit-maximizing discriminating monopolist allocates his output between two markets and charge different prices?
16. Show graphically the determination of profit maximizing equilibrium of discriminating monopolist. Is price discrimination socially desirable?
17. (a) Explain how profit maximization by a monopoly firm reduces public welfare vis-à-vis a competitive firm.
    (b) Why is price discrimination under monopoly considered to be economically desirable?
18. Suppose a simple monopolist is in equilibrium. At the point of equilibrium, the coefficient of price elasticity is – 2 and marginal cost is Rs 4.0. Calculate monopoly's equilibrium price. How will this price be affected by an increase in the fixed cost of the monopolist?
19. Calculate the ratio of prices charged by a discriminating monopolist in two markets, *A* and *B*, having price-elasticities of demand as – 0.5 and –1.5, respectively.
20. (a) Show the circumstances under which a per unit tax imposed on a monopolist raises the price by more than the tax.
    (b) Show that with a given supply curve and a given equilibrium point, the lower the elasticity of the demand curve, the greater the burden of a per unit tax on the consumer.
21. (a) A monopolist is always able to shift the entire excise tax burden on to the consumers. Do you agree with this statement? Give reasons.
    (b) Explain why does a lump-sum tax does not affect monopoly equilibrium.
22. How does a subsidy provided by the government to a monopoly affect its equilibrium price and output? Does a monopolist pass the entire benefits of subsidy to the consumers? Illustrate your answer graphically.

23. By using a suitable diagram, compare the effects of a unit subsidy on the equilibrium output and price of a monopolist and a competitive firm.
24. Why should the government control a monopoly price? Under what conditions is monopoly economically desirable? What are the criteria for price control?
25. What is meant by monopoly power? What are the methods of measuring the degree of monopoly power?
26. Write notes on the following criteria of monopoly power.
    (a) Concentration ratio,
    (b) Excess profitability criterion, and
    (c) Cross-elasticity criterion.
27. Which of the following statements are correct?
    (a) A monopolist can charge any price to maximize profits.
    (b) A monopoly firm can fix its price anywhere along the demand curve.
    (c) If monopoly's $MC = 0$, it fixes its price where $e = 0$.
    (d) The slope of monopoly's MR curve is twice that of AR curve.
    (e) A monopolist is in equilibrium where $MC = MR$.
    (f) A necessary condition for monopoly's long-run equilibrium is $AC = AR = MC = MR$.
    (g) A monopolist produces always less than its optimum capacity.
    (h) There is no unique relationship between price and supply under monopoly.
    (i) Equilibrium price of a monopolist is always higher than that of a competitive firm.
    (j) Price discrimination is possible only when demand curves are identical in two markets.
    (k) A monopoly firm can always pass the entire tax on to the consumers.

[**Ans.** (d) (e) (h) (i)]

28. Suppose market demand function for monopoly firm is given by = 100 – 5*P*. Find the following.
    (a) Price function or reverse demand function for the monopolist;
    (b) *AR*-function of the monopolist;
    (c) *MR*-function of the monopolist;
    (d) *TR-function* of the monopolist.
29. Suppose a monopoly firm sells it product in two different markets with their respective demand functions given as follows.

$$Q_1 = 500 - P_1,$$
$$Q_2 = 300 - P_2$$

Firm's total cost function is given as

$$TC = 50000 + 100Q$$

Find:

(a) profit maximizing output,
(b) profit maximizing price,
(c) prices for the two markets, and
(d) total profit at equilibrium.

30. Suppose demand function and total cost function for a monopoly firm are given as follows.

$$\text{Demand function: } Q = 101.25 - 0.25P$$

and

$$TC\text{-function: } TC = 40 + 5Q + Q^2$$

Find:

(a) profit maximizing output,
(b) profit maximizing price,
(c) total revenue function, and
(d) average revenue function.

31. Suppose demand function for a monopolist is given as $Q = 100 - 5P$ and its MC has been estimated as $MC = 10$. Find (a) TR-function; (b) MR-function and (c) profit maximizing output.

ENDNOTES

1. A close substitute is one whose cross-elasticity is positive and close to 1 or even greater than 1.
2. C.E. Ferguson, *Microeconomic Theory*, 2nd edn, *op. cit.*, p. 286.
3. A price function can be derived directly from the demand function.
4. The TR-function can be derived by using the price function as follows. Suppose demand function for the monopoly firm is given as

$$Q = a - bP$$

from the demand function, price function can be derived as

$$P = a/b - Q/b$$

Since $TR = P \cdot Q$, by substituting price function for P in the demand function, we get TR as

$$TR = (a/b - Q/b)\,Q = (aQ - Q^2)/b$$

Price function has been derived from the demand function as follows. Given the demand function as

$$Q = 100 - 0.2P,$$

price function can the expressed as

$$0.2P = 100 - Q$$

$$P = \frac{100 - Q}{0.2} = 500 - 5Q.$$

5. Pigou, A.C. (1949), *The Economics of Welfare*, p. 279.
6. John Robinson calls it 'perfect discrimination' from a monopolist point of view.

7. Readers interested in algebraic treatment of third-degree price discrimination are referred to the appendix to this chapter.
8. See Lipsey, R.G. *An Introduction to Positive Economics, op. cit.*, 7th edn, pp. 227–228.
9. Lipsey, R.G, *ibid.*
10. Harberger, A.C. 'Monopoly and Resource Allocation', *American Economic Review*, 44 (May 2954).
11. Samuelson, P.A. (1955), *Economics*, 15th edn, (New york, NY: Macmillan), p. 175.
12. Stigler, G.J. (1956), 'The Statistics of Monopoly and Merger', *Journal of Polymer*, 64 (February).
13. Kamerschen, David R. (1966), "An Estimation of the 'Welfare Losses' from the Monopoly in the American Economy", *Wester: Economic Journal*, 4 (Summer).
14. Musgrave, R.A. and P.B. Musgrave (1989), *Public Finance in Theory and Practice*, 5th edn, (New York, NY: McGraw-Hill International), p. 265.
15. Hunter, Alex (1970), *Measurement of Monopoly Power in Monopoly and Competition* (London: Penguin Books), p. 92.
16. Maclup, Fritz (1952), *The Political Economic of Monopoly* (Baltimore, MD: The Johns Hopkins Press), p. 470.
17. Hunter, A., *op., cit.*, p. 101.
18. Ibid.
19. Maclup, Fritz, *op. cit.*, p. 477.
20. Hunter, A., *op. cit.*, p. 102
21. Lerner, A.P. (1934), 'The Concept of Monopoly and the Measure of Monopoly Power', *Review of Economic Studies*, June, 1934.
22. Fritz Machlup, *op. cit.*, p. 515.

FURTHER READINGS

Bain, J.S. (1953), *Pricing Distribution and Employment* (New York: Holt Rhine), Chapters 5 and 9.

Basankso, D.A. and Braeutigam, R.R. (2002), *Microeconomies: An Integrated Approach* (New York: John Wiley & Sons, Inc.), Chapters 11 and 12.

Blaug, M. (1970), *Economic Theory in Retrospect* (Homewood, IL: Richard D. Irwin).

Browning, K.E. and Browning, J.M. (1986), *Microeconomics: Theory and Applications* (New Delhi: Kalyani Publishers), 2nd Edn., Chapters 11 and 12.

Herberger, A.C. (1954), 'Monopoly and Resource Allocation', *American Economics Review.*

Koutsoyiannis, A. (1979), *Modern Microeconomics* (London: Macmillan), Chapters 6 and 7.

Lerner, A.P. (1943), 'The Concept of Monopoly and Measurement of Monopoly Power', *Review of Economic Studies*, 157–175.

Marshall, A. (1920), *Principles of Economics* (London: Macmillan), 8th Edn., Book V, Chapter 14.

Perloff, J.M. (2001), *Microeconomics*, (New York, NY: Addison Wesley), 2nd Edn., Chapters 11 and 12.

Pigou, A.C. (1920), *The Economics of Welfare* (London: Macmillan).

Pindyck, R.S. and D.L. Rubinfeld (2001), *Microeconomics* (London: Prentice Hall International), 5th Edn., Chapters 10 and 11.

Robinson, J. (1933), *The Economics of Imperfect Competition* (London: Macmillan), Chapters 2, 3, 15 and 16.

Chapter 4

Price and Output Determination Under Monopolistic Competition

CHAPTER OBJECTIVES

The objective of this chapter is to explain the theory of price and output determination under the condition of monopolistic competition among the firms. This chapter understand you helps the following aspects:

- Meaning and characteristics of monopolistic competition and how it differs from perfect competition;
- Chamberlin's theory of price and output determination under monopolistic competition;
- What is the nature of competition among the firms under monopolistic competition;
- How firms under monopolistic competition determine the price and output of their product;
- How firm's equilibrium is affected when firms incur *selling costs*; and
- How valid is Chamberlin's theory of price and output determination under monopolistic competition.

INTRODUCTION

In two preceding chapters, we have discussed the theory of price and output determination under perfect competition and monopoly. The "theories of perfect competition and monopoly constituted the 'classical' microeconomic theory from Marshall to Knight"[1] and dominated the theory of value till the early 1920s. After the WW-I, however, there was rapid economic growth—generally in war-affected countries—accompanied by a drastic change in market structure. The change in market structure was reflected by the disappearance of perfect competition and monopolies and emergence of a different market structure dominated by *monopolistic competition*. With this kind of change in market structure, the relevance of the pricing theories based on perfect competition and monopoly declined gradually. Therefore, in the late 1920s and the early 1930s, economists expressed their dissatisfaction with perfect competition and pure monopoly models, as these models did not represent the real world business behaviour that prevailed at that time. In reality, there were very few monopolies because there were very few commodities for which there were no close substitutes, and there were very few perfectly competitive markets because there were very few homogeneous products. In today's business world, perfect competition and monopoly represent only two extreme and uncommon market structures. Such as it is, theories of perfect competition and monopoly could be applied to only two small segments of the markets at two opposite extremes—not to the major part of the market structure.

Piero Shraffa[2] was one of the first to point out the limitations of perfect competition and pure monopoly models. He was followed by Hotelling[3] and Zeuthen[4] who claimed that (i) neither perfect competition nor monopoly represents the real business world and (ii) most common markets fall between the perfect competition and the monopoly. It was in this background that Edward H. Chamberlin[5] of Harvard University made a path-breaking contribution to the theory of value in 1933. Another important contribution to the theory of value, as an alternative to Chamberlin's theory, was made by Joan Robinson[6] of the Cambridge University—six months later the same year. It is said that Chamberlin spent a lot of time and labour in pointing out the difference between his own and Joan Robinson's work so much so that Joan Robinson expressed her regret for Chamberlin's hard work—'I'm sorry I ruined his life.'[7] Chamberlin's theory is, however, considered to be superior for its, at least, two significant contributions: (i) he introduced firms' practice of 'product differentiation' and its effect on the demand curve and the theory of pricing and (ii) he included selling cost in his analysis as an element of competition and its effect on firm's cost curves and equilibrium.

In this chapter, we will explain the basic elements of the theory of price and output determination as expounded by Chamberlin. Let us begin by looking at analytical framework used by Chamberlin in formulating his theory.

MONOPOLISTIC COMPETITION: DEFINITION AND CHARACTERISTICS

Definition of Monopolistic Competition

By definition, monopolistic competition refers to a market structure in which a large number of sellers sell differentiated products, which are close substitutes for one another. Incidentally, a close substitute is one whose cross-elasticity is close to unity or greater. Monopolistic competition combines the basic elements of both perfect competition and monopoly.

The *element of monopoly* in monopolistic competition arises from the fact that each firm has an absolute right to produce and sell a *branded* or *patented* product. Other firms are prevented by laws from producing and selling a branded product of other firms. This gives a firm *monopoly power* over production, pricing and sale of its own-banded product. For example, consider toilet soap industry. There are a number of brand names available in the market, e.g., Lux, Liril, Palmolive, Fairglow, Pears, Fa, Rexona, Lifebuoy, Carmel, Godrej, Cinthol, Ponds, Dove, Dettol and so on. Each of these branded toilet soaps is produced and sold by a company having monopoly power over the product. Similarly, Maruti Udyog Limited has monopoly power for producing and selling cars under the brand name Maruti. No other car manufacturing company can produce and sell cars under this brand name. So is the case with all other car manufacturing companies.

The *element of competition* comes from the fact that each branded product has several close substitutes and firms selling branded products of the same generic category have to compete for the market share. Considering again our example of toilet soaps,, all the companies producing and selling these branded toilet soaps are in intensive competition for capturing the largest possible market share. One index of the competition between them is the amount that they spend advertising their product. These features of the toilet soap industry make it monopolistically competitive. Toothpaste industry with a number of branded product names (e.g. Binaca, Colgate, Close-up, Pepsodent, Forhans, Cibaca, Neem, Meswak, Signal, Promise, Prestige and so on) is another example of monopolistic competition. So is the case with major industrial products in India, e.g., electrical tubes and bulbs, TV sets, refrigerators, air conditioners, personal computers, textile goods, tea, coffee, cigarettes, soft drinks, cold creams, shampoos, detergents, shaving blades, shaving cream, hair oils, hair dyes, shoes, wrist watches, steel, cement, mobile phones and so on.

Some of the industries looking monopolistically competitive may be *oligopolistic* in which there are only a few sellers selling differentiated or homogenous products. The question as to what makes a market monopolistically competitive or oligopolistic will be taken up in the next chapter which deals with *oligopoly markets*. Let us now know look at the general characteristics of monopolistic competitions.

Characteristics of Monopolistic Competition

As mentioned earlier, monopolistic competition combines the elements of both perfect competition and monopoly power. Therefore, the main characteristics of monopolistic competition are the blend of perfect competition and monopoly. The main features of monopolistic competition *vis-à-vis* perfect competition and monopoly are described below.

1. ***Product Differentiation***. Product differentiation is the basis of and the main distinctive characteristic of monopolistic competition that distinguishes it from monopoly and perfect competition. In case of monopoly, there is only one product and only one seller of the product, and under perfect competition, a large number of sellers sell *homogeneous product*. Under monopolistic competition, the firms differentiate their products from one another in respect of their shape, size, colour, design, minor qualitative differences, efficiency in use, some extra facility, packaging, after-sale-service, guarantee and warrantee and so on. Product differentiation may be real or fanciful and spurious.[8] The basic purpose of product differentiation is to make the consumers believe that a product is different from others and, thereby, to create brand loyalty of the consumers. Product differentiation affects firm's demand curve in a significant way.
2. ***Large Number of Sellers***. Under monopolistic competition, the number of sellers is *large*. How large? It is difficult to specify number of firms: it may be 10, 20 or more depending on the size of the market. However, the question 'how large' can be answered in conceptual terms with reference to perfect competition. Under perfect competition, the number of sellers is so large that a firm becomes a *price taker*. In contrast, under monopolistic competition, the number of firms is only so large that a firm retains its power to be a *price maker*. The monopolistically competitive firms have the power to set the price of their product depending on the objective of the firm.
3. ***Free Entry and Free Exit***. As in case of perfect competition, there is no barrier on the entry of new firms and exit of old ones from the industry. New firms are free to enter the monopolistically competitive industry and to quit at will. Entry of new firms reduces the market share of the existing ones and exit of firms does the opposite. These consequences of free entry and

free exit lead to intensive competition among the firms for retaining as well as increasing their market share.

4. ***Selling Costs.*** Unlike firms under perfect competition and monopolies, firms under monopolistic competition make heavy expenditure on advertisement and other sales promotion schemes for their product. This is an important feature that distinguishes monopolistic competition from perfect competition and monopoly. *Selling costs* include all the expenditure on advertisement, sales promotion schemes and salaries of sales personnel. Selling costs and their effect of firm's equilibrium will be discussed below in detail.
5. ***Downward Sloping Demand Curve.*** As in case of monopoly, a monopolistically competitive firm faces a downward sloping demand curve. The reason is that a monopolistically competitive firm can, by exercising its monopoly power, increase its price and still retain some buyers with brand loyalty and can increase the demand for its product by decreasing the price because of a relatively higher cross-elasticity of the competitive product.

CHAMBERLIN'S THEORY OF MONOPOLISTIC COMPETITION

Basic Elements of Chamberlin's Theory

In the rest of this chapter, we will be concerned with Chamberlin's theory of monopolistic competition. For a better comprehension of his theory, it is essential to understand the implications of the following three basic elements of monopolistic competition as defined by Chamberlin.

1. Product differentiation and firm's perceived demand curve;
2. Selling costs and firm's cost structure and
3. Product differentiation and the concept of industry.

These aspects of monopolistic competition are briefly discussed below.

Product Differentiation and Firm's Perceived Demand Curve

Product differentiation is the basis of competition among the monopolistically competitive firms. Chamberlin has defined *product differentiation* in the following words:

A general class of product is differentiated if any significant basis exists for distinguishing the goods (or services) of one seller from those of others. Such a basis may be real or fancied, as long as it is of any importance to buyers, and leads to a preference for one variety of product over another. Differentiation may be based upon certain characteristics of the product itself, such as exclusive patented features, trademarks, trade names, peculiarities of the package or container, if any, of singularity in quality, design, colour or style. It may also exist with respect to the conditions surrounding its sales. In retail trade, these conditions include such factors as the convenience of the seller's location, the general tone or character of his establishment, his way of doing business, his reputation for fair dealing, courtesy, efficiency and all the personal links, which attach his customers either to himself or to those employed by him.[9]

Thus, the basic purpose of product differentiation is to make customers distinguish the product of a firm from those of the others in the industry and to develop a preference or band loyalty. Once brand loyalty is developed, it alters the course of the demand curve for the product. In the ultimate analysis, *product differentiation aims at changing the slope and position of the demand curve for the product and converting it from a horizontal demand line (as under perfect competition) to a downward sloping demand curve.* The downward sloping demand curve gives the firm power to use its discretion in fixing the price of its product.

The Preview Demand Curve Under monopolistic competition with product differentiation, each firm perceives that the demand curve for its own product is more elastic than that of the rival firms. This aspect is illustrated in Figure 4.1. Suppose industry's demand curve (i.e. market demand curve) is given by the curve D_M. If industry demand is proportionately divided between the firms, each firm is supposed to have a demand curve shown by D_F.

However, firms under monopolistic competition do not take D_F to be the demand curve for their individual product. Each firm perceives that the demand curve for its own product is *more elastic* than that of the other firms. Its *perceived demand curve* is shown by the demand curve D_P. Note that the *perceived demand curve*, D_P, is more elastic than the demand curve D_F. The basis of the perceived demand curve is the firm's belief that if it changes the price of its own product, it will go unnoticed by the other firms and they will not react to change the price of their products. The reason for this assumption is the firm's belief that the number of firms is so large that price changes made by a single firm is very much likely to go unnoticed by the rival firms.

The concept and derivation of the *perceived demand curve* can be explained as follows. Given the industry demand curve D_M in Figure 4.1, if price for the industry (the 'product group') is given at OP_2, the demand for the industry as a whole will be OQ_1 and each firm will be selling an equal quantity, OQ_E. Given this price–quantity combination, an individual firm perceives that if it cuts down the price of its own product to OP_1, the other firms will not change their price, and then the demand for its product will increase by Q_EQ_P. The additional increase in the demand for its product is the result of cross-elasticity,

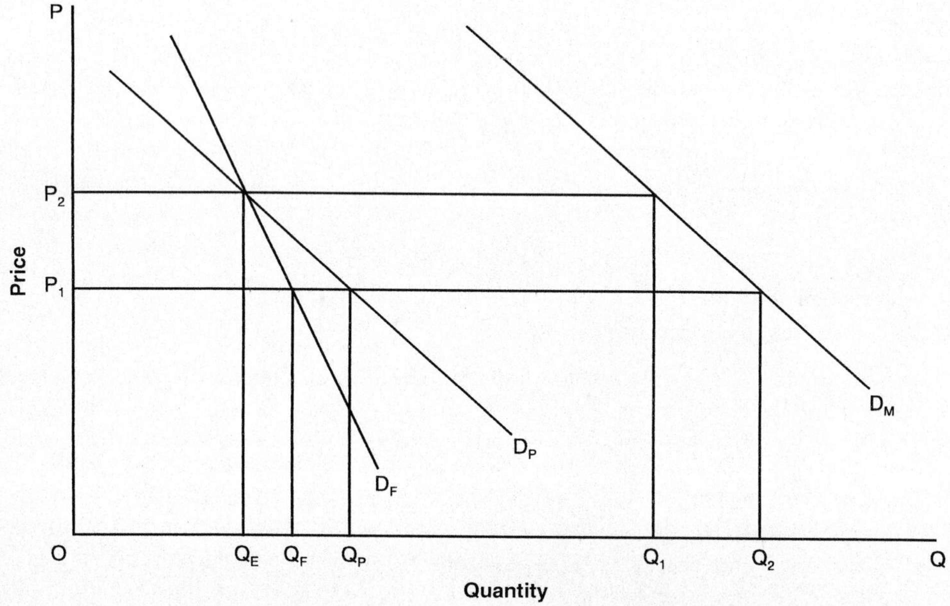

Figure 4.1 *Demand Curves for the Industry and the Firms*

i.e., when one firm decreases its substitute price and other firms do not, its substitute product becomes relatively cheaper. Since products of all the firms are close substitutes for one another, some customers will switch over from the constant-price products to the product which has a lower price. Similarly, if only one firm increases its price, it looses its customers to other firms. As a result, demand for its product decreases more than indicated by the demand curve D_F. This holds for all price changes and gives rise to a perceived demand curve D_P. The perceived demand curve plays a significant role in price and output determination in Chamberlin's theory of monopolistic competition with price competition. This aspect is discussed further in a subsequent section. Let us first look at another aspect of Chamberlin's theory, i.e., selling cost.

Selling Costs and Firm's Cost Structure

The selling cost incurred by the firms under monopolistic competition and its impact on their cost structure is another important aspect of Chamberlin's theory of monopolistic competition. Introduction of selling costs in the theory of price and output determination under monopolistic competition is another innovative contribution made by Chamberlin. He defines *selling costs* as 'costs incurred in order to alter the position or the slope of the demand curve for a product'.[10] Chamberlin's concept of selling costs is not exactly the same as advertisement cost:[11] it is advertisement cost plus. By Chamberlin's definition, selling costs include:

1. Cost of advertisement;
2. Expenditure on sales promotion schemes (including gifts and discounts to buyers);
3. Salary and commission paid to sales personnel;
4. Allowance to retailers for displays and
5. Cost of after-sale-services.

Also, Chamberlin distinguishes *selling costs* and *production cost* on the basis of their basic purpose and functions. According to Chamberlin, costs that are incurred to create a product or service of utility and making it available to the consumers are *production costs*. In Chamberlin's perception, production cost includes also the cost of transportation. The basic function of the production cost is to create a commodity and to make it available to the consumers. The selling costs, on the other hand, perform the following functions:

1. Informing potential buyers about the availability of the product;
2. Increasing demand for the product by attracting customers of the rival products and
3. Making the demand curve shift upward.

What is more important in price and output determination is the effect of selling costs on the total cost that figure in pricing decisions. In his model of monopolistic competition, Chamberlin assumes the traditional U-shaped cost curves—*AC*, *AVC* and *MC*—and also a U-shaped *average selling cost* (*ASC*) curve. *ASC* is defined as *SC*/*S* (where *SC* = *selling costs* and *S* = *sales*). The U-shaped *ASC* curve is illustrated in Figure 4.2.

As Figure 4.2 shows, the *ASC* first decreases until it reaches its minimum and then begins to increase. In the beginning, it is very high because a little selling cost (or advertisement cost) is not effective enough to promote sales. With increase in selling costs, however, sales increase at a rate higher than the rate of increase in selling costs. As a result, *ASC* decreases. The decrease in *ASC* is attributed to 'increasing

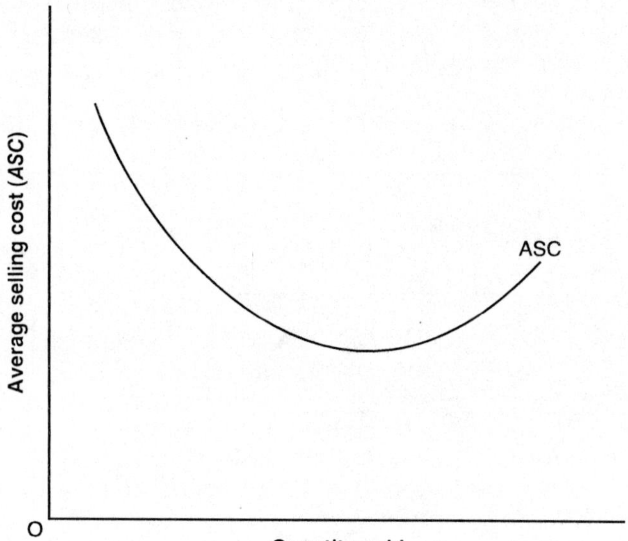

Figure 4.2 *The Average Selling Cost Curve*

returns' to advertising and *economies of scale* in advertisement cost.[12] It must, however, be noted that returns to selling cost are determined by the following factors:

1. ***Price of the product.*** A high price makes selling cost less effective;
2. ***Price of the substitute.*** A lower price of the substitutes makes selling cost less productive;
3. ***Buyers' income.*** Advertising a costly product in low-income society has no pay-off and
4. ***Buyers' loyalty to rival brands.*** The stronger the loyalty to rival brands, the lower the cross-elasticity and the less effective the selling cost.

However, even if all these factors are favourable, a stage is finally reached when returns to selling costs, especially to advertisement cost, tends to become constant. This is the stage of saturation. The stage of saturation may be marked by the size of the market and/or competitive advertisement by the rival firms. Increasing selling costs or advertisement cost at the stage of saturation tends to become less and less effective in attracting more buyers. Therefore, sales increase at a much lower rate than the increase in the selling costs. Consequently, *ASC* begins to increase and goes on increasing. This is how *ASC* gets its U-shape, as shown in Figure 4.2. The *ASC* curve is added to the *AC* curve in determining the profit-maximizing level of output and price. This aspect is discussed in the next section.

What is the Optimum Level of Advertising Cost? Given the nature of the *ASC* curve (in Figure 4.2), a question arises: What is the optimum level of advertising cost? The optimum level of advertising cost is determined by the objective of the firm—whether it is profit maximization, retaining market share or countervailing the advertisement by the rival firms. Optimization of advertising expenditure is illustrated in Figure 4.3 under the following assumptions.

1. Objective of the firm is to maximize its profit;
2. Price of the product is given;[13]

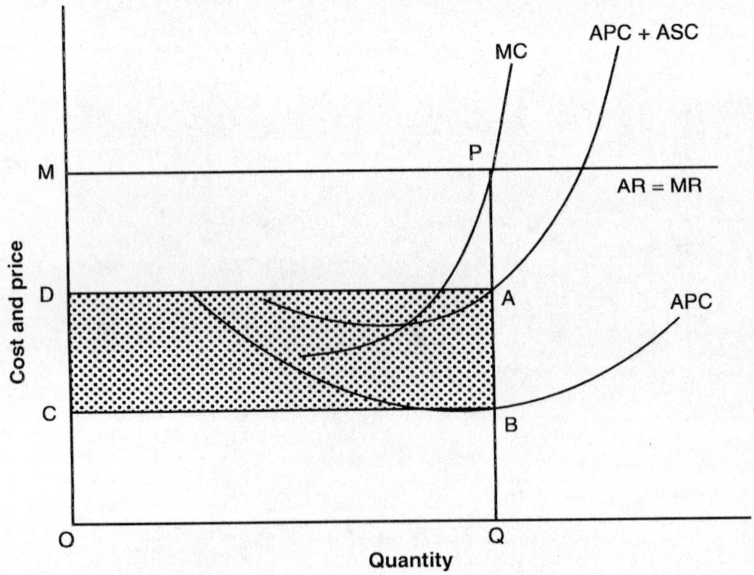

Figure 4.3 *Optimization of Selling Cost*

3. Average production cost (*APC*) and *MPC* curves are given and
4. Average selling cost (*ASC*) curve is also known.

Under these conditions, the optimum level of selling cost is determined where the firm's overall marginal cost (*MC*) including 'marginal cost of production' (*MCP*) and marginal cost of advertising (*MCA*) equals the price. Since price is given by assumptions, *price* = *AR* = *MR*. Thus, the condition for the optimum selling cost can be expressed as $MC = MPC + MAC = AR = MR$.

The determination of the optimum selling cost is illustrated in Figure 4.3. The price of the product is given at *OM* and firm's *APC* is shown by the curve *APC*. The firm's *APC* curve added vertically with *ASC* curve (not given in the figure) is shown by the curve labeled *APC* + *ASC*. The vertical distance between the *APC* and *APC* + *ASC* gives the measure of the *average selling cost* (*ASC*). For example, at output *OQ*, the *ASC* equals *AB*. Finally, firm's overall *MC* (associated with *APC* + *ASC*) is shown by the *MC* curve.

As Figure 4.3 shows, price line, $AR = MR$, and *MC* curve intersect at point *P* determining the equilibrium price at *OM*. An ordinate drawn from point *P* to the quantity axis determines the profit-maximizing output at *OQ*. Once profit-maximizing output is determined, the optimum level of all costs (given the cost curves) is automatically determined. It can be seen in Figure 4.3 that at profit-maximizing output *OQ*, price equals $OM = PQ = BQ + AB + AP$. Note that at output *OQ*, average selling cost (*ASC*) equals *AB*. That is, at the profit-maximizing level of output, average advertising cost equals *AB*. Therefore, *AB* is the *optimum average selling cost* (*ASC*). The total optimum selling cost or advertisement expenditure can be obtained by multiplying *ASC* with output *OQ*. That is, *total optimum advertisement expenditure* = $OQ \times AB$. Since $OQ = CB$, the total optimum selling cost can be written as $CB \times AB = DABC$, as shown by the shaded area.

Concept of Industry and Product Groups

Chamberlin pointed out also a conceptual problem in defining an industry under monopolistic competition. Recall that an industry under perfectly competitive conditions is defined as a group of firms producing a homogeneous product. But, this concept of industry cannot be applied to the cases where products are differentiated. Where products are differentiated—slightly or substantially—each firm is, in a sense, an industry in itself, exactly as a monopoly firm is an industry in itself. The heterogeneity of the products, therefore, causes a problem in analytical treatment of the industry. Problem arises because *industry demand curve under monopolistic competition is not the same as under perfect competition.* Since under perfect competition, product is homogeneous, demand curve for an industry can be obtained by adding individual demand curve of individuals firms. But, under monopolistic competition, product is made heterogeneous through product differentiation techniques and in case of heterogeneous products, the demand for individual products cannot be added to obtain market demand and supply curves.

For the reason given above, Chamberlin defines the monopolistically competitive industry as a 'group' of firms producing a 'closely related' commodity, called *product group.* The products of the 'group' must be *close, technological and economic substitutes.* The two products are *technological substitutes* for each other if they technically satisfy the same want. For example, different brands of soaps, cigarettes, toothpastes, automobiles, TV sets, etc. satisfy the same want. The two products are considered as *economic substitutes* for each other when they satisfy the same want and have *more* or *less* the same price. For example, all simple mobile phones of different brands are economic substitutes for one another. But simple mobile phones are not economic substitutes for mobile phone with camera and other facilities because their prices are widely different but they are technological substitutes.

Operationally, the *product group* may be defined as the group of firms whose products have between themselves high *price elasticity* and high *cross-elasticities.* This definition, although theoretically plausible, involves the problems of measuring cross-elasticities and of determining its degree that can make a commodity admissible to the group. Determining the product group, therefore, involves subjective judgment.

FIRM'S EQUILIBRIUM UNDER MONOPOLISTIC COMPETITION

Having described the analytical framework, we now proceed to discuss Chamberlin's theory of price and output determination under monopolistic competition and how firms in monopolistic competition find their equilibrium. Chamberlin prefaces his theory with a comparison of price and output choices under pure competition and monopoly and under monopolistic competition. He points out that under pure competition, firms selling homogeneous products are given a price at which they can sell any quantity they can. Advertising by the individual firm is of no consequence: it is rather a waste. On the other hand, a monopoly firm faces a downward sloping demand curve and it has the power of discretion in respect of determining the price and quantity to be sold. In general, a monopoly firm fixes a price that maximizes its total profit. Advertising by a pure monopoly is of little consequence. Under monopolistic competition, however, a firm can alter its sales prospects by the following *three methods*:

1. By changing the price of its product;
2. By changing 'the nature of the product' and
3. By incurring the advertisement outlays.

As regards to changing price, since a firm under monopolistic competition faces a downward sloping demand curve with elasticity less than infinity, it has the option to change the price. In regard to changing the nature of the product, a firm can do it by changing the quality of its product by making technical changes, by introducing a new design, by using superior material, by making a new style of packaging, by establishing a close link with buyers and so on. As regards the methods of sales promotion, a firm can increase its sales by prompt and courteous service, credit facilities and by enhancing expenditure on advertisement. While making changes in price and output is a short-run phenomenon, changing the quality of the product and attracting larger number of buyers are long-run phenomena. Therefore, Chamberlin's theory of price and output determination is discussed under *short-* and *long-run* conditions. In what follows, we will discuss Chamberlin's theory of price and output determination under the short- and long-run conditions. Let us begin by looking at the *assumptions*, Chamberlin made to develop his theory of monopolistic competition.

Assumptions

Chamberlin has made the following *explicit* and *implicit* assumptions to develop his theory of monopolistic competition.

1. There are a large number of firms selling slightly differentiated products, which are close substitutes for one another.
2. The number of firms in a product group is so large that their activities, especially, manoeuvring of price and output, go unnoticed by the rival firms.
3. Demand and cost curves for all the products and for all the firms of the group are uniform, i.e., firms face identical demand (including *perceived* one) and cost curves.
4. Consumer's preferences are evenly distributed among the different products and product differentiations are not such that they make a difference in cost.[14]

The last two assumptions are called rather 'heroic' in the sense that these are unrealistic. However, it can be assumed, for theoretical convenience, that the differences, wherever they are, are not significant enough to influence the price and output decisions of the rival firms. Given the assumptions, let us discuss first the *short-run equilibrium of the firm*. Firm's *long-run equilibrium* will be discussed in the next section.

Short-run Equilibrium of the Firm

The *short-run equilibrium* of the firm under monopolistic competition is illustrated in Figures 4.4 and 4.5. Figure 4.4 illustrates how firms in the state of disequilibrium adjust their price and output to move to the state of equilibrium. Figure 4.5 presents the final position of the firm's equilibrium and also the determination of equilibrium prices and output.

In Figure 4.4, the firm's perceived and proportional market demand curves are given by the curves D_p and D_H, respectively. The MR_p curve shows their *marginal revenue* curve corresponding to their perceived demand curve (D_p) and their *marginal cost curve* is shown by the curve *MC*. Now suppose that in the short-run market price is given at OP_3 determined by the firms themselves or by 'custom',[15] and all the firms are at point *A*, each one selling output OQ_1. Incidentally, OQ_1 equals D_M/n (where D_M is the total market demand for the industry as a whole and *n* is the number of firms.

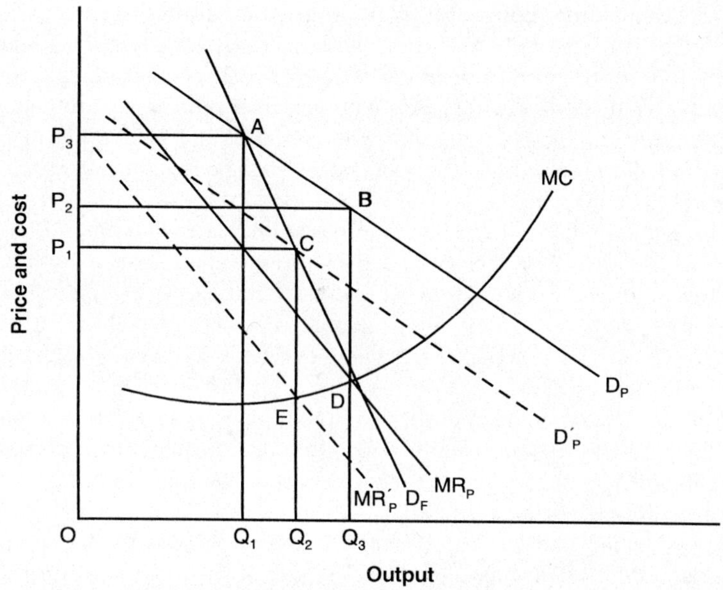

Figure 4.4 *Price and Output Adjustments in the Short-run*

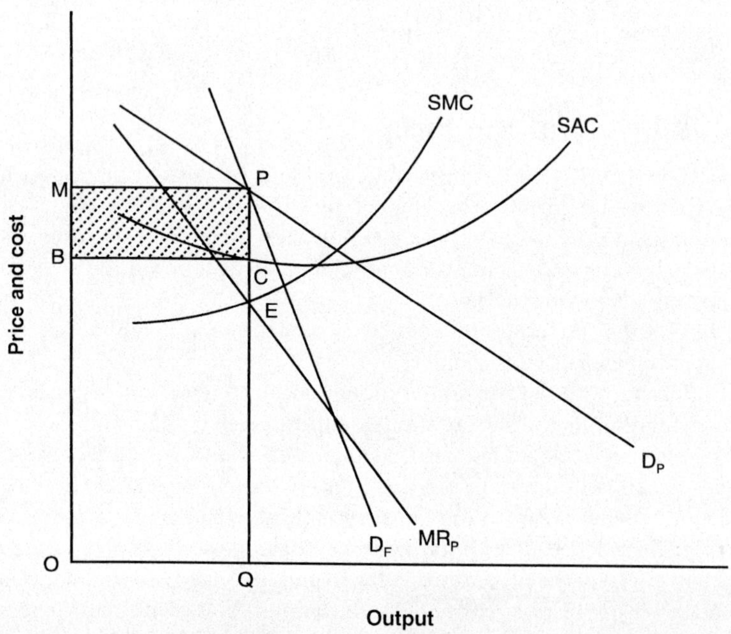

Figure 4.5 *Short-run Equilibrium of the Firm Under Monopolistic Competition*

Under monopolist competition, however, this position is *not* stable because each firm, given its perceived demand curve (D_p), expects to sell more by cutting down the price of its product. Therefore, they cut down their price in anticipation of increase in their sales. They continue to cut down their price until price and output reach the level at which they maximize their profits. The profit-maximizing quantity and price is determined in Figure 4.4 at point *D*, the point of intersection between firms' *MC* and *MR* (perceived) curves. Point *D* determines the profit-maximizing output at OQ_3 and price at OP_2. That is, each firm produces OQ_3, and charges price at OP_2.

It can be seen in Figure 4.4 that total production based on perceived demand has increased very heavily—by ($Q_1Q_3 \times n$). The firms find that there is excess production even at a lower price. In order to get rid of their surplus production, the firms begin to cut down their price. As a result, their perceived demand curve (D_p) shifts downward as shown by the dashed perceived demand curve (D'_p). This shift continues until the firms reach the level of final demand curve (D'_p) and they reach their final equilibrium through point *E* in Figure 4.4.

The *final short-run equilibrium* position of the firm under monopolistic competition is illustrated in Figure 4.5. In this figure, the firm's perceived demand curve and the corresponding marginal revenue curve are shown by D_p and MR_p curves, respectively, its short-run average and marginal cost curves are shown by the *SAC* and *SMC* curves, respectively.

As Figure 4.5 shows, the *MR* and *MC* curves intersect at point *E* determining the profit-maximizing output at *OQ* and price at *M*. Each firm produces *OQ* and sells at price *PQ*. At this price and output, the firms maximize their short-run profit. The firms are, therefore, in short-run equilibrium at point *E*. Their maximum pure profit equals $BC \times PC = MPCB$ as shown by the shaded area. Any other price and output will reduce their total profit. Therefore, firms have no incentive to change their price and output. Note that the final price is determined at the point of intersection between D_p and D_F curves.

This, however, should not mean that all the firms in monopolistic competition make pure profits in the short run. Chamberlin does not rule out the possibility of some firms making losses.

Long-run Equilibrium of the Firm

The long-run conditions differ from the short-run conditions because in the long run: (i) new firms enter the industry, (ii) firms indulge in price competition, (iii) changes (i) and (ii) take place simultaneously and (iv) firms advertise their product more vigorously. Chamberlin has used a sequence of *four models* to analyse the long-run equilibrium with these changes. The four models present, in fact, the four different levels of analysis. Following the general practice, however, we present here only the final form of his model of long-run equilibrium under monopolistic competition. A detailed analysis of Chamberlin's four models is given in *Appendix* to this chapter.

The long-run equilibrium of the firms under monopolistic competition is illustrated in Figure 4.6. The revenue and cost curves in Figure 4.6 are similar to those given in Figure 4.5. To analyse the process of adjustment, let us have a re-look at Figure 4.5. As Figure 4.5 shows, each firm makes a pure or supernormal profit of *PC* per unit of output, i.e., to the extent of the difference between the price and *SAC*. Supernormal profit attracts new firms to the industry as there is no barrier to entry. With the entry of new firms, the existing firms loose a part of their market share to the new entrants. As a result, the proportional demand curve (D_p) of the firms shifts leftward and perceived demand curve (D_p) shifts downward. This shift continues until firms reach a new equilibrium point with their perceived $MR_p = MC$. This stage is shown by point is *M* when *MC* intersects with MR_p. Point *M* determines the equilibrium output at OQ_A and price at PQ_A. Note that at point *P*, demand curve D_p is tangent to *LAC* curve and

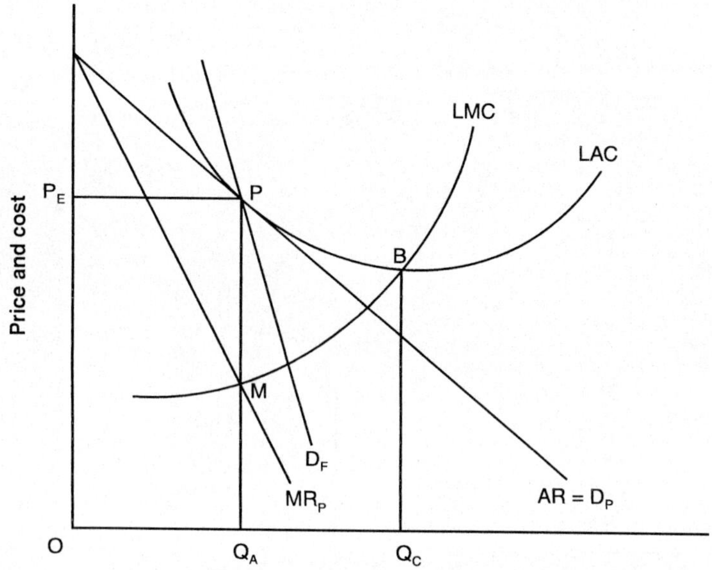

Figure 4.6 *Long-run Equilibrium of Firms Under Monopolistic Competition*

demand curve D_p intersects with them. Since price equals *LAC* at point *P*, no firm is making pure profit. There is, therefore, no incentive for new firms to enter the industry nor is there any disincentive for the existing ones to quit the industry. The firms are, therefore, in the state of their long-run equilibrium at point *P*.

It is important to note here that point *P* is not imaginary or coincidental. It is determined by the intersection of the *MR* and *MC* curve determining profit-maximizing output at OQ_A and price at PQ_A. At their equilibrium, firms produce and sell quantity OQ_A at price $PQ_A = OP_E$. This is how, according to Chamberlin, monopolistically competitive firms reach their equilibrium in the long run. An important outcome of this analysis is that, in the long run all firms in monopolistic competition make only normal profit.

EXCESS CAPACITY UNDER MONOPOLISTIC COMPETITION

As in case of monopoly, there is excess capacity or idle capacity under monopolistic competition. The excess capacity or unutilized capacity is a social waste. In this section, we will discuss (a) concept and measure of 'ideal output' and excess capacity and (b) non-price competition and excess capacity.

Ideal Output and Excess Capacity

'The excess capacity of a firm is defined as the difference between the 'ideal output' and the 'actual output' attained in the long run. What is 'ideal output'? The economists[16] from Marshall down to Kahn,[17] Harrod,[18] and Cassels[19] defined *ideal output* as the output that can be produced at the minimum *long-run average cost (LAC)*. This concept of 'ideal output' is linked to social optimality of production. *Excess capacity* is also called as 'idle capacity' and 'unused capacity'.

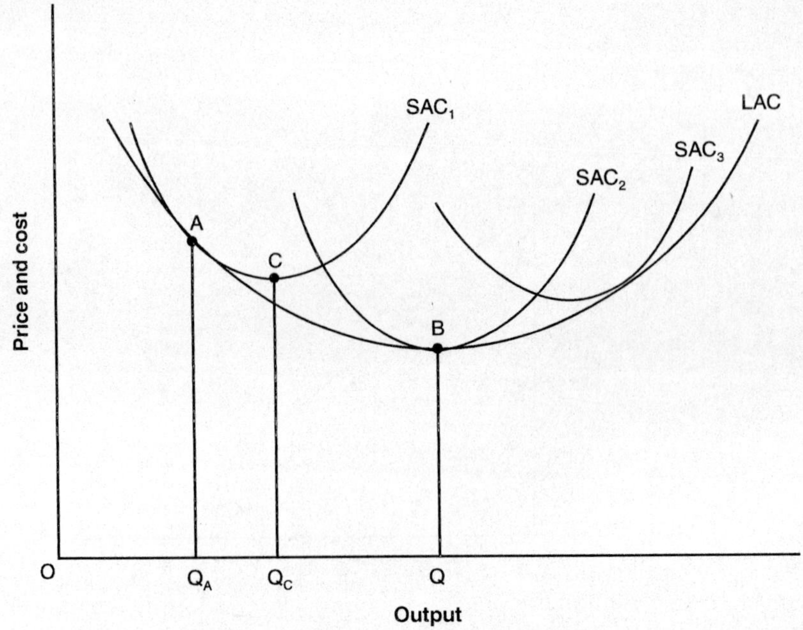

Figure 4.7 *Ideal Output and Excess Capacity*

The existence of excess capacity under monopolistic competition can be seen in Figure 4.6. The firm is in equilibrium at point *P*. Its *actual output* at equilibrium is OQ_A. As regards the 'ideal output', note that *LMC* intersects *LAC* at point *B* which marks, as a matter of rule, the minimum point at the *LAC* curve. Point *B* determines the 'ideal output' at OQ_C. Thus 'actual output' is OQ_A and 'ideal, output' is OQ_C. The difference between the actual output OQ_A and the ideal output OQ_C equals Q_AQ_C. Thus Q_AQ_C is the 'excess capacity' under monopolistic competition.

Cassels[20] has divided excess capacity in two parts on the basis of what is optimum from the view points of individual firms and the society. The two parts of the excess capacity are illustrated in Figure 4.7. Suppose a firm is optimally placed at point *A* (where SAC_1 is tangent to its *LAC*) whereas its ideal but put is given by point *C*—the point of minimum SAC_1. The firm produces OQ_A whereas ideal output is OQ_C. The difference between OQ_A and OQ_C, i.e., Q_AQ_C, is the *first part* of the excess capacity.

The *second part* of excess capacity is associated with what is socially optimum size of the firm. A firm in monopolistic competition can expand its scale of production to point *B* which marks the minimum of both *SAC* (i.e., SAC_2) and *LAC*. That is, socially optimum output is given by point *B* at OQ_B. But a firm in monopolistic competition does not use enough resources of the society to produce at point *B*. Assuming that the firm produces at point *A*, the firm leaves out the prospects producing an additional output Q_CQ. This is the *second part* of the excess capacity.

However, Chamberlin argues that 'ideal output' conforming to the minimum *LAC*, as shown by point *B* in Figure 4.6, is not an attainable ideal output in monopolistic competition because product distinctiveness is a necessity and it affects both demand and cost conditions. The distinctiveness of the product makes demand curve a downward sloping one whereas attaining point *B* requires that demand curve must be a horizontal flat line. It affects cost conditions because cost of distinctiveness added to the cost of production makes the minimum point of *LAC* plus shift to the left and above point *B*.

Non-price Competition and Excess Capacity

According to Chamberlin, excess capacity in monopolistic competition arises in the long run when there is free entry but *absence of active price competition* between the firms. It implies that if monopolistic competition is characterized by free entry and active price competition, there would be no excess capacity. Chamberlin attributed the excess capacity to the absence of active competition. Firms may abstain from active price competition for such policy reasons as 'formal or tacit agreements, open price association, trade association activities building up an espirit de corps 'price maintenance', the imposition of uniform prices on dealers by manufacturers, and excessive differentiation of the product in the attempt to turn attention away from price' (Chamberlin, p. 106). The other factors may be 'customary prices', 'professional ethics', fear that price cutting might give a wrong signal to the consumers about quality of the product (p. 107), and avoiding problems arising out of price competition.

Chamberlin's view that excess capacity is the result of non-price competition is illustrated in Figure 4.8. As usual, the *LAC* curve represents the *long-run average cost* curve which is the same for all the firms and their *perceived* and *proportional* demand curves are shown by D_P and D_F curves, respectively. If there is *free entry with price competition*, the firms will be in equilibrium at point *P* where the firms' perceived demand curve D_P is tangent to the *LAC* curve and their proportional demand curve D_P intersects both the curves D_F and *LAC*. At equilibrium point *P*, firms produce OQ_C at price OP_C. The reason for the firms being in equilibrium at point *P* is given in Figure 4.6. Note that point *P* in Figure 4.8 corresponds to point *P* in Figure 4.6. If firms adopt an aggressing price competition, point *P* will shift closer to point *M*, the point of perfectly competitive equilibrium.

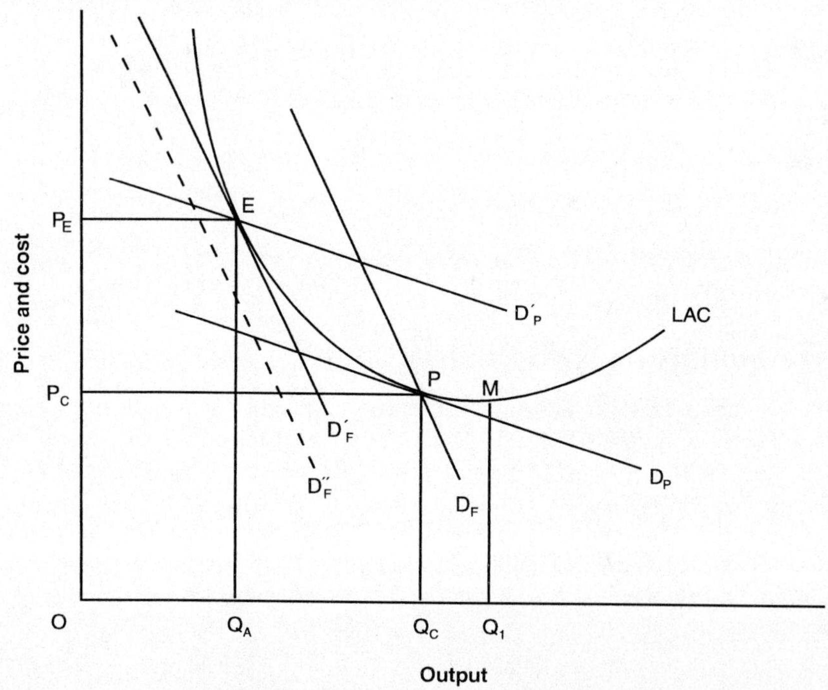

Figure 4.8 *Long-run Equilibrium: Non-price Competition and Excess Capacity*

Let the *price competition now be eliminated from the monopolistic competition.* If there is no price competition, the *perceived demand curve* D_P has no existence. The firms are left with its *proportional demand curve* D_F. In the absence of active price competition, entry of new firms makes the demand curve D_F shift leftward because market share of each firm decreases. New firms continue to enter the industry until the demand curve D_F shifts to the position of D'_F which is tangent to the *LAC* curve. Any further entry of firms will make the D'_F shift further to the left and away from the *LAC* curve as shown by the dashed demand curve D''_F. In that case, all the firms will make losses forcing some of the firms to quit the industry. As a result, the dashed demand curve D''_F shifts rightward to D'_F which is tangent to the *LAC* curve. Therefore, all the firms are making only normal profit and, hence the entry of new firms stops at point *E*. It means that point *E* marks the point of long-run equilibrium where long-run output is OQ_A and price is $EQ_A = OP_E$.

Now, by comparing equilibrium output OQ_C corresponding to *free entry with active competition,* and equilibrium output OQ_A corresponding *to free entry with no active price competition,* we get Chamberlin's measure of excess capacity. Chamberlin's excess capacity can be obtained as $OQ_C - OQ_A = Q_AQ_C$.

According to Chamberlin, 'excess capacity' may exist even 'under pure competition, owing to miscalculation on the part of the producers or to sudden fluctuations in demand or cost conditions'. But in the long run, excess capacity 'is the peculiarity of the monopolistic competition' which is a 'waste' caused by the 'monopoly element in monopolistic competition' and for it 'there is no automatic corrective.[21]

SELLING COST AND FIRM'S EQUILIBRIUM: NON-PRICE COMPETITION

The meaning and purpose of selling costs, returns to the selling costs, the shape of average selling cost (*ASC*) curve, its effect on the total cost (i.e., average production cost *plus* selling costs), and optimization of selling coat, as enunciated by Chamberlin, have already been discussed in detail in Section 4.3.2 of this chapter. In this section, we confine our discussion to the effect of selling costs on the equilibrium of firms under monopolistic competition. Chamberlin has developed his theory of value under monopolistic competition with selling costs at two levels: (i) the case of 'individual equilibrium', i.e., the equilibrium of an individual firm assuming *other firms do not advertise their products* and (ii) the case of 'group equilibrium', i.e., when all the firm adopt a competitive advertising. We present here a brief description of Chamberlin's analysis of 'individual equilibrium' and 'group equilibrium'.

Individual Equilibrium with Selling Cost

Chamberlin has enunciated equilibrium of an individual firm under the following three conditions: (a) determination of the optimum selling cost with price given; (b) determination of equilibrium price with a given amount of selling cost and (c) determination of price and selling costs simultaneously. Case (a) is already illustrated in Figure 4.3. Given our limited purpose here, we will confine to case (b) and case (c). We begin our analysis with case (c) in which a firm facing a downward sloping demand curve and a U-shaped *ASC* curve has to find equilibrium price and selling costs. This covers the case (b) also.

The equilibrium of an individual firm under conditions (b) and (c) is explained below under the following *assumptions*:

1. The firm seeks to maximize its profit;
2. It is free to adjust its price, output, and selling cost to maximize its profit;

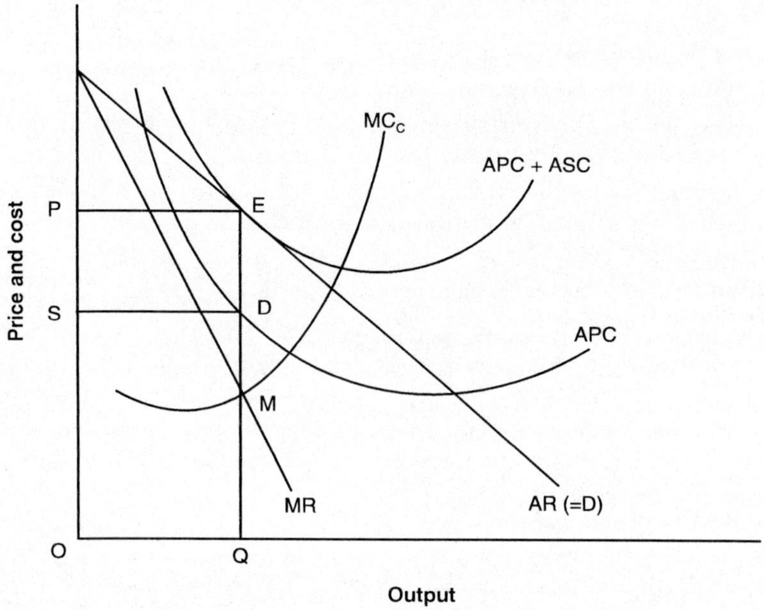

Figure 4.9 *Firm's Equilibrium with Variable Price and Selling Costs*

3. 'Price, products, and selling policies of all competitors' are given and
4. There is no interdependence between the firms.

The equilibrium of the individual firm is illustrated in Figure 4.9. Firm's downward sloping demand curve is given by the curve D (= AR) and its marginal revenue curve by the curve MR. Its average production cost curve is given by the curve APC; its overall cost is shown by the curve labelled $APC + ASC$; and its *combined marginal cost* by the curve MC_C. Firm's MR and MC_C curve intersect at point M determining the equilibrium output at OQ. Given the demand curve, equilibrium price is determined at $OP = EQ$. That is, firm's profit-maximizing output is OQ and price is OP. At the equilibrium level of output, its average selling cost (ASC) equals ED and its total selling cost equals $ED \times OQ$. Since $OQ = SD$, firm's total selling cost equals $ED \times SD = SDEP$. This is *optimum selling cost*. The total revenue of the firm equals its output × price $= OQ \times OP = OPEQ$. Since firm's demand curve and overall average cost curves are tangent to one another at point E, selling price equals the overall average cost, i.e., $APC + ASC$. The firm is therefore making only normal profit. This is the general case of firm's individual equilibrium provided there is no competition. However, if firm's demand curve lies above the $APC + ASC$ curve, the firm will make pure profit, but only in the short run.

Group Equilibrium

Chamberlin has developed his 'group equilibrium' model taking into account, as in case of individual equilibrium, a variety of conditions pertaining to product, price, selling cost, price and selling cost taken together, action and reaction of competitors and constant and variable price and selling costs. We present here only the final form of his model of group equilibrium. His group equilibrium model is based on the following explicit and implicit assumptions.

Assumptions

1. There is a group of firms all aiming at maximization of profits.
2. Price for the group product is given by custom or otherwise.
3. 'Demand curves, production cost curves, and selling cost curves are uniform for all the products in the group'—'the drastic assumption'[22]
4. The firms make competitive advertisement either to increase the demand for their product or to prevent the fall in their market share due to advertisement by competitors or to recapture their lost market share.
5. All of the firms face the identical demand and cost curves.

The group equilibrium of the firms in monopolistic competition is illustrated in Figure 4.10 under the assumptions given above. The curve *APC* represents the average production cost of the firms. Price of the group product is given at OP_3 and, at the given price, the price line for all the firms is given by the line labelled $AR = MR$. None of the firm is incurring any selling cost. Under these conditions, according to Chamberlin, all the firms are shown to be in equilibrium at point *E* where they all make only normal profits. Now suppose that one of the firms incurs selling cost so that its *APC* added with average selling costs (*ASC*) rises to the position shown by the curve $APC + ASC_1$ and its total sale increases to OQ_4. At output OQ_4, the firm makes supernormal profits of P_3PMP_2. This profit is, however, possible only so long as other firms do not advertise their own products. If other firms do advertise their products and incur the same amount of selling cost, the initial advantage to the firm advertising first will disappear and its output will fall to OQ_2. In fact, all the firms reach equilibrium at point *A* and produce OQ_2 units. But their short sightedness impels them to increase their selling cost because they expect to reduce their *APC*

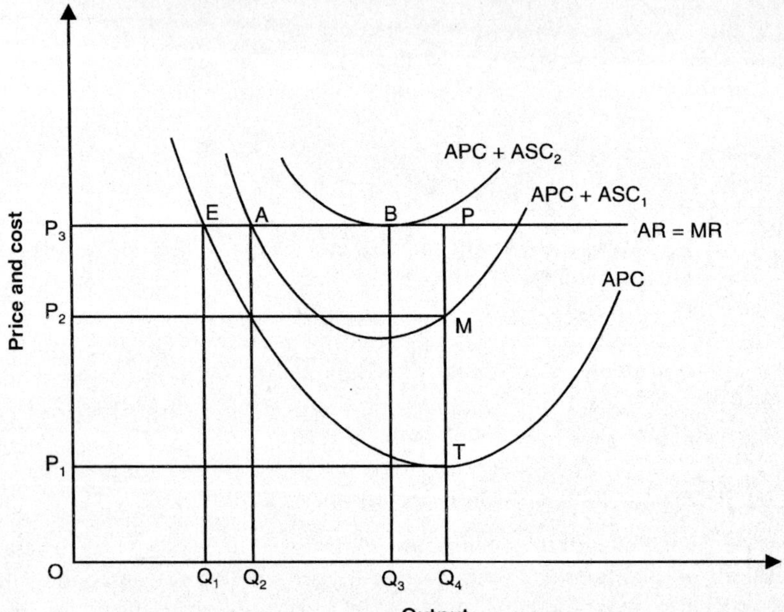

Figure 4.10 *Selling Costs and Group Equilibrium*

by expanding their output. With increased selling cost, their *APC* + *ASC* curve shifts further upward. This process continues until $APC + ASC_2$ becomes tangent to the *AR* = *MR* line, as shown by point *B*. Beyond point *B*, advertising is of no avail to any firm. The equilibrium will be stable at point *B* where each firm produces OQ_3 and makes only normal profit.

MONOPOLISTIC COMPETITION VERSUS PERFECT COMPETITION: A COMPARISON

As mentioned earlier, the monopolistic competition as perceived by Chamberlin, is characteristically closer to perfect competition. There are, however, significant differences between the two kinds of markets. This section presents a comparison of monopolistic competition and perfect competition is respect of (i) the number of firms, (ii) the nature of products, (iii) the nature of competition, (iv) efficiency in production and (v) capacity utilization.

1. ***The Number of Firms.*** The number of firms in both monopolistic competition and perfect competition is very large. But the number of firms under perfect competition is much larger than that under monopolistic competition. Though number cannot be specified numerically, there is significant conceptual difference. The number of firm in perfect competition is so large that an individual firm has absolutely no control on the price of its product: price is determined by the market forces and is given to the firm. Under monopolistic competition, however, the number of firms is only so large that an individual firm does have power to change price of its product especially under the condition of product differentiation. A firm can increase the price of its product and still retain some of its buyers (which are not possible under perfect competition) and if a firm cuts down the price of its product, it captures a part of the market of the rival firms. On the contrary, if a firm in perfect competition cuts down the price, it goes out of the market itself.
2. ***The Nature of the Product.*** Under perfect competition, product is *homogeneous* and, therefore, the product of each seller is treated as a *perfect substitute* for the product of other firms. Under monopolistic competition, on the other hand, there is *product differentiation* and the product of each firm is a *close substitute* for that of the others. As discussed earlier, *product differentiation* adds the *element of monopoly* and the scope for competition, making the market monopolistically competitive.
3. ***The Nature of Competition.*** Under perfect competition with homogeneity of products, there is *virtually no competition*. Each firm faces a horizontal demand curve and sells any quantity without affecting the market share of other firms. Under monopolistic competition, on the contrary, the firms face a downward sloping demand curve due to product differentiation. Competition between the firms may take the form of *price competition* or *non-price competition*. The basis of *price competition* is the firm's perception that the demand curve for its product (i.e., the *perceived demand curve)* is more elastic than the market demand curve. So the firms can cut down the price of its product and increase its sales. This leads to price competition. More important is the *non-price competition. Non-price competition* takes the form of *competitive advertising*[23] of the product by the firms.
4. ***Efficiency in Production.*** Efficiency in production under monopolistic competition and perfect competition is compared on the basis of their equilibrium output. Although rules for profit

maximization are the same for the firms in both the kinds of the markets (i.e., $MR = MC$ with MC rising), equilibrium output under perfect competition is higher than that under monopolistic competition. For illustration, refer to Figure 4.6. The equilibrium of a firm in monopolistic competition is determined at point P with output OQ_A and equilibrium of a firm under perfect competition will be at point B where equilibrium output is OQ_E. Recall that the firms under perfect competition face a horizontal demand curve passing though the minimum point of the LAC curve, i.e., point B. Thus, the equilibrium output under monopolistic competition in OQ_A and equilibrium output under perfect competition is OQ_C. It can be seen in Figure 4.6 that $OQ_C > OQ_A$. It means that production under perfect competition is more efficient than under monopolistic competition.

5. ***Capacity Utilization***. Related with equilibrium output is the issue of capacity utilization. In continuation with the issue of efficiency in production, it can be shown that capacity utilization under monopolistic competition is lower than that under perfect competition. Referring again to Figure 4.6, full capacity utilization lies at point B conforming to equilibrium output OQ_C under perfect competition. Under monopolistic competition, however, firms produce OQ_A which is lower than full-capacity output. It means that under monopolistic competition, there is underutilization of capacity. That is, there is *excess capacity* under monopolistic competition whereas there is none under perfect competition.

CRITICISM OF CHAMBERLIN'S THEORY OF MONOPOLISTIC COMPETITION

Chamberlin's theory of monopolistic competition was received enthusiastically as a path-breaking contribution to the theory of value as it sought to analyse the determination of price and output in the market structure other than monopoly and pure competition. In later years, however, Chamberlin's theory was criticized by the economists on both theoretical and empirical grounds. Major criticisms of Chamberlin's theory are briefly given below.

1. ***Chamberlin's Theory has Low Predicting Power***. The test of the validity of an economic theory lies in its power to predict the effect of changes in economic conditions. On this test, Chamberlin's theory has been found to have low predicting power. Critics claim that his model of monopolistic competition is not significantly different from traditional models of perfect competition and pure monopoly. Where models of perfect competition and pure monopoly do not apply in predicting the price and output, *oligopoly models* apply better than Chamberlin's model of monopolistic competition. Therefore, his model has not been found useful for making predictions.
2. ***Chamberlin's Model is Challenged on Theoretical Grounds***. In monopolist competition, product differentiation makes the product, in reality, heterogeneous in terms of quality, price, use, distinctive appearance, consumers' liking, etc. Chamberlin has, therefore, devised the concept of 'product group', i.e., the group of firms selling products which are very close substitutes for one another. Stigler,[24] a Nobel Laureate, has, however, criticized Chamberlin's definition of the 'product group'. He argues that products are so heterogeneous that grouping them under a category of very close substitutes is not reasonable and dependable. In fact, the concept of 'product group' is *ambiguous*. For example, look at the so-called car industry. The number of brand names and variety of cars with significantly different prices and use is so large that it is

difficult to group certain brands as a 'product group'. An attempt to group them under different product groups will violate the concept of industry as each brand name of certain size will make a different industry. Under these conditions, it is extremely difficult to find a demand curve for the product group.

3. ***Chamberlin's Model Makes Unrealistic Assumptions***. Chamberlin's theory has also been criticized for making unrealistic assumptions. The arguments against three of his basic assumptions are as follows:
   (a) ***Assuming identical cost and revenue curves are not justified***. Critics argue that Chamberlin's *heroic assumption* that firms have *identical* or 'uniform' cost and revenue curves is questionable. Under monopolistic competition, products are so widely differentiated that each product makes an industry in itself and has a different demand curve. Also, where product differentiation is very significant, it does make a difference in the cost of production. Therefore, assuming identical demand and cost curves is unrealistic.[25]
   (b) ***Assuming no interdependence is not reasonable***. Chamberlin assumes that the number of firms in monopolistic competition is so large that pricing and selling strategies adopted by an individual firm go unnoticed by the competitors and, therefore, there is no *interdependence* between the firms. This assumption has been questioned on the ground that rival firms are bound to be affected by the pricing and selling strategies adopted by a firm because their products are deemed to be close substitutes. Therefore, rival firms are bound to react and adopt a countervailing policy. It is, therefore, not reasonable to assume *absence of interdependence*.
   (c) ***Assuming that firms do not learn is not correct***. Chamberlin's model of price output determination assumes implicitly that firms do not learn from their mistakes and experience. Cohen and Cyert[26] question the validity of this assumption. They argue that it is puzzling to accept that firms repeat the mistake of cutting down the price of their products time and again even if price reduction results in no gain. Therefore, firms cannot be supposed to continue to stick to their belief that their *perceived demand curve* provides them with real opportunities. If this argument is accepted, Chamberlin's model of price competition breaks down.
4. ***Chamberlin's Measure of Excess Capacity is Logically Inconsistent***. Harrod[27] has questioned the logic of Chamberlin's measures of the excess capacity. He argues that it is logically *inconsistent* because Chamberlin uses *long-run MC* curve with *short-run MR* curve to determine the actual output. Consistency requires that *with long-run MC curve, only long-run MR curve should be used*. If long-run *MR* curve is used, the actual output will be larger than Chamberlin's output because the long-run demand and *MR* curves will be more elastic. In that case, the measure of excess capacity will be lower than one suggested by Chamberlin. Also, Chamberlin's measure of excess capacity is not corroborated by empirical evidence.
5. ***Chamberlin's Model Lacks Empirical Validity***. Cohen and Cyert[28] claim that it is difficult to find any example in the real world to which Chamberlin's model of monopolistic competition is relevant. According to them, most markets that exist in the real world may be classified as perfect competition, pure monopoly, oligopoly or monopoly (pp. 229–230) and none under monopolistic competition. These critics hold the view that Chamberlin's model of monopolistic competition is not a useful addition to economic theory as it does not pertain to any real market.

Despite these damaging criticisms, Chamberlin's theory of monopolistic competition is regarded as a significant contribution to the theory of value and remains a subject matter of microeconomics for analytical rigour and insight that it provides in analysing a monopolistically competitive market.

APPENDIX

Long-run Equilibrium of Firms Under Monopolistic Competition

As already mentioned in the text, long-run changes in monopolistic competition include (i) new firms enter the industry, (ii) firms indulge price competition and (iii) firms make vigorous advertisement with a view to enhancing their market share or to retain their market share especially when there is entry of new firms into the industry or the product group. These changes affect the market share of the rival firms which leads to intensive competition. Chamberlin has used three models to analyses the effects of these changes on firm's equilibrium. His three models present, in fact, the three different stages of analysis. In this first model, he analyses firm's equilibrium with free entry of new firms into the industry, all other things given. His second model analyses the effect of price competition between the firms on their equilibrium, with no entry or exit. His third model presents a combined analysis of free entry and price competition on the firm's equilibrium. These models are discussed below in the same sequence.

Model I: Long-run Equilibrium with Free Entry of New Firms

The long-run equilibrium of the existing firms with free entry of new firms, other things remaining the same, is illustrated in Figure 4.1A. The *LAC* and *LMC* curves are the cost curves faced by the firms. The initial *AR* and *MR* curves (i.e., prior to the entry of new firms) are given by $AR = D_1$ and MR_1, respectively. Given the cost and revenue curves, the firms would be in short-run equilibrium at price OP_2 and output OQ_2. The firms are making supernormal profit to the extent of *EB* per unit of output.

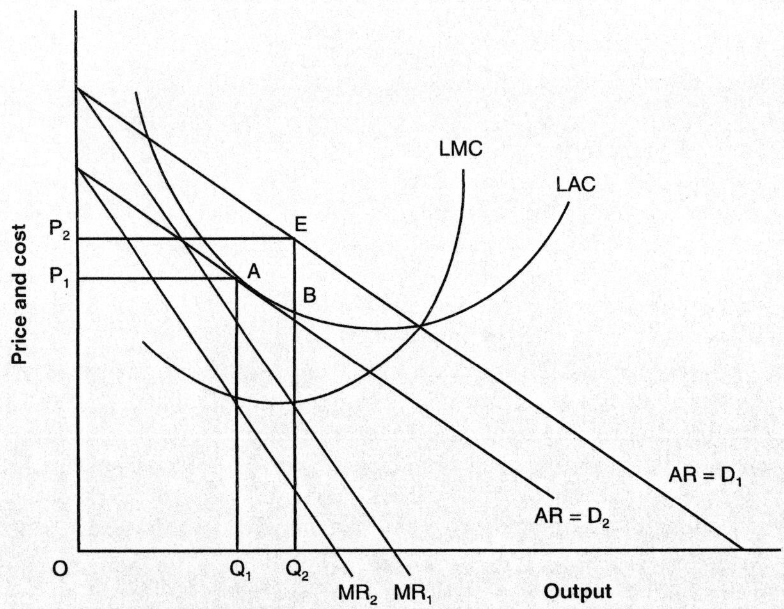

Figure 4.1A *Long-run Equilibrium with Free Entry*

The existence of supernormal profit attracts new firms to the product group. With the entry of new firms, the sale of each firm in the group decreases. Consequently, the demand curve (i.e., *AR* curve) for the old firms shifts downward. Therefore, firms adjust their price and output to the new *AR* and *MR* conditions, cost conditions remaining the same. This process continues until the demand curve is tangent to the *LAC*, as shown by the demand curve $AR = D_2$ and all the firms earn only normal profits. The final equilibrium position of the firms in the long run under monopolistic competition is shown at point *A*, where price is OP_1 and output OQ_1. At this price and output, all firms make only normal profit. Therefore, there is no incentive for the new firms to enter the industry. The equilibrium will, thus, be stable at point *A*.

Model II: Long-run Equilibrium with Price Competition

In his model of long-run equilibrium with price competition, Chamberlin assumes (i) that the number of existing firms in the product group is optimal, i.e., the number of firms is compatible with long-run equilibrium of the industry and (ii) there is no entry or exit of the firms. Given these assumptions, he analyses the long-run equilibrium with price competition in two stages. In the first stage, he traces the perceived or the expected demand curve resulting from the change in price, assuming that rival firms do not react to the price changes. In the second stage, he traces the long-run equilibrium under the conditions of optimal number of firms and price competition.

Chamberlin's first stage of analysis, i.e., the derivation of the perceived demand curve is shown in Figure 4.2A. Let us assume that demand curve for the product of all the firms is identical and is given by DD_1 and that all the firms are in equilibrium at point *E*, with price *OP* and output *OQ*. Now suppose that

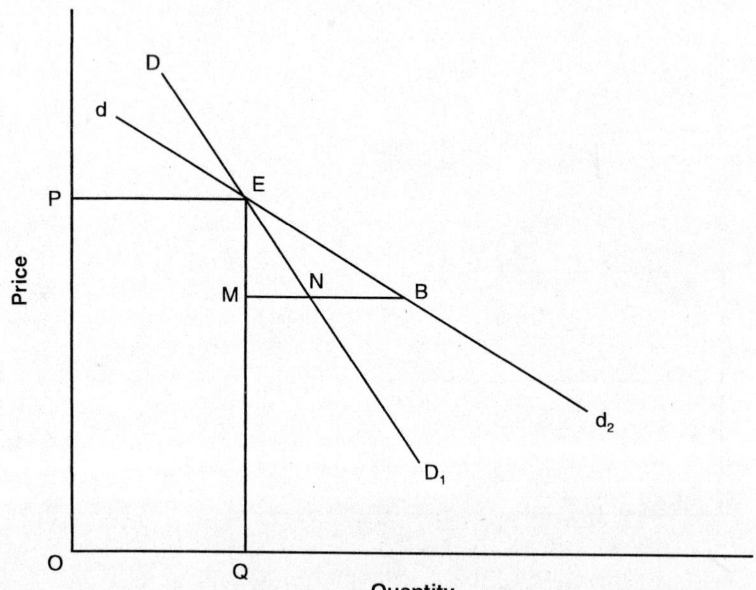

Figure 4.2A *Introduction of Perceived Demand Curve*

one of the firms contemplates a price reduction assuming that the rival firms will not react to its price reduction, By reducing its price, the firm expects to expand its sales on account of two factors: *first*, the demand for its product is elastic, and *secondly*, the consumers of other products will switch over to the product of this firm if other firms do not simultaneously reduce their prices. This is *substitution effect*. Thus, the firm can expect a substantial increase in its total sales. For example, if the firm *reduces* its price by *EM*, it expects the demand for its product to increase by *MB*. Of this, *MN* is due to the elasticity of its original demand DD_1 and *NB* is due to the substitution effect. Similarly, if the firm raises its price, and the rival firms do not raise their prices, it looses its market partly because its demand curve is elastic and partly because its customers switch over to other products which become automatically cheaper. Thus, the firm expects a different and more elastic demand curve for its product, as shown by dd_2. This is called as the *perceived demand curve*. But, if all the firms change their prices simultaneously this advantage to an individual firm is lost and entire firm return to the original demand curve DD_1.

Having introduced the perceived demand curve, let us now discuss the second stage of Chamberlin's analysis of long-run equilibrium of a firm with price competition. The long-run equilibrium with price competition is presented in Figure 4.3A. The curves DD_1 and dd_1 are the firm's normal and perceived demand curves, respectively, and *LAC* is the long-run average cost curve of a 'typical' firm of the group. Let the initial short-run equilibrium of the firms of the group be at point *P* where price is OP_2 and output is OQ_1. At this price and output, the firm makes the total supernormal profit represented by the area $CMPP_2$.

Let us now introduce price competition and analyse its effect on firm's equilibrium. Competition begins with the firms' belief that DD_1 is market (or group) demand curve and dd_1 is the demand curve for their own product. Note that dd_1 is more elastic than DD_1. Therefore, each firm thinks that it can increase its profit by cutting down its price and increasing the demand for its product. In an attempt to

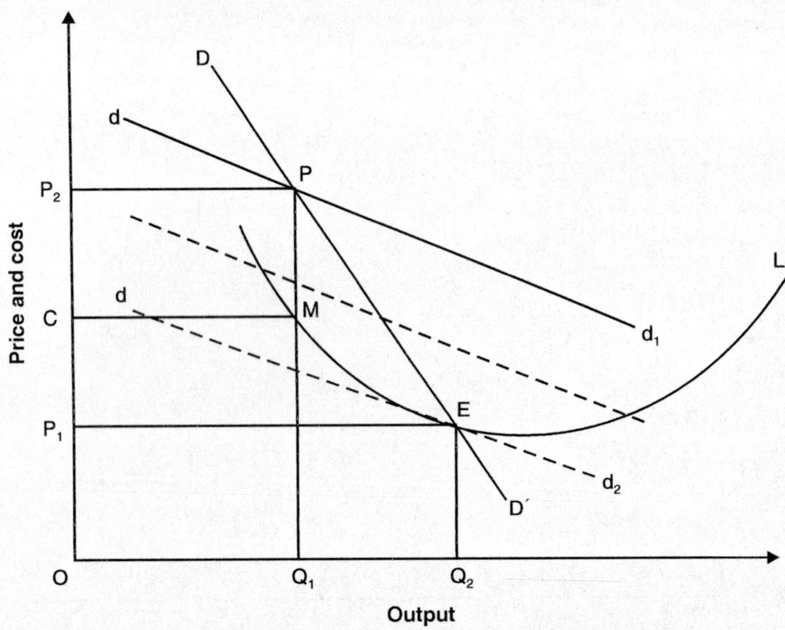

Figure 4.3A *Long-run Equilibrium: Price Competition*

increase profits, each firm reduces its price expecting to move along the demand curve dd_2. But, instead of moving along dd_2 the firms move along the market demand curve DD_1 because all of them reduce their prices simultaneously.

Why do firms not realize this phenomenon? According to Chamberlin, *the firms do not learn from their past experience* and each firm sticks to its own belief that price reduction will make the demand curve for its product more elastic than the market demand curve (DD_1), as shown by demand curve dd_1. Therefore, the firms go on reducing their prices independently and their assumed demand curve (dd_1) slides downward along the curve DD_1. This process continues until the downward shift in dd_1 makes it tangent to the *LAC* curve at point *E*, as shown by dd_2, in Figure 4.3A. Here price is OP_1. A further reduction in price will make firms incur losses. Therefore, reduction in price below OP_1 is not desirable. Thus, long-run equilibrium of firms takes place at point *E*, *where each firm produces* OQ_2 and fixes its price at OP_1.

Model III: Long-run Equilibrium with Free Entry and Price Competition

We have explained above separately the equilibrium of the firm with free entry and with price competition. In this model, we bring together the two equilibrium analyses and explain Chamberlin's *third and the final model of equilibrium* of firms under monopolistic competition.

According to Chamberlin, the ultimate equilibrium under monopolistic competition can be achieved through an integrated analysis of effects of free entry and price adjustments. The integrated analysis of equilibrium is presented in Figure 4.4A. In this figure, DD_1 is assumed to represent in initial demand curve and *LAC* to represent the long-run average cost curve. Let us suppose that the firms are initially in equilibrium at point *B*, where output is OQ_5 and price is BQ_5. Here firms make abnormal profits

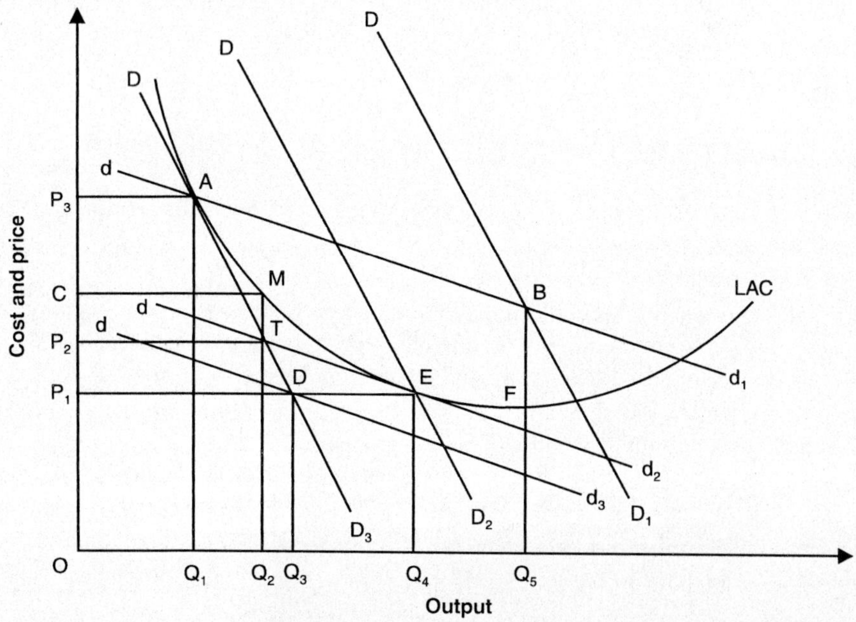

Figure 4.4A *Long-run Equilibrium with Free Entry and Price Competition*

per unit of sale to the extent of *BF*. Since entry to the 'product group' is free, new firms are attracted to the industry by the abnormal profit. When new firms enter the product group with slightly differentiated products, the share of each existing firm in the market is reduced. Hence, their demand curves DD_1 shifts leftward. Given the *LAC*, the leftward shift in the demand curve will continue until it becomes tangent to *LAC* at point *A*, as shown by DD_3 in Figure 4.4A. For, till this point is reached, firms will make abnormal profits and new firms will continue to enter the 'product group'.

It appears from this part of analysis that the long-run equilibrium is attained at point *A* with output OQ_1 and price OP_3. This is however not the case. This is only half of the story, i.e., the influence of free entry on firms' equilibrium. Let us now consider the competitive maneuvering of price and its role in determining the long-run equilibrium. When abnormal profits disappear, firms get levelled up at normal profits. Here begins the price-war. As shown above, each firm thinks, that its demand curve is dd_1, not DD_3. Each firm believes that it can increase its profit by reducing the price and thereby increasing the sales. Therefore, in their attempt to increase their profits, they reduce prices of their product one after another because each firm has the same incentive to do so. As a result, firms move down along DD_3 whereas they had expected to move down along dd_1. In this process, they incur losses. For example, if price is reduced to OP_2, the total loss equals the rectangle $CMTP_2$.

It might seem that the firms could eliminate their loss by reducing the price to OP_1. But, when all the firms reduce their price to OP_1 their subjective demand curve dd_2 slides further down to dd_3. As a result, the firms make ever-increasing losses. A temporary equilibrium will be attained at point *D* with output OQ_3. Here all firms incur heavy losses. Consequently, the firms which are unable to sustain losses eventually leave the industry. The remaining firms find their share in the market increasing. Therefore, demand curve DD_3 moves to the right and dd_3 shifts upward. This process continues until DD_3 shifts to DD_2 and dd_3 shifts upward to the position of dd_2. Note that the demand curve dd_2 is tangent to *LAC* at point *E*. The demand curve DD_2 too passes through the point *E*. Point *E* is therefore the point of long-run equilibrium. Thus, the long-run equilibrium is attained at point *E* which, according to Chamberlin, is stable because all firms earn only normal profits and, therefore, there is no entry or exit of the firms.

REVIEW QUESTIONS AND EXERCISES

1. What is monopolistic competition? How does it differ from perfect competition and monopoly?
2. Monopolistic competition is the middle ground between perfect competition and monopoly. Explain the statement.
3. Theories of monopolistic competition and monopoly do not represent the real business world whereas theory of monopolistic competition offers an explanation to price and output determination in a real business world. Explain and justify the statement.
4. What are the characteristics of monopolistic competition? Compare the characteristics of monopolistic competition with those of perfect competition?
5. There is an element of monopoly in monopolistic competition. What factors give monopoly power to a firm in monopolistic competition?
6. What is meant by product differentiation? What is the purpose of product differentiation? How does it affect firm's demand curve?

7. In monopolistic competition, firms think that the demand curve for their individual product is different from that of the industry as whole. Illustrate graphically firm's perception of their individual demand curve.
8. What is meant by selling costs? How is selling cost different from advertisement cost? Why do firms in monopolistic competition incur selling costs?
9. According to Chamberlin, average selling cost (*ASC*) curve is U-shaped. What factors determine the shape of the *ASC*? Illustrate graphically how selling costs affect the overall cost structure of the firm.
10. The purpose of selling cost is to increase the demand for the product and to make demand curve more elastic. But there is limit to it. How can a firm find the optimum level of selling cost? Explain by using appropriate diagrams.
11. What is Chamberlin's concept of 'product group'? How is the concept of 'product group' different from the traditional meaning of industry?
12. How does a monopolistically competitive firm adjust its price and output to arrive at its equilibrium? Explain and illustrate how a firm in monopolistic competition reaches its equilibrium in the short run? Does a firm in equilibrium in monopolistic competition always make a super-normal profit?
13. Suppose market demand curve is given $Q = 500 - 0.5P$. Work out the proportional demand curve for a firm assuming there are 50 firms in the industry. Is the elasticity of the proportional demand curve at a given price is the same as that of the market demand curve or different?
14. How are the long-run conditions different from short-run conditions for a firm in monopolistic competition? Illustrate and explain the long-run equilibrium of firm in monopolistic competition? How is firm's long-run equilibrium different from its short-run equilibrium?
15. What is meant by 'ideal output' and 'excess capacity'? Illustrate Chamberlin's measure of excess capacity. How does Harrod's measure of excess capacity differ from Chamberlin's measure?
16. What are the wastages of monopolistic competition? Is the 'traditional' concept of excess capacity an overstatement of one of the wastages of monopolistic competition? Give reasons in support of your answer.
17. What is the usual form of non-price competition in monopolistic competition? Explain and illustrate the firm's long-run equilibrium under non-price competition. Why do firms involved in non-price competition make only normal profit in the long run?
18. What does Chamberlin mean by 'group equilibrium'? How does selling cost affect the group equilibrium? Illustrate firm's equilibrium with selling costs.
19. Group equilibrium shows that firms incurring selling costs make only normal profit in the long run. It implies that selling cost is a waste. Do you agree with this statement? Give reason for your answer.
20. What are the drawbacks of Chamberlin's theory of monopolistic competition? What is the merit of his theory in spite of its drawbacks?
21. Write a note on the critical evaluation of Chamberlin's theory of monopolistic competition? Why is his theory not in use even though it is analytical sound?

ENDNOTES

1. C.E. Ferguson, *Microeconomic Theory*, 2nd edn (Homewood, IL: Richard D. Irwin), p. 317.
2. Piero Shraffa, 'The Laws of Returns under Competitive Conditions', *Economic Journal*, 1929, pp. 41–57.
3. Harold Hotelling, 'Stability and Competition', *Economic Journal*, 1929, pp. 41–57.
4. Zeuthen, A., *Problems of Monopoly and Economic Welfare* (London: Routledge, 1930).
5. Edward Hasting Chamberlin, The Theory of Monopolistic Competition: A Re-Orientation of the Theory of Value (Cazmbridge, MA: Harvard University Press, 1933).
6. Joan Robinson, *The Economics of Imperfect Competition* (London, Macmillan, 1933).
7. Quoted in Maddala, G. S. and Miller, E., *Microeconomics: Theory and Application* (New York, NY: McGraw-Hill, 1989), p. 375.
8. For example, toothpaste companies make high claims of removing bad breath, strengthening gums, making teeth sparkle and so on whereas dentists claim that brushing teeth with plain water is as good as brushing with any toothpaste. Similarly, in spite of high claims of anti-dandruff shampoos, no body is known to have got rid of dandruff even after using the costliest ones year after year.
9. Chamberlin, E.D., Theory of Monopolistic Competition: A Re-Orientation of the Theory of Value (OUP), 7th edn, 1956, p. 56.
10. Chamberlin, A.D, *op.cit.*, p. 56.
11. However, in Ch. VII of his book (*op. cit.*), he has used 'advertising' often as 'Synonymous with Selling Cost' (see p. 130, fn. 1).
12. Chamberlin E.D., *op.cit.*, pp. 132–33.
13. This assumption is made to avoid complications arising out of change in price due to price competition (see Chamberlin, pp. 130–131).
14. Chamberlin (1956), *op. cit.*, p. 82.
15. Assumed by Chamberlin (1956), p. 140.
16. Quoted in John P. Gould, Jr. and Edward P. Lazear, *Microeconomic Theory* (Richard D. Irwin, Homewood, IL), 6th edn, 1933, p. 359.
17. R.F. Kahn, 'Some Notes on Ideal Output', *Economic Journal*, 45 (1934).
18. R. Harrod, 'Doctrines of Imperfect Competition', *Quarterly Journal of Economics*, 49 (1934–35).
19. J.M. Cassels, 'Excess Capacity and Monopolistic Competition', *Quarterly Journal of Economics*, 51, May 1937.
20. Op. cit.
21. Chamberlin, (1956), p. 109.
22. Chamberlin has himself called this assumption as 'the drastic assumption'. He has however, defended it in the following words, '...let us not exaggerate the drastic nature of this assumption. Markets are often fairly uniform in composition, consumer's preferences fairly evenly distributed, difference between products [is] such as to give rise to no marked differences in costs, and selling methods [are] stable and unsensational. Where these things are true, our assumptions are sufficiently realistic to make the results of some direct applicability' (p. 150).

23. Advertising is of two types: (i) informative and (ii) persuasive. *Informative advertising* aims at providing information to the potential buyers about the product, its quality and price, and location of availability. *Persuasive advertising* aims at attracting customers of the other firms which leads to intensive advertising of the product. For example, Pepsi and Coca-Cola companies have been involved in aggressive advertising of their product over a decade without making profits. This is a non-price competition for market share.
24. Stigler, G.J., *Five Lectures on Economic Problems* (London, Longmans, 1949).
25. Chamberlin has himself called this assumption as 'the drastic assumption'. He has however defended his assumption. To quote him again '...let us not exaggerate the drastic nature of this assumption. Markets are often fairly uniform in composition, consumer's preferences fairly evenly distributed, difference between products [are] such as to give rise to no marked differences in costs, and selling methods [are] stable and unsensational. Where these things are true, our assumptions are sufficiently realistic to make the results of some direct applicability' (p. 150).
26. K.J. Cohen and R.M. Cyert, *Theory of the Firm*, 2nd edn (New Delhi, Prentice Hall of India, 1976).
27. R.F. Harrod, *Economic Essays* (New York, NY: Harcourt Brace, 1952).
28. Theory of the Firm, op. cit., p. 230.

FURTHER READINGS

Bain, J.S. (1971), 'Chamberlin's Impact on Microeconomic Theory', in R.E. Kuenne (ed), *Monopolistic Competition Theory: Studies in Impact—Essays in Honour of E.H. Chamberlin* (NY: Wiley Eastern, 1966), reprinted in H. Townsend (ed.), *Readings in Price Theory* (Middlesex, England: Penguin).

Browning, E.K. and Browning, J.M. (1994), *Microeconomic Theory and Applications* (New Delhi: Kalyani Publishers), 2nd Edn., Chapter 13.

Chamberlin, E.H. (1956), *The Theory of Monopolistic Competition* (Cambridge, MA: Harvard University Press), 7th Edn.

Cohen, K.J. and Cyert, R.M. (1976), *Theory of the Firm* (New Delhi: Printice-Hall of India), Chapter 11.

Dempetz, H. (1959), 'The Nature of Equilibrium in Monopolistic Competition', *Jl. Pol. Eco.*, November.

Gould, J.P. and Lazear, E.P. (1993), *Microeconomic Theory* (Homewood, IL: Richard D. Irwin), 6th Edn., Chapter 12.

Koutsoyiannis, A. (1979), *Modem Microeconomics* (London: Macmillan), 2nd Edn., Chapter 8.

Maddala, G.S. and Miller, E. (1989), *Microeconomics: Theory and Applications* (New York, NY: McGraw-Hill Book Co.), Chapter 13.

Robinson, J. (1953), *The Economics of Imperfect Competition*, (Macmillan, 1953) and 'Imperfect Competition Revised,' *Eco. Jl.*, (1953).

Shraffa, P. (1926), 'The Laws of Returns under Competitive Conditions,' *Eco. J.* Reprinted in *Readings in Price Theory*, Am. Eco. Assn, 1944.

Stigler, G.J. (1949), 'Monopolistic Competition in Retrospect', *Five Lectures on Economic Problems* (Longmans: Green).

Triffin, R. (1939), *Monopolistic Competition and General Equilibrium* (Cambridge, MA: Harvard University Press).

Chapter 5

Price and Output Determine Oligopoly

CHAPTER OBJECTIVES

The objective of this chapter is to explain the various theories formulated by the economists in regard to price and output determination by the firms under *oligopoly*—a market of few sellers. This chapter helps you learn:

- The nature and working of oligopolistic market;
- The factors that lead to the emergence of oligopolistic markets;
- The three famous models of oligopoly developed by economists, viz., Cournot, Chamberlin and Sweezy;
- The theoretical methods of price and output determination under collusive oligopoly—the oligopoly in which firms form a Cartel, a union type of organization, for determining mutually the price and output for each of them;
- The method of price determination by the leading firm of the oligopoly;
- Baumol's theory of price and output determination; and
- The game theory of oligopoly firms based on prisoners' dilemma.

INTRODUCTION

In the previous chapter, we have discussed Chamberlin's theory of price and output determination under monopolistic competition, a market organization in which there is *a large number of sellers* selling differentiated products. In this chapter, we will discuss the theory of price and output determination under *oligopoly*,[1] a market organization in which there are few sellers.

The first oligopoly model (in the form a duopoly model) was developed by a classical economist, Augustin Cournot, as early as 1838. Over nearly a century, however, the economists had devoted little attention to theory of oligopoly. During this period, only two other economists, viz., Edgeworth and Bertrand, had contributed a little to the theory of oligopoly. It was in 1933, that Chamberlin had formulated his theory of monopolistic competition under the condition of a large number of monopolistic sellers. But his critics found that his theory was not logically sound and empirically verifiable. Then economists' attention was drawn towards oligopoly and a number of complex theories were developed over time to analyse price and output determination in an oligopolistic market. This, however, added more complications and confusions to the subject rather than offering a non-controversial theory. In this chapter, however, we limit our discussion to theories considered to have made significant contribution to the theory of oligopoly. We begin our discussion with meaning and characteristics of oligopoly.

OLIGOPOLY: A MARKET OF FEW SELLERS

Definition of Oligopoly

Oligopoly is the market structure in which there are a few sellers selling homogeneous or differentiated products. However, economists do not specify what number of sellers make the market oligopolistic. In fact, it depends on the market size. However, two sellers is the *limiting case* of oligopoly. When there are only two sellers, the market is called *duopoly*.

In any case, if oligopoly firms sell a homogeneous product, it is called *pure* or *homogeneous oligopoly*. For example, industries producing bread, cement, steel, petrol, cooking gas, chemicals, aluminium and sugar are industries characterized by *homogeneous* oligopoly. And, if firms of an oligopoly industry sell *differentiated products*, it is called *differentiated* or *heterogeneous oligopoly*. Automobiles, television sets, soaps and detergents, refrigerators, soft drinks, computers, cigarettes, etc., are some examples of industries characterized by *differentiated* or *heterogeneous oligopoly*.

In the opinion of some authors, 'oligopoly is the most prevalent form of market organization in the manufacturing sector of the industrial nations…'[2] In non-industrial nations like India also, a majority of big and small industries have acquired the features of oligopoly market. The market share of 4–10 firms in 84 big and small industries[3] of India is given in Table 5.1.

As the data presented above shows, in India, in 50 out of 84 selected industries, i.e., in about 60 per cent industries, 4–10 firms have a 75 per cent or more market share. This gives a *concentration ratio*[4] of 0.500 or above. All such industries can be classified under oligopolies.

Factors Causing Oligopoly

The main factors that lead to the growth of oligopoly are described here briefly.

1. ***Huge Capital Investment***. Some industries are by nature capital intensive, e.g., firms manufacturing automobiles, aircraft, ships, TV sets, refrigerators, steel and aluminium goods, etc., and hence

Table 5.1 *Distribution of Market Share*

Market Share (%) of 4–10 Firms	Number of Industries
1–24.9	8
25–49.9	11
50–74.9	15
75–100	50
Total	84

require huge investment. Therefore, only a few firms can enter these kind of industries. In fact, a huge investment requirement works as a natural barrier to entry to the oligopolistic industries.

2. ***Economies of Scale***. By virtue of huge investment and large scale production, large units enjoy *absolute cost advantage* due to economies of scale in their purchase of industrial inputs, acquiring external finance, and in sales organization. This gives the existing firms a comparative advantage over new firms, especially in price competition. This works not only as a deterrent for the entry of new firms, but also causes exit of high cost firms.
3. ***Patent Rights***. In case of *differentiated oligopoly*, firms get their differentiated product patented which gives them monopoly power, i.e., an exclusive right to produce and market the patented commodity. This prevents other firms from producing the patented commodity. Therefore, unless new firms have something new to offer and can match the existing products in respect of quality and cost, they cannot enter the industry. This keeps the number of firms limited.
4. ***Control over Certain Raw Materials***. Where a few firms acquire control over almost the entire supply of important inputs required to produce a certain commodity, new firms find it extremely difficult to enter the industry. For example, if a few firms acquire the right from the government to import certain raw materials, they control the entire input supply.
5. ***Merger and Acquisition***. Merger of rival firms or takeover of rival firms by the bigger ones with a view to protecting their joint market share or to put an end to waste of competition is an important factor creating oligopoly. In fact, in modern times, this is the most important factor that gives rise to oligopolies and strengthens the oligopolistic tendency in modern industries.

Features of Oligopoly

Let us now look at the important characteristics of oligopolistic industries.

1. ***Small Number of Sellers***. As already mentioned, there is a small number of *sellers* under oligopoly. How small the number of sellers is not given precisely: it depends largely on the size of the market. Conceptually, however, the number of sellers is so small that the market share of each firm is so large that a single firm can influence the market price and the business strategy of its rival firms. The number may vary from industry to industry. Some examples of oligopoly industries in India and market share of the *dominant* firms[5] in 1997–1998 is given in Table 5.2.
2. ***Interdependence of Decision Making***. The *most striking feature* of an oligopolistic market structure is the *interdependence* of business decision of oligopoly firms. The characteristic fewness of firms under oligopoly brings the firms in keen competition with each other. The competition between the firms takes the form of action, reaction and counteraction in the absence of collusion between the firms. Since the number of firms in the industry is small, the business decision and strategy of each firm in respect of pricing, advertising, product modification is closely watched by the rival firms and it evokes retaliatory actions. What is equally important in strategic business decisions is that firms initiating a new business strategy anticipate and take into account the counteraction by the rival firms. This is *called interdependence* of oligopoly firms.

   An illuminating example of strategic maneuvering is cited by Robert A. Meyer.[6] To quote the example, one of the US car manufacturing companies announced in one year in the month of September[7] an *increase* of $180 in the price list of its car model. Following it, a second company announced a few days later an increase of $80 only and a third announced an increase of $91. The first company made a counter move: it announced a *reduction* in the enhancement in the list price from $180 to $71. This is a pertinent example of interdependence of firms in business

Table 5.2 *Market Share of Firms in Some Selected Industries*

Industry	Number of Firms	Total Market Share (%)
Ice-cream	4	100.00
Bread	2	100.00
Infant milk food	6	99.95
Motorcycles	5	99.95
Passenger cars	5	94.34
Cigarettes	4	99.90
Fruit juice, pulp & cone.	10	98.21
Fluorescent lamps automobile	3	91.84
Tyres	8	91.37

*Currently only two firms—Maruti Suzuki (60%) and Hyundai (25%)—together account for about 85% of the total sales of passenger cars in India.

Source: CMIE, Industries and Market Share, August 1999.

decisions under oligopolistic market structure. In India, when Maruti Udyog Limited (MUL), announced a price cut of Rs 24,000 to 36,000 in early 1999 on its passenger cars, other companies, specifically Hyundai, followed the suit and cut down their price by Rs 18,000–22,000. However, *price competition* is not the major form of competition among the oligopoly firms as price war destroys the profits. A more common form of competition is *non-price competition* on the basis of product differentiation, vigorous advertising and provision of services.

3. ***Barriers to Entry***. Barriers to entry to an oligopolistic industry arise due to such market conditions as (i) huge investment requirement to match the production capacity of the existing ones, (ii) economies of scale and absolute cost advantage enjoyed by the existing firms, (iii) strong consumer loyalty to the products of the established firms based on their quality and service and (iv) resistance by the established firms by price cutting. However, the new entrants that can cross these barriers can and do enter the industry, though only a few, that too mostly the franchise branches of MNC*s*.
4. ***Indeterminate Price and Output***. Another important feature, though controversial, of the oligopolistic market structure is the indeterminateness of price and output. The characteristic fewness and interdependence of oligopoly firms makes derivation of the demand curve a difficult proposition. Therefore, price and output are said to be indeterminate. However, price and output are said to be determinate under collusive oligopoly. But, collusion may last long or it may breakdown. *An opposite view is that price under oligopoly is sticky*, i.e., if price is once determined, it tends to stabilize.

THE OLIGOPOLY MODELS: AN OVERVIEW

As already mentioned, under oligopolistic conditions, rival firms adopt an intricate pattern of actions, reactions and counteractions showing a variety of behavioural patterns. The uncertainty arising out of unpredictable behaviour, actions and reactions of oligopoly firms makes systematic analysis of oligopoly an extremely difficult task. As Baumol puts it,

Under [these] circumstances, a very wide variety of behaviour pattern becomes possible. Rivals may decide to get together and cooperate in the pursuit of their objectives, ... or, at the other extreme, may try to fight each other to death. Even if they enter an agreement, it may last or it may breakdown.[8]

Economists have, therefore, found it extremely difficult to make a systematic analysis of price and output determination under oligopoly.[9] The complexity of the problem, however, could never deter the economists from their efforts to find a reasonable solution to the problem.

In accordance with the wide variety of behaviour patterns, economists have developed a variety of analytical models based on different behavioural assumptions. The widely quoted models of oligopoly include Cournot's duopoly model (1838), Bertrand's duopoly model (1880), Edgeworth's duopoly model (1897), Stackelberg's model (1933), Sweezy's kinked demand curve model (1939), Neumann and Margenstern Game Theory model (1944), and Baumol's sales maximization model (1959). None of these models, however, provides a universally acceptable analysis of oligopoly, though these models do provide an insight into oligopolistic behaviour.

In this chapter, we will discuss oligopoly models with the purpose of showing the behaviour of oligopoly firms and working of the oligopolistic markets. The analytical models discussed here show how price and output are determined under price competition, cartel system and the dilemma that oligopoly firms face in their price and output decision.

The oligopoly models discussed here can be classified as follows.

1. Duopoly models of oligopoly
   (a) Cournot's duopoly model,
   (b) Bertrand's duopoly model,
   (c) Edgeworth's duopoly model and
   (d) Stackelberg's duopoly model.
2. Oligopoly models
   (a) Non-collusive models
      (i) Chamberlin's small-group model and
      (ii) Sweezy's kinked demand curve model.
   (b) Collusive models
      (i) Cartel models and
      (ii) Price leadership models.
3. Baumol's sales revenue maximization model.
4. Game theory of oligopoly: prisoners' dilemma.

Let us now discuss these oligopoly models in the same order.

DUOPOLY MODELS OF OLIGOPOLY

Cournot's Duopoly Model

Augustine Cournot,[10] a French economist, was first to develop a formal oligopoly model in 1838 in the form of a duopoly model. To develop his model, Cournot made the following assumptions:

1. There are only two firms, each owning an artesian water well;
2. Both the firms operate their wells at zero marginal cost (*MC*);

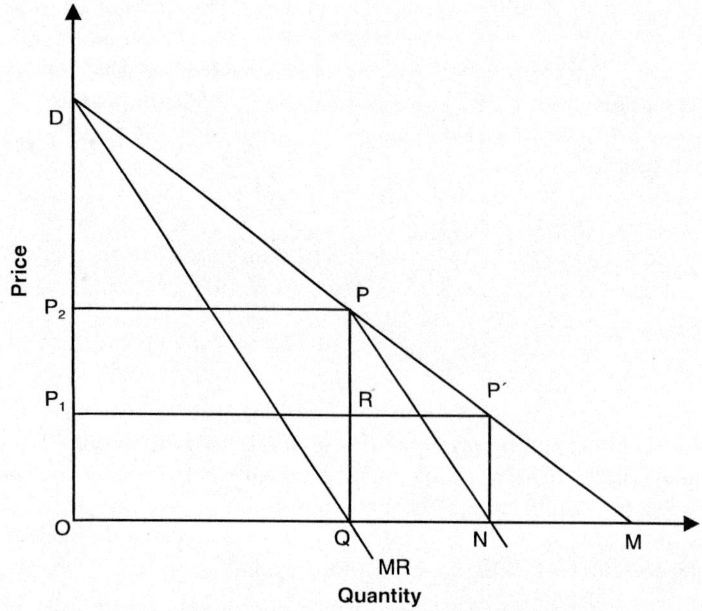

Figure 5.1 *Price and Output Determination Under Duopoly: Cournot's Model*

3. Both the firms face a demand curve with constant negative slope and
4. Each firm acts on the assumption that its competitor will not react to its decision to change its output —Cournot's behavioural assumption.

Cournot's duopoly model, based on the above assumptions, is presented in Figure 5.1. Suppose that the market demand curve is given by the *DM* curve, note that the demand curve represents also the *AR* curve. Given the *AR* curve, the *MR* curve is drawn and given by curve *DQ*. To begin the analysis, let us suppose that firm *A* is the only seller of mineral water in the market. By assumption, its $MC = 0$. Following the profit maximizing rule, firm *A* sells quantity *OQ* where its $MC = 0 = MR$, at price OP_2. Its total profit is OP_2PQ.

Now let firm *B* enter the market. Firm *B* finds that the market open to it is *QM* which is *half of* the total market. That is, firm *B* can sell its product in the remaining half of the market. But, the question for firm *B* is: what quantity to sell and at what price? In determining its sale, the firm *B* assumes that firm *A* will not change its *output* because it is making maximum profit. Specifically, *B* assumes that *A* will continue to sell *OQ* at prices OP_2. Thus, the market available to *B* is *QM* and the relevant part of the demand curve is *PM*. Given the demand curve *PM*, the *MR* curve is given by the curve *PN* which bisects *QM* at point *N* where $QN = NM$. In order to maximize its revenue, firm *B* sells *QN* at price OP_1. *B*'s total revenue is maximum at *QRP′N* which equals its total profit. Note that *B* supplies only $QN = 1/4 = (1/2)/2$ of the market.

Let us now see how *A*'s profits is affected by the entry of *B*. With the entry of *B*, price falls to OP_1. Therefore, *A*'s expected profit falls to OP_1RQ. Faced with this situation, *A* assumes, in turn, that firm *B* will not change its output *QN* and price OP_1 as *B* is making maximum profit. Since $QN = 1/4$th of the market, firm *A* assumes that it has 3/4 (=1 – 1/4) of the market available to him. To maximize its profit, *A* supplies 1/2 of (3/4) of the market i.e., 3/8 of the market. It is noteworthy that *A*'s market share has fallen from

1/2 to 3/8. Note that *A* and *B* supply only half of the market available to them. Thus, with *B*'s entry, *A*'s price and output go down. But *A* has to accept the situation unless market conditions change again.

Now it is *B*'s turn to react. Following Cournot's assumption, *B* assumes that *A* will continue to supply only 3/8 of the market and the market open to it equals 1 – 3/8 = 5/8. To maximize its profit under the new conditions, *B* supplies 1/2 × 5/8 = 5/16 of the market. It is now for *A* to reappraise the situation and adjust its price and output accordingly.

This process of action and reaction continues in successive periods. In the process, *A* continues to lose market share and *B* continues to gain. Eventually, a situation is reached when their market shares equal 1/3 each. Any further attempt to adjust output produces the same result. The firms, therefore, reach their equilibrium position where each one supplies 1/3 of the market and both charge the same price.

The actions and reactions and equilibrium of the sellers *A* and *B*, according to Cournot's model, are presented in Table 5.3.

Cournot's equilibrium solution is stable. For the given action and reaction, it is not possible for any of the two sellers to increase their market share as shown in the last row of the table.

Cournot's model of duopoly can be extended to a general oligopoly model. For example, if there are three sellers in the industry, each one of them will be in equilibrium when each firm supplies 1/4 of the market. The three sellers together supply 3/4 of the total market, 1/4 of the market remaining unsupplied. Similarly, when there are four firms each one of them supply l/5th of the market and 1/5th of the market remains unsupplied. The formula for determining the share of each seller in an oligopolistic market is given as

$$Q - (n + 1)$$

where Q = market size, and n = number of sellers.[11]

Table 5.3 *Determination of Market Share by Action and Reaction*

Period	A	B
I	$\frac{1}{2}(1) = \frac{1}{2}$	$\frac{1}{2}\left(\frac{1}{2}\right) = \frac{1}{4}$
II	$\frac{1}{2}\left(1 - \frac{1}{4}\right) = \frac{3}{8}$	$\frac{1}{2}\left(1 - \frac{3}{8}\right) = \frac{5}{16}$
III	$\frac{1}{2}\left(1 - \frac{5}{16}\right) = \frac{11}{32}$	$\frac{1}{2}\left(1 - \frac{11}{32}\right) = \frac{21}{64}$
IV	$\frac{1}{2}\left(1 - \frac{21}{64}\right) = \frac{43}{128}$	$\frac{1}{2}\left(1 - \frac{43}{128}\right) = \frac{85}{256}$
...	...	...
...	...	...
N	$\frac{1}{2}\left(1 - \frac{1}{3}\right) = \frac{1}{3}$	$\frac{1}{2}\left(1 - \frac{1}{3}\right) = \frac{1}{3}$

Note: Arrows show the direction of actions and reactions of sellers *A* and *B*.

An Algebraic Solution Cournot's model can also be presented algebraically. Let us suppose that the market demand function is given by linear function as

$$Q = 90 - P \tag{5.1}$$

and that

$$MC = AC = 0$$

As noted above, under zero cost condition, profit is maximum where $MC = MR = 0$ and when $MR = 0$, the profit maximizing output is 1/2(Q).

Let us suppose that when seller *A* is the only seller in the market, his profit-maximizing output is (Q_A) determined by the profit maximizing rule under zero-cost condition. Given the demand function, *A*'s market share $Q_A = 1/2(Q)$ can be determined as

$$Q_A = 1/2(90 - P) \tag{5.2}$$

When seller *B* enters the market, his profit maximizing output is determined as follows.

$$Q_B = 1/2[1/2(90 - \text{P})] \tag{5.3}$$

Thus, the respective shares of seller *A* and *B* are fixed at Q_A and Q_B, respectively.

The division of market output may be expressed as

$$Q = Q_a + Q_B = 90 - P \tag{5.4}$$

The demand function for *A* may now be expressed as

$$Q_A = (90 - Q_B) - P \tag{5.5}$$

and for *B* as

$$Q_B = (90 - Q_A) - P \tag{5.6}$$

Given the demand function (5.5), the market open to *A* (at $P = 0$) is $90 - Q_B$. The profit maximizing output for seller *A* can be worked out as

$$Q_A = \frac{90 - Q_B}{2} \tag{5.7}$$

and for seller *B*, as

$$Q_B = \frac{90 - Q_A}{2} \tag{5.8}$$

Equations (5.7) and (5.8) represent the reaction functions of sellers *A* and *B*, respectively. For example, consider Eq. (5.7). The profit maximizing output of *A* depends on the value of Q_B, i.e., the output which *B* is assumed to produce. If *B* chooses to produce 30 units, (i.e., $Q_B = 30$), then *A*'s output = [(90 – 30)1/2] = 30. If *B* chooses to produce 60 units, *A*'s output = (90 – 60)/1/2 = 15. Thus, Eq. (5.8) is *A*'s reaction function. It can similarly be shown that Eq. (5.8) is *B*'s reaction function.

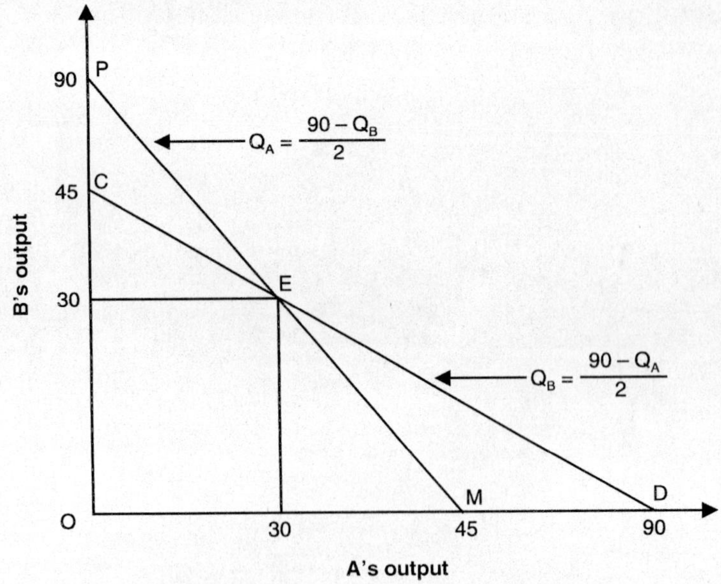

Figure 5.2 *Reaction Functions and Equilibrium: Cournot's Model*

The reaction functions of sellers *A* and *B* are graphed in Figure 5.2. The reaction function *PM* shows how *A* will react on the assumptions that *B* will not react to changes in his output once *B's* output is fixed. The reaction function *CD* shows a similar reaction of *B*. The two reaction functions intersect at point *E*. It means that the assumptions of *A* and *B* coincide at point *E* and here ends their action and reaction. Point *E* is, therefore, the point of stable equilibrium. At this point, each seller sells only 30 units, given the demand function. The same result can be obtained by equating the two reaction Eqs. (5.7) and (5.8). Cournot's equilibrium is often compared with Nash equilibrium (discussed later).

The market slope of sellers *A* and *B* can be obtained by equating *A's* and B's reaction functions (5.7) and (5.8), respectively. That is, market equilibrium lies where

$$\frac{90 - Q_B}{2} = \frac{90 - Q_A}{2}$$

Since, $Q_B = (90 - Q_A)/2$, by substitution, we get first term as

$$Q_A = \frac{90 - (90 - Q_A)/2}{2}$$

$$Q_A = 30$$

Thus, both the sellers are in equilibrium at their respective output of 30. The market output will be 60 units. Given the market demand curve, market price will be $P = 90 - Q = 90 - 60 =$ Rs 30.

Criticism of Cournot's Model As we have seen earlier, Cournot's model is logically sound and yields a stable equilibrium solution. His model has, however, been criticized on the following grounds.

First, Cournot's behavioural assumption, specifically the assumption that sellers assume that the rival firm will not change its output is said to be naive as it implies that firms continue to make wrong calculations about the behaviour of the rival firms even though their calculations are proved wrong. For example, each seller continues to assume that his rival will not change his output even though he finds frequently that his rival does change his output.

Secondly, Cournot assumed zero cost of production, which is not realistic. However, even if his assumption is dropped and a constant $MC > 0$ is assumed, Cournot's results are not affected.

Bertrand's Duopoly Model

Betrand,[12] a French mathematician, criticized Cournot's model and developed his own model of duopoly in 1883. Bertrand's model differs from Cournot's model in respect of its behavioural assumption. While Cournot postulates in his model that each seller assumes his rival's output to remain constant, Bertrand assumes in his model that each seller determines his price on the assumption that his rival's price, rather than his output, remains constant.

Bertrand's model concentrates on price competition. His analytical tools are reaction functions of the duopolists. Reaction functions of the duopolists are derived on the basis of iso-profit curves. An iso-profit curve, for a given level of profit, is drawn on the basis of various combinations of prices charged by rival firms. To explain it further, let us suppose there are two firms *A* and *B*. The derivation of their reaction curves are shown in Figures 5.3 and 5.4, respectively. The two axes of the figures measure one each the prices of the two firms. The reaction curves of the two firms are drawn through their iso-profit curves. Iso-profit curves of the two firms are convex to the respective price axis, as shown in Figures 5.3. and 5.4. Iso-profit curves of firm *A* are convex to it price axis P_A (Figure 5.3) and those of firm *B* are convex to P_B (Figure 5.4).

To explain the implication of an iso-profit curve, consider curve *A* in Figure 5.3. It shows that firm *A* can earn a given profit from the various combinations of its own and its rival's price. For example, price combinations at points *a, b* and *c* on iso-profit curve A_1 *yield* the same level of profit. If firm *B* fixes its price P_{B1}, firm *A* has two alternative prices, P_{A1} and P_{A2}, to make the same level of profits. When firm *B* reduces its price, firm *A* may either raise its price or reduce it. Firm *A* will reduce its price when it is at

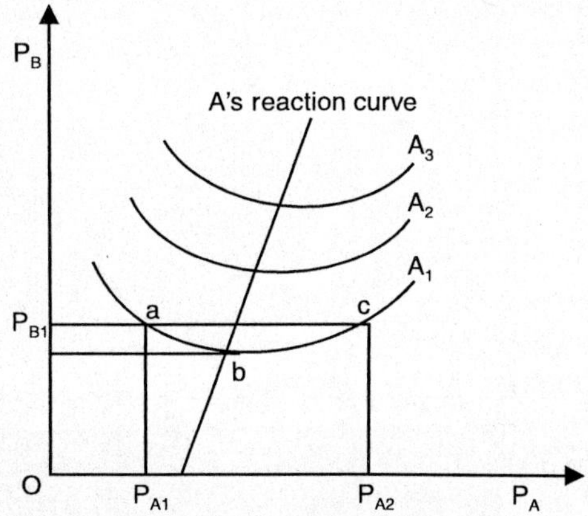

Figure 5.3 *A's Reaction Curve*

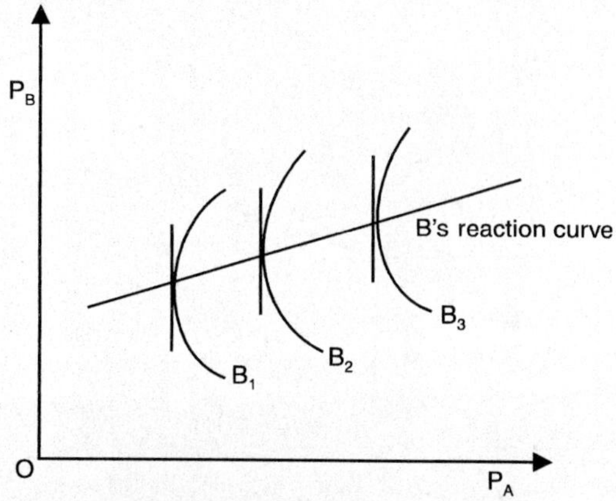

Figure 5.4 *B's Reaction Curve*

point c charging price P_{A2} and it will raise its price above P_{A1} when it is at point a. But there is a limit to which this price adjustment is possible. This point is given by point b. So there is a unique price for firm A to maximize its profits. This unique price lies at the lowest point of the iso-profit curve. By joining points a, b and c, we get a curve A_1. The profit all along the curve A_1 is the same. The same analysis applies to all other iso-profit curves. If we join the lowest points of the iso-profit curves A_1, A_2 and A_3, we get A's reaction curve. Note that A's reaction curve has a rightward slant. This is so because iso-profit curve tend to shift rightward when firm A gains market from its rival firm B.

Following the same process, B's reaction curve may be drawn as shown in Figure 5.4. The equilibrium of duopolists suggested by Bertrand's model may be obtained by putting together the reaction curves of the firms A and B as shown in Figure 5.5. The reaction curves of firm A and B intersect at point E where their expectations materialize. Point E is therefore the equilibrium point. According to Bertrand, this equilibrium is stable. For, if anyone of the firms deviates from the equilibrium point, it will generate a series of actions and reactions between the firms which will lead them back to point E.

Criticism Bertrand's model has however been criticized on the same grounds as Cournot's model. Bertrand's implicit behavioural assumption that firms never learn from their past experience is naive. Furthermore, if cost is assumed to be zero, price will fluctuate between zero and the upper limit of the price, instead of stabilizing at a point.

Edgeworth's Duopoly Model

Edgeworth[13] developed his model of duopoly in 1897. Edgeworth's model follows Bertrand's assumptions that each seller assumes his rival's price, instead of his output, to remain constant and that cost of production is zero. His model is illustrated in Figure 5.6.

Let us suppose that there are two sellers, A and B, in the market and the size of the entire market is given $M'M$. The entire market $M'M$ in Figure 5.6 is equally divided between the two seller as $M'M/2 = OM + OM'$. Given their market share, the two sellers face identical demand curves. Seller A faces demand curve as D_A and seller B as D_B. Let us also assume that seller A has a maximum capacity of output OM and seller B has a maximum output capacity of OM'. The ordinate OD measures the price.

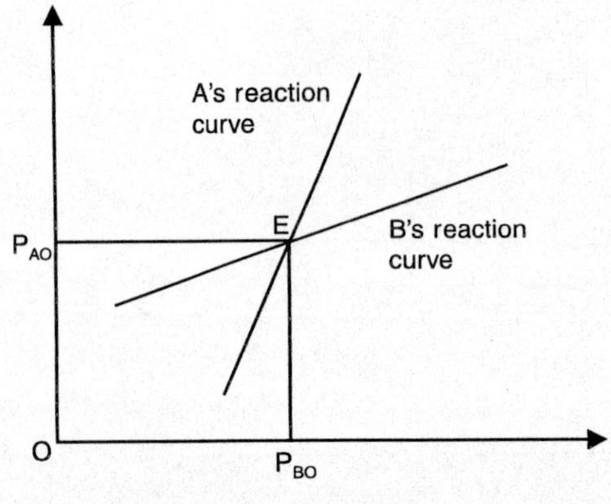

Figure 5.5 *Duopoly Equilibrium: Berland's Model*

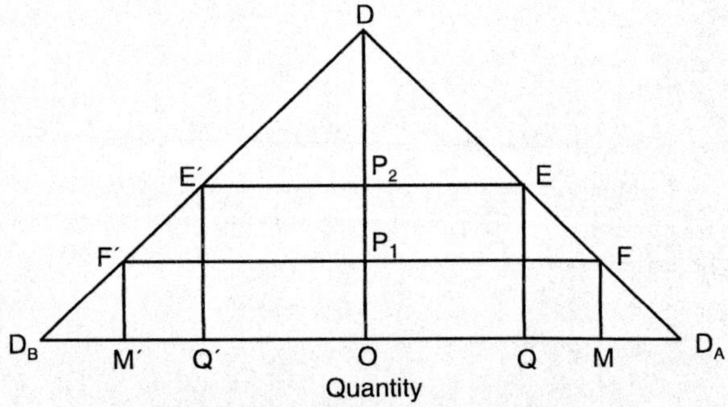

Figure 5.6 *Edgeworth's Model of Duopoly*

To begin the analysis of Edgeworth's model, let us suppose that *A* is the only seller in the market. Following the profit-maximizing rule of a monopoly seller, he sells *OQ* and charges a price, OP_2. His monopoly profit, under zero cost condition equals OP_2EQ. Now, seller *B* enters the market and assumes that *A* will not change his price since he is making maximum profit. With this assumption, *B* sets his price slightly below *A*'s price (OP_2) and is able to sell his total output and also to capture a substantial part of *A*'s market.

Seller *A* now realizes the reduction in his sale. In order to regain his market, *A* sets his price slightly below *B*'s price. This leads to price war between the sellers. The price war takes the form of price cutting which continues until price reaches OP_1. At this price, both *A* and *B* are able to sell their entire output. *A* sells *OM* and *B* sells *OM′*. The price OP_1 could, therefore, be expected to be stable. But, according to Edgeworth, price OP_1 should not be stable.

The reason for instability of the price is that, once price OP_1 is set in the market, the sellers observe an interesting fact. That is, each seller realizes that his rival is selling his entire output and he will, therefore, not change his price, and each seller thinks that he can raise his price to OP_2 and can make pure profit. This realization forms the basis of their action and reaction. For example, let seller *A* take the initiative and raise his price to OP_2. Assuming *A* to retain his price OP_2, *B* finds that if he raises his price to a level slightly below OP_2, he can sell his entire output at a higher price and make greater profits. Therefore, *B* raises his price according to his plan.

Now it is *A's* turn to appraise the situation and react. Seller *A* finds that his price is higher than *B*'s price. His total sale falls. Therefore, assuming *B* to retain his price, seller *A* reduces his price slightly below *B*'s price. Thus, the price war between *A* and *B* begins once again. This process continues indefinitely and price keeps moving up and down between OP_1 and OP_2. Obviously, *according to Edgeworth's model of duopoly, equilibrium is unstable and indeterminate* as price and output are never determined. In the words of Edgeworth, 'There will be an indeterminate tract through which the index of value will oscillate, or, rather vibrate irregularly for an indefinite length of time.'[14]

Edgeworth's model, like Cournot's and Bertrand's model, is based on a naive assumption i.e., each seller continues to assume that his rival will never change his price or output even though they are proved repeatedly wrong. But, Hotelling remarked that Edgeworth's model is definitely an improvement upon Cournot's model in that it assumes price, rather than output, to be the relevant decision variable for the sellers.

Stackelberg's Leadership Model

Stackelberg,[15] a German economist, developed his leadership model of duopoly in 1930. His model is an extension of Cournot's mode. Stackelberg assumes that one of the duopolist (say, firm *A*) is sophisticated enough to play the role of a leader and the other (say, firm *B*) acts as a follower. The leading duopolist firm *A* recognizes that its rival firm *B* has a definite reaction function which firm *A* uses for its his own profit function and maximizes its profits.

Suppose market demand function is given as in Eq. (5.1), i.e., $Q = 90 - P$ and *B*'s reaction function is given as in Eq. (5.9), i.e.,

$$Q_B = \frac{90 - Q_A}{2} \tag{5.9}$$

Now, let firm *A* incorporate firm *B*'s reaction function into the market function and formulate its own demand function as given below.

$$Q_A = (90 - Q_B) - P \tag{5.10}$$

Since Q_B=(90–Q_A)/2, Eq. (5.10) may be written as

$$Q_A = 90 - \frac{90 - Q_A}{2} - P$$

or

$$Q_A = 45 - (Q_A/2) - P$$

or

$$2Q_A = 90 - Q_A - 2P \tag{5.11}$$

$$Q_A = 90 - 2P$$

Thus, by knowing *B*'s reaction function, firm *A* is able to determine its own demand function. Following the profit maximization rule (under zero cost condition), firm *A* will fix its output at 45 units (=90/2), i.e., half of the total demand at zero price.

Now, if firm leading *A* produces 45 units and the follower firm *B* sticks to its own reaction function, it will produce

$$Q_B = \frac{90 - 45}{2} = 22.5 \text{units.} \tag{5.12}$$

Thus, the industry output will be

$$45 + 22.5 = 67.5.$$

Stackelberg's model does not show the determination of equilibrium price. It implies that price set by the leading firm will be the market price. Another problem with Stackelberg's model is that it does not determine as to which of the firms will act as leader (or follower). If each firm assumes itself to be the leader and the other to be the follower, then Stackelberg's model will be indeterminate with unstable equilibrium.

OLIGOPOLY MODELS

In this section, we move to explain some important theories of price and output determination under oligopoly—a kind of market in which the number of sellers is more than two but only a few. As mentioned earlier, there are two kinds of oligopoly models: (i) non-collusive models and (ii) collusive models. We will first discuss the non-collusive models and then proceed to discuss collusive models. The non-collusive models of oligopoly explain the price and output determination in a free market structure in which oligopolists recognize their interdependence. Chamberlin's non-collusive model of oligopoly, i.e., 'small group' model, is considered as a major contribution to the theory of oligopoly. Another famous model of this category is Sweezy's *kinked demand curve model.* We begin our discussion on oligopoly models with Chamberlin's non-collusive model.

Non-Collusive Models of Oligopoly

Chamberlin's Model of Oligopoly: The 'Small Group' Model The *classical* models of duopoly—models developed by Cournot. Bertrand, Edgeworth and Stackelberg—assumed independent action by the rival firms in their attempt to maximize their profits. Chamberlin rejected the assumption of independent action by the competing firms. He developed his own model of oligopoly assuming *interdependence* between the competitors. He argued that firms do not act independently. They do recognize their mutual interdependence. Firms are not as 'stupid' as assumed in the models of Cournot, Edgeworth and Bertrand. In his own words, 'When a move by one seller evidently forces the other to make a counter move, he is very stupidly refusing to look farther than his nose if he proceeds on the assumption that it will not. '[16] Chamberlin suggests that each seller seeking to maximize his profit reflects well and looks into the consequences of his move.[17] The total consequence of a seller's move consists of both its direct and indirect effects. The *direct effects* are those which result from a seller's own action, rival sellers not reacting to his action. The *indirect effects* are those which result from the reaction of the rival sellers to the moves made by a seller.

Chamberlin suggests in his oligopoly model that, if rival firms are assumed to recognize their mutual interdependence and act accordingly, a stable equilibrium can be reached where each firm charges a monopoly price and shares equally the monopoly equilibrium output. When all firms are in equilibrium, industry profit is maximized. Since Chamberlin follows Cournot to develop his own model, Chamberlin's oligopoly model of 'small group' can be best understood if presented in the framework of Cournot's duopoly model.

Cournot's model used by Chamberlin is reproduced in Figure 5.7, added with ordinate *AB*. Suppose, there are two firms, *A* and *B* and let the firm *A* enter the market first as a monopolist. Following the profit maximization rule, firm *A* produces *OQ* and charges monopoly price OP_2 (=*PQ*). When the firm *B* enters the market, it considers that *PM* is its demand curve. Under Cournot's assumption, firm *B* will sell output *QN* at price OP_1. As a result, market price falls from OP_2 to OP_1. It is now *A's* turn to appraise the situation. At this point, Chamberlin *deviates from Cournot's model.* While Cournot's model assumes that firm *A* does not recognize *the interdependence* between them and acts independently, Chamberlin

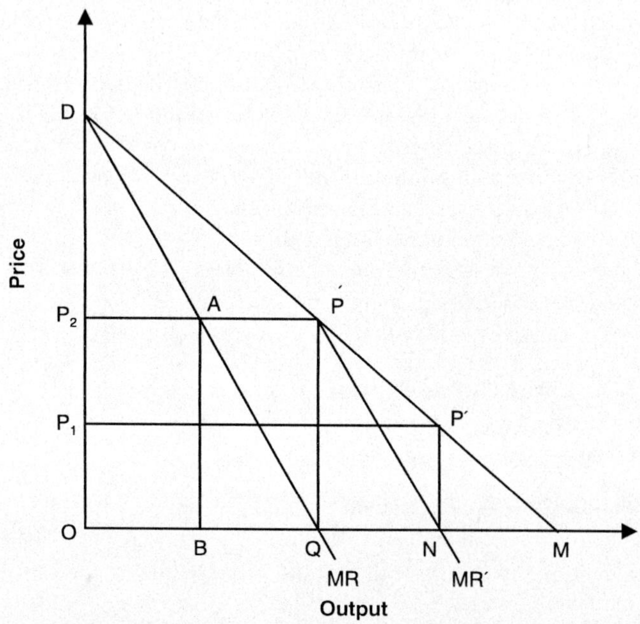

Figure 5.7 *Chamberlin's Model of Stable Equilibrium*

assumes that firm *A* does recognize the interdependence between them and it does recognize the fact that *B* will react to its decisions. Therefore, firm *A* decides to compromise with the existence of firm *B* and decides to reduce its output to *OB* which is half of the monopoly output, *OQ*. Its output *OB* equals *B*'s output *QN* (=*BQ*). In its turn, firm *B* also recognizes their interdependence. Firm *B* moves from point *P*' to point *P*. It realizes that *BQ* is the most profitable output for it. Thus, the industry output is *OQ* which is shared equally by firms *A* and *B*. The total output *OQ* equals *monopoly output* and market price is OP_2(=*PQ*) which equals *monopoly price*. Thus, by recognizing their interdependence, the firms reach a stable equilibrium. This equilibrium is stable because under the condition of interdependence, firms do not gain by changing their price and output.

As discussed earlier, in case of Cournot's model, Chamberlin's duopoly model can be extended to oligopoly.

Criticism Chamberlin's model is regarded as an improvement over the earlier models, at least in respect of its behavioural assumption of interdependence. His model has, however, been criticized on the grounds that the idea of joint profit maximization implicitly assumes that demand and cost functions are known which, in reality, may not be. Unless demand and cost functions are fully known to the competitor, joint profit maximization is doubtful.

Sweezy's Model of Oligopoly: Kinked-Demand Curve Model

The concept and form of the kinked-demand curve was first developed and used by Chamberlin in his theory of monopolistic competition.[18] Later, Hall and Hitch[19] used kinked-demand curve to explain rigidity of prices in oligopolistic market. But, neither Chamberlin nor Hall and Hitch used kinked-demand curve as a tool of analysis in their respective theories. It was Paul M. Sweezy[20] who used the kinked-demand curve in his model of price stability in oligopolistic market. Sweezy's model is described below.

The kinked-demand curve model developed by Paul M. Sweezy has features common to most oligopoly pricing models. This is the best-known model to explain, relatively more satisfactorily, the behaviour of the oligopolistic firms. It must, however, be noted at the outset that *kinked-demand* curve *analysis does not deal with price and output determination*. Rather, it seeks to establish that once a price–quantity combination is determined, an oligopoly firm does not find it profitable to change its price even when there is a considerable change in the cost of production and change in demand for the product.

The logic behind this proposition is as follows. An oligopoly firm believes that if it reduces the price of its product, the rival firms would follow and neutralize the expected gain from price reduction. But, if it raises the price, the firms would either maintain their prices or even go for price cutting, so that the price-raising firm loses a part of its market to the rival firms. This behaviour is true of all the firms. The oligopoly firms would, therefore, find it more desirable to maintain the prevailing price and output. Let us now see how Sweezy has proved this point of view by using kinked demand curve technique.

Sweezy's Kinked-Demand Curve Model In order to analyse the effects of possible reactions of the rival firms on the demand for the product of the firm initiating the change in price, let us make the following assumptions.

1. There are four oligopoly firms—*A*, *B*, *C* and *D*;
2. Market demand is divided between the firms and all the firms face a uniform demand curve and
3. All the firms are in equilibrium at a point of time, all maximizing their profit.

Sweezy's kinked-demand curve model is presented in Figure 5.8 on the basis of these assumptions. Let us suppose that the individual demand curve is given by the curve *MN* and the price is initially fixed

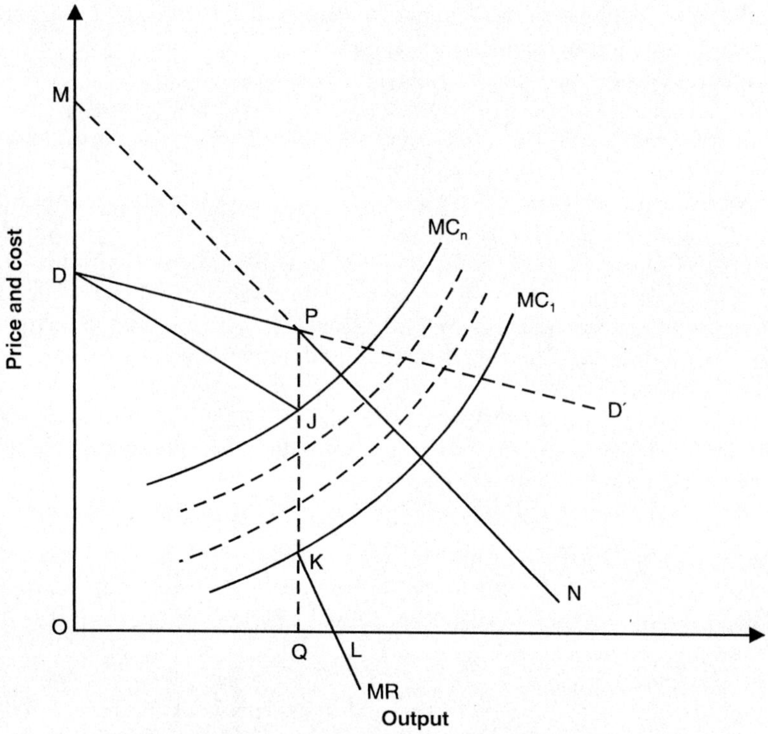

Figure 5.8 *Kinked-Demand Curve Analysis*

at *PQ*. Given the price at *PQ*, let firm *A* take the lead in changing its price. Let us now examine the effect of various kinds of possible reactions of the rival firms on demand for *A*'s product.

- **Reaction (i)**. When firm *A* increases or decreases its price, the rival firms follow the suit. Then, firm *A* finds itself moving along the demand curve *MN′*. It does not gain or lose.
- **Reaction (ii)**. If rival firms do not react to price changes made by the firm *A*, its demand curve will be *DD*'. To explain it further, when firm *A* raises its price and rival firms do not follow, firm *A* loses part of its market to the rival firms and moves along the *PD* part of the demand curve. But, when firm *A* cuts its price down and rival firms do not follow, then it captures a part of the rival's market share and finds itself moving along the *PD′* part of the demand curve. This is what firm *A* would like to achieve. Note that *PD′* part of demand curve is more elastic than *DP*.
- **Reaction (iii)**. When firm *A* raises its price and rival firms do not follow, then firm *A* loses a part of its market share to the rival firms. Then the relevant demand curve for firm *A* is *DP*. But, when firm *A* decreases its price, rival firms react by cutting down their own prices by an equal amount or even more. This counter move by the rival firms prevents firm *A* from taking any advantage of price cut. Therefore, firm *A* is forced to move along the *PN* part of the demand curve.

Thus, the two relevant segments of demand curve for firm *A* (below point *P*) is *PN* and *PD* beyond point *P*. When the two relevant segments of the two demand curves (*MN* and *DD′*) are put together, the demand curve for *A*'s product takes the form of the curve *DPN*. The demand curve *DPN* has a *kink* at point *P*. It is, therefore, called *a kinked-demand curve*.

Consider now the relationship between *AR* and *MR*. We know that $MR = AR - AR/e$. The *MR* curve, drawn on the basis of this relationship, will take a shape as shown by *DJKL* in Figure 5.8. It is discontinuous between points *J* and *K*, at output *OQ*. The segment *DJ* of the *MR* curve corresponds to *DP* segment of the demand curve and *KL* segment of *MR* curve corresponds to *PN* segment of the demand curve.

Now let us see why price gets stabilized at *PQ* even when there is change in cost curves. Suppose *MC* curve of the firms is given as MC_1 which intersects *MR* at point *K*, Point *K* satisfies the necessary condition for profit maximization ($MR = MC$). Therefore, oligopoly firms are in equilibrium at output *OQ* and they are making maximum profit at price *PQ*. Now, if *MC* curve shifts upwards to MC_n or to any level between points *J* and *K*, their profit would not be affected because profit maximization condition remains undistributed. Therefore, they have no motivation for increasing or decreasing their price. It is always beneficial for them to stick to the price *PQ* and output *OQ*. Thus, both price and output are *stable*. The oligopoly firms would think of changing their price and output only if *MC* rises beyond point *J* or falls below point *K* (in Figure 5.8).

To conclude, the basic point that Sweezy's model establishes is the rigidity of price in oligopolistic market. As shown in Figure 5.8, once price is determined in oligopoly, it remains rigidly fixed because profit maximizing firms have no incentive to change price even if *MC* curve shifts upwards or downwards within the range between points *J* and *K*. Therefore, price remains constant over a period of time.

Firm's Equilibrium in a Buoyant Market: The Sellers' Market The kinked-demand curve analysis presented above is relevant mainly to those oligopolistic industries which are working under static or normal business conditions. A similar analysis can be performed for the oligopolistic industries enjoying buoyant business conditions. A buoyant market is one in which demand tends to expand. It is also known as *sellers' market*.

The relevant kinked-demand curve under buoyant business conditions is given by the curve *DPd′* in Figure 5.9. It has been drawn on the assumption that when an oligopoly firm raises its price above *P*,

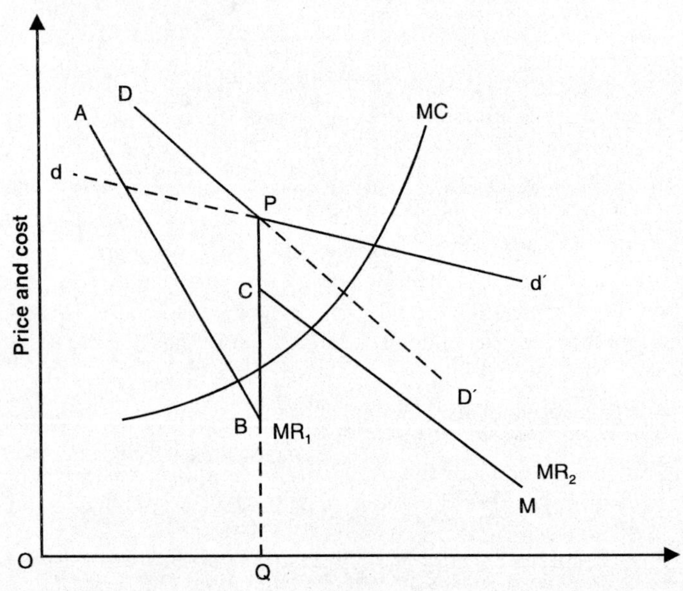

Figure 5.9 *Equilibrium of Oligopoly Firms Under Buoyant Conditions*

other firms also raise their prices by an equal amount, but when it reduces its price below *P*, rival firms do not reduce their prices because their sales are not affected significantly in a buoyant market. Since rival firms follow price rise, only *DP* segment of the demand curve *DD′* is relevant. But, since rival firms do not follow price cut, the price-reducing firm retains its (perceived) individual demand curve *Pd′* under buoyant market conditions. The two segments, *DP* and *Pd′* put together make the demand curve for the product of the price-cutting oligopolist, as shown by *DPd′*. The firm's *MR* curve is shown by the curve *ABCM*. Despite the difference in prices, the market price would tend to stabilize. It is obvious from the figure that *MC* intersects both *MR* curves, *AB* and *CM* marked as MR_1 and MR_2, respectively. It means that some firms equalize their *MC* and *MR* at MR_1 and some firms at MR_2. So the firms of both the categories maximize their profits under buoyant business conditions.

However, these very conditions may create instability in price and output. Since *MC* intersects both the *MR* curves, it implies that profits increase irrespective of rise or fall in price. Therefore, while some firms would like to raise their price, others would prefer to reduce their price. This kind of firm's behaviour makes the market condition unstable, and determination of prices and outputs uncertain. It is, therefore, not possible to make any generalizations about oligopoly price and output under buoyant market conditions.

Criticism of Sweezy's Model As mentioned earlier, Sweezy's model is considered to be the best-known model that explains relatively more satisfactorily the behaviour of the firms in oligopoly. On the face it, it appears to be logically sound and realistic. However, economists have criticized Sweezy's model on both theoretical and empirical grounds, which are summarized below.

1. ***Sweezy's Model does not Explain Price Determination***. The basic function of price theory is to explain price and output determination in a particular kind of market. Sweezy's model, however, does not explain price and output determination. His model only assumes the price to be given at a point to time. It explains only why price once determined tends to be sticky even if there are changes in cost conditions to a certain extent. Sweezy's model is, therefore, regarded as an *ex-post rationalization* rather than *ex-ante* explanation of market equilibrium.
2. ***This Model does not Determine the Point of Kink***. This is a criticism related to non-determination of price. The kinked-demand curve analysis explains why 'kink' appears on the demand curve. It does not explain how and at what level of price and output, the point of kink is determined. George Stigler"[21] doubts even the existence of the kinked demand curve. Stigler's view is supported by Julian Simon.[22] This makes the model a purely hypothetical one, not as realistic as it appears on the face of it.
3. ***Price Rigidity is not Supported by Empirical Facts***. Sweezy's claim of price rigidity in oligopoly does not stand the test of empirical verification. Empirical facts reveal a surprising lack of price stability in oligopoly markets. Empirically, monopoly prices have been found to be more stable than oligopoly prices. Economists' opinion is, however, divided on the issue of price rigidity in oligopoly. While Stigler[23] has questioned price rigidity in oligopoly market, Liebhafsky[24] finds considerable evidence of price rigidity in oligopolistic industries of the US. Cohen and Cyert argue that kink in the demand curve and price rigidity may exist for a short period, for lack of inter-firm information, especially when new and unknown rivals enter the market. They are of the opinion that kink is clearly not a stable long-run equilibrium.[25]
4. ***Sweezy's Conclusion Conflict with Marginal Productivity Theory***. In Sweezy's model, *MC* curve can shift up and down (say, between finite points *J* and *K* in Figure 5.8), while *MR* remains the same. This argument is in conflict with *marginal productivity theory* of factor pricing as this means that factor prices do not necessarily equal the marginal revenue (*MR*) productivity.

COLLUSIVE MODEL OF OLIGOPOLY

The oligopoly models discussed in the previous sections are based on the *assumption* that the oligopoly firms act *independently*; they are in competition with one another; and there is *no collusion* between the firms. The oligopoly models of this category are called *non-collusive models*. In reality, however, oligopoly firms are found to be in some kind of collusion or agreement—open or secret, explicit or tacit, written or unwritten, and legal or illegal—with one another for at least *three major reasons*.

First, collusion eliminates or reduces the degree of competition between the firms and gives them some monopolistic powers in their price and output decisions.

Secondly, collusion reduces the degree of uncertainty surrounding the oligopoly firms and ensure profit maximization.

Thirdly, collusion creates some kind of barriers to the entry of new firms.

The models that deal with the collusive oligopolies are called *collusive oligopoly models*. Collusion between firms may take many forms depending on their relative strength and objective of collusion, and on whether collusion is legal or illegal.[26] There are, however, two major forms of collusion between the oligopoly firms: (i) cartel, i.e., firms' association and (ii) price leadership agreements.

Accordingly, collusive oligopoly models can be classified as:

1. Cartel models and
2. Price leadership models.

In this section, we will discuss these two types of oligopoly models.

What is a Cartel Form of Collusion?

A *cartel* is a formal collusion of the oligopoly firms in an industry with a purpose. A general purpose of cartels is to centralize certain managerial decisions and functions of individual firms of the industry, with a view to promoting common benefits. Cartels may be in the form of *open* or *secret collusion*. Whether open or secret, cartel agreements are *explicit* and formal, in the sense, that agreements are enforceable on member firms not observing the Cartel rules or dishonouring the agreements. Cartels are, therefore, regarded as *the perfect form of collusion*. Cartels and cartel-type agreements between the firms in manufacturing and trade are illegal in most countries. Yet, cartels in the broader sense of the term exist in the form of trade associations, professional organizations and the like.

A cartel performs a variety of functions for its members. The two services of central importance are:

1. Fixing price for joint profit maximization and
2. Market sharing between its members.

Let us now discuss price and output determination under cartel system.

Joint Profit Maximization by the Cartel Let us suppose that a group of firms producing a homogeneous commodity forms a cartel aiming at joint profit maximization. The firms constitute a cartel management board with powers to take decisions on the following aspects.

1. The total quantity to be produced;
2. The price at which it must be sold and
3. The share of each firm in the total output.

The cartel board is provided with cost data of individual firms. Besides, it is supposed to obtain the necessary data required to formulate the market demand (*AR*) curve. The cartel board calculates the *MC* and *MR* for the industry. In a sense, the cartel board holds the position of a multi-plant monopoly. It determines the price and output for each firm in the manner a multi-plant monopoly determines the price and output for each of its plants.

The model of price and output determination for each firm is presented in Figure 5.10. For the sake of analytical convenience, let us suppose that there are only two firms, *A* and *B*, in the cartel. Their respective cost curves are given in the first two panels of Figure 5.10. In the third panel, *AR* and *MR* curves represent the revenue conditions of the *industry*. The *MC* curve in the industry panel is the summation of *mc* curves of the individual firms, i.e., $MC = MC_A + MC_B$. The *MC* and *MR* curves intersect at point *C* determining the industry output at *OQ*. The market price is determined at $PQ = OP_C$. The industry output *OQ* is so allocated between firms *A* and *B* that their individual $MC = MR$. The share of each firm in the industry output, *OQ*, can be obtained by drawing a line from point *C* and parallel to *X*-axis through MC_B and MC_A. The points of intersection C_A and C_B determine the level of output for firms *A* and *B*, respectively. Thus, the share of firms *A* and *B*, is determined at OQ_A and OQ_B, respectively, where $OQ_A + OQ_B = OQ$. At these outputs, they maximize their respective profits.

A Numerical Illustration of Joint Profit Maximization by the Cartel[27] To illustrate price and output determination numerically by the cartel, let us assume that there are only two firms, F_1 and F_2 forming the cartel for joint profit maximization under the following conditions.

1. Market demand function: $Q = 50 - 0.5P$ Price (the reverse demand) function: $P = 100 - 2Q$
2. Cost functions $F_1 : C_1 = 100 + 20Q_1 + Q_1^2$
   $F_2 : C_2 = 48 + 36Q_2 + 2Q_2^2$

Total joint profit (II) is the sum of individual profits of the two firms. That is,

$$\Pi = \Pi_1 + \Pi_2$$

where Π_1 denotes profit of firm F_1 and Π_2 denotes profit of firm F_2.

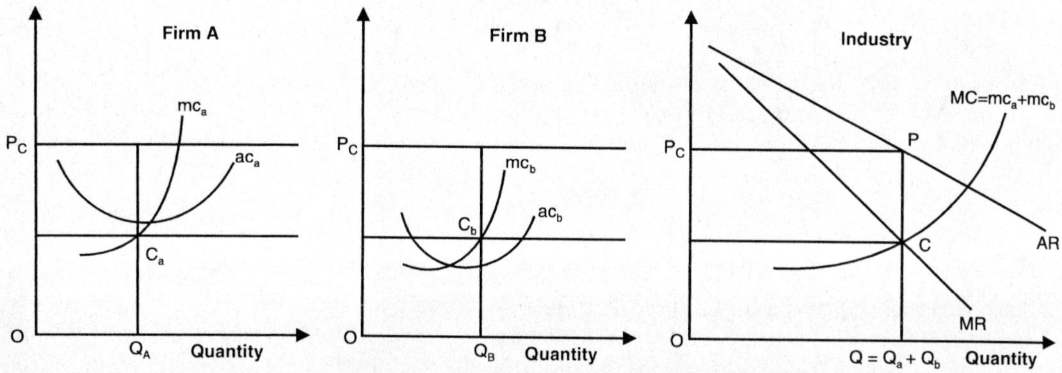

Figure 5.10 *Price and Output Determination Under Cartel*

The measure of the profit of the individual firms can be expressed as

$$\Pi_1 = R_1 - C_1$$

and

$$\Pi_2 = R_2 - C_2$$

where R_1 = total revenue of F_1 and R_2 = total revenue of firm F_2.

Since $R_1 = P \cdot Q_1$ and $R_2 = P \cdot Q_2$, by substitution, total joint profit can be redefined as

$$\begin{aligned}\Pi &= P \cdot Q_1 + P \cdot Q_2 - (C_1 + C_2)\\ &= P(Q_1 + Q_2) - (C_1 + C_2) \qquad (5.13)\end{aligned}$$

By substituting price and cost functions into the profit equation (5.13), we get

$$\begin{aligned}\Pi &= \left[100 - 2(Q_1 + Q_2)\right](Q_1 + Q_2) - \left(100 + 20Q_1 + 2Q_1^2 + 48 + 36Q_2 + 2Q_2^2\right)\\ &= 100Q_1 - 2Q_1Q_2 - 2Q_1^2 + 100Q_2 - 2Q_2^2 - 2Q_1Q_2 - 148 - 20Q_1 - 36Q_2 - 2Q_2^2\\ &= 80Q_1 + 64Q_2 - 4Q_1^2 - 4Q_2^2 - 4Q_1Q_2 - 148 \qquad (5.14)\end{aligned}$$

Since $\Pi = \Pi_1 + \Pi_2$, profit maximization requires that Π_1 and Π_2 are maximized. The first-order condition of profit maximization requires that partial derivative of the individual profit functions, i.e., $\partial\Pi/\partial Q$, is equal to zero. Although, individual profit functions are not known, the partial derivative of the individual firm's profit function can be obtained by differentiating profit function (5.14) with respect to Q_1 and Q_2 and setting them equal to zero as shown below.

$$\frac{\partial\Pi}{\partial Q_1} = 80 - 8Q_1 - 4Q_2 = 0 \qquad (5.15)$$

and

$$\frac{\partial\Pi}{\partial Q_2} = 64 - 8Q_2 - 4Q_1 = 0 \qquad (5.16)$$

Equations (5.15) and (5.16) are two simultaneous equations with two unknowns (Q_1 and Q_2) which can be solved for Q_1 and Q_2 as follows. Equations (5.15) and (5.16) can be written, respectively, as follows.

$$8Q_1 + 4Q_2 = 80 \qquad (5.17)$$

$$4Q_1 + 8Q_2 = 64 \qquad (5.18)$$

By solving these equations for Q_1 and Q_2, we get $Q_1 = 8$ and $Q_2 = 4$.

This means that cartel will maximize profit by dividing the market between firms F_1 and F_2 in proportion of 8 and 4. This will maximize their joint profit. Maximum profit can be obtained by substituting 8 and 4 for Q_1 and Q_2, respectively, in profit function (5.14), reproduced below.

$$\Pi = 80Q_1 + 64Q_2 - 4Q_1^2 - 4Q_2^2 - 4Q_1Q_2 - 148$$

By substitution,

$$\begin{aligned}\Pi &= 80(8) + 64(4) - 4(8)^2 - 4(4)^2 - 4(8)(4) - 148\\ &= 640 + 256 - 256 - 64 - 128 - 148\\ &= 300\end{aligned}$$

Thus, joint profit is maximized at 300 with firm F_1 producing and selling 8 units and firm F_2 producing and selling 4 units. Thus, joint output equals 12. By substituting 12 for Q in price function, we get the common price at Rs 76. By substituting 8 and 4 units in TR and TC functions of firms F_1 and F_2, one can obtain firms' individual share in total profit: it is 220 for F_1 and 80 for F_2 and 220 + 80 = 300.

Problems in Joint Profit Maximization Although the solution to joint profit maximization by cartel appears to be theoretically sound, William Fellner[28] gives the following reasons why profits may not be maximized jointly.

First, it is difficult to estimate market demand curve accurately because each firm thinks that the demand for its own product is more elastic than the market demand curve as its product is a perfect substitute for the product of other firms.

Secondly, an accurate estimation of industry's MC curve is highly improbable for lack of adequate and correct cost data. If industry's MC is incorrectly estimated, industry output can be only incorrectly determined. Hence joint profit maximization is doubtful.

Thirdly, cartel negotiations take a long time. During the period of negotiations, the composition of the industry and its cost structure may change. This may render the estimates irrelevant, even if they are correct. Besides, if the number of firms increases beyond 20 or so, cartel formation becomes difficult, or even if it is formed, it tends to break down soon or it becomes ineffective.

Fourthly, there are 'chiselers' who have a strong temptation to give hidden or undisclosed concessions to their customers. This tendency in the cartel members reduces the prospect of joint profit maximization.

Fifthly, if cartel price, like monopoly price, is very high, it may invite government attention and interference. For the fear of government interference, members may not follow the cartel price agreement.

Sixthly, another reason for not charging the cartel price is the fear of entry of new firms. A high cartel price which yields monopoly profit may attract new firms to the industry. To prevent the entry of new firms, some firms may decide on their own not to charge the cartel price.

Finally, yet another reason for not charging the cartel price is the desire to build a public image or good reputation. Some firms may, to this end, decide to charge only a fair price and realize only a fair profit.

Non-Price Competition and Market Sharing by Cartel The market-sharing cartels are more common because this kind of collusion permits a considerable degree of freedom in respect of style of the product, advertising and other selling activities. There are two main methods of market allocations: (a) non-price competition agreement and (b) quota system.

1. ***Non-price Competition Agreement.*** The non-price competition agreements are usually associated with loose cartels. Under the non-price competition agreement between the firms, a uniform price is fixed and each firm is allowed to sell as much as it can at the cartel price. The only obligatory condition is that firms are not allowed to reduce the price below the cartel price.

The cartel price is a bargain price. While low-cost firms press for a low price, the high-cost firms press for a higher price. But the cartel price is so fixed by mutual consent that all member firms are able to make some profits. However, firms are allowed to compete with one another in the market on a non-price basis. That is, they are allowed to change the style of their product, innovate new designs and to promote their sales without reducing their price below the level of cartel price.

Whether this kind of agreement works or breaks down depend on the cost conditions of the individual firms. If some firms expect to increase their profits by violating the price agreements, they will indulge in cheating by charging a lower price. This may lead to a price war and the cartel may break down.

2. ***Quota System***. The second method of market sharing is *quota system*. Under this system, the cartel fixes a quota of market share for each firm. There is no uniform principle by which quota is fixed. In practice, however, quota for each firm is determined on the basis of the following factors.
   (a) Bargaining ability of a firm and its relative importance in the industry,
   (b) The relative sales or market share of the firms in pre-cartel period and
   (c) Production capacity of the firms on the base period. The choice of the base period depends on the bargaining ability of the firm.
3. ***Fixation of Quota*** is, however, a difficult problem. Nevertheless, some theoretical guidelines for market sharing are suggested as follows. A reasonable criterion for ideal market sharing can be to share the total market between the cartel members in such proportions that the industry's *MC* equals the *MC* of individual firms. This criterion is illustrated in Figure 5.11 assuming an oligopoly industry consisting of only two firms, *A* and *B*. The *AR*, *MR* and *MC* curves of the two firms are given in panels (a) and (b), respectively. The summation of their *AR*, *MR* and *MC* curves are given in panel (c). There curves make the industry *AR*, *MR* and *MC* curves as shown by the AR_M, MR_M and *MC* curves in panel (c). The MR_M and *MC* curves intersect at point *C* determining the profit maximizing output of the industry at *OQ*. The quota for each firm is

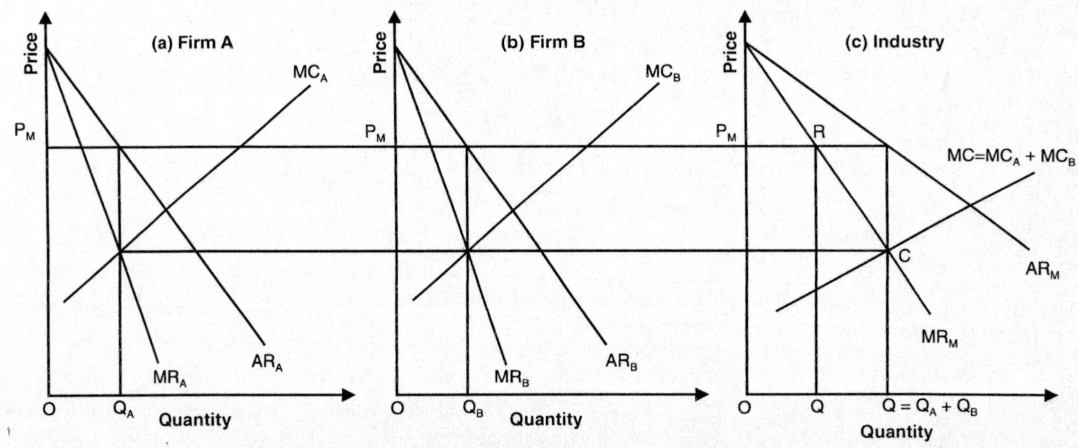

Figure 5.11 *Quota Allocation Under Cartel Agreements*

determined by finding the output of each firm at which their individual MR is equal to industry MC. A horizontal line drawn form point C thought MR_B and MR_A determines their quota. As panel (a) shows market share for firm A is determined at OQ_A and panel (b) shows market share of firm B at OQ_B. Thus, the industry output OQ is shared between the two firms A and B, as OQ_A and OQ_B, respectively. Note that $OQ = OQ_A + OQ_B$. At output OQ_A, MC of firm A equals industry's marginal cost, MC, and at output OQ_B, MC of firm B equals industry's MC. Thus, under quota system, the quota for firms A and B would be fixed as OQ_A and OQ_B, respectively. As Figure 5.11 shows both the firms fix the same price, OP_M. However, given the quota allocation, the firm may set different prices for their product depending on the position and elasticity of their individual demand curves. This criterion is identical to the one adopted by a multiplant monopolist in the short run, to allocate the total output between the plants.

Another reasonable criterion for market sharing under quota system is *equal market share for equal firms*. This criterion is applicable where all firms have *identical* cost and revenue curves. This criterion also leads to a monopoly solution. It resembles Chamberlin's duopoly model.

To illustrate equal market sharing through quota allocation, let us assume that there are only two firms, A and B. Suppose their AR, MR and MC curves are given as in Figure 5.11(a) and (b), respectively, the market revenue and cost curves, which are obtained by summing the individual revenue and cost curves, are presented in part (c) of the figure. As shown in panel (c) of Figure 5.11, MR_M and MC intersect at point C. Thus, the industry equilibrium output is determined at OQ. The share of each firm, which maximizes their profits, is so determined that $OQ = OQ_A + OQ_B$. Given the identical cost and revenue conditions, $OQ_A = OQ_B$. That is, market is divided equally between firms A and B. This result can be obtained also by drawing an ordinate from the point where price line (P_M) intersects the MR_M, i.e., from point R. The market output OQ is divided equally between firms A and B.

It may be noted at the end that cartels do not necessarily create the conditions for price stability in an oligopolistic market. Most cartels are loose. Cartel agreements are generally not binding on the members. Cartels do not prevent the possibility of entry of new firms. On the contrary, by ensuring monopoly profits, cartels, in fact, create conditions which attract new firms to the industry. Besides, 'chiselers' and 'free-riders' create conditions for instability in price and output.

Price Leadership Models

Price leadership is an imperfect form of collusion between oligopoly firms. Price leadership is an informal position given to or attained by a firm in an oligopolistic setting to lead other firms in pricing. This leadership may emerge spontaneously due to technical reasons or out of tacit or explicit, agreements between the firms to assign leadership role to one of the firms.

The *spontaneous price leadership* may be result of such technical reasons as size, efficiency, economies of scale and firm's ability to control the market. The most typical case of price leadership is the leading role played by the dominant firm of the industry. The dominant firm takes lead in price changes and the smaller ones follow. Sometimes price leadership is *barometric*. In the barometric price leadership, one of the firms, not necessarily dominant one, takes lead in announcing change in price, particularly when such a change is due but is not brought into effect due to uncertainty in the market.

The price leadership is possible under the conditions of both *product homogeneity* and *product differentiation*. There may, however, be price differentials on account of product differentiation. Price differentials may also exist on account of cost differentials.

Another important aspect of price leadership is that it often serves as a means to price discipline and price stabilization. Achievement of this objective establishes an effective price leadership. Such a price leadership can, however, exist effectively only under the following conditions.

1. Number of firms is small;
2. Entry to the industry is restricted;
3. Products are, large and homogeneous;
4. Demand for industry is inelastic or has a very low elasticity and
5. Firms have almost similar cost curves.

As mentioned earlier, there are three common types of price leaderships:

1. Price leadership by a low-cost or most efficient firm;
2. Price leadership by the dominant firm and
3. Barometric price leadership.

Let us discuss price and output determination under the three kinds of price leaderships.

Price Leadership by a Low-Cost Firm

The price and output decisions under price leadership of a low-cost firm are illustrated in Figure 5.12. Suppose all the firms face identical revenue curves as shown by *AR* and *MR* curves. But the largest firm or the low-cost firm has its cost curves as shown by AC_1 and MC_1, whereas all the rival firms, smaller in size, have their cost curves as shown by AC_2 and MC_2. The largest firm has greater economies of

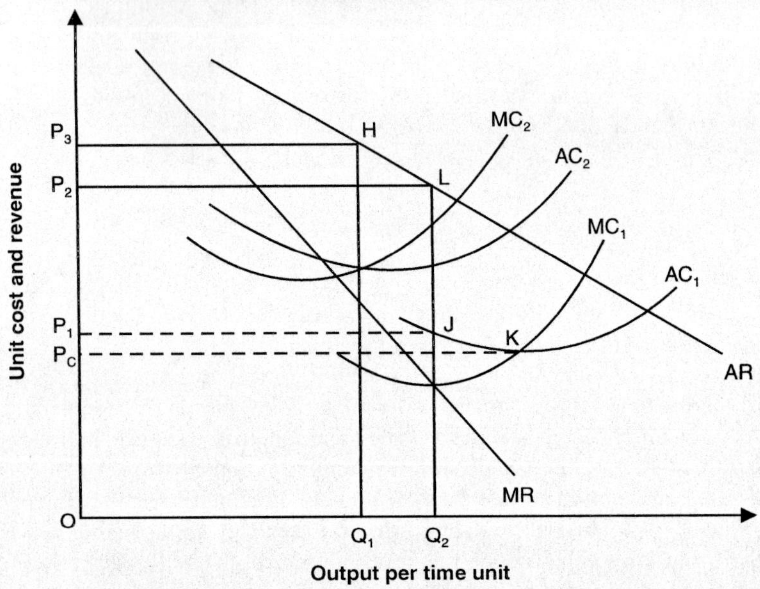

Figure 5.12 *Price Leadership by a Low-Cost Firm*

scale and, therefore, its cost of production is lower than that of the other firms. Given the cost and revenue conditions, the low-cost firm would find it most profitable to produce and sell OQ_2 and fix its price at OP_2 (=LQ_2). Since at this level of output, its $MC = MR$, its profit is maximum. On the other hand, the high-cost firms would be in a position to maximize their profit at price OP_3 and quantity OQ_1. But, if they charge a higher price, OP_3 they would lose their customers to the low-cost firm. The high-cost firms are, therefore, forced to accept the price OP_2 and recognize the price leadership of the low-cost firm.

Note that the low-cost firm can eliminate other firms and become a monopolist by cutting the price down to OP_1 (=JQ_2). The low-cost firm can sell its entire output OQ_2 at price OP_1 and make only normal profit. If necessary, it can cut its price further down to OP_0 and still make normal profits. It will, however, not do so as it would avoid falling under anti-monopoly laws. This is how price leadership of the low-cost firm is established.

Numerical Illustration Suppose there are two oligopoly firms—Firm 1 and Firm 2—selling homogeneous products and, therefore, they face the same demand curve. These demand curves are, however, expressed with different notations for the sake of computational convenience. Suppose demand curves of Firm 1 and Firm 2 and their reverse demand functions (i.e., the price function) are given as follows.

$$\text{Firm 1: } Q_1 = 50 - 0.5P_1\text{: } P_1 = 100 - 2Q_1 \tag{5.19}$$

$$\text{Firm 2: } Q_2 = 50 - 0.5P_2\text{: } P_2 = 100 - 2Q_2 \tag{5.20}$$

Suppose also that Firm 1 is a low-cost firm and Firm 2 is a high-cost firm. Their respective cost functions are given as follows.

$$\text{Firm 1: } TC_1 = 100 + 20Q_1 \cdot 2Q_1^2 \tag{5.21}$$

$$AC_1 = TC_1/Q_1 = \left(100 + 20Q_1 + 2Q_1^2\right)/Q_1$$

$$= 20 + 2Q + 100/Q \tag{5.22}$$

$$\text{Firm 2: } TC_2 = 48 + 36Q_2 + 2Q_2^2 \tag{5.23}$$

$$AC_2 = TC_1/Q_1 = \left(48 + 36Q_2 + 2Q_2^2\right)/Q_2$$

$$= 36 + 2Q_2 + 48/Q_2 \tag{5.24}$$

Let us now see how oligopoly firms will set their price and output independently acting as monopolies. Like all other firms, Firm 1 will determine its output at the level which maximizes its total profit, Π_1. Total profit is maximum, where

$$\Pi_1 = TR_1 - TC_1 \text{ is maximum}$$

For Firm 1, TC_1 is given in Eq. (5.21). What we need now is to find its TR_1.

$$TR_1 = P_1 \cdot Q_1$$

$$= (100 - 2Q_1)Q_1$$

$$= 100Q_1 - 2Q_1^2 \tag{5.25}$$

By substituting TR_1 and TC_1 into the profit equation, we get the profit function for Firm 1 as

$$\Pi_1 = 100Q_1 - 2Q_1^2 - \left(100 + 20Q_1 + 2Q_1^2\right)$$
$$= 80Q_1 - 4Q_1^2 - 100 \tag{5.26}$$

Profit maximizing output for Firm 1 can be obtained by taking the first derivative of its profit function (5.26) and setting it equal to zero. Thus,

$$\frac{\partial \Pi_1}{\partial Q_1} = 80 - 8Q_1 = 0 \tag{5.27}$$

By solving Eq. (5.27), we get $Q_1 = 10$.

Alternatively, Q_1 can be obtained by finding and equating MC_1 and MR_1 functions. MC_1 can be obtained by differentiating TC_1 function (5.21) and MR by differentiating TR_1 function (5.25).

Profit maximizing price (P_1) and average cost (AC_1) of Firm 1 can be obtained by substituting 10 for Q in price function (5.19) and AC function (5.22), respectively. Thus,

$$P_1 = 100 - 2Q_1$$
$$= 100 - 2(10)$$
$$= \text{Rs } 80$$

and

$$AC_1 = 20 + 2Q + 100/Q$$
$$= 20 + 2Q + 100/Q = \text{Rs } 50$$

Firm 2 will also set its output at the level which maximizes its profit, Π_2

$$\Pi_2 = \text{tr}_2 - \text{tc}_{2.}$$

The TC_2 of Firm 2 is given in Eq. (5.23). Its TR, i.e., TR_2 can be obtained as follows

$$TR_2 = P_1 \cdot Q_2$$
$$= (100 - 2Q_2)Q_2$$
$$= 100Q_2 - 2Q_2$$

By substitution, we get profit function as

$$\Pi_2 = 100Q_1 - 2Q_1^2 - \left(48 + 36Q_2 + 2Q_2^2\right)$$
$$= 64Q_2 - 4Q_2^2 - 48 \tag{5.28}$$

As in case of Firm 1, profit maximizing output of Firm 2 can be obtained by setting the first derivative of its profit function (5.28) equal to zero. Thus,

$$\frac{\partial \Pi_2}{\partial Q_2} = 64 - 8Q_2 = 0. \tag{5.29}$$

By solving Eq. (5.29), we get $Q_2 = 8$.

Profit maximizing price (P_2) and average cost (AC_2) of Firm 2 can now be obtained by substituting output 8 for Q_2 in price function (5.20) and AC function (5.24), respectively. Thus,

$$P_2 = 100 - 2Q_2$$
$$= 100 - 2(8) = \text{Rs } 84$$

and

$$AC_2 = 36 + 2Q_2 + \frac{48}{Q_2}$$
$$= 36 + 2 \times 8 + \frac{48}{8}$$
$$= \text{Rs } 58$$

To summarize, given the market demand function and individual cost functions, the two firms will set their price and output in the absence of collusion between them as follows.

$$\text{Firm 1: } Q_1 = 10 \text{ and } P_1 = 80$$

and

$$\text{Firm 2: } Q_2 = 8 \text{ and } P_2 = 84$$

Under the *price leadership model*, however, Firm 1, a low-cost firm, acting as price leader will set the price of its product at Rs 80 and Firm 2 will also set the price of its product at Rs 80, the price set by Firm 1. Note that per unit profit of Firm 2 is reduced from Rs 26 ($=P_2 - AC_2 = 84 - 58$) to Rs 22 ($=80 - 58$). But this happens only when a high-cost firm has to accept the price leadership of the low-cost firm.

Price Leadership by the Dominant Firm

Price leadership by a dominant firm is found to be more common than by a low-cost firm. In the analysis of price leadership by a dominant firm, it is assumed that there exists a large size firm in the industry, which supplies a large proportion of the total market.[29] The dominance of the large firm is indicated by the fact that it could possibly eliminate all its rival firms by price cutting. In that case, the large firm gains the status of a monopoly which may invite legal problems. The dominant firm, therefore, compromises with the existence of the rival firms in the market. It uses its dominance to set its price so as to maximize its profit. The smaller firms recognize their weak position and behave like a firm in a perfectly competitive market, i.e., smaller firms accept the price set by the dominant firm.

The price leadership and market sharing between the dominant firm and the rival small firms as a group is illustrated in Figure 5.13. Suppose that the market demand curve is given by DD_M and the supply curve of the small firms is given by the curve S_S in panel (a) of the figure. The problem confronting the dominant firm is to determine its price and output that will maximize its profit, leaving the rest of the market to be jointly supplied by the small firms. To solve this problem, the dominant firm finds its demand curve by deducting the quantity supplied jointly by the small firms at different prices from the corresponding market demand. The dominant firms consider the residual of the market share as the

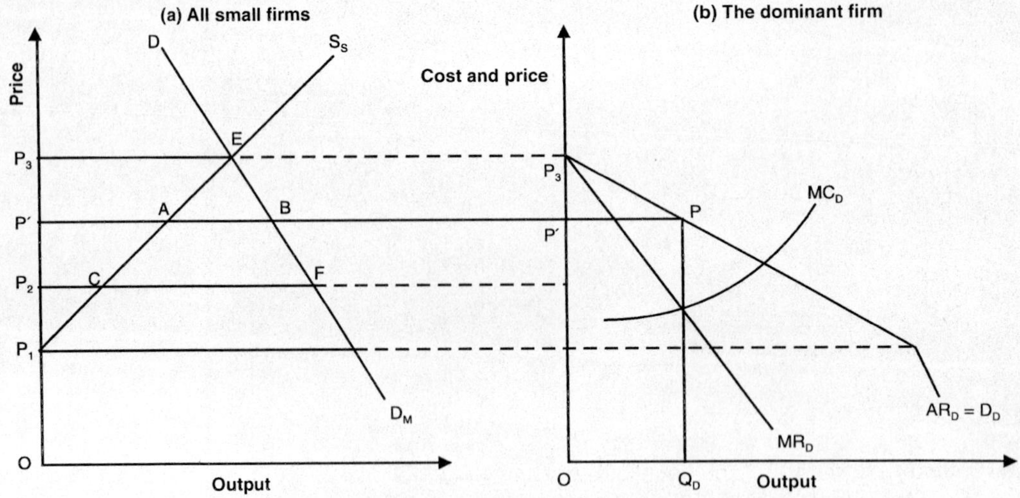

Figure 5.13 *Price Leadership by a Dominant Firm*

demand for its own product. Thus, at a given price the market share of the dominant firm equals the market demand *less* the share of small firms.

For example, when market price is set at OP_3, the total supply by the smaller firms is P_3E which equals the market demand. Therefore, at price OP_3, the market left for the dominant firm is zero. When price falls to OP_2, the demand for dominant firm's product is $CF = P_2F - P_2C$. Following this process, the market share of the dominant firm at other prices can be easily obtained.

Note that the gap between demand curve DD_M and supply curve P_1S_S below point E in Figure 5.13(a) measures the demand for the dominant firm.

The demand so derived and plotted graphically gives P_3D_D as the demand curve for the dominant firm [Figure 5.13(b)]. Since the relation between AR and MR is known, the MR curve for the dominant firm can be derived as MR_D [Figure 5.13(b)]. If MC curve of the dominant firm is assumed to be given as MC_D, its profit maximizing output will be OQ_D and price PQ_D.

Once the dominant firm sets its price at $PQ_D = OP'$, the small firms have to accept this price, and then their joint market demand curve is the horizontal straight line PB [in Figure 5.13(a)], because they can sell at this price as much as they can produce. But, in order to maximize their joint profits, small firms will produce jointly only $P'A$. For small firms, therefore, profit maximizing joint output is $P'A$.

Numerical Illustration Suppose there are five firms—one of them being dominant—in an industry supplying a nearly homogeneous product. Suppose also that market demand function for the product of all the five firms is given as

$$Q_M = 100 - 2P \tag{5.30}$$

and the combined supply function of four small firms is given as

$$Q_S = 10 + P. \tag{5.31}$$

Given the demand and supply functions (5.30) and (5.31), respectively, the market equilibrium without the dominant firm can be obtained by equating the demand and supply functions. Thus, the market for small firms is in equilibrium where

$$Q_S = Q_M$$
$$10 + P = 100 - 2P$$
$$P = 30$$

The market supplied by the four small firms together can be obtained by substituting 30 for P in either the demand or supply function. Using the supply function,

$$\begin{aligned} Q_S &= 10 + P \\ &= 10 + 30 \\ &= 40 \end{aligned}$$

This means that five small firms jointly supply 40 units at $P = 30$.

Now, let us see how the dominant firm works out the demand function for its product and sets its price. The demand function for the dominant firm can be obtained by deducting the quantity ($Q_S = 40$) supplied by the small firms from the market demand function (5.30). Thus,

$$\begin{aligned} Q_D &= Q_M - Q_S \\ &= (100 - 2P) - 40 \\ &= 60 - 2P \end{aligned} \tag{5.32}$$

The dominant firm's profit maximizing output (Q_D) and price (P_D) can be obtained by finding and equating its MC_D and MR_D functions. Suppose its total cost function (TC_D) is given as

$$TC_D = 50 + 6Q_D + 0.25Q_D^2 \tag{5.33}$$

The marginal cost function (MC_D) of the dominant firm can be obtained by differentiating the TC_D function (5.33). Thus,

$$MC_D = \frac{\partial TC_D}{\partial Q_D} = 6 + 0.5Q_D \tag{5.34}$$

The TR function (TR_D) of the dominant firm can be obtained as follows: Given the Q_D function (5.32), the price function or the reverse demand function (P_D) can be estimated as

$$P_D = 30 - 0.5Q_D \tag{5.35}$$

Given the price function (5.35), TR_D ($=P_DQ_D$) can be obtained as

$$\begin{aligned} TR_D &= (30 - 0.5Q_D)Q_D \\ &= 30Q_D - 0.5Q_D^2 \end{aligned} \tag{5.36}$$

Dominant firm's MR function can be obtained by differentiating the TR function (5.36), as

$$MR_D = \frac{\partial TR_D}{\partial Q_D} = 30 - Q_D$$

Now that the dominant firm's MC_D and MR_D functions have been obtained, the profit maximizing Q_D and P_D can be worked out as follows. At equilibrium,

$$MC_D = MR_D$$
$$6 + 0.5Q_D = 30 - Q_D$$
$$1.5Q = 24$$
$$Q = 16$$

Having obtained the equilibrium output ($Q_D = 16$), equilibrium price P_D can be obtained by substituting 16 for Q_D in its price function (5.32). That is,

$$P_D = 30 - 0.5$$
$$= 22 \text{ (Rs)}$$

To conclude, the dominant firm fixes its output at 16 and price at Rs 22. This price has to be accepted by the small firms. Thus, $P_D = 22$ becomes the market price (P) common for both the dominant and the small firms, i.e., $P = 22$. The final market share of the dominant and small firms can be worked out as follows. The total demand at price $P = 22$ can be obtained by substituting 22 for P in the market demand function (5.30).

$$\text{Total demand} = 100 - 2(22)$$
$$= 56$$

Of the total demand of 56 units at price Rs 22, only 16 units will be supplied by the dominant firm and the remaining part of the market, i.e., 56 – 16 = 40, will be shared by the four small firms.

Critical Appraisal The dominant-firm price leadership model, as presented above, yields a stable solution to the problem of price and output determination under oligopoly only if the small firms faithfully follow the leader. That is, small firms produce the right quantity and charge the price set by the dominant firm. Besides, the model requires that the dominant firm should be both large and a low-cost firm. For, if a firm does not enjoy the advantage of large size and, consequent upon it, the advantage of low cost, it cannot act as a price leader.

In practice, however, one finds many cases of price leadership by a firm which is neither large nor a low-cost firm. But such cases are found mostly under recessionary conditions when a relatively smaller firm reduces its price, to survive in the market.

Furthermore, if the dominant firm loses its cost advantages, it also loses its leadership. Such cases are frequent in the real business world. Leadership also changes following the innovation of products and techniques of production by the relatively small firms.

Besides, where there are many large firms of equal size and have some cost advantage, price leadership by any firm or group of firms becomes less probable, particularly when the number of small firms is smaller than that of larger firms. Under such conditions, barometric leadership emerges.

Lastly, it is assumed that the entry of new firms is prevented either by low cost of the existing firms or by initial high cost of new firms. In practice, however, many firms having the capacity to diversify their products enter the industry with relatively initial low cost.

For these reasons, dominant-firm leadership model is not considered to be a realistic one.

The Barometric Price Leadership

Another form of price leadership is *barometric price leadership*. In this form of price leadership, a firm initiates well-publicized changes in price which are generally followed by the rival firms. This kind of price leadership may not necessarily come from the largest firm of the industry. The barometric firm is, however, supposed to have a better knowledge of the prevailing market conditions and has an ability to predict the market conditions more precisely than any of its competitors. These qualities of the barometric firm should have been established and recognized over time by the rival firms. The firm having the qualifications of price leadership is regarded as a barometer, which reflects the changes in business conditions and environment of the industry. The price changes announced by the barometric firm serve as a barometer of changes in demand and supply conditions in the market.

The barometric leadership evolves for various reasons, of which the major ones are the following.

First, the rivalry between the large firms may lead to cut-throat competition to the disadvantage of all the firms. Also, rivalry between the larger firms may make them unacceptable as a leader. So, a firm which has better predictive ability emerges as the price leader.

Secondly, most firms in the industry may have neither the capacity nor the desire to make continuous calculations of cost, demand and supply conditions. Therefore, they find it advantageous to accept the price changes made by a firm which has a proven ability to make reasonably good forecasts.

Thirdly, Kaplan *et al.*[30], observe that barometric price leadership often develops as a reaction to a long economic warfare in which all the firms are losers.

The Nature of Non-Price Competition in Oligopoly Markets It is obvious from the foregoing discussion that oligopolists may be reluctant to wage price war and encroach upon each other's market share. There is, therefore, generally an absence of price competition in the oligopolistic market structure. The absence of price competition should not mean the absence of competition among oligopoly firms. In fact, the competition among oligopoly firms takes the form of *non-price competition*. The forms of non-price competition are diverse. Yet, there are two important techniques of non-price competition.

First, non-price competition involves product differentiation. The product differentiation may take any or many of such changes as improvement of quality, design, appearance, attractiveness, size, after sale service, warranty, cost-wise affordability and additional facilities. Product differentiation is intended to attract new customers by enhancing preferability of the product.

Secondly, perhaps the most important technique of non-price competition is advertisement. The primary objective of advertising is to make the demand curve for the product shift upward. The sellers try to capture on the market of other sellers through advertising. Advertising is also necessary to retain market share in the face of tough competition between the firms.

BAUMOL'S THEORY OF SALES MAXIMIZATION: AN ALTERNATIVE THEORY

Baumol's theory of sales maximization is an important alternative theory of the firm's behaviour in oligopoly. The basic premise of this theory is the *sales maximization*, rather than *profit maximization*. In Baumol's own words, 'My hypothesis … is that oligopolists typically seek to maximize their sales to a minimum profit constraint.'[31] He argues that there is no reason to believe that all firms seek to maximize their profits. Business firms, in fact, pursue a number of incompatible objectives and it is not easy to single out one as the most common objective pursued by the firms. However, from his experience as a consultant to many big business houses, Baumol finds that most managers seek to maximize sales revenue rather than profits. He argues that in modern business, management is separated from ownership and managers enjoy discretion to pursue goals other than profit maximization. Their discretion eventually falls in favour of sales maximization.

According to Baumol, business managers pursue the goal of sales' maximization rather than profit maximization for the following reasons.

First, financial institutions consider sales as an index of performance of the firm and are willing to finance the firm with growing sales.

Secondly, while profit figures are available generally at the end of the financial year whereas sales figures can be obtained periodically and more frequently to assess the performance of a management. Maximization of sales is more satisfying for the managers than the maximization of profits which go to the pockets of the shareholders.

Thirdly, the routine evaluation of managers' performance, salaries and slack earnings of the top managers are linked more closely to sales than to profit.

Fourthly, the routine personnel problems are more easily handled with growing sales. Higher payments may be offered to employees if sales figures indicate better performance. Profits are generally known after a year. To rely on profit figures means, therefore, a longer waiting period for both employees and management.

Fifthly, if profit maximization is the goal of the firm and if profit rises in one period to an unusually high level, this becomes the standard profit target for the shareholders, which managers find very difficult to maintain in the long run.

Finally, sales growing more than proportionately to market expansion indicate growing market share and a greater competitive strength and bargaining power of a firm in a collusive oligopoly.

To formulate his theory of sales maximization, Baumol[32] has developed two basic models: (i) Static Model and (ii) Dynamic model, each with and without advertising. Baumol's dynamic model falls outside the purview of this look. Hence, we confine to his static model. His static models with and without advertising are discussed below.[33]

Baumol's Model without Advertising

Baumol assumes cost and revenue curves to be given as in conventional theory of pricing. Suppose that the total cost (*TC*) and the total revenue (*TR*) curves are given as shown in Figure 5.14. The total profit curve, *TP*, is obtained by measuring and plotting the difference between the *TR* and *TC* curves. The *TP* curve gives the measure of $TR - TC$. Profit is zero where $TR = TC$. Given the *TR* and *TC* curves, there is a unique level of output at which total sales revenue is maximum. As a rule, total sales revenue is maximum where elasticity of demand equals one (i.e., $e = 1$) and the slope of the *TR* curve (i.e., $MR = \partial TR/\partial Q$) is equal to zero. Such a point lies at the highest point of *TR*. The point *H* on the *TR* in Figure 5.14 represents the total maximum revenue, HQ_3. In Baumol's theory, the *profit maximizing rule*, $MR = MC$, is replaced by *sales maximization* rule.

At output OQ_3, the firm maximizes its total revenue and makes profit $HM = TQ_3$. If this profit is enough or more than enough to satisfy the stockholders, the firm will produce output OQ_3 and charge a price determined as TR/Q, where Q = quantity sold. In Figure 5.14, $TR = HQ_3$ and $Q = OQ_3$. So, the price $= HQ_3/OQ_3$. But, if profit at output OQ_3 is not enough to satisfy the stockholders,[34] then the firm's output must be changed to a level at which it makes a satisfactory profit. Suppose shareholders fix a minimum profit target at $OP_2 = LQ_2$. Then, the manager will set output target at OQ_2 which yields a profit $LQ_2 > TQ_3$.

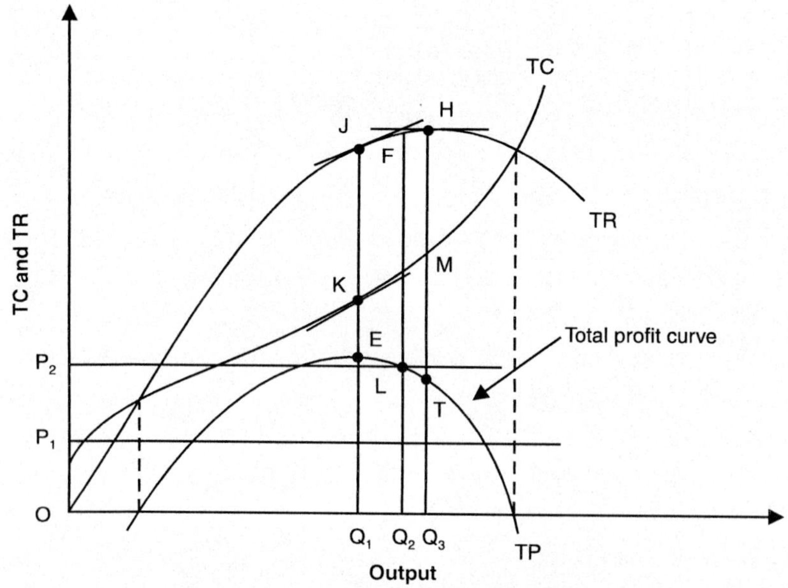

Figure 5.14 *Sales Revenue Maximization*

Thus, there are two types of equilibrium which appear to be possible. The *first* equilibrium criterion is one in which the profit constraint does not provide an effective barrier to sales maximization. This equilibrium is associated with output OQ_3 and total revenue HQ_3. The *second* equilibrium is one in which profit maximization does provide an effective barrier to sales maximization. In the second type of equilibrium, the firm will have to produce an output which yields a satisfactory profit. It may be any output between OQ_1 and OQ_3. For example, if minimum required profit is OP_1, then the firm will stick to its sales maximization goal and produce output OQ_3 which yields a profit much greater than the required minimum.

Profit Constraint and Revenue Maximization Since actual profit (TQ_3) is much greater than the minimum required, the minimum profit constraint is not operative. But, if required minimum profit level is OP_2, output OQ_3 will not yield sufficient profit to meet the requirement. They will, therefore, have to produce an output which yields the required minimum level of profit OP_2 ($=LQ_2$). Thus, the firm will produce OQ_2 where its profit is just sufficient to meet the requirement of minimum profit. This output OQ_2 is less than the sales maximization output OQ_3. Evidently, the profit maximization output, OQ_1 is less than the sales maximization output OQ_2 (with profit constraint).

Baumol's Model with Advertising

We have explained above Baumol's model of price and output determination in a static single-period model without advertising. In an oligopolistic market structure, however, prices and output are subject to non-price competition. Baumol considers, in his model, *advertising* as the typical form of non-price competition and suggests that the various forms of non-price competition may be analysed on similar lines.

In his analysis of advertising, Baumol makes the following assumptions.

1. Firm's objective is to maximize sales, subject to a minimum profit constraint;
2. Advertising causes an upward shift in the demand curve and, hence, the total sales revenue (TR) increases with increase in advertisement expenditure (A), i.e., $\partial TR/\partial A > 0$;

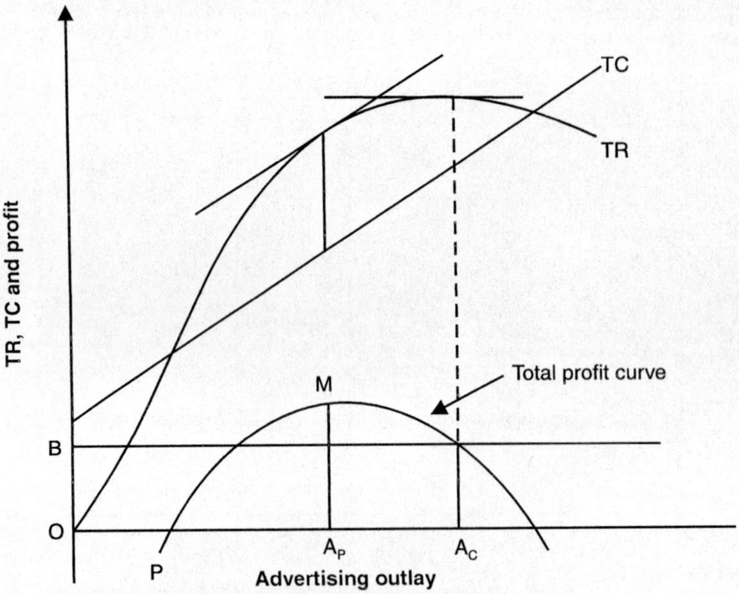

Figure 5.15 *Baumol's Model with Advertising*

3. Price remains constant—a simplifying assumption; and
4. Production costs are independent of advertising. This, too, is an unrealistic assumption since increase in sales may put output at a different cost structure.

Baumol's model with advertising is presented in Figure 5.15. The *TR* and *TC* are measured on the *Y*-axis and total advertisement outlay on the *X*-axis. The *TR* curve is drawn on the assumption that advertising increases total sales in the same manner as price reduction.

The *TC* curve includes both production cost and advertising outlays. The total profit curve *PP′* is drawn by subtracting the *TC* from the *TR*. As shown in Figure 5.15, profit maximizing advertisement expenditure is OA_p, where the maximum profit is MA_p. Assuming that minimum profit required is *OB*, the sales maximizing advertisement outlay would be OA_C. This implies that a firm increases its advertisement outlay until it reaches the profit constraint level, i.e., until profits are reduced to the minimum acceptable level. This also means that sales maximizing firms advertise no less, rather more, than the profit maximizers.

Criticism of Baumol's Theory First, it has been argued that in the long run, Baumol's sales maximization hypothesis and the conventional hypothesis would yield identical results, because the *minimum required* level of profits would coincide with the *normal* level of profits.

Secondly, Baumol's theory does not distinguish between firm's equilibrium and industry equilibrium. Nor does it establish industry's equilibrium when all the firm's are sales maximizers.

Thirdly, it does not clearly bring out the implications of inter-dependence of firm's price and output decisions. Thus, Baumol's theory ignores not only actual competition between the firms but also the threat of potential competition in an oligopolistic market.

Finally, Baumol's claim that his solution is preferable to the solutions offered by the conventional theory, from social welfare point of view, is not necessarily valid.

THE GAME THEORY

In the preceding sections, we have discussed the classical models of strategic action and reaction among the oligopoly firms and the cartel system of price and output determination. We have also discussed Baumol's theory of sales maximization. We have also noted that none of the models explains satisfactorily the strategic actions and reactions of the oligopoly firms nor do they offer a lasting solution to their profit or sales maximization objective. But, the search for a reasonable solution to this problem does not end there. Classical theories show, in fact, only the beginning of the economists' effort to analyse the determination of the profit maximizing price and output in an oligopolistic market setting.

In this section, we discuss another approach, i.e., the *game-theory approach*, to explain the strategic interaction among the oligopoly firms. The game-theory approach uses a mathematical technique to show how oligopoly firms play their game of business. The first systematic attempt in this field was made by Von Neumann and Margenstern.[35] Although their work was followed by many others, Martin Shubik[36] is regarded as the 'most prominent proponent of the game-theory approach' who 'seems to believe that the only hope for the development of a general theory of oligopoly is the games theory'.[37] Though not much seems to be contributed by further works in this area, the usefulness of game theory in revealing the intricate behavioural pattern of the oligopoly firms cannot be denied. Here, we present an elementary description of the game theory as applied to oligopoly.[38] We will first illustrate the nature of the problem faced by the oligopoly firms in their strategy formulation.

The Nature of the Problem: Prisoners' Dilemma

The nature of the problem faced by the oligopoly firm is best explained by the *Prisoners' Dilemma Game*. To illustrate *prisoners' dilemma*, let us suppose that there are two bookies, Ranga and Billa, who are partners in an illegal activity of match fixing. On a tip-off, the CBI arrests Ranga and Billa on suspicion of their involvement in fixing cricket matches. They are arrested and lodged in separate jails with no possibility of communication between them. They are being interrogated separately by the CBI officials with the following conditions disclosed to them in isolation.

1. If you confess your involvement in match fixing, you will get a five-year imprisonment.
2. If you deny your involvement and your partner denies too, you will be set free for lack of evidence.
3. If your partner does not confess and you confess and turn approver, then you get two-year imprisonment, and your partner gets 10-year imprisonment.

Given these conditions, each suspect has two options open to him: (i) to confess, and (ii) not to confess. Now, both Ranga and Billa face a dilemma on how to decide whether or not to confess. While taking a decision, both have a common objective, i.e., to minimize the period of imprisonment. Given this objective, the option is quite simple that both of them deny their involvement in match fixing. But, there is no certainty that if one denies, the other will also deny: the other may confess and turn approver. With this uncertainty, the dilemma in making a choice still remains. For example, if Ranga denies his involvement, and Billa confesses (settles for a two-year imprisonment), and turn approver, then Ranga gets a 10-year jail term. So is the case with Billa. If they both confess, then they get a five-year jail term each. Then what to do? That is the dilemma. The nature of their problem of decision making is illustrated in the following Table 5.4 in the form of a 'pay-off matrix'. The pay-off matrix shows the pay-offs of their different options in terms of the number of years in jail.

Table 5.4 *Prisoners' Dilemma: The Pay-off Matrix*

Ranga's Options	Billa's Options			
Confess Deny	Confess		Deny	
Confess	Ranga	Billa	Ranga	Billa
	5	5	2	10
Deny	Ranga	Billa	Ranga	Billa
	10	2	0	0

Given the conditions, it is quite likely that both the suspects may opt for 'confession', because neither Ranga knows what Billa will do, nor Billa knows what Ranga will do. When they both confess, each gets a five-year jail term. This is the second best option. For his decision to confess, Ranga might formulate his strategy in the following manner. He reasons out: if I confess (though I am innocent), I will get a maximum of five year's imprisonment. But, if I deny (which I must) and Billa confesses and turns approver, I will get 10 year's imprisonment. And, that will be the worst of the worst. It is quite likely that suspect Billa also reasons in the same manner, even if he too is innocent. If they both confess, they would avoid 10 year's imprisonment, the maximum possible jail term under the law. This is the best they could achieve under the given conditions.

Relevance of prisoners' dilemma in oligopoly: The prisoners' dilemma illustrates the nature of problems oligopoly firms are confronted within the formulation of their business strategy with respect to strategic advertising, price cutting and cheating in case of a cartel. Look at the nature of the problems an oligopoly firm is faced with when it plans to increase its *advertisement* expenditure (ad-expenditure for short). The basic issue is whether or not to increase the ad-expenditure. If the answer is 'do not increase', then the questions are: Will the rival firms increase ad-expenditure or will they not? And if they do, what will be the consequences for the firm under consideration? And, if the firms answer is 'increase', then the questions that arise are: What will be the reaction of the rival firms? Will they increase or will they not increase their ad-expenditure? What will be the pay-off if they do not and what if they do? If the rival firms do increase their advertising, what will be the pay-off to the firm? Will the firm be a net gainer or a net loser? The firm will have to find answer to these questions under the conditions of uncertainty. To find the answer, the firms will have to anticipate actions, reactions and counteraction by the rival firms and chalk out its own strategy. It is in case of such problems that the case of prisoners' dilemma becomes an illustrative example.

Application of Game Theory to Oligopolistic Strategy

Let us now apply the game theory to our example of 'whether or not to increase ad-expenditure', assuming that there are only two television companies, Sony and Samsung i.e., the case of a duopoly. We know that in all the games, the players have to anticipate the move made by the opposite player(s) and formulate their own strategy to counter the different possible moves by the rival. To apply the game theory to the case of 'whether or not to increase ad-expenditure' a company needs to know or anticipate:

1. The counter moves by the rival company in response to increase in ad-expenditure by this company and
2. The *pay-offs* of this strategy when (a) the rival company does not react and (b) the rival company does make a counter move by increasing its ad-expenditure.

Table 5.5 *Pay-off Matrix of the Ad-Game (Increase in Sales in Million Rs)*

Sony's Strategy	Samsung's Options			
	Increase Ad		Don't Increase	
Increase Ad	A	B	A	B
	20	10	30	0
Don't increase	A	B	A	B
	10	15	15	5

After this data is obtained, the company will have to decide on the best possible strategy for playing the game and achieving its objective of, say, increasing sales and capturing a larger share of the market. The best possible strategy in game theory is called the 'dominant strategy'. A *dominant strategy is one that gives optimum pay-off, no matter what the opponent does*. Thus, the basic objective of applying the game theory is to arrive at the dominant strategy.

Suppose that the possible outcomes of the ad-game under the alternative moves are given in the pay-off matrix presented in Table 5.5. In the figure, A indicates Sony's gain and B indicates Samsung's gain in terms of increase in sales.

As the matrix shows, if Sony decides to increase its ad-expenditure and Samsung counteracts by increasing its own ad-expenditure, Sony's sales go up by Rs 20 million and that of Samsung by Rs 10 million. And, if Sony increases its advertisement and Samsung does not, then Sony's sales gain is Rs 30 million and no gain to Samsung. One can similarly find the pay-offs of the strategy 'Don't increase' in case of both of firms.

Given the pay-off matrix, the question arises as to what strategy should Sony choose to optimize its gain from extra ad-expenditure, irrespective of moves of the rival Samsung. It is clear from the pay-off matrix that Sony will choose the strategy of increasing the ad-expenditure because, no matter what Samsung does, its sales increase by at least Rs 20 million. This is, therefore, the *dominant strategy* for Sony. A better situation could be that when Sony increases its expenditure on advertisement, Samsung does not. In that case, Sony's sales could increase by Rs 30 million and sales of Samsung do not increase. But there is a greater possibility that Samsung will go for counter advertising, in anticipation of losing a part of its market to Sony in future. Therefore, a strategy based on the assumption that Samsung will not increase its ad-expenditure involves a great of uncertainty.

Nash Equilibrium In the preceding section, we have used a very simple example to illustrate the application of game theory to an oligopolistic market setting, under the following simplifying assumptions that:

1. Strategy formulation is a one-time affair,
2. One company initiates the competitive warfare and other companies only react; and
3. There exists a *dominant strategy*—a strategy which gives an optimum solution.

The real-life situation is, however, much more complex. There is a continuous one-to-one and tit-for-tat kind of warfare. Actions, reactions and counteractions are regular phenomena. Under these conditions, a *dominant strategy* is often found to be non-existent. To analyse this kind of situation, John Nash,[39]

Table 5.6 *Pay-off Matrix of the Ad-Game (Sales Figures in Million Rs)*

A's Strategy	B's Options			
	Increase Ad		Don't Increase	
Increase Ad	Sony	Samsung	Sony	Samsung
	20	10	30	0
Don't increase	Sony	Samsung	Sony	Samsung
	10	15	25	5

an American mathematician, developed a technique, known as *Nash equilibrium. Nash equilibrium technique* seeks to establish that each company does the best it can, given the strategy of its competitors. By definition, *Nash equilibrium implies a situation in which none of the players can improve their pay-off given the strategy of the other players.* In case of our example, Nash equilibrium can be defined as one in which none of the companies can increase its pay-off (sales) given the strategy of the rival company.

The Nash equilibrium can be illustrated by making some modifications in the pay-off matrix given in Table 5.5. Now we assume that action and counter action between Sony and Samsung is a regular phenomenon and that the pay-off matrix that appears finally is given in Table 5.6. The only change in the modified pay-off matrix is that if neither Sony nor Samsung increases its ad-expenditure, then pay-offs change from (15, 5) to (25, 5).

It can be seen from the pay-off matrix (Table 5.6) that Sony has no more a *dominant strategy*. Its optimum decision depends now on what Samsung does. If Samsung increases its ad-expenditure, Sony has no option but to increase its advertisement expenditure. And, if Sony reinforces its advertisement, Samsung will have to follow the suit. On the other hand, if Samsung does not increase its ad-expenditure, Sony does the best by increasing its ad-expenditure. Under these conditions, the conclusion that both the companies arrive at is to increase ad-expenditure if the other company does so, and 'don't increase', if the competitor 'does not increase'. In the ultimate analysis, however, both the companies will decide to increase the ad-expenditure. The reason is that if none of the companies increases advertisement, Sony gains more in terms of increase in its sales (Rs 25 million) and the gain of Samsung is much less (Rs 5 million only). And, if Samsung increases advertisement expenditure, its sales increase by Rs 10 million. Therefore, Samsung would do best to increase its ad-expenditure. In that case, Sony will have no option but to increase its ad-expenditure. Thus, the *final conclusion* that emerges is that both the companies will go for advertisement war. In that case, each company finds that it is doing the best, given what the rival company is doing. This is the Nash equilibrium.

However, there are situations in which there can be more than one Nash equilibrium. For example, if we change the pay-off from (25, 5) to (22, 8) each firm may find it worthless to wage advertisement war and may settle for 'don't increase' situation. Thus, there are two possible Nash equilibrium.

CONCLUDING REMARKS

What we have presented above is an elementary introduction to the game theory. It can be used to find equilibrium solution to the problems of oligopolistic market setting under different assumptions regarding the behaviour of the oligopoly firms and market conditions.[40] However, despite its merit of revealing the nature and pattern of oligopolistic warfare, game theory often fails to provide a determinate solution.[41]

REVIEW QUESTIONS AND EXERCISES

1. What are the characteristics of oligopoly? How is an oligopoly market different from monopolistically competitive market in respect of price and output determination? Is price determinate in an oligopoly market?
2. What are the assumptions of theory of oligopoly? How are these assumptions different from those of theory of monopolistic competition?
3. Explain Cournot's model of duopoly. Illustrate graphically whether price is determinate and stable in Cournot's model of duopoly. Show that his model of duopoly can be applied to oligopoly?
4. Suppose a demand function is given as $Q = 100 - 2P$. Using Cournot's model, find the equilibrium output and price. Is equilibrium of the firm stable in Cournot's model?
5. Explain and illustrate Chamberlin's model of oligopoly (small group). How is Chamberlin's model different from Cournot's model of oligopoly? Which of the two models offers a more realistic explanation of oligopoly markets?
6. What are the assumptions behind the existence of kinked demand curve? How does it reflect behaviour of the oligopoly firms? Why do rival firms react to a price cut but not to price rise in oligopoly markets?
7. Kinked demand curve model establishes that price once determined in oligopoly does not change even if there is change in cost of production. Using kinked demand curve model show that change in cost of production does not lead to change in price in oligopoly.
8. Explain and illustrate graphically Sweezy's kinked demand curve theory of rigidity in oligopoly. Are prices in oligopoly really sticky? What are the weaknesses of this model?
9. Using kinked demand curve model, show that price remains rigid at its current level in an oligopoly market even if there is an upward shift in the market demand curve. What happens to the price in a buoyant oligopoly market?
10. What is meant by cartel? Why do firms in an oligopoly market form cartel? Illustrate and explain joint profit maximization by the cartel. Does cartel system work efficiently?
11. Suppose there are only two firms in an oligopoly industry, F_1 and F_2, facing the demand and cost functions given as follows.

    Demand function: $Q = 25 - 0.5P$

    Cost function F_1: $C_1 = 50 + 10Q + Q_1^2$

    Cost function F_2: $C_2 = 24 + 10Q_2 + Q_2^2$

    Find the profit maximization output for firms F_1 and F_2 and maximum joint profit.
12. Suppose an industry is characterized by oligopoly and is dominated by a large firm. The supply curve for the small firms in an oligopoly market is perfectly elastic. Does the dominant firm have any role in this kind of market? Does it still have a scope to determine its price like a monopolist?
13. Suppose there are only two firms in an oligopolistic industry, F_1 and F_2. While F_1 is a low cost and F_2 is a high cost firm. The firm F_1 acts as a price leader. Using an appropriate price-leadership model, explain and illustrate graphically price determination by the low-cost firm. Should F_2 accept the price leadership of F_1? Give reasons for your answer.

14. How does a firm in oligopoly market gain the status of a dominant firm? Suppose there are four firms, *A, B, C* and *D*, in an oligopoly market, firm *D* being the dominant one. Explain and illustrate price determination by the dominant.
15. Suppose in an oligopoly market, the joint demand curve for small firms *A, B* and *C* is given as $Q = 100 - 2P$ and their joint supply curves is given as $Q = 5 + 2P$. Derive the demand curve for the dominant firm, *D*. Find the price determined by the dominant firm assuming its *MC* function given as $MC = 5 + 0.5Q$.
16. The demand curve for oligopoly firms is given by the demand function

$$D_1 = 50 - 0.5P_1$$

The firms however believe that their individual demand function is

$$D_2 = 80 - P_2$$

Their identical cost function is given as

$$TC = 150 + 10Q + 0.05Q^2$$

   (i) Find the initial level of price and output and
   (ii) What is the range of variation in *MC* which will not affect the price and output?
17. Suppose there are two oligopoly firms—Firm 1 and Firm 2. Firm 1 is a low-cost firm whereas Firm 2 is a high-cost firm. Both the firms face an identical demand curve given by the demand function as

$$Q = 50 - 0.5P$$

The cost functions of the two firms are given, respectively, as

$$TC_1 = 100 + 20Q_1 + 2Q_1^2$$

and

$$TC_2 = 48 + 36Q_2 + 2Q_2^2$$

Find the following:
   (a) Price and output of Firm 2 prior to Firm 1 working as the price leader and
   (b) Price and output of Firm 2 after it accepts the price leadership of Firm 1.
18. Suppose there are five firms in an oligopoly market, one of them being a dominant one. The market demand function is given as

$$Q_M = 200 - 2P$$

and the supply function of 4 small firms together is given as

$$Q_S = 20 + P$$

The cost function of the dominant firm reads as follows.

$$TC_D = 100 + 12\,Q + 0.25Q^2$$

Find the following:

(a) Total supply by 4 small firms and their supply price before the dominant firm fixes its own price,

(b) Price and output of the dominant firm, and

(c) Total market share of four small firms after dominant firm fixes its price.

19. Explain and illustrate Baumol's theory of sales revenue maximization assuming (i) there is no advertisement by the firms, and (ii) firms do advertise their products. What are the shortcomings of Baumol's model?
20. The game theory explains the behaviour of oligopoly firms better than the classical oligopoly models. Do you agree with this statement? Give reasons for your answer.
21. Explain 'prisoners' dilemma' through an appropriate example. How can the model of 'prisoners' dilemma' be applied to explain the problems in price and output determination in oligopoly markets?

ENDNOTES

1. The word 'oligopoly' has been derived from Greek word '*oligi*' meaning 'few' and '*polien*' meaning 'sellers'.
2. Salvatore, D. (1989), *Managerial Economics* (New York, NY: McGraw Hill), p. 475.
3. On the basis of data published by the CMIE in August 1999 issues of its *Industries and Market Share*.
4. The 'concentration ratio' is the percentage share of 4–12 dominant firms in the total sale of the industry. The US Census of Manufacturing uses 4, 8 and 12 firms for working out the concentration ratio for different industries.
5. Market shares of individual firms in an industry vary to a great extent. For example, in 1997–1998, Hindustan Lever had a share of 74% of the ice cream market; Surva Roshini had 61% share in fluorescent lamp market; MUL had 76.1% market share in passenger cars; and *ITC* had 75.38% market share in cigarettes.
6. *Microeconomic Decision* (Houghton Miflin Company, Boston, 1976), p. 249.
7. The month in which automobile manufacturers introduce new models.
8. Baumol, W.J. (1985), *Economic Theory and Operations Analysis* (New Delhi: Prentice Hall of India), 4th Edn., p. 410.
9. Baumol, W.J., *op.it.*, p. 410.
10. Cournot, A., (1907), *Research into the Mathematical Principles of the Theory of Wealth*—translation by Nathaniel T. Bacon (New York: Macmillan).
11. Note that where $MR = 0$, price-elasticity of demand $(e) = 1$, *i.e.*, $PM/PD = 1 = QM/OQ$. This means, $PM = PD$ and $QM = OQ$.
12. Bertrand, J. (1983), 'Theorie Mathematique de la Richasse Sociale,' *Journal des Savatits*, Paris, p. 499.
13. Edgeworth, F.Y. (1925), wrote his paper in 1897. Its English translation 'The Pure Theory of Monopoly' was reprinted in *Edgeworth: Papers Relating to Political Economy* (London: Macmillan).
14. Edgeworth, F.Y. *op. cit.*, p. 118.

15. Von Stackelberg, H. (1952), *The Theory of the Market Economy*, translated by A.T. Peacock (New York: Oxford University Press).
16. Chamberlin, E.H. (1929), *Qly. J. Eco.*, November.
17. Chamberlin, E.H., *The Theory of Monopolistic Competition*, 7th Edn., pp. 46–47.
18. See his *The Theory of Monopolistic Competition 'op. cit.' Chapter* 17, Section Long-run Equilibrium: Price Competition.
19. Hall, R.L. and Hitch, C.I. (1939), 'Price Theory and Business Behaviour,' *Oxford Economic Papers*, 12–45.
20. Sweezy, P.M. (1939), 'Demand under Conditions of Oligopoly,' *Journal of Political Economy*, 568–573.
21. Stigler, G.J. (1947), 'The Kinky Oligopoly Demand Curve and Rigid Price', *Journal of Political Economy*, 55. Reprinted in *Readings in Price Theory, ed.* by George J. Stigler and Kenneth E. Boulding (Homewood, IL: Richard D. Irwin, 1952), pp. 410–439. For a summary of this paper, see Cohen and Cyert, *op. cit.* pp. 254–255.
22. Simon, J. (1969), 'A Further Test of the Kinky Oligopoly Demand Curve', *Am. Eco. Rev.*, December 1969, 971–975.
23. Ibid.
24. Liebhafsky, H.H. The Nature of Price Theory.
25. Cohen and Cyert, *op. cit.*, pp. 255–258.
26. For a detailed classification of collusion, see Fritz Machlup, *The Economics of Sellers' Competition* (Baltimore, MD, Johns Hopkins, 1952).
27. Students of graduate courses may skip this section.
28. William Fellner (1949), Competition among the Few: Oligopoly and Similar Market Structure.
29. For example, according to market data collated by Nielson, a market researcher, the market share of some dominant companies in FMCG in some specific product in April 2010 was as follows: HUL—soaps (43.8 per cent), Shampoo (48.9 per cent), Skincare (45.4 per cent); Dabur—Chyawanprash (80.9 per cent); Nestle—Coffee (41.8 per cent), Noodles (62.2 per cent); Colgate—Toothpaste (51.2 per cent).
30. Kaplan, A.D.H., Dirlam, J.B. and Lanzillotti, R.F. (1958), *Pricing in Big Business* (Washington, DC: The Brookings Institution), p. 206. Quoted in Cohen and Cyret, *op. cit.*
31. Baumol, W.J. (1958), 'On the Theory of Oligopoly', *Economica*, New Series, 15.
32. Baumol, W.J. (1959), *Business Behaviour, Value and Growth* (New York, NY: Macmillan), Revised edition, Harcourt Brace and World, Inc., 1967.
33. As summarised in his *Economic Theory and Operations Analysis*, op, cit., 4th edn.
34. According to Baumol, the minimum acceptable profit is determined by such 'long run consideration' as profit must be high enough to provide for future investment and a sufficient dividend to shareholders for future issue of stocks.
35. Von Neumann, J. and Margenstern, O. (1953), *Theory of Games and Economic Behaviour* (Princeton, NJ: Princeton University Press).
36. See Martin Shubik, *Strategy and Market Structure*, (John Wiley, 1959), and his *Game Theory in the Social Sciences* (Cambridge, MA: MIT Press, 1982).

37. Koutsoyiannis, A. (1979), *Modern Macroeconomics* (London: Macmillan), 2nd Edn., p. 404.
38. For a comprehensive discussion on the game theory and its application to oligopolistic behaviour, see James W. Friedman, *Game Theory with Application to Economics* (New York, NY: Oxford University Press, 1990), David Krepps, A *Course in Microeconomic Theory* (Princeton, NJ: Princeton University Press, 1990). For a brief discussion on and application of game theory to oligopoly, see Robert S. Pindyck and Daniel L. Rubinfeld, *Microeconomics* (New Delhi: Prentice Hall of India, 1995), Third edn, Chapter 18, and F.M. Scherer, *Industrial Market Structure and Economic Performance* (Chicago, IL: Rand McNally, 1980), pp. 160–164.
39. 'Nash equilibrium' was developed by John Nash, an American Mathematician, in 1951, to find equilibrium where there is no dominant strategy.
40. The interested reader may refer to the advanced references (see Bibliography).
41. Browning, E.K. and Browning, J.K. (1989), *Microeconomic Theory and Application* (London: Scott, Foresman and Co.), 3rd Edn., p. 413.

FURTHER READINGS

Bain, J.S. (1960), 'Price Leaders, Barometers and Kinks', *Journal of Business.*

Bishop, R.L. (1960), 'Duopoly: Collusion or Warfare?' *American Economic Review.*

Browning, E.K. and Browning, J.M. (1986), *Microeconomic Theory and Applications* (New Delhi: Kalyani Publishers), 2nd Edn., Chapter 13.

Chamberlin, E.H. (1933), *The Theory of Monopolistic Competition* (Cambridge, MA: Harvard University Press), 8th Edn.

Cohen, KJ. and Cyert, R.M. (1976), *Theory of The Firm* (New Delhi: Prentice-Hall of India), Chapter 12.

Fellner, W.J. (1949), *Competition Among the Few: Oligopoly and Similar Market Structure* (New York: Alfred A. Knopf).

Gould, J.P. and E.P. Lazeur (1993), *Microeconomics Theory* (Homeswood, IL: Richard D. Irwin), 6th Edn., Chapter 13.

Hall, R.L. and Hitch, C.J. (1939), 'Price Theory and Business Behaviour', *Oxford Economic Papers.*

Henderson, J.M. and Quant, R.E. (1974), *Microeconomic Theory: A Mathematical Approach* (New York: McGraw-Hill).

Kaplan, A.D.H., Dirlam, J.B. and Lanzillotti, R.F. (1958), *Pricing in Big Business* (Washington, DC: The Brookings Institutions).

Koutsoyiannis, A. (1979), *Modern Microeconomics* (London: Macmillan), 2nd Edn., Chapters 9 and 10.

Lanzillotti, R.F. (1957), 'Competitive Price Leadership: A Critique of Price Leadership Model', *Rev. Eco. and Stat.*

Machlup, F. (1952), *The Economics of Sellers's Competition* (Baltimore, MD: John Hopkins).

Rothschil, K.W. (1949), 'Price Theory and Oligopoly', *Economic Journal*, LVII.

Stigler, G.J. (1947), 'The Kinked Oligopoly Demand Curve and Rigid Prices,' *Journal of Political Economy*, LV.

Stigler, G.J. (1964), 'A Theory of Oligopoly,' *Journal of Political Economy*

Sweezy, P.M. (1939), 'Demand Under Conditions of Oligopoly,' *Journal of Political Economy*, 568–573.

Part II

Factor Market and Factor Pricing

Chapter 6

The Factor Market: Factor Demand and Supply

CHAPTER OBJECTIVES

This part of the book deals with the theory of factor price determination. The term 'factor' refers to factors of production, viz., labour, land and capital. Like price of a product is determined by its demand and supply, the price of a factor input is also determined by the demand for and supply of the factor input. But the factors that determine the demand for an input (say, labour) and its supply are different from those that determine the demand for and supply of a product. This chapter explains the determinants of the demand for and supply of a factor input and also the derivation of the factor demand and supply curves. By going through this chapter, you learn:

- What determines the demand for a factor input;
- What is marginal productivity of a factor input;
- How marginal productivity determines the demand for a factor input;
- How demand curve for a factor input is derived;
- What determines the supply of a factor input, especially labour;
- How labour supply curve is derived; and
- How price of a factor input is determined in a perfectly competitive market.

INTRODUCTION

In this part of the book, we move on from the *theory of product pricing* to the *theory of factor pricing*, i.e., how prices of factors of production are determined. The factors of production are conventionally classified as *labour, land, capital* and *entrepreneurship*. However, *labour, land* and *capital* are the three basic factors of production[1] and their respective prices are *wages, rent and interest rates*. The question that we are concerned in the part of the book is: *How are rates of wages, rent, interest and profits determined in different kinds of factor markets?* The answer to this question is provided by the *theory of factor pricing*. This is the subject matter of this part of the book.

This chapter presents a detailed discussion on the nature and working of the factor market. Like product markets, factor markets too work on the principles of demand and supply. We have first explained the derivation of the factor demand curve on the basis of the *marginal productivity theory* and then the derivation of the labour supply curve on the basis of the *wage-work offer curve*. Finally, we have used the factor demand and factor supply curve to show how factor prices are determined in a simplified economy model.

It is important to note here that the derivation of factor demand curve and factor supply curve and the determination of the factor price have been explained with reference to *labour* as the only variable input. But the same logic applies, at least theoretically, to all other factors of production. However, the different theories of rent, interest rate and profit propounded by the economists of different ages have been discussed in the subsequent chapters.

It may be added at the outset that the *theory of factor pricing* is a by product of the *classical theory of distribution*. Therefore, before we proceed to discuss the theory of factor pricing, let us have a glance at the *theory of distribution* which provides the origin and the basic foundation of the factor pricing theory.

THE THEORY OF DISTRIBUTION AND FACTOR PRICING: AN OVERVIEW

The theory of factor pricing has its origin in the *classical theory of distribution*. The theory of distribution explains how national income (output) is distributed among the various factors of production. Distribution of national income between the factors of production is called *functional distribution* of national income, i.e., distribution of national income on the basis of economic functions of the people. Classical economists, Adam Smith, Ricardo and Marx were concerned with the functional distribution of national income. The basic classical proposition in this regard is that the share of a factor of production in the national income equals the *average price* of a factor multiplied by its *total employment*. For example, assuming there are only two factors, labour (L) and capital (K) with a given wage rate (w) and interest rate or capital rental (r), the share of labour and capital in the national output (Q) can be determined as follows.

$$\text{Share of labour} = \frac{w \cdot L}{Q}$$

$$\text{Share of capital} = \frac{r \cdot K}{Q}$$

and

$$\frac{w \cdot L}{Q} + \frac{r \cdot K}{Q} = Q$$

In determining the functional distribution of national income, classical economists had to find how *factor price* and *employment* are determined. This led to the emergence of classical theories of *factor pricing* and *employment*. In this part of the book, we will discuss the theories of factor pricing. Before proceeding further, let us have an overview of the theory of factor pricing.

Peculiarities of Factor Demand and Supply

The theory of factor pricing is not fundamentally different from the theory of product pricing. Both product and factor prices are essentially determined by the interaction of demand and supply forces. In case of factor pricing, demand and supply forces refer to demand for and supply of factors of production. As in case of product pricing, the basic function of the theory of factor pricing is to explain the determinants of demand for and supply of a factor and to show how demand and supply interact to determine the price of a factor. However, both demand and supply of factors have *certain peculiarities* as compared to demand for and supply of goods. The fact is that the peculiarities of factors of production necessitate formulating separate theories of factor pricing. Let us look at some basic peculiarities of factors of production.

On the demand side, there is a difference between the demand for a product and the demand for a factor. While demand for consumer goods is, in general, *autonomous demand*, demand for factor services is a *derived demand*. This aspect is discussed below in detail.

On the supply side, factors of production—labour, land and capital—differ in their character in respect of their supply, especially land and labour. Land is a gift of nature and labour is partly a natural and partly a man-made factor. Capital is a man-made factor. For this reason, perhaps, early economists developed theories of factor pricing with respect to each factor separately, known as: (i) theory of wages, (ii) theory of rent, (iii) theory of interest and (iv) theory of profit.

Development of Theories of Factor Pricing

The theories of factor pricing were developed by different classical economists at different points of time, and are, therefore, different in approach to factor price determination. *Theory of wages*, often called as *marginal productivity theory of wages*, is attributed to John Bates Clark, an American economist, popularly known as J.B. Clark. J. B. Clark had developed the marginal productivity theory in his book, *The Distribution of Wealth* (1899, p. VIII). However, several other economists had earlier hinted at the concept of marginal productivity, including Von Thunen in his *Der Isolierte Staat* (1826), Longfield in his *Lectures on Political Economy* (1834), and Henry George in his *Progress and Poverty* (1879). Besides, in 1880s and 1990s, many other economists had made important contributions to the concept of *marginal productivity*—W. Stanley Jevons in his '*The Theory of Political Economy*'; Philip Wicksteed in his '*An Essay on the Coordination of the Theory of Distribution*'; Alfred Marshall in his '*Principles of Economics*'; Stuart Wood in his '*The Theory of Wages*'. (AEA, No 4, 1889); Leon Walras in his '*Elements d'economie politique pure*' and some others.[2] 'The classical theory of rent' was propounded by David Ricardo. Several classical economists have contributed to 'The Theory of Interest'.[3] Similarly, several classical economists, including J.B. Clark, have contributed to 'The Theory of Profit'.

In this chapter, we will discuss the *marginal productivity theory of wages*. Theories of rent, interest and profit will be discussed in three subsequent chapters. To begin with, let us look at the factors that determine the demand for a factor. In our analysis of demand for factors, we will consider *demand for labour*. But the analysis can be applied to other factors also.

FACTOR DEMAND: WHY A FACTOR IS DEMANDED

As noted earlier, the price of factor is determined by its demand and supply. Before we discuss the theory of factor price determination, let us know: (i) why a factor of production is demanded and (ii) what determines the demand for a factor. These aspects are discussed here briefly.

Factor Demand is a Derived Demand

A factor of production is demanded because it is productive and what it produces is demanded by the people, the consumers and producers. A factor, which is not productive be it land, labour or capital, is not demanded for its own sake. For example, infertile land is not demanded for cultivation; an uneducated labour is not demanded for teaching and an outdated machinery is not demanded because it cannot produce goods and services in demand.

However, productivity of a factor alone is not sufficient for its demand. For example, a labour may be very skilled and efficient in making hand fans but its service is not demanded in cities because hand fans are not demanded there. Similarly, services of a computer software expert in MS DOS are no more in demand because this software has been replaced by Windows. It means that it is equally important that *what a factor can produce must be in demand.* That is why *demand for a factor is said to be a derived demand:* it arises out of the demand for goods and services it can produce. For example, farm labour is demanded because people demand wheat, rice, sugar and other farm products; construction labour is demanded because people demand house and so on.

Marginal Revenue Productivity: The Basic Determinant of Factor Demand

The productivity of a factor and demand for its product create the demand for the factor. But these factors do not determine the *quantity demanded* of a factor. From the viewpoint of a profit-maximizing firm, the quantity demanded of a factor is determined by the revenue it yields to the user. From factor demand point of view, what matters is its *marginal revenue productivity (MRP)* and *the price of the factor. MRP* of a factor can be defined as *the revenue that a firm can earn by employing one additional unit of a factor*. The concept of *MRP* can be clarified further with reference to a specific factor, e.g., labour. When a firm employs an additional unit of labour, it produces a certain quantity of a good. The quantity produced by the marginal labour is called *marginal physical productivity of labour* (MPP_L). Now, the *MRP* of labour (MRP_L) can be defined as follows.

$$MRP_L = MPP_L \cdot \bar{P}$$

where MPP_L = *marginal physical productivity of labour*, and $\bar{P}$ = constant price of the product.

Here, we present a simplified version of the MPP_L curve and show the derivation of MPP_L, under the following assumptions.

1. Labour is the only variable factor of production and
2. MPP_L is subject to diminishing return.

Table 6.1 shows the computation of and relation between *MPP* and *MRP*, assuming diminishing returns to a variable factor (labour). As the table shows, as more and more units of labour are employed, total production (*TP*) increases but at diminishing rates, i.e., marginal physical productivity (MPP_L) of labour decreases with increase in employment of labour. Column 3 shows the diminishing MPP_L. Column 4 shows the constant price and column 5 shows the marginal revenue productivity (MRP_L).

Table 6.1 *Marginal Physical and Revenue Productivity of Labour*

Variable Factor (*L*)	Total Production (*TP*) (units)	MPP_L (units)	*P* (Price) (constant)	$MRP_L = MPP \times P$ (Rs)
(1)	(2)	(3)	(4)	(5)
1	20	20	5	100
2	38	18	5	90
3	52	14	5	70
4	58	6	5	30
5	58	0	5	0

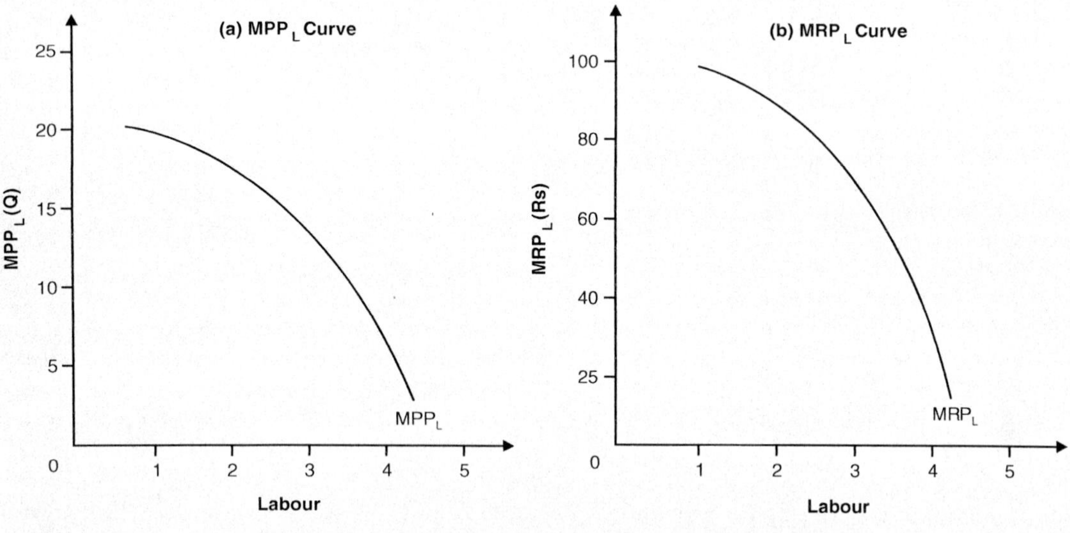

Figure 6.1 *Derivation of* MPP_L *and* MRP_L *Curves*

The MPP_L and MRP_L, curves can be derived by using the MPP_L and MRP_L data in Table 6.1 as shown in Figure 6.1(a) and (b), respectively. As the figures show, on the assumption of diminishing returns, both MPP_L and MRP_L curves have a downward slope. The MRP_L curve provides the basis of derivation of the demand curve of labour. That is why the *marginal productivity theory* is called the theory of factor demand. We now move on to discuss the derivation of demand curve for a factor of production (labour) through marginal productivity theory.

MARGINAL PRODUCTIVITY AND FACTOR DEMAND

In this section, we show the use of the *MRP* curve to derive the labour demand curve (D_L). According to the classical theory of demand for a factor, say labour, a profit-maximizing firm demands labour until $MRP_L = W$ (wage rate). Based on this rule, the classical theory of marginal productivity forms the basis of demand for a factor (labour). An elementary theory of factor demand based on

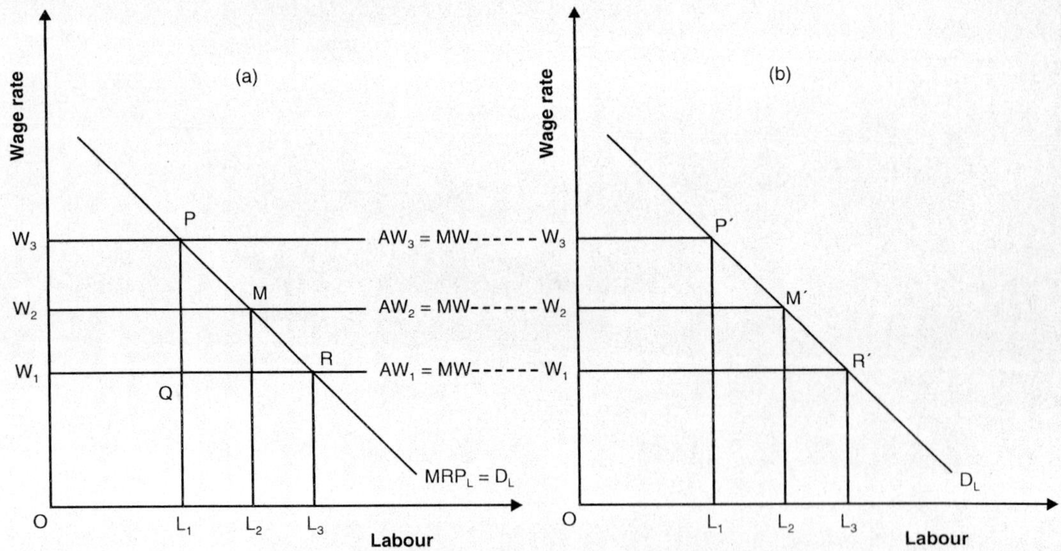

Figure 6.2 *MRP_L, Wages and Labour Demand*

the marginal productivity theory is illustrated in Figure 6.2 assuming labour to be the only factor of production.

The *MRP* curve of labour is given by the MRP_L curve in panel (a) of Figure 6.2. Given the MRP_L curve, the number of workers to be employed will be determined by the point where MRP_L = wage rate. For example, if wage rate is given at OW_3 a profit-maximizing firm will employ labour where $OW_3 = MRP_L$. This condition is fulfilled at point *P*. Point *P* indicates that at wage rate OW_3 only OL_1 number of workers will be employed. When wages go down to OW_2, demand for labour increases from OL_1 to OL_2 and when wage rate goes further down to OW_1, labour demand increase to OL_3. Note that as wage rate goes on declining, the demand for labour goes on increasing. When wage rate goes down, more workers are employed, because it pays to employ more workers. For example, if wages go down from OW_3 to OW_1, and firms still employ only OL_1 workers, they will lose possible revenue equal to the area, *PQR*. Therefore, demand for labour increases as wages go down. This relationship between wages and employment is called *marginal productivity theory* of factor demand. It is on the basis of this theory that factor demand curve is derived. In fact, the MRP_L curve represents the factor demand curve.

The derivation of labour demand curve is illustrated in panel (b) of Figure 6.2. In panel (b), points *P′*, *M′* and *P′* corresponds to points *P*, *M* and *R* in panel (a). By joining the points *P′*, *M′* and *R′*, and extending it further we get the labour demand curve (D_L).

FACTOR SUPPLY: SUPPLY OF LABOUR

Demand side of the labour market has been discussed in the preceding section. In this section, we will discuss the supply side of the labour market. As a general rule, factor supply increases with increase in factor price. But this rule does not apply to labour supply at all the levels of wage rate. Our main task here is to derive the labour supply curve. The supply of labour has some peculiarities in contrast to supply of other factors. Derivation of labour supply curve, therefore, requires a detailed analysis. The derivation of labour supply curve is presented below.

Derivation of Individual Labour Supply Curve

Here, we will explain briefly the technique of deriving the labour supply curve under the following assumptions.

1. All labour is homogeneous;
2. Labour units are identical and
3. Unlike other factors, labour finds a trade-off between hours of work and leisure and income—this is a unique feature of labour supply.

Figure 6.3 illustrates the derivation of labour supply curve. Money income is measured on the vertical axis and the hours available to a worker per time unit (per day or per week) are measured on the horizontal axis. One can read also the hours of work on the horizontal axis. The hours of work (H_w) equals the total hours (H_T) *minus* the hours of leisure (H_L), i.e., $H_w = H_T - H_L$. Let us now suppose that the total number of hours (H_T) available to an individual labour is *OH* in Figure 6.3, which he can use either for leisure or for work. Given the wage rate, if he works for *OH* hours and enjoys no leisure, he will earn an income equal to OM_1.

If labour enjoys his entire time *OH* as leisure, he has a zero income. And, if he divides his time between work and leisure, he has a combination of income and leisure. The income–leisure combination is given by the line M_1H—when one increases, the other decreases. The line M_1H is called *income–leisure trade-off* line.

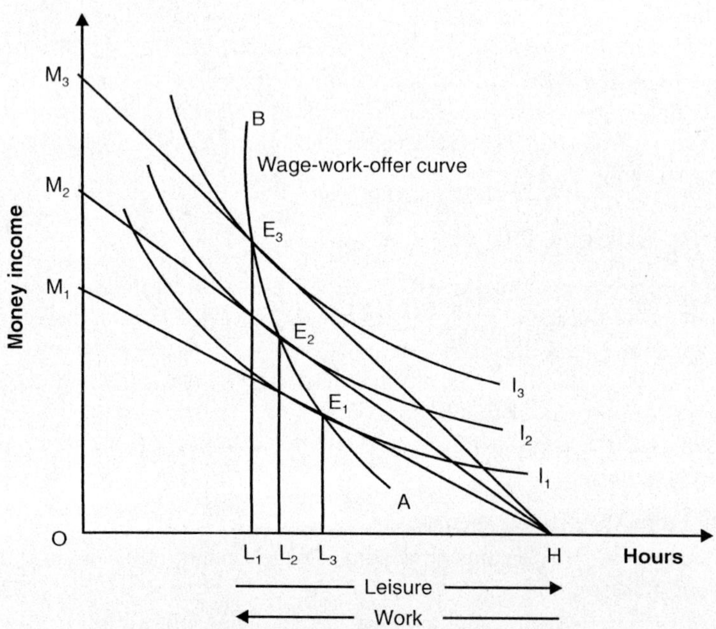

Figure 6.3 *Derivation of Wage-Work-Offer Curve*

A question arises here: How does a labour find his optimum combination of leisure, work and income? The answer to this question can be found by introducing labour's leisure–income indifference curve and combining it with his leisure–income trade-off line. In Figure 6.3, the indifference curve I_1, I_2 and I_3 represent the leisure–income preference function of the individual labour at different levels of wage rates. These curves are called as *leisure–income indifference* curves. The negative slope of the leisure–income indifference curve shows substitution between leisure and income, worker's total satisfaction remaining the same.

Given the wage rate, (say, $W_1 = OM_2/OH$), the individual is in equilibrium at point E_1 by working for HL_3, hours and enjoying a leisure for OL_3 hours. When the wage rate rises to W_2 ($= OM_2/OH$), the individual moves to a new equilibrium point E_2. At this equilibrium point, he works for HL_2 hours, has leisure of OL_2 hours, and earns an income E_2L_2. Similarly, when wage rate increases further to W_3 ($= OM_3/OH$) the individual moves to equilibrium point E_3 where he works for HL_1 hours, reduces his leisure from OL_2 to OL_1. By joining the equilibrium points E_1, E_2 and E_3, we get a curve called *wage-work offer curve.* It shows preference for work in relation to wages. The wages-work offer curve *AB* provides the basis for deriving the *labour supply curve*, as it gives labour supply at different wage rates, as in the following table.

Equilibrium Point	Wage Rate	Labour Supply
E_1	$OM_1/OH = W_1$	HL_3
E_2	$OM_1/OH = W_2$	HL_2
E_3	$OM_3/OH = W_3$	HL_1

Information contained in the table above may be graphed to obtain the normal labour supply curve. The derivation of labour supply curve is illustrated in Figure 6.4(a). The curve *SS′* is the normal labour supply curve[4] with a positive slope. If wage-rate continues to increase, the labour supply curve *SS′* will bend backward shown by curve *SL* in Figure 6.4(b). This is so because higher wages create disincentive for longer hours of work and incentive for increasing hours of leisure. This phenomenon can be verified from Figure 6.3. As the figure source, with the subsequent increase in the wage rate, the wage-offer curve (*AB*) tends to bend rightward which indicates fall in hours of work after increase in the wage rate beyond a certain level. This trend produces a *backward bending labour supply curve*. We have, however, used the labour supply curve *SS′* of Figure 6.4(a) in our further analysis.

Market Labour Supply Curve

The market labour supply curve is the horizontal sum of individual labour supply curves. The economists, however, disagree on the shape of the market supply curve of labour. Different shapes have been suggested for short and long runs, depending on the occupational mobility, the type of labour used and level of economic growth. In the *short run*, if a firm uses specific type of labour, 'nothing can be said about the slope or shape of the labour supply curve. It may be negative, or it may have segments of positive and negative slope'.[5] In the *long run*, however, the market supply curve of specialized labour is likely to be a positively sloping one. The reasons are:

1. occupational mobility of labour increases;
2. with the increase in population and expansion of education and training facilities, supply of all types of labour increases and
3. with the increase in information about job market, young people are able to plan their education and career.

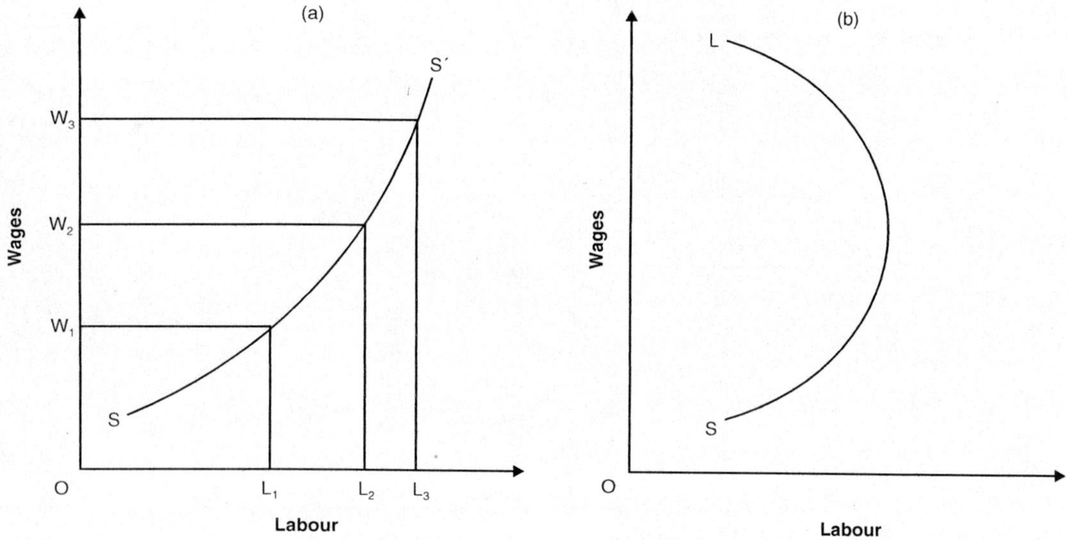

Figure 6.4 *Labour Supply Curve*

In case of non-specialized labour, however, the shape of labour supply curve is generally predictable. It has a positive slope for two reasons.

First, industries which plan to employ more labour can draw it from other industries by offering higher wages. Hence, the labour supply to such industries increases only at higher wage rates.

Secondly, some industries lose their labour and hence their output falls. The fall in the output of such industries lead to a rise in the price of their products causing an upward pressure on the demand price of labour. Therefore, such industries too obtain a larger supply of labour at increasing wage rates only. For these reasons, the industries attempting to employ larger units of labour must face a labour supply curve with a positive slope.

There is, however, a likelihood that *the market labour supply curve in an affluent country is a backward-bending one.* The reason is when individual become richer and richer, they begin to prefer smaller number of working hours, longer holidays and fewer hours of work per day, and so on, as they need longer time to enjoy their high earnings. This likelihood would, however, be limited to the rich nations in which the scope for further expansion is limited. It is, therefore, generally believed that *labour supply curve in the long run must have a positive slope.*

DETERMINATION OF MARKET WAGE RATE: A SIMPLE THEORY

We have derived above the market demand and supply curves for labour. These tools may now be straight away applied to illustrate the determination if wage rate in a competitive market. Figure 6.5 shows the determination of wage in a competitive market. The labour demand curve (D_L) and labour supply curve (S_L) intersect at point *P*. At this point, demand and supply of labour are equal at *OL*, and wage rate is determined at *OW*. This wage rate will remain stable in a competitive market as long as demand and supply conditions do not change.

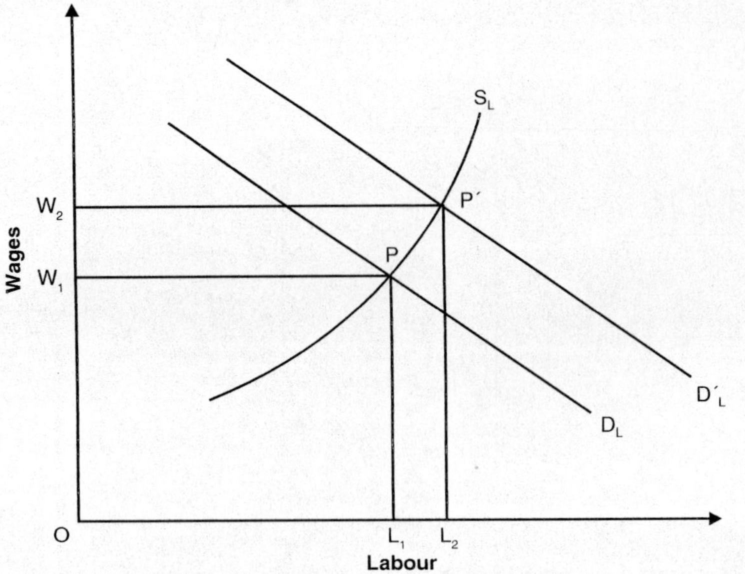

Figure 6.5 *Determination of Wages in a Perfectly Competitive Market*

Shift in Factor Market Equilibrium and its Stability

As mentioned earlier, the demand and supply conditions remaining the same, the factor market will remain in equilibrium and factor price will remain stable. For example, given the labour demand curve (D_L) and labour supply curve (S_L), wage rate is determined at OW_1. This wage rate will remain stable if D_L and S_L do not change. However, if there is a change in the demand for and supply of labour, demand and supply curves may shift upward or downward setting up a new equilibrium in the labour market at a higher or lower wage rates. For example, if labour demand curve shifts upwards, labour supply curve remaining the same, as shown by the D'_L curve in Figure 6.5, the labour market equilibrium shifts upward from point *P* to point *P*′ at a higher level of labour employment (OL_2) and a higher wage rate (OW_2). The labour market equilibrium at point *P*′ will remain stable unless there is further change in labour demand curve or a shift in the labour supply curve.

The model of wage rate determination presented above is a simplified model. In real life, however, market conditions are not as simple as assumed here. The diversity of the labour market conditions lead to the formulation of a different theory of wage determination. The theory of wage determination under different kinds of market conditions are presented in the forthcoming two chapters.

REVIEW QUESTIONS AND EXERCISES

1. Explain that demand for a factor is a derived demand. How is demand for a factor different from demand for commodity?
2. What is *MRP*? What role does it play in the derivation of demand curve for a factor of production?

3. Explain the derivation of demand for a factor of production assuming that (i) only labour is demanded and (ii) both labour and capital are demanded.
4. What is meant by the interdependence of factor demand? What problems does it create in deriving a factor demand curve?
5. Explain the substitution and output effects of a change in price of a factor on its demand.
6. Derive a wage-offer curve and explain its role in deriving the labour supply curve?
7. Why is labour supply curve backward bending? Does it bend backward for all kinds of labour?
8. Explain the determination of the price of a factor under perfect competition in both factor and product markets.
9. Given the following production schedule of a firm, where L is the number of workers hired per day (the only variable factor) and Q is the quantity of a commodity produced per day and the constant commodity price of P = Rs 5 is assumed.

L	1	2	3	4	5	6
Q	0	10	18	24	28	30

   (a) Find the marginal revenue product of labour.
   (b) How many workers per day will the firm hire, if the wage rate is Rs 40.00?
10. Explain the marginal productivity theory of factor pricing. What are the shortcomings of this theory of factor pricing?
11. How is price of a factor determined when both product and factor markets are perfectly competitive? Is the factor price so determined stable?

ENDNOTES

1. Although *entrepreneurship* is also treated traditionally as a factor of production, its cost is *risk*, not *profit*. Profit is the reward for entrepreneurship—the desire and motivation for taking risk in business. However, we will discuss also *theory of profit*—the concept, source and the determinants of profit.
2. For greater details, see Blaug, M. (1983), *Economic Theory in Retrospect* (Vikas Publishing House), 3rd Edn., Chapter 11.
3. J.M. Keynes and J.K. Hicks made a significant contribution to interest theory. Their theories are however studied in Macroeconomics.
4. Note that in Figure 6.4(a), OL_1, OL_2, and OL_3 are equal to HL_3, HL_2 and HL_1, respectively.
5. Ferguson, C.E. *Microeconomic Theory*, *op. cit.*, p. 408.

FURTHER READINGS

Carter, A.M. (1959), *Theory of Wages and Employment* (Homewood, IL: Richard D. Irwin).
Carter, A.M. and Marshall, F.R. (1972), *Labour Economics, Employment and Trade Unionism* (Homewood, IL: Richard D. Irwin).
Clark, J.B. (1905), *The Distribution of Wealth* (New York: Macmillan).
Douglas, P.H. (1934), *The Theory of Wages* (New York: Macmillan).

Dunlop, J.T. (1944), *Wage Determination under Trade Union* (New York: Macmillan).
Hicks, J.R. (1932), *The Theory of Wages* (New York: Macmillan).
Kaldor, N. (1955–1956), 'Alternative Theories of Distribution', *Rev. Eco. Stud.*, XXIII (2): 83–100.
Koutsoyiannis, A. (1978), *Modern Microeconomics* (New York: Macmillan), 2nd Edn., Chapter 12.
Lipsey, R.G. and Chrystal, K.A. (1999), *Principles of Economics* (Oxford: Oxford University Press) Chapter 14.
Perlman, R. (1969), *Labour Theory* (London: Wiley).
Roninson, J. (1933), *The Economics of Imperfect Competition* (New York: Macmillan), Chapter 25.

Chapter 7

Wage Determination Under Perfect Competition

CHAPTER OBJECTIVES

The objective of this chapter is to elaborate on the theory of determination of wage rate and labour employment under perfect competition in both the product market and the labour market. This chapter explains the following aspects of the theory:

- How demand curve for labour for an individual firm is derived when the firm uses labour as the only variable factor, capital remaining constant;
- How demand curve for labour for an individual firm is derived when the firm uses both labour and capital as variable factors;
- What is the difference between *marginal revenue productivity* (*MRP*) and the *value of marginal product* (*VMP*) of a factor;
- How is wage rate determined under the condition of perfect competition in both product and labour markets;
- How change in wage rate results in substitution of capital for labour, called *substitution effect*;
- What is the meaning of and the nature of *heterogeneity* of labour; and
- Why there are wage differentials even under perfect competition.

INTRODUCTION

The basic theory of factor pricing has already been discussed in Chapter 6. However, the simplified version of the factor-pricing theory is based on certain explicit and implicit unrealistic assumptions. The assumptions made there include (i) labour is the only factor of production, (ii) all labour is homogeneous and (iii) *MRP* of a factor is the only determinant of its demand. In reality, however, labour is not the only factor of production; all labour is not homogeneous, and apart from *MRP*, there are other determinants of factor demand. For these reasons, the simplified version of the theory of factor pricing cannot be applied to the different kinds of product and labour market conditions. The economists have, however, developed factor-pricing theory, especially wage determination, under different kinds of market conditions. In this chapter, we are concerned with the theory of wage determination. The theory of wage determination developed under different kinds of market conditions are generally classified as under.

1. Wage determination under perfect competition and
2. Wage determination under imperfect conditions.

In this chapter, we discuss the factor pricing under perfect competition. Factor-pricing theory under imperfect conditions will be discussed in the next chapter.

WAGE DETERMINATION IN A PERFECTLY COMPETITIVE MARKET

As already noted in Chapter 6, wage rate is determined by demand for and supply of labour. The demand for labour under simplified labour market conditions has already been discussed there. But, in a perfectly competitive market with a large number of firms, the labour demand by individual firms may be different—different from what is assumed in the simplified model. The difference in demand for labour under perfect competition arises because (i) there are a large number of firms with different size and (ii) all firms may not have the same *marginal physical productivity* (MPP_L) and, therefore, not the same *MRP* (MRP_L). Therefore, individual firms may have different MRP_L curve and hence a different labour demand curve. Besides, under perfect competition, product price is subject to variation due to change in demand and supply conditions. For these reasons, MRP_L may be different at different levels of prices. In order to account for this possible difference, the economists use different term, *value of marginal product* (VMP_L) in place of MRP_L, though the two terms are conceptually the same.[1] For these reasons, it becomes necessary to derive the labour demand curve for individual firms. Recall that the sum of the labour demand by individual firms makes the market demand for labour. Therefore, in order to explain the determination of wage rate under perfect competition, we begin by explaining the derivation of labour demand curve by an individual firm under perfect competition.

Derivation of Labour Demand Curve

The demand for labour by an individual firm depends on MRP_L. Another factor that plays an important role in demand for labour by an individual firm is whether the firm uses labour as a *single variable factor* or whether it uses both labour and capital as the variable factors of production. Accordingly, firm's labour demand curve is derived under two different conditions:

1. The firm uses labour as a single variable factor, with capital constant.
2. The firm uses both labour and capital as variable factors.

The derivation of a firm's labour demand curve under these conditions is explained below.

Demand for Labour as a Single Variable Factor The labour demand curve of an individual firm is derived under the following assumptions.

1. Firm's objective is to maximize its profit;
2. The firm uses labour as a single variable factor, capital remaining constant;
3. Labour market is perfectly competitive and wage rate is given;

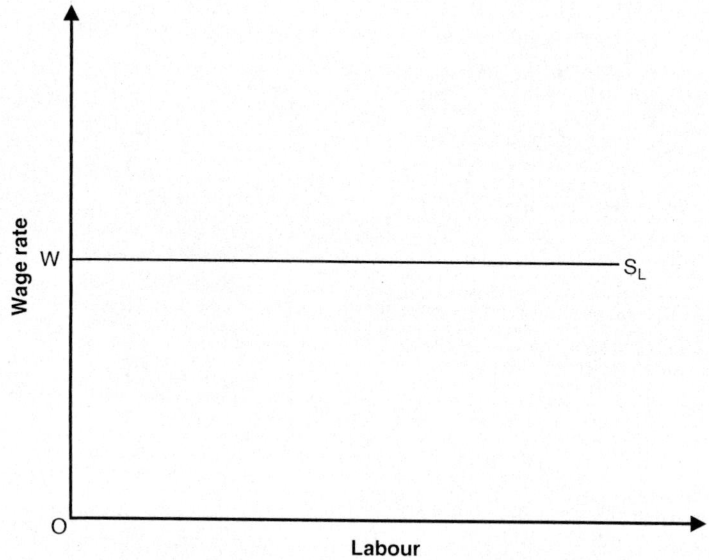

Figure 7.1 *Labour Supply for an Individual Firm*

4. Labour-supply curve for the firm is perfectly elastic and is given by a horizontal line as shown in Figure 7.1 and
5. The firm produces a single commodity, X, with its given price, P_X.

Given the assumptions, demand for labour by an individual firm would depend on the *MRP* of labour. In the analysis of labour demand under *perfect competition*, however, *MRP* is given a different name[2]—***the*** *VMP*, though the numerical value of VMP_L at a constant price of the product is the same as of MRP_L. The VMP_L is expressed as

$$VMP_L = MPP_L \cdot \overline{P}_X = MRP_L$$

Note that under perfect competition with a constant price, the numerical value of MRP_L and VMP_L is the same. Let us now derive the labour demand curve.

Application of VMP_L for Deriving Labour Demand Curve We have already derived the MPP_L in Chapter 6 and illustrated in Figure 6.1(a) and MRP_L curve in Figure 6.1(b) assuming constant price of the product (see Table 6.1). As noted earlier, if price is constant, $MRP_L = VMP_L$ and MRP_L curve is the same as VMP_L curve. The MRP_L curve in Figure 6.1(b) is reproduced in Figure 7.2 as VMP_L curve in its general form. The VMP_L curve represents demand for labour by an individual firm in a perfectly competitive market. This can be shown as follows.

We know that a profit maximizing firm produces quantity of output at which $MR = MC$. Going by the profit maximization rule, a *profit maximizing firm employs labour to the extent at which the marginal cost of labour, i.e., wage rate, (w), equals the value of its marginal product* (VMP_L). In other words, a profit maximizing firm employs labour up to a number at which $w = VMP_L$. Given this rule, demand for labour by a profit maximizing firm is illustrated in Figure 7.2. The VMP_L curve shows the *VMP* of labour at different levels of its employments and S_L lines present the labour-supply curves for an individual firm

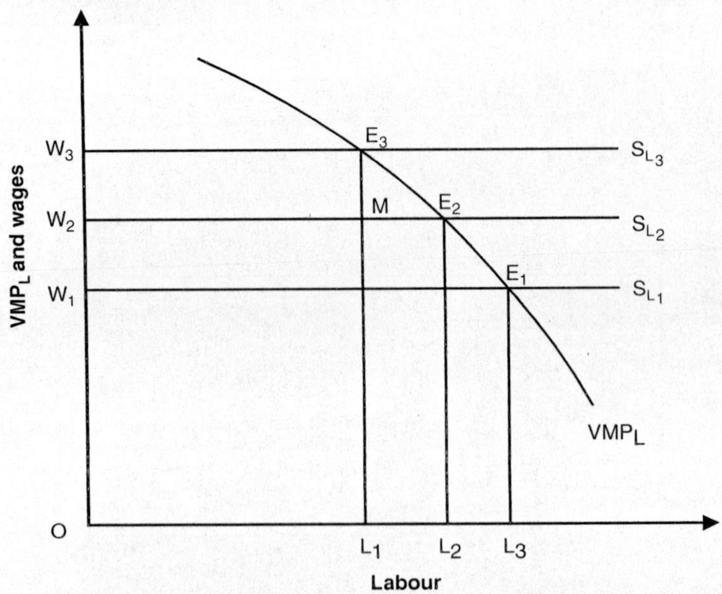

Figure 7.2 *Short-run Employment of Labour: Single Variable Factor*

[assumption (c)], at different constant wage rates. Given the wage rate at OW_3, the line S_L represents the labour-supply curve for an individual firm. It implies that the firm can employ any number of labour at wage rate OW_3. The VMP_L curve and the line S_L intersect at point E_3. At point E_3, $VMP_L = OW_3$. The profit maximizing firm will therefore employ OL_1 units of labour. Any additional employment of labour will make $OW_3 > VMP_L$ and hence the profit will decrease by $OW_3 - VMP_L$. And, at any employment less than OL_1, the total earning of the firm will be lower than the maximum. Thus, given the VMP_L and S_L, a profit maximizing firm will demand only OL_1 units of labour.

If wage rate falls to OW_2, firm's factor–demand equilibrium point shifts from point E_3 to E_2 and firm's demand for labour increases from OL_1 to OL_2. Similarly, when wage rate falls to OW_1, firm's equilibrium shifts downward to E_1 showing an increase in the demand for labour to OL_3. Obviously, as wage rate falls, demand for labour increases. This relationship between the wage rate and labour demand gives a usual downward-sloping demand curve for labour. Thus, the VMP_L curve gives the demand curve for labour under perfect competition in both product and labour markets. Thus, *VMP_L curve is the same as labour demand curve* under the condition that a single variable factor is used. It may now be concluded that firm's *individual demand* curve for a single variable factor (e.g., labour) is given by its *VMP* curve (VMP_L).

Demand for Labour with more Variable Inputs: The Interdependence of Factor Demand We have illustrated above the derivation of demand curve for a factor of production assuming that labour is the only factor demanded. This is somewhat unrealistic assumption or relevant to only short run. In real-life situation, demand for one factor is linked to or creates demand for other factors. For example, when there is demand for labour, there is a demand also for capital because labour with empty hands is unproductive. Labour without capital can work only as a porter, a watchman or guide and so on. In another case, when there is demand for capital, there is demand for labour because capital—a passive agent of production—cannot produce any thing on its own—a fully automatic machinery is a rarity. This means *demand for factors of production is interdependent in case more than one variable input is used.*

The interdependence of factor demand complicates the derivation of factor demand curve. It implies that, in the context of demand for labour, the interdependence of demand for labour and capital creates problem in deriving the demand for labour and *vice versa*. The problem arises for two reasons:

1. When two factors—labour and capital—are being used to produce a commodity, it is very difficult to measure the contribution of each factor. As William Petty put it, 'labour is the father of product and land, the mother. We cannot say which is more essential in producing a baby—a mother or a father'.[3] In the words of Samuelson and Nordhaus, '...it is generally impossible to say how much output has been created by any one of the different inputs taken by itself'.[4] Clearly, measuring output effect of change in a factor is a difficult proposition.[5]
2. Change in the price of one factor changes the demand for the other factor also. For instance, decrease in wage rate decreases the demand for capital because firms tend to substitute cheaper labour for costlier factor, capital. This change is known as *substitution effect*.

Due to interdependence of inputs, change in the price of one variable factor causes a change in the demand for the other factor due to three effects—*substitution effect, output effect* and *profit effect.* To derive the demand for labour under the condition of two variable factors, it is essential to understand how these effects arise and how they affect the demand for labour. We begin with the explanation *of the substitution and output effects*, as these effects arise simultaneously.

Substitution and Output Effects *Substitution* and *output effects* arise directly from the change in factor prices. When price of one factor changes, prices of other factors remaining constant, the relative price of all factors changes too. While one factor becomes relatively cheaper, the other factors become relatively costlier. For example, in the context of labour and capital, when labour price (wage rate) decreases, capital price (interest rate) remaining the same, capital becomes relatively costlier. As a result, profit maximizing firms, substitute labour for capital. This is called *substitution effect of change in labour price. The substitution effect may cause an upward shift in the VMP_L curve. It means that VMP_L is not the final labour demand curve in case more than one input are being used in the process of production.*

As regards the *output effect*, with change in labour price, the optimal combination of labour and capital to maximize output also changes. This may necessitate hiring more labour in addition to substitution effect. This effect is called *output effect*. The substitution and output effects of change in labour price are explained below graphically.

The *substitution* effect of a change in factor price on the demand for a variable factor can be explained more clearly by using *isoquant* and *isocost* curves. For the sake of convenience, let us assume that (i) there are only two variable factors, labour (L) and capital (K) used in the production process of a commodity; (ii) the initial price of labour, i.e., wage rate, and price of capital (r) are given and (iii) initial isocost is given by AB and initial isoquant is given by isoquant I_1 in Figure 7.3.

Under the assumptions given above, firm's optimum combination of inputs (labour and capital) lies at point P, where it uses OL_1 of labour and OK_3 of capital to produce output represented by isoquant I_1. Now let the wage rate fall, price of capital remaining the same, so that the new isocost is AD. Consequently, the firm moves on to a new optimum input which is equal to combination point R at a higher isoquant I_2. The movement from P to R indicates increase in use of labour by L_1L_3. This increase in labour demand is the result of price effect. The price effect consists of *substitution* and *output effects.*[6] Thus, the movement from P to R can be decomposed into *substitution* and *output effects*. The two effects can be split by

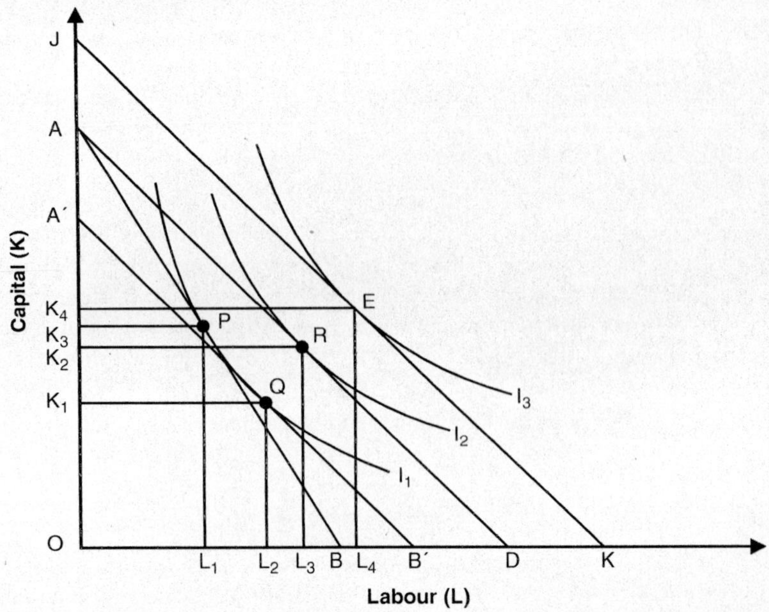

Figure 7.3 *Substitution and Output Effects of Change in Wage Rate*

drawing an imaginary isocost ($A'B'$) parallel to the isocost AD and tangent to the initial isoquant I_1. The significance of the isocost $A'B'$ is that it eliminates the *output effect* of the fall in wage rate and gives the measure of the *substitution effect*. It tells how much of labour can be substituted for how much of capital. As can be seen from Figure 7.3, the movement from P to Q on the initial isoquant I_1 means substitution of L_1L_2 of labour for K_1K_3 of capital. It is clear that L_1L_2 is the *substitution effect* of decrease in price of labour. The *output effect* of change in labour employment can now be obtained as follows.

$$\text{Output effect} = \text{Price effect} - \text{Substitution effect}$$
$$= L_1L_3 - L_1L_2 = L_2L_3$$

Thus, the movement from Q to R gives the *output effect* of decrease in wage rate, i.e., how much labour (in addition to substitution effect) is demanded to increase the output. Since the firm ultimately settles at equilibrium point R, it will use more of both labour and capital. The increase in capital employment with the increase in use of labour increases marginal product of labour. Consequently, the VMP_L shifts upward to the right due to output effect.

Profit Maximization Effect of Change in Wage Rate Let us now return to the *profit maximization effect*. The movement from point P to R (Figure 7.3) accounts for only *substitution* and *output effects*. These effects do not account for the *profit effect* of fall in wage rate. The profit effect is illustrated in Figure 7.4. The profit effect arises from the downward shift in the MC curve due to fall in wage rate (Figure 7.4). For example, suppose that commodity price is given at OP and marginal cost curve by the curve MC.

The MC curve and MR line intersect at point E, which determines the profit maximizing output at OQ which, let us suppose, is the output indicated by isoquant I_2 (Figure 7.3). When wage rate falls, the MC

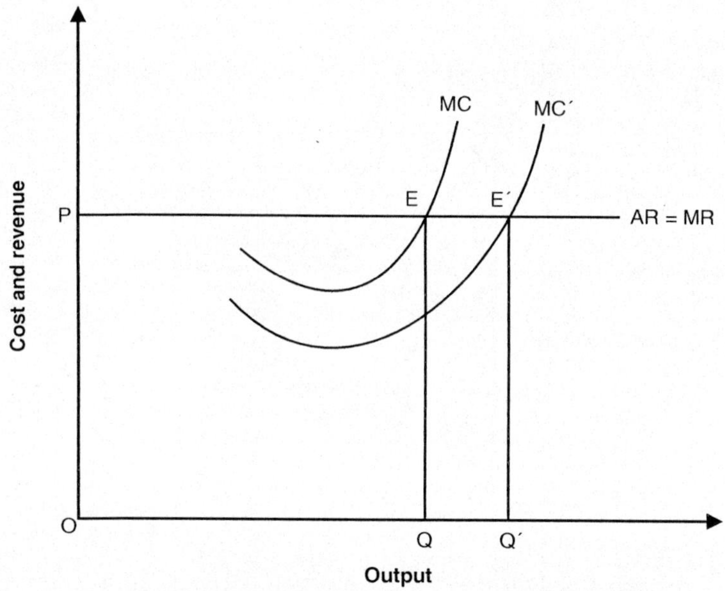

Figure 7.4 *Profit Effect of Change in Wage Rate*

curve shifts downward to the position of *MC*′. The equilibrium point shifts from point *E* to point *E*′and the profit maximizing output increases from *OQ* to *OQ*′. A profit maximizing firm will, therefore, increase its output by *QQ*′. The expansion of output requires an additional expenditure on both labour and capital.

The increase in expenditure made by the firm to maximize its output will make the isocost *AD* shift upward to *JK* (Figure 7.3), and the firm finally reaches equilibrium at point *E* on isoquant I_3. At equilibrium point *E*, the total demand for labour OL_4. As Figure 7.3 shows, the additional labour demand equals $L_2L_4 = L_2L_3 + L_3L_4$. Of this increase in labour demand, L_2L_3 is the additional demand for labour caused by the *output effect* and L_3L_4 is the *profit maximization effect*. The output and profit maximization effects, both being positive, lead to additional employment of capital. Thus, the employment of both labour and capital increases simultaneously as a result of output and profit maximization effects. The increase in capital together with labour leads to increase in the marginal physical product of labour (MPP_L) causing a rightward shift in the VMP_L curve.

Derivation of Labour Demand Curve with Two Variable Inputs

We now turn to derive the demand curve for the variable factor, labour, under the condition of interdependence of factor demand. The demand for labour under the condition of factor–demand–interdependence is illustrated in Figure 7.5. Given the VMP_L curve and labour-supply curve, S_{L_2}, if wage rate is given at OW_2, the firm will employ OL_1 units of labour. If wage rate falls to OW_1, the new labour-supply line for the individual firm shifts downward to S_{L_1}. Had labour been the only variable factor, the firm would have employed OL_2 units of labour. But, under the condition that both the factors, labour and capital, are variable and that their demand is interdependent, the fall in wage rate creates a much larger demand for labour—larger than L_1L_2. The reason is employment of additional labour (L_1L_2) creates additional demand for capital. With the use of more capital, labour productivity increases. As a result, VMP_L curve shifts to the right to the position of VMP'_L. The VMP'_L curve intersects the new labour-supply curve SL_1

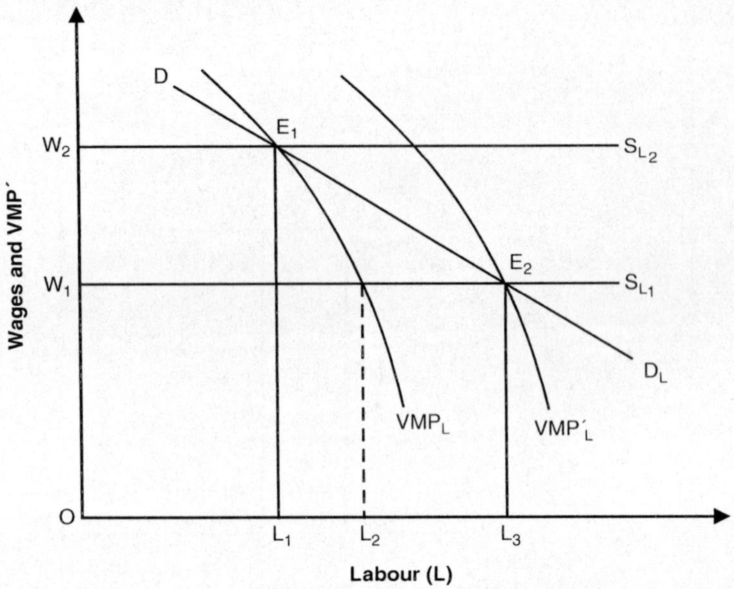

Figure 7.5 *Labour Demand Curve when Both L and K Are Variable*

at point E_2. Point E_2 is, therefore, the new equilibrium point after the fall in wage rate. A similar analysis may be performed for further fall in the wage rate. By joining the equilibrium points E_1 and E_2, we get the demand curve, DD_L, representing labour demand curve under the condition of interdependence of factor demand, when two variable inputs (labour and capital) are used for the production of a commodity.

Industry Demand Curve for a Variable Factor: Labour

The industry demand for a variable factor should, in general, be the horizontal summation of the demand curves of the individual firms for the factor. However, a straightforward horizontal summation of individual demand curves for a factor does not yield the industry demand curve for the factor because this process ignores the *market* or *external* effects of change in the factor prices on factor demand. The external effects are the effects of change in price of the variable factor on the price of the commodity which it produces and its repercussions on the demand for the factor. In a purely competitive market, when the price of a variable factor (say, labour) decreases, all the firms employ more of labour and hence the supply of the commodity increases demand remaining the same. As a result, price of the commodity falls. The fall in price causes a decrease in the VMP_L which causes a downward shift in the VMP_L curve. It means that a fall in factor price (wages) that should have increased demand for labour causes a decline in labour demand due to downward shift in VMP_L curve. Therefore, market demand curve for a variable factor cannot be obtained directly by summing the individual factor-demand curves.

The derivation of industry demand curve for labour is illustrated in Figure 7.6. Suppose that the curve dd_1 in Figure 7.6(a) is a typical individual firm's demand curve for labour, and the initial wage rate is given at OW_2. Given the demand curve and wage rate, a profit maximizing firm employs OL_1 unit of labour. Supposing all firms employ the same (OL_1) units of labour, the market demand for labour can be obtained by multiplying OL_1 with the number of firms. Suppose $OL_1 \times$ Number of firms equals ON_1 as shown in Figure 7.6(b). Thus, at wage late OW_2 we get point J as one point on the industry demand curve

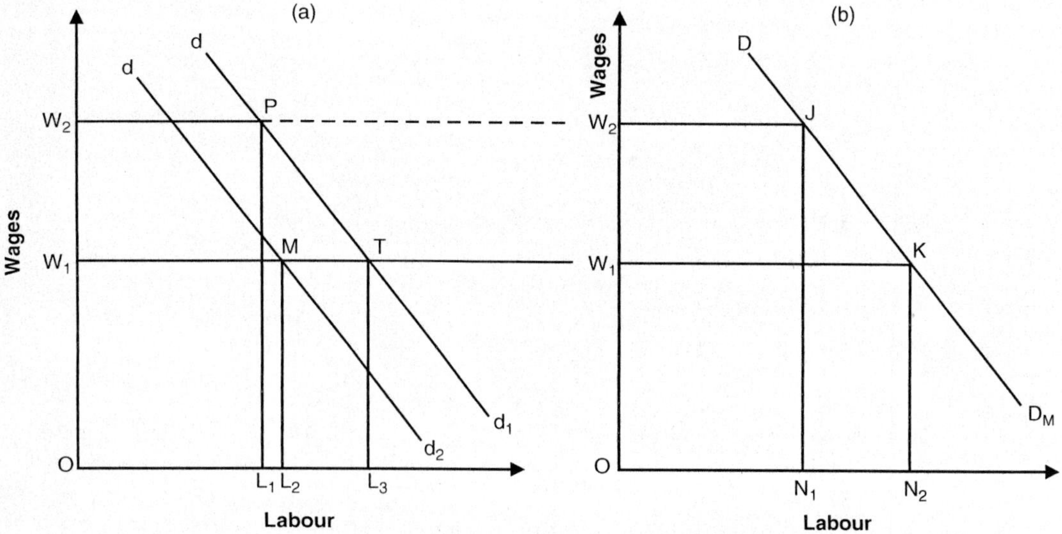

Figure 7.6 *Derivation of Industry Labour Demand Curve*

for labour. Now let the wage rate fall to OW_1 [Figure 7.6(a)]. All other things remaining the same, the firm would move down to point T on demand curve dd_1, and their employment of labour will increase to OL_3. But, *other things do not remain the same.* The increase in labour employment by all the firms—each using L_1L_3 additional labour—the total supply of the commodity increases. Consequently, commodity price decreases. The fall in commodity price causes a fall in the VMP_L. As a result, the labour demand curve for an individual firm shifts leftward from dd_1 to dd_2, as shown in Figure 7.6(a). So, the new labour demand curve is dd_2 and the new equilibrium point is M where demand for labour is OL_2. Thus, industry demand for labour will be equal to OL_2 multiplied by the number of firms. Note that at wage rate OW_1, industry labour demand equals $OL_2 \times$ Number of firms. For example, let us suppose that $OL_2 = 20$ and the number of firms is 10, then industry labour demand equals $OL_2 \times 10 = 20 \times 10 = 200$. Let this industry labour demand of 200 be represented by ON_2 in panel (b) of Figure 7.6. It means that at wage rate OW_1, industry labour demand is ON_2. The wage–labour-demand combination is represented by point K. By joining points J and K in panel (b) of Figure 7.6, we draw the industry labour demand curve as shown by the curve DD_M.

Determination of Market Wage Rate

As in case of the product market, the wage rate in a perfectly competitive product and labour market is determined by the demand for and supply of labour. Derivation of labour demand curve has been, discussed elaborately in the preceding sections. Derivation of labour-supply curve has already been discussed in detail in Chapter 6. In this section, we present the final form of the theory of wage determination under the condition that both product and labour markets are perfectly competitive.

The determination of wage rate under perfect competition is illustrated in Figure 7.7. The labour demand and supply curves are shown by D_L and S_L curves, respectively. The labour demand curve D_l and labour-supply curve S_L intersect at point E determining the market wage rate at OW and labour employment at $OL = WE$. At wage rate OW and employment at OL, the labour market is in equilibrium.

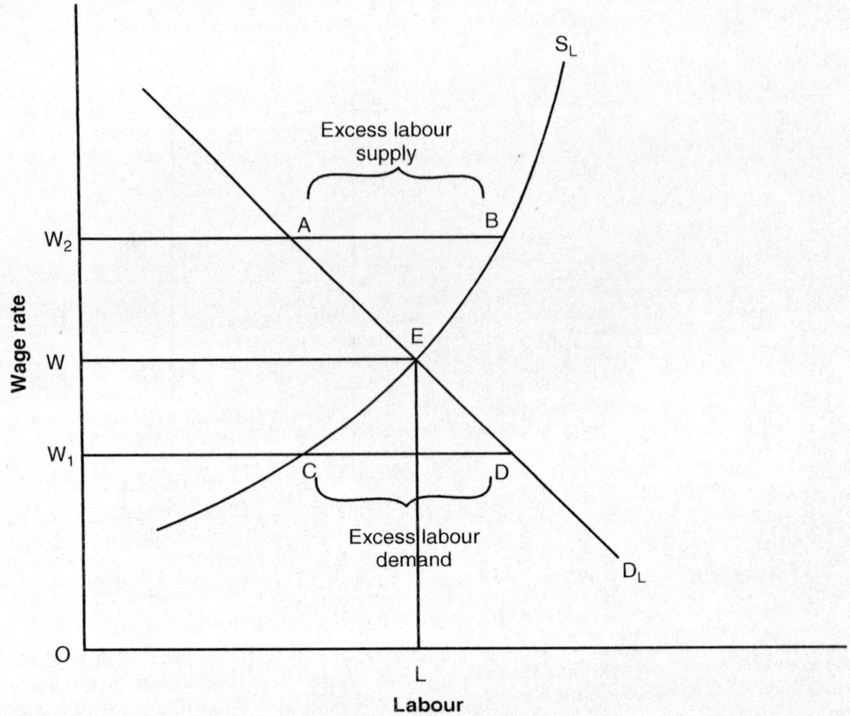

Figure 7.7 *Determination of Wage Rate under Perfect Competition*

If for some reason, say, due to labour union pressure, wage rate is fixed at OW_2, labour demand would decrease to W_2A and labour supply would increase to W_2B. It means that labour supply would exceed the labour demand and there would be unemployment to the extent of *AB*. Under perfect competition, however, excess labour supply would force wage rate to decrease and hence labour demand would increase. This process would continue until market equilibrium is not regained at point *E*. Similarly, if wage rate falls down, for some reason, labour demand would increase and labour supply would decrease, labour demand exceeding the labour supply by *CB*. The market process will push the wage rate up to the equilibrium level, *OW* and employment at *OL*.

NON-HOMOGENEOUS LABOUR AND WAGE DIFFERENTIALS

The theory of labour pricing discussed so far assumes that labour is homogeneous. If labour is homogeneous, and non-monetary advantages are the same in all jobs, then the price of labour tends to be the same in a perfectly competitive market. In the real world, however, labour is not homogeneous. Nor are the different kinds of labour paid the same wages. In this section, we will discuss the reasons for wage differentials.

There are two kinds of wage differentials:

1. Dynamic wage differentials and
2. Static wage differentials

Dynamic Wage Differentials

Dynamic differentials in factor prices arise due to disequilibrium in commodity and factor markets from time to time. The dynamic-factor-price differentials act on the demand and supply conditions of the factor to restore the equilibrium and, thereby, remove the factor price differences. Such differentials are, therefore, temporary and exist only until the disequilibrium persists. For example, suppose that there are only two industries, *A* and *B*, in a country, which use only one factor of production, labour (*L*). Both industries are in equilibrium and pay the same wage rate (*W*) to the labour. Suppose, for some reason, the demand for product of industry *B* decreases. As a result, *B*'s price falls and hence VMP_L curve shifts leftward, causing a fall in the wages paid by industry *B*. Industry *B* pays a lower wage while industry *A* continues to pay the same wages (*W*). Wage rate in industry *B* will be lower than that in industry *A*. *This is the dynamic type of wage differential—wage differentials arising out of changing market conditions.*

The dynamic wage differentials are self-adjusting. The process of wage adjustment work as follows. Due to lower wage rate in industry *B*, labour tends to move to industry *A* in which wages are relatively higher. So the supply of labour to industry *A* increases. This causes a fall in wages in industry *A*. Shift of labour to industry *A* continues until wages in industry *A* fall to the level of industry *B*. Thus, in due course of time, the wage differentials disappear.

Whether a new equilibrium is reached and wage differentials disappear depends on the *factor mobility*. If labour is immobile, the wage differentials persist. If labour is mobile, the wage differentials disappear over time. How long does it take for wage differentials to disappear? It depends on the degree of factor mobility. The greater the labour mobility, the quicker the wage equalization in various industries, and *vice versa*.

Static Wage Differentials

The static wage differentials are those that persist in the state of equilibrium. Such differences are not removed by the competitive forces of the market. Wage differentials of this type arise mainly due to the following reasons.

1. Qualitative differences in labour, i.e., heterogeneity of labour;
2. Difference in the nature of occupations;
3. Differences in the prices of product which various kinds of labour produce and
4. Market imperfections.

We will explain first the static wage differentials caused by *qualitative differences in labour* in some detail and then discuss briefly the wage differentials caused by *other factors*.

Wage Differentials due to Heterogeneity of Labour

Labour is the most heterogeneous factor of production. Therefore, wage differentials are far more common than the other factor price differentials. Wage differentials between the two broad groups of labour—*skilled* and *unskilled*—are more obvious than those within the groups. The nature of wage differentials between the skilled and unskilled labour is illustrated in Figure 7.8(a) and (b). The total supply of both unskilled and skilled labour is assumed to be perfectly *inelastic*. The supply curve of unskilled labour is shown by S_u line in Figure 7.8(a) and that of skilled labour by S_s line in Figure 7.8(b). The market demand curve[7] for unskilled and skilled labour are, respectively, shown by D_u and D_s curves. Consider first Figure 7.8(a). Given the D_u and S_s curves, the unskilled labour, market is in equilibrium at point E_u,

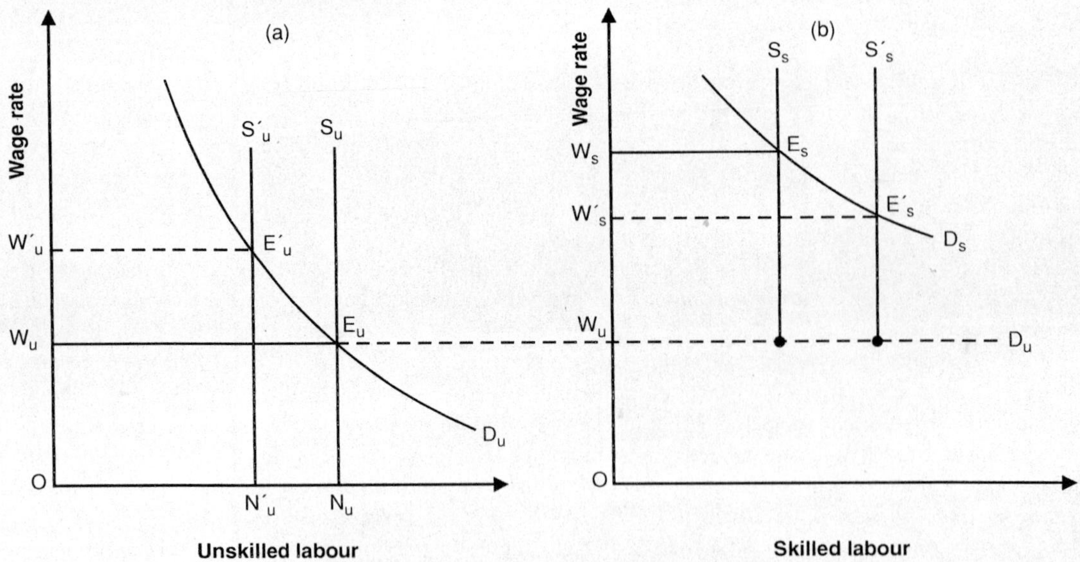

Figure 7.8 *Wage Differential: (a) Unskilled and (b) Skilled Labour*

and wage rate for unskilled labour is determined at OW_u. At this wage rate (OW_u), the total employment of unskilled labour is ON_u.

Let us now look at the case of skilled labour. Note that at wage rate OW_u [Figure 7.8(b)], the supply of skilled labour is there but no skilled labour offers to work at this wage rate. That is, at wage rate OW_u, there is no supply of skilled labour. The wage rate for skilled labour will be determined at a level much higher than that for unskilled labour. Given the demand curve D_s and supply curve S_s, the market wage rate for skilled labour is determined at OW_s. This wage rate is greater than the wage rate (OW_u) for unskilled labour. This kind of wage differential between the skilled and unskilled labour is of *static* nature–static in the sense that it persists even if there are changes in skilled and unskilled labour markets.

The wage differentials may narrow down or widen over time. If higher wage rates for skilled labour encourage people to acquire skill through training and education, the supply of skilled labour will increase. As a result, supply curve will shift rightward to S'_s [(Figure 7.8(b)], and wage rate will tend to settle at equilibrium point E'_s with wage determined at W'_s provided there is no barrier to entry into the skilled labour market. This will reduce the wage differential. On the other hand, if supply of skilled labour increases because workers of unskilled group acquire training and skill, the labour-supply curve of unskilled labour [Figure 7.8(a)] will shift leftward causing a rise in the unskilled labour rate, towards point E'_u pushing the wage rate up to OW'_u. This will further reduce the wage differentials. Note that the difference between unskilled-labour-wage rate OW_u and skilled-labour-wage rate OW_s, narrows down in Figure 7.8(b). As shown in Figure 7.8(a), wages for unskilled labour increases from OW_u to OW'_u and in Figure 7.8(b), wages for skilled labour decreases from OW_s to OW'_s. This trend reduces the wage differentials.

However, whether wage differentials narrow down depends on market conditions. If labour unions and associations of professionals restrict the entry to the skilled labour market and the demand curve for unskilled labour shifts rightward the wage differentials may widen. On the other hand, government policy of promoting skilled manpower through scholarships, student loans, free education and training, creation of educational and training facilities and so on, may increase the supply of skilled manpower which may narrow down the wage differentials between skilled and unskilled labour.

Some wage differentials may still persist between the broad groups of skilled and unskilled labour. The wage differentials between the individuals of each broad group may also exist. Let us now look into the nature and causes of wage differentials that persist.

The Nature and Causes of Persisting Wage Differentials

In this section, we explain the persistent wage differentials caused by other factors. The wage differentials that persist over time are of two kinds: (i) compensating or equalizing and (ii) non-compensating differentials.

Compensating Wages Differentials Compensating wage differentials account for the non-monetary gains or costs that are associated with various kinds of jobs. The compensating wage differentials arise from the following factors.

1. ***Cost of Training***. While some jobs, e.g., medical, engineering and managerial professions require heavy monetary investment in education and training, some others require low investment. Also, some jobs require a longer duration of training than the others. The jobs needing greater investment in terms of money and time are generally highly paid. Higher salaries include compensation for high cost of training and education.
2. ***Risk in Performing Jobs***. Some jobs by nature involve risk to life and body. Among risky jobs, some are riskier than the others. Highly risky jobs, e.g., jobs of mining workers and engineers, aeroplane pilots and so on, are more highly paid than the less and non-risky jobs. Higher payments include compensation for the risk of job. Some jobs, like teaching and white-collar jobs do not involve any risk and hence are low-paid.
3. ***Hours of Leisure***. People in the teaching profession and research, generally, enjoy longer leisure hours than people in medical and engineering professions and in business management. That is why, perhaps, doctors and engineers are paid higher salaries than the university and college teachers. (Longer leisure hours compensate for wage differences.)
4. ***Cost of Living***. Cost of living varies from area to area and from city to city. Therefore, labour posted in costly cities (Grade A) in India is paid higher salaries than those posted in less costly cities (Grade B and C).
5. ***Other Factors***. The other factors which contribute to the persistent wage differentials are: (i) cost of tools and equipments required for performing the job; (ii) pleasantness or unpleasantness of the job; (iii) job security; (iv) nature of employment (i.e., whether contractual or permanent); (v) working conditions and environment of working place and (vi) social prestige associated with job and so on.

Non-compensating Wage Differentials

The non-compensatory wage differentials are those for which there is no compensating (or equalizing) factor. Such wage differentials arise because of the following factors.

1. ***Individual Qualities of Labour***. Individuals are born with different mental and physical abilities and endowments which determine their work efficiency, and the nature of jobs to which they are best suited. Such differences in individual labour exist in all kinds of labour—skilled and unskilled. The differences in individual abilities and expertise cause differences in their

productivity. Therefore, there would be differences in the reward which they can earn in the market for their services. One can find a number of such cases of wage differentials in the cadre of professional managers in the corporate sector.

2. ***Market Imperfections***. If labour market conditions are imperfect, and generally, they are, then workers lack adequate information regarding the opportunities open to them. This restricts the mobility of labour to higher-paid jobs and places. Immobility of labour due to market imperfections may cause low wage in some areas and high wages in others. Besides, discrimination in employment on the basis of colour, sex, religion and caste and so on, also causes non-compensating wage differentials. For instance, women workers are generally paid low wages for the same kind and hours of work.
3. ***Differences in Prices of Products***. The market value of a commodity produced by a labour is one of the most important causes of wage differences. Labour employed in industries producing low-price goods tends to get lower wages than those employed in the industries of highly priced goods. The reason is that the *MRP* of labour in case of low-price goods is lower than that of highly priced goods. For example, *bidi* workers get low wages than the workers of a cigarette company.

SUMMARY

Under perfect competition, wage rate, or any factor price for that matter, is determined by market demand for and the overall supply of labour. In general, labour demand and wage rate are inversely related—when wages decreases, labour demand increases. However, this general rule does not apply straight away to perfectly competition markets. The reason is that a change in wage rate causes three effects—*substitution effect, output effect* and *profit effect*. These effects reduce the effect of change in wage rate on the labour demand under perfect competition with large number of firms. Therefore, labour demand curve has to be derived by accounting for these effects. In fact, these effects reduce the increase in labour demand expected from decrease in wage rate under normal conditions and *vice versa*. Once demand curve is derived, given the supply function, the wage rate is determined by the intersection of labour demand and supply curves.

REVIEW QUESTIONS AND EXERCISES

1. Distinguish between *MRP* and *VMP*. How are these concepts applied to factor-price determination under perfect competition and imperfect competition in product and factor markets?
2. What is meant by interdependence of factor demand? How does interdependence of factor demand affect the factor demand?
3. What is meant by interdependence of factor demand? How does interdependence of factor demand affect the factor demand?
4. What is meant by interdependence of factor demand? How does interdependence of factor demand affect the factor demand?
5. Define perfect competition and imperfect competition in both product and factor market. How is wage rate determined under perfect competition in both product and factor markets?
6. What is meant by interdependence of factor demand? Suppose there are only two factors, labour and capital. How does decrease in wage rate affect the demand for labour and capital?

7. What is meant by substitution effect, output effect and profit effect of change in the price of a factor? Explain how can these effects of decrease in wage rate be measured, price of capital remaining constant? Illustrate your answer graphically.
8. Explain and illustrate the derivation of demand curve for labour under the conditions (i) labour is the only variable factor and (ii) both labour and capital are variable inputs.
9. When labour is the only variable factor, industry's demand curve for labour is the sum of individual firm's demand for labour at different wage rate. Does this rule apply when both labour and capital are variable factor? How is industry's demand for labour derived under the condition that both labour and capital are variable factors?
10. What is meant by homogeneity and heterogeneity of labour? What are the reasons for wage differentials in the labour market? Distinguish between dynamic and static wage differentials.
11. When price of a factor changes, factor proportion changes due to:
    (a) Substitution effect,
    (b) Output effect,
    (c) profit effect, or
    (d) all of above?

ENDNOTES

1. The difference between MRP_L and VMP_L will be explained in detail with numerical example and graphical illustration in Chapter 8.
2. In case of imperfect competition, however, *MRP* and *VMP* are defined differently as given below.

$$MRP_L = MPP_L \cdot MR$$
$$\text{and } MRP_L = MPP_L \cdot P(= AR)$$

   The significance of the difference in nomenclature and its application will be clarified further when we discuss wage determination in imperfectly competitive markets in the next chapter.
3. Quoted by Paul A. Samuelson and William D. Nordhaus, in their book, *Economis* (New York, NY: McGraw-Hill, 15th International Edition), p. 206.
4. Ibid.
5. Although output effect of change in a factor of production can be measured by using production function, provided it has already been estimated. But production function does not capture the *X*-efficiency of the two factors. So the measurement of the out effect of change in a single factor is not accurate.
6. We will return later to the third effect of change in wage rate, i.e., *profit effect*.
7. Derived from the summation of the VMP_L curves of the individuals.

FURTHER READINGS

Carter, A.M. (1959), *Theory of Wages and Employment* (Homewood, IL: Richard D. Irwin).
Carter, A.M. and Marshall, F.R. (1972), *Labour Economics, Employment and Trade Unionism* (Homewood, IL: Richard D. Irwin).

Clark, J.B. (1905), *The Distribution of Wealth* (New York: Macmillan).
Douglas, P.H. (1934), *The Theory of Wages* (New York: Macmillan).
Dunlop, J.T. (1944), *Wage Determination under Trade Union* (New York: Macmillan).
Hicks, J.R. (1932), *The Theory of Wages* (New York: Macmillan).
Kaldor, N. (1955–1956), 'Alternative Theories of Distribution', *Rev. Eco. Stud.*, XXIII (2): 83–100.
Koutsoyiannis, A. (1978), *Modern Microeconomics* (New York: Macmillan), 2nd Edn., Chapter 12.
Lipsey, R.G. and Chrystal, K.A. (1999), *Principles of Economics* (Oxford: Oxford University Press) Chapter 14.
Perlman, R. (1969), *Labour Theory* (London: Wiley).
Roninson, J. (1933), *The Economics of Imperfect Competition* (New York: Macmillan), Chapter 25.

Chapter 8

Wage and Employment Determination Under Imperfect Competition

CHAPTER OBJECTIVES

This chapter presents a discussion on wage and employment determination under imperfect competition in both product and labour markets. Imperfectly, competitive market is characterized by the existence of monopoly in both product and labour markets—monopoly in labour market is created by formation of labour unions that restrict the supply of labour. When a monopoly firm hires labour from the unionized labour market, i.e., monopolized labour market, it makes the monopoly firm a monopsonist—the single demander of labour. By going through this chapter, you know:

- How wage rate is determined when there is monopoly in the product market and perfect competition in the labour market;
- How and under what conditions a monopoly firm exploits labour when labour market is perfectly competitive;
- How wage rate is determined when there is monopoly in the labour market and perfect competition in the product market;
- How wage rate is determined if there is monopoly in both product and labour markets, i.e., the case of *bilateral monopoly*; and
- Why there is a need *for minimum wage laws* and how minimum wage acts affect the labour and employment of labour.

INTRODUCTION

The theory of wage determination and employment in imperfectly competitive markets is basically the same as one applicable to the perfectly competitive markets. However, the imperfections in the commodity and labour markets necessitate some modification in the theory. The need for modification arises for *two reasons*. First, average revenue (AR) and marginal revenue (MR) in an imperfectly competitive market are different from, those in perfectly competitive markets. In a perfectly competitive product market, $AR = MR$, and this revenue condition is represented by a straight horizontal line, whereas AR and MR curves in an imperfect commodity market slope downward to the right. Recall that VMP_L curve derived on the basis of constant AR represents labour demand curve under perfect competition. But, the VMP_L curve of a variable factor (labour) is not a relevant under imperfect market conditions. Secondly, the imperfections in the factor market alter the supply conditions of variable factor (labour).

From wage determination point of view, the imperfect markets may be classified as:

1. Monopoly in commodity market and perfect competition in labour market;
2. Monopoly in product market and monopsony in competitive labour market;
3. Perfect competition in commodity market and monopoly in labour market and
4. Bilateral monopoly—monopoly in both product and labour markets.

Determination of wages and employment under these categories of imperfect markets are discussed below. Our analysis is confined to a single variable factor (labour).

WAGE DETERMINATION UNDER PRODUCT MONOPOLY AND PERFECT COMPETITION IN LABOUR MARKET

In this section, we discuss wage determination under the market conditions in which a monopolist[1] in the product market (X) buys the services of a variable factor (labour) in a perfectly competitive labour market. As noted above, in case of product monopoly, VMP_L is not the basis of monopolists labour demand curve. The reason is VMP_L is calculated at a constant price, i.e., $VMP_L = MPP_L P_X$ where $P_X = MR$, whereas under product monopoly $P_X > MR_X$ because a monopolist faces a downward sloping demand curve. The equilibrium condition for monopoly is given as $MC = MR$. Where labour cost (W) is the only cost, $MC = MW$ (where MW is marginal wage cost). The monopolist reaches equilibrium with respect to variable labour employment where $MRP_L = MW$ (where $MRP_L = MPP_L \cdot MR_X$). Since $P_X > MR_X$ under product monopoly, $VMP_L > MRP_L$. The difference between MRP_L and VMP_L is illustrated in Table 8.1

Table 8.1 *The MRP_L and VMP_L Schedules*

Units of Labour	Total Output (Q)	Marginal Product (MPP_L)	Selling Price (P_X)	Total Revenue ($TR = Q \cdot P_X$)	$\Delta TR = TR_n - TR_{n-1}$	Marginal Revenue ($MR = \Delta TR/MPP_1$)	$MRP_L =$ ($MPP_L \times MR$)	$VMP_L =$ ($MPP_L \cdot P_X$)
(1)	(2)	(3)	(4)	(5)	(6)	(7)	(8)	(9)
1	10	10	15	150	150	15	150	150
2	19	9	14	266	116	13	117	126
3	27	8	13	351	85	11	88	104
4	34	7	12	408	57	8	56	84
5	40	6	11	440	32	5	30	66
6	45	5	10	450	10	2	10	50

Note: Figures in the 7th column onwards are rounded up.

Derivation of MRP_L Curve under Product Monopoly

Having noted the reason why *AR* and *MR* curves under product monopoly are different from those under perfect competition in the product market, let us now derive the MRP_L curve under product monopoly.

It can be seen in columns (8) and (9) of Table 8.1 that, except at the initial stage, MRP_L is not the same as VMP_L. While both MRP_L and VMP_L tend to decrease with increase in labour, MRP_L falls at a much faster rate than the VMP_L. The difference between MRP_L and VMP_L is brought out more clearly by graphical presentation of MRP_L and VMP_L data given in columns (8) and (9) of Table 8.1, as shown in Figure 8.1. It can be seen that VMP_L curve lies above the MRP_L curve at all the levels of labour employment. The reason why MRP_L fall at a higher rate than VMP_L is obvious. Recall that $MRP_L = MPP_L \times MR$ and $VMP_L = MRP_L \times P_X$. Note that MPP_L is a common factor in the calculation of the values of MRP_L and VMP_L. So, the rate of change in MRP_L and VMP_L depends on the rate of change in *MR* and P_X. It can be seen in Table 8.1 that *MR* falls at a much faster rate than the P_X. Therefore, MRP_L falls at a much faster rate than VMP_L.

Having derived the MRP_L and VMP_L curves for a product monopoly, let us now derive the labour demand curve for a product monopoly. The labour demand curve of a product monopoly is derived on the basis of the MRP_L curve under the following two conditions.

1. The monopoly firm uses only labour as a variable factor and
2. The monopolist uses both labour and capital as variable factors.

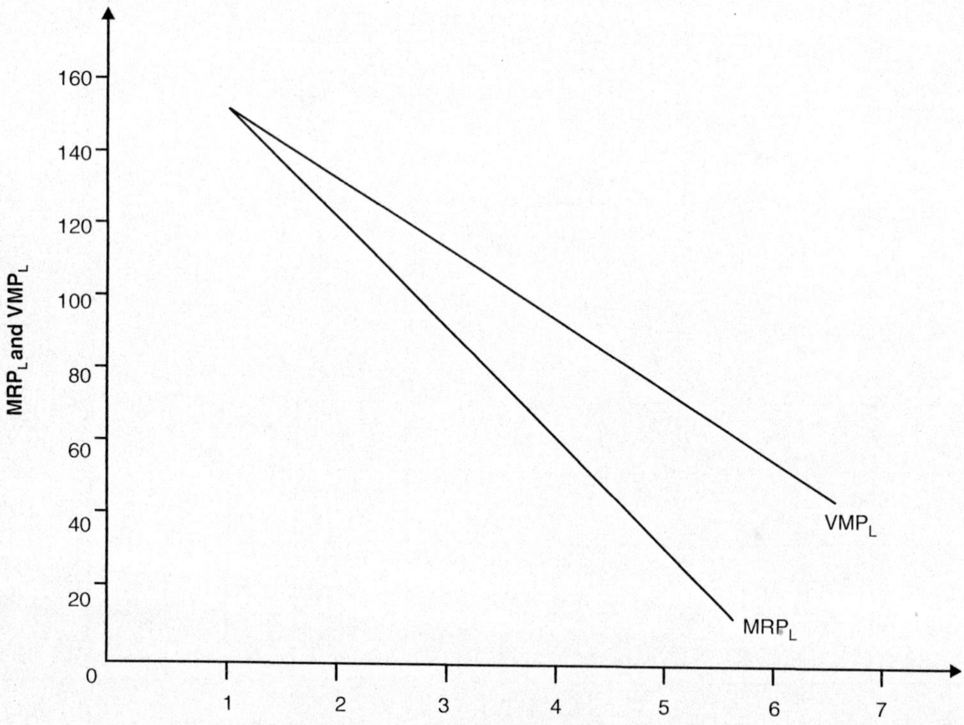

Figure 8.1 *MRP_L and VMP_L Curve*

Monopoly's Demand for Labour—Single Variable Factor Let us recall the assumption that the monopolist hires labour from a perfectly competitive labour market. Since labour market is perfectly competitive, a monopoly firm faces a perfectly elastic labour supply curve, as shown by the S_L curves in Figure 8.2. As regards the monopoly firm's demand for labour, the curve MRP_L represents its labour demand curve. A profit-maximizing monopoly firm will hire labour up to the point where marginal revenue productivity of labour (MRP_L) equals the marginal cost of labour (MC_L), i.e., where $MRP_L = MC_L$. If wage rate in a perfectly competitive labour market is given, Q, then the profit-maximizing monopolist will employ labour up to the point, where $MRP_L = MC_L$.

The deviation of monopoly's labour demand curve is illustrated in Figure 8.2. As panel (a) of Figure 8.2 shows, MRP_L and S_{L3} curves intersect at point E_3. At this point, $MRP_L = W_3 = MC_L$. Point E_3, therefore, determines the equilibrium demand for labour at OL_1. In other words, the profit-maximizing monopoly will employ OL_1 units of labour because this level of employment satisfies the profit-maximizing condition, i.e., its $MRP_L = MC_L = W_3$. By employing OL_1 units of labour, the monopolist maximizes its profits at point E_3. When wage rate decreases to OW_2, the monopolist employs OL_2 units of labour. Similarly, when wage rate decreases to OW_1, the firm will employ OL_3 units of labour. It is thus clear that as the wage rate decreases, the demand for labour increases along the MRP_L curve. Thus, the MRP_L curve represents monopoly's demand curve for labour, where labour is the only variable factor used the monopoly firm.

However, monopolist's labour demand curve can be derived directly by graphing the wage–labour data revealed by the panel (a) of Figure 8.2. The wage–labour data revealed by the panel (a) can be listed as follows.

Wage Rate	Labour Demand
W_3	L_1
W_2	L_2
W_1	L_3

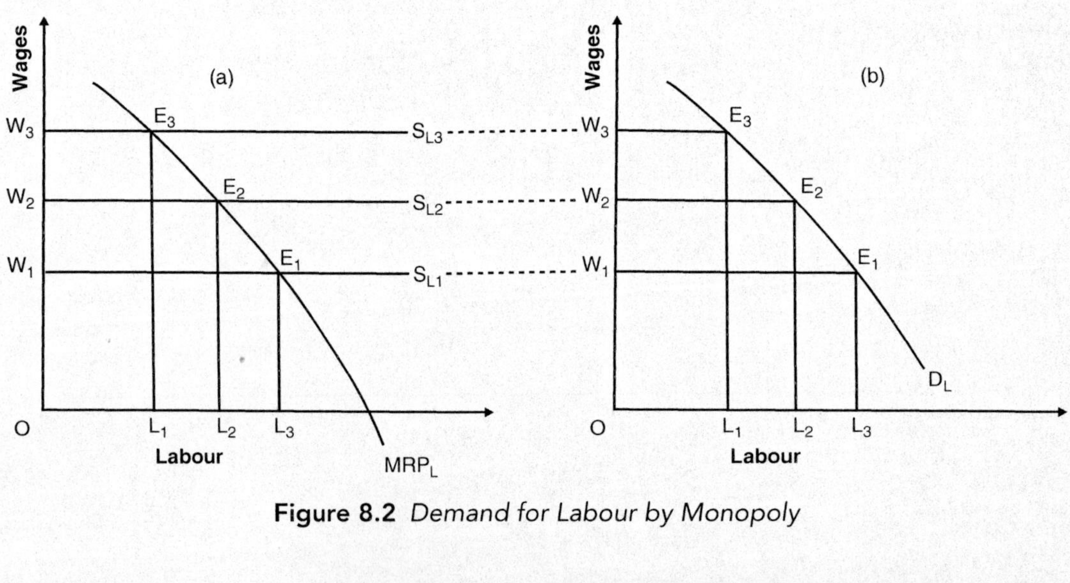

Figure 8.2 *Demand for Labour by Monopoly*

This wage–labour demand data is presented graphically in panel (b) of figure. Points E_3, E_2 and E_1 are located by connected the labour demand at different wage rates. By joining the points E_3, E_2 and E_1 by a curve, we drive the labour demand curve as shown in panel (b) of Figure 8.2.

Monopoly Firm's Demand for Labour with Two Variable Factors As noted earlier, when more than one variable input or factor is used in the process of production, the VMP_L or the MRP_L curve does not represent the demand curve for labour. The same logic applies to the monopoly demand for labour too. To put it more specifically, as shown in Figure 8.2, when a monopolist uses one variable input (labour), the MRP_L curve represents its labour demand curve. But, *when a monopolist uses more than one variable input, its marginal revenue product curve (MRP_L) is not its demand curve for labour.* The reason for this is given in Section 7.2 (see Figure 7.4). The process of deriving monopoly demand curve for labour when the monopolist uses more than one variable input is also the same as discussed in Section 7.2.1 (ii). The process is briefly repeated here.

Let us suppose that monopolist's MRP_L curve and labour supply curve (S_L) are initially given by MRP_{L1} and S_{L2}, respectively, in Figure 8.3. Given the wage rate OW_2, the monopolist is in equilibrium at point E_1, where the monopolist employs OL_1 units of labour. Now let the wage rate fall to OW_1, all other things remaining the same, the monopolist should have moved down along the MRP_{L1} to point E. But other things do not remain the same because of interdependence of factor demand. The fall in the wage rate from OW_2 to OW_1 causes three kinds of effects: *substitution effect, output effect* and *profit-maximization effect*. The output and profit-maximization effects cause a rightward shift in the MRP_L curve. Suppose the MRP_{L1} curve shifts to the position of MRP_{L2} (Figure 8.3), the MRP_{L2} intersects S_{L1} at point E_2. Therefore, the profit-maximizing monopolist moves to a new equilibrium point E_2. By joining the equilibrium points E_1 and E_2, we get the monopolist's demand curve for labour under the condition

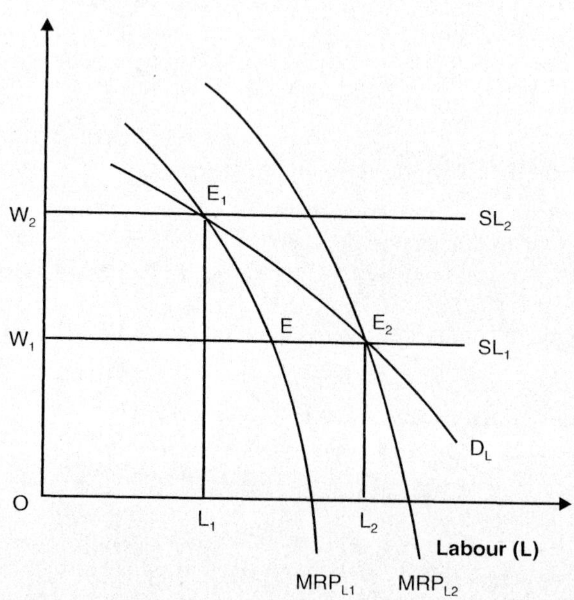

Figure 8.3 *Derivation of Monopoly Demand for Labour with Two Variable Inputs*

that the monopolist uses two or more inputs. The curve D_L represents the monopoly's demand curve for labour, when both labour and capital are the variable factors.

Market Demand for Labour under Monopoly and Monopolistic Competition Recall that market demand curve for a variable factor (labour) in a competitive market is the horizontal sum of the individual demand curves. In case of a monopolized industry, however, there is no external or industry effect resulting from a decrease in the price of labour. Since a monopolist is the sole supplier of the product, the external effect of expanded output on the product price is automatically taken into account in the marginal revenue product curve. Therefore, in case of a monopoly firm buying labour in a competitive market, the market demand curve for labour is the same as monopoly's demand curve for labour.

But in case of oligopolistic and monopolistic competitors, the market demand curve for a variable input is the summation of the individual demand curves for it. The reason is that when all oligopolistic and monopolistic firms expand their output, the market price of the output falls. As a result, the individual demand curve and marginal revenue curve for the commodity shift to the left. Due to leftward shift in the demand and marginal revenue curves, the individual demand curves for the variable input shifts leftward. Such as it is, the procedure of deriving market demand curve for a variable factor is exactly the same as in case of perfectly competitive industry.

Determination of Factor Price and Employment When product market is characterized by monopoly or monopolistic competition and the variable factor market is perfectly competitive, the *factor price and employment* are determined in the same way as they are determined in a perfectly competitive market. That is, *market equilibrium of factor price and employment of a variable factor is determined by the intersection of market demand curve for and market supply curve of the factor*. Thus, whether product market is monopolistic or perfectly competitive, the analysis of equilibrium price of a variable factor and its employment is the same. (For details, see Chapter 7, Section 7.2: Wage Determination in a Perfectly Competitive Market) There is, however, one important difference between the two types of market competition. In case of perfectly competitive product market, the market demand curve for labour is based on its VMP_L, whereas in case of monopoly and monopolistic competition, the market demand curve for labour is based on its MRP_L.

Exploitation of Labour by Monopoly

When there is monopoly or monopolistic competition in the product market and perfect competition in the labour market, then the monopolist or monopolistic firms tend to exploit labour by paying wages less than their *VMP*. In this subsection, we explain and illustrate the exploitation of labour by monopoly and monopolistic firms.

Monopolistic exploitation of labour is analysed here under the following two conditions.

1. Exploitation of labour by a monopoly firm and
2. Exploitation of labour under monopolistic competition.

Exploitation of Labour by a Monopoly Firm The monopolistic exploitation of labour is caused by the fact that market demand curve for labour by a monopoly firm in product market is based on MRP_L rather than on its VMP_L. There is exploitation because labour is paid wages equal to its *MRP* which is lower than its *VMP*. According to Joan Robinson,[2] a productive factor is exploited if it is paid a price less than the value of its marginal product (*VMP*). Robinson's analysis of monopolistic exploitation of labour is presented below.

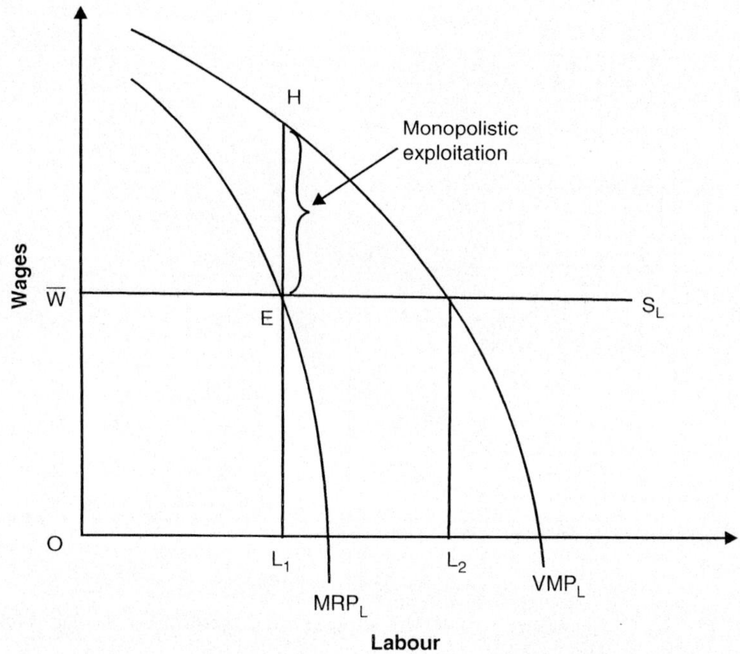

Figure 8.4 *Exploitation of Labour Under Product Monopolist*

The monopolistic exploitation of labour (a variable factor) by a monopoly firm is illustrated in Figure 8.4. In Figure 8.4, the MRP_L curve represents monopoly's demand curve and S_L line represents the labour supply. In Figure 8.4, given the MRP_L and S_L curves, a profit-maximizing monopolist will employ OL_1 units of labour determined by point E and pay wage $O\overline{W}$ ($= EL_1$). But, under perfect competition in the product market, VMP_L is the relevant labour demand curve. Under this condition, if only OL_1 unit of labour is demanded, the wage rate will be HL_1. Thus, the difference between monopoly wage rate (EL_1) and competitive wage rate (HL_1), i.e., ($HL_1 - EL_1 = HE$) is the extent of *monopolistic exploitation* of labour.

Not only there is exploitation of labour, but also there is another big social disadvantage caused by the monopoly in product market. The social disadvantage of monopoly reflects in the form of loss of employment and the consequent loss of output. The monopolist restricts employment of labour to OL_1 units whereas the perfectly competitive firm would employ OL_2 units of labour. The lower level of employment by a monopolist results in loss of output.

Exploitation of Labour under Monopolistic Competition Figure 8.5 illustrates the exploitation of labour under monopolistic competition at *the market level.* In this figure, curve D_M represents the market demand curve for labour by the monopolistic firms based on MRP_L; curve D_C represents the market demand curve for labour by the perfectly competitive firms based on VMP_L; and curve S_L represents the market supply curve of labour. Under monopoly and monopolistic competition, labour market will be in equilibrium at point E_M; wage rate will be OW_M; and employment will be OL_M units of labour. But, in case product market is perfectly competitive, labour market will be in equilibrium with wage rate OW_C and employment OL_C units of labour. Obviously, imperfect competition in the

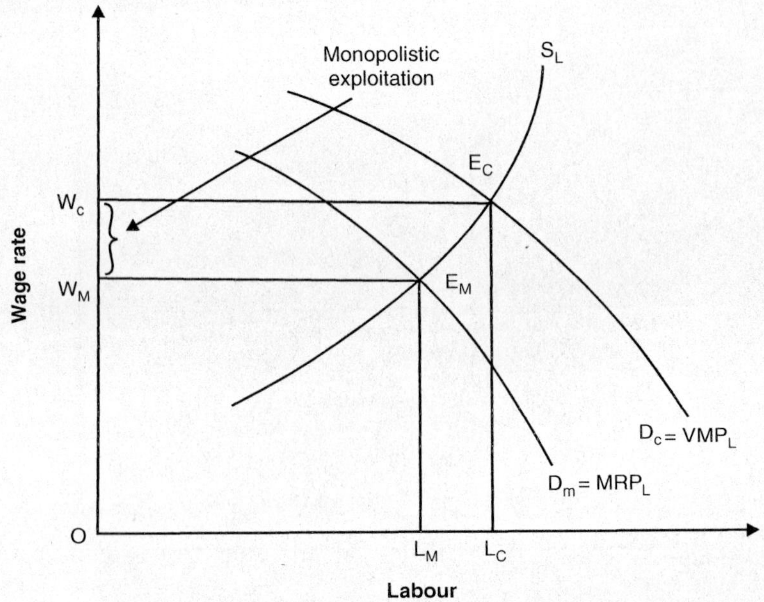

Figure 8.5 *Exploitation of Labour Under Monopolistic Competition*

product market causes wage rate to be lower than the value of marginal product (VMP_L) as is the case in a perfectly competitive product market. Thus, according to Joan Robinson, $OW_C - OW_M = W_CW_M$ is the extent of *exploitation* under monopolistic competition.

Criticism Joan Robinson's view on monopolistic exploitation of labour has, however, been questioned on the ground that lower wage payment is inevitable because of divergence between MRP_L and VMP_L. The MRP_L is lower than VMP_L (at all levels of employment) not because of monopoly powers of the monopolistic sellers but because of *product differentiation*. Product differentiation creates brand loyalty which makes the demand curve slope downward to the right. In case of a downward sloping demand curve, there is bound to be a difference between the price (AR) and the marginal revenue (MR), marginal revenue being lower than the price. Since all firms, whether in perfect or imperfect market, attempt at profit maximization, a monopolistic firm will have to pay labour a wage rate that equals MRP_L Therefore, the difference between OW_C and OW_M cannot be considered as exploitation. The difference arises due to the market conditions. However, if product differentiation is excessive and commodities are imposed on the consumers by the monopolistic sellers, then the argument of monopolistic exploitation may be acceptable.

WAGE DETERMINATION UNDER PRODUCT MONOPOLY AND FACTOR MONOPSONY

In this section, we discuss wage determination in another kind of market setting. In this market setting, there is monopoly in the commodity market and monopsony in the input (labour) market. When there is a single buyer of an input (say, labour), there exists *monopsony* in the labour market. Thus, in the present model, the product monopolist is also a monopsonist in the labour market while labour supply is competitive. The analysis of determination of wage rate and employment under the conditions of monopoly in the commodity market and monopsony in the labour market is relevant also for monopolistic competition and oligopoly in the commodity market, and monopsony and oligopsony in the factor market.

Wage and employment determination in the market setting described above is discussed under two different assumptions that: (i) only a single variable factor (labour) is used and (ii) more than one variable factor is used, i.e., both labour and capital are in demand. Before we analyse the determination of wage rate and employment, let us explain the *concept of marginal cost of labour* (MC_L)—a concept used in the analysis of factor price determination.

Marginal Cost of a Variable Factor (Labour)

Factor price and employment under the conditions of monopoly in the commodity market and monopsony in the labour market are determined by intersection of labour demand curve and the marginal cost of labour[3] (MC_L) curve. The monopsonist's demand curve for labour is MRP_L curve as derived in the preceding section. There the labour supply curve faced by a monopsonist was supposed to be perfectly elastic. However, the labour supply curve faced by the monopsonist is not perfectly elastic: it is a usual upward sloping supply curve. It implies that more and more labour is supplied only at increasing wage rate. With the increase in wage rate, the supply of labour increases yielding a positively sloping labour supply curve.

In case the labour supply curve has a positive slope, there is a divergence between the average cost and marginal cost of labour. The monopsonist must therefore consider his *marginal cost of labour* to decide on the units of labour to be employed. The marginal cost of the variable input, (labour), may be computed as shown in Table 8.2.

It is obvious from the table that marginal cost of labour (MC_L) is greater than the average wage rate (AW) at all levels employment. The numbers in the 2nd and 4th columns, when graphed with reference to labour units, as shown in Figure 8.6, give the labour supply curve (AW) and the marginal cost of labour (MC_L) curve for the monopsonist. The AW curve represents the labour supply curve for the monopsonist. Obviously, the labour supply curve faced by a monopsonistic monopoly is different from one faced by the simple monopoly.

Table 8.2 *Total and Marginal Cost of Labour*

Units of Labour	Average Cost of Labour (AW) (Rs)	Total Labour Cost (TC_L) (Rs)	Marginal Cost of Labour ($MC_L = TC_L$) (Rs)
1	5	5	5
2	6	12	7
3	7	21	9
4	8	32	11
5	9	45	13
6	10	60	15
7	11	77	17

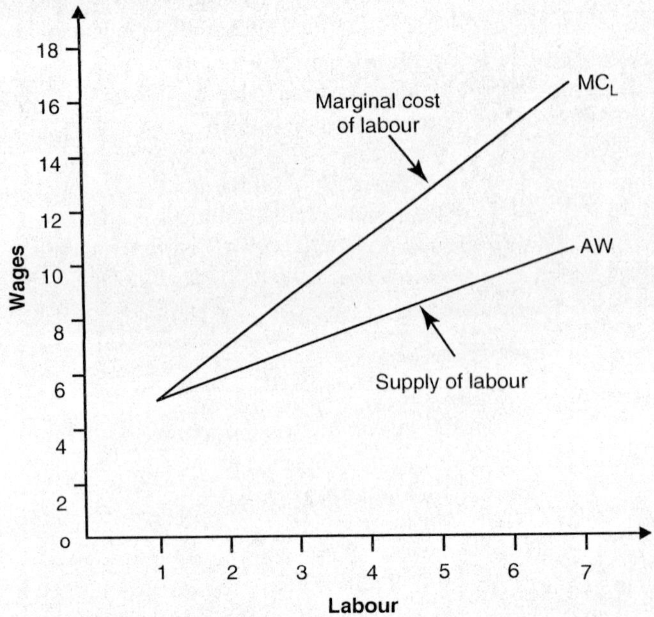

Figure 8.6 *Marginal Cost of Labour and Labour Supply Curve*

Wages and Employment under Monopsony: Single Variable Factor (Labour)

As mentioned earlier, factor price and employment under monopsony are determined by the intersection of monopsonist's demand curve for labour and marginal labour cost curve (MC_L). When monopsony–monopoly firm uses only one variable factor (labour), MRP_L curve is its demand curve for labour and its labour supply curve (S_L) is the same as *AW* curve, as shown in Figure 8.6. Given the monopsonist's labour demand curve (MRP_L) and labour supply curve (MC_L), let us now explain and illustrate the wage and employment determination under monopsony.

Figure 8.7 illustrates the determination of wage rate and employment under monopolist's monopsony when a single variable factor (labour) is used. The MRP_L curve represents monopsonist's demand curve for labour and MC_L curve represents its marginal cost. A monopsonist employs labour up to the point at which the marginal revenue product of labour (MRP_L) equals its marginal cost of labour (MC_L), i.e., where $MRP_L = MC_L$. In Figure 8.7, the MRP_L and MC_L curves intersect at point *E* at which $MRP_L = MC_L$. The monopsonist finds, therefore, its equilibrium at point *E*, where he employs *OL* units of labour. Thus, *OL* is the equilibrium level of labour employment. As the figure shows, ordinate *EL* intersects labour supply curve (S_L) at point *M*, which determines the equilibrium wage rate corresponding to the equilibrium level of employment (*OL*) at *OW* (= *ML*).

Factor Price and Employment under Monopsony: Two Variable Factors Case

When a monopsonist firm uses more than one variable factor, its demand for a variable factor (labour) is determined by the principle of least-cost combination of variable factors. If a competitive firm uses two variable factors, labour (*L*) and capital (*K*), the least-cost criterion is given by

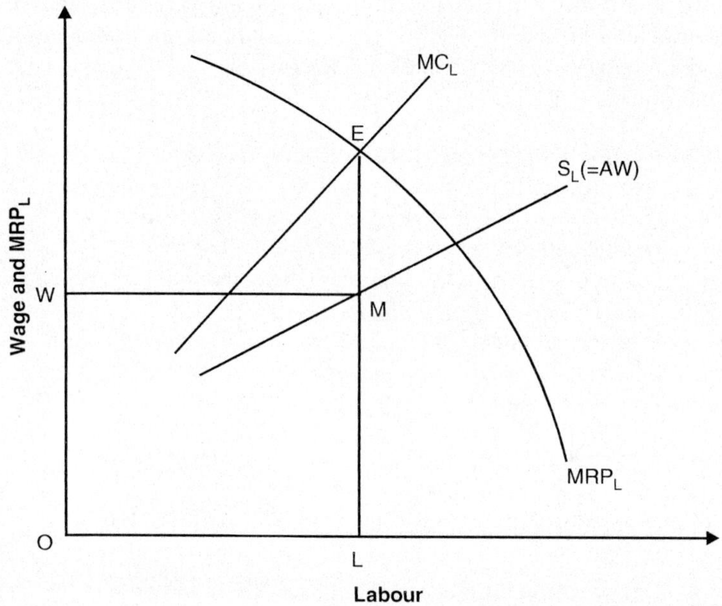

Figure 8.7 *Price and Employment Determination Under Monopsony*

$$\frac{MP_L}{MP_K} = \frac{P_L}{P_K} \text{ or } \frac{MP_L}{P_L} = \frac{MP_K}{P_K}$$

where MP_L = marginal physical product of labour; MP_K = marginal physical product of capital; P_L = wage rate (W) and P_K = price of capital (interest).

For a monopsonist, however, the criterion for the least-cost combination of variable factor is somewhat different from one that applies to the perfectly competitive firms. The reason is that if both commodity and factor markets are perfectly competitive, changes in labour demand by a firm leave factor prices unchanged. In simple words, P_L and P_K remain unchanged, and hence average cost of labour (AW) equals its marginal cost (MW). But, if labour market is monopsonistic, changes in labour employment by a monopsonist cause changes in wage rate. Changes in wage rate create a divergence[4] between average wage cost (AW) and its marginal wage cost (MW). The profit-maximizing monopsonist must, therefore, consider marginal cost of labour rather than the average price of labour (AW). Thus, the least-cost criterion for the monopsonist may be expressed as

$$\frac{MP_L}{MC_L} = \frac{MP_K}{MC_K}$$

or

$$\frac{MP_L}{MP_K} = \frac{MC_L}{MC_K}$$

where MC_L = marginal cost of labour (MW), and MC_K = marginal cost of capital.

This analysis shows that a profit-maximizing monopsonist will employ a variable factor until the ratio of its marginal product to its marginal cost is equal to that of other variable inputs. Given the cost minimization rule, we can now proceed to discuss the determination of wage rate and also exploitation of labour by the monopsonist.

Wage Determination and Exploitation of Labour The determination of factor price (wage rate) and monopsonist exploitation of labour are analysed here simultaneously. We have shown in Figure 8.4 that the existence of monopoly in the commodity market leads to *monopolistic exploitation* of labour. The *monopsonistic exploitation* arises for the reasons similar to monopolistic exploitation. But monopsonistic exploitation is greater than the monopolistic exploitation. A monopsonist pays wages to labour which is less than not only its VMP_L but also less than its MRP_L. This gives rise to the *monopsonistic exploitation. The extent of monopsonistic exploitation of labour may be measured by comparing the wage rate in perfectly competitive commodity and labour markets with the wage rate under monopolistic product market and monopsonistic labour market conditions.* A comparative analysis of the two wage rates is presented in Figure 8.8

When both product and labour markets are perfectly competitive, the VMP_L curve represents the industry or market *demand curve* for labour,[5] and the curve S_L (= AW) represents the market *supply of labour*. Labour demand and supply curves intersect at point P determining the wage rate at OW_3, which equals VMP_L, i.e., $AW = VMP_L$.

Let us now look at wage determination assuming that there is monopoly in the commodity market while labour market remains *perfectly competitive* and market demand curve for labour is given by MRP_L curve in Figure 8.8. The MRP_L intersects the labour supply curves, S_L, at point M, determining wage rate at OW_2. Thus, under monopoly, labour market reaches a new equilibrium point (M) where wage rate is determined at OW_2. Note that monopoly wage rate OW_2 is less than the competitive wage rate OW_3.

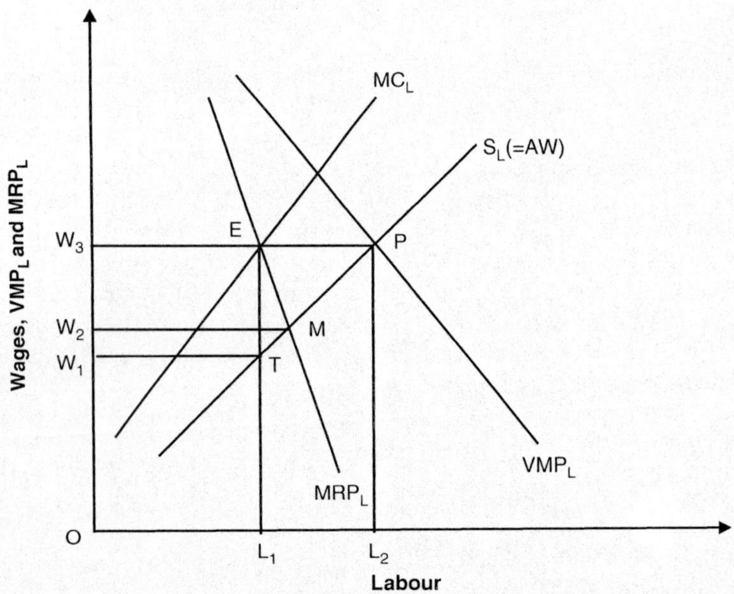

Figure 8.8 *Monopsonistic and Monopolistic Exploitation of Labour*

The difference between OW_3 and OW_2 (i.e., $OW_3 - OW_2 = W_2W_3$) is the *monopolistic exploitation* of labour. Besides, when there is monopoly in the product market, not only the wage rate is lower but also employment of labour decreases from W_3P *to* W_2M. Thus, monopolistic exploitation is accompanied by a lower level of employment and at a lower wage rate.

Finally, let the product monopolist have *monopsony* in the labour market. This is the kind of market setting with which we are concerned mainly in this section. The monopsonist must employ labour until $MRP_L = MC_L$, the marginal cost of labour. As Figure 8.8 shows, MRP_L and MC_L curves intersect at point E which determines the equilibrium level of employment at OL_1. The ordinate EL_1 intersects the labour supply curve S_L at point T, which determines the equilibrium wage rate for the monopsonist at OW_1. Thus, the wage rate under monopsony in labour market goes further below the competitive rate, even below the monopoly level. The difference between the competitive wage rate (OW_3) and the monopsony wage rate (OW_1) measure of the *monopsonistic exploitation* of labour, i.e.,

$$\text{Monopsonistic exploitation} = OW_3 - OW_L = W_1W_3$$

The monopsonistic exploitation of labour to the extent of W_LW_3 may be split into two parts—W_2W_3 and W_LW_2. The exploitation to the extent of W_2W_3 is attributable to monopoly power in the commodity market. This part of factor exploitation is not unique to the monopsonist. But the remaining part, W_LW_2, is unique to the monopsonist. Thus, the main feature of the monopsonistic exploitation is that each factor is paid a price less than even its *MRP*.

PERFECT COMPETITION IN COMMODITY MARKET AND MONOPOLY IN LABOUR MARKET: THE CASE OF LABOUR UNION

In the analysis of wage determination, so far, we have assumed perfect competition in the labour market. In general, however, labour market is not perfectly competitive because of formation of *labour unions* and heterogeneity of labour. In this section, we assume that *labour union* has control over the labour supply to an industry. This makes the labour market monopolistic. Here, we explain wage determination assuming monopoly in the factor market and perfect competition in the commodity market.

The determination of wage rate under the condition of monopoly in the labour market and perfect competition in product market is illustrated in Figure 8.9. The monopoly labour supply curve is shown by curve $S_L = MC_L$. Note that the curve $S_L = MC_L$ in Figure 8.9 represents the marginal cost of labour, not the average cost of labour. The curve $D_L = VMP_L = AR_L$ represents the demand curve for labour by the competitive firms. This curve serves also as firm's average revenue curve for the labour union. Under competitive conditions, the equilibrium wage rate would be determined by point E at OW_1 and equilibrium employment OL_2.

Now suppose that labour market is unionized and labour supply monopolized by the union and also that union bargains for higher wage rate and succeeds raising wage rate to OW_2, the supply of labour at this wage rate is OL_3. Thus, the rise in wage rate creates a perfectly elastic labour supply curve up to W_2K units. Thus, the new labour supply curve is W_2KS_L. With the emergence of the new supply curve, the new equilibrium takes place at point J—the point of intersection between the labour demand curve (D_L) and labour supply curve W_2KS_L. At point J, the equilibrium level of employment is OL_1. As is clear from Figure 8.9, the union has succeeded in raising the wage rate above its competitive level (OW_1) but

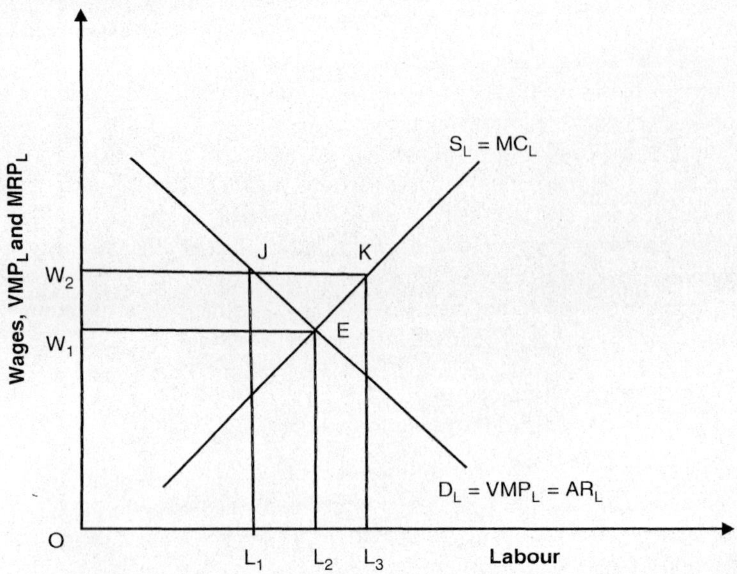

Figure 8.9 *Wage Rate Under Monopoly in Labour Market*

at the same time, it has caused a fall in employment from OL_2 to OL_1. Since union creates excess supply of labour to the extent of $JK = L_1L_3$, and the unemployed labour (JK) would be prepared to work at a wage rate lower than the union wage rate (W_2), there is a possibility of wage cutting. But labour union would not allow the unemployed to accept a lower wage rate. So a higher wage rate at OW_2 would remain stable.

WAGE DETERMINATION UNDER BILATERAL MONOPOLY: THE CASE OF COLLECTIVE BARGAINING

The case of a bilateral monopoly[6] is said to exist in the factor market when there is a single buyer (the product monopolist being the monopsonist) and a single seller of a factor (the labour union). This section analyses the determination of wage rate and employment in a simplified model. The model assumes that *labour is supplied by monopolist (the labour union) and is demanded by a monopsonist* (the product monopolist). It is also assumed that all buyers of a factor (labour) buy it from an employers' union which acts as a monopolist in the labour market. On the supply side, labour is organized in a labour union which acts as a monopolist. This kind of market situation is generally analysed under *collective bargaining.*

Equilibrium under Bilateral Monopoly is Indeterminate

Let it be noted at the outset that economic theory does not predict a precise outcome of collective bargaining. The outcome of collective bargaining is not certain. *The solution to bilateral monopoly situation is, in fact, indeterminate.* The economic analysis of bilateral monopoly (or collective bargaining) does, however, bring out the upper and lower limits within which wage rate can be determined through the process of collective bargaining. The determination of wage rate depends ultimately on a number of factors, e.g., bargaining powers and skills, economic and political power of labour unions and employer's association, the effect of government intervention, etc.

We will first show the *indeterminateness* of equilibrium under bilateral monopoly and then analyse the effects of labour unions in respect of *monopsonistic exploitation.*

Indeterminateness of Bilateral Monopoly

The indeterminateness of equilibrium under bilateral monopoly is illustrated in Figure 8.10. The monopsonist's demand curve for labour is given by $D_L = MRP_L$. The monopolist (i.e, the labour union) considers MRP_L curve as its average revenue (AR_U). Given the AR_U curve, the marginal revenue curve of the labour union may be derived as MR_L—like *AR* and *MR* curves are drawn. The labour supply curve from the monopsonist's point of view is given by $S_L = AW_M = MC_U$ and its marginal cost of labour curve is given by MC_L.

Let us consider the situation from monopsonist point of view. The monopsonist firm must employ labour where $MRP_L = MC_L$ in order to maximize its profit. Thus, given the MC_L and MRP_L curves, the monopsonist firm finds its equilibrium at point *E*, where it would employ OL_U units of labour and pay wages OW_M as determined by the labour supply curve, S_L.

On the Other hand, the labour union[7] maximizes its gains (earning per unit of time) where its marginal cost (MC_U) equals its marginal revenue (MR_L). The MC_U curve, from labour union's point of view, is the same are S_L curve. The MR_L and S_L curves intersect at point E_U. Thus, labour union's equilibrium condition is fulfilled at point E_U. At this point, employment is OL_M. Given the labour demand curve D_L, the labour union would press for wage rate OW_U.

This analysis shows that there are two possible wage rates—OW_M offered by the monopsonist and OW_U demanded by the labour union. These are the two lower and upper limits of possible wage

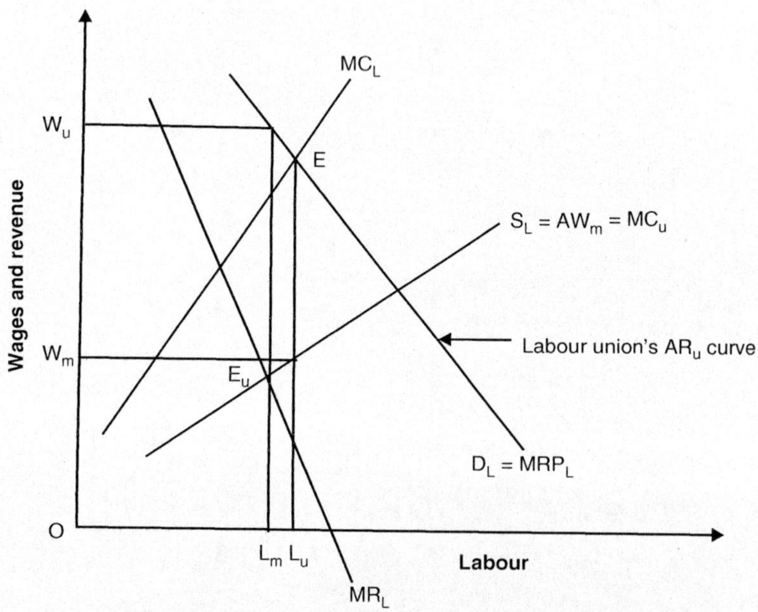

Figure 8.10 *Indeterminate Bilateral Monopoly*

rates, respectively. There is no compromise point between these two wage rates. Therefore, if monopsonist can force the monopolist (the labour union) to behave like a competitive seller, the wage rate will be fixed at OW_M. And, if labour union, the monopolist, can force the monopsonist to behave like a competitive buyer, the wage rate will be OW_U. Whether monopsonist firm succeeds in keeping the wage rate at OW_M or labour union is strong enough to force the wage rate to go up to OW_U is *uncertain*. Under bilateral monopoly, therefore, determination of wage rate remains *indeterminate*.

Economic analysis does not offer a determinate solution to wage rate determination under bilateral monopoly.[8] Whether a compromise wage rate is settled is a matter of bargaining power of the two parties. Bargaining power of labour unions depends on their financial ability to sustain strikes, weaknesses of employers, labour laws, quality of leadership and political patronage, and bargaining power of the employers depends on their ability to sustain losses, their hold on the government and their approach towards and ability to buy the union leaders. This aspect of analysis goes beyond the scope of this book.

Labour Union and Monopsonistic Exploitation

As noted above, labour union may succeed in raising the wage rate to OW_U. But labour union can do so at the cost of employment. As shown in Figure 8.10, if labour union succeeds in pushing the wage rate up from OW_M to OW_U, employment of labour decreases from OL_U to OL_M. It means loss of job to the extent of $L_M L_U$. So, when there is gain in terms of increased earnings per time unit for union members, other workers pay for it in terms of loss of their jobs. This, however, should not mean that labour unions cannot benefit their unemployed fellowmen. If labour unions act rationally, they can eliminate *monopsonistic exploitation* in the monopsonistic or oligopsonistic labour market and can increase both wage rate and employment. Let us now explain these effects of labour unions in some detail.

In Figure 8.11, $D_L = MRP_L$ curve represents the demand curve for labour, $S_L = AW$ is the labour supply curve and MC_L curve represents the marginal cost of labour. To begin the analysis, let us assume

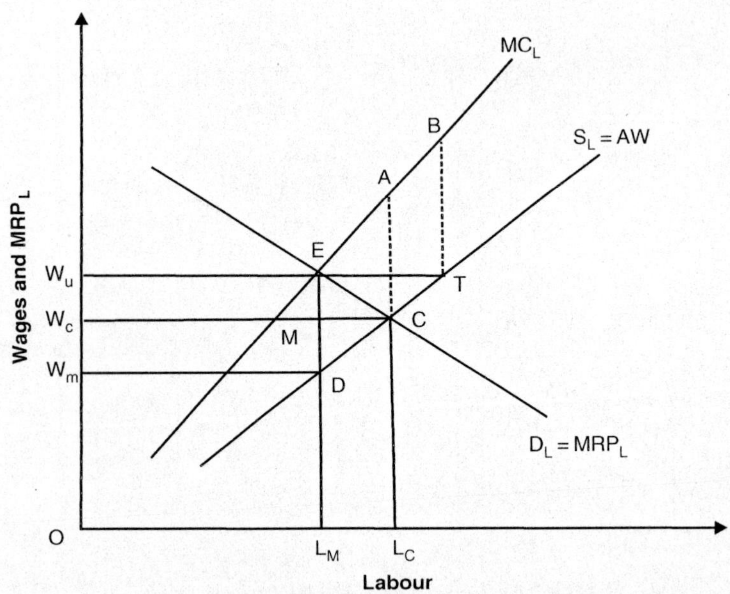

Figure 8.11 *The Effects of Labour Union in Monopsonistic Labour Market*

that initially labour market is not unionized, i.e., there is no labour union. Thus, we have a case in which labour is supplied competitively and demanded monopsonistically. In that case, equilibrium will take place at a point where $MRP_L = MC_L$. The equilibrium is thus attained at point E in Figure 8.11. The equilibrium wage rate is OW_U and equilibrium employment is OL_M where wage offered by the monopolist is OW_M.

Let us assume now that labour market is unionized. What labour union will do depends on what it wants to achieve—maximum employment or maximum wage rate and labour income.

Let us suppose first that the labour union attempts to maximize employment for its members. The maximum level of employment is given by the competitive equilibrium at point C where employment is OL_C. Therefore, if union attempts to maximize the total employment, it must negotiate for wage rate OW_C. This makes the labour supply curve as $W_C CS_L$, and the corresponding. MC_L curve as $W_C CA$. By negotiating for wage rate OW_C, the union succeeds in raising wage rate from OW_M to OW_C and employment from OL_M to OL_C. As a corollary, the total wage bill also increases.

What is more important to note is that at equilibrium point C, each worker is paid wages equal to his $MRP_L = OW_C$. Recall from Figure 8.8 that monopsonistic exploitation would otherwise equal $W_M W_C$. Since wage rate OW_C covers $W_M W_C$, the union succeeds in eliminating a part of monopsonistic exploitation to the extent of $W_M W_C$. However, it cannot eliminate monopolistic exploitation which equals $OW_U - OW_C = W_C W_U$.

Let us now suppose that the labour union chooses to maximize wage bill at the initial level of employment OL_M. It will then force for wage rate OW_U. Then the labour supply curve will be $W_U TS_L$, and the corresponding marginal cost curve (MW) will be $W_U \cdot TB$. The MRP_L equals MC_L at point E, and hence equilibrium level of employment remains at its initial level, OL_M. But wage rate goes up to OW_U which is the maximum attainable wage rate without reducing the employment below the pre-union level.

We have discussed two extreme cases of choice between maximum employment and maximum wage rate. The union may act to achieve an intermediate objective, i.e., some increase in both wage rate and employment. The range of intermediate objective lies between points D and C on the S_L curve. Thus, labour union can eliminate only a part of total exploitation that can be uniquely attributed to the monopsony power in the factor market. The union can in no way eliminate the exploitation attributed to monopoly power in the commodity market.

APPLICATION OF THE WAGE DETERMINATION THEORY

In the preceding sections, we have discussed the theory of wage determination in different kinds of market settings in product and labour markets. In this section, we will discuss the application[9] of the theory of wage determination to examine the wage and employment effects of the *minimum wage law* implemented in most countries. The minimum wage law fixes the minimum wage that must be paid to labour by the employer.

The basic purpose of the minimum wage law[10] is to protect the interest of labour when

1. Market determined wage rate is found to be much less than what is required to meet the basic needs of labour including medical care and basic education;
2. Market conditions open the possibility of exploitation of unorganized, unskilled and unemployed labour and
3. Government adopts a policy to improve economic condition of labour living in abject poverty.

We will examine here the effects of minimum wage law on the wage rate and labour employment under the following market conditions:

1. There is perfect competition in both product and labour markets and
2. There is monopsony and trade union monopoly in the labour market.

Effects of Minimum Wage Laws in Perfectly Competitive Markets

Economists have, in general, found that *minimum wage law increases wage rate but decreases employment.* Also, it prevents the wage rate from falling below a certain level but prevents the possibility of increase in employment. The effects of minimum wage law on wages and employment is illustrated in Figure 8.12. Suppose that labour demand and labour supply curves are represented by D_L and S_L curves, respectively, in the absence of minimum wage law. If product and labour markets were perfectly competitive, wage rate and employment will be determined at point E which is the point of labour market equilibrium. At equilibrium, wage rate is determined at OW_0 and total labour employment at OL_2.

Now, suppose that the wage rate OW_0 is found to be unreasonably low and minimum wage law is enacted which fixes minimum wage rate at OW_M. With the fixation of minimum wage rate at OW_M, demand for labour decreases from OL_2 to OL_1 and supply of labour increases from OL_2 to OL_3. That is, as a consequence of minimum wage fixed at OW_M, labour supply exceeds labour demand by $L_1L_3 = OL_3 - OL_1$. Obviously, minimum wage law causes an *unemployment* equal to L_1L_3. The implementation of minimum wage law causes unemployment on two counts.

1. Unemployment due to decrease in demand for labour by L_1L_2 and
2. Unemployment due to increase in supply of labour by L_2L_3.

$$\text{Total unemployment} = L_1L_2 + L_2L_3 = L_1L_3$$

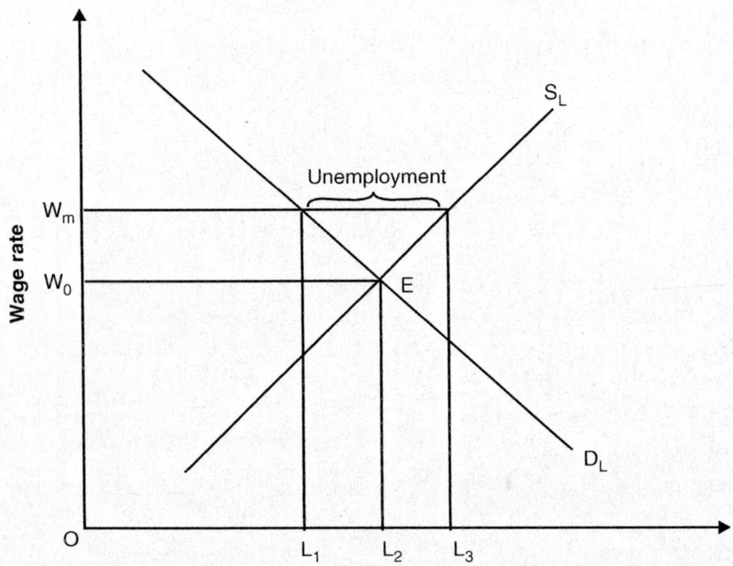

Figure 8.12 *Effects of Minimum Wage Law on Wages and Employment*

Whether major part of unemployment is caused by fall in demand or by increase in labour supply depends on the *wage-elasticities of demand for and supply of labour*. The simple rule is: given the elasticity of labour supply *the greater the wage-elasticity of demand for labour, the greater the share of fall in demand in causing unemployment, and vice versa*. Similarly, *given the elasticity of labour demand, the higher the elasticity of labour supply, the higher the share of increase in labour supply in increasing unemployment, and vice versa*.

The relative importance of elasticities of labour demand and supply in causing unemployment is illustrated in Figure 8.13(a) and (b). Figure 8.13(a) illustrates the case of labour supply being more wage-elastic than labour demand. In this figure, labour supply curve (S_L) is shown to be more elastic (flatter) than labour demand curve (D_L). In free market, wage rate would be determined at OW_0 and employment at OL_2. With the fixation of minimum wage at OW_M, unemployment increases by L_1L_3. Of this total unemployment, L_1L_2 is caused by the decrease in labour demand and L_2L_3 caused by the increase in labour supply. Note that $L_2L_3 > L_1L_2$. Thus, unemployment caused by increase in labour supply, L_2L_3, is much greater than the unemployment (L_1L_2) caused by the decrease in labour demand.

Figure 8.13(b) illustrates the case of demand for labour being more wage-elastic than the supply of labour. In panel (b), labour demand curve (D_L) is shown to be more elastic (flatter) than labour supply curve (S_L). Therefore, unemployment caused by decrease in labour demand, L_1L_2, is much greater than unemployment caused by the increase in labour supply, L_2L_3.

However, what is more *important* from policy point of view is the decrease in demand for labour due to increase in wages as shown in panel (b) of Figure 8.13. It may be added here that decrease in employment caused by a non-economic, legal or a social factor is a serious matter that makes the minimum wage law questionable. Increase in unemployment due to increase in the supply of labour is of secondary importance, from policy point of view.

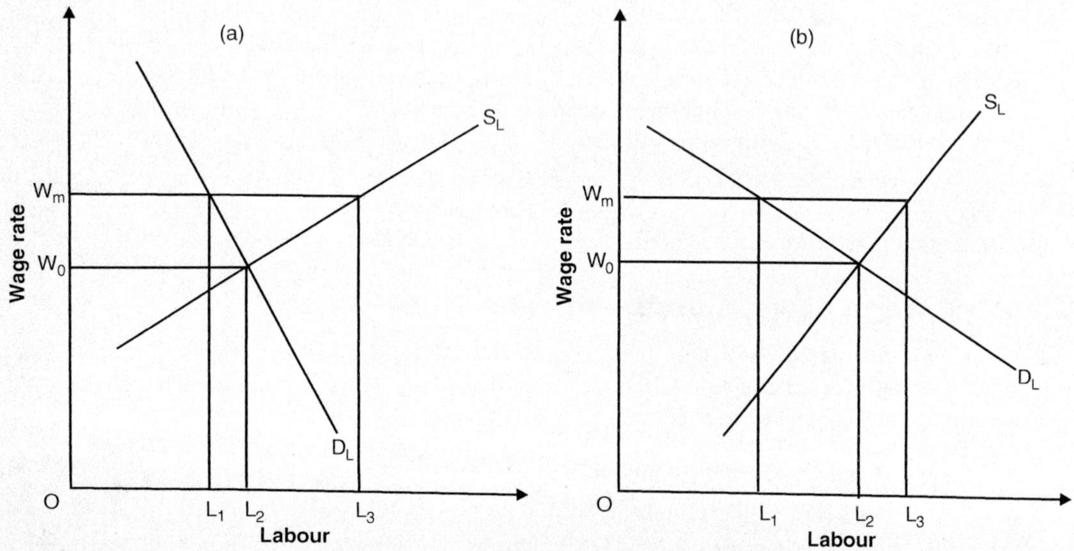

Figure 8.13 *Elasticities of D_L and S_L Curves and Effect of Minimum Wage Law on Unemployment*

Why is Minimum Wage Law Justified?

We have noted above that minimum wage law causes unemployment. Yet, most countries have minimum wage law. The question now arises: What is the justification for enacting and implementing the minimum wage law? The minimum wage law is justified on the following grounds.

- First, the foregoing analysis of employment effect of minimum wage law makes an implicit assumption that the entire labour supply consists of homogeneous, unskilled and unorganized low-paid workers. This gives a somewhat exaggerated view of unemployment caused by the minimum wage law. In reality, labour supply is heterogeneous consisting of unskilled, skilled, highly specialized and educated labour. All other categories of labour—other than unskilled and unorganized labour—are paid wages generally much higher than the minimum wage fixed by the law. Therefore, the negative unemployment effective of the minimum wage law is confined to the category of unskilled labour. Thus, the employment cost of minimum wage law of protecting the interest of the weaker section of labour is not as high as projected above.
- Secondly, the negative employment effect of the minimum wage law is mitigated by the positive employment effect of higher wage earnings. Higher wage incomes lead to higher consumption. Increase in demand for consumer goods, increases demand for labour and also open up new opportunities for employment. There is, therefore, justification of the minimum wage law.
- Thirdly, inflation has become a common feature of most economies in modern times. A significantly high rate of inflation results in erosion of the real income and real wage. Therefore, even if wage rates were fairly higher than what is justified under the minimum wage law, inflation causes a decrease in the real wage rate. The existence of minimum wage law provides an opportunity and need for upward revision of the wage rate.
- Fourthly, one major objective of the minimum wage law is to promote social equity through a more equitable distribution of income. Whether this objective is achieved in a highly corrupt society, like we have in India, is a different matter. It is sometimes argued that minimum wage law is not implemented effectively and, therefore, this law is infructuous. This, however, does not reduce the justification for the minimum wage law.
- Finally, in a country where there is large supply of labour and a monopolistic setting in the product market, there is massive exploitation of labour. This leads to poverty, on the one hand, and unequal distribution of national income, on the other. This is socially undesirable.

Minimum Wage Laws, Monopsony and Trade Unions

We have noted in the preceding section that, in perfectly competitive product and labour markets, the minimum wage law increases wages but decreases employment. In case of monopsony in labour market, however, minimum wage can be so fixed that:

1. It increases wage rate without affecting the employment or
2. It increases both wages and employment.

These cases are illustrated in Figure 8.14. This figure is almost a reproduction of Figure 8.7 which shows wage determination and labour exploitation under monopsony in labour market. Recalling the analysis in Section 8.3.2, a monopsonist will be in equilibrium at point *A* in Figure 8.14, where its

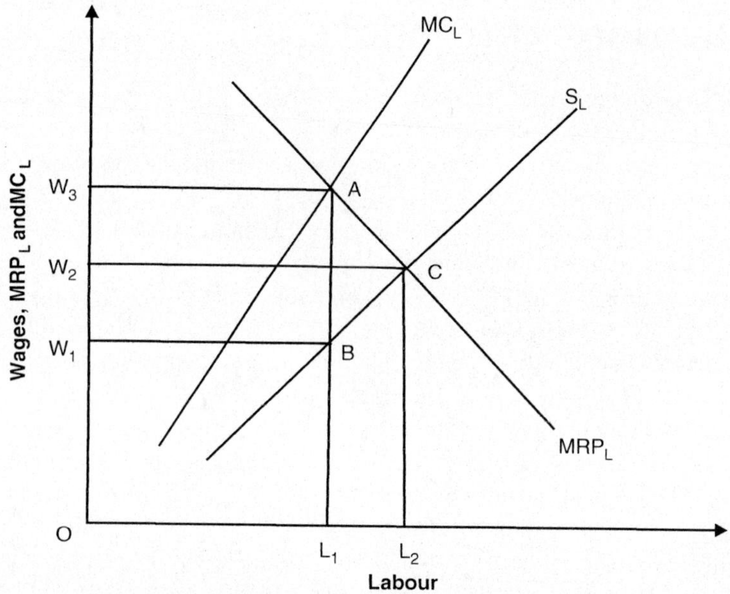

Figure 8.14 *Minimum Wage Law in Monopsony and Employment*

profit-maximizing labour employment is OL_1. Given the labour supply curve, S_L, the monopsonist pays wage rate OW_L as indicated by point *B*. The extent of labour exploitation by the monopsonist equals *AB* or W_LW_3. In the absence of minimum wage law, maximum employment will be OL_1, wage rate OW_1 and there will be exploitation of labour to the extent of W_1W_3.

Now, let us introduce minimum wage law and examine its effect on wages and employment. If minimum wage law is enforced to eliminate total exploitation without affecting employment the minimum wage rate will be fixed at OW_3. Note that wage rate, OW_3, eliminates exploitation leaving the total employment unaffected at OL_1. Alternatively, minimum wage law can be used to eliminate exploitation and also to increase employment. The appropriate equilibrium point for this purpose is given by point *C*, the point of intersection between the MRP_L curve and labour supply curve S_L. The equilibrium point, *C*, determines wage rate OW_2 and employment at OL_2. Under the given conditions, this is the maximum possible employment that can be achieved by applying the minimum wage law.

Conclusion The minimum wage law is universal. Most developed and less developed countries have enacted and implemented the minimum wage law with the basic purpose of preventing exploitation of labour by the business firms. The economists have, however, pointed out the adverse effect of the minimum wage law on the society as it leads to unemployment. Nevertheless, the minimum wage law may be formulated in the manner that minimize the scope of unemployment and at the same time prevent the exploitation of labour—the weaker section of the society. This point of view has been illustrated in Figure 8.14.

This takes us to the end of our discussion on the theory of wage and employment determination under different kinds of market settings. In the next chapter, we will discuss the theory land rent.

REVIEW QUESTIONS AND PROBLEMS

1. How is the theory of wage determination in imperfectly competitive product and labour markets different from that in perfectly competitive product and labour markets?
2. Explain the theory of wage and employment determination under the condition that a monopolist in product market is monopsonist in a perfectly competitive labour market.
3. What is meant by exploitation of labour? Under what kind of market conditions, labour is exploited? What gives the measure of labour exploitation?
4. How is wage rate determined if there is perfect competition in the product market and monopoly in the labour market? Is the labour employment under these conditions less than the employment under perfectly competitive market? Illustrate your answer graphically.
5. Why is wage rate and employment indeterminate when a firm is a monopsonist in the labour market and there is monopoly in the labour market?
6. Is it possible for a labour union to raise wages without reducing employment under the condition of perfect competition in the labour market and monopsony in the product market?
7. Suppose that labourers face a monopsonistic buyer of labour and that labour is the only variable factor for this monopsonist. The MRP_L and labour supply curve are given by the following equations:

$$MRP_L = 70 - 5Q_L$$
$$P_L = 10 + 5Q_L$$

   (where P_L = price of labour and Q_L = quantity of labour)

   (i) Determine the wage rate and the level of employment when the monopsonist maximizes total profit.
   (ii) What is the wage rate if the labourers form a union and maximize the level of employment for its members?
8. The minimum wage law reduces the level of employment. Do you agree with the statement? Give reasons for your answer.
9. If minimum wage law causes unemployment why do most countries enact this law? How does this law protect the interest of labour?
10. Illustrate graphically that minimum wage law causes unemployment. Does this theoretical conclusion hold under all the conditions of the labour market?
11. Suppose there is monopsony in the labour market, explain and illustrate graphically that minimum wage law can be used to eliminate exploitation of labour and also to increase labour employment.
12. Explain the effect of fixation of minimum wage on employment in a monopsonistic labour market. How can the unemployment effect of minimum wage be minimized?

ENDNOTES

1. The analysis carried out with respect to a monopoly firm applies also to firms under monopolistic competition and oligopoly.

2. Joan Robinson (1993), *The Economics of Imperfect Competition* (London: Macmillan), pp. 281–291.
3. Marginal cost of labour (MC_L) means, what Koutsoyiannis calls, marginal expense on labour (ME).
4. For divergence between AW and MW, see Table 8.2 and Figure 8.6.
5. The VMP_1 curve is not the horizontal sum of individual labour demand curves, but it does represent the VMP_L of the industry.
6. The term 'bilateral monopoly' means, in fact, a market situation in which there is a single seller and a single buyer of a product.
7. The behaviour of labour union in Figure 8.10 can be understood better if one looks at labour unions behaving as a commodity seller.
8. Koutsoyiannis. A, *op. cit., p.* 465.
9. The theory of wages can be applied to a wide range of wages and unemployment problems. However, given the study needs of the graduate students, we will confine to application of wage theory to wage and employment problems under perfectly competitive and monopsonistic labour markets.
10. The 'minimum wage act' was enacted in India in 1948, and has been modified from time to time.

FURTHER READINGS

Carter, A.M. (1959), *Theory of Wages and Employment* (Homewood, IL: Richard D. Irwin).

Carter, A.M. and Marshall, F.R. (1972), *Labour Economics, Employment and Trade Unionism* (Homewood, IL: Richard D. Irwin).

Clark, J.B. (1905), *The Distribution of Wealth* (New York: Macmillan).

Douglas, P.H. (1934), *The Theory of Wages* (New York: Macmillan).

Dunlop, J.T. (1944), *Wage Determination under Trade Union* (New York: Macmillan).

Hicks, J.R. (1932), *The Theory of Wages* (New York: Macmillan).

Kaldor, N. (1955–1956), 'Alternative Theories of Distribution', *Review Economic Studies*, XXIII (2): 83–100.

Koutsoyiannis, A. (1978), *Modern Microeconomics* (New York: Macmillan), 2nd Edn., Chapter 12.

Lipsey, R.G. and Chrystal, K.A. (1999), *Principles of Economics* (Oxford: Oxford University Press) Chapter 14.

Perlman, R. (1969), *Labour Theory* (London: Wiley).

Roninson, J. (1933), *The Economics of Imperfect Competition* (New York: Macmillan), Chapter 25.

Chapter 9

Theory of Rent

CHAPTER OBJECTIVES

Although the *marginal productivity theory of* factor pricing applies to rent, this chapter discusses a prominent classical theory of rent, popularly known as the *Ricardian theory of rent*. By going through this chapter, you will learn the following aspects of the rent theory:

- The historical background in which Ricardo had formulated his theory of rent;
- The basics of the Ricardian theory of rent;
- Marshall's contribution to the theory of rent;
- The application of modern concepts 'opportunity cost' and 'economic rent' to the theory of rent; and
- The purpose and effects of controlling rent by law.

INTRODUCTION

Rent is the payment made for the use of land and other kinds of rentable assets. The basic theory of factor pricing, i.e., the *marginal productivity theory* applies to land rent also. However, much prior to the formulation of modern theory of factor pricing, many classical economists have used different concepts and have formulated different theories for different factor prices. So is the case with the theory of rent. Ricardo had formulated a theory of rent, which is widely known as the *classical theory of rent*. After Racardo, Marshall made some significant contributions to the concept of rent, e.g., the concept of *quasi-rent* and *economic rent*. Modern economists have made some important contributions to the concept and applicability of the rent theory. The basic conceptual difference between the Ricardian and the modern theories of rent is that Ricardo considered rent as a '*surplus produce of land*', modern economists interpret rent as '*economic surplus*', the concept which applies to other factors of production with fixed supply in the short run also. This chapter deals with different aspects of the rent theory in detail. Let us begin by looking at how economists interpret land as a factor of production.

LAND AS A FACTOR OF PRODUCTION

The classical economists treated land as a 'free gift of nature'. Land was treated as a special factor of production distinct from man-made means of production including capital, technology and desert reproducible human labour. Land as a means of production has been used in three different senses: (a) the dry and desert area of land within the territory of a country; (b) the area of fertile land available for cultivation and (c) natural resources underground and on the surface of land.

When the term 'land' is used in sense (a), the supply of land is traditionally assumed to be absolutely *inelastic*. Ricardo considered land as a non-reproducible means of production. But, his view applies to land only in its physical sense and not in economic sense. In economic sense of the term, 'land' is defined as 'cultivable fertile area' and as a 'basket of natural resources', which can be exhausted and replenished to some extent. Land is thus not much different from man-made resources and its supply is subject to variable[1] Maintaining the supply of land, defined as fertile cultivable area, requires a considerable amount of effort and cost on the improvement of land, maintenance of the fertility of soil (e.g., cost of manuring and soil conservation) and creation of irrigation facilities and so on. Otherwise, the supply of cultivable land will decrease. The supply of cultivable land can be increased by means of land reclamation, soil conservation, fertilization and expansion of irrigation facilities.

On the other hand, supply of cultivable land tends to decrease when cost of soil conservation and so on. goes up and *vice versa*. Similarly, if land is defined to include all the natural resources underground and on the surface of land, the exploitation of resources and converting them into usable intermediate goods, requires a heavy cost. Since the magnitude of natural resources, available in or on the land of a country's territory is limited, their supply can be increased by increasing cost of exploiting natural resources. For example, water resources, forest resources, minerals, petroleum and natural gas and so on, are available in a limited supply, scattered over the territory of a country. Besides, exploitation of natural resources is subject to diminishing returns, i.e., their supply can be increased but at an increasing cost. Thus, the supply of land, in the economic sense, is not perfectly inelastic. Land supply is, however, less elastic than the supply of man-made means of production.

HISTORICAL BACKGROUND OF RENT THEORY

The classical theory of rent, as formulated by David Ricardo, has an interesting antecedent. In the early 19th century, food prices in Britain had increased heavily partly due to Napoleanic War and partly due to increase in population and the consequent increase in demand for food. The rise in food prices caused a great deal of anxiety to the British government. Therefore, both the House of Lords and the House of Commons appointed a committee to investigate the causes of rise in food prices. The committee reported that '*food prices were high because rents were high*'. The contemporary economists, namely, West, Torrens, Malthus and Ricardo disagreed to this suggestion. They offered, separately, alternative explanations to the problem. In their opinion, *food prices were high not because rents were high, instead rents were high because food prices were high.*[2] According to them, food prices had gone up due to Napoleanic War and increase in population causing increase in demand for food. Scarcity of food led to increase in food prices which, in turn, increased profitability of cultivation. This resulted in increase in demand for cultivable land, which caused rise in rents. Ricardo added that the landed aristocracy (the landlords) was thriving on the misfortune of the rest of the society and causing misery to the tenant farmers. For defending his view, Ricardo was criticized as being anti-landed aristocracy. Ricardo expounded a theory of rent in his efforts to establish his argument. The Ricardian theory of rent is discussed below.

THE RICARDIAN THEORY OF RENT

Ricardian Definition of Rent

Ricardo had defined rent as 'that portion of the produce of the earth which is paid to the landlord for the use of the *original* and indestructible powers of the soil'.[3] Ricardo considered payment of rent as an indication of *niggardliness* of nature. This was contrary to the opinion of French economists, known as 'Physiocrats' who considered rent as the result of *bounty* of nature. By niggardliness of nature, Ricardo meant 'fixed supply' of land with different levels of productivity. Given the fixed supply of land, it proves to be scarce with the growth of population. Growth of population forces extension of cultivation to inferior lands. According to Ricardo, the need for the payment of rent arises due to differences in surplus accruing to the cultivators of different grades of land. The reason for the difference in surplus product is the difference in the fertility of soil of different grades of land.

The Ricardian Theory of Rent

Ricardian theory of rent is based on the principle of demand and supply of land. If supply of land in a country exceeds the total demand for land, no rent will be paid, like nothing is paid for the use of air. In Ricardo's words, 'If all lands had the same properties, if it were unlimited in quantity, and uniform in quality, no charge could be made for its use, unless where it possessed peculiar advantages of situation.'[4] Rent is chargeable '...because land is not unlimited in quantity and uniform in quality and because [due to increase in population], land of an inferior quality, or less advantageously situated, is called into cultivation...'.[5] Ricardo has observed that, with increase in demand for food, land may be used extensively and intensively and that *rent arises in both extensive and intensive cultivation of land.*

Extensive cultivation means extending cultivation to inferior grades of land with the same amount of capital and labour applied to all grades of land. When cultivation is extended from superior to inferior lands, then superior land bears a rent. The rent on superior land equals the difference between the produce of the superior land and that of the most inferior land. Suppose there are three grades of land—*A*, *B* and *C*—suitable for wheat cultivation but land *A* is of the best quality and land *C* of the worst quality. If an equal amount of capital and labour is used to cultivate an equal area of each grade of land, then the respective yields are 100, 80 and 70 quintals of wheat. If, in a country, the supply of *A*-grade land is greater than what must be cultivated to meet the food requirement of the entire population, no rent is payable on the land of *A* grade. When population increases, demand for food increases and, therefore, demand for land increases. And, if cultivation has to be extended beyond grade-*A* land, then the land of grade *B* will be brought under cultivation. But, compared to yield from land *A* (i.e., 100 quintals), land *B* yields only 80 quintals of wheat, with the same quantities of capital and labour. According to the Ricardian theory of rent, the difference in the yields from lands of category *A* and *B* gives rise to rent on land of grade *A*. The rent on land *A* equals 100 – 80 = 20 quintals of wheat. Similarly, when population increases further, land of grade *C* is also brought under cultivation. The *C*-grade land yields only 70 quintals of wheat. This gives rise to a rent on land *B* and raises rent on land *A*. The rent on the three grades of land can be computed as follows:

$$\text{Rent on land } A = 100 - 70 = 30 \text{ quintals of wheat}$$

$$\text{Rent on land } B = 80 - 70 = 10 \text{ quintals of wheat}$$

$$\text{Rent on land } C = 70 - 70 = 0 \text{ quintals of wheat}$$

If the value of capital and labour used in cultivation equals the value of 70 quintals of wheat, the land of grade C will not bear any rent. Land C is, therefore, called '*marginal land*' or '*no-rent land*'. According to Ricardo, the land of grade C will remain a no-rent land until cultivation is extended to land of grade D, if any.

In case of *intensive cultivation*, as Ricardo observed, it is often found that before land B is brought under cultivation, additional capital is employed to increase productivity of land A. But, it is quite likely that when capital expenditure on land A is doubled, output is not doubled. It may yield only 95 quintals (instead of 100 quintals) of wheat. Note that the yield from A-grade land is still greater than the yield expected from land B. The cultivators would, therefore, intensify cultivation of land A, instead of employing their capital on land B or any inferior land. In this case, the rent on land A would be 5 quintals (= 100 – 95 quintals) of wheat. Thus, in case of intensive cultivation, additional capital will be employed on land A till the yields from subsequent units of capital used on land A are greater than that of land B without using extra capital and labour. As more and more units of capital and labour are employed on land A, the yield from the successive units of capital and labour decreases. When yield from additional units of capital equals the yield from land B (without extra capital), then the cultivators may continue to cultivate land A or move on to land B, depending on their choice on non-economic considerations. This has two repercussions: (1) rent on land A increases and (2) the inferior land, i.e., land B, is brought under cultivation. It shows that Ricardian concept of rent is based on the *law of diminishing returns*. This is, in brief, the Ricardian theory of rent determination.

Criticism

Ricardian theory of rent has been criticized on the following grounds.

First, Ricardo's concept of rent is based on the assumption that powers of soil are 'original and indestructible'. This view can hardly be accepted. 'Powers of soil', i.e., productivity of land, can be created through techniques of soil conservation and land reclamation, and can be destroyed through continuous and intensive use of land, soil erosion, spread of desert, flood and so on. Destruction of 'power of soil' by flood and spread of desert is widely known.

Secondly, Ricardo's idea that rent is peculiar to land as a factor of production has been questioned by the modern economists. The differential surplus as rent accrues also to other factors—labour, capital and entrepreneurship—as well as to land.

Thirdly, Ricardo assumed only one use of land, i.e., growing corn, and hence, there is no transfer earning. So, all that is paid in the name of rent becomes *economic rent*. There are, however, alternative uses of land. There are, therefore, *transfer earnings*, and the total rent cannot be economic rent.

Finally, Ricardo considered land supply to be fixed because he considered land of the economy as a whole. For an individual cultivator, however, the supply of land has an elasticity greater than zero. This alters the concept of rent as envisaged by Ricardo.

In spite of these points of criticism, the Ricardian theory of rent holds the ground. The reason is that criticism of the theory is not strong enough to refute it altogether. For instance, whatever one says, the productivity of land is original and natural, though it can be increased or decreased. Similarly, one can apply the Ricardian concept of rent to other factors also but it does not challenge the original concept. So is the case with the supply of land. Although land supply can be increased, it is limited to the boundary walls of a nation.

TRANSFER EARNING AND ECONOMIC RENT: THE MODERN APPROACH

The two other important concepts that are used in modern economic analysis of factor prices are the concepts of 'economic rent' and what Marshall called 'transfer earning'. In modern economist's perception, these two concepts constitute the actual factor earning. Thus, the factor price at equilibrium consists of two components:

1. Transfer earning and
2. Economic rent.

The *transfer earning* is also known as *opportunity cost* and 'reservation price'. Suppose a factor has alternative uses and it is put to its best use. It will not be transferred till its earning is equal to the earning expected from the second best use. Thus, transfer earning is defined as the *amount that a factor must earn to remain in its present occupation*. Alternatively, the transfer earning can be defined as the amount that a factor expects to earn if transferred to its *second best use*. For example, if wheat cultivation on an area of land yields Rs 60,000 annually and when used for running a school it yields Rs 80,000 annually, the land will be used for running a school. In that case, the transfer earning of land is Rs 60,000—the earning expected from wheat cultivation.

Consider the case of a labour. Suppose a doctor earns Rs 50,000 per month from his private practice, the alternative available to him is to serve in a hospital as an employee where he expects to earn Rs 30,000 per month. Thus, doctor's *transfer earning* is Rs 30,000 per month. He must earn a minimum of Rs 30,000 per month to remain in his private practice. So long as he earns Rs 30,000 per month from his private practice, he has no incentive to join a hospital as an employee.

Economic rent (*ER*) is the excess of *actual earning* (*AE*) of a factor over its transfer earning (*TE*). Economic rent may thus be defined as $ER = AE - TE$. In our example of land, the use of land for running a school yields an economic rent of Rs 20,000 = Rs 80,000 – Rs 60,000. Similarly, doctor's monthly economic rent is the difference between his actual earning and his opportunity cost, i.e., doctor's economic rent equals Rs 50,000 – 30,000 = Rs 20,000.

Note that the term 'economic rent' has a different meaning compared to the term 'rent' used in common parlance. In its common usage, the term 'rent' means the *actual* payment to the landlord, i.e., contractual rent, much of which is transfer earning. But, when an economist uses the term 'rent', he means 'economic rent', i.e., the difference between the actual earning and the transfer earning.

Elasticity of Factor Supply and Economic Rent

The existence of economic rent depends on the elasticity of factor supply. Economic rent may be zero or equal to transfer earning depending on whether factor supply is *perfectly elastic* or *perfectly inelastic* or it has elasticity between zero and infinity. Let us explain this aspect of economic rent in some detail.

1. ***If Factor Supply is Perfectly Elastic, Economic Rent is Zero.*** A perfectly elastic factor supply (i.e., $e_s = \infty$) means that a factor owner can supply a factor in any quantity at *a given price*. This kind of factor supply has been shown the line *PS* in Figure 9.1. In such a case, *the whole price paid to the factor* equals its *transfer earning*. Therefore, there is no excess payment over the transfer earning. As shown in Figure 9.1, the factor price is determined at $OP = EN$, i.e., the actual earning of the factor. No unit of factor is paid in excess of *OP*. Hence *economic rent is zero.*
2. ***When Factor Supply is Perfectly Inelastic (i.e., $e_s = 0$) Economic Rent Equals Actual Earning.*** When factor supply is fixed and factor has only one use, the factor owners accept whatever market offers. Even if factor owners are not satisfied with what the market offers, they cannot transfer their factors to other uses, since there is none. Therefore, in such cases, *transfer earning* is zero. Thus, the whole factor price is *economic rent*. This case is illustrated in Figure 9.2. The market price is fixed at $OM = EN$, which equals economic rent.

3. ***When Factor Supply Curve is Positively Sloping, Economic Rent Equals Factor Price Less Transfer Earning.*** Consider the factor supply curve, *S*, given in Figure 9.3. It has a positive slope with elasticity greater than zero and less than one. It implies that factor supply increases with increase in factor price. Given the demand curve, *D*, the market factor price is determined at OP_3 where equilibrium supply of factor is *ON*. Note that, given the supply curve, all but one unit of *ON* (i.e., *ON* – 1) of factor are willing to remain in this industry at factor prices lower

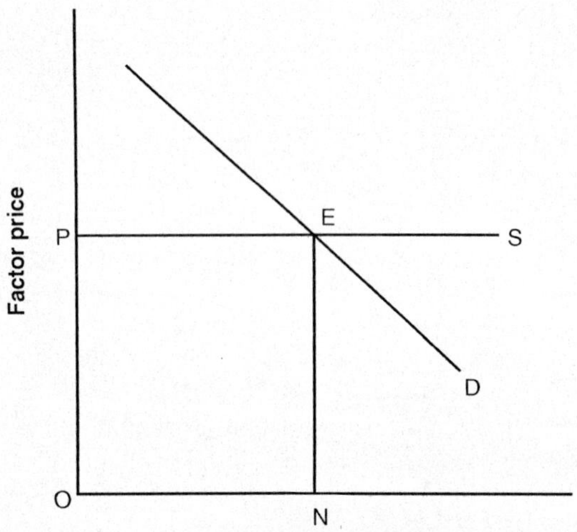

Figure 9.1 *Zero Economic Rent*

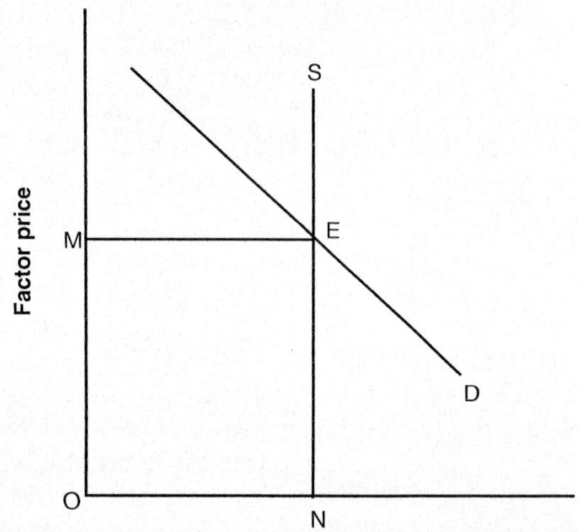

Figure 9.2 *Zero Transfer Earning*

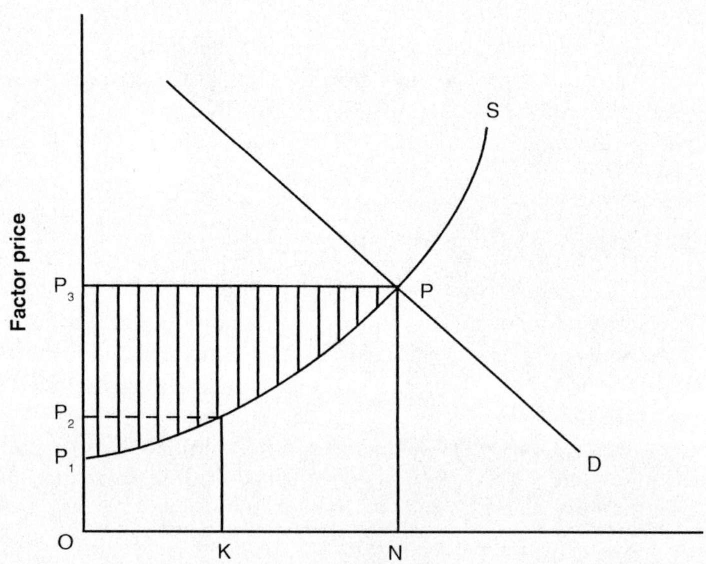

Figure 9.3 *Economic Rent*

than OP_3. That is, minimum payment that must be made to all but the last factor unit, in order to prevent the transfer of factors to alternative uses, is less than the equilibrium price OP_3. In other words, the transfer earning of all factor units, *excepting the last one*, is less than their actual earning. For example, the *transfer earning* of *OK*th unit of factors is only OP_2 whereas the actual earning, i.e., the market factor price, is OP_3. Thus, economic rent earned by the *OK* units is $OP_3 - OP_2 - P_2O_3$. The same exercise may be performed for all the *ON* factor units to compute their economic rent. The shaded area, $P_1P_2P_3$, represents the *total economic rent* of *ON* units. Note that the *ON*th unit, i.e., the last unit of the factor, does not earn economic rent because its actual earning equals its transfer earning. The total transfer earning is shown by area OP_1PN.

QUASI-RENT: THE SHORT-TERM EARNING OF FIXED FACTORS

The concept of *quasi-rent* was introduced by Marshall[6] to analyse the short-term earnings of man-made factors including machinery and other capital equipments. An important feature of capital equipments is that their *supply is inelastic in the short-run* and *elastic in the long run*. The short-term earning of man-made factors may be termed, to begin with, as the *surplus of total revenue after the payment to variable factors*. In Marshall's view, short-run earning of man-made factors cannot be called 'rent' (in usual sense of the term) because, unlike rent, it is subject to fluctuation in the short run. Short-run variation in factor payment depends on the change in the price of the goods they produce. If demand for the product increases in the short run, its price goes up. But more of capital equipments cannot be hired to increase production because their supply in the short run is fixed. Therefore, price of the goods remains high. This increases the total revenue. Consequently, surplus of total revenue over the cost of variable factors increases. As a result, the surplus accruing to man-made factors exceeds their *normal earnings*, i.e., their rentals. Similarly, when demand for the product decreases, its price goes down. As a result, total revenue goes down. Therefore, the surplus over the variable cost goes down, reducing the earning of the man-made factors. It may go below the normal rate of rentals. That is, short-term earnings sometimes exceed the normal rentals and sometimes go much below it. That is why, perhaps, Marshall did not find it appropriate to use the term 'rent' for the short-run earnings of the man-made factors. Marshall coined a new term '*quasi-rent*' for the short-term earnings of the man-made factors in inelastic supply, in the short run.

Graphical Illustration of Quasi-rent

The concept and measurement of quasi-rent are illustrated in Figure 9.4. Suppose a firm hires a machine (a fixed factor) and labour (a variable factor) to produce a commodity, for machine, it pays monthly rentals and labour, its wages. Rentals are fixed which make firm's *AFC* and its wages are variable costs which make its *AVC*. Firm's $AC = AFC + AVC$). If firm's *AC* and *AVC* curves are given, as shown in Figure 9.4, its *AFC* is given by the vertical difference between *AC* and *AVC* curves.

Given the firm's cost curves, let us suppose that price of its commodity in the short run is given at *OA* and the firm faces a horizontal demand curve as shown by the line AD_1. Since price is fixed, firm's $AR = MR = OA$. Given the price, the firm finds its equilibrium at point *B* where its $MR = MC$ and its profit maximizing output is *OM*. At this price and output, the firm is making 'abnormally high profits' which equal $BM - FM = BF$.

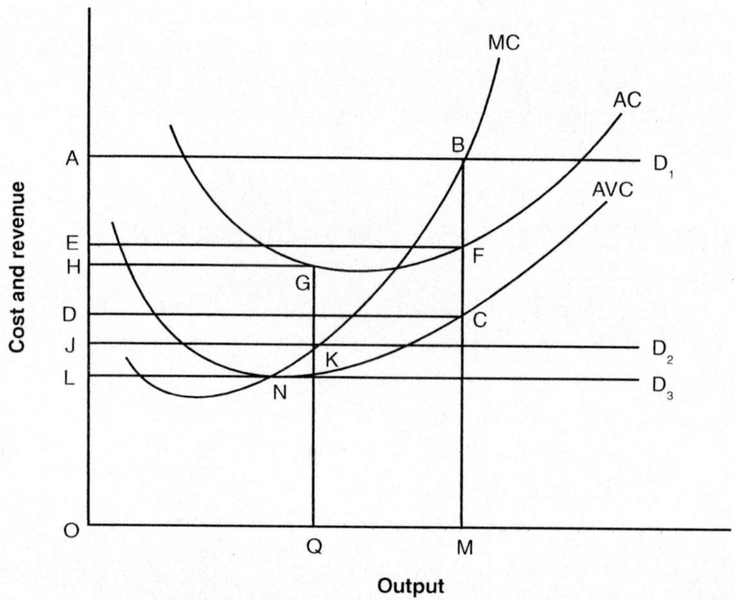

Figure 9.4 *Determination of Quasi-Rent*

Now, firm's quasi-rent, as conceived by Marshall, can be defined as

$$\text{Quasi-rent} = TR - TVC$$

Firm's $TR = OA \times OM = OABM$ and its TVC = total variable cost, i.e., wage bill $= OM \times CM = OMCD$. Now quasi-rent can be obtained as

$$\text{Firm's Quasi-rent} = TR - TVC$$
$$= OABM - OMCD = DABC$$

It can be seen in Figure 9.4 that Marshallian quasi-rent has two components: (i) total rentals which equals total fixed cost (*TFC*) and (ii) a pure profit. Firm's $TFC = EFCD$ and its short-run pure profit = *ABFE*. Thus,

$$\text{Quasi-rent} = \text{fixed cost (rentals)} + \text{pure profit}$$
$$= DABC = EFCD + ABFE$$

The pure profit part of the quasi-rent available to a firm is short-run phenomenon. For, in the long run, supply of capital equipments becomes elastic and more of it can be hired. As a result, product supply increases and its price goes down. When price goes down, demand curve shifts downward. Suppose demand curve AD_1 shifts downward to JD_2, in that case, firm's equilibrium point ($MR = MC$) at point *B* shifts downward to point *K* and quasi-rent, as defined earlier, falls to *JKGH* which is smaller than earlier one, *DABC*. If the price goes further down to *OL* and demand curve shifts down to LD_3, the firm recovers only its *AVC*; the capital equipment earns zero rentals and the firm makes losses to the extent of *TFC*. At this point, it pays the firm to close down. It means that quasi-rent cannot be negative. In the long run, however, supply of product decreases; product price goes up; demand curve shifts upwards and capital equipments begin to earn their normal rentals. Whether quasi-rent will emerge again depends on how demand and price behave.

IS RENT PRICE DETERMINED OR PRICE IS RENT DETERMINED?

A Classical Controversy

Different classical economists held different views on the question *whether rent is price determined or price is rent determined.* In other words, the issue is whether rent enters into the cost of production (see also Section 9.2 of this chapter). Some classical economists held the view that 'food prices were high because rents were high'. It implies that rent does constitute a part of the cost of production. 'John Stuart Mill was first to admit that the rent that land could earn in one use forms a cost that must be paid when it is used for some other purpose'. Following John Stuart Mill, Jevons showed that land has a supply price like any other factor and its price cannot be less than what it can earn in its most remunerative *alternative use*, what is now called *transfer earning*. And, transfer earning does constitute a part of the cost of production.

On the contrary, Ricardo held an opposite view. He said, 'Corn price is high not because rent is high; rent is high because corn is high'. This statement of Ricardo implies that rent is not a part of cost of production. He argued that the price was determined on the basis of cost of production from 'marginal land 'or' no-rent land'. Since no rent is paid on the marginal land, rent does not constitute a part of cost of agricultural produce. Besides, Ricardo considered land as a unique factor, fixed in supply, having no alternative use than cultivation. It has, therefore, no transfer earning. It implies that *rent is price-determined, not price is rent-determined.*

Modern View

The modern view is not categorical in this regard. In the opinion of the modern economists, rent *may or may not be considered as a part of* the cost of production depending on the 'viewpoint' one takes of rent. In this regard, modern economists view 'transfer earning' and 'economic rent' from different angles and answer this question from the viewpoint of an individual firm and from the viewpoint of the society as a whole. The following two points of view represent the modern view.

1. 'The earnings of any input in excess of its transfer price constitute rent; from the viewpoint of the firm hiring the productive agent, rents are part of the cost of production. If the supply of [a factor] is fixed and its services are specific to one use, transfer earnings are zero and the whole of its reward is rent both from the individual and social point of view'.[7]
2. In simple words, economic rent does constitute a part of the cost of production from both individual's and society's point of view. For example, all specialized professionals have zero transfer earning. Consider the case of university professors of highly specialized nature. They have zero transfer earnings for all practical purposes. Therefore, their entire salary is their economic rent and is a part of the university's cost of producing educated manpower.

3. 'From the point of the view of the industry or of society as a whole [economic rents] are price determined', not price determining[8].

The modern view is a very slippery one. If applied to the real-life situations, numerous difficulties are encountered. For example, suppose that a business manager is earning Rs 90,000 a month in a company and, in his own business, he expects to earn only Rs 80,000 a month. His economic rent is Rs 10,000 a month. But his employer, the firm, does not consider only Rs 10,000 as his monthly cost on a manager.

RENT CONTROLS: AN APPLICATION OF RENT THEORY

Controlling rent on land and building, i.e., fixing rent by law, has been a permanent feature of the Indian society[9]. In this section, we will show the *application of rent theory* and examine the consequences of controlling rent by law on urban housing. It may be recalled here that the theory of rent determination is based on the theory of demand for and supply of rentable property. It is the same theory which will be applied here to analyse the effect of rent control.

The theoretical consequences of rent control are illustrated in Figure 9.5. The curves labelled D_H and S_H represent the long-run demand for and supply of housing in a city like Delhi. In the absence of Rent Control Act, house rent (per standard housing unit) will be determined at point *E*, the point of intersection between the demand and supply curves. The market determined house rent is OR_2 and the number of houses/flats demanded and supplied is equal to OH_2 and the house market is in equilibrium.

Suppose market determined rent OR_2 is found to be very high and unaffordable by a large section of the city population. Therefore, the government fixes upper limit of rent at OR_1 which is considerably lower than the market determined house rent OR_2. As Figure 9.5 shows, fixation of maximum rent at OR_r increases demand for housing from OH_2 to OH_3 but causes a decline in the supply of houses from

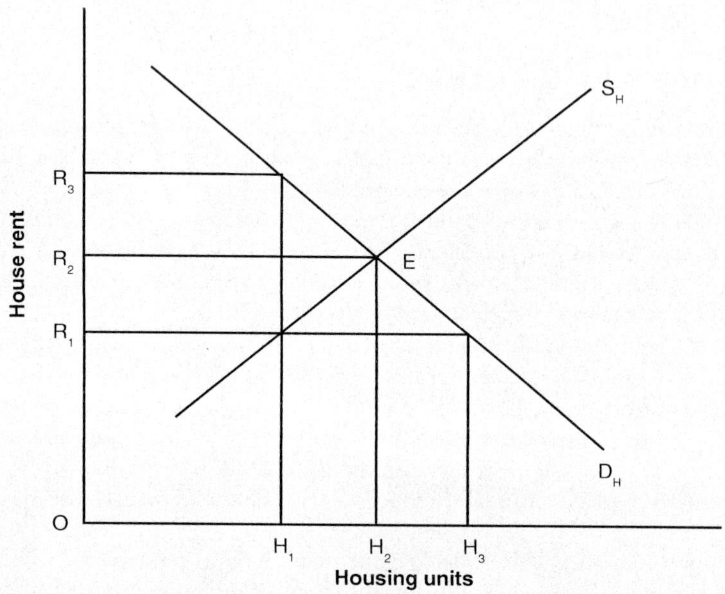

Figure 9.5 *Effects of Rent Controls*

OH_2 to OH_1. The result is *shortage of houses*. This is an obvious consequence of rent control. The supply of houses declines because return on investment in housing declines and landlords shift their investment to more remunerative non-housing investment avenues[10].

Does This Happen in Reality?

We have seen above that rent control causes shortages of houses in a perfectly competitive real estate market. In reality, however, real estate market, like any other market, is not perfectly competitive. Apart from rent control being added as one element of market imperfection, landlords devise a number of ways to circumvent the Rent Control Act especially where tenants are willing to pay higher rents, as shown in Figure 9.5. For example, tenants may be willing to pay OR_3 as rent for OH_1 number of houses.

Some common ways[11] of circumventing the rent law are:

1. Tenant are required to deposit heavy sums, refundable or non-refundable, at the time of making rent agreements—the interest on the refundable, deposit makes up for the loss in the market rent;
2. The responsibility of maintenance—repairs and white washing and so on—is put on the tenants which reduces the loss of market rent and
3. Where ejecting old tenants is not permitted by law, house is left unmaintained and unrepaired over the years so that house becomes dilapidated and uninhabitable as has been the case Mumbai.

For these reasons, rent control is generally not effective in meeting its objectives. Therefore, the shortage of houses as projected above does not take place in reality. For instance, capital city Delhi has its own Rent Control Act. Yet house construction in this city has proliferated over the past three decades at an unprecedented rate because of ever increasing demand for houses, regularization of unauthorized colonies, growth of builders and colonizers, leading to construction boom. There are at least two possible reasons: (i) house is a basic necessity and (ii) investment in real estate is still considered to be the safest with a fair rate of return.

'Who Loses and Who Benefits?'

It is difficult to give a judgement on 'who loses and who gains' from rent control. It is said, at least theoretically, that *landlords* are the losers in the initial stage of the enactment and implementation of the Rent Control Act. But, as has been shown above, house owners do not lose over time: they find ways and means to recover their loss and make a reasonable earning from investment in housing.

As regards the *tenants*, economists are 'skeptical' on the gain to the tenants. Some 'economists believe that tenants, on average, are worse off under rent controls.'[12] The benefits of lower rents are lost due to other changes in the house market, especially low quality of housing.

One big disadvantage of rent control to tenants is that it leads to non-pricing rationing by the landlord to the disadvantage of the tenants. For example, house owners become selective about the tenants, especially in a market where demand for house exceeds its supply. Some house owners prefer tenants with small size of family or families without children and pets, tenants with stable job and high incomes, tenants of some particular profession, area or community.

Another disadvantage of rent control is the reduction in the house tax base. House or property tax is one of the most important source of revenue for the municipal corporations. Rent control lowers both the market value of the property and its ratable value. Whether market value or ratable value is the tax base, both go down due to rent laws that reduce rentals below the market rate. However, lower house tax works as an incentive for construction of houses in a larger number which compensates over time for the loss of revenue.

For these reasons; it is difficult to generalize whether rent control is advantageous to the landlords or to tenants. Generalization becomes more difficult when some classes of tenants benefit and some lose, and among those who benefit, some benefit more and some less.

REVIEW QUESTIONS AND EXERCISES

1. How land as a factor of production is different from other factors? How does this difference matter in the determination of rent?
2. Explain the Ricardian concept of rent and his theory of rent. Can Ricardian theory of rent be applied to the pricing of other factors of production? Give reasons for your answer.
3. Ricardian concept of rent applies to only extensive cultivation, not to intensive cultivation. Do you agree with this statement? Explain your view with example.
4. Examine critically the Ricardian theory of rent. What modifications does modern theory of rent make to this theory of rent?
5. Is rent price determined or price rent determined? Explain in this regard the Ricardo's view.
6. Explain the difference between the modern and Ricardian theories of rent. Can modern productivity theory of factor pricing be applied to rent determination? If yes, how?
7. Explain the concept of quasi-rent and distinguish between rent and quasi-rent. Why is quasi-rent said to be short-run phenomenon?
8. Explain the concept of transfer earning and economic rent. Can economic rent exist in the long run? Explain the conditions under which the whole price paid to a factor is economic rent.
9. What is the role of elasticity of demand for and supply of a factor in determining the economic rent of the factor. Explain and illustrate graphically.
10. How does Rent Control Act affect the supply of and demand for housing? How does it affect the house owners and the tenants?
11. Explain the effects of rent control on the demand for and supply of houses. Who benefits from rent control—landlords or tenants?
12. Which of the following statements is correct and why?
    - (a) Rent enters the cost of production.
    - (b) Rent does not enter the cost of production.
    - (c) Only economic rent enters the cost of production.

ENDNOTES

1. Given the national territory of a country, the land in economic sense can be increased by leveling of land, converting non-cultivable land into convertible land and increasing facilities like irrigational facilities and by converting bushy land into cultivable land.
2. This issue has been discussed in detail ahead in Section 9.6.
3. Ricardo, D. (1951), in P. Sraffa (ed.), *On the Principles of Political Economy* (Cambridge, MA: Cambridge University Press), p. 67.
4. *Ibid.*, p. 70.

5. *Ibid.*
6. Marshall, A. (1949), *Principles of Economics* (New York: Macmillan), 8th Edn., p. 74.
7. Blaug, M. (1983), *Economic Theory in Retrospect* (New Delhi: Vikas Publishing House), 3rd Edn., p. 85.
8. Blaug, M. *op. cit.*, p. 85.
9. Fixing rent on agricultural land by law has been there since Moghal period. Control of house rent was introduced during the British period. In capital city, Delhi, the rent control law was in practice till 2006.
10. Even otherwise when returns on investment in real estate is lower than on investment in stocks or in other avenues, a many landlords dispose of their rented houses/flats and invest in stock and other way round. Untill recently, it has been a common practice in Delhi.
11. In cities like Delhi, *goondas* are hired, along other methods, to evict the old tenants not meeting the demand of the landlords.
12. Browning, E.K. and Browning, J.M. (1986), *Microeconomic Theory and Applications, op. cit.*, 2nd Edn., p. 293.

FURTHER READINGS

Blaug, M. (1983), *Economic Theory in Retrospect* (New Delhi: Vikas Publishing House), 2nd Indian Edn.

Lipsey, R.G. and Chrystal, K.A. (1999), *Principles of Economics* (Oxford: Oxford University Press), 9th Edn., Chapter 14, pp. 232–234.

Marshall, A. (1922), *Principles of Economics* (London: Macmillan), Book IV, Chapter 2 and 3; and Book V, Chapter 9 and 19.

Ricardo, D. (1951), in P. Sraffa (ed.), *On the Principles of Political Economy and Taxation* (Cambridge, MA: Cambridge University Press), Chapter II.

Chapter 10

Theories of Interest and Investment Decisions

CHAPTER OBJECTIVES

In this chapter, we move from the theory of rent to the theories of interest rate determination. The objective of this chapter is to explain:

- What is concept and meaning of capital as a factor of production;
- What is the essence of interest as a cost of capital;
- How early economists conceived the need for payment of interest and their theories of interest and its determination;
- What are the classical and modern theories of interest—how is the market rate of interest determined; and
- How investment decisions are taken given the rate of interest.

INTRODUCTION

The basic activity in the financial market of a country is borrowing and lending of money. The lender charges and the borrower agree to pay an amount in addition to the amount lent and borrowed. This excess amount is called, in common usage, *interest*. In economic terminology, like rent and wages, interest is a factor payment. Interest is paid for the services of capital as a factor of production. In economic sense of the term, interest is the cost of capital per unit of time.

The term 'capital' is used in two senses: (i) money or financial capital, i.e., loanable or investible stock of money and (ii) physical assets, e.g., land, building, plant and machinery and so on. Money capital in the form of bank term deposits, shares and debentures and so on. yield different forms of incomes—interest and dividend. Investment in physical capital yields income called 'return on capital'. Money capital finally takes the form of physical capital and interest paid on money capital takes the form of 'cost of capital'. Based on the two concepts of capital, there are two types of interest theories: (i) monetary theories of interest and (ii) real theories of interest, entwined with the Theory of Capital. A comprehensive treatment of theories of category (ii) falls outside the purview of this book. Our discussion in this chapter is, therefore, confined to the *monetary theories of interest* and the role of interest in *investment decisions*. Since interest is the cost of capital, let us first describe of capital, as a factor of production and its peculiarities.

CAPITAL AS A FACTOR OF PRODUCTION

It may be noted at the outset that the theoretical problems associated with capital and interest are much more complicated than those pertaining to other factors and factor prices. The complications arise for at least three reasons. *First*, unlike land and labour, physical capital is a man-made factor—a produced means of production. The supply of capital is, therefore, under human control. It is produced only when it is needed. Production of each capital asset is a matter of economic decision. Besides, there are various types of capital assets with varying productivity.

Secondly, another peculiarity of capital is that producing capital goods requires investment. Availability of funds for investment depends on savings. Given the income, additional saving requires cutting the present consumption. Cutting present consumption with the purpose of having a higher level of income and consumption in future is the matter of making choice between the present and future consumption. Making choice between the present and future consumption brings in the question of *time preference*.

Thirdly, production of capital is a 'round about process' which is time consuming. For example, to produce tractors requires steel, which requires mining of iron ore. To mine iron requires mining machinery and equipment, and the process goes on. Thus, tractor production takes a long time. Besides, capital goods generally have a long productive life but are subject to wear and tear and obsolescence. This necessitates maintaining capital intact and replacement of obsolete capital. It, therefore, requires a near-accurate prediction of timings of expenditure on capital goods and returns from them. All these considerations are taken into account in the theory of interest and investment decisions.

SOME EARLY THOUGHTS ON INTEREST THEORY

The earliest form of interest theory appeared in the writings of John Locke, William Petty and Stuart Law in the 18th century. These authors considered interest to be a monetary phenomenon and believed that interest varies inversely with supply of money: the larger the availability of money, the lower the interest, and *vice versa*. They argued that when money supply increases, purchasing power of money decreases, demand for money decreases and, hence, interest decreases. David Hume was first to criticize the early theory of interest. Following Hume, Adam Smith also criticized this theory. He argued that interest is merely a ratio of two sums of money—amount of loan and amount of loan repayment—which remains unaffected by the change in money supply.

However, Cantillon, Hume and Turgot criticized the monetary theory of Locke *et al.* more profoundly. They argued that when money supply increases, prices rise and investors are, therefore, required to borrow a larger sum to finance a given project. Hence, interest rises with the rise in money supply. They themselves believed that interest depends on the demand for investment goods. This belief marks the beginning of real theories of interest. However, a logically consistent theory of interest was not formulated until recently. The classical economists, Adam Smith and David Ricardo, could offer no real solution to the problems of interest determination.[1] In fact, they did not provide a consistent theory of profits or pure interest at all.[2] They treated rate of interest simply as the rate of return on capital invested.[3]

Senior was the first to offer a broad outline of modern theory of capital and interest. According to Senior's theory, the rate of interest, i.e. the price of capital, is determined by the forces of demand for and supply of capital goods. Capital goods are demanded because they are productive and can produce goods and services that are in demand. Thus, he suggested the idea that demand for a factor is a derived demand. In his view, the supply of capital goods depends on the consumer's willingness to abstain from consumption and to save a part of resources that could be used to produce capital goods. According to Senior, creation of capital goods required abstinence from consumption and the interest was the 'reward for abstinence'. Senior's theory was later improved by J.S. Mill which came to be known as 'abstinence theory of interest'.

The 'abstinence theory of interest' was, however, found to be an incomplete theory of interest as it considers only supply of saving and does not explicitly relate demand for capital to its productivity.[4] Marx objected to the abstinence theory on the ground that it is mostly the rich who can save and rich make no sacrifice by abstaining from current consumption. According to him, rich are not required to forego their current consumption as they possess surplus income. He argued also that many owners of productive assets might have inherited the assets rather than procured by reducing their consumption.

However, Senior argued that income from inherited property is of the nature of rent, not interest. To avoid such criticism, Marshall substituted a neutral word, 'waiting', for the term 'abstinence'. The term 'waiting' implies that an investor has to wait until he receives the returns from his investment. If the present value of the total expected returns is greater than the cost of investment, it yields a surplus to the investor. This surplus is a reward for 'waiting'. Thus, according to Marshall, interest was treated as a reward for 'waiting'.

Having looked at some early thoughts on the meaning and the source of interest, we turn now to discuss the formal theories of interest rate determination.

THEORIES OF INTEREST

Bohm-Bawerk's Theory of Interest[5]

Bohm-Bawerk, an Austrian economist, propounded a theory of interest in 1884, which is widely known as *Austrian theory of interest*, is one of the most profound early theories of interest. Bohm-Bawerk emphasized that land and labour are 'original' or primary factors of production, while 'capital' is an intermediate factor whose supply depends on land and labour used for its production.[6] This distinction is fundamental to Bohm-Bawerk's theory of interest and is the source of 'origin of interest'.

According to Bohm-Bawerk, *interest is paid in the process of lending present income against the promise of future income*. Interest arises because people prefer present consumption of goods to their future consumption. They are, therefore, willing to pay a premium on present goods for the privilege of spending it when they want to spend. Or, conversely, they discount the future goods, the people would, therefore, be willing to lend a certain quantity of present goods only if they are sure of being repaid with a greater quantity of goods of the same kind and quantity. It is this time preference which forms the basis of interest.

Bohm-Bawerk gave *three reasons* for why people prefer the present consumption to the future. First, *the circumstances and the intensity of and provision for the present wants are higher than the future wants.* If income rises continuously, it becomes subject to the law of diminishing marginal utility. If individuals act so as to maximize the sum of utilities of all future incomes, they would be willing to pay a premium on present goods (when income is rising). The reason for this is that increase in present consumption adds more to the total utility than the increase in the future consumption. That is why people prefer present goods to future goods.

Secondly, *people underestimate future* because of (a) deficiency of imagination, i.e., myopia in respect of future; (b) limited will-power and (c) the shortness and uncertainty of life. These factors lead to discounting of future wants.

Thirdly, *present capital goods are economically superior to future ones*. This is so because 'present goods can be invested now and reinvested as they accrue tomorrow, but available tomorrow can be invested tomorrow' only. Besides, present goods invested today in round-about method of production yield a larger physical output in future than an equal quantity invested in future either in direct or in round-about production. The reason for this is, even if other things remain the same, yields from investment today compound over a longer period per time unit. This is a very strong reason why people prefer present goods to future ones and why they are willing to pay a premium on present goods and discount on future goods. This third reason, according to Bohm-Bawerk, constitutes an independent ground for a positive rate of interest.

Irving Fisher, however, argued that any one reason is not sufficient to make interest rate positive. It is in fact the interaction of the three reasons which is fundamental to the interest being greater than zero. As Mark Blaug remarks, Bohm-Bawerk's three 'reasons' and their interaction provide an exhaustive explanation of the existence of interest in a stationary as well as in a dynamic economy.[7]

According to Bohm-Bawerk's theory, the rate of interest is determined by the demand for and supply of funds. The demand for funds comes solely from the capitalists and supply comes primarily from the retained earning. The total capital consists of subsistence wages paid to the workers, which is fixed. The marginal productivity of this part of capital decreases over time. The rate of interest is determined where present value of expected marginal product equals the wage rate.

Fisher's Theory of Interest[8]: The Time Preference Theory

Fisher's notion of interest is the same as that of Bohm-Bawerk. According to Fisher, interest arises because people prefer present to future income. The rate of interest, according to Fisher's theory, equals the price that people are willing to pay for income now rather than income at some future date. This price (or the rate of interest) is determined by the interaction of 'willingness to give up present consumption in favour of a larger consumption in future, and 'opportunity' to invest.' The opportunity to invest is measured by the rate of return over cost. Here, 'cost' means the loss of income due to withdrawal from an income stream and 'return' means the gain in the forms of returns from a new income stream. Fisher's 'rate of return over cost' is that critical discount rate at which two or more alternative investment opportunities have the same present net values.

Fisher's theory of interest determination is presented in Figure 10.1. Horizontal axis measures *income today* and vertical axis measures *income tomorrow*. The 45° line represents a constant flow of income, i.e., income available today is available tomorrow also. The indifference curves, I_1, I_2 and I_3, represent the people's willingness curve which shows their time preference with respect to income today and income tomorrow. The convexity of indifference curves implies the diminishing marginal utility of present and of future income.

A very important aspect of the indifference curve (i.e., willingness curve) is its slope ($\Delta Y/\Delta X$) at the point where it intersects the constant income streamline, e.g., point M on I_1 as it reflects the people's time preference for income. If slope of the indifference curve at the point of intersection is greater than 1, it reflects a positive time preference; if slope = 1, time preference is neutral; and if slope < 1, time preference is negative. It may be observed in Figure 10.1 that the slope ($\Delta Y/\Delta X$) of $I_1 > 1$, $\Delta Y/\Delta X$ of $I_2 < 1$, and $\Delta Y/\Delta X$ of $I_3 = 1$. Thus, indifference curve I_1 shows positive time preference, i.e., present income is

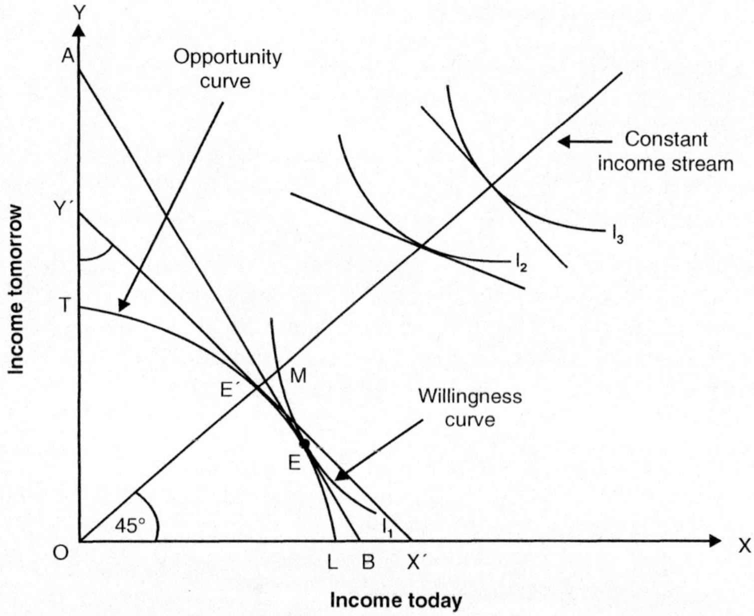

Figure 10.1 *Interest Determination: Fisher's Theory*

preferred to future income. The indifference curve I_2 shows negative time preference, i.e., future income is preferred to present income; and indifference curve I_3 shows equal time preference for present and future income.

The opportunity curve or technical transformation curve is shown by the *TL* curve. It reveals the rates at which present income can be transformed into future income. Thus, it reveals the net productivity of capital. The concavity of the opportunity curve implies diminishing returns to capital, i.e., present income converted into investment. In other words, the concavity of opportunity curve indicates diminishing marginal productivity of capital.

The rate of interest is determined at point *E* where the willingness curve, I_1, and opportunity curve, *TL*, are tangent with one another. At point *E*, the slopes of I_1 and *TL* curves are equal, the slope of willingness curve being positive. The interest rate is therefore positive and equals the slope of the line *AB*. If, at the point of tangency, slope of transformation curve (i.e., the opportunity curve) and that of the indifference curve are equal to unity, the rate of interest will be equal to zero because, at point *E*, net productivity of capital is zero and time preference is neutral.

Criticism

The economists have pointed out several *weaknesses* in Fisher's theory.

First, it places too much emphasis on consumption rather than on output.

Secondly, it ignores the influence of banking system on the rate of interest.

Thirdly, Fisher's theory ignores also the role of expectations.

Schumpeter has, however, commended Fisher's theory as 'the peak achievement' of 'perfection' in interest theory within its framework.

The Classical Theory of Interest

The classical theory of interest refers, according to Keynes, to the theories (or views) of Marshall, Cassel, Tausig and Walras and so on. In fact, *none of these economists, whom Keynes groups at modern classical school, has given a precise or an explicit account of the interest theory.*[9]

Keynes has, however, reconstructed the classical theory of interest himself which is presented here. According to the classical theory, the rate of interest is determined by the *demand for investment* and *willingness to save*. In the words of Keynes,

> Investment represents the demand for investible resources; saving represents the supply, and the rate of interest is the 'price' of investible resources at which the two are equated. Just as the price of a commodity is necessarily fixed at that point where the demand for it is equal to the supply, so the rate of interest necessarily comes to rest under the play of market forces at the point where the amount of investment at the rate of interest is equal to the amount of saving at the rate.[10]

In simple words, rate of interest is determined by demand for investible funds and the supply of investible funds, i.e., supply of savings. The rate of interest is determined where demand for investible funds equals the supply of savings. The classical theory of interest is presented in Figure 10.2. The investment demand schedule is inversely related to interest as shown by I_1 and I_2—the investment demand schedules. In contrast, the supply of savings schedule, *S*, is positively related to interest. The investment demand schedule, I_1, intersects with the supply of savings schedule at point *E*. The rate of interest is thus determined at *OR* by the point of intersection of the two schedules. At this rate of interest, the demand for investible funds, *OQ*, equals the supply of funds. The interest rate *OR* is therefore the equilibrium rate of interest. The equilibrium rate of interest will be disturbed only when there is a change in the demand

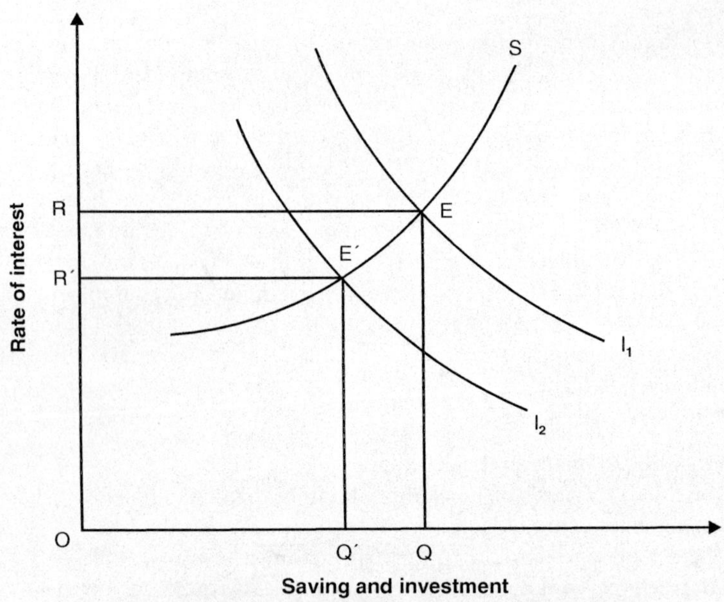

Figure 10.2 *The Classical Theory of Rate of Interest*

for investible funds and in the supply of savings. But, investment and savings will automatically adjust themselves to a new equilibrium rate of interest. For instance, given the saving supply schedule, *S'*, if investment demand schedule shifts downward to I_2, intersecting *S*-schedule at *E'*, a new (lower) rate of interest will be determined at *OR'*.

Keynes' Criticism of Classical Theory

Keynes himself criticized the classical theory of interest on the following grounds.

First, classical theory implicitly assumes *income to be given* and saving to be a unique function of interest, i.e., $S = f(i)$. Keynes, however, argues that the classical assumption of constant *income* implies that there exists an important relationship between saving and income, i.e., $S = f(Y)$ also. Savings are, thus, not the function of interest alone but also of income, i.e., not only $S = f(i)$, but also $S = f(Y)$. But the classical school neglects this important relationship between income and savings, which leads to a theoretical error in the classical theory of interest.

Secondly, in spite of its theoretical error, classical theory of interest concludes that, given the investment and saving schedule, interest will be determined by the investment demand and saving schedules. It implies that interest rate will be determined even if there is a shift in the investment demand schedule. But interest rate is indeterminate. This point is illustrated in Figure 10.3. Suppose that rate of interest was initially determined at Or_3 by intersection of I_1 and S_1 schedules at point E_1. If investment demand schedule shifts leftwards to I_2, due to say, a fall in the marginal efficiency of capital, according to the classical theory, interest rate will be determined at Or_1 by intersection of S_1 and I_2 curves at point E_2. Similarly, if both investment demand and savings schedules shift leftward, interest will be determined at Or_2 by point E_3. As Keynes puts it, 'the classical theory of rate of interest seems to suppose that, if the demand curve for capital shifts or if the curve relating the rate of interest to the amount saved out of a

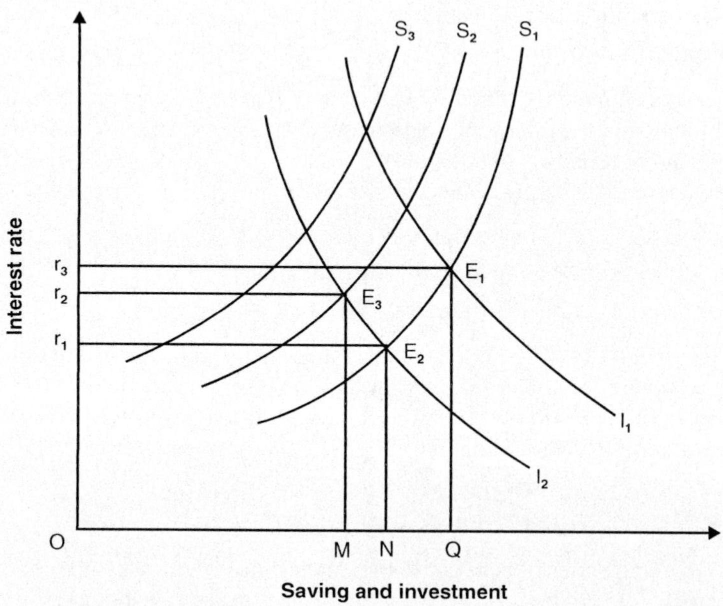

Figure 10.3 *Change in Interest Rate and Levels of Income*

given income shifts or if both these curves shift, the new rate of interest will be given by the point of intersection of the new position of the two curves' (Keynes, p. 179). 'But this,' according to Keynes, 'is nonsense theory.' The error in classical theory lies in its assumption that investment demand schedule (I) can shift without causing a shift in the saving schedule (S). In fact, when investment schedule shifts, it means a change in investment. Change in investment causes a change in income (Y) because $Y = f(I)$. When income changes, savings change too because $S = f(Y)$. For instance, if investment schedule I_1 shifts downward to I_2 (S_1 remaining the same), investment falls by QN. Since $Y = f(I)$, incomes will fall due to fall in investment. Since $S = f(Y)$, savings will also fall due to fall in income and saving schedule S_1 shifts backward to S_2. As a result, interest rises from Or_1 to Or_2 and investment falls further by NM (Figure 10.3). This fall in investment will again generate a chain of adjustments.

It is, therefore, inconsistent to assume that investment demand and saving schedules can shift independent of each other. A shift in investment demand schedule does cause a shift in saving schedule. If investment demand and saving schedules keep shifting from one position to another, the whole classical scheme of interest determination breaks down. Interest rate cannot find its equilibrium. Thus, according to Keynes *classical theory of interest is indeterminate.*

The Loanable Fund Theory of Interest

A variant of classical theory is the loanable fund theory of interest, also called the *neo-classical theory of interest.* The economists who have contributed to the growth of this theory include Wicksell, Ohlin, Robertson, Pigou and Viner. According to the loanable fund theory, rate of interest is determined by the intersection of demand and supply schedules of *loanable funds.*

According to the loanable fund theory of interest, the *demand for loanable funds* consists of:

1. investors' demand for funds (I_D);
2. consumers' demand for funds (C_D); and
3. demand for funds for hoarding (H_D).

All the three kinds of demand for funds are inversely related to the interest as shown in Figure 10.4. The horizontal summation of the three kinds of demand curves gives the aggregate demand for loanable funds (D_L) as shown by the schedule D_L in Figure 10.4.

According to Robertson, the *supply of loanable funds* consists of:

1. voluntary savings (V_s), i.e., savings out of disposable income;
2. bank credits (B_C), i.e., the supply of credits by banks; and
3. activated idle balances or dishoardings (D_h).

All the three components of the supply of loanable funds are positively related to interest. A horizontal summation of the schedules V_s, B_c and D_h gives the aggregate supply schedule of loanable funds (S_L) as shown in Figure 10.4. The demand schedule for loanable funds (D_L) intersects the supply schedule of loanable funds (S_L) at point P, determining interest rate at OR.

Classical vs Neo-Classical Theory of Interest

The neo-classical theory of interest is superior to the classical theory in so far as it considers the demand for funds other than the demand for investment, and also the other sources of fund supply than voluntary savings. Besides, the loanable fund theory, as presented in Figure 10.4, reveals important information that

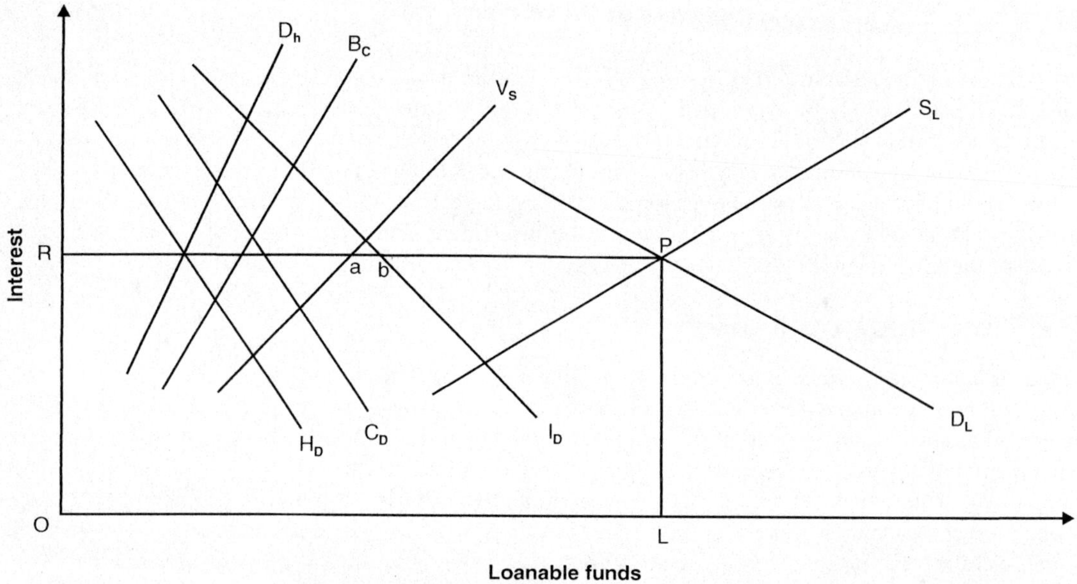

Figure 10.4 *Loanable Fund Theory of Interest*

planned savings may not be equal to the planned investment at equilibrium rate of interest. The planned savings are represented by the schedule V_s and planned investment by the schedule I_D. As Figure 10.4 shows, at equilibrium rate of interest, *OR*, planned savings, *Ra*, is less than planned investment, *Rb*.

Criticism

Keynes's criticism of classical theory of interest applies to the loanable fund theory also. According to Keynes, like classical theory of interest the *loanable funds theory* is also *indeterminate*. In the loanable fund theory, supply of investible funds include voluntary savings, bank money and the dishoarding of idle balances. Of the three components of the total supply of inventible fund, 'savings' accounts for the largest proportion in the total and savings are functions of the 'disposable incomes'. In fact, almost entire supply of investible funds depends on the disposable incomes. Therefore, interest cannot be known unless income is known; income cannot be known unless investment is known and investment cannot be known unless interest is known. As in classical theory, the error in the neo-classical theory lies in the implicit assumption that demand for and supply of investible funds can vary independent of each other.

It is, however, suggested that Keynes's criticism of classical theory does not apply to the neo-classical theory. For, unlike classical theory, the neo-classical theory considers savings to be the function of the preceding year's income which is known and cannot be influenced by the current investment.[11]

Having criticized the classical theories of interest, Keynes propounded his own *Liquidity Preference Theory of Interest*. Keynesian theory of interest is a purely monetary theory of interest. Also, it considers aggregate demand for and aggregate supply of money in the determination of interest rate. Therefore, Keynesian theory of interest is discussed in a macro-monetary framework. Since this book is concerned with only micro analysis, Keynesian theories of interest and later development in interest theory have been omitted.

INTEREST AND INVESTMENT DECISIONS

The classical and neo-classical theories of interest, discussed in the preceding sections, might or might not explain convincingly how rate of interest is determined in the money market. But, one thing is certain: in all market economies, there does exist an interest rate structure at which people borrow and lend money. The rate of interest plays a decisive role in determining the level of investment in a country. In this section, we will answer the question: How does interest rate figure in investment decisions and how does the market rate of interest influence the investment decisions? The *time value of money* is central to the investment decisions. Let us, therefore, first look into the time value of money.

The Time Value of Money

Money is demanded because it has a value, a purchasing power. But money has a time value also in the sense that money today is preferable to money expected tomorrow. It means that money has a present value and a future value. Its present value is what it can buy today in the market and its future value is what it can buy in future. The present value of money is certain, but its future value is uncertain. The fundamental rule is that one bird in hand is better than two in bush. That is why people prefer to have money today rather than to have it tomorrow. But then, why do people spend money on the assets which yield income in future? They do so because they expect that the future volume of their money will be higher than its present value. In other words, they expect that the investment will yield an income which will buy a larger amount of goods and services that it can buy today. That is why people save and invest.

Investments are made to enhance the income in future. However, income to be received in future involves an *opportunity cost*, i.e., the loss of interest. The loss of interest arises because had the money not been invested, it could have been lent on interest. Since the money is invested for a higher income in future, the investor loses the interest. That is why if the receipt of an expected income is deferred for some future date, the investor loses interest on the expected incomes. Therefore, the present value of future income is less than its money worth. A question arises here as to how to find the *present value of future incomes*. The present value of a future income is obtained by discounting the expected future income at the current market rate of interest. This is how interest rate enters the investment decisions.

Having explained the concept of the time value money, we proceed to discuss the method of computing the *present value* of a future income, its *net present value* (*NPV*) and their implication in investment decisions. In addition, we will discuss also the concept of *internal rate of return* (*IRR*)—an alternative determinant of investment—and compare its role with that of interest rate in investment decisions.

Present Value and Investment Decisions

The *present value* of a future income may be defined as the sum of money which must be invested at a compounding interest rate to get the same amount in future. In other words, the present value of a future income is its value discounted at the market rate of interest. To explain the concept of present value, let us suppose that a sum, X_0, is invested for a period of one year at an annually compounding interest rate, r. At the end of the year, the total receipt, say X_1, can be calculated as follows.

$$\begin{aligned} X_1 &= (X_0 + rX_0) \\ &= X_0(1+r) \qquad (10.1) \end{aligned}$$

Equation 10.1 shows that X_0 *increases* at the rate of $(1 + r)$ to take the value X_1 after one year. It implies that if X_1 is discounted at the interest rate, *r*, we get its *present value* (*PV*). Thus, computing *PV* is a reverse process of computing the future value of an investment. The formula for measuring the present value (*PV*) of a future income is given as

$$PV \text{ of } X_1 = \frac{X}{(1+r)} = X_1\left(\frac{1}{1+r}\right) \quad (10.2)$$

In Eq. (10.2), the term $1/(1 + r)$ is the discount rate for one year. Now given the rate of interest, i.e., the actual value of *r*, any income receivable after one year can be discounted to obtain its present value. For example, the present value of an income of Rs 1100 expected after one year from now, given the rate of interest as 10 per cent per annum, can be calculated as follows.

$$PV = 1100\left(\frac{1}{1+0.1}\right) = 1000$$

It means that the present value of Rs 1100 expected after one year, hence, is Rs 1000, if the rate of interest is 10 per cent per annum.

The *discount rate* (*D*) for an income receivable after two years will be $1/(1 + r)^2$, and for an income receivable after 3 years, $D_3 = 1/(1 + r)^3$ and so on. The formula for discount rate for the *n*th year is

$$D_n = \frac{1}{(1+r)^n} \quad (10.3)$$

The formula for calculating present value (*PV*) of an amount (X_n) receivable in the *n*th year is

$$PV = X_n\left[\frac{1}{(1+r)^n}\right] \quad (10.4)$$

The formula for calculating the *total present value* (*TPV*) of a stream of annual returns $R_1, R_2, R_3 \ldots R_n$ of an equal amount over *n* years is given as

$$TVP = R_1\frac{1}{(1+r)} + R_2\frac{1}{(1+r)^2} + R_3\frac{1}{(1+r)^3} + \cdots + R_n\frac{1}{(1+r)^n}$$

or

$$TVP = \frac{R_1}{(1+r)} + \frac{R_2}{(1+r)^2} + \frac{R_3}{(1+r)^3} + \cdots + \frac{R_n}{(1+r)^n} \quad (10.5)$$

$$= \sum_{j=1}^{n} R_n \frac{1}{(1+r)^n}$$

or

$$= \sum_{j=1}^{n} \frac{R_n}{(1+r)^n} \tag{10.6}$$

NPV and Investment Decision

After having noted the concept and the method of calculating present value of a future income, let us now see how investment decisions are taken on the basis of present value of a future income. In fact, the investment decisions—accepting or rejecting the project—are based on *NPV*. The *NPV* may be defined as the difference between the present value expected in the *n*th year and the cost of lump-sum investment (*C*), i.e.,

$$NPV = PV - C$$

By substituting Eq. (10.6) for *PV* in the above equation, *NPV* can be expressed as

$$NPV = \sum_{j=1}^{n} R_n \left[\frac{1}{(1+r)^n} \right] - C \tag{10.7}$$

In Eq. (10.7), *C* represents the total investment or the cost of project without any recurring expenditure. If investment does involve a recurring expenditure, the total present cost (*TPC*) for *n* years can be calculated in the same manner, as present value, i.e.,

$$TPC = \sum_{j=1}^{n} \frac{C_n}{(1+r)^n} \tag{10.8}$$

The *NPV* can then be computed as

$$NPV = \sum_{j=1}^{n} \frac{R_n}{(1+r)^n} - \sum_{j=1}^{n} \frac{C_n}{(1+r)^n}$$

$$= \sum_{j=1}^{n} \frac{R_n - C_n}{(1+r)^n} \tag{10.9}$$

Once *NPV* of a future income is calculated, *investment decision* becomes a simple matter. The decision rule is that if the *NPV* is positive (i.e., $NPV > 0$), the project is worth investment; if $NPV < 0$, reject the investment proposal; and if $NPV = 0$, the project may be accepted or rejected on the basis of non-economic considerations. Anyway, if $NPV > 0$, the firm can borrow any amount at the existing interest rate (*r*) and invest it. Where a choice between a number of alternative projects has to be made, the one with higher *NPV* would be chosen.

IRR and Investment Decision

Recall that the *NPV* criterion of investment decision is based on total values of *PV* and *TPC*. Keynes has suggested an alternative method of investment decision based on only the rate of interest (*r*) and the *IRR*—internal in the sense that it is relevant to a particular firm or the decision maker, not to all. The *IRR* criterion of investment decision, or what Keynes called *marginal efficiency of investment* (*MEI*) is defined as 'the rate of interest or return which renders the discounted present value of its expected future marginal yields exactly equal to the investment cost of project'. In other words, *IRR is the rate of return* (*r*) at which the discounted present value of receipts and expenditures are equal. The *IRR* may also be defined in terms of Eq. (10.9). That is, *IRR* is the rate (*r*) at which

$$\sum_{j=1}^{n} \frac{R_n}{(1+r)^n} = \sum_{j=1}^{n} \frac{C_n}{(1+r)^n} \tag{10.10}$$

In Eq. (10.10), the factor *r* represents the *IRR*. The *IRR* criterion tells that so long as *IRR* (*r* in Eq. (10.10)) is greater than the market rate of interest (*i*), it is always worthwhile to borrow and invest. However, in a perfectly competitive market $r = i$. It implies that in a perfectly competitive market, firm's *IRR* always equals the market rate of interest.

*IRR*s vs Present Value

From Eq. (10.10), it may be inferred that *IRR* and *NPV* criteria lead to the same conclusion or yield the same decision. There are situations, however, where the two criteria give the conflicting results. For example, suppose that a firm has to make a choice between Project *A* and Project *B*, each having a productive life of two years. The stream of net income[1] at the end of the year from the two projects and their respective costs are presented in Table 10.1.

Let us now calculate the *NPV* for both the projects, assuming a 10 per cent rate of interest, and compare the result with *IRR* or *MEI*. Recall that $NPV = PV - C$.

Project A

$$PV = 0 + \frac{140}{(1+0.10)^2} = 115.70$$

and

$$NPV = 115.70 - 100$$
$$= 15.70$$

Since *NPV* is positive (Rs 15.70) at 10 per cent rate of interest, Project *A* is acceptable. But, if we raise the rate of interest to 20 per cent, Project *A* will not be acceptable. For, at this rate of interest, *NPV* is negative (–2.78), calculated as below:

$$NPV = 0 + \frac{140}{(1.20)^2} - 100$$
$$= 97.22 - 100$$
$$= -2.78$$

Table 10.1 *Flow of Net Incomes*

Project	Cost of Project	1st Year	2nd Year
Project *A*	100	0	140
Project *B*	100	130	0

Project B

$$PV = \frac{130}{(1+.10)} + 0 = 118.18$$

and

$$NPV = 118.18 - 100$$
$$= 18.18$$

Project *B* is acceptable at 10 per cent rate of interest because *NPV* (= Rs 18.18) is positive. It will be acceptable even at the interest rate of 20 per cent because *NPV* will be Rs 8.33.

The investment decisions based on *NPV* may now be concluded as Project *A* is acceptable at interest rate of 10 percent but not at 20 percent whereas Project *B* is acceptable at both the rates of interest. Let us now calculate *MEI* for both the projects and compare the results.

By definition, the *MEI* is the rate of return (*r*) which, if used to discount the income stream, renders the *NPV* equal to zero. Using the definition in Eq. (10.10), the *IRR*, (denoted by *r*) for Project *A*, may be calculated as below. The *r* should be such that

$$NPV = 0 + \frac{140}{(1+r)^2} = 100$$

$$(1+r)^2 = \frac{140}{100} = 1.40$$

$$(1+r) = \sqrt{1.40}$$

$r = 0.183$ or 18.3 per cent

In case of Project *B*, the *IRR* (*r*) can be worked out as follows.

$$NPV = \frac{130}{(1+r)} + 0 = 100$$

$$(1+r) = \frac{130}{100} = 1.30$$

$r = 0.30$, or 30 per cent

We find that *MEI* of Project *A* is 18.3 per cent and of Project *B*, it is 30 per cent. The information generated above may now be tabulated as given in Table 10.2.

Table 10.2 *NPV and MEI of Projects A and B*

Project A		Project B	
r	NPV	r	NPV
0.0	40.00	0.00	30.00
10.0	15.70	10.00	18.18
18.3 = *MEI*	0.00	20.0	8.33
20.00	−2.78	30.00 = *MEI*	0.00

The conflict between the two criteria may be shown by plotting the information given in Table 10.2, as shown in Figure 10.5. The plotted figure gives lines showing relation between *NPV* and *r* with respect to each project. The two lines corresponding to the two projects intersect at point *P*. The value of *r* at point *P* is 7.7 per cent. This value of *r* (= 7.7%) is common to both the projects.

The value of *r* common to both the projects can also be calculated as follows.

Let *r* be such that $NPV_A = NPV_B$.

$$NPV_A = 0 + \frac{140}{(1+r)^2} - 100$$

and

$$NPV_B = \frac{30}{(1+r)} + 0 - 100$$

The common value of *r* can be found by the equating NPV_A and NPV_B. Thus,

$$0 + \frac{140}{(1+r)^2} - 100 = \frac{130}{(1+r)} + 0 - 100$$

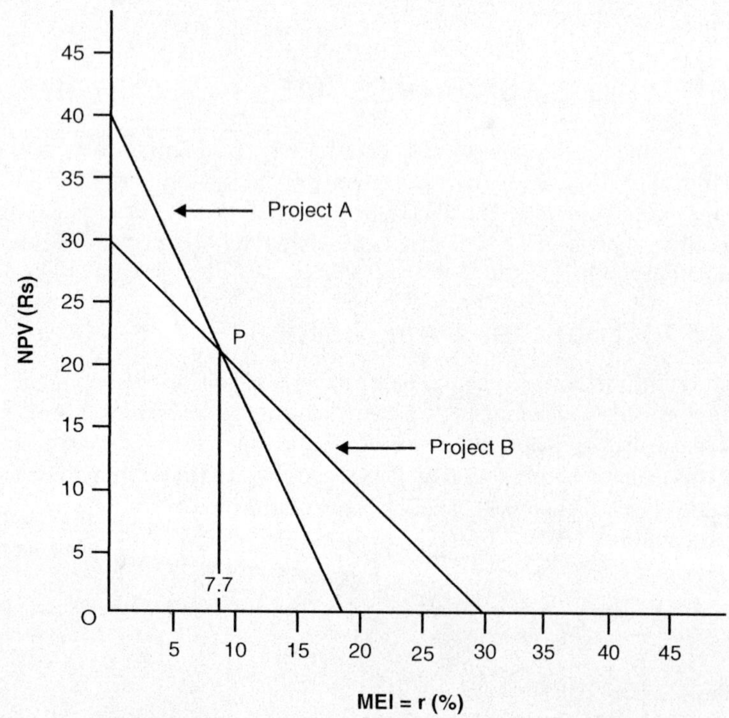

Figure 10.5 *NPV and MEI of Project A and B*

or

$$\frac{140}{(1+r)^2} = \frac{130}{(1+r)}$$

$$\frac{(1+r)^2}{(1+r)} = \frac{140}{130}$$

or

$$(1 + r) = 1.077$$
$$\therefore r = 0.077 \text{ or } 7.7 \text{ per cent}$$

From the foregoing calculations, we infer that at 7.7 per cent rate of return (or interest) both the projects are equally acceptable or rejectable. If rate of return is less than 7.7 per cent, Project *A* is preferable because its *NVP* is higher than that of Project *B*. But, if the rate of return is greater than 7.7 per cent, Project *B* is preferable because its *NPV* is higher than that of Project *A*. It follows that a firm paying interest below 7.7 per cent will prefer Project *A*, even though it will have to wait longer to recover its initial cost. Thus, the choice between the two projects will be based on pay-off period.

Furthermore, if firms consider *IRR* or *MEI*, Project *B* should be preferable since its $IRR = r = 30$ percent is greater than that of Project *A* at $IRR = r = 18.5$ percent. Obviously, the two criteria, *NPV* and *IRR* provide conflicting conclusions in regard to choice between the two projects. In actual practice, however, the firms are guided by their objective. The *NPV* is in either case preferable.

RISK, UNCERTAINTY AND INVESTMENT DECISIONS

Our discussion on investment decisions so far is based on the assumption that there is full certainty about the returns. In reality, however, there is uncertainty about the future events and, therefore, there is risk involved in the expected return. The uncertainty and risk play a crucial role in most investment decisions. In this section, therefore, we have briefly discussed the important methods[12] of risk adjustment in the investment decisions.

Risk-Adjusted Discount Rate Approach

A common, though crude, method of accounting for the risk factor in investment decisions is to use a *risk-adjusted discount rate* in the assessment of present value of future returns. In this method, the discount rate (r) used in calculating the present value is increased so as to cover the risk factor. The present value calculated in this manner is treated as *risk-free present value* of future streams of cash flows. If risk-adjusted present value is greater than the cost of investment, the project is accepted, otherwise rejected. The risk-adjusted discount rate (D) is expressed as

$$D = \frac{1}{1 + r + u}$$

where u denotes the degree of risk.

For example, if $r = 0.07$ or 7 percent and degree of risk (u) is 3 per cent or 0.03, then the risk-adjusted discount rate (D) is obtained as

$$D = \frac{1}{1 + 0.07 + 0.03}$$
$$= \frac{1}{1.1} = 0.91$$

It may be noted that lower the risk, the lower the risk-adjusted discount rate and the lower the discounted present value.

Properties

The risk-adjusted discount rate approach has certain desirable properties.

First, the discount rate can be adjusted for the varying degrees of risk in different years, simply by increasing or decreasing the risk factor (u) in calculating the risk-adjusted discount rate.

Secondly, the method of discounting is such that the higher risk factor in the remote future is accounted for automatically since the denominator in the risk-adjusted discounting factor [$1/(1 + r + u$] is raised to higher powers (i.e., by the number of years considered). For example, the discounting factor for the 10th year will be as

$$D = \frac{1}{(1 + r + u)^{10}}$$

This method of discounting reduces automatically the present value drastically and provides for the risk a decade hence.

Thirdly, the method is easy to handle in comparison with other methods.

But, the basic *weakness* of this method is that it does not provide any guideline for estimating the risk factor, i.e., the value of u. This method, therefore, requires to be supplemented with some other method of calculating risk factor, individual judgement or intuition of the decision maker.

The Mean–Standard Deviation Method

The *mean–standard deviation* method provides a straightforward method of incorporating risk into discounted present value. In this method, the discounted present value of future stream of returns is calculated on the basis of their mean value, instead of actual cash flows. The use of mean value of cash flows brings into consideration the dispersion—the difference between the mean value and the actual value. Therefore, standard deviation which is an explicit reflection of the risk becomes an important element in investment decisions. Once the discounted present value of mean of the future stream of returns and the standard deviation are computed, the decision makers are equipped with the necessary data required for investment decisions. They can now easily decide whether the expected return is worth taking the risk.

The major *weakness* of the method, however, is that it assumes certainty about the mean return. Also, this method has no use if expected stream of return is uniform over the life time of the project.

The Finite-Horizon Method

Under the finite-horizon method, a final date of return is fixed even if the project is expected to yield returns thereafter. This method is similar to pay-back method applied under the condition of certainty. In this method, a terminal date is fixed and in the decision making, only the expected returns or gains prior to the terminal date are considered. The gains or benefits expected beyond terminal date are ignored—the gains beyond the terminal date are simply treated as non-existent. The logic behind this approach is that the developments during the period under consideration, might render the gains beyond terminal date of no consequence. For example, a hydel electricity project might go out of use say, after 30 years of its installation, when atomic or solar energy becomes available in abundance and at lower cost. Even if the project continues to yield returns after 30 years, its finite horizon is taken to be 30 years.

Drawback

The drawback of this method lies in its assumption. Adopting this method means treating two projects as equal even if one really terminates at or around the terminal date, while the other yields considerable gains for quite some time thereafter. The latter is clearly preferable. The gains from such long-run public projects as soil conservation and flood control systems beyond the arbitrarily decided terminal point cannot be justifiably ignored. This method is therefore considered as deficient in dealing with long-term project as it deals with the problem with imperfect foresight.

The Probability Theory Approach

We have so far discussed the investment decisions under the condition that there is no uncertainty about the returns expected from the project. In this section, we discuss the approach adopted in investment decision under the condition that there is risk and uncertainty about the returns from the project under consideration. The degree of certainty is measured in terms of probability rate, i.e., the probability of riskless return. This approach is called, the *probability theory of investment*. The *probability theory method* considers a whole range of possible risk–return combinations, which can adequately represent the full range of alternative outcomes of a risky undertaking. Therefore, it is necessary to consider a large number of alternative cash flows and the associated probabilities, for each time period under consideration. The process is illustrated in Table 10.3.

As the table shows, given the alternative cash flows and the associated probabilities, the expected returns with probability 1 are Rs 1850 in the first year, Rs 1600 in the second year, and Rs 1300 in the third year. These expected returns may now be discounted to their present value. Rest of the decision procedure would be the same as in case of discounted present value criterion.

Table 10.3 *Alternative Cash Flows and Associated Probabilities*

Cash Flows (Rs)	1st Year		2nd Year		3rd Year	
	Probability	Risk Adjusted Return (Rs)	Probability	Risk Adjusted Return (Rs)	Probability	Risk Adjusted Return (Rs)
1000	0.50	500	0.50	500	0.70	700
2000	0.25	500	0.40	800	0.30	600
3000	0.15	450	0.10	300	0.00	0
4000	0.10	400	0.00	0.00	0.00	0
Total	**1.00**	**1850**	**1.00**	**1600**	**1.00**	**1300**

As regards its *applicability*, the probability theory method can be applied only if a large number of similar investments are to be undertaken and if one project fails to yield the expected return, others fare so well that the loss is more than compensated, as it happens in the case of insurance policies. Among the insurance policy holders only a few die before the terminal date of insurance policy. Only in these cases, the insurance company suffers a loss. But, since most policy holders survive till the maturity date of the policy, the insurance company makes profit which more than compensate for the loss caused by the death of some policy holders before the policy matures.

Markowitz has shown that this method has a great deal of application to the problem of portfolio selection of securities, i.e., in determining the optimum combination of stocks, bonds, government securities and other financial instruments. The application of this method to the problem of portfolio selection is an exemplary case. The Markowitz method of project choice is illustrated in Figure 10.6. In this figure, the curve marked *RR* is the *risk–return probability curve* and I_1, I_2 and I_3 curve are investor's *risk–return indifference curve*. The *RR′* curve shows the various combinations of the risk and return. The derivation of the *RR′* curve needs some explanation given below.

In his approach to drive the *RR′* curve, Markowtiz has utilized two focal measures: (i) an index of expected returns and (ii) an index of risk.[13] The index of expected returns can be constructed by computing the average expected earning.[14] The index of risk is constructed on the basis of standard deviation of the expected earning. Then, a series of combination of risk and return can be formed for different kinds of financial instruments. These combinations when graphed give a risk–return probability, i.e., the *RR′* curve, showing the various rates of returns and the associated risk, as shown by the curve *RR′* in Figure 10.6. This curve shows the various combinations of return rates and the associated risk.

The curve *RR′* may also be called as *risk-earning possibility curve*—to use Baumol's expression.[15] The various points on the curve *RR′* represent, in a sense, the optimal combinations of risk and return: *the lesser the risk, the lower the return, and the higher the risk, the higher the return.* As such, an *a priori*

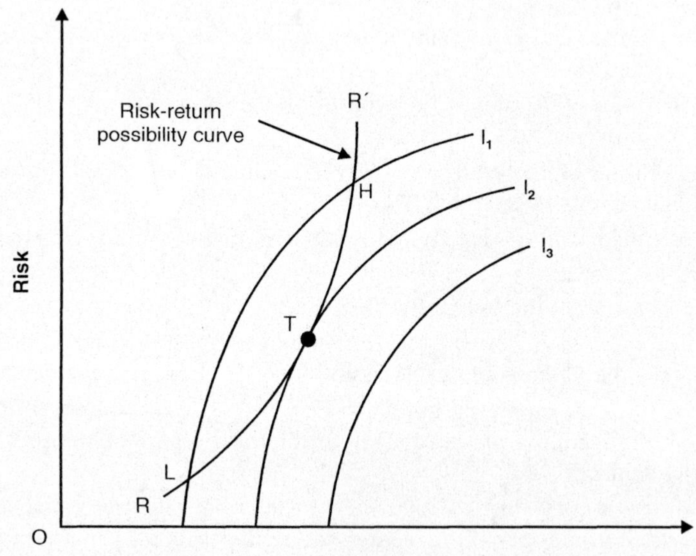

Figure 10.6 *Risk–Return Combinations*

choice of a particular point will be arbitrary. Those who prefer lesser risk and lower return would choose a point on the lower part of the curve, e.g., point *L*, and those who prefer high risk and high return would choose point *H*. This pattern of portfolio selection does not provide an optimal combination of stocks and securities and so on.

The *optimal combination of portfolio* can, however, be determined by superimposing a risk–return indifference map on Figure 10.6, as shown by curves, I_1, I_2 and I_3. It is important to note here that risk–return indifference curves I_1, I_2 and I_3 are inverted ones as compared with standard indifference curves used in consumer analysis or isoquant curves used in the analysis of optimal input combination. Contrary to the isoquant, the risk–return indifference curves (I_1, I_2 and I_3) have a positive slope because as the risk increases, a relatively higher rate of return must be associated with it to keep the investor indifferent between the lower and higher risk–return combinations.

As a general rule, the optimal combination of portfolios is decided by the point of tangency between the risk–return possibility curve (*RR′*) and the risk–return indifference curves, I_2. The optimal combination is shown by point *T* in Figure 10.6. This proposition is however only a theoretical solution to the problem of portfolio selection. In practice, it depends, by and large, on the risk-taking attitude of the investors.

This takes us to the end of our discussion on theory of interest and investment decisions as per the scope of this chapter. In the next chapter, we will be concerned with concept, source and theories of profit.

REVIEW QUESTIONS AND EXERCISES

1. How is capital as a factor of production different from land and labour? How does capital earn a payment for its services?
2. What is meant by 'time preference' in the context of interest theory? What is the importance of this concept in charging and paying interest?
3. Why is interest charged and paid? Will interest accrue in an economy in which there is excess idle supply of savings?
4. Discuss Austrian theory of interest. Do you think it is a complete theory of interest? Give reasons for your answer.
5. Explain Fisher's theory of interest. In what way it is an improvement on Bohm-Bawerk's theory of interest? What are its shortcomings?
6. Discuss classical theory of interest rate determination. Why is this theory said to be indeterminate?
7. Discuss loanable theory of interest? Is this theory superior to the classical theory? Is this theory determinate?
8. Examine critically the classical and neo-classical theories of interest rate determination.
9. Define present value. Compute the present value of an income stream of Rs 80 in the first year, Rs 100 in the second year, and Rs 120 in the third year, assuming a rate of interest of 10 per cent per annum.
10. Given the choice, will you prefer Rs 100 receivable after one year from today or Rs 110 receivable after two years from today, if the market rate of interest is 5% per annum? Give reason for your choice.

11. The anticipated cash flows from a certain project are Rs 100 in the first year and Rs 125 in the second year. What is its present value when the interest rate is 10%? What is the highest rate of interest at which the project should be undertaken?
12. Given the projects *A* and *B*, which project has the maximum net discounted present value if market rate of interest is 10% given the following conditions?
    (a) Project *A* yields an income of Rs 100 per year perpetually; and
    (b) Project *B* yields Rs 400 per year for only two years.
13. Suppose the rate of interest is 5%. A certain investment is expected to yield Rs 500 at once, Rs 1400 at the end of one year; and Rs 900 at the end of second year. What amount in perpetuity is equal in present value to the discounted present value of the above investment?
14. What is *IRR*? Is there any conflict between *NPV* and *IRR* criteria for project selection? How is the conflict resolved?
15. What is risk-adjusted discount rate? Find the present value of Rs 1000 expected after 2 years from now assuming a rate of interest of 10% and a risk probability of 8%.
16. Define 'risk–return probability curve' and 'risk–return indifference curve'. How do they help in investment decisions?
17. What is the probability theory of investment? How does this theory help in finding an appropriate combination of risk and return in investment decisions?

ENDNOTES

1. This is what is revealed by their writings. In fact in their days, interest was taken to be as rent for money borrowed.
2. Blaug, M. *Economic Theory in Retrospect, op. cit.*, p. 42.
3. Bronfenbrenner, M. (1971), '*Income Distribution Theory*' (Chicago: Aldine).
4. Blaug, M. *Economic Theory in Retrospect, op. cit.*, 1973, p. 509.
5. For a detailed *discussion*, see Blaug, M. *Economic Theory in Retrospect, op. cit.*, Chapter 12.
6. In Bohm-Bawerk's view, capital based production is 'round about' method of production whereas land and labour based production is 'direct method' of production. Bohm-Bawerk assumed that 'round about' method of production (i.e., the use of capital in the process of production) is more productive (though at diminishing rates), than the direct method of production, i.e., by the direct use of primary factors (labour and land) to produce final goods. But the 'round about' method is more time consuming than the direct method.
7. Blaug, M. *Economic Theory in Retrospect, op. cit.*, p. 508.
8. Propounded first in his *Rate of Interest* (1907) and later revised in his *Theory of Interest* (1930).
9. Keynes, J.M. *General Theory*, p. 175. Keynes found it difficult to state the classical theory of interest precisely or to discover an explicit account of it in the leading treatise of the classical school.
10. Ibid.
11. Halm, G.N. *Monetary Theory*, 2nd Edn., p. 147.

12. Given the scope of this book, some methods are excluded. The excluded methods include 'Hurdle rate' Method, Simulation Sensitivity Analysis, Decision Tree, and the Shackle Approach.
13. For details, see Baumol, W.J. (1984), *Economic Theory and Operations Analysis* (New Delhi: Prentice Hall of India), 4th Edn., pp. 619–625.
14. Expected earnings can be obtained by extrapolating on the basis of past earnings of similar securities or on the basis of expert opinion.
15. Baumol, W.J. '*Economic Theory and Operations Analysis*', *op. cit.*, p. 622.

FURTHER READINGS

Baumol, W.J. (1985), *Economic Theory and Operations Analysis* (New Delhi: Prentice Hall of India), 4th Edn., Chapter 25.

Blaug, M. (1983), *Economic Theory in Retrospect* (New Delhi: Vikas Publishing House), 3rd Indian Edn., Chapters 12 and 14.

Bronfenbrenner, M.J. (1971), *Income Distribution Theory* (Chicago, IL: Aldine).

Fisher, I. (1930), *The Theory of Interest* (New York, NY: Macmillan).

Halm, G.N. (1955), *Monetary Theory*, 2nd Edn.

Hansen, A. (1953), *A Guide to Keynes* (New York, NY: McGraw-Hill), Chapter 17.

Hawtrey, R.G. (1937), 'Alternative Theories of Rate of Interest', *Eco. Jl.*, (September).

Keynes, J.M. (1946), "'The Theory of the Rate of Interest" in *Readings in Theory of Income Distribution*', *Am. Eco. Assn.*

Keynes, J.M. (1961), *The General Theories of Employment, Interest and Money* (London: Macmillan), Chapter 14.

Robertson, D.H. (1937), 'Alternative Theories of the Rate of Interest', *Eco. Jl.*, (September).

Chapter 11

Theories of Profit

CHAPTER OBJECTIVES

In this chapter, we move on to discuss the theories of profit. The concept and source of profit have been a debatable issue. By going through this chapter, you learn:

- What is meant by profit and pure profit;
- What are the different sources of profit;
- How economists look at the different sources of profit;
- How risk bearing, business dynamism, inventions and innovations give rise to profit;
- Does profit arise due to any one of these factors or due to a combination of different factors giving rise to profit; and
- Whether profit enters the cost of production in general economic analysis of cost structure.

INTRODUCTION

It has been pointed out that *marginal productivity theory applies* to all factors of production. However, all factors of production have certain unique features determining their demand and supply. That is why, perhaps, that the economists, right from the so-called classical economists to modern economists, have expressed their own opinion on the meaning and source of the profit. As regards the theories of profit, according to the 'marginal productivity theory', in the long-run competitive equilibrium, the reward for each factor, including the reward for 'entrepreneurship' equals the value of its marginal product. It implies that 'profit', which is the reward for 'entrepreneurship', is the marginal value of product resulting from entrepreneurship. There are, however, a number of other concepts of profit and profit theories developed by economists over time. In this chapter, we briefly review some important profit theories. Let us first have a brief look into the meaning of 'pure profit' and answer the question as to whom pure profit belongs to. Let us now look how economist look at profit.

MEANING OF PURE PROFIT

The meaning and source of 'profit' have always been a matter of controversy. 'The word 'profit' has different meanings to business men, accountants, tax collectors, workers and economists ...'[1] For example, 'profit to a layman means all income that go to the capitalist class'. To an accountant, profit means the excess of revenue, which is over all paid-out costs including both manufacturing and overhead expenses. For all accounting purposes, businessmen also use this definition of profit. But on the question as to whether a businessman should stay in his present business or move to another, accounting profit is not a relevant guide. The term 'profit' in the accounting sense does not include the *opportunity cost* that a businessman bears to earn a given profit in his present occupation. But a businessman does consider his *opportunity cost* in his calculation of his satisfactory profit that must be large enough to cover his opportunity cost. The 'opportunity cost' includes all the incomes which he might earn from the second best alternative use of his *own resources*—labour and capital. Let us now look how economists look at 'profit'.

Economists' concept of profit is of *pure profit*. It is also called '*economic profit*' or 'just profit'. 'Pure profit' is a return over and above the opportunity cost, i.e. the payment that would be 'necessary to draw forth the factors of production from their most remunerative alternative employment'. Pure profit may thus be defined as 'a residual left over after all contractual costs have been met, including the transfer costs of management, insurable risks, depreciation, and payments to shareholders sufficient to maintain investment at its current level'.[2] In other words, *pure profit* equals *net profit*[3] less opportunity costs of management, insurable risk, depreciation of capital, necessary minimum payments to shareholders that can prevent them from withdrawing their capital from its current use.

The pure profit, so defined, may not necessarily be positive for a single firm in a single year; it may be a negative profit (i.e. loss). What is important is the return over time. In the long run, in a competitive system, however, pure profit is presumed to be equal to zero. That is, pure profit is non-existent in the long run.

To discover whether such profit exists, take the revenue for the firm and deduct the costs of all factors of production other than capital. Then deduct the pure return on capital and any risk premium necessary to compensate the owner of capital for the risk associated with its use in this firm and industry. Anything that remains is pure profit.[4]

An important question regarding 'pure profit' is 'to whom does it belong and in what form?' It is stated as a common knowledge that pure profit belongs to the entrepreneur, the owner of the firm. But the question arises: how does it accrue to the entrepreneur? For, if an entrepreneur is treated as a separate factor of production, pure profit must equal the value of its marginal product. But marginal value of product cannot be logically equated to pure profit, because as concluded above, pure profit is a 'residual'.[5]

In fact, this problem has been the source of controversy and the various profit theories. The important theories of profit are discussed as follows.

PROFIT THEORIES: WHAT ARE THE SOURCES OF PROFITS?

In this section, we will discuss the various theories of profit. The theories of profit, in fact, bring out the *sources of profit* and the *determinants of profit*, not the determination of the profit rate or the rate of return on capital investment. The sources of profit pointed by early economists are as much relevant today as they were centuries ago.

Walker's Theory of Profit: Profit Is Rent of Ability

One of the most widely known theories advanced to explain the nature of profit was formulated by F.A. Walker. According to him, profit is the rent of the superior abilities of an entrepreneur in comparison with the least efficient entrepreneur. Just as rent on land is the difference between the yields of the most and the least fertile lands, pure profit is the difference between the earnings of the most and the least efficient entrepreneurs.

In formulating his profit theory, Walker visualized a state of perfect competition in which all firms (or entrepreneurs) are presumed to possess equal managerial ability or entrepreneurship. Assuming no barrier to prevent the entry of new firms to the industry, he argued that the number of firms would increase until the remuneration of firms was just enough to keep them in the industry. Each firm would then receive only the *wages of management* which, in Walker's view, forms a part of (pure) profit. He regarded *wages of management* as *ordinary wages*. Thus, under perfectly competitive conditions, there would be no pure profits.

However, when one departs from the realm of perfect competition, one finds in almost all industries that while some firms are making only a bare living or a normal profit, other firms in the same industry are making pure profits. Walker argued that pure profits of profit-making firms arise from what a more efficient firm is able to produce over and above what the least efficient firm is able to produce with the same amount of capital and labour.[6] Walker attributed this surplus wholly to the greater efficiency of a firm, which distinguishes itself from the least efficient ones.

Thus, to Walker, profit is akin to rent paid for exceptional business ability over and above the ordinary ability required for management and organization which could be rewarded by a wage or salary. Just as rent is a reward for higher productivity, so is the profit reward for superior managerial ability of an entrepreneur.

Does Pure Profit Enter Cost of Production? A natural corollary of this view is that pure profit does not enter the cost of production as is the case with rent. Therefore, according to Walker, profit does not enter the price determination. The logic that Walker gives for his argument runs as follows. Market price is determined by the cost of production of that portion of supply which is produced by the least efficient firms. Prices so determined make allowance for only wages of management, not the surplus that accrues to the firms with greater efficiency.

Clark's Theory of Profit: Profit Is Reward for Dynamic Entrepreneurship

The dynamic entrepreneurship theory of profit is associated with the name of J.B. Clark.[7] He propounded his theory of profit in 1900. According to Clark, profits accrue in a dynamic world, not in a static word. It does not exist in a static world.

According to Clark, a *static world* is one in which there exists absolute freedom of economic activity and competition; population and capital are stationary; there are no inventions; production process does not change and goods continue to remain homogeneous. Besides, in a static state, there is perfect mobility of factors of production but there is no movement of factors because marginal productivity of labour and capital is the same in all groups of industries. Furthermore, in a static state, there is no uncertainty and hence, no risk. If some risks do arise due to natural calamities, etc., they are insurable. In Clark's view, in a static world, entrepreneurs earn only wages of management.

To show how profits are eliminated in a *static state*, Clark draws a distinction between the work of an entrepreneur and that of a manager of a business. He believed that the task of a manager could be described as managerial labour which can be paid for by wages.[8] In a static state, profit would not arise because competition would not permit any business manager to earn more than his actual wages which equals marginal value of his product. Therefore, there would be no surplus which could be called *profit*.

On the other hand, a *dynamic world* is one in which, factors that remain constant in a static world undergo a process of change. Clark indicated certain *generic changes* that mark the transition of a society from a static to a dynamic state. Briefly speaking, generic changes include

1. increase in population;
2. increase in capital;
3. improvement in production techniques;
4. changes in forms of business organization and
5. multiplication of consumer's wants.

In Clark's view, the major function of an entrepreneur in a dynamic society is to take the advantage of generic changes to promote his business, to expand sales and to reduce cost of production. The typical changes which emerge out of this special effort of some entrepreneurs are inventions, innovation and improvement in the methods of production. These changes lead to increase in production given the costs or to reduction in costs given the output. This results in emergence of profits to the initial inventors.

Such *profits are*, however, *temporary*, i.e. a short-run affair. For, with the passage of time, the profits resulting from the inventions and improvements in production method tend to disappear. What happens, in fact, is that competition between firms forces other entrepreneurs to imitate and adopt the new technology. This leads to a rise in demand for labour and capital. Consequently, wages and interest rate rise increasing the cost of production. On the other hand, with larger employment of labour and capital, production increases leading to fall in product prices. The ultimate result is that profits disappear. In Clark's own words, 'profit is an elusive sum which entrepreneurs grasp but cannot hold. It slips through their fingers and bestows itself on all members of the society'.

This, however, should not mean that, in a dynamic society, profits arise only to disappear and never to emerge again. In fact, in a dynamic society, the generic changes continue to take place: change is a continuous process. The process of dynamic change gives entrepreneurs opportunities time and again to adjust their business to the changing conditions, make inventions and to improve production methods with a view of making pure profits. In fact, emergence and disappearance of profits is a continuous process too.

On the question of *risk* involved in making inventions and improving production methods, Clark was of the view that profit does not arise due to risk. If risk is there, it affects capitalist because risk-income accrues to them. Profit, on the other hand, is the result of entrepreneurial functions under dynamic conditions. Therefore, profit does not result from risk bearing.

To sum up, according to J.B. Clark, profit is a reward for inventing products and production techniques and for coordinating functions of entrepreneurs under dynamic conditions. It is a reward for dynamic entrepreneurship. It is not a reward for risk bearing. Pure profit, according to him, is a residue that remains after interest and wages are paid. That is, the difference between the gross receipts and payments for wages plus interest represents profit.

Criticism of Clark's Theory Clark's theory, though logically valid, has failed to win unqualified acceptance. It has been criticized on the following grounds.

First, to some economists, the division of firm's earning between the wage of 'management' and 'profits' is not acceptable. It has been contended, for instance, that even the routine conduct of a business calls for judgement and administrative ability just as these qualities are called for in the exploitation of a new invention or in any other manifestation of economic change. Clark's definition was, therefore, a matter of phraseology and no clear line could be drawn to show the functions which give 'wages of management' and those which were remunerated by 'profits'.

Secondly, even if it is accepted that profits are accounted for by the coordinating functions of entrepreneurs, it poses special difficulties in explaining the profits in the practical world. For instance, profits of companies are paid mainly to the shareholders who do not exercise any co-ordinating functions. Therefore, one may say for the sake of argument that what shareholders receive is only a fair interest on their investment and that the profit is what remains after paying this 'interest'. Still, the surplus over the 'interests' paid to shareholders would continue to be their property, because they are the owners of retained earnings. Making a distinction between 'interest' and 'dynamic reward' is a difficult proposition in practice.

Thirdly, the basic tenet of Clark's theory is that profits result from certain generic changes and Clark's entrepreneur is the pioneer of such changes. But, in practice, one finds that profit also exists under different conditions. There are many profitable business organizations engaged in forms of activity in which dynamic stage is long since past, and in which no change takes place and business has settled down to almost routine conditions, and yet profits continue to be made despite competition. So, to say that profit arises out of only generic changes is not always true.

Finally, it has been argued by Frank H. Knight that all changes would not give rise to profits. Some changes are predictable and some are not. So far as predictable changes are there, they pose no managerial problems or uncertainty. Therefore, such changes cannot give rise to profit. Only the unpredictable changes would require the use of managerial talent and give rise to uncertainty. Clark's theory, thus, misses an important element of uncertainty, risk and their relation to profit.

Hawley's Risk Theory of Profit: Profit Is Reward for Risk Bearing

The risk theory of profit was propounded by F.B. Hawley in 1893. Hawley regarded risk taking as an inevitable accompaniment of dynamic production, and those who take risk have a sound claim to a separate reward, known as *profit*. Thus, according to Hawley, profit is simply the price paid by society for assuming business risk. In his opinion, businessmen would not assume risk without expecting an adequate compensation in excess of *acturial value*. That is, the entrepreneur would always look for a return in excess of the expected losses. The reason why Hawley regarded *profit to exist only over and above the acturial risk is that taking risk is irksome; it gives rise to trouble, anxiety and disutilities of various kinds, which gives a claim to reward for all these pains in excess of acturial value of risk*. Profit, according to Hawley, consists of two parts: *one* part represents compensation for acturial or average loss incidental to the various classes of risks necessarily assumed by the entrepreneur and the *second* part represents an inducement to suffer the prospect of being exposed to the risk.

Hawley recognized the importance of coordination function which Clark had talked of in his theory. But Hawley found that Clark's profit could be called profit only when coordination happens to be an incident of ownership and that profit arises from ownership only so long as ownership involves risk. Thus, risk has to be assumed by the trim to qualify for profit. If an entrepreneur shifts his risks by insuring against them, he would cease to be an entrepreneur and would not receive any profit. It is in connection with uninsured risks that profits arise, and until the uncertainty ends with the sale of entrepreneur's products, the amount of the reward cannot be determined. Profit, is therefore, a residue and *Hawley's theory is a residual theory of profit*.

Hawley was conscious that his theory does not offer a full explanation of all the gains arising from business activities. In monopoly undertakings, for example, many a time profit could not be attributed to the risks. Profits of monopoly firms arise from the very fact of not undertaking the risks. Thus, monopoly gains fall outside his theory. In order to make up for this drawback in his theory, he placed monopoly gains in a separate category of business gains which might arise to other factors also. According to his view, monopoly gains could also occur to labour, landlords and capital suppliers. But, since their respective incomes—wages, rent and interest—do not arise from the operation of productive forces, these are merely *economic gains*.

Criticism of Risk-Bearing Theory Perhaps no other theory of profit has attracted more attention and generated a prolonged debate than *Hawley's Risk Theory of Profit*. It ranks today as one of the most widely accepted theories of profits. Nevertheless, Hawley's risk theory of profit has been criticized on the following grounds.

First, in his reaction to risk theory of profit, Clark remarked that the profit visualized by Hawley is nothing but an interest on capital. Risk, in Clark's view, is risk of loss of capital. As such the reward for assuming this risk is interest and not profit.

Secondly, it has also been argued that, although Hawley stressed on the risk in terms of loss of capital, he did not give due consideration to the fact that risks also arise in the use of factors of production other than capital.

Thirdly, Hawley's theory of profit concentrates only on risk-bearing element of business and ignores other entrepreneurial functions, viz. organization and coordination, which also lead to emergence of profit.

Fourthly, Hawley fails to make a distinction between predictable and unpredictable risks. While predictable risks are insurable, unpredictable risk are not. Since predictable risks can be insured, such risks do not give rise to profit because the risk is shifted on to the insurer. As Knight put it, it is, in fact, the uninsurable risk that gives rise to profit. Thus, in his view, profit is a reward for uncertainty bearing rather than a reward for risk bearing.

Fifthly, Carver observed that profits are reward for avoiding risk and not for bearing risk because only those entrepreneurs who are able to avoid risk make profits.

Finally, if profits were the reward for risk bearing, then the greater the risk undertaken, the greater the profits. But there is no empirical support to this inference which can be drawn from Hawley's theory.

Knight's Theory of Profit: Profit Is a Return to Uncertainty Bearing

Frank H. Knight[9] treated profit as a residual return to uncertainty bearing, not to risk bearing. Obviously, Knight made a distinction between *risk* and *uncertainty*. He divided risks into calculable and incalculable risks. Calculable risks are those whose probability of occurrence can be statistically calculated on the basis of available data, e.g. risks due to fire, theft, accidents, etc. Such risks are insurable. There remains, however, an area of risk in which probability of risk occurrences cannot be calculated. For instance, there may be certain element of cost which may not be accurately calculated and the strategies of the competitors may not be accurately assessed and predicted. The risk element of such incalculable events is not insurable. The area of incalculable risks is, thus, marked by 'uncertainty'. It is in this area of uncertainty that decision becomes a peculiar responsibility of an entrepreneur. If his decisions are proved to be correct by the subsequent events, the entrepreneur makes profit, and vice versa. The profits may arise as a result of

1. decisions concerning the state of market;
2. decisions which result in increasing the degree of monopoly;
3. decisions regarding holding stocks that give rise to windfall gains stock when stock prices increases and
4. decisions taken to introduce new techniques or innovations that give rise to profit.

Criticism of Knight's Theory of Profit The following objections have been raised against Knight's theory of profit.

First, it has been contended that Knight's uncertainty theory lacks scientific precision. Uncertainty is a difficult concept to handle. Tausig has shown that certain risks are undoubtedly in the area of uncertainty, many are not. For example, suppose that a person is betting in a horse race. If he has the knowledge of age, training, rearing, etc. of different horses and their jockeys, he would be operating in the region of *risk*. And, if he does not have the knowledge about the horses and jockeys participating in the race, he would be regarded as operating in the area of *uncertainty*. But, if he has some knowledge about the horses and jockeys, it will be difficult to decide whether the person is operating in the area of risk or in the area of uncertainty.

Secondly, by considering profit as a reward exclusively for uncertainty bearing, Knight has implicitly accorded it (uncertainty bearing) the status of a factor of production whereas it is simply an element of real cost as distinguished from money cost. Therefore, uncertainty bearing cannot be accepted as a factor of production, and hence, the sole cause of profit.

Thirdly, Knight's attempt to explain profits only by 'uncertainty' makes his theory unconvincing if one examines it in the light of real experience of the business world. If his theory is accepted, it would mean that the greater the degree of uncertainty, the greater the profits, and vice versa. *But* there are enterprises, e.g. agriculture, which are known for their high uncertainty and low returns.

Schumpeter's Innovation Theory of Profit: Profit Is Reward for Innovations

The innovation theory of profit was developed by Joseph A. Schumpeter[10] in 1934. Throughout his life as an economist, he was preoccupied with the study of economic evolution and development in capitalist system. He was of the opinion that issues like interest, profit, trade cycles and many others were only incidental to a distinct process of economic development and the principles which could explain this process would also explain these economic variables. His theory of profit is, thus, embedded in his theory of economic development.

To explain the phenomenon of economic development (and therefore, of profit), Schumpeter starts from the state of stationary equilibrium which is characterized by full equilibrium in all the spheres. He assumes a closed, commercially organized, and a capitalist economy in which it is *legal to hold* private property and there are divisions of labour and free competition. Everybody sells all his products, and in so far as he himself consumes, he is his own customer. The productive services may also be included in the same category of marketable things. Anyone who wants to purchase the goods or productive services must also have his own products or services to offer. This is the case of a barter economy in which all goods and services are exchanged for one another. 'Hence, it follows that somewhere in the economic system a demand is, so to say, ready awaiting every supply, and nowhere in the system are there commodities without complements....'[11] Therefore, it follows that sellers of all the commodities also appear as buyers to acquire the goods. This maintains their consumption and also productive capacity in the next period at the existing level. As a result, there emerges, 'an unchanging economic process which flows on at constant rates in time and merely reproduces itself'.[12]

Under these conditions of stationary equilibrium, total receipts from the business are exactly equal to the total outlays—there is no profit. Profit can be made by introducing innovations in manufacturing and methods of supplying the goods. Innovations include

1. introduction of a new good or a new quality of good;
2. introduction of a new method of production;

3. opening up or finding out a new market;
4. finding and using new sources of raw material and
5. organizing the industry in a different and more efficient manner.

When an entrepreneur introduces an innovation, it generates a surplus over cost of innovation, provided following conditions are fulfilled:

1. When new supply comes forth as a result of innovation, the price of commodity does not fall to such an extent that it eliminates all gains from the larger product.
2. The unit cost of output with new technique is less than that of older methods.
3. The increase in demand for the productive services due to innovation does not lead to rise in average cost of production higher than the rise in revenue per unit.

If these conditions are fulfilled, the surplus realized becomes *ipso facto* a *net profit*. However, these profits exist only for a short period. This is so because when an entrepreneur introduces an innovation, others are likely to imitate it for its profitability. First a few and then many entrepreneurs follow the lead and produce the commodity by the same technique. This causes a keen competition for the productive inputs and services to be employed with the new techniques. The inputs supply remaining constant, factor prices tend to increase. As a result, cost of production increases. On the other hand, when other firms adopt the innovation, supply of goods and services increases resulting in a fall in their prices. Thus, on the one hand, cost per unit of output goes up and, on the other, revenue per unit decreases. Ultimately, a time comes when the difference between cost and receipts disappears and thus the profit disappears. In the process, however, the economy reaches a higher level of stationary equilibrium.

It is, however, quite likely that profit exists in spite of the process of profits being wiped out. Such profits are in the nature of *quasi-rent* arising due to some special characteristics of productive services. Furthermore, where profits arise due to factors like patents, trusts, cartels, etc. such profits would be in the nature of monopoly revenue rather than entrepreneurial profits.

It may be inferred from the above that *profit is the child as well as victim of economic development*. Economic development consists of increase in national output. When innovations occur the national output increases because the same output can be produced at lower costs, or what is the same thing, with the same amount of resources greater output can be produced. But producing at lower cost or producing more output with the same cost results in profits. Thus, *economic development gives birth to profits*. But, when other producers also adopt the technique introduced by the innovator, the total national output increases, i.e. economic development catches pace. The widespread use of innovation, however, wipes out the profits, as explained earlier. Hence, economic development itself is responsible for the disappearance of profits.

Criticism of Innovation Theory of Profit The major criticism against Schumpeter's innovation theory of profit is that it ignores the risk and uncertainty, the two major sources of profit as pointed out in the traditional theories of profits. Although in his book *Capitalism, Socialism and Democracy*, he admits that innovations are made by the risk-taking entrepreneurs, he ignores uncertainty altogether. Besides, it has also been argued that innovation is not the only function of the entrepreneurs. As delineated in the dynamic theory of profit, entrepreneur's functions also include organizational and co-ordination activities in response to the changing conditions and needs of the society.

DOES PROFIT ENTER THE COST OF PRODUCTION?

From the above description of profit theories, one is tempted to infer that profits do not enter the cost of production. In fact, profits enter the cost of production depends on the concept of profit under reference. Generally, two different concepts of profits are used in economic literature, viz. *normal profit* and *pure profit*. Before we answer the question, let us look into these concepts of profit.

The meaning of *pure profit* has already been explained. We describe briefly here the meaning of *normal profit. Normal profit* is the minimum rate of return that a firm must earn to remain in the industry. In other words, normal profit equals the *transfer earning*. Normal profit is also defined as the *wages of management*. Marshall calls it the supply price of average business ability. The concept of normal profit is related to the concept of long run. It refers to the long-term earning of the entrepreneurs under competitive conditions. Under competitive conditions, in the long run, the earnings of the entrepreneurs of an industry tend to be equal. Besides, the concept of normal profit is also related to the state of equilibrium in which there is no risk or uncertainty involved. Nor is there any tendency of firms to enter or to leave the industry. That is, in a static equilibrium, all firms earn only normal profit or what Knight calls, the wages of management.

Let us now return to the question whether profits enter the cost of production. When reference is made to normal profit, it does enter the cost of production, in the same way as rent, interest and wages. The simple reason is that normal profit is treated simply as the *wages of management*. But, when reference is made to *pure profit*, it does not enter the cost of production. Pure profit is rather a surplus over and above the cost of production.

REVIEW QUESTIONS AND EXERCISES

1. What is 'pure profit'? How does pure profit differ from gross profit?
2. 'The modern theory of profits regards the entrepreneur's contribution to the process of production as that of bearing non-insurable risks and uncertainties.' Explain and discuss.
3. 'Profit is a dynamic surplus.' Discuss.
4. Write a note on the following:
    (a) Uncertainty and profits.
    (b) Profits as a dynamic surplus.
5. Discuss Walker's theory of profit. How is this theory similar to the theory of rent?
6. What is Clark's theory of profit? What are the drawbacks of this theory?
7. What is the difference between a static and a dynamic economy? What are the generic changes in a dynamic world? How does dynamic system create opportunity for profit?
8. In a dynamic society profits appear to disappear. Explain the statement.
9. Explain Hawley's theory of profit? Why is his theory regarded as the theory of residual profit?
10. How is Schumpeter's innovation theory of profit different from Hawley's risk-bearing theory of profit? Which of these two theories of profit explain better the source of profit?
11. Profits are reward for uncertainty bearing. Discuss.
12. 'Profits are a reward for risk bearing, innovation or a result of monopoly power'. Comment.
13. 'There can be no profit in the stationary state.' Discuss.

14. 'Profit is an illusive sum which entrepreneurs grasp but cannot hold.' Explain.
15. Does profit enter the cost of production?

ENDNOTES

1. Dean, J. (1960), *Managerial Economics* (Bombay: Asia Publishing House), Indian Edn., p. 36.
2. Blaug, M., *op. cit.*, p. 467.
3. Defined as total sales revenue *minus* all contractual payments.
4. Lipsey, R.C. (1985), *An Introduction to Positive Economics* (London: Oxford), 5th Edn., pp. 208–209.
5. According to Lipsey, pure profit belongs to the owner of the firm 'as an additional return on the capital' (p. 209, fn. 4).
6. Walker, F.A. (1887), 'The Source of Business Profits', *The Quarterly Journal of Economics*, April.
7. Clark, J.B. (1965), *The Distribution of Wealth* (New York: Augustus M. Kelly). Reprinted in *Economic Classics.*
8. ——(1891), 'Distribution as Determined by Law of Rent', *The Quarterly Journal of Economics*, April.
9. Knight, F.H. (1957), *Risk, Uncertainty and Profit* (Boston and New York: Houghton Mifflin Co.).
10. Schumpeter, J.A. (1934), *Theory of Economic Development* (Cambridge, MA: Harvard University Press).
11. Schumpeter, J.A., *op. cit.*, p. 8.
12. ——(1939), *Business Cycles* (New York and London: McGraw Hill Book Company, Inc.).

FURTHER READINGS

Blaug, M. (1968), *Economic Theory in Retrospect* (London: Heinmann), pp. 466–477.
Clark, J.B. (1891), 'Distribution as Determined by Law of Rent', *The Quarterly Journal of Economics*, April.
Clark, J.B. (1965), *The Distribution of Wealth* (New York: Augustus M. Kelly).
Dean, J. (1960), *Managerial Economics* (Bombay: Asia Publishing House), Indian Edn., Chapter 1.
Hawley, F.B. (1893), 'The Risk Theory of Profit', *The Quarterly Journal of Economics*, July.
Knight, F.H. (1957), *Risk, Uncertainty and Profit* (Boston and New York: Houghton Mifflin Co.).
Schumpeter, J.A. (1938), *Theory of Economic Development* (Cambridge, MA: Harvard University Press).
Walker, F.A. (1887), 'The Source of Business Profits', *The Quarterly Journal of Economics*, April.

Chapter 12

Product Exhaustion Theorem

CHAPTER OBJECTIVES

Having elaborated on the various theories of factor price determination, we now move to look at the final form of the theory of distribution, i.e., theories and theorems that explain the determination of the factor share in the national output. This chapter tells you:

- What determined the factor share in the national output;
- Whether adding up factor shares give the national output;
- What is Euler's theorem and what it proves;
- What is Clark–Wicksteed–Walras theorem and what are its applications; and
- How change in relative factor prices affects the share of a factor in national output.

INTRODUCTION

In the preceding five chapters, we have discussed the marginal productivity theory of factor pricing – the general theory of factor pricing – and the various theories of factor pricing pertaining to different factors as formulated by the economists of different era. What these theories explain is the determination of price per unit of a factor, not the share of each factor in the total production. As mentioned earlier, the ultimate aim of the *theory of distribution* is to explain how the share of factors of production in total national output is determined. This part of the distribution theory is discussed in this chapter.

There has been a controversy on as to how the share of each factor in the national income is determined. The controversy is known as '*Adding-up Controversy*'. This controversy is here discussed first to focus on the nature of the problem. This is followed by Euler's theorem of distribution and then relative factor share. Finally, the issue of technological process and income distribution is discussed.

THE ADDING-UP PROBLEM

When marginal productivity theory gained the general acceptance by the end of the 19th century, a controversy arose whether distribution of national income among the various factors of production according to their marginal productivity was equitable and morally justifiable. In the course of the debate, there arose another question as to whether the sum total of labour and capital incomes based on their marginal productivity equals the total national product. Or, if each factor is paid the value of its marginal product (*VMP*), does this mean that the entire output is exhausted and nothing is left that falls into the hands of exploiting capitalist?

Some economists attempted to show that if each factor is paid a price equal to its *VMP*, the distribution of income under free enterprise (or capitalist) system must be equitable. Also, they demonstrated that if labour (*L*) and capital (*K*) are the only factors, then

$$Q = (MP_L)L + (MP_K)K \tag{12.1}$$

and, in terms of value,

$$P \cdot Q = (MP_L \cdot P)L + (MP_k \cdot P)K \tag{12.2}$$

where *P* is price of the product and *Q* denotes total output.

Eq. 12.2 proves that sum of the value paid to labour and capital on the basis of their marginal productivity equals the total national output. It can also be proved that since $MP_L \cdot P = VMP_L$ and $MP_k \cdot K = VMP_k$,

$$P \cdot Q = VMP_L + VMP_k \tag{12.3}$$

One of the earlier proofs to this identity was provided by a Swiss mathematician, Leonard Euler (1707–1783), which is known as Euler's theorem. Euler's theorem is discussed below.

EULER'S THEOREM

Euler's theorem demonstrates that if production function is homogeneous of degree one (which reveals constant returns to scale), then

$$Q = \frac{\partial Q}{\partial L} \cdot L + \frac{\partial Q}{\partial K} \cdot K \tag{12.4}$$

Since $\partial Q/\partial L = MP_L$ and $\partial Q/\partial K = MP_K$, Eq. (12.4) takes the form of Eq. 12.1, i.e.,

$$Q = MP_L \cdot L + MP_K \cdot K$$

This may be proved as follows. Suppose aggregate production function of an economy conforms to Cobb–Douglas production function of homogeneous type.[1] A production function, $Q = f(L, K)$, is homogeneous of degree *v* if

$$f(\lambda L, \lambda K) = \lambda^V \cdot f(L, K) \tag{12.5}$$

By differentiating Eq. (12.5) with respect to λ, we get

$$L\frac{df}{dL}+K\frac{df}{dK}$$
$$=v\lambda^{(v-1)}f(L,K)$$

When there is constant return to scale, $v = 1$, then Eq. (12.5) may be written as

$$L\,(MP_L) + K(MP_k) = f(L, K)$$

Thus,

$$Q = MP_L(\mathrm{L}) + MP_k(K)$$

Multiplying MP by the price of product, P, we get

$$P\cdot Q=(MP_L\cdot P)L+(MP_k\cdot P)K$$
$$=VMP_L\cdot L+VMP_k\cdot K$$

If $VMP_L = w$ and $VMP_k = r$, then

$$P\cdot Q = TR = w\cdot L + r\cdot K$$

It is thus proved that if each factor is paid a sum equal to its *VMP*, the total value of product is exhausted.

THE CLARK–WICKSTEED–WALRAS THEOREM

Euler's product exhaustion theorem, given above, assumes a homogeneous production function, i.e., constant returns to scale. Clark, Wicksteed and Walras have, however, shown jointly that the assumption of homogeneous production function is not necessary for the product exhaustion theorem. It holds for all types of production functions. Their theorem is known as Clark–Wicksteed–Walras product exhaustion theorem. A graphical proof of Clark–Wicksteed–Walras theorem of product exhaustion is given in Figure 12.1.

Let us assume (i) that an economy consists of n number of identical firms, (ii) each firm employs the same number of homogeneous labour (*OH*) and the same stock of capital and (iii) the marginal physical product of labour is given by the curve MP_L in Figure 12.1. Given the MP_L curve, the output of each firm is represented by the area *OMBH*. Suppose also that each labour is paid a real wage *OQ* (= *BH*) and that the total wages equal the area *OQBH*.

That is, the share of labour in total output (*OMBH*) is given by *OQBH*. The residual (*OMBH* – *OQBH* = *QMB*) goes to capital as the share of capital income. The rent so computed is merely a residual. But Clark and others provided that *QMB* is not merely a residual: it is also the marginal physical product of capital. By proving this, they had established their own product exhaustion theorem. Note that, given n firms, the total output of industry is $n \times OMBH$. Now suppose that the number of firms increases to $n + 1$, the number of workers remaining the same, i.e., $n \times OH$. The new firm gets its labour supply from the existing firms. Suppose $n \times OH$ workers are so distributed between $n + 1$ firms that each firm again has the same number of workers, say *OH*. Note that number of workers employed by each firm decreases from *OH* to *OL*, so that $(n + 1) \times OL = n \times OH$.

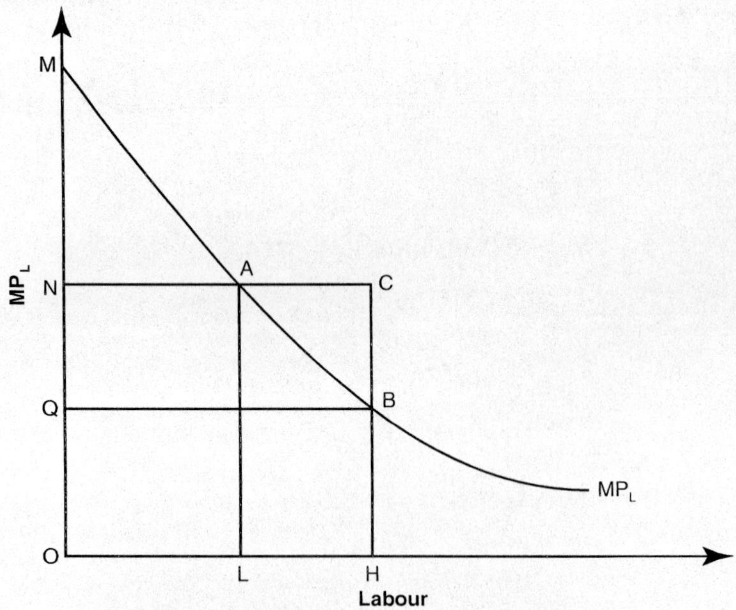

Figure 12.1 *Product Exhaustion Theorem*

Suppose each firm $n + 1$ employs OL workers and output per firm is $OMAL$. In that case, the total output of the industry can be worked out as

$$(n+1)\ OMAL = n \cdot OMAL + OMAL \tag{12.6}$$

The initial output of the industry with n firms may be written as

$$n(OMBH) = n(OMAL) + n(LABH) \tag{12.7}$$

The difference between Eqs. (12.6) and (12.7) is the marginal product of capital (MP_k). That is,

$$\begin{aligned} MP_K &= (n \cdot OMAL + OMAL) - (n \cdot OMAL - n \cdot LABH) \\ &= \text{OMAL} - n \cdot LABH \end{aligned} \tag{12.8}$$

As can be seen from Figure 12.1,

$$OMAL = NMA + ONAL \tag{12.9}$$

and

$$LABH = LACH - ABC \tag{12.10}$$

By substituting Eqs. (12.9) and (12.10) in Eq. (12.8), we get

$$\begin{aligned} MP_k &= NMA + ONAL - n(LACH - ABC) \\ &= NMA + ONAL - n \cdot LACH + n \cdot ABC \end{aligned} \tag{12.11}$$

Since $n \cdot LACH = ONAL$,[2] by substituting, we can write Eq. (12.11) as

$$\begin{aligned} MP_k &= NMA + ONAL - ONAL + n(ABC) \\ &= NMA + n(ABC) \end{aligned} \tag{12.12}$$

Consider the last term, $n(ABC)$. As $n \to \infty$, the share of each firm in the given supply of labour tends to be zero. Therefore, the last term $n(ABC) \to 0$. Consequently,

$$MP_k = NMA = \text{capital income}$$

It is the same *residual* as calculated earlier to show the capital income of each firm employing *OL* number of labour. Thus, Clark–Wicksteed–Walras theorem is proved.

CHANGE IN RELATIVE FACTOR SHARES AND INCOME DISTRIBUTION

In this section, we discuss how a *change* in relative factor prices affects the relative factor shares and income distribution. When relative factor prices change, one factor becomes relatively cheaper and the other relatively costlier. This impels the profit maximizing firms to substitute the cheaper factor for the costlier one. As a result, factor ratio changes. For example, suppose there are only two variable factors, labour (L) and capital (K), and factor ratio is given as K/L. This factor ratio changes at margin when one factor is substituted for another. When factor ratio changes, relative factor share in output also changes. The change in *relative factor* share depends on the *elasticity of factor substitution.* Let us now see how elasticity of factor substitution determines the factor share with change in factor prices.

The Elasticity of Factor Substitution and Relative Factor Shares

The extent to which relative factor share in income is affected by the change in relative factor prices depends on the *elasticity of factor substitution*, generally denoted by σ. The concept of the elasticity of factor substitution was developed by J.R. Hicks.[3] The elasticity of factor substitution is regarded as the foundation of the modern neo-classical theory of distribution and relative factor share. Ferguson[4] remarks that the concept of *elasticity of substitution* lies at the heart of the neo-classical theory of distribution. The *elasticity of substitution* (σ) is defined as

$$\sigma = \frac{\partial(K/L)/(K/L)}{\partial(MRTS)/(MRTS)} \tag{12.13}$$

Recall that in a perfectly competitive input market, a firm is in equilibrium where *MRTS* is equal to the factor-price ratio (w/r), i.e., where

$$MRTS_{L,K} = \frac{w}{r} \tag{12.14}$$

where w = price of labour (wage rate) and r = price of capital (interest).

Since at optimum combination of inputs, $MRTS = w/r$, the elasticity of factor substitution given in Eq. (12.13) can be expressed by substituting as

$$\sigma = \frac{\partial(K/L)/(K/L)}{\partial(w/r)/(w/r)} \tag{12.15}$$

The elasticity of substitution (σ) is always positive, though in some cases, $\sigma = 0$. Thus, *the value of σ ranges from zero to infinity*. The value of σ yields useful information regarding the degree of substitutability between the factors. If $\sigma = 0$, it means that substitution between labour and capital is impossible, i.e., the two factors can be used only in a fixed proportion. In that case, the isoquant curve is *L* shaped.

The positive range of σ may be classified and interpreted as follows:

1. $\sigma < 1$ means **Inelastic substitution:** the degree of substitutability between the two factors is very low.
2. $\sigma = 1$ means **Unit elasticity of substitution:** the two factors can be substituted at a constant rate for one another (see properties of Cobb–Douglas production function).
3. $\sigma > 1$ means **Highly elastic substitutability:** one factor can substitute another to a large extent.
4. $\sigma = \infty$ means **Perfect substitutability:** one factor can substitute another to any extent.

Let us now examine the relationship between the value of σ and the relative shares of factors in the total output. Consider the two-factor model in which the total income $P \cdot Q$ is the sum of labour share ($w \cdot L$) and capital share ($r \cdot K$). That is,

$$P \cdot Q = w \cdot L + r \cdot K \tag{12.16}$$

The relative share of *labour* in the total value of the output is given by

$$\frac{w \cdot L}{P \cdot Q}$$

Similarly, the relative share of capital in the total value of the output is given by

$$\frac{r \cdot K}{P \cdot Q}$$

Thus, the *ratio* of relative share of *L* and *K* in *P. Q* can be written as

$$= \frac{w \cdot L}{P \cdot Q} / \frac{r \cdot K}{P \cdot Q}$$

$$= \frac{w \cdot L}{r \cdot K} \tag{12.17}$$

$$= \frac{w/r}{K/L} \tag{12.18}$$

Equation (12.18) can be used to show the effect of change in relative factor price (w/r) on the relative shares of *L* and *K* in the value of total output.

Suppose w/r increases by 10 per cent, i.e., labour becomes costlier by 10 per cent. This will lead to a substitution of capital (the relatively cheaper factor) for labour (the relatively costlier factor). The extent of substitution depends on the value of σ (i.e., the elasticity of substitution). Suppose $\sigma = 0.5$, i.e., $\sigma < 1$. Then a 10 per cent increase in w/r will result in a 5 per cent increase in the capital–labour ratio (K/L). This will alter the relative shares of K and L.

The *new relative factor shares* can be obtained as

$$\left(\frac{w \cdot L}{r \cdot K}\right)^{*} = \frac{(w/r)}{(K/L)} \cdot \frac{(1+0.10)}{(1+0.05)}$$

$$= \frac{1.10}{1.05} \cdot \frac{(w/r)}{(K/L)} \tag{12.19}$$

where (∗) denotes the new relative factor share.

Equation (12.19) reveals that

$$\left(\frac{wL}{rK}\right)^{*} < \left(\frac{wL}{rK}\right)$$

It means that new relative factor–share ratio is greater than the initial ratio. By the same reasoning it can be proved that if $\sigma > 1$ and other things remain the same, then

$$\left(\frac{wL}{rK}\right)^{*} < \left(\frac{wL}{rK}\right)$$

There is a two-way causation in the change in relative factor share caused by a change in relative factor prices. Changes in the relative supply position of factors change the relative factor prices which, in turn, change the factor ratios depending on the value of σ. This leads to a change in the relative shares on the factors in the total output. Thus, the change in relative factor prices causes change in the share of each factor in the national output. It is thus clear that the concept of elasticity of substitution plays a very important role in neo-classical theory of income distribution.

TECHNOLOGICAL PROGRESS AND INCOME DISTRIBUTION

So far, the analysis of factor price determination and relative factor shares has been based on a tacit assumption that the production function is given, and production technology remains unchanged over the reference period. In the real world, however, technological progress does take place. Technological progress means that a given quantity of output can be produced with less quantity of inputs or a given quantity of inputs can produce a larger quantity of output. This means a downward shift in the production function (i.e., isoquant) towards the origin.

Technological progress is graphically shown in Figure 12.2. A given level of output is shown by isoquants I, I' and I''. That is, all the three isoquants—I, I' and I''—represent the same level of output.

The downward shift in an isoquant from the position of I to I' and from I' to I'' means that a given level of output can be produced with smaller quantities of labour and capital represented by points a, b and c. The slope of the ray, OP, shows the constant capital labour ratio.

According to J.R. Hicks, technological progress may be classified as (i) *neutral technological progress,* (ii) *capital deepening* and (iii) *labour deepening technological progress.*

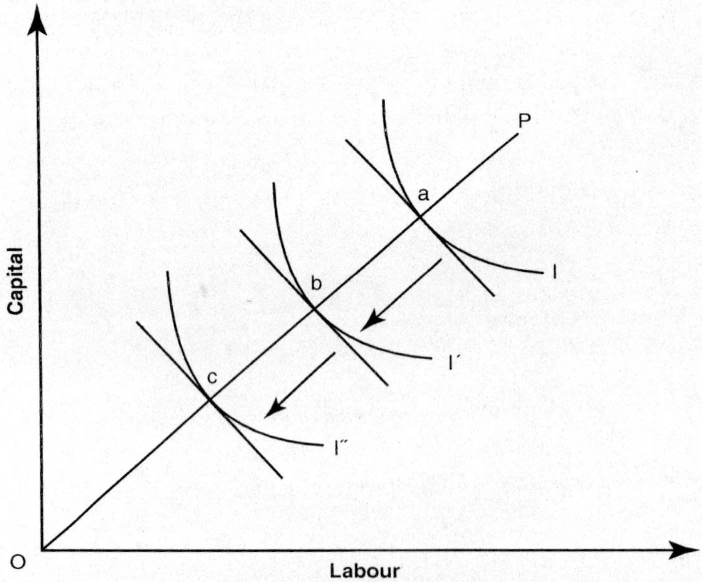

Figure 12.2 *Neutral Technological Progress*

Neutral Technological Progress

Technological progress is neutral if, at constant *K/L*, the marginal rate of technical substitution of capital for labour (i.e., $MRTS_{k,\,L}$) remains constant. The neutral technological progress is illustrated in Figure 12.2. At each equilibrium point, $MRTS_{L,\,k} = w/r$. When technological progress is neutral, both *K/L* and *w/r* remain unchanged.[5] It follows that relative factor share remains unchanged under neutral technological progress.

Capital Deepening

Technological progress leading to capital deepening is illustrated in Figure 12.3. Technological progress is capital deepening when, at a constant capital/labour ratio (*K/L*), $MRTS_{k,\,l}$ declines. It implies that, MP_k increases at constant *K/L*, relative to MP_1. Therefore, at each equilibrium point, *w/r* declines, as *r* increases relative to *w*.

Consequently, the relative factor share changes in favour of *K*. That is, share of capital in the total output increases while that of labour decreases. This change indicates the capital deepening.

Labour Deepening

Technological progress is labour deepening when, at a given *K/L*, the $MRTS_{l,\,k}$ increases. Labour deepening technological progress is illustrated in Figure 12.4. Following the above reasoning, it can be proved that under labour-intensive technological progress, the share of labour in the total output increases while that of capital decreases.

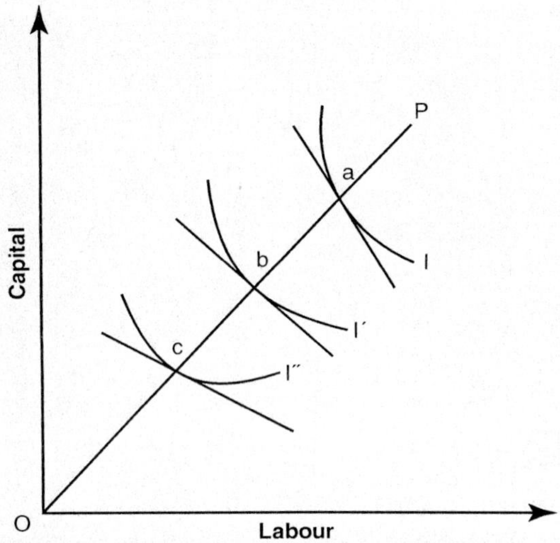

Figure 12.3 *Capital Deepening Technological Progress*

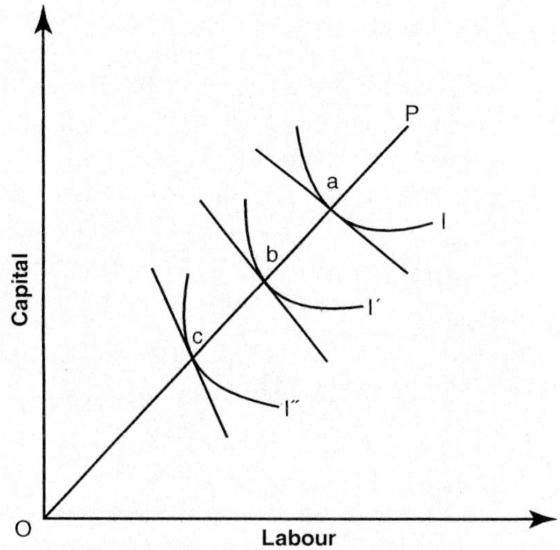

Figure 12.4 *Labour Deepening*

REVIEW QUESTIONS AND EXERCISES

1. What is adding-up controversy? How does Euler's theorem resolve the controversy?
2. State and explain Euler's theorem? How does it explain the distribution of national income?
3. The marginal productivity theory of distribution states that if all of productive agents are rewarded in accordance with their marginal product, then the total output will be exhausted. Explain.
4. What is Clark–Wicksteed–Walras theorem of output distribution? How does it differ from Euler's theorem?
5. Assuming a homogeneous production function of Cobb–Douglas type, prove that if factors of production are paid according to their marginal value of productivity, the output will be exhausted.
6. How does a change in the elasticity of factor substitution affect the relative share of factors in the total output? Suppose elasticity of substitution equals 0.5, and wages/interest ratio changes by 10 per cent, what will be the change in the share of labour in the total output?
7. What is meant by the change in relative factor price? How does the change in relative factor price change the factor share in the national output?
8. What is meant by technological progress? How does technological progress affect the relative share of labour and capital in national output?
9. What are the symptoms of neutral technological progress? Suppose technological progress in a country is of neutral nature, how does it affect the factor share in national output?

ENDNOTES

1. For a detailed discussion on Cobb–Douglas production function, see Ch. 12, sec, 12.9.v.
2. It follows from the equal division of labour, that is, $n(LH) = OH$. Therefore $(LH \cdot AL) = LACH$ and $n \cdot LACH = ONAL$.
3. Hicks, J.R. (1963), *The Theory of Wages* (London: Macmillan and Co. Ltd.), 2nd Edn.
4. Ferguson, F.E., *Microeconomic Theory* (Illionosis: Richard D. Irwin, Inc.), 2nd Edn., p. 416.
5. It is evident from Figure 12.2 that budget lines are parallel.

FURTHER READINGS

Blaug, M. (1968), *Economic Theory in Retrospect* (London: Heinmann), pp. 466–77.

Clark, J.B. (1891), 'Distribution as Determined by Law of Rent', *Qtly. Jl. Eco.*, (April).

——— (1965), *The Distribution of Wealth* (New York: Augustus M. Kelly).

Dean, J. (1960), *Managerial Economics* (Bombay: Asia Publishing House), Indian Edn., Chapter 1.

Howley, F.B. (1893), 'The Risk Theory of Profit', *Q. J. E.*, (July).

Knight, F.H. (1957), *Risk, Uncertainty and Profit* (Boston, NY: Houghton Mifflin Co.).

Schumpeter, J.A. (1938), *Theory of Economic Development* (Cambridge, MA: Harvard University Press).

Walker, F.A. (1887), 'The Source of Business Profits', *Qtly. Jl. Eco.*, (April).

Part III

General Equilibrium and Welfare Economics

Chapter 13

General Equilibrium Analysis

CHAPTER OBJECTIVES

We have so far discussed the conditions of *partial equilibrium analysis*. In this chapter, we proceed to discuss the general equilibrium analysis. This chapter helps us learn:

- What is the meaning and purpose of general equilibrium;
- How all the consumers of all the products reach the state of equilibrium simultaneously;
- How all the producers of all the goods reach the state of equilibrium simultaneously;
- How all the factors of production attain equilibrium in all professions and in all the industries at the same point of time; and
- How an economy reaches the state of general equilibrium.

INTRODUCTION

The economic analysis that we have presented so far is called *partial equilibrium analysis*. It is partial in the sense that the economic analysis was related to the analysis of a micro part of the economy. It analyses the behaviour of an individual decision-making unit – a consumer, a producer and an individual factor owner. In market analysis, it explains the price determination of a single commodity and a single production factor. Be it the analysis of the decision-making behaviour of a consumer or of a producer or of a factor owner or the analysis of a product and factor price determination, the entire analysis is based on the assumption that *all other factors remain constant* or the change in other factors, if any, do not affect the decision of the decision maker. For example, in the analysis of consumer equilibrium, it is assumed that consumer's decision regarding the consumption of a commodity is not affected by change in prices of other goods, his income and so on. Similarly, in the analysis of firm's equilibrium, it is assumed that the change in demand, supply and price of other products does not affect the firm's choice of equilibrium price and output. This is justifiable in building microeconomic models and in the formulation of microeconomic theories. But this makes only a *partial analysis* of the economy, not of the economic system as a whole.

In reality, however, markets are *interrelated and interdependent. In fact, in an economy, everything depends on everything else.* A change in one product or factor affects market, directly or indirectly, the equilibrium of all related markets. For example, spread of cable TV in India, particularly in major cities, has reduced the demand for cinema tickets; introduction of mobile phones has affected the demand for government telephone services; increase in petrol price affects the demand for car and so on. This kind of inter relationship between the markets is not captured in *partial equilibrium analysis*. As a matter of methodological necessity, partial equilibrium analysis assumes away relationships and interdependence between the economic units and markets by *ceteris paribus assumption*. To that extent, partial equilibrium analysis presents a microscopic picture of the economy.

In contrast, *general equilibrium analysis* aims at analysing working of economic system as a whole in an integrated manner by recognizing and integrating interrelationships and mutual interdependence between the input and output markets. The basic purpose of *general equilibrium analysis* is to develop an analytical framework and specify the conditions for the general equilibrium in the economy. *General equilibrium* can be defined as *a state of economy in which all individual economic units–consumers, producers and factor owners–and all markets are in equilibrium*. An economy is said to be equilibrium when all economic units are simultaneously in equilibrium, each firm is in equilibrium, each product and factor market is in equilibrium, i.e. quantity demanded is equal to quantity supplied in each product and factor market. When an economy attains and remains in this state of general equilibrium over a period, the economy is said to be in *static general equilibrium*. The conditions for static general equilibrium are discussed in a section ahead.

In this chapter, we present elementary treatment of the *general equilibrium analysis*. Dealing with general equilibrium analysis at length falls outside of the purview of this book. We will, therefore, confine to the basic elements of general equilibrium analysis. We will first show the interrelationship and interdependence of different markets is a simple model. This will be followed by a general equilibrium analysis of production and exchange. We will finally present a simplified Walrasian general equilibrium model.

INTERRELATIONSHIP AND INTERDEPENDENCE OF MARKETS

Interrelationship between the Markets

To appreciate the significance of general equilibrium analysis, it is essential to understand the interrelatedness and interdependence of the various markets of the economic system. Suppose demand for housing increases, as it is happening in Delhi and Mumbai, supply falling short of demand, at some point of time in an economy. Realty prices and house rents go up and profitability of the housing industry increases. This invites new investment in the housing industry. Therefore, the demand for land, labour, capital and also the demand for construction materials—steel, cement, bricks, timber and paints increases. In order to meet the increasing demand the firms producing intermediate goods increase their demand for factor inputs—land, labour and capital. Consequently, supply of houses increases, on the one hand, and larger factor incomes flow to the households, on the other. When household income increases, demand for other consumer goods and services increases and creates another chain of action and reaction between household and product markets, and between product markets and factor markets. The whole economic system functions in a complex manner. The complexity is further increased due to change in relative prices of products and factors which causes, respectively, product substitution and factor substitution. Such changes affect the markets of substitute goods. The various markets, thus, act and react in response to changes in the interconnected markets in innumerable ways. A simple case of interrelatedness of markets is illustrated through a simple model presented in Figure 13.1.

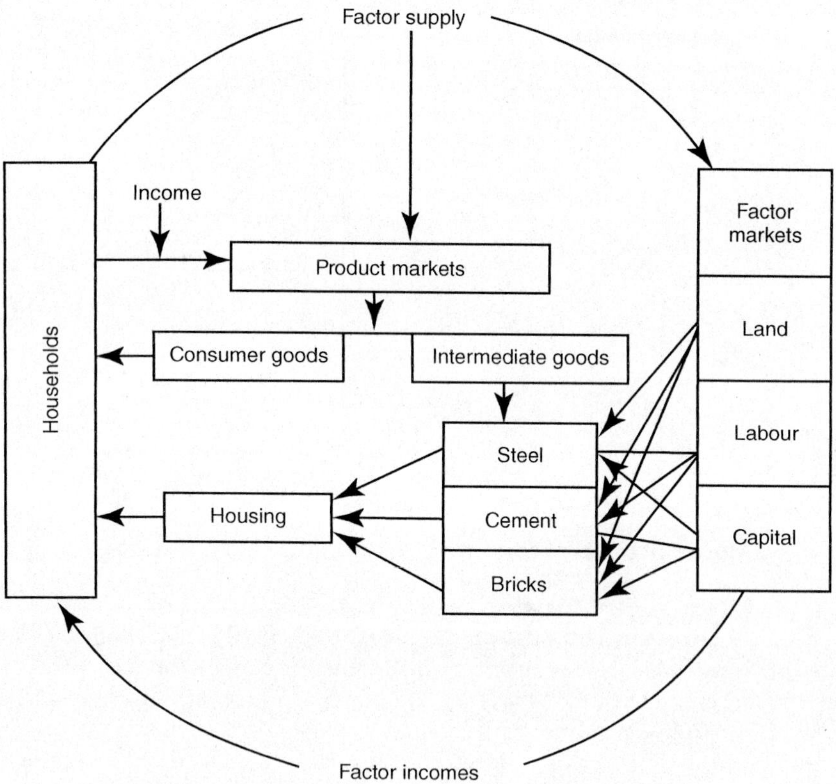

Figure 13.1 *Interrelationship between Markets*

Interdependence of Markets

We have shown above, by using a simple example of demand for housing, how markets are interrelated and interconnected. We will now show the *interdependence of markets* by using a simple example of two substitute goods, tea and coffee. Figure 13.2 illustrates the interdependence of tea and coffee markets. It shows how change in price of tea affects the price and production of coffee. Panel (a) of Figure 13.2, presents demand and supply conditions of the tea market and panel (b) those of the coffee market. Suppose, at a point of time, tea market is in equilibrium at point *A*, the point of intersection between the demand curve D_T and supply curve S_T. Equilibrium price of tea (per kg) is determined at P_{T1} with demand and supply at OT_2. Similarly, suppose coffee market is in equilibrium at point *E*, the point of intersection between coffee demand curve D_c and supply curve S_c. At equilibrium, price of coffee (per kg) is determined at P_{c1} and output at OC_1.

When two markets are in equilibrium, any exogenous change in any one of the two markets will disturb the equilibrium of the other market. To illustrate this, let us suppose that government imposes excise duty on tea so that tea supply curve, S_T, shifts upward to S'_T. With the shift in the supply curve, tea market equilibrium shifts from point *A* to point *B* which determines new equilibrium tea price at P_{T2} with tea demand and supply at OT_1. In partial equilibrium analysis, market analysis ends here. But, general equilibrium analysis looks into the effect of changes in tea market and the coffee market.

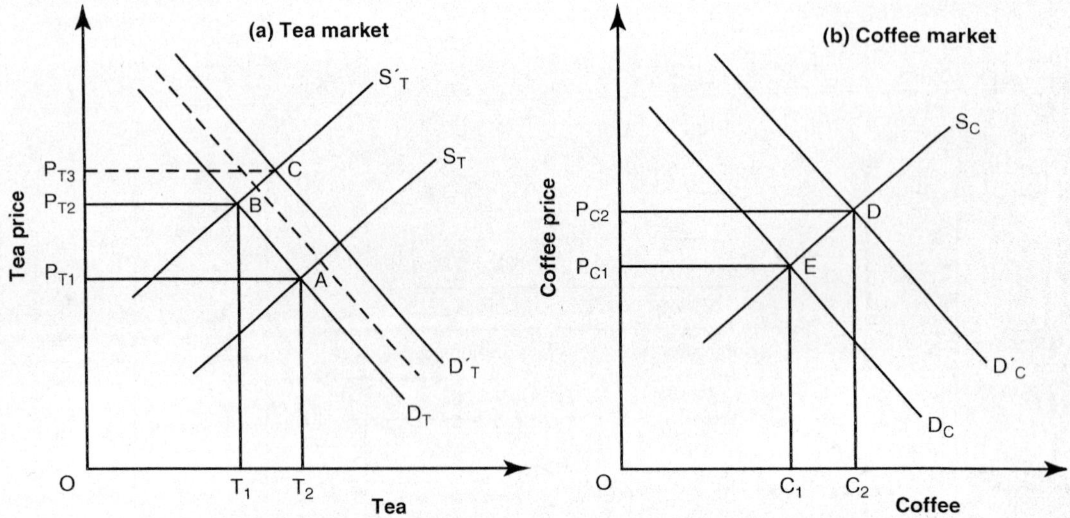

Figure 13.2 *Interdependence of Markets: Tea and Coffee*

How does Excise Duty on Tea Affect the Coffee Market? Since coffee is a substitute for tea, a rise in tea price causes a substitution effect which shifts a part of demand from tea to coffee. As a result, the demand for coffee increases. As a result, coffee demand curve shifts from D_c to D'_c as shown in panel (b) of Figure 13.2. Consequently, coffee price increases from P_{c1} to P_{c2}. Recall that the shift in coffee demand curve and increase in coffee price depend on cross elasticity of demand for coffee. The process of action and reaction between these two markets does not end here. When coffee price increases to P_{c2}, some consumers find it relatively costlier than tea even with tax. Therefore, they switch over back to tea. Consequently, tea demand curve shifts upwards, say to D'_T, pushing tea price further up to P_{T3}. The rise in tea price will send some consumers back to coffee. As a result, tea demand curve shifts downwards as shown by the dashed demand curve in panel (a) of Figure 13.2. This process continues until both tea and coffee markets reach their final point of equilibrium.

This description shows the interdependence of the markets. The process of adjustment discussed above fits to all the goods and services. The process of market adjustment in both product and related input markets continues until the whole economy reaches the point of general equilibrium. The final conditions of the general equilibrium are given in the following section.

THE CONDITIONS OF STATIC GENERAL EQUILIBRIUM

Before we proceed to discuss how an economy reaches the state of general equilibrium, let us first look at the conditions of static general equilibrium with respect to consumers, producers and factor owners.

The Condition for Consumers' General Equilibrium

Recall from the analysis of consumer's equilibrium that a consumer with a given income and prices of goods and services is in equilibrium when he/she allocates his/her total consumption expenditure in such proportions that he/she derives the same marginal utility (MU) per unit of expenditure from each commodity. This condition for consumer's equilibrium is expressed as follows

$$\frac{MU_1}{P_1} = \frac{MU_2}{P_2} = \frac{MU_3}{P_3} = \ldots = \frac{MU_n}{P_n}$$

This condition applies to each and every consumer. When all the consumers satisfy this condition, they are in general equilibrium.

The Condition for Production General Equilibrium

The condition for general equilibrium in the production sector requires that, given the technology and input prices, inputs (labour and capital) are so combined in production of each good that ratio of *marginal revenue productivity* (MRP) of inputs is equal to their factor-price ratio ($P_L P_k$) in case of all the goods. The MRP is given by MP_L/MP_k. Thus, the general equilibrium condition for production can be expressed as

$$\frac{MRP_L}{MRP_K} = \frac{P_L}{P_K}$$

For the production sector to be in general equilibrium, this condition must apply to the production of all goods.

The Condition for Producers' General Equilibrium

According to the theory of firm's equilibrium, a firm is in equilibrium where its marginal revenue (MR) is equal to the marginal cost (MC) of its product with increasing MC, of course. That is, a firm is in equilibrium where its

$$MR = MC$$

When all the firms of the economy satisfy this equilibrium condition, the producers are in general equilibrium.

The Condition for Factor Owners' General Equilibrium

As discussed earlier (Chapters 7–9), a factor owner is in equilibrium where its *marginal revenue productivity* (MRP) is equal to its *opportunity* cost (OC), i.e. a factor owner is in equilibrium where its

$$MRP = OC = MC \text{ of' factor}$$

When all these equilibrium conditions are satisfied, the economy is in the state of general equilibrium. Of these general equilibrium conditions, *the general equilibrium in exchange* between two consumers and *general equilibrium in production* of two goods are the most important aspects the general equilibrium analysis. Therefore, these two cases are discussed below in detail by using *Edgeworth box diagram.*

GENERAL EQUILIBRIUM IN EXCHANGE

Having shown market interdependence, let us now discuss the general equilibrium in a sectoral framework. We will first show the *general equilibrium in exchange*, i.e. exchange of goods between the individuals, so that each has the same utility from the goods. The general equilibrium in exchange requires that consumer goods are so distributed between the consumers that each consumer is in equilibrium with *MRS* being equal to commodity price ratio and that the total product is exhausted. For the purpose of our analysis, we will use a simple case of two consumers (*A* and *B*) and two goods (food and clothing). A popular technique used to show the general equilibrium in exchange (and also in production) is *Edgeworth box diagram*. We will first describe the formation of the *Edgeworth box diagram*[1] then use it to show how consumers (*A* and *B*) arrive at the general equilibrium.

Edgeworth Box Diagram

The Edgeworth box diagram is a graphical technique for illustrating optimum allocation of a given quantity of two goods between two consumers and of a given quantity of two inputs between two industries. Here, we use this technique to illustrate the general equilibrium in exchange—the exchange of two goods by two individuals, so that both are in equilibrium and total utility is maximized. Let us first show the formation and the application of the Edgeworth box diagram.

Figure 13.3 illustrates the Edgeworth box assuming that there are only two goods, *food* and *clothing*, and two consumers, *A* and *B*, and that the maximum quantity of food and clothing are given. In the Edgeworth box, the point of origin for consumer *A* is given at south-west end by O_A and for consumer *B* at the north-east end by O_B. Horizontal axis measures the maximum quantity of food, and vertical axis measures the maximum quantity of clothing. What is important to note is that for consumer *B*, quantity of food is to be read leftwards from the point of origin O_B as shown by the arrow and the quantity of clothing is to be read downwards from the point of origin. In case of consumer *A*, quantities are measured in the usual manner. The terminal points of the box mark the maximum availability of the two goods.

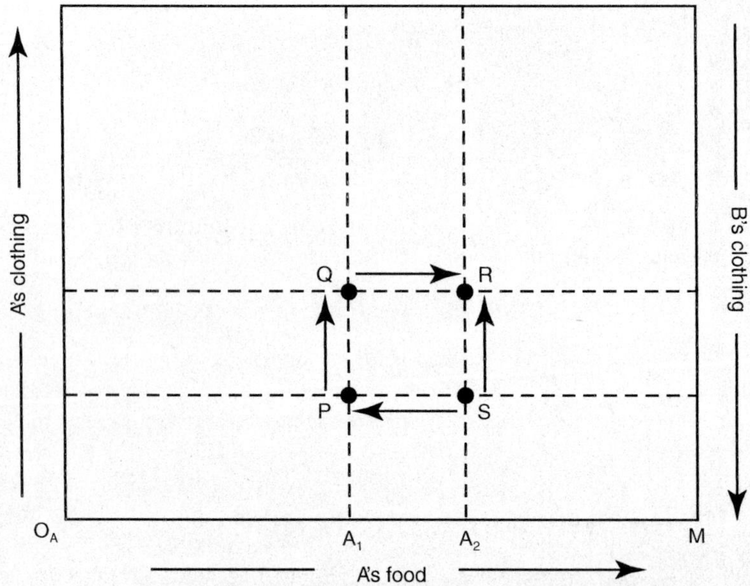

Figure 13.3 *Exchange in Edgeworth Box*

Each point inside the box shows a combination of food and clothing available to consumers *A* and *B*. For example, at point *S*, consumer *A* has $O_A A_2$ of food and SA_2 of clothing, and consumer *B* has SB_1 of clothing and $O_B B_1$ of food. With this distribution, the total stock of food and clothing is exhausted. The consumers can move to any other point only by exchanging food and clothing between them. For example, if *A* has to move from point *S* to point *Q*, he will have to exchange *SP* of food for *PQ* of clothing. After the exchange, both *A* and *B* are placed at point *Q*. This exchange possibility shows that, given their choices and preferences, consumers *A* and *B* may reach a point where they have no incentive for further exchange of the goods.

It is *important* to note here that consumers' shift from corner points and from border lines towards a point in the central area makes them both better off. Thus, consumers' shift from *S* to *Q* makes them both better off. However, Figure 13.3 does not reveal whether both the consumers are in equilibrium at point *Q*, or, in other words, it does not show whether there is general equilibrium. This task is accomplished below.

The Condition for General Equilibrium in Exchange

The general equilibrium in exchange requires that food and clothing are so allocated between *A* and *B* that *marginal rate of substitution* between the two goods is the same for both the consumers, i.e.

$$MRS^A_{f,c} = MRS^B_{f,c}$$

This condition is illustrated in Figure 13.4 by introducing *indifference curves* to the Edgeworth box diagram. *A*'s indifference curve are drawn in an usual manner whereas *B*'s indifference curves are drawn up side down with base O_B. An alternative way can be to draw *B*'s indifference map in the usual manner and rotate it by 180° and then superimpose it over *A*'s indifference map with the ends of axes meeting

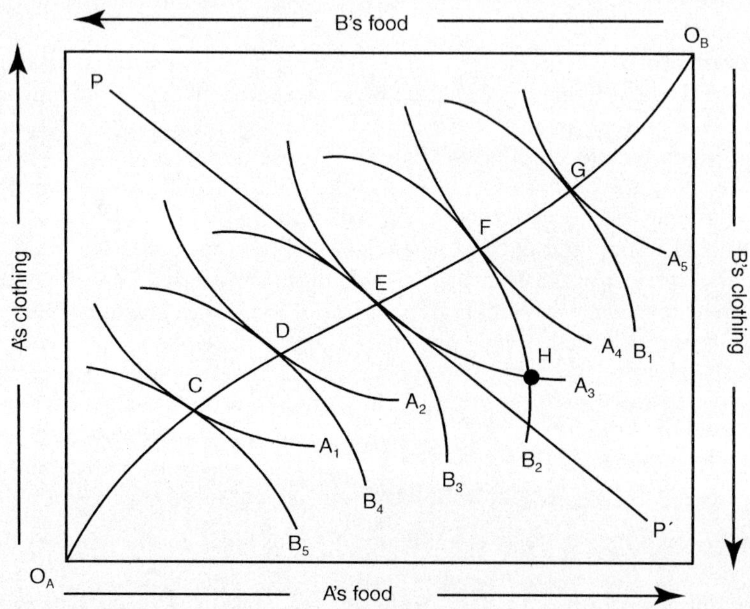

Figure 13.4 *Edgeworth Box Diagram: General Equilibrium in Exchange*

together. This makes the *Edgeworth's box diagram* with indifference curves of consumers *A* and *B*, as shown in Figure 13.4. This Edgeworth box diagram is called *Edgeworth's exchange box diagram*.

Figure 13.4 is full of *A*'s and *B*'s indifference curves but only five indifference curves each of consumers *A* and *B* have been used to show the method of locating point of general equilibrium. Note that each indifference curve of *A* is tangent to one of the indifference curves of *B*. The equilibrium condition of consumers *A* and *B* (i.e. $MRS^A_{F,C} = MRS^B_{F,C}$) is satisfied at the points of tangency between *A*'s and *B*'s indifference curves. By joining the points of tangency *C*, *D*, *E*, *F* and *G* by a curve and extending it to the points of origin, we get a curve called the *contract curve*. The *contract curve* is a locus of points that gives the pathway of the general equilibrium in exchange of food and clothing between *A* and *B*.

Efficient Allocation of Goods

The contract curve O_AO_B in Figure 13.4 gives not only the possible points of general equilibrium but also the points of efficient allocation of the two goods between consumers *A* and *B*. The efficient allocation of goods requires that goods are so distributed between the two consumers that no consumer can be made better off without making the other worse off. This condition is not satisfied at any other point than the points on the *contract curve*. For example, point *H*, the point of intersection between *A*'s indifference curve A_3 and *B*'s indifference curve B_2 satisfies the equilibrium condition as at this point $MRS^A_{F,C} = MRS^B_{F,C}$. However, such points are *not the point of efficient allocation* of food and clothing between *A* and *B* for it is always possible at such points to make one consumer better off without making the other worse off. For example, consumer *A* can be moved on to a higher indifference curve A_4 along the curve *HF* keeping *B* on her indifference curve B_2. Similarly, *B* can be moved to a higher indifference curve B_3 along the curve *HE* keeping *A* on his indifference curve A_3. But, once they reach any point on the *contract curve*, say, point *C*, *D*, *E* or any other point, one cannot be made better off by exchange of goods without making the other one worse off. Thus, it is only the *contract curve* which gives the efficient allocation of the two goods between *A* and *B*.

It is *important* to note here that the *contract curve* gives only the possible points of efficient allocation, i.e. the point of general equilibrium in exchange between two goods, with price and income distribution unknown. The movement from point O_A towards point O_B along the contract curve shows increase in total utility of consumer *A* and decrease in total utility of consumer *B*. Similarly, movement from point O_B towards point O_A along the contract curve shows increase in total utility of consumer *B* and decrease in total utility of consumer *A*. *The contract curve does not give the unique point of most efficient allocation* of the two goods, i.e. the point that maximizes the utility of both the consumers simultaneously. This point will be discussed further in the next chapter. For our limited purpose here, however, the most efficient allocation can be obtained by assuming (i) price line or the budget line to be given by the line *PP*′, and (ii) both the consumers have the same income and their total income is sufficient to buy the entire output. Under these assumptions, point *E* is the point at which indifference curves of *A* and *B* are simultaneously tangent with the price line or the budget line. Therefore, point *E* is the point of most efficient allocation of the two goods. Point *E* satisfies the equilibrium condition given as

$$MRS^A_{f,c} = MRS^B_{f,c} = P_F/P_C$$

where P_F = price of food, P_C = price of clothing and P_F/P_C is given by the slope of the curve *PP*′ in Figure 13.4.

This illustration of Edgeworth's box diagram shows how total social utility, or what is called social welfare, can be maximized by exchanging consumer goods between the individuals.

GENERAL EQUILIBRIUM IN PRODUCTION

The condition for the general equilibrium in production is that factor inputs are so allocated among the industries that *marginal rate of technical substitution* (*MRTS*) between the inputs is the same for all the industries. The method of analysing general equilibrium in production is essentially similar to one used in general equilibrium analysis of exchange. The technique used is the same, i.e. the Edgeworth box diagram called *Edgeworth production box diagram*. The general equilibrium in production is analysed under the following simplifying assumptions:

1. There are only two consumer goods, e.g. food (F) and clothing (C);
2. There are only two inputs, labour (L) and capital (K), available in fixed supply;
3. Input prices, i.e. price of labour (P_L) and price of capital (P_K), are given and
4. Production technology is given.

Given the assumptions, we now introduce Edgeworth production box diagram showing possible allocations of labour and capital to the production of food and clothing industries. The Edgeworth production box diagram for the purpose is illustrated in Figure 13.5. The method of making Edgeworth production box is similar to Edgeworth exchange box diagram. In Figure 13.5, point O_F marks the origin of food production and point O_C that of cloth production. The horizontal axis measures the units of labour, and vertical axis measures the units of capital used in production of food. In case of clothing production, however, labour is read leftwards from the point origin O_C and capital downwards, as shown by the arrows.

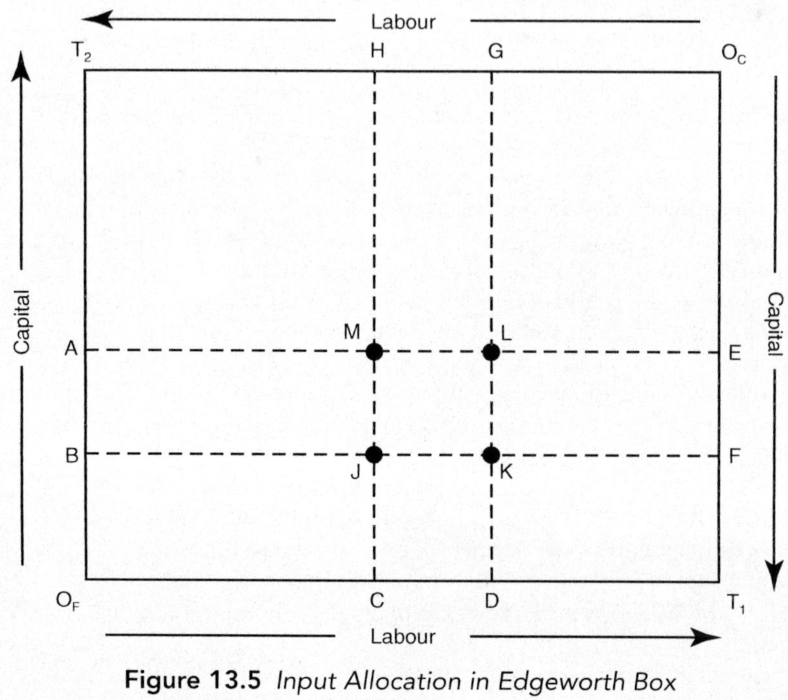

Figure 13.5 *Input Allocation in Edgeworth Box*

Each point inside the box shows all the possible combinations of labour and capital that can be used in the production of food and clothing. For example, point M means that O_FC units of labour and O_FA units of capital are available for food production. Given the labour–capital combination for food production, the remaining labour ($CT_1 = O_CH$) and capital ($O_CE = HM$) go to production of clothing. In other words, with reference to point M, labour–capital combination available for production of clothing is given as O_CH units of labour and O_CE units of capital. It can be verified from the figure that with these combinations of labour and capital for food and clothing production, total labour and capital are fully employed.

Figure 13.5 shows also that if more of labour and capital is used for any one of the products, less of them will be available for the other commodity. For example, movement from point M to K means that more of labour (JK) and less of capital (JM) are allocated to food production and share of clothing in labour and capital changes to the same extent. Besides, the figure shows also the possibility of substitution between labour and capital. For example, movement from point K to M implies substitution of JK of labour for JM of capital in food production. One can similarly locate a number of points inside the box and examine their implications with reference to one another.

The Condition for General Equilibrium in Production

As mentioned above, the general equilibrium in production requires that factor inputs are so distributed among the various industries that their marginal productivity in each industry is the same and each industry produces maximum output. The technical condition for general equilibrium in production is that *marginal rate of technical substitution* ($MRTS$) between the inputs in each industry is the same. With reference to our two-industry-and-two-input model, the condition for general equilibrium in production can be specified as follows:

$$MRTS_{L,K}^{F} = MRTS_{L,K}^{C}$$

The $MRTS$ is given by the slope of the *production isoquants*, given the production function. To show the general equilibrium in production, we need therefore to introduce isoquants to Figure 13.5. It may be recalled here that Figure 13.5 shows only the possible combinations of inputs (labour and capital) to produce a certain quantity of food and clothing—it does not show the quantity combination of food and clothing that can be produced with different combinations of inputs. The introduction of isoquants to the Edgeworth production box diagram reveals both possible input combinations and the corresponding production of food and clothing. This is accomplished in Figure 13.6. Note that the isoquants pertaining to food production are shown in the usual manner whereas those pertaining to clothing production are shown in an inverted form (as in case of indifference curves in Figure 13.4). Isoquants F_1, F_2, F_3 and F_4 represent food production and, isoquants C_1, C_2, C_3 and C_4 represent production of clothing.

Given the isoquants, various combinations of inputs and corresponding production of each commodity can be found in Figure 13.6. For example, point A shows that if L_F units of labour and K_F units of capital are employed in food production, then F_1 quantity of food can be produced. Reading the diagram from origin O_C tells that L_C units of labour and K_C units of capital can produce C_4 units of clothing.

Having explained the properties of Edgeworth production box diagram, we return to the question how general equilibrium in production is determined. The general equilibrium condition for production, i.e. $MRTS_{L,K}^{F} = MRTS_{L,K}^{C}$ is given by the points of tangency between the isoquants and at the points of their intersection. However, only the points of tangency, e.g. points A, B and C in Figure 13.6 represent the efficient allocation of labour and capital in production of food and clothes. Although the

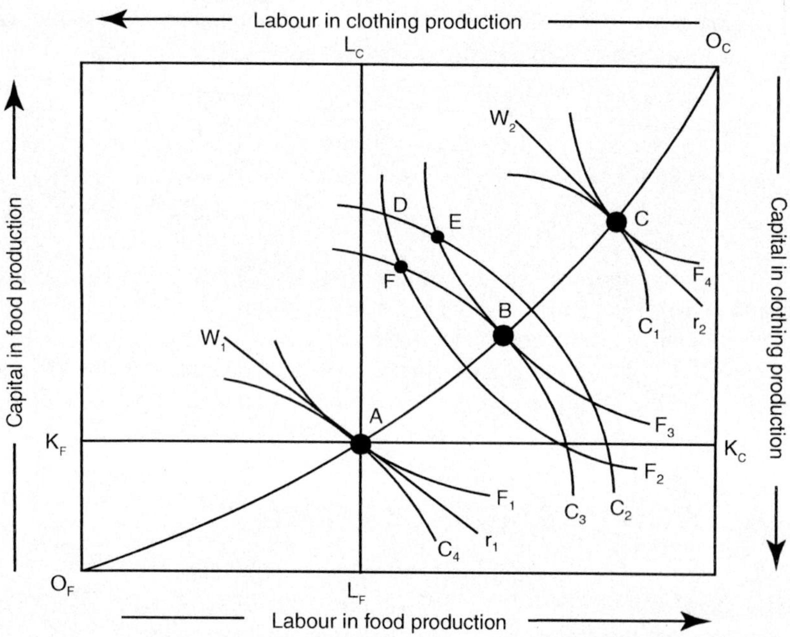

Figure 13.6 *General Equilibrium in Production*

general equilibrium condition is satisfied also at point *D*, this point does not represent an efficient allocation of resources because production of food (or clothing) can be increased by reallocating labour and capital without reducing the production of clothing (or food). For example, if labour and capital are so reallocated that point *E* is reached, production of food increases from isoquant F_2 to F_3, production of clothes remaining the constant at C_2. Similarly, if resources are reallocated as indicated by point *F*, production of clothes increases from isoquant C_2 to C_3, production of food remaining constant at isoquant F_2. Note that an efficient reallocation of labour and capital between food and clothing production will finally lead to point *B*. By joining the tangential points from origin O_F to O_C, e.g. points *A*, *B* and *C*, we get the *production contract curve*. The production contract curve gives all the possible combinations of labour and capital and the corresponding output of food and clothing. *Each point on the production contract curve represents efficient production and gives the point of general equilibrium in production.*

Producer's Equilibrium in a Competitive Input Market

The *production contract curve* gives only the possible points of efficient production, not the *most efficient allocation* of labour and capital. This issue is discussed in detail in the next chapter. For limited purpose here, this problem can be resolved by looking at producer's equilibrium. A cost minimizing firm employs labour and capital in a combination at which the ratio of *marginal product* (*MP*) of labour and capital is equal to the factor-price ratio (P_L/P_K), i.e.

$$MP_L/MP_K = MP_K = P_L/P_K$$

We know that marginal product ratio (MP_L/MP_K) equals the *marginal rate of technical substitution* (*MRTS*). Therefore, firm's optimum combination of inputs is given by the condition

$$MRTS_{L,K} = P_L/P_K$$

While $MRTS_{L,K}$ is given by the slope of the isoquants, factor-price ratio (P_L/P_K) is given by the slope of the factor-price line labelled w_1r_1 and w_2r_2. As shown in Figure 13.6, at point *A*,

$$MRTS^F_{L,K} = MRTS^C_{L,K} = P_L/P_K = w/r$$

Therefore, point *A* gives the optimum combination of inputs and producer's equilibrium. A similar situation is shown at point *C*. The point at which firms end up ultimately combining labour and capital depends on the *demand for goods*. If consumers prefer more of food than clothing, one possible equilibrium point is *C* and if they prefer more of clothing than food, a possible equilibrium point is *A*. One can similarly locate a number of other points of producers' equilibrium on the production contract curve.

THE PRODUCTION POSSIBILITY FRONTIER

In Section 13.4, we have discussed *general equilibrium condition in exchange* assuming that total supply of goods is given, and in Section 13.5 we have discussed the *general equilibrium condition in production*, i.e. optimum allocation of factor inputs in the production of consumer goods assuming that all that is produced will be consumed. For the economy to be in general equilibrium, the general equilibrium condition for exchange and production must hold at the same level of consumption and production. Furthermore, these conditions must match with production possibilities of the economy. What we need now is to integrate the general equilibrium conditions of exchange and of production to present a complete picture of the general equilibrium in the economy. This requires integrating *production possibilities* with *demand possibilities*. In this section, we will show the derivation of the *production possibility curve*, also called *production possibility frontier* (*PPF*).

The *production possibility frontier* (*PPF*) shows the various alternative combinations of two goods (food and clothing) that can be produced with a given quantity of inputs (labour and capital), assuming production technology to be given. *The production possibility frontier* for food and clothing is illustrated by curve *PF* in Figure 13.7. This *production possibility frontier* is derived from the *production contract curve* in Figure 13.6 *by plotting the various combinations of food and clothing that can be produced, given the supply of labour and capital*. For example, point O_C, on the production contract curve in Figure 13.6 shows an extreme production combination in which the entire labour and capital is used to produce only food and no clothing. This point is shown by point *F* on the *production possibility frontier* in Figure 13.7. Similarly, point O_F in Figure 13.6 shows another extreme, that the entire labour and capital is used to produce only clothing and no food. This point is shown by point *P* on the production possibility frontier in Figure 13.7. Likewise, intermediate points (e.g. points *A*, *B* and *C*) on the *production contract curve* in Figure 13.6 are represented by the intermediate points (points *A*, *B* and *C*) on the *production possibility frontier*. In fact, many such points on the production contract curve can be located and a smooth and continuous production possibility frontier can be drawn as shown in Figure 13.7. The production possibility frontier (*PPF*) as shown by the curve *PF* indicates that all the combinations of two goods (food and clothing) represented by a point on or inside the frontier can be produced, given the supply of inputs.

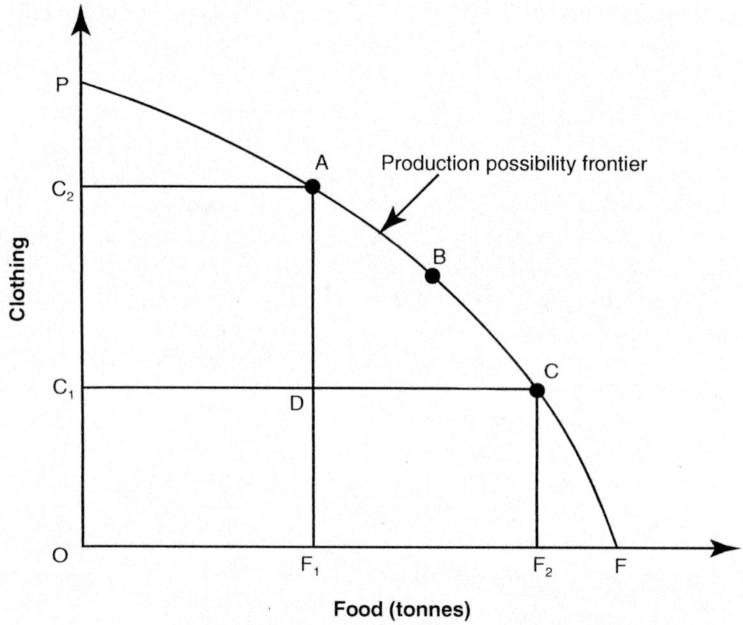

Figure 13.7 *Production Possibility Frontier*

The Slope of *PPF* and Marginal Rate of Transformation (*MRT*)

An *important feature* of the production possibility frontier (*PPF*) is that it is *concave to origin*. Concavity implies that its *slope* goes on increasing as one moves down or up along the production possibility frontier. The slope of the production possibility frontier gives the rate at which one commodity (say, food) can be transformed into another (clothings) at different levels of production. This rate is called, in economic jargon, *the marginal rate of transformation* (*MRT*). The *MRT* can be defined as the *rate at which one commodity can be transformed into another*. For example, in Figure 13.7, movement from point *P* to *A* on *PPF* means that PC_2 of clothing can be transformed into C_2A of food. It implies that if PC_2 of clothing is not produced, some labour and capital are spared and if this labour and capital are put to food production, C_2A of food can be produced. Similarly, movement from point *A* to *C* means that *AD* of clothing can be transformed into *DC* of food. Thus, the slope of the *PPF* gives the *MRT*.

The increasing slope of the *PPF* means increasing *MRT*. The *MRT* can be converted into *marginal cost ratio*, as follows. As *PPF* shows, movement from point *P* to point *A* means that if PC_2 of clothing is not produced, some cost is saved. Let us call it cost of clothing (*CC*). If the same cost is incurred to produce food, C_2A of food can be produced. Let us call it cost of food (*CF*). The *cost ratio* can now be expressed as *CC*/*CF*. By dividing *CC* by PC_2, we get marginal cost of clothing (MC_C) and by dividing CF by C_2A, we get marginal cost of food (MC_F). Thus, the *cost ratio* (*CC*/*CF*) can be converted into *marginal cost ratio as* MC_C/MC_F. The cost-ratio (*CC*/*CF*) and *marginal cost ratio* (MC_C/MC_F) are both given by the slope of the *PPF*. The slope of the *PPF* gives the measure of MRT. In terms of cost,

$$MRT = MC_C/MC_F$$

Thus, increasing *slope* of *PPF* means increasing *MRT* and therefore increasing marginal cost. That is why *PPF* is concave to origin.

GENERAL EQUILIBRIUM IN COMPETITIVE PRODUCT MARKET

Having introduced the *production possibility frontier* (*PPF*), we are now in a position to illustrate, general equilibrium in a two-good and two-input economy assuming perfect competition. The general equilibrium in this kind of economy takes place where the conditions of the *general equilibrium in exchange* and *in production* are satisfied at the same level of output and employment. The general equilibrium in a competitive output market is illustrated in Figure 13.8. The production possibility frontier, *PP*′, is the same as one given in Figure 13.7. To this has been added the most efficient exchange equilibrium (corresponding to position *E* in Figure 13.4) indicated by point *E* with price line *ff*′ and also a product price line *pp*′. The price line *pp*′ is parallel to price line *ff*′ determining the equilibrium of consumers *A* and *B* at point *E*′. Price line *pp*′ has the same slope as *line ff*′. The general equilibrium in a competitive output market is shown at point *E*. Point *E* satisfies the equilibrium conditions of both the exchange and production. This can be proved as follows.

The slope of the *PPF* curve equals *MRT* and slope of the price line *pp*′ equals the price ratio of clothing and food (P_C/P_F). Note that *pp*′ is tangent to PPF at point *E*. Therefore, at point *E*,

$$MRT = P_C/P_F$$

We know that a consumer is in equilibrium where commodity price ratio equals MRS. Therefore, at consumer's equilibrium, $P_C/P_F = MRS$. It means that at point *E*

$$MRT = MRS$$

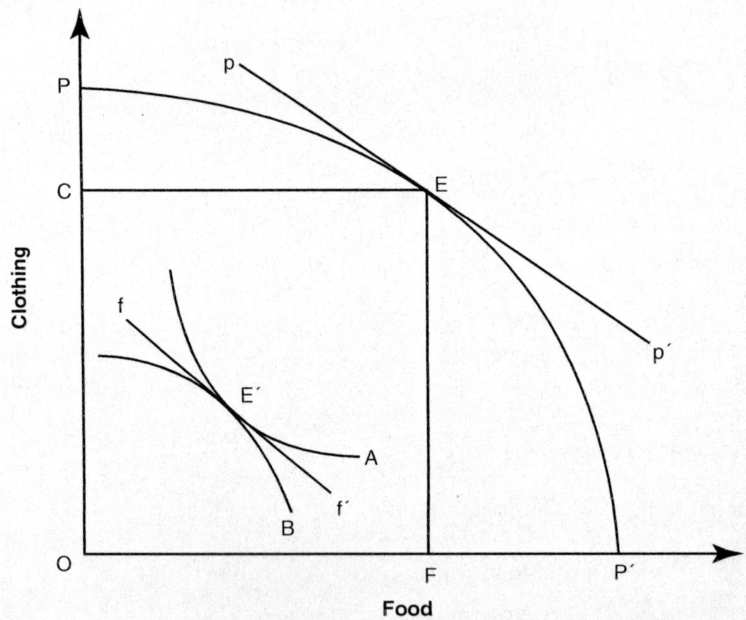

Figure 13.8 *General Equilibrium in Competitive Output Market*

This equation satisfies the condition that production possibility matches with consumers' demand. What about factor prices and employment? We also know that in competitive output and input markets, prices of goods equal their marginal cost. Therefore, $P_C = MC_C$ and $P_F = MC_F$. Thus,

$$P_C/P_F = MC_C/MC_F$$

Therefore, at point E,

$$MRT = MRS = MC_C/MC_F$$

This satisfies the general equilibrium condition.

REVIEW QUESTIONS AND EXERCISES

1. Distinguish between partial equilibrium and general equilibrium analyses. In what sense does partial equilibrium analysis provide a partial economic analysis?
2. What is meant by the interdependence of markets? Illustrate how a change in one market affects the equilibrium of another related market.
3. What is Edgeworth box diagram? How is Edgeworth exchange box diagram different from Edgeworth production box diagram?
4. What is contract curve in Edgeworth exchange box diagram? How is it derived and what is its significance in general equilibrium analysis?
5. What will be the shape of exchange contract curve if (a) indifference curves of both the consumers are identical and (b) indifference curves are not identical?
6. What is meant by the general equilibrium in production? How is the path of general equilibrium in production determined? Illustrate your answer.
7. Why is input combination at any point other than those on the production contract curve is inefficient? Explain and illustrate your answer.
8. Define production possibility frontier. How is production possibility frontier derived?
9. Suppose production function for goods is such that it gives constant returns to scale. What is the likely shape of the production possibility frontier?
10. Suppose in an economy there are two consumers consuming two goods. How can general equilibrium be defined?
11. Why is production possibility frontier concave to origin? Is production possibility frontier always concave to origin? If not, what is its other possible shape?
12. What is meant by marginal rate of transformation? What is the measure of the marginal rate of transformation? Why does it increase along the production possibility frontier?
13. Production possibility frontier shows all the possible combinations of two goods that can be produced with fixed factor inputs but all combinations are not equally efficient. How is the most efficient combination of the goods determined? Illustrate and explain.
14. Using production possibility frontier and Edgeworth exchange box diagram, show the point of general equilibrium in a competitive output market.

15. The marginal rate of transformation is obtained from which of the following?
    (a) isoquants,
    (b) indifference curve,
    (c) production possibility frontier, or
    (d) production contract curve.

ENDNOTE

1. Here, we discuss the Edgeworth box diagram in detail because this technique will be used frequently in this and the next chapter.

FURTHER READINGS

Blaug, M. (1968), *Economic Theory in Retrospect* (London: Heinemann), 2nd Edn., Chapter 13.

Cohen, K.J. and Cyert, R.M. (1975), *Theory of the Firm: Resource Association in a Market Economy* (Englewood Cliffs, NJ: Prentice Hall), Chapter 11.

Hansen, B. (1970), *A Survey of General Equilibrium Systems* (New York: McGraw-Hill).

Johnson, H.G. (1971), *Two-Sector Model of General Equilibrium* (New York: Aldine Press).

Koutsoyiannis, A. (1979), *Modern Microeconomics* (London: Macmillan), Chapter 22.

Kuenne, R.E. (1967), *The Theory of General Economic Equilibrium* (Princeton: Princeton University Press), 2nd Edn.

Quirk, J.R. and Saposnic, K. (1968), *Introduction to General Equilibrium and Welfare Economics* (New York: McGraw-Hill).

Simpson, D.M. (1975), *General Equilibrium Analysis* (London: Black Well).

Weintraub, E.R. (1974), *General Equilibrium Theory* (London: Macmillan).

(Note: Most of these readings are advanced and highly mathematical.)

Chapter 14

Welfare Economics: Pareto Optimality

CHAPTER OBJECTIVES

Having explained the conditions for the general equilibrium, we move now to discuss the welfare economics. By going through this chapter, you learn:

- What is meant by social welfare;
- What is welfare economics and what it deals with;
- What are the measures of social welfare;
- How social welfare is measured in economic sense;
- What is Pareto optimality—the basic foundation of welfare economics;
- What are the conditions of Pareto optimality;
- How Pareto optimality maximizes the social welfare; and
- What are the limitations of the Pareto optimality condition.

INTRODUCTION

We have discussed in Parts I the positive aspects of microeconomic theory. Our main objective was to discuss how individual economic entities optimize allocation of their resources, i.e. how individual consumers maximize their *utility function* and firm their *profit function*. From the analysis of economic behaviour, it may appear that if all individual firms optimize their resource allocation, the total output of goods and services available to the society will be maximum. And, when all individual consumers optimize their resource allocation to maximize their utility function, then the total utility enjoyed by the society as a whole will be maximum. In other words, if both, firms and consumers maximize their respective objective functions, the total economic welfare of the society will be maximum. However, the conditions of general equilibrium do not exist in reality. Markets are not perfectly competitive. Resource allocations are not as efficient as perceived in the theory of general equilibrium. Decisions of individual consumers and producers are not perfectly rational. Decisions taken by individual consumers and producers create *negative* and *positive externalities*. The risk and uncertainties prevailing in human life make right decision-making a difficult proposition. Resources and incomes are inequitably distributed. Therefore, optimization of resource allocation from individual's point of view may not conform to the tests of maximization of social welfare. Positive microeconomics does not answer the question as how to maximize social welfare and what policy measures can maximize the economic well-being of the society as a whole. The branch of economics which deals with these problems is called *welfare economics*. The welfare economics imparts economic science a *normative character*. Before we proceed further, let us have a view of definition and nature of welfare economics.

DEFINITIONS AND NATURE OF WELFARE ECONOMICS

Definition of Welfare Economics

Welfare economics is the study of conditions that maximize economic welfare of the society as a whole. In the words of Oscar Lange, 'Welfare economic is concerned with the conditions which determine the total economic welfare of a community.'[1] Reder defines 'welfare economics as that branch of economic science that attempts to establish and apply the criteria of propriety to economic policies.'[2] In his *survey of welfare economics*, Mishan defines theoretical welfare economics, as 'that branch of study which endeavours to formulate propositions by which we may rank on the scale of better and worse, alternative economic situations open to society.'[3] The function of welfare economics is to evaluate alternative economic situations and determine whether one economic situation yields greater economic welfare than others. Welfare economics may also be defined as that branch of economic science which evaluates alternative patterns of resource allocations from the viewpoint of maximizing economic welfare of the society as a whole.

Is Welfare Economics a Positive or a Normative Science?

Economists differ on the question *whether welfare economics is a positive or a normative science*. Although welfare economics has been regarded as positive economics right from its inception, 'at one point in economic thought, it was felt that welfare economics was unscientific; that it was normative and was hence a branch of Ethics....'[4] It was also argued that welfare economics is concerned with 'what ought to be' and, hence, it is 'normative' in character. This view has, however, been disputed with reference to Pigou's *Economics of Welfare*. It has been argued that Pigou was concerned, in his *Economics of Welfare*, with the causes and conditions of economic welfare—he did not make any policy recommendation. Pigou's *Economics of Welfare* is, therefore, a positive study.[5] Nevertheless, if one goes by Baumol's opinion that 'welfare economics (is) concerned ... mostly with policy issues which arise out of the allocation of resources...'[6] between various commodities and between various consumers, welfare economics is a normative science.

In spite of the controversy on the issue, a widely held view on this issue is that *welfare economics is both a positive and a normative science*. Welfare economics is a *positive science* insofar as it attempts to examine and predict the welfare implications of the functioning of the economic system. Welfare propositions 'may be subjected to test in the same way as those of positive economics,' though testing welfare propositions is much more difficult than the propositions of general positive economics. The information gained through positive analysis is useful in devising appropriate policy measures to maximize the welfare of the society. Welfare economics is a *normative science* in that it provides guidelines for policy formulations to maximize social welfare. Maximization of economic welfare of a society presumes a social welfare function which consists essentially of value judgements. Given the welfare function, welfare economics, as a normative science, provides guidelines for appropriate policy measures.

In this chapter, we will discuss briefly the welfare economics including concept and measurement of social welfare and Pareto's optimality conditions for maximizing economic welfare which lays down the foundation of welfare economics. Let us begin with the concept of social welfare.

THE CONCEPT AND MEASUREMENT OF SOCIAL WELFARE

The term 'welfare' has been defined in diverse ways, perhaps, because it is extremely difficult to give it a precise meaning. The difficulty arises from the fact that welfare of an individual or of a group of individuals depends on many *immeasurable* social, political and economic factors. Besides, it depends also on the philosophical attitude of the people towards life and society. In economics, however, the concept of welfare is used in a narrow sense: it is limited to only *economic welfare*. Even the term 'economic welfare' eludes a precise definition. Nevertheless, economists have tried to give it a precise meaning for the purpose of economic analysis.

Some Early Concepts of Welfare

Jeremy Bentham defined *social welfare* as 'the sum total of the happiness (or welfare) of all the individuals in society.'[7] Following Benthamite doctrine, Pigou defined social welfare as the arithmetic sum of the individual welfare. In nutshell, social welfare was regarded by the economists of cardinal utility tradition as the arithmetic sum of the utility gained by the individual members of society.

This concept of social welfare has, however, met with certain serious *objections. First*, it is argued that utility cannot be *cardinally* measured and, hence, cannot be added to obtain the social welfare. It is, therefore, meaningless to define social welfare as the sum of the individual utilities. This objection is universally accepted. *Second*, it is also widely accepted that since even *ordinal* measurement of utilities is not possible, neither inter-product nor interpersonal comparison of utilities is not possible, in an objective or scientific manner. It would, therefore, not be possible to determine how a change in existing pattern of resource allocation would affect the aggregate welfare unless it is unrealistically assumed that all individuals have identical income utility and commodity utility functions.

Owing to these problems, Benthamite and Pigovian concepts of social welfare had become impracticable, in the sense that it cannot be used objectively in any policy formulation. Therefore, the cardinal utilitarian thesis that the welfare of different individuals could be added up to arrive at the welfare of society had to be abandoned.

Pareto's Concept of Welfare

It was Vilfredo Pareto, an Italian economist, who deviated from the cardinal utility tradition and gave a new orientation to welfare economics. He did not attempt to define social welfare. Instead, he suggested a condition for maximization of social welfare irrespective of whether it is measurable or not measurable. For the purpose, Pareto introduced a new concept, i.e., the concept of *social optimum*. This concept is central to Pareto's welfare economics. According to Pareto, although it is not possible to measure and add up utilities of individuals to arrive at the total social welfare, it is possible to determine whether social welfare is optimum. Conceptually, social welfare is said to be *optimum* when nobody can be made better-off without making somebody worse-off. In the words of Boulding, 'a social optimum is defined as a situation in which nobody can move to a position which he prefers without moving somebody else to position which is less preferred.'[8] In simple words, social welfare is *optimum* when it is not possible to make even a single person better-off by reallocating productive resources and consumer goods and services, without making someone else worse off.

It is important to note that Pareto's concept of social optimum does neither define nor suggest a measure of the magnitude of optimum social welfare. Pareto was concerned with the question whether social welfare from a given economic situation can be or cannot be increased by changing the allocation of resources. The test of increase in social welfare is that at least one person should be made better-off without making anybody else worse-off.

Having introduced the welfare economics and the concept of economic welfare, we will now discuss various theories of welfare and welfare criteria devised by welfare economists. It may be noted here that it is very difficult to point out the period in the history of economic thoughts which marks the beginning of welfare economics. Nor is it easy to attribute the emergence of welfare economics with any particular economist because 'welfare economics does not appear at any time to have wholly engaged the labours of any one economist.'[9] Some believe that Pigou's book *Wealth and Welfare* and his later work *Economics of Welfare* mark the emergence of welfare economics as a separate branch of economics. Hla Myint has, however, pointed out, in his *Theories of Welfare Economics*, that the classical economist had a great deal to say on a subject which could reasonably be brought within the compass of welfare economics. Following the general tradition, however, we commence our discussion on welfare economics with Pareto's welfare economics.

PARETO'S WELFARE ECONOMICS

Vilfredo Pareto's *Manual of Political Economy* (1906) represents a landmark in the history of subjective welfare economics. Pareto broke away from the traditional utilitarian economics. He rejected the hypotheses based on cardinal utility and also the additive utility function. His welfare propositions do not require any interpersonal comparison whatsoever.[10] Some have, therefore, called Pareto's welfare economics as *new welfare economics*. In this section, we discuss (i) the concept of Pareto optimality and (ii) marginal conditions of Pareto optimality.

Pareto Optimum: Definition

Pareto optimum is also called *Pareto Efficiency, Pareto Unanimity Rule, Pareto Criteria and Pareto Social Optimum*. Pareto optimum is defined as a position from which it is not possible to improve welfare of any one by any reallocation of factors or of goods and services without impairing the welfare of someone else. In other words, a Pareto optimum position is attained when it is not possible, through any reallocation of resources, to make anyone move on to a higher indifference curve without making someone move to a lower indifference curve. From this concept of Pareto optimum is derived *Pareto Criterion of Welfare*. According to Pareto criterion, *any change that makes at least one person better-off without making someone else worse-off makes definitely an improvement in social welfare*. Conversely, any change that makes at least one person worse-off and no one better-off causes a decrease in social welfare.

Pareto's concept of 'social optimum' is definitely an improvement over cardinal utility approach in that it is free from the problems of additive utility function and interpersonal comparison of utility. Pareto's concept of social optimum has, however, been criticized on the following grounds.

First, Pareto optimum does not define a unique optimum economic situation. As Winch has pointed out, There are three aspects of optimum performance of an economic system, associated respectively with the three basic functions (the transformation function, the utility function and the welfare function). The unique optimum economic situation requires perfect performance in all three respects, but the term

Pareto Optimum has come to mean the simultaneous fulfilment of the first two regardless of the third.[11] There are, therefore, an infinite number of Pareto optima that satisfy Pareto optimality condition. The Pareto optimum, however, does not determine the *optimum optimorum*— the best of the best. In fact, each Pareto optimum (as defined above) is sub-optimum. It is, therefore, quite likely that an optimum situation which corresponds to a bad distribution of income may be worse than a sub-optimum position corresponding to a good distribution of income.[12] It means that a situation in which Pareto optimality conditions are fulfilled may well be inferior to a number of other situations in which they are not fulfilled.[13] It means that Pareto optimum does not guarantee the maximization of social welfare.

Second, any point on production possibility curve, given the factor prices and technology, may satisfy Pareto efficiency in production. But (as we will show), all points do not represent the maximum social welfare. It is, therefore, alleged that Pareto optimum, as it is defined, offers only a necessary but not a sufficient condition of welfare maximization.

Third, Pareto optimum raises the question of payment of compensation because it is difficult to imagine an economic change that benefits at least one person without harming another. If interpersonal comparisons are rejected, then we cannot say whether gains of the person who benefits from the change is greater than, equal to or less than the loss of the person who suffers from the change. It may thus be said that Pareto optimum does not offer a measure to evaluate the change that makes some persons better-off and some others worse-off.

In spite of its conceptual deficiencies in *Pareto optimum*, as pointed out by the economists, it remains the foundation of welfare economics. No discussion on welfare economies begins without reference to Pareto optimality conditioner. Given its theoretical importance, let us look at the conditions of Pareto optimality.

Pareto Optimality Conditions

Pareto optimality conditions can be classified under two categories:

1. Marginal conditions and
2. General conditions.

The two kinds of Pareto optimality conditions are briefly discussed here.

Marginal Conditions of Pareto Optimum The marginal conditions are the *first-order conditions* that must be satisfied to attain the maximum social welfare in accordance with Pareto optimality. Hicks calls these conditions as *marginal conditions of maximum welfare*. The marginal conditions of Pareto optimality have been set out by Hicks,[14] Lerner[15] and Lange.[16]

The marginal conditions of maximum welfare have been derived directly from the definition of maximum social welfare. As mentioned above, maximum social welfare is achieved when it is impossible to make any one better-off, by reallocating resources, without making someone else worse-off. Achieving maximum social welfare in this sense is possible only when allocation of productive factors between the various commodities, allocation of commodities between the consumers and allocation of productive factors between the firms are all optimum. Pareto optimality is therefore also called as *allocative efficiency*.

We now turn to explain the *marginal condition* or the *first-order conditions* of Pareto optimality in welfare maximization under the following categories[17]:

1. *Pareto optimality in exchange*, i.e., optimum allocation of products among the consumers.
2. *Pareto optimality in production*, i.e., optimum allocation of inputs between the goods, and between the firms, i.e. optimum specialization.

3. *General optimality of production and exchange*, i.e., simultaneous fulfilment of production and exchange optimality conditions.
4. Total optimality conditions of welfare maximization.

Assumptions

In order to explain the marginal conditions of welfare maximization, let us set out the model and the assumptions under which marginal conditions of Pareto optimality are specified.

The model used for explaining the Pareto optimality conditions consists of two commodities (*X* and *Y*), two consumers (*A* and *B*), two factors (capital, *K*, and labour, *L*) and two firms (F_1 and F_2). Given the model, the following assumptions are made to analyse Pareto optimalities:

1. Consumers maximize their utility function which are independent of each other.
2. Factors, *K* and L, are homogeneous, perfectly divisible, available in fixed quantities and are exogenously determined. Both factors are used in the production function of each good.
3. Production functions for both goods are given.
4. There is perfect competition in both product and factor markets.

Having specified the model and the assumptions of the model, we will now discuss

1. Pareto optimality in exchange,
2. Pareto optimality in production,
3. optimality distribution of goods between the firms and
4. the general optimality conditions.

Pareto Optimality in Exchange

The Pareto optimality (or efficiency) in exchange requires that marginal rate of substitution (MRS) between any two products must be the same for every consumer of both the products. This marginal condition in exchange, with reference to two-commodity (*X* and *Y*) and two-consumer (*A* and *B*) model, may be expressed as

$$MRS^{A}_{x,y} = MRS^{B}_{x,y}$$

The Pareto optimum allocation of the two goods among the consumers is illustrated by using Edgeworth box diagram[18] as presented in Figure 14.1. As assumed earlier, there are only two consumers, *A* and *B*, and only two commodities *X* and *Y*. The point of origin for consumer *A* is O_a and O_b for consumer *B*. Indifference curves from A_1 to A_5 represent *A*'s scale of preference and indifference curves from B_1 to B_5 represent *B*'s scale of preference. The Edgeworth contract curve, *CC*′, represents the points that satisfy the Pareto optimality condition of exchange, i.e.

$$MRS^{A}_{x,y} = MRS^{B}_{x,y}$$

Distribution of goods, *X* and *Y*, between consumers *A* and *B* represented by any point away from the *CC*′ curve is inefficient. Therefore, movement from a point away from the *CC*′ curve towards a point on *CC*′ curve improves the satisfaction level of either both the consumers or of at least one of them without

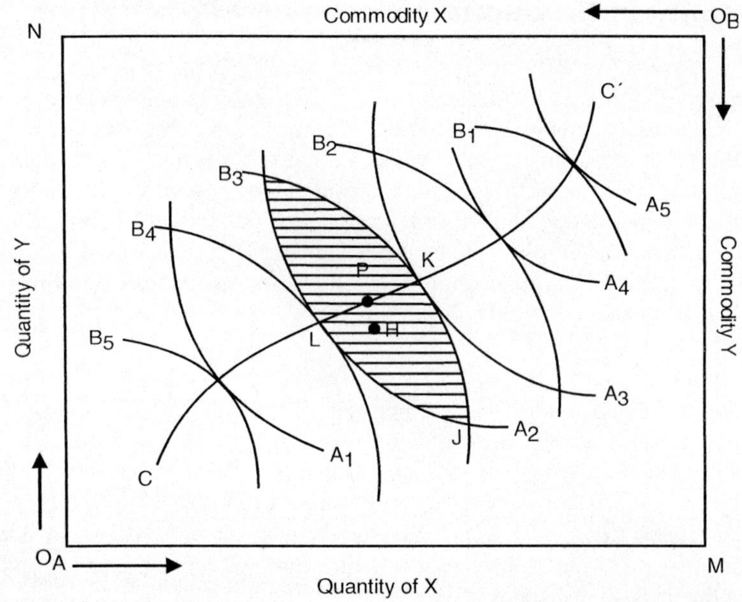

Figure 14.1 *Edgeworth Box Diagram: Pareto Efficiency in Exchange*

affecting the satisfaction of the other. For example, suppose both the consumers are at point *J*. Movement along the curve *JK* increases the satisfaction of *A* as he moves on to a higher indifference curve, say A_3, while *B* remains on the same indifference curve, B_3. Similarly, movement from point *J* towards point *L* increases the satisfaction of *B*, without reducing *A*'s satisfaction. Any point in the shaded area, say *H*, indicates the increase in the satisfaction of both *A* and *B*, as both move on to their higher indifference curves. Thus, movement towards the contract curve from any other point shows the improvement in the total welfare. Recall that the contract curve, *CC′*, is formed by joining the tangential points of *A*'s and *B*'s indifference curves and at each point of tangency marginal rates of substitution ($MRS_{X,Y}$) between the two goods, *X* and *Y*, is the same for both the consumers. Therefore, each point on the contract curve satisfies the Pareto optimality condition of exchange. The following inferences may be drawn from Figure 14.1.

1. Since there are infinite points on the contract curve, *CC*', that satisfy the optimality condition, there are infinite Pareto optima.
2. Given the subjective nature of indifference curves, it is not possible to conclude that every Pareto optimum solution indicates greater social welfare than that indicated by every non-optimal point. For example, we cannot compare an optimal point *K* with a non-optimal point *H* because while *A* will prefer optimal point *K* with non-optimal point *H*, *B* will prefer a non-social optimal point, *H*. Thus, without an explicit interpersonal comparison of utilities it will not be possible to judge which of the two points (*K* or *H*) is social optimum.[19]
3. An upward movement on the contract curve *(CC')* makes *A* better-off and *B* worse-off. Similarly, a downward movement makes *B* better-off and *A* worse-off. Therefore, it cannot be said that every point on the *CC'* curve represented *optimum optimorum*.

Pareto Optimality in Production: Optimum Allocation of Factor Inputs

The second marginal condition of Pareto optimality is related to optimal allocation of resources between the goods, *X* and *Y*. Pareto optimality in allocation of resources requires that factors (*L* and *K*) are so allocated to the production of two goods, *X* and *Y*, that it is not possible to increase the output of one commodity, by reallocating factors, without causing a decrease in the production of the other. The marginal condition that must be fulfilled to achieve Pareto optimality in resource allocation is that *marginal rate of technical substitution* (*MRTS*) between *L* and *K* is the same for both the goods, *X* and *Y*, produced by firms F_1 and F_2. It means that resources are so allocated that for all producers of *X* and *Y*,

$$MRTS^X_{L,K} = MRTS^Y_{L,K}$$

Pareto optimality in the allocation of factors between the two products and also between the two firms is presented graphically in Edgeworth box diagram in Figure 14.2. The analysis is analogous to one developed to show Pareto optimality in exchange of goods between the consumers in Figure 14.1.

In Figure 14.2, horizontal axis represents the total amount of labour ($O_X W$) and vertical axis represents the total quantity of capital ($Q_X M$) available for production of commodities *X* and *Y*. Isoquant map for *X* is given by isoquants from X_1 to X_5 with origin O_X. Isoquant map for *Y* is given by isoquants from Y_1 to Y_5. Following the method of Edgeworth box diagram, the isoquant map of *Y* (with origin at Q_Y) is

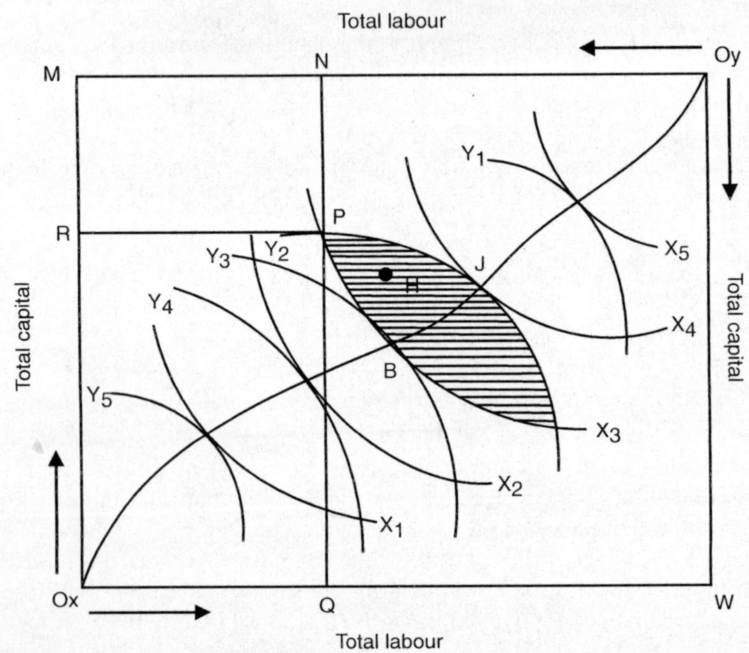

Figure 14.2 *Edgeworth Box Diagram: Pareto Efficiency in Production*

inverted and superimposed on the isoquant map of X. The curve joining the two points of origin, O_X and O_Y, is obtained by connecting tangential points of isoquants for X and Y. This curve is called *production contract curve*. It is the locus of tangential points of the isoquants of the two firms F_1 and F_2 both producing goods X and Y. At each point of tangency, the *MRTS* for both the goods are the same, that is,

$$MRTS^X_{L,K} = MRTS^Y_{L,K}$$

Therefore, only those points that lie on the production contract curve (O_XO_Y) represent the Pareto optimality in production or Pareto efficient production. Any other point that satisfies the above condition is not efficient. For example, point P, the point of intersection of isoquants X_3 and Y_2, satisfies the Pareto optimality condition but production is not Pareto efficient. At point P, labour O_X $Q(=MN)$ is allocated to the production of X and QW $(=O_Y N)$ of labour to the production of Y. And, PQ of capital is allocated to X while PN of capital goes to the production of Y. This allocation of L and K between X and Y is not Pareto efficient because point P falls away from the contract curve, O_X O_Y. Therefore, any movement towards the contract curve, through the shaded area, will improve the efficiency in resource allocation for both the goods. For example, factor allocation represented by point H will increase the production of both, X and Y, as both products would move onto higher isoquants.

To explain the point further, the movements along the ridge lines of the shaded area improves the output of one of the commodities without reducing production of the other. Therefore, any point on the ridge lines indicates a more efficient allocation of L and K, than point P. For example, movement along PJ indicates reallocation of factors which lead to increase in the production of X without reducing production of Y. Similarly, movement along PB increases production of Y without affecting output of X. But, once a point on contract curve is reached, it will not be possible to increase the production of any commodity without reducing that of the other. Thus, each point on the production contract curve (O_X O_Y) represents optimal allocation of K and L between goods X and X in Paretian sense.

It may be noted here that *Pareto optimality condition of production does not offer a unique solution*. It may be inferred from Figure 14.2 that there are infinite points on the contract curve of production that satisfy the marginal condition of Pareto optimality in production. By a reasoning analogous to one applied to consumption-exchange-optimality condition shown in Figure 14.1, it is not possible to say which point on the production contract curve represents optimum optimorum.

Optimum Distribution of Goods Between Firms: Optimum Specialization of Firms

Another condition that must be satisfied for Pareto optimality in production is optimum degree of specialization by the firms. It means, that the production of goods X and Y is so divided between the firms that no reallocation of output among the firms can increase the output of any of the two goods without reducing the output of the other. A necessary condition that must be fulfilled is that *marginal rates of transformation (MRT)*[20] between X and Y must be the same in all the firms producing them both. This is, however, not a sufficient condition. Sufficient condition requires that this condition is satisfied at the point of tangency of *MRT* curves of firms F_1 and F_2—not at the points of intersection. If this condition is not fulfilled it will always be possible to increase the total social product by reallocating goods between the firms. For example, if firm F_1 can produce one additional unit of X at the

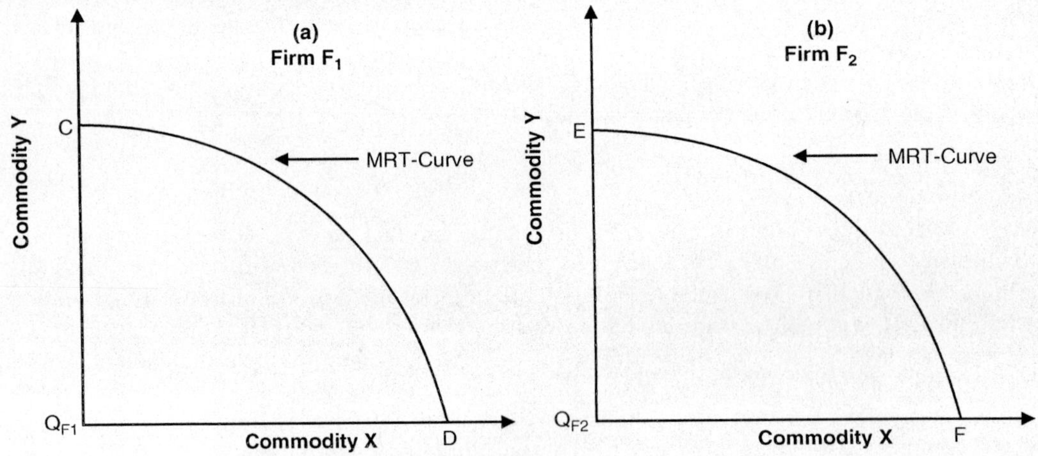

Figure 14.3 *Marginal Rate of Transformation Curves*

cost of 3 units of Y, and firm F_2 can produce 2 units of Y at the cost of one unit of X, then MRT for F_1 is $1X = 3Y$, and for F_2, it is $2Y = 1X$. It means that if F_1 is made to produce one unit less of X and F_2 to produce one additional unit of X, then production of Y can be increased by one unit, without reducing the production of X.

This point is illustrated in Figures 14.3 and 14.4. Suppose that the marginal rates of transformation (MRT) curves of firm F_1 and F_2 for products X and Y are, respectively, given as CD and EF in Figure 14.3(a) and (b). If we invert the panel (b) shifting its origin O_{F2} to north-east corner and superimpose it over panel (a), the picture that emerges can be shown as in Figure 14.4. The MRT curves CD and EF intersect each other at two points P_1 and P_2.

In Figure 14.4, at points P_1 and P_2, MRT of firm F_1 equals MRT of firm F_2. But none of these points optimizes the output of the two firms. Nor does it maximize the output of X and Y. This can be proved as follows. Suppose two firms settle at point P_2 where firm F_1 produces MP_2 of X and QP_2 of Y, and firm F_2 produces NP_2 of X and RP_2 of Y. By adding the output of each commodity produced by each firm, we can obtain the total output of X and Y as given below:

$$\text{Total output of } X = MP_2 + NP_2 = MN$$

$$\text{Total output of } Y = QP_2 + RP_2 = RQ$$

Thus, if the two firms settle at point P_2 the maximum total output of X will be MN and that of Y will be RQ. One can similarly find the total output of X and Y at point P_1.

It can, however, be proved that point P_2 or point P_1 in Figure 14.4 is not the point of maximum possible output of X and Y. Note that if the firms are required to move from point P_2 towards P_1 (or from point P_1 towards P_2) along their respective MRT curves, production of both X and Y increases up to a certain level. The maximum output of X and Y can be obtained by shifting the inverted MRT curve of firm F_2 further north-eastward until its MRT curve EF is tangent to MRT curve CD of firm F_1.

As shown in Figure 14.4, the MRT curve EF is shifted upwards till a point is reached where MRT curves, CD and $E'F'$ are tangent to each other. The tangential point is point P. This point satisfies both *necessary* and *sufficient conditions of Pareto optimality* of specialization between the firms for output mix.

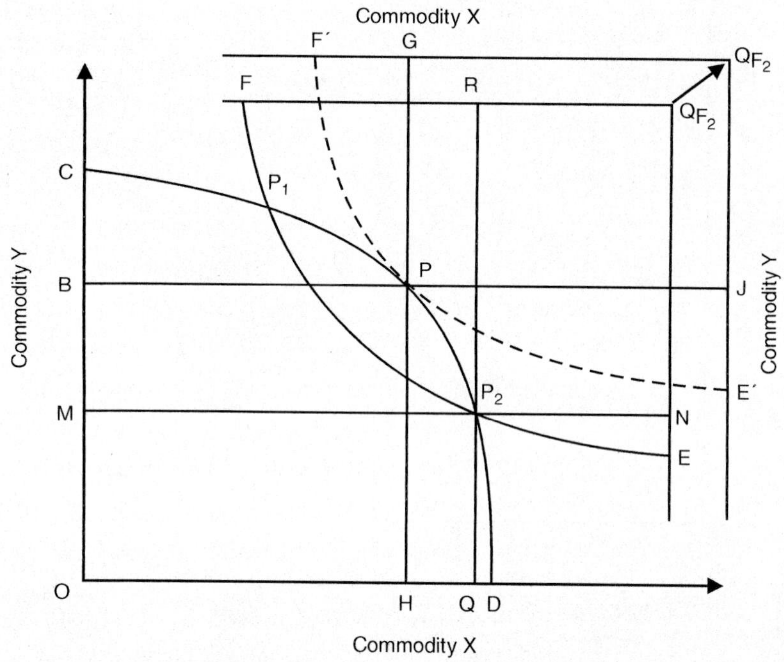

Figure 14.4 *Optimum Specialization of Firms in Production*

At point P, firm F_1 produces PH of Y and PB of X and firm F_2 produces PJ of X and GP of Y. The total output of X and Y at point P may now be compared with that at point P_1 as shown below:

$$\text{Total output of } X = BP + PJ = BJ,$$

and

$$\text{Total output of } Y = PH + PG = GH$$

It can be seen in Figure 14.4 that $BJ > MN$ and $GH > RQ$. It means that output at points P_1 and P_2 is not maximum. It is only the point P where output is maximum. At point P, the output GH of X and BJ of Y is maximum that can be produced given the factors. Also, the output mix of the two firms is optimum.

General Optimality of Production and Exchange The *third necessary condition* that must be fulfilled for social welfare to be optimum in the Pareto's sense is that the bundle of factors used and the bundle of goods produced in the economy are so distributed that increasing production of one good and increasing satisfaction of one person is impossible without decreasing that of another.[21] For increasing production and consumers' satisfaction, it is necessary that optimality conditions of both production and exchange are fulfilled simultaneously and at the maximum level of output of various goods. That is, the optimum output mix must coincide with the optimum demand mix. This is called also as 'Top Level' optimality condition of welfare maximization. The fulfilment of the top level Pareto Optimality condition requires (in our $2 \times 2 \times 2$ model) that the MRT between the two products (X and Y) must be equal to the MRS between the two products for the two consumers (A and B). That is,

$$MRT_{x,y} = MRS^A_{x,y} = MRS^B_{x,y}$$

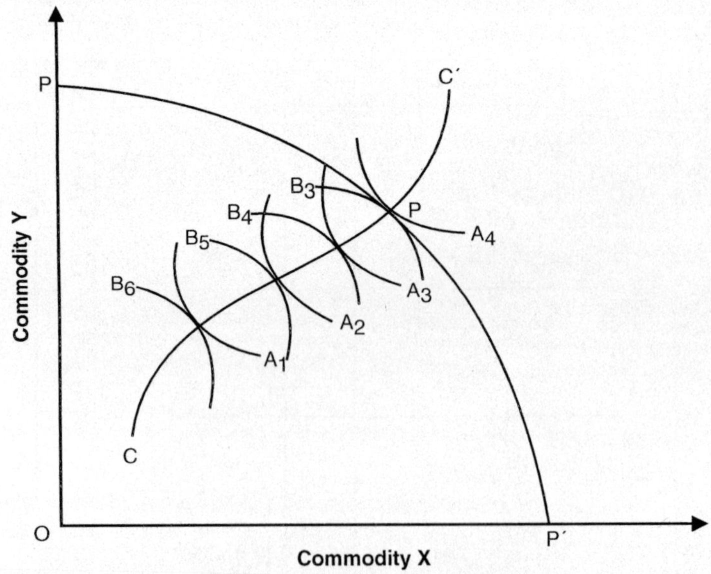

Figure 14.5 *General Optimality of Production and Exchange*

The fulfilment of this condition is graphically illustrated in Figure 14.5. The curve *PP′* is the production possibility (or product transformation) curve for products *X* and *Y*. Let us also assume that *MRT* curve (*PP′*) applies to both the firms,[22] F_1 and F_2. The slope of curve *PP′* gives the *MRT*. The indifference curves of consumer *A* are given by A_1, A_2, A_3, ... and those of consumer *B* are given by B_3, B_4, ... (for details see Figure 14.1). The curve *CC′* is the contract curve of exchange. The production transformation curve *PP′* is intersected by the contract curve of exchange *CC* at point *P*. We know that at each point on *CC′* curve,

$$MRS^A_{x,y} = MRS^B_{x,y}$$

As noted earlier, product transformation curve *PP′* shows the *MRT*, i.e. the marginal rate at which one commodity can be transformed into the other, given the technology. The *MRT* is different at different points of the transformation curve *PP′*. What is important to note here is that, at point *P*,

$$MRT = MRS^A_{x,y} = MRS^B_{x,y}$$

Point *P*, therefore, satisfies the third Pareto optimality condition of welfare maximization.

Summary of Pareto Optimally Conditions

The basic marginal conditions of Pareto optimality are summarized as follows:

Marginal Condition of Exchange Optimality

$$MRS^A_{x,y} = MRS^B_{x,y}$$

It means that the marginal rate of substitution (*MRS*) between any pair of goods must be the same for all the consumers.

Marginal Condition for Production Optimality

$$MRTS^X_{L,K} = MRTS^Y_{L,K}$$

It means that the marginal rate of technical substitution (*MRTS*) between any pair of factors must be equal for all commodities and all firms.

Marginal Condition of General Optimality

$$MRTS_{x,y} = MRS^A_{x,y} = MRS^B_{x,y}$$

It means that the marginal rate of transformation (*MRT*) between any pair of goods must be equal to the marginal rate of substitution between them for any pair of consumers.

Some Additional Conditions of Pareto Optimality

In addition to the optimality conditions (a) and (b), the following marginal conditions must also be simultaneously satisfied.

First, the owner of a factor is always in a position to use it for personal satisfaction or to rent it out for income, or put it partly for personal use and rent it partly for earning income. If it is rented out, the reward that is paid to the owner for renting the marginal unit of a factor must be equal to the value of the marginal physical product of the factor unit. Pareto calls this as *optimum allocation of factor-unit time.*

Secondly, the marginal rate of substitution between resource control or ownership at any two points of time (t_1 and t_2) is the same for every pair of individuals or firms, including pairs in which one member is a firm and the other is an individual. This condition relates to optimum control of resources through time by individuals and firms. This is *inter-temporal condition* of maximum welfare.

Thirdly, Boulding[23] has pointed out two other conditions relating to time-preference which have not been explicitly stated in the literature: *one*, that owner's rate of *time preference* for any one individual for two commodities must be the same; and *two*, that the rate of *time preference* for an individual must be equal to the rate of *time substitution* in production for every commodity.

Total Conditions of Pareto Optimality

There is another 'set of conditions', what Hicks calls 'total condition' that must be satisfied in order that social welfare is maximized. The 'total conditions' may be stated as 'it must be impossible to increase welfare by producing a product not otherwise produced (or produced by only one firm); or by using a factor not otherwise used (or used by only one firm).'[24]

Thus, in order that social welfare is maximum all the conditions *first order, second order and total conditions* must be simultaneously satisfied. But this maximum will not be unique. The reason is that it presupposes a given distribution of income which is not determined by the optimality conditions of welfare maximization. If income distribution (presumed arbitrarily to be given) changes, it will cause a change in welfare maximizing output and factor allocations.

PERFECT COMPETITION AND PARETO OPTIMALITY

A necessary condition for the Pareto optimality is the existence of perfect competition in both product and factor markets. This is, in fact, one of the basic assumptions of Pareto optimality. Let us see how perfect competition leads to Pareto optimality in exchange of consumption and production.

Efficiency in Exchange

Pareto optimality in exchange requires that marginal rate of substitution between any two goods must be the same for the two consumers, i.e.

$$MRS^{A}_{x,y} = MRS^{B}_{x,y}$$

We know that every utility maximizing consumer attains his equilibrium (or the level of maximum satisfaction) where

$$MRS_{x,y} = \frac{P_x}{P_y}$$

where P_X and P_Y are prices of commodities, X and Y, respectively.

We also know that under perfect competition, P_X and P_Y are the prices that are paid by each consumer at equilibrium. Therefore, at equilibrium,

$$MRS^{A}_{x,y} = MRS^{B}_{x,y} = P_x/P_Y$$

Under perfect competition, this condition holds for any pair of goods for all the consumers. Perfect competition, therefore, ensures optimality in exchange.

Efficiency in Production

Pareto efficiency (or optimality) in production requires that *MRTS* between any two factors must be the same for all the commodities. With reference to two products, *X* and *Y*, and two factors, *L* and *K* in our model, this condition is expressed as

$$MRTS^{X}_{L,K} = MRTS^{Y}_{L,K}$$

Profit maximizing firms are in equilibrium with respect to *X* where

$$MRTS^{X}_{L,K} = \frac{P_L}{P_K} = \frac{w}{r}$$

where $P_L = w =$ wages, and $P_K = r =$ price of capital.

When factor market is perfectly competitive, P_L and P_K are the same for all the firms. Therefore,

$$MRTS^{X}_{L,K} = MRTS^{Y}_{L,K} = P_L/P_K$$

This shows that perfect competition ensures also the optimality in production, i.e. the first-order condition of maximum welfare.

Efficiency in Production and Exchange

The third condition of Pareto optimality requires that *MRS* must be equal to *MRT* for all products. We have already shown that

$$MRS_{x,y} = \frac{P_x}{P_y}$$

Under perfect competition, a profit maximizing firm sets its optimum combination of its output *X* and *Y* where

$$MRS_{x,y} = \frac{\Delta Y}{\Delta X} = \frac{MC_x}{MC_y}$$

Also, in a perfectly competitive market, $MC_X = P_X$ and $MC_Y = P_Y$. Therefore,

$$MRT_{x,y} = \frac{MC_x}{MC_y} = \frac{P_x}{P_y}$$

Since

$$MRS_{x,y} = \frac{P_x}{P_y}$$

therefore,

$$MRS_{x,y} = \frac{P_x}{P_y} = MRT_{x,y}$$

It is, thus, established that it is only the perfect competition that ensures the maximization of social welfare provided the first- and the second-order conditions are simultaneously satisfied.

Some Exceptions

It is shown above that perfect competition is a necessary condition for attainment of Pareto optimality in exchange and production. There are, however, certain cases in which perfect competition is neither a necessary nor a sufficient condition for maximizing welfare in the Paretian sense. Besides, there are certain other factors which cause non-optimization of welfare even if first-order conditions are satisfied under perfect competition. Some important cases of these categories are discussed below.

Satiety of Consumers *Pareto optimality in exchange may not be attained under perfect competition if one or more consumers are satiated.* A consumer is said to be satiated (or has reached the maximum level of his satisfaction), when his $MU = 0$ for all goods that he consumes. If a consumer is satiated, goods may be diverted from him, without reducing his total satisfaction, to those whose $MU > 0$. This results in increase in the total satisfaction of the society. Therefore, one additional condition of Pareto optimality under perfect competition is that no consumer is satiated.

Corner Solution In some cases, under perfect competition, Pareto optimality may be represented by a corner solution, as shown by point *C* in Figure 14.6. In such cases, marginality condition is not satisfied. However, such an optimum solution represents minimum rather than maximum welfare. In such cases, perfect competition offers a solution which represents only minimum welfare, because only commodity *Y* will be produced and consumed.

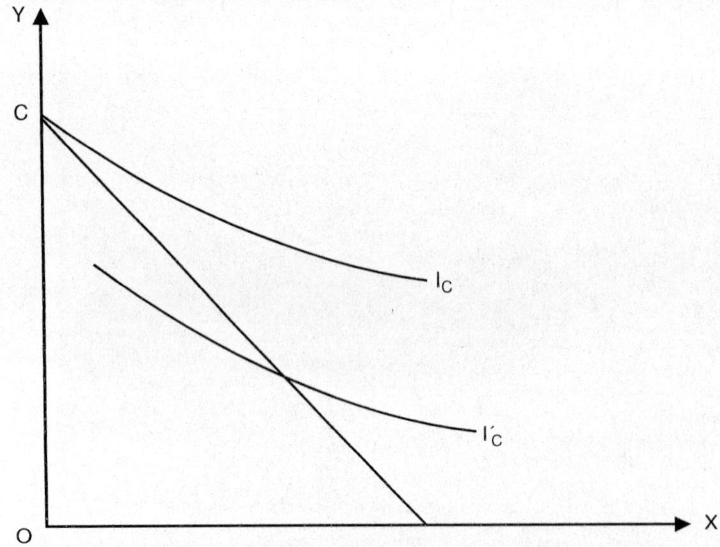

Figure 14.6 *Corner Solution of Pareto Optimality*

EXTERNALITIES AND PARETO OPTIMALITY

The foregoing conclusion that perfect competition leads to Pareto optimality is based upon the assumption that there are no external effects on or from consumption and production. This assumption implies (i) that production function of each producer is independent of others and (ii) utility function of each individual is independent of others. In reality, however, production by one firm is affected by production by other firms and consumption of one consumer affects the consumption of other consumers and producers. Such effects are known as *external effects* or *externalities.* The term *externalities* refer to the external economies and diseconomies that arise due to the activities of others. For example, if people use pollution free cars, it benefits the others. This is the case of external economy. Similarly, if smokers smoke in public place, it results in passive smoking which damages the health of non-smokers. This is the case of external diseconomy. *External economies* are the *gains* that arise from the activities of an economic unit—consumer or producer—and accrue to other members of the society for which they cannot be charged through the market price system. Similarly, *external diseconomies* are the cost that are imposed on some members of the society by the economic activities of the others for which market system does not provide a compensation to those who suffer. External economies and diseconomies arise in both production and consumption. When there are externalities in production and consumption, Pareto optimality may not be attained even under the conditions of perfect competition.

Let us now examine the effects of externalities—external economies and diseconomies—in production and consumption on welfare maximization.

Externalities in Production

Production of a commodity may involve both (i) external economies and (ii) diseconomies. Let us first discuss the nature and effects of external economies.

External Economies in Production

To understand the *external economies* in production consider the following examples:

1. When an irrigation facility is extended to non-irrigated areas, productivity of land increases and land values go up. The land owners, who gain, are not required to bear the cost of irrigation programmes.
2. When new firms are set up in an industry, the demand for inputs increases. This increase in demand for inputs might give an opportunity to the input suppliers to expand their production. The expansion of production might reduce the cost of input production to economies of scale. As a result, the input-prices for *all the users* of inputs decrease. This is an external gain to the input users.
3. The education and training programmes of the government increases the supply of skilled labour to the industrial units. But industrial units do not bear the cost of education and training. A part of this gain to the industrial units may percolate down to the consumers in terms of lower price.
4. Construction of roads and railways reduces the cost of transportation in terms of both money and time. The advantage accrues to the industrial units which do not bear the cost of road and railway construction.
5. Afforestation schemes increase rainfall and oxygen gas in the air; reduce air pollution; and maintain ecological balance. These effects of afforestation benefit the citizens in general and farmers in particular. But they do not bear the cost of afforestation.

This kind of external economies in production create a divergence between private and social gains. The divergence between the private and social gains results in non-optimization of production. Under perfect competition, a firm producing a commodity (say, X) is in equilibrium where

$$MC_x = P_x$$

As shown in Figure 14.7, $MC_X = P_X$ at point E_1. This point is the point of firm's production equilibrium. The firms produce OQ which maximizes their profits. In the absence of external economies in production, the price and output will be Pareto optimum.

In reality, however, external economies do exist which result in social benefits. The price, P_x, which consumers pay equals only their private benefits (PB), i.e. $PB_X = Q_X \cdot P_X$. This does not include their social gains. If, by some means, social benefits of external economies are measured and added to the P_X the marginal social benefit (MSB_X) will exceed $Q_X \cdot P_X$. Let us suppose that with external benefit P_X rises to P_X. There is thus a divergence between private and social benefits. The difference between P_X and P'_X (or between PB_X and MSB_X) gives the measure of the divergence of MSB_X from PB.

As shown in Figure 14.7, when social benefits of external economies are added to P_X, it rises to MSB_X. In that case, profit maximizing output will be OQ', which is greater than OQ. Thus, Pareto optimum (OQ) is less than the socially optimum output (OQ') when external economies are accounted for in social pricing. It means that the exclusion of social benefits (when $SB > 0$) leads to under production. It may, therefore, be concluded that, in the presence of external economies in production, Pareto optimality may not be realized even under perfect competition.

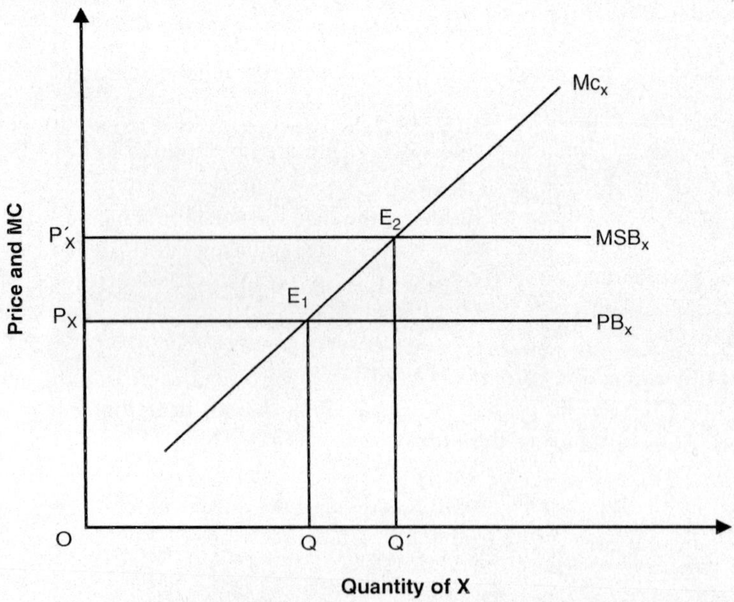

Figure 14.7 *Divergence between Private and Social Benefits and Optimum Output*

External Diseconomies in Production

Some widely known diseconomies of industrial production are: (i) environment and air pollution caused by factory smoke and emissions of transport vehicles; (ii) water-pollution caused by discharge of industrial effluents and wastes; and (iii) concentration of industries in an area creates industrial slums which breed diseases and criminals. The environment, air and water pollution are health hazards and pose threat to human, animal and plant lives. Due to these health hazards, medical expenses of the inhabitants of the area go up or they suffer from poor health. This is an external cost to the society resulting from the *external diseconomies* of production. All such costs incurred by the society, individually or collectively, to prevent the ill-effects of production of a commodity, are included in the *external social cost* (*ESC*). The external social cost is not included in the private cost of production. The total social cost (*TSC*) includes both private cost (*PC*) and social cost (*SC*) of a product, i.e.

$$TSC = PC + SC$$

There, is obviously, a divergence between private cost and total social cost. That is, $TSC > PC$, if SC is greater than 0. By definition, therefore, marginal social cost (*MSC*) exceeds the marginal private cost, *MC*.

Since there is a divergence between private and social costs, Pareto-optimum is not optimum in production. This point is illustrated in Figure 14.8. Given the MC_X curve and price OP_X, the Pareto optimal output is determined by point *E* at OX_1, i.e. the level of output where

$$MC_x = P_x\ (=MR_x)$$

If it were possible to measure the marginal external cost (MEC_X) and firms were made to pay for the full social costs, their MC_X curve will shift to MSC_X curve. Note that the vertical distance between MC_X

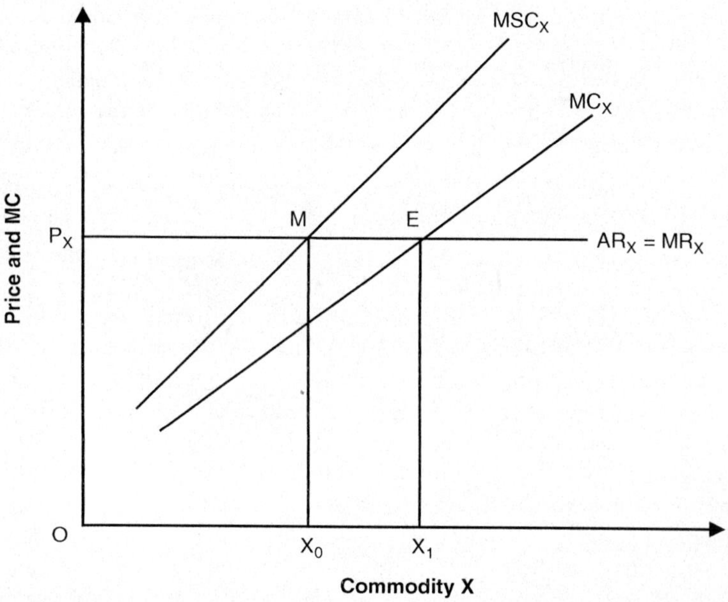

Figure 14.8 *Divergence between Private Social Costs and Optimum Output*

and MSC_X measures the external cost of production of commodity X. Given the MSC_X and P_X profit maximizing firms will be in equilibrium at point M and will produce OX_0 of X. Obviously, if external costs are included, Pareto optimal output will decrease from OX_1 to OX_0. It implies that exclusion of external costs (when $SC > 0$) leads to a larger production which is socially non-optimal.

However, in case social benefits and social costs of production cancel out each other, the Pareto optimality can be realized under perfect competition. The equality of social cost and benefits is, however, not guaranteed.

Externalities in Consumption

Interdependence of utility functions. Like externalities in production, there are externalities in consumption also. Externalities in consumption prevent the realization of Pareto optimality in consumption. We have shown below how external economies and diseconomies in consumption affect Pareto optimality under competitive conditions.

External Economies in Consumption

When a housewife replaces her traditional charcoal-stove with a gas-stove, her neighbours benefit because air-pollution caused by smoke is reduced. Similarly, if a person plants trees around his house or decorates his courtyard with flower pots, his neighbours benefit from the oxygen produced by the trees and also from the beautiful greenery around. A well-maintained car improves the safety of the people on the road and reduces air-pollution. Expenditure on education by some gives people benefit of an educated society.

All such external benefits imply that utility functions of some individuals are dependent on the consumption of others. Interdependence of utility functions violates one of the marginal conditions of Pareto optimality, i.e. it affects the condition that *MRS* between any pair of goods must be the same for all consumers. Since utility of one consumer increases because of increase in the consumption of another consumer, it is always possible to redistribute the goods and increase total social utility.

External Diseconomies in Consumption

Analogous to diseconomies in production, there are diseconomies in consumption too. Diseconomies in consumption arise when consumption of a commodity by an individual decreases the total utility of others. For example, (i) smoking cigarette in a bus, railway compartment, theatre or restaurant causes disutility to non-smokers; (ii) neighbours' colour TV reduces the utility of owners of black and white set; (iii) Veblen and snob effects also cause diseconomies in consumption; (iv) using automobiles causes air-pollution and breathing problems also to non-users and (v) playing radio and tape-recorder, and using loud-speakers for religious and marriage ceremonies cause disutility to others. Such diseconomies of consumption imply interdependence of utility functions, since utility of a commodity for a consumer depends on the consumption of that commodity by others.

The interdependence of consumers' utility functions affects Pareto optimality. The effect of interdependence of utility functions on Pareto optimality is illustrated graphically in Figure 14.9(a) and (b) Let us suppose (i) that there are two consumers, *A* and *B* of two commodities *X* and *Y*; (ii) that indifference maps of *A* and *B* are given as in Figure 14.9(a) and (b), respectively, (iii) that utility level of *A* is not affected by *B*'s consumption; and (iv) that utility level of *B* is affected by *A*'s consumption of *X*, but not of *Y*.

To begin the analysis, let us assume that *A* is at points *J* in panel (a) and *B* is at point *R* in panel (b). Suppose also that at these points $MRS^A_{X,Y} = MRS^B_{X,Y}$. Given this condition, let the distribution of commodities be changed in such a way that consumer *A* moves to point *L* where his consumption of commodity

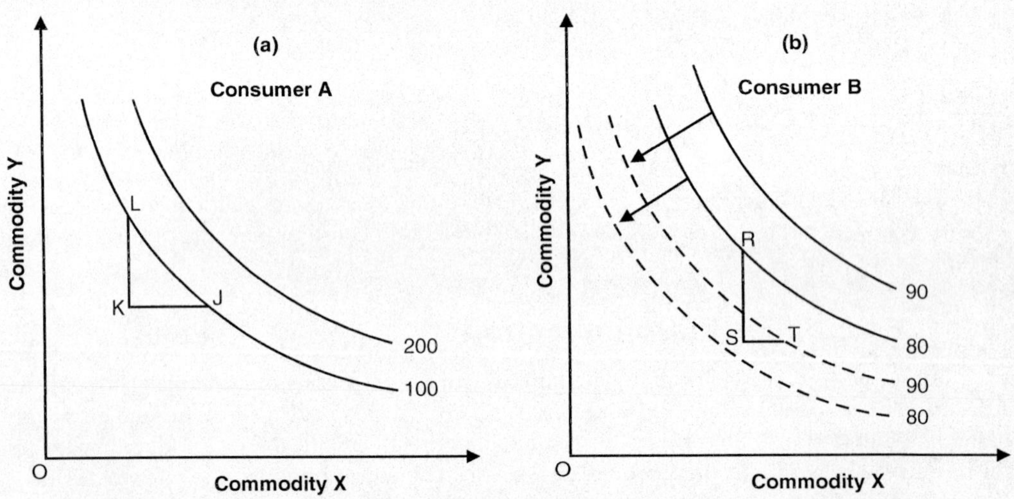

Figure 14.9 *Interdependence of Utility Functions and Pareto Optimality*

X decreases by JK and of Y increases by LK. Since A remains on the same indifference curve his total utility remains unchanged.

What about consumer B? Since consumer B's utility is dependent also on A's consumption of X (which has decreased), his indifference map shifts downwards due to fall in consumption of X by consumer A. It is so because of external costs (say, due to demonstration effect) borne by B due to A's consumption of X. The downward shift of B's indifference map implies that she gains the same utility from a smaller basket of goods. The downward shifts[25] are denoted by the dashed indifference curves [Figure 14.9(b)]. Assuming that consumer B moves from point R to point T, his index of total social satisfaction increases from 80 to 90. As a result of this shift, the total social satisfaction index increases from 180 (=A's 100 + B's 80) to 190 (=A's 100 + B's 90). Note also that at new equilibrium of A and B, $MRS^A_{X,Y} = MRS^B_{X,Y}$. It may thus be concluded that when externalities exist, equality of MRS between any pair of goods for any two consumers does not ensure realization of Pareto optimality. For, utility level of one consumer (B) can be increased without reducing utility level of the other consumer (A).

Externalities of Public Goods

We have so far discussed Pareto optimality in respect of *private goods* and the effects of externalities in their production and consumption. Here, we discuss optimality conditions in respect of public goods and externalities that arise due to consumption of public goods.

A pure public good is one to which *exclusion principle* of market cannot be applied. The important characteristics of a pure public good are following.

1. *Non-excludability of Consumers.* Nobody can be excluded from its consumption, nor can consumers be forced to pay for their benefit, e.g. for pollution control measures.
2. *Joint Consumption.* Its consumption is collective and all consumers are supplied with it jointly, e.g. pollution free environment.
3. Non-rival Consumption. A larger consumption of a public good by some does not affect the share of others, nor is their satisfaction level affected, e.g. telecast service.
4. *Zero Marginal Cost.* Marginal cost of supplying a public good is zero, i.e. if number of consumers increases, cost of supply of a public good, e.g. broadcasting and telecast services, does not increase.
5. *Non-appropriation.* No individual can appropriate a public good for his personal use.

Some standard examples of public goods are (a) Radio and TV transmission; (b) improved sanitary system of town; (c) air-pollution control programmes; (d) road safety-measures and (e) tree-plantation on the road sides and green-belts of a city. Some of these goods may, however, turn to be non-public goods beyond a certain number of consumers. Pareto optimality conditions are not valid to this category of goods. Public goods, therefore, require formulation of new rules. The rule for optimum output of public goods is that the sum of its marginal benefits must equal its marginal cost.[26] The marginal benefit of an individual from a public good, X, equals in theoretical terms, the amount of money that the individual is willing to pay for his benefit, i.e. in terms of his marginal rate of substitution between X and money (m).[27] Thus, the marginal benefit of an individual from X,

$$= \frac{MU_x}{MU_m} = MRS_{x,m}$$

The sum of marginal benefits of individuals from (1, 2, 3, …, *n*) *X* may thus be expressed as

$$\frac{MU_x^1}{MU_m^1}+\frac{MU_x^2}{MU_m^2}+\cdots+\frac{MU_x^n}{MU_m^n}$$

The optimum output condition for the public good (*X*) is then

$$\frac{MU_x^1}{MU_m^1}+\frac{MU_x^2}{MU_m^2}+\cdots+\frac{MU_x^n}{MU_m^n}=MC_x$$

In an economy, however, a public good exists along with many private goods. Under this condition, a Pareto optimum can be realized only by equating the *MRT* between the public goods and any other good with the sum of *MRS* between the same pair of goods for all the individuals. That is, Pareto optimality in case of a public good, *X*, and a private good, *Y*, is realized when

$$MRT_{x,y}=MRS_{x,y}$$

There remains, however, the problem of discovering individual utility functions. The knowledge of individual utility functions is necessary to obtain the sum of *MRS* of all the individuals.

Indivisibility and Pareto Optimality

One of the assumptions of Pareto optimality conditions is that commodities and inputs are perfectly divisible. In reality, however, one comes across many indivisible goods and services in both consumption (e.g. a car) and production processes (e.g. a machinery). If indivisibilities are introduced, perfect competition may not lead to optimal allocation of resources. Consider a few examples. Suppose there are two types of technology: one used by small-scale firms and the other used by large-scale firms. The large-scale firms enjoy the economies of scale and, therefore, have lower average cost of production than the small-scale firms. If large-scale technology is indivisible, then perfect competition does not ensure optimum allocation of resources. Nor does it lead to maximization of welfare.

Suppose also that a large number of firms are in competitive equilibrium and $MRT = MRS$ for all firms and consumers. Assume also that production process is indivisible and that economies of scale that accrue to the large firms are not available to the small firms. On the other hand, a few large firms can produce goods more efficiently. It means that if all inputs are used only by small number of large firms, production possibility curve will shift upwards. It may thus be concluded that if indivisibilities exist, production by small firms turns out to be in optimal, even if marginal conditions are satisfied under perfectly competitive conditions.

CONCLUSION

The welfare economics deals with the conditions under which economic welfare of the society can be maximized. It was Pareto who suggested certain conditions, called 'optimality conditions' for the maximization of welfare. The Pareto optimality conditions lay the foundation of the Welfare Economics.

According to Pareto, the existence of the following conditions is necessary for maximization of economic welfare:

1. Consumer goods and services are optimally distributed between all the consumers;
2. Factor inputs or factors of production are optimally allocated between the goods and service for their production;
3. Production of goods and services are optimally allocated between the firms;
4. All the optimality conditions are satisfied simultaneously.

However, the modern economists have pointed out certain deficiencies in economic system that may prevent the application of Pareto optimality conditions for maximization of economic welfare of the society. This has created condition for further contributions to welfare economics. This has led to the emergence of New Welfare Economics. The New Welfare Economics has been discussed in the forthcoming chapter.

REVIEW QUESTIONS AND EXERCISES

1. What welfare economics is about? Is it positive or normative in character?
2. Distinguish between:
   - (i) Classical and neoclassical welfare economics,
   - (ii) Neoclassical and Paretian welfare economics,
   - (iii) Paretian and new welfare economics.
3. State and explain the marginal conditions of Paretian optimum in consumption and production. What is total condition of Paretian optimum?
4. What are the conditions that must be fulfilled to achieve Pareto optimality in exchange and production under perfect conditions?
5. An equal division of income is an optimum division of income'. Elucidate.
6. 'A cake is divided between two individuals. Pareto optimality requires that they receive equal share'. Do you agree with the statement? Why?
7. In any economy producing two goods, if one of the goods is a pure public good, how will you modify the Pareto-optimality conditions to arrive at the optimum?
8. Pareto optimality is a necessary but not a sufficient condition for welfare maximization. Examine this statement in the context of a given social welfare function and grand utility possibility frontier.
9. State the marginal conditions for Pareto optimality. How are the conditions affected by the presence of:
   - (i) externalities in production,
   - (ii) externalities in consumption, and
   - (iii) public goods?
10. What are the Paretian optimality conditions? Are they necessarily achieved under perfect competition?
11. 'The Pareto criterion does not give us a sufficient basis for ordering states. The Kaldor-Hicks-Scitovsky criteria do not carry us much farther. 'Examine the statement critically.

12. State the conditions of Pareto optimality. How are these conditions affected in the presence of (i) social cost, and (ii) public goods?
13. (a) State and explain graphically the marginal conditions of a Pareto-optimal distribution of goods and resources in a two-commodity-two-consumer-two-input model.
14. (b) How can the Kaldor-Hicks-Scifovsky criteria be considered as an improvement over the Pareto criterion?
15. If $MRT_{X,Y} = 2/3$, while $MRS_{X,Y} = 2$ for individuals A and B, should the economy produce more of X or more of Y to reach equilibrium of production and exchange simultaneously? Why?
16. What is meant by externalities in consumption and production? How does the existence externalities affect the achievement of Pareto optimum?
17. The concept of 'social optimum' was introduced to welfare economics by
    (a) A.C. Pigou,
    (b) J. Bentham,
    (c) Vilfred Pareto,
    (d) Adam Smith.
18. Pareto optimality in exchange is gained under which of the following conditions?
    (a) $MRS^A_{x,y} = MRS^B_{x,y} = MRT_{x,y}$
    (b) $MRT^L_{A,B} = MRT^K_{A,B}$
    (c) $MRTS^X_{L,K} = MRTS^Y_{L,K}$
    (d) $\dfrac{MU_x}{P_x} = \dfrac{MU_y}{P_y}$
19. Pareto optimality in production is gained in which of the following conditions?
    (a) $MRTS^X_{L,K} = MRTS^Y_{L,K}$
    (b) $MRS^A_{x,y} = MRS^B_{x,y}$
    (c) $MRT^k_{x,y} = MRT^L_{x,y}$
    (d) $\dfrac{MP_L}{P_L} = \dfrac{MP_K}{P_K}$
20. General Pareto optimality exists where
    (a) $MRTS^X_{L,K} = MRTS^Y_{L,K}$
    (b) $MRT_{x,y} = MRS^A_{x,y} = MRS^B_{x,y}$
    (c) $MRTS^L_{x,y} = MRTS^K_{x,y}$

    Or

    (d) $\dfrac{MP_L}{MP_K} = \dfrac{P_1}{P_K}$?
21. In a model consisting of two individuals (A and B), two goods (X and Y), and two factors (L and K), the total Pareto optimality requires which of the following conditions?
    (a) $MRS^A_{x,y} = MRS^B_{x,y}$
    (b) $MRS^A_{x,y} = MRS^B_{x,y} = MRT_{x,y}$

(c) $MRTS^X_{L,K} = MRTS^Y_{L,K}$

(d) All the above at the same point?

[**Ans.** 21 (c), 22 (a), 23 (a), 24 (b), 25 (d)]

ENDNOTES

1. Lange, O. (1942), The Foundations of Welfare Economics,' *Econometrica*, 10, Reprinted in Arrow, K.J. and Scitovskv, T. (eds.), *Readings; in Welfare Economics* (London: George Allen and Unwin), pp. 26–28.
2. Reder, M.W. (1947), *Studies in the Theory of Welfare Economics* (New York: Colombia University Press), p. 13.
3. Mishan, E.J. (1965), *A Survey of Welfare Economics, Survey of Economic Theory* (London: Macmillan), Vol. I, p. 156.
4. Reder, *op. cit.*, p. 13.
5. I.M.D. Little has, however, shown in his *A Critique of Welfare Economics* (Oxford University Press, 1957) that Pigou's *Economics of Welfare* cannot be regarded as a purely objective study of the causes of welfare.
6. Baumol, W.J. *Economic Theory and Operation Analysis, op. cit.* p. 496.
7. Quoted in Little, I.M.D. (1957), *A Critique of Welfare Economics* (Oxford University Press), 2nd Edn., p. 70.
8. Boulding, K.E. (1952), Welfare Economics, in Haley, B.P. (ed.), *A Survey of Contemporary Economics*, Vol. II by (Richard D.Irwin, Inc), p. 12.
9. Mishan, *op. cit.*, p. 154.
10. Mark, B., *op. cit.*, p. 618.
11. Winch, D.M. (1971), *Analytical Welfare Economics* (Penguin), p. 77.
12. Little, I.M.D., *op. cit.*, p. 84.
13. Dobb, M. (1973), Theories of Value and Distribution Since Adam Smith, 1973.
14. Hicks, J.R. (1939), The Foundations of Welfare Economics', *Econ. J.*, (December).
15. Lerner, A.P. (1944), *The Economics of Control* (London: Macmillan), Chapter III.
16. Lange, O. (1942), The Foundation of Welfare Economics, *Econometrica*, (July–October).
17. Reder, W.M. has analysed marginal conditions under seven categories. But, as he himself has said, his second, third and fourth conditions can be reduced to one following Hicksian convention of treating factors (inputs) as negative output. His sixth and seventh conditions and also some of those suggested by Boulding (*op. cit.*) have been summarized, in this chapter under 'Total Optimality Conditions'.
18. Edgeworth's box diagram has been explained in Chapter 13.
19. However, the Pareto optimality point of exchange can be obtained by introducing the price line or the budget line. For graphical proof, see Figure 13.4 in Chapter 13.
20. Recall that *MRT* is the rate at which one product can be transformed into another. For example, suppose if one unit of *X* is not produced, then *k* units of capital and *L* units of labour are saved. If factors saved $(k + l)$ can produce 2 units of *Y*, then $MRT = \Delta Y/(-)\Delta X = 2$.

21. Winch, D.M., *op. cit.*, p. 80.
22. One can assume different *MRT* curves for firms F_1 and F_2 and use a diagram like Figure 14.4, making sure that their *MRT* curves are tangent to a point *P* in Figure 14.5.
23. Boulding, K.E., *op. cit.*, p. 23.
24. Reder, *op. cit.*, p. 37.
25. Downward shift implies that *B* gains the same utility even when she consumes less of *X* or *Y* or of both because she gains from the fall in *A*'s consumption of *X*.
26. Henderson and Quant, *op. cit.*, pp. 290–298.
27. Baumol, W.J., *op. cit.*, p. 522.

FURTHER READINGS

Arrow, K.N. (1951), *Social Choice and Individual Values* (New York: John Wiley and Sons, Inc.).
Bator, F.M. (1957), 'The Simple Analytics of Welfare Maximisation', *Am. Eco. Rev.*, 47, 22–59.
Baumol, W.J. (1952), *Welfare Economics and the Theory of the State* (London: Longmans, Green and Co. Ltd.).
——— (1964), 'External Economies and Second-order Conditions', *Am. Eco. Rev.*, LIV: 358–372.
——— (1980), *Economic Theory and Operations Analysis* (New Delhi: Prentice Hall of India), 4th Edn., Chapter 21.
Bergson, A. (1938), 'A Reformulation of Certain Aspects of Welfare Economics', *Q. J. Econ.*, 52 (February), reprinted in *Readings in Economic Analysis* (Cambridge, MA: Addison-Wesley), R.V. Clemence (ed.), (1950).
Davis, O.A. and Whinston, A.B. (1965), 'Welfare Economics and the Theory of Second Best', *Rev. Econ. Stud.*, 32: 1–14.
Graff, J.De.V. (1957), *Theoretical Welfare Economics* (New York: Cambridge University Press).
Hicks, J.R. (1939), 'The Foundation of Welfare Economies', *Eco. Jl.*, XLIX.
Kaldor, N. (1939), 'Welfare Propositions in Economics and Interpersonal Comparisons of Utility', *Econ. J.*, XLIX: 549–552.
Koutsoyiannis, A. (1979), *Modern Macroeconomics* (London: Macmillan), 2nd Edn., Chapter 23.
Lange, O. (1942), 'The Foundations of Welfare Economics', *Econometrica*, vol.10.
——— (1969), *Welfare Economics: An Assessment* (Amsterdam: North Holland).
Lerner, A.P. (1946), *The Economics of Control* (New York: The Macmillan Co.).
Lipsey, R.G. and Lancaster K. (1956–1957), 'The General Theory of Second Best', *Rev. Eco. and Stud.*, XXIV: 11–32.
Little, I.M.D. (1957), *A Critique of Welfare Economics* (London: Oxford University Press), 2nd Edn.
Mishan, E.J. (1960), 'A Survey of Welfare Economics, 1939–1959', *Econ. J.*, LXX.
Mishan, E. (1964), *Welfare Economics* (New York: Random House).
Myint, M.H. (1948), *Theories of Welfare Economics*.
Pareto, V. (1906), *Manual of Political Economy* (Paris: Giard, V. and Bre're, E.), published in English in 1909.
Pigou, A.C. (1932), *The Economics of Welfare* (London: Macmillan, and Co.).
Quirk, J. and Saposnik, R. (1968), *Introduction to General Equilibrium Theory and Welfare Economics* (New York, NY: McGraw-Hill).
Reder, M.W. (1947), *Studies in the Theory of Welfare Economics* (New York: Columbia University Press).

Samuelson, P.A. (1948), *Foundations of Economic Analysis* (Cambridge, MA: Harvard University Press), Chapter VIII.

——— (1956), 'Social Indifference Curves', *Q. J. Econ.*, 70.

——— (1942–1943), 'A Reconsideration of Theory of Tariffs', *Rev. Eco. Stud.*, IX. Reprinted in American Economic Association (1949) *Readings in the Theory of International Trade* (New York: McGraw-Hill).

Scitovsky, T. (1941–1942), 'A Note on Welfare Propositions in Economics', *Rev. Eco. Stud.*, IX.

Winch, D.M. (1971), *Analytical Welfare Economics* (London: Penguin).

Chapter 15

New Welfare Economics

CHAPTER OBJECTIVES

The new welfare economics refers to the developments in welfare economics beyond Pareto welfare economics. The objective of this chapter is to discuss the developments that have taken place in welfare economics after Pareto's contribution. By going through this chapter, you will know:

- What major contributions are made to welfare economics by the modern economists;
- What is Kaldor–Hicks principle of compensation for welfare maximization;
- What are Scitovsky's double criteria for welfare maximization;
- What is Bergson's welfare function and how it can be maximized;
- What is 'Grand Utility Possibility Frontier' and how is it applied for welfare maximization; and
- What is the 'Theory of Second Best' in the analysis of welfare economics.

INTRODUCTION

According to Pareto optimality conditions, as discussed in the preceding chapter, economic welfare of the society is maximized when consumer goods are optimally allocated between the consumers, production inputs are optimally allocated for the production of goods and services, and production of goods is optimally allocated between the firms. Optimum allocation of resources implies that any reallocation of resources between consumers and producers will reduce the economic welfare and it is not possible to make some one better-off without making some one worse-off. However, modern economists are of the view that this kind of Pareto optimality is practically unachievable. In general, the resources are so distributed among the members of the society that it is always possible to reallocate the resources to maximize the welfare. In the opinion of the modern economists, especially, Kaldor, Hicks and Scitovsky, it is difficult to think of a change in reallocation of resources that can make some one better-off without making some one worse-off. Any change in the allocation of resources will make some one better-off and some one worse-off. But, it is always possible to increase the social welfare so long as the persons who gain from the change are able and willing to compensate those who lose from the change and yet remain better-off. This thought of the modern economists gave birth to a new principle, called *principle of compensation*. The *principle of compensation* forms the basis of *New Welfare Economics*.

The new welfare economics is founded on the 'compensation principle'. To understand compensation principles, let us recall the Pareto criteria for welfare judgement. As noted above, according to Pareto criterion, social welfare increases if reallocation of resources makes at least one individual better-off without making any other individual worse-off. It is, however, difficult to imagine an economic change or implementation of a policy measure that does not affect any individual adversely. In reality, most economic changes make some people better-off and some worse-off, and gains and losses of the individuals do not always cancel out. Pareto criterion does not evaluate such economic changes. The economists, namely Kaldor, Hicks and Scitovsky, have, however, devised compensation criteria[1] in their attempt to overcome the limitations of the Pareto criteria of maximum social welfare. This has come to be called *New Welfare Economics.*

In this chapter, we explain the *compensation criteria* proposed by Kaldor, Hicks and Scitovsky and also the contributions made by other economists.

THE KALDOR–HICKS COMPENSATION CRITERION

Although Kaldor[2] and Hicks[3] proposed their compensation criteria in their separate articles in 1939, their criteria are conceptually very much similar. Their individual criteria are, therefore, jointly referred to as *Kaldor–Hicks Criterion.* There is, however, a minor difference between their criteria which must be noted at the very outset. While Kaldor evaluates compensation from gainers' point of view, Hicks does it from losers' angle. According to Kaldor, if an economic change makes some people gain and some others lose, and gainers are able to compensate the losers and yet they are better-off, then the change increases social welfare. According to Hicks, if an economic change makes some people gain and some others lose, and losers are not able to compensate the gainers to prevent them from voting for the change, then the change is socially desirable. Although both criteria are essentially the same, Hicks' criterion gives a definitive measure of compensation.

The Kaldor–Hicks criterion may be stated as follows: if gainers of a proposed economic change (or reallocation of resources) evaluate their gains as G and losers evaluate their losses as L, and if $G > L$, then gainers would be able to compensate the losers and yet retain a net gain. Under this condition, the proposed change will increase the social welfare.

The Kaldor–Hicks compensation criterion is graphically illustrated in Figure 15.1 Vertical axis measures B's utility and horizontal axis measures A's utility. Figure 15.1 presents two utility possibility curves—UP and WD—with and without change in resource allocation, respectively. The curve UP is the utility possibility curve obtained by graphing combinations of utilities of A and B as represented by various points on the consumption contract curve in Edgeworth box diagram of exchange (see Figure 15.1). The curve UP shows the various combinations of utility received by A and B, in the utility space, when the economy is in the state of general equilibrium. Recall that at each point on UP curve, $MRS^A_{x,y} = MRS^B_{x,y}$. Likewise, the curve WD represents the possible utility combinations from a proposed economic change.

Now, consider first the utility possibility curve UP. All points on this curve (e.g. points J and K) represent the alternative distribution of utilities with the existing distribution of resources. The movement along the UP curve gives the measure of utility lost and gained by A and B. The movement from point U towards point P shows the utility lost by B and utility gained by A. For example, a movement from point J to K indicates that B loses utility JM and A gains utility MK and vice versa. It is important to note that a change from J and K implies that A (the gainer) can compensate B (the

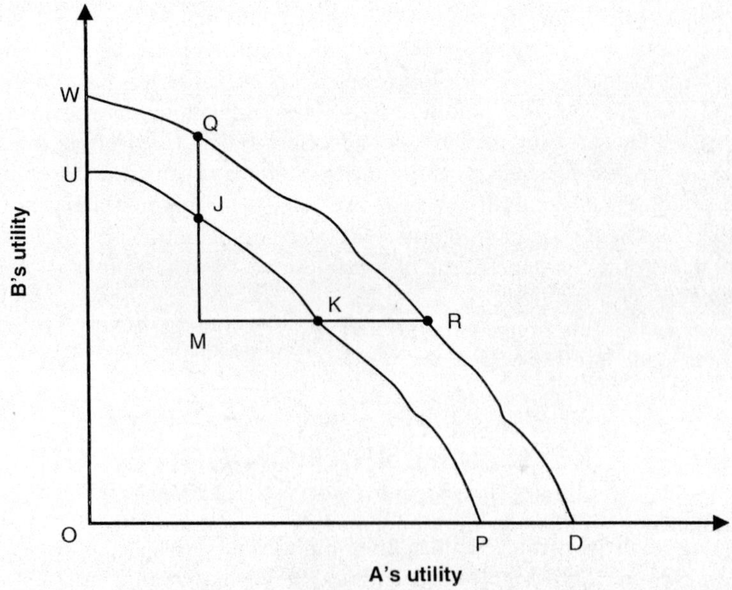

Figure 15.1 *Utility Possibility Curves and Kaldor–Hicks Criterion*

loser) without retaining any net gain, since *A*'s gain equals *B*'s loss. Pareto optimality condition can be applied to evaluate this change. But a movement from point *J* on the curve *UP* to the point *R* on the upper curve *WD* due to an economic change would make *A* better-off and *B* worse-off. This change cannot be evaluated by Pareto criterion. On the Kaldor–Hicks criterion, however, movement from *J* to *R* is an improvement in welfare, because *A* can compensate *B* for her loss and yet be better-off than his position at *J*. *A*'s movement from point *J* to *R* indicates *B*'s loss of utility by *JM* and *A*'s gain of utility by *MR*. Note that $MR = MK + KR$ and *MK* is just sufficient to compensate *B* because $MK = JM$. After compensating *B* for her loss, *A* is left with a net gain of *KR*. This shows an improvement in social welfare. The Kaldor–Hicks criterion applies also to movement from point *K* to *Q*.

Whether compensation is actually paid or not is, in Kaldor's opinion, a matter of political or ethical decision. In the welfare criterion, compensation is simply a measure of difference between gainer's gain and loser's loss. In formulating his criterion for judging the social desirability of an economic change, Kaldor merely suggests that the gainers must be potentially able to compensate the losers and yet retain some gains to themselves. The Kaldor–Hicks criterion is, therefore, considered to be a superior criterion and an important improvement in welfare economics.

Shortcomings of Kaldor–Hicks Criterion

Although Kaldor–Hicks criterion is considered to be an important contribution to welfare economics, it has its own shortcoming.

First, the fundamental problem in compensation criterion is that it refers to only potential rather than the actual compensation. There is a world of difference between a potential and an actual compensation.

If losers are actually compensated for their loss, then no problem arises. It satisfies the Kolder–Hicks criterion, i.e. at least one person is better-off and no person is worse-off. But, if the potential compensation is not actually paid, then what happens to the measure of welfare? In that case, welfare has to be measured only in terms of feelings. It requires that the individual preference pattern is also known. This means 'interpersonal comparison of utility'.[4] But this issue is still unresolved. The Kaldor–Hicks criterion, therefore, does not provide a test free from value judgement.

Secondly, another problem with Kaldor–Hicks criterion is the use of money value of gains and losses in evaluating the economic efficiency of a change. But the value of money itself varies from person to person. This results in a serious shortcoming in compensation criterion, as it does not give the real value of gains and losses. If gainers are highly rich, the real value of their monetary gain (even if it far exceeds the loss of losers) may be insignificant compared to the real loss to the poor (even if monetary loss is much less than gainers' monetary gain). In that case, the gainer may not be able to compensate the loser.

Finally, Scitovsky has pointed out a *contradiction* in Kaldor–Hicks criterion. The contradiction is illustrated in Figure 15.2. Suppose a proposed economic change affects not only the utility of each individual (*A* and *B*) but also shifts simultaneously the utility possibility curve (*UP*) in such a manner that it intersects *WD*, as shown in Figure 15.2. It means that a change from *J* and *K* not only changes utilities of *A* and *B*, but also it makes the utility possibility curves intersect. Note that *WD* intersects *UP*. There is no reason why the utility possibility curves should not intersect.

To illustrate the *contradiction*, let us begin by considering a policy change that makes *A* and *B* to move from point *J* to *L* or to *M* or to any point (e.g. *Q*) between *L* and *M*. Such a movement satisfies Pareto criterion. However, Pareto criterion cannot evaluate a situation that results due to a move from point *J* to *R*, because, in this case, *A* gains at the cost of *B*. This situation can however be evaluated on the basis of Kaldor–Hicks criterion, simply by asking *A* how much he would like to pay to have the change and by

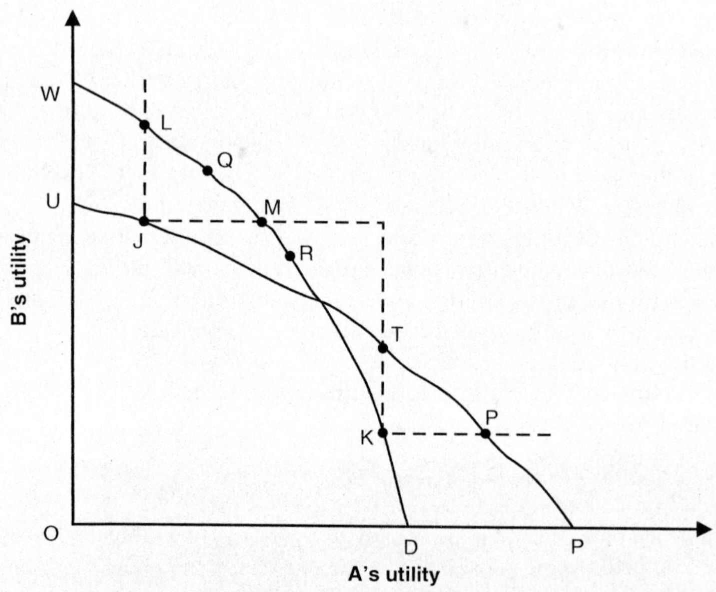

Figure 15.2 *Contradiction in Kaldor–Hicks Criterion*

asking B how much she would pay to prevent the change. Suppose A puts his amount at M_a and B puts it at M_b. If $M_a > M_b$, the policy change makes an improvement in welfare. But, it is difficult to evaluate social welfare implication of a movement from J to K, on the Kaldor–Hicks criterion. The same argument can be applied to the change from point K back to J. Note that in the change from J to K, point K can be regarded a superior point. But in a change from K to J, point J is a superior point and K an inferior point. Thus, Kaldor–Hicks criterion is self-contradictory.

THE SCITOVSKY DOUBLE CRITERIA

As mentioned above, Scitovsky pointed out a contradiction in Kaldor–Hicks criterion. He then proposed his own criterion, called *double criterion.*[5] His criterion may be stated as follows: A change in economic situation of individuals would increase welfare only if (i) the change improves welfare on Kaldor–Hicks criterion and (ii) losers are not capable of bribing the gainers for voting against the change. Obviously, Scitovsky's criterion is rather stringent.

Scitovsky's criterion is based on the premise of Kaldor–Hicks criterion. In fact, one of his double criteria is the same as Kaldor–Hicks criterion. It can, therefore, be said that most of criticism against Kaldor–Hicks criterion apply also to Scitovsky's double criterion. In addition, there are only a few changes in real life that would meet the Scitovsky double criterion. In fact, if the double criterion is to be satisfied for an increase in welfare, the general welfare should not be affected by change in expenditure pattern and in income distribution.[6]

THE BERGSON CRITERION: THE SOCIAL WELFARE FUNCTION

It may be concluded from the foregoing discussion that the attempts to devise a value-free-welfare criterion have not yielded satisfactory results. It is not possible to evaluate a change which makes some persons better-off and some worse-off without making some implicit value judgement about the deservingness of an individual or a group. Recognizing the inevitability of value judgement, Bergson[7] suggested that the only way out to resolve this problem is to formulate a set of explicit value judgement which enables the analyst to evaluate the situation. The value judgements may be set by the analyst himself, government authorities, legislators, social reformers or an individual or a group of the society. Bergson suggests that value judgements may be explicitly formulated in the form of a social welfare function. A social welfare function is an indifference map which ranks different combinations of individual utilities according to a set of explicit value judgements about the distribution of income. It is analogous to the utility function of a consumer. More precisely, a social welfare function is an ordinal index of welfare of the society and is a function of the utility levels of all individual members. It may be expressed as

$$W = f(u_1, u_2, \ldots, u_n)$$

where W denotes social welfare and $u_1, u_2, \ldots$ are utility index of an individual.

Assuming an economy of two persons, A and B, the social welfare function may be written as

$$W = F(U_A, U_B)$$

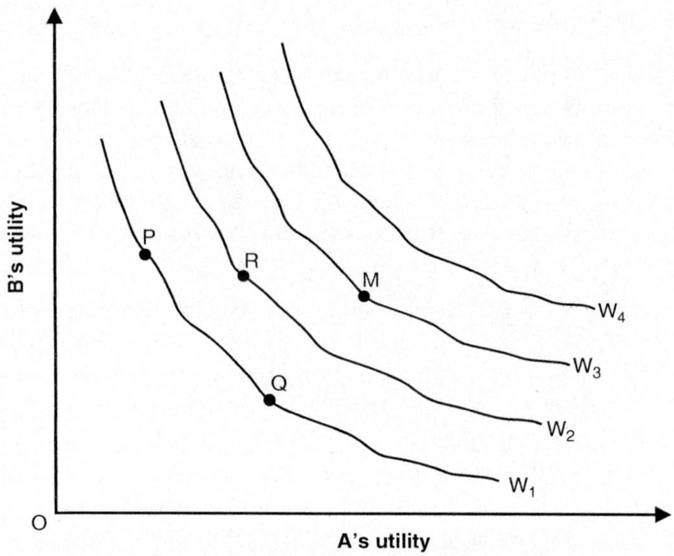

Figure 15.3 *Bergson's Social Welfare Function*

This function may be represented by a set of social indifference curves, as shown in Figure 15.3. Each social indifference curve (such as W_1, W_2, … , W_n) in utility space is the locus of combination of utilities of individuals *A* and *B*, which yields the same level of social welfare. The social welfare function as mapped in Figure 15.3 permits an analyst to judge unambiguously whether a proposed policy change is or is not an improvement in welfare. For example, a change from *P* to *R* or to *M* improves social welfare since these points are on higher social indifference curves. But a change from *P* to *Q* does not improve social welfare as *Q* lies on the same social indifference curve.

Weakness of Bergson Criterion

Although Bergson's criterion has been well received by economists, it has its own *weaknesses.*

First, Bergson's criterion requires explicit value judgements. Value judgements of different categories of judges may differ. Economists' value judgement may be different from those of the legislators, electorates or a committee assigned with the task of policy making. Bergson does not offer a solution to resolve such difference in value judgements.

Secondly, there is no easy method of constructing social welfare function. Bergson's criterion does not come out with necessary instructions for making welfare judgements which are required in the formulation of welfare function. Thus, the most difficult problem of this criterion remains unsolved. As Mishan has pointed out, 'Although the social welfare function had received continual mention since Bergson's 1938 formulation, no instruction in the drafting of this grandiose design had been hazarded.'[8]

Thirdly, construction of social welfare function on the basis of ordinal preferences of the individuals leads to contradictions if majority rule is applied. If majority votes for a non-essential commodity, the essential ones may not be adequately produced.

ARROW'S THEOREM OF DEMOCRATIC GROUP DECISION

As noted above, Bergson's criterion runs into difficulty when it comes to formulating the social welfare function, i.e. translating individual choices into group decisions. Arrow[9] has attempted to formulate social preferences. In this section, we briefly describe the Arrow's theorem of social choices.

Arrow's Axioms. Social preferences may be formulated on the basis of individual preferences by legislators or by policy makers by majority rule applied to group choices. Not all methods are equally desirable or sensible. Arrow has stated axioms which social choices must meet in order to be acceptable to maximum number of people:

1. Social choices must be transitive. It means that if an event *A* is preferred to event *B* and *B* is preferred to event *C*, then *C* is not preferred to *A*.
2. Social choices must not be dictated by anybody within or without the group.
3. Social choices must reflect the majority individual preferences and must not change in opposite direction, i.e. a choice which would have been made by the majority must not be rejected just because some people favour it more than others. Furthermore, if no individual prefers *A* to *B* and at least one person prefers *B* to *A*, society must prefer *B* to *A*.
4. The ordering of social choices must not change so long as individuals do not change their own ordering of alternatives. But, when individual ranking changes, the ranking of social choices must change.

Problems in Arrow's Theorem

Arrow's axioms are said to be reasonable as his axioms provide an appropriate set of conditions for making democratic choices. However, Arrow's axioms have *two serious problems.*

First, Arrow has himself demonstrated that it is not possible to formulate social preferences that satisfy all the axioms. Baumol[10] has illustrated the difficulties that arise in formulating social choices. The standard procedure of making a social decision is to go by the majority rule. But the majority rule may lead to social choices which are not transitive even if individual preferences are transitive. For example, suppose there are three individuals, *X, Y* and *Z* (each with 6 votes) to make choice from three alternatives, *A, B* and C, and their voting pattern for the three alternatives is given in the following table.

	Alternatives		
Individual	*A*	*B*	*C*
X	3	2	1
Y	1	3	2
Z	2	1	3

As the table reveals, *X* and *Z* prefer *A* to *B; X* and *Y* prefer *B* to *C* and *Y* and *Z* prefer *C* to *A*. Obviously, majority (i.e. two of three individuals) prefers *A* to *B* and *B* to *C*, and *they also prefer C* to *A*. Thus, majority rule leads to intransitive social choices, i.e. it is difficult to find majority choice.

Secondly, Arrow's fourth axiom is more restrictive than it appears. This axiom considers only the ranking, not the intensity of feelings. For example, suppose 50 per cent population of a city prefers a flyover while the remaining 50 per cent prefer houses for homeless. But the feeling of those who prefer house for homeless may be much more intensive. Arrow's fourth axiom ignores this fact, although there is no measure of feeling.

Despite these shortcomings, however, Arrow's contribution is regarded as an important addition to economists' analytical tools.

GRAND UTILITY POSSIBILITY FRONTIER AND WELFARE MAXIMIZATION

Another important contribution to welfare analysis of Pareto tradition was made by F.M. Bator.[11] He has combined the concept of social welfare function with Pareto's optimality condition in production and consumption to arrive at the *point of bliss*, i.e. the point of *optimum optimorum*. Assuming that there does exist a social welfare function, he derives a *grand utility possibility frontier* from Edgeworth's box diagrams for efficiency in consumption and production as described below.

Derivation of Grand Utility Possibility Frontier

Recall our two-consumer, two-good, two-firm and two-input model along with its assumptions. Using this model, we have shown that optimality in consumption and production mix of two commodities, X and Y, requires that $MRS^A_{x,y} = MRS^B_{x,y} = MRT^B_{x,y}$, where superscripts A and B denote two consumers. The production possibility curve is shown by the curve PP' in Figure 15.4. Let us suppose that the point that satisfies optimality condition is point K in Figure 15.4. At point K, output mix is $O_A X_1 + O_A Y_1$. The distribution of

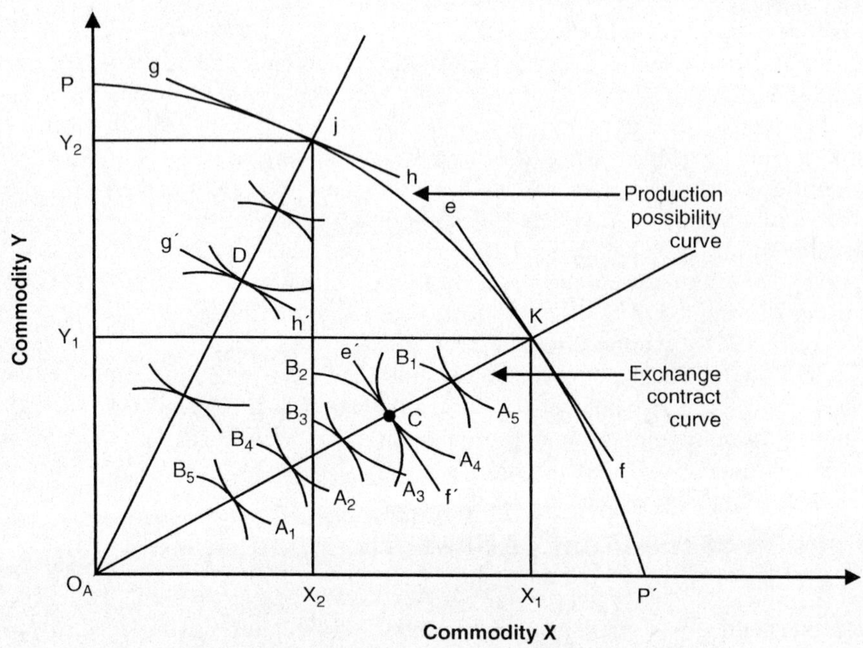

Figure 15.4 *Pareto Optimality in Product Mix*

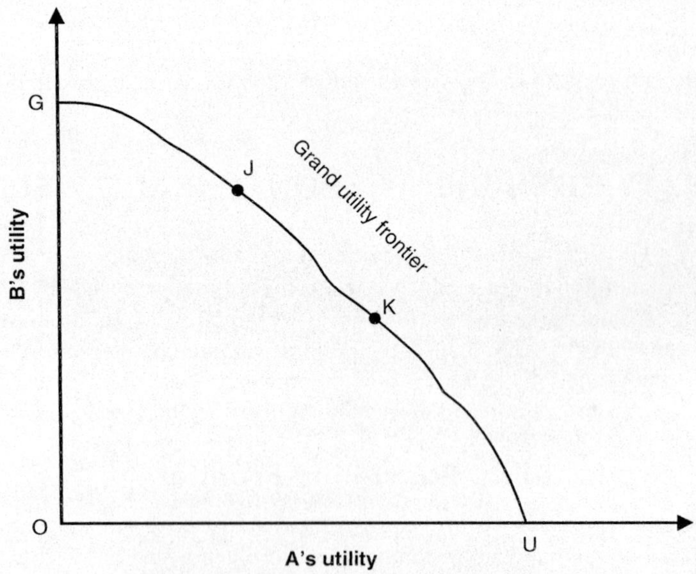

Figure 15.5 *Grand Utility Possibility Frontier*

O_AY_1 (between consumers *A* and *B*) will be somewhere on the *exchange contract curve*, O_AK, at the point of tangency between *A*'s and *B*'s indifferent curves.

Let the distribution of two goods between the two individuals take place at point *C*. It can be shown that point *C* satisfies the optimality condition, i.e. $MRS^A_{x,y} = MRS^B_{x,y} = MRT^B_{x,y}$ because line *e'f'* is parallel to the line *ef* which is tangent to the *PP'* curve at point *K*—point *K* gives the $MRT_{X,Y}$. The distribution of O_AX_1 and O_AY_1 at point *C* yields some utility to consumer *A* and some utility to consumer *B*. Suppose by plotting their utility on a utility surface, we get point *K* in Figure 15.5. Point *K*, therefore, represents the point of *grand utility* available to the society of two persons, *A* and *B*

This procedure can be repeated for each point on the production possibility curve (i.e. the transformation curve). For example, if point *J* in Figure 15.4 gives the product-mix (i.e. $O_AX_2 + O_AY_2$), and point *D* gives the distribution of O_AX_2 and O_AY_2 between *A* and *B*, the *grand utility* is represented by point *J* in Figure 15.5. If we continued to repeat this procedure for other points on the transformation curve, we get a curve *GU* through points *K* and *J*, as shown in Figure 15.5. This curve is known as *Grand Utility Possibility Frontier*. At each point on the grand utility possibility frontier, $MRS^A_{x,y} = MRS^B_{x,y} = MRT$. The grand utility possibility frontier shows the maximum utility available to the society, given the production possibility frontier.

Determination of the Point of Bliss: The Point of Maximum Social Welfare

Figure 15.6 presents the grand utility possibility frontier (*GU*) combined with social welfare function shown by a set of social indifference curves, W_1, W_2 and W_3. One thing is certain that the point of maximum welfare lies on the *grand utility possibility curve* (*GU*). Any point (e.g. point *N*) which lies

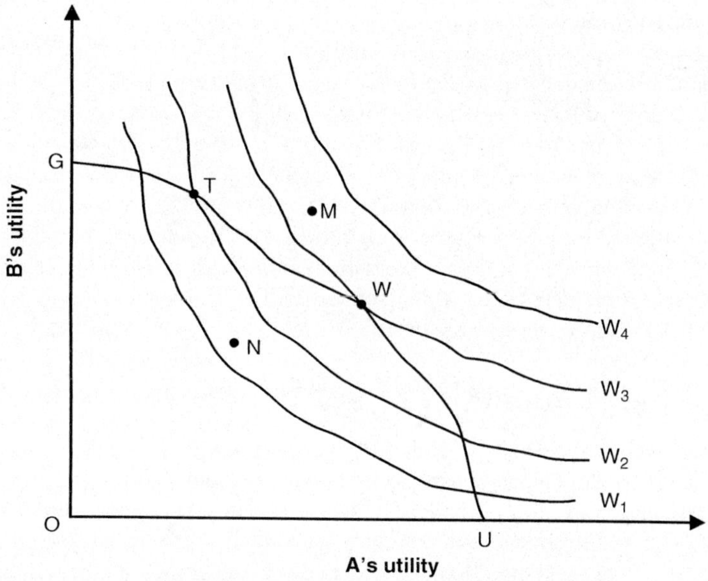

Figure 15.6 *Maximization of Social Welfare: The Point of Bliss*

below the *GU* curve represents a less than maximum welfare and any point (e.g. point *M*) which lies beyond the *GU* curve represents an unattainable level of welfare. Furthermore, not all points on the *GU* curve represent maximum welfare. There is only one specific point of maximum welfare. This point lies where the grand utility possibility curve (*GU*) is tangent with the highest possible social indifference (W_S) as shown by point *W* in Figure 15.6. This point is called the *point of bliss* as it represents the maximum possible attainable social welfare. Any other point on *the grand utility frontiers curve* (*GU*) even the points of intersection of *GU* curve and social indifference curves, say at point *T*, is inferior because it lies on a lower social indifference curve.

It is important to note here that Figure 15.6 establishes only the necessary conditions of Pareto optimality, not the sufficient conditions. Each point on the *grand utility possibility curve* (*GU*) satisfies the first three marginal conditions. But, each point on *GU* curve is not Pareto optimal.

THE THEORY OF SECOND BEST

The basic idea underlying the *theory of the second best* was conceived and used by different economists in different contexts. The principle of *second best* was, however, generalized for the first time by Richard G. Lipsey and Kelvin Lancaster[12] though they themselves refuted this theory. The theory of second best as formulated by Lipsey and Lancaster is briefly described here.

The basic idea behind the theory of *second best* is as follows. The *first best* solution to welfare maximization is obtained only when all the marginal conditions of Pareto optimality are simultaneously satisfied. However, if any of the marginal conditions is not satisfied somewhere in the economy, the first best solution (i.e. the Pareto optimum solution) cannot be obtained. And, there are reasons to believe that, because of institutional constraints (like monopolies and imperfect market conditions, etc.), externalities and indivisibilities, one or more of the first-order conditions may not be satisfied. This would mean that the first best solution is not attainable. However, for a long time, economists believed that, if one or more of the first-order conditions of Pareto optimality are not fulfilled for some reason, it is still desirable to satisfy the remaining conditions to have a solution as close as possible to Pareto optimum. This is the *theory of second best*. Henderson and Quandt[13] have summarized the second best theory in following words: '[where] the best welfare position is unattainable ..., it is relevant to enquire whether a second-best position can be attained by satisfying the remaining Pareto conditions.' Economists believed that the greater the number of conditions satisfied, the closer would be the solution to Pareto optimum. This belief prevailed for a long time and found application to the fields like public finance and international trade[14] until Lipsey and Lancaster refuted the belief.

Lipsey–Lancaster Refute the Second Best Theory

Lipsey and Lancaster suggested that if ' ... one of the Paretian optimum conditions cannot be fulfilled, then an optimum situation can be achieved only by departing from all the other Paretian conditions.' In other words, if any of the Pareto optimality conditions is not satisfied, the attempt to reach Pareto optimum—the first best solution—must be abandoned, and the second best solution should not be attempted. Thus, according to Lipsey and Lancaster, if one or more of the necessary conditions for Pareto optimality cannot be satisfied in general, it is neither necessary nor desirable to satisfying the remaining conditions.

In their *theory of second best*, Lipsey and Lancaster have proved that if the first best solution is not realized, then there is nothing to choose between the second best or the third best and so on. This conclusion is contrary to the earlier belief that if the *first best* is unattainable, then the *second best* may be attained even if some Pareto optimality conditions are not satisfied. The implications of Lipsey–Lancaster argument for traditional welfare economics are devastating as their theory effectively questions the desirability of attaining Pareto optimality through various policy measures on piecemeal basis.

CONCLUSION

Welfare economics begins with Pareto optimality conditions. However, economists found analytical deficiencies and problems in the application of Pareto optimality conditions. This led to the formulation of other theories of welfare maximization. The new theories of welfare maximization came to be known as *new welfare economies*. The foundation of the new welfare economics lies in the introduction of the *principle of compensation*. The modern economists found that the fulfillment of Pareto optimality condition is only a purely theoretical proposition, rather hypothetical, under the condition that prevail in the economy. In general, resources are allocated inoptimally; there is no perfect competition; and cardinal measurement of utility is not possible. Therefore, it is always possible to adopt policy measures to reallocate the resources so that welfare can be maximized. Besides, in the opinion of the modern economists, it is difficult to think of a policy measure which benefits some people without harming any body. In general, a policy measure benefits some and harms some others. As long as those who benefit from the change and are willing and able to compensate those who lose, change is desirable as it increases the social welfare. This gave emergence to the *compensation principle* conceived by Kaldor and Hicks. However, the theories and welfare maximization criteria based on the compensation principle were also found to be deficient in many respects. Another economist, Bergson, came out with the idea of formulating social welfare function and its maximization. But his approach was found to have its own deficiencies and drawbacks. Later, Bator introduced the concept of *grand utility possibility frontier* for the maximization of social welfare. This concept was found to have its own problems. Finally, a new theory, called the *theory of second best* was formulated. The essence of this theory is that if best is not available, go for the second best. However, this theory was also found to be unworkable. In conclusion, the welfare economics, like other aspects of economic theories, remains an unfinished part of economic science.

REVIEW QUESTIONS AND PROBLEMS

1. What lies in foundation of the New Welfare Economics? Do theories classified under the new welfare economics resolve the problems confronted under Pareto optimality conditions?
2. What is the basis of compensation principle? How do you think introduction of compensation principle makes a significant improvement over Pareto optimality conditions?
3. What is Kaldor–Hicks compensation criterion? Illustrate graphically the derivation and application of Kaldor–Hicks compensation criterion. What are its shortcomings?
4. How is Bergson–Samuelson social welfare function derived? What purpose does it serve in maximization of social welfare?
5. What is meant by *Bliss Point*? Illustrate graphically how bliss point of allocation of consumer goods and production factors can be arrived at.
6. How is Grand Utility Possibility Frontier derived? How can it be applied to find the point at which social welfare is maximized?
7. Explain the Theory of the Second Best. Does this theory serve any useful purpose in solving the problems in welfare maximization?

ENDNOTES

1. The idea of compensation was originated by E. Barone, in his article 'The Ministry of Production in the Collectivist State', published in 1908, English translation printed in F.A. Hayek (ed.), *Collectivist Economic Planning*, London, 1935.
2. Kaldor, N. (1939), 'Welfare Propositions in Economics and Interpersonal Comparisons of Utility', *Economic Journal*, 49.
3. Hicks, J.R. (1939), 'The Foundations of Welfare Economics', *Economic Journal*, 49.
4. Blaug, M., *op. cit.*, p. 622.
5. Scitovsky, 'A Reconsideration of the Theory of Tariff', *The Review of Economic Studies*, IX(2): 1942–43. See also his 'A Note on Welfare Proposition in Economics', *The Review of Economic Studies*, IX, November 1941.
6. Blaug, M. *op. cit.*, p. 625.
7. Bergson, A. (1938), 'A Reformulation of Certain Aspects of Welfare Economics', *Quarterly Journal of Economics*, 52, February.
8. Mishan, E.J. (1960), 'A Survey of Welfare Economics, 1939–1959', *The Economic Journal*, reprinted in his *Welfare Economies: Five Introductory Essays* (1964) and in *Surveys of Economic Theory, Vol. I* (London: Macmillan, 1965), p. 169.

9. Kenneth, J.A. (1951), *Social Choice and Individual Values* (Cowless Commission Monograph No. 12, New York, and John Wiley and Sons, Inc.).
10. Baumol, *op. cit.*, pp. 532–34.
11. Bator, F.M. (1957), 'The Simple Analytics of Welfare Maximization', *The American Economic Review*, 47, March.
12. Lipsey, R.G. and Lancaster, K. 'The General Theory of Second Best', *The Review of Economic Studies*, XXXIV(1): 1956–57.
13. Henderson, J.M. and Quandt, R.E. (1989), *Microeconomics Theory—A Mathematical Approach* (London: McGraw-Hill), p. 316.
14. Nath, S.K. (1969), *A Reappraisal of Welfare Economics* (London: Routledge and Kegan Paul).

Chapter 16

Market Failures and Public Goods

CHAPTER OBJECTIVES

The analysis and theories of welfare maximization are based on the assumption that market system works efficiently. In reality, however, market system does not work as efficiently as presumed in welfare economics. In general, markets are not perfectly competitive and do not work efficiently. Besides, there are *public goods* whose production does not fall under the purview of private firms. Therefore, the case of public goods needs to be included in the analysis of welfare maximization. This chapter helps you understand:

- What is meant by market failures;
- What factors lead to market failures;
- How growth of monopolies lead to market failures;
- How public goods create problems in welfare maximization;
- What is meant by *externalities* and how externalities arise in economic system;
- How externalities affect the process of welfare maximization;
- What is meant by 'public goods' in contrast to 'private goods'; and
- How production of public goods can be maximized to maximize the economic welfare.

INTRODUCTION

A necessary condition for the maximization of social welfare, i.e. achievement of Pareto optimality in exchange and production, in a free economy, is the existence of perfect competition in both product and input markets. But, as noted earlier, perfect competition as envisaged in economic theory does not exist in reality. Most markets are imperfectly characterized by monopoly, monopolistic competition and oligopolies. Therefore, markets fail to ensure optimum allocation of goods between the consumers, optimum allocation of factor inputs between various productive activities and optimum distribution of incomes. Due to imperfectness of the market system, markets fail to ensure optimal allocation of resources. This is called *market failures*. The major factors responsible for market failures are following:

1. Growth of monopoly powers;
2. Incomplete information;
3. Existence of public goods and
4. Externalities.

In this chapter, we will discuss (1) how these factors contribute to *market failure*, (2) how public authorities can optimize the production of public goods and (3) how tax and subsidy measures can be used to correct externalities.

GROWTH OF MONOPOLY POWER AND MARKET FAILURE

Monopoly powers in product markets grow over time for reasons, such as (i) patent rights, (ii) legal restrictions on the entry of new firms, (iii) production efficiency and (iv) mergers and acquisition. In input markets, especially in the labour market, monopoly powers grow due to politicization of labour force and formation of labour unions. Growth of monopoly powers distorts the competitive structure of the markets. Market distortion results in inefficient allocation of resources among the industries and of consumer goods among the consumers. How monopoly power in product markets causes market failure is discussed below.

Let us recall our example of food and clothing in the previous chapter. Suppose that both food and clothing markets are perfectly competitive. Also, recall from our earlier analysis of product pricing that in perfectly competitive food market, the price of food (P_F) equals its marginal cost (MC_F). Therefore, in competitive food market,

$$P_F = MC_F$$

and in its competitive clothing market, the price of clothing (P_C) equals its marginal cost (MC_C), i.e.,

$$P_C = MC_C$$

This means that both the markets work efficiently because product–price ratio equalled the input–price ratio; i.e.

$$P_C/P_F = MC_C/MC_F$$

Now let the clothing industry be monopolized, remaining food industry competitive. In this case, $P_C > MC_C$. Therefore, the relative product price is no more equal to relative factor price. The relative price relationship is now given as

$$P_C/P_F > MC_C/MC_F$$

The change in relative price ratio distorts the *product mix*. The distortion in product mix can be explained as follows. Since clothing industry is monopolized and profit-maximizing monopoly output is less than the competitive output, some factors are spared and are transferred to food industry. This situation is illustrated in Figure 16.1.

Let us suppose that prior to monopolization of clothing industry, the two-sector economy was in equilibrium at point *A* on the production possibility frontier *PF*. As Figure 16.1 shows the relative factor price line *PT* is tangent to production possibility frontier *PF* at point *A*. Therefore, at point *A*,

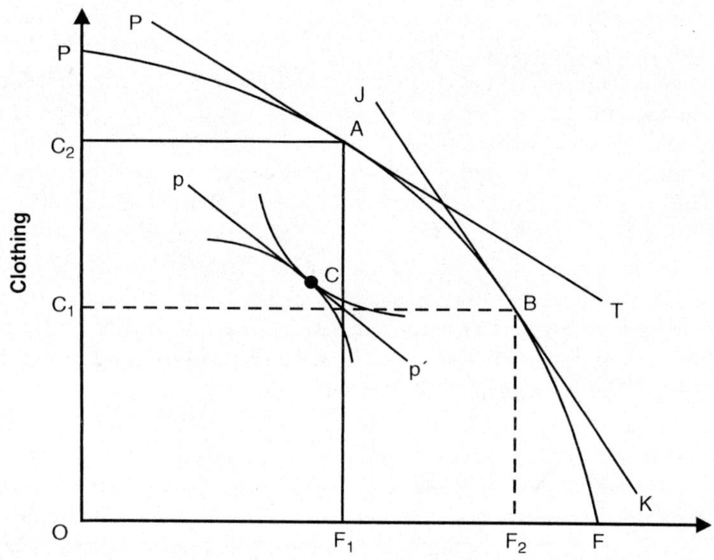

Figure 16.1 *Monopoly and Inefficient Output Mix*

$$P_C/P_F = MC_C/MC_F = MRT$$

After monopolization of clothing industry, however, $P_C/P_F > MC_C/MC_F$. Therefore, the relative factor price line *PT* shifts to *JK*, and a new equilibrium is reached at point *B*. Note that at point *B*, the slope of the factor–price line changes—line *JK* is steeper than line *PT*. What is *important* to note here is that change in relative product price has changed the *product mix*. Prior to monopolization of clothing industry, product mix included OF_1 of food and OC_2 of clothing. Note that the consumers are in equilibrium at point *C* and the product–price line *PP* is parallel to factor–price line *PT*. Therefore, *MRS* = *MRT*. This is Pareto optimality condition. After monopolization of clothing industry, the production of clothing decreases from OC_2 to OC_1 and the food production increases from OF_1 to OF_2. Now the product mix combines OF_2 of food and OC_1 of clothing. This means a larger production of food and a smaller production of clothing compared to their competitive levels of output. As a result P_F decreases and P_E increases, and hence relative product–price changes. This disturbs the equilibrium condition *MRS* = *MRT*. This is how monopoly powers cause market failures in respect to resource allocation.

IMPERFECT MARKET INFORMATION

One of the basic conditions for the market system to work efficiently is 'perfect knowledge'. For efficient allocation of resources, the consumers require complete information about market price of the products and their quality, and the producers need to have full information about market size, demand for the product, availability of inputs, input prices and their productivity, the cost conditions and so on. In the absence of complete and reliable information about the market, neither consumers nor producers can optimize the allocation of resources. For lack of complete and correct information, consumers may spend more on some goods and less on others than required to maximize their utility; producers may produce some goods in excess of demand and some goods much less than the prevailing demand; and workers may not be able to find right wages and right place for their employment.

In general, market system works with *imperfect, incomplete* and *inaccurate information*. The major sources of information regarding *market price* of consumer goods are retailers, friends, neighbours and relatives, and news media. All these sources produce incomplete information. Besides, almost all prices are negotiable. What consumers pay depends on their bargaining power. This causes uncertainty regarding the price. As regards the quality of the products, there is a greater degree of uncertainty. Producers are supposed to have full knowledge about the quality of the inputs, though not necessarily, where large-scale production is involved. Product designing and its attributes are determined by the designers; production is carried out by production department; quality of the product is controlled by quality control department, all with their own limitations and intentions. The quality that is projected in the market through advertisement media is not what it actually is: it is highly exaggerated. In simple words, *consumers are misinformed about the quality of the product*.

Things are much worse in countries like India because of proliferation of duplicate and imitated goods; called 'local'. It is difficult to name a product in India, which is not adulterated or is not substandard. Name any food item, it is adulterated. You name any consumer good whether in higher-price range goods as computers or low-price goods as electrical bulbs and tubes, their indistinguishable duplicates are available in India's consumer market. There is virtually no or little information about the quality. A large number of pending cases with consumer courts is evidence of uncertainty about the quality of the product. Under these conditions, market cannot work efficiently. We know that markets are working and people are getting whatever they want. But neither production nor consumption is efficient. This is *failure of the market* caused by imperfect market information.

EXISTENCE OF PUBLIC GOODS

Market system does work, though inefficiently, in providing *pure private goods*. But, it fails altogether in making an efficient provision for *pure public goods*. Here, we explain briefly why market system fails to provide provision for pure public goods and why government is required to make provision for goods of this category. Let us first look at the concept and characteristics of *pure public goods*. The basic characteristics of pure public goods have already been noted in Chapter 14. Here, we discuss them in detail.

What Are Public Goods?

Economists have defined 'public goods' in different terms, emphasizing some unique features thereof. Samuelson[1] has defined a 'pure public good' as one whose total production at equilibrium equals the quantity consumed by each consumer, and each consumer consumes the same amount. That is, a good is a public good if its total output $Q_T = C_A = C_B = C_C = \ldots = C_N$ (where Q_T is total production of a pure public good and C_A, C_B, C_C and C_N are the quantity of the pure public goods consumed by consumers *A*, *B*, *C* till *N*th consumer. Samuelson's definition emphasizes that consumption of a pure public good by each consumer equals its total output.

According to another economist, 'A pure public good is defined as one whose benefits are consumed by all members of a community as soon as it is produced for, or by, any one member.'[2] More appropriately, a pure public good can be defined as one which is *consumed jointly* by all the members of a society even if it is produced by an individual, and no one can be *excluded* from its consumption even if one does not pay for the good. Production of a *pure public good* generates external benefits and costs which go to all the members of a society whether intended or not. National defence, law and order system, flood control, control of epidemics and pollution-free atmosphere are some of the classic examples of *pure public goods.*

Characteristics of Pure Public Goods

It is easier to identify a pure public good by its characteristics rather than to define it in specific terms. As mentioned earlier (Chapter 14), there are three basic characteristics of public goods, viz. (i) collective consumption, (ii) non-rival consumption and (iii) non-exclusion. These three characteristics stem from the other features of pure public goods, i.e. its indivisibility forcing their *joint consumption.* Let us discuss these characteristics of pure public goods in comparison with *pure private goods.*

Collective or Joint Consumption A pure private good is consumed individually. For example, a shirt cannot be put on by two or more persons simultaneously. In contrast, a pure public good (air) is consumed jointly by all the members of a society because of its *indivisibility.* In simple words, a pure public good cannot be divided into parts or apportioned in accordance with the consumer's need. For example, national defence and pollution-free air cannot be divided into parts and made available to the people in accordance with their need. Because of their indivisibility, pure public goods have to be consumed *jointly* and *simultaneously* by all members of a society. An important property of pure public goods is that the demand for a public good cannot be determined on the basis of choices and preference function of an individual. Demand for a public good is determined by collective choice of all the consumers.

Non-Rival Consumption There is rivalry in the consumption of private goods in the sense that, given the supply of a product, if one consumer consumes more of a commodity, it reduced the share of others. For example, if you occupy larger number of houses, the number of houses available (given the supply) to other residents of the city is reduced, and if you consume larger quantity of petrol, my share is reduced. In contrast, consumption of a pure public good is *non-rival. This is a unique feature of pure public goods. Non-rivalry in consumption means that consumption by one does not prevent consumption by others and a larger consumption by one does not reduce the share of others and increase in the number of consumers does not reduce the amount available to other consumers.* For example, if some persons of the society benefit more from a pollution-free atmosphere, it does not reduce the share of others. This is called *non-rivalry in consumption of pure public goods.* It is equally *important* to note that *marginal cost of distribution of a pure public good to additional consumers is zero*, though marginal cost of production may be positive. For example, if population of a city increases, the cost of pollution control may increase but not the marginal cost of distribution.

Non-Excludability In case of pure private goods, a person who does not pay for the commodity can be excluded from the use of that commodity. For example, if you do not pay taxi fare, you may be excluded from using the taxi service and if you do not pay for a laptop, you may be excluded from its use. In contrast, in case of a pure public good it is not technically feasible to exclude a consumer from its consumption, if he or she is unwilling to pay for it. For example, it is technically not feasible to exclude an individual from the benefits of expenditure on national defence and control of air pollution if he or she does not or cannot pay for defence services. This characteristic along with others, assumes a special significance with regard to the provision of pure public goods through market system. Because of non-excludability of consumers, the *exclusion principle*[3] *of market system* does not apply to pure public goods. Therefore, market system fails to provide for pure public goods.

Public Goods and Market Failures

The market failure in respect of public goods has already been noted in Chapter 14. Let us now look in some detail how pure public goods cause market failure.

Market Failure Due to Non-Rival Consumption Due to non-rivalry in consumption, consu-mers of a pure public good have no reason for revealing their preference or willingness to pay for the good. No body is willing to pay for a commodity which can be obtained free of cost. Under these conditions, the market system does not produce necessary signals for the profit-maximizing producers to determine the quantity to be produced and the price to be charged. For example, all the residents of the city of Delhi, nick-named as 'gas chamber', feel the urgency of checking air pollution, but no body would be willing to pay the cost on his or her own because once air pollution is controlled it is freely available to all the residents.

Besides, there is a practical problem in determining the efficient production of a public good. Efficient production requires that $MC = MR$. If a pure public good has to be provided efficiently by the market system, this condition has to be fulfilled. But marginal cost of admitting an additional consumer to a public good is zero. Therefore, excluding a consumer by some mechanism or charging him or her a price would be neither socially desirable nor ethical, nor even efficient. However, where producing an additional unit of a pure public good does involve additional cost (MC), the cost of production has to be recovered. For example, when some new families settle in the catchment area of a TV tower, no additional cost will be required, i.e. $MC = 0$. Therefore, no price is chargeable. But, if catchment area has itself to be extended, it will involve additional cost, i.e. $MC > 0$. Now the question arises as whom to charge and what price to charge. Since exclusion is not desirable, cost cannot be recovered. That is, where $MR = 0$ or $MC = 0$ or $MR = 0 = MC$, market system cannot work.

Market Failure Due to Non-Excludability Market system works on the 'principle of exclusion', i.e. those who do not pay for a commodity are excluded from its consumption. For example, if you do not pay your telephone bill, your telephone line is disconnected; if you do not pay your electricity bill, your electricity supply line is disconnected; if you do not pay your house rent, you will be ejected from the house; and so on. This principle allows the producers to produce only for those who are willing to pay for a good and to charge a price which covers their cost and profits. Wherever this rule breaks down, the market system breaks down. In simple words, market system fails to work where exclusion principle cannot be applied. In case of most pure public goods, application of exclusion principle is simply not feasible and where it is, the cost of exclusion may be prohibitive. For example, given the present state of technology, no citizen can be excluded from the benefit of such pure public goods as national defence, pollution control, control of epidemics, law and order system or internal security system, etc. even if one does not pay for them. In case of some public goods, e.g. TV and radio broadcasting services, one may think of devising a jamming device to prevent non-paying users from the use of these services, but the cost of exclusion may prove prohibitive.

Problem of Free Riders Another factor which causes market failure in case of public goods is the problem of 'liars' and 'free rider'. 'Liars' are those who, given the opportunity, do not reveal their preferences honestly or correctly for a public good. 'Free riders' are those who take the benefit of a good or service but do not pay for it even though they are supposed or required to pay, voluntarily or otherwise, e.g. travellers without ticket and beneficiaries of pollution control. To explain the problem further, let us suppose that people living on the bank of Yamuna River are asked (i) to reveal their preference for an embankment along the river to protect them from floods and (ii) whether they are willing to pay for it voluntarily. What would happen, generally, people would reveal a high preference for the embankment. But on the question of payment, many would understate their preference. They are the 'liars'. Let us suppose that the embankment is constructed expecting cost to be recovered through the voluntary payment. Since payment is voluntary, many would not make the payment but cannot be excluded from the benefit of the embankment. They are 'free riders'.

Now let us look at how liars and free riders cause market failure. When understated preferences and voluntary payment offers are added up, this would give an underestimate of the aggregate demand for protection from flood. If actual cost of the embankment is much higher than the sum of the revealed preference, then there are two possibilities: (i) embankment is not constructed at all and (ii) an inefficient protection against flood is provided. In either case, market system fails to work efficiently.

EXTERNALITIES AND MARKET FAILURE

Another reason for market failure is the existence of *externalities* in both production and consumption. *Externalities* refer to the costs people have to pay and the benefits they enjoy due to production and consumption by others. For example, air pollution caused by industrial units located inside the city of Delhi and about 5 million cars running on Delhi roads cause health problems like breathing problem, asthma, bronchitis and lung infection; industrial units polluting Yamuna River are all the *cases* of *negative externalities*. This is called *external cost* to the society. There are *positive externalities* also. For example, private cost of immunization against contagious diseases and car owners getting their cars regularly checked for pollution, benefit the people who do not pay it. Such benefits are called *external benefits*. External costs and benefits are together called *externalities* or *spillovers*. Market system fails to work efficiently where externalities exist because private entrepreneurs take into account only their private explicit cost, and there is no way to compensate the losers and to charge the gainers. Externalities lead in non-optimal allocation of resources from social welfare point of view: they create divergence between social and private costs and between private and social benefits. The market system does not provide a mechanism to account for such social costs and benefits. Therefore, market fails to work efficiently.

PUBLIC PROVISION OF PUBLIC GOODS

We have discussed in the previous section that how existence of public goods causes market failure and why private firms abstain from producing and supplying pure public goods. But public goods have to be provided for the benefit of the society as whole. In this section, we discuss how government can make an *efficient provision of public goods*.

Suppose that public authorities plan to construct a road in a suburb area of the city. Road is a public good in the sense that their benefits are equally distributed and no resident can be excluded. All the persons living in the area would benefit, but only two persons, say, truck owners, *A* and *B*, are willing to reveal their benefits and preferences for it. The benefits which they derive from the road are shown by their demand curves, *AA′* and *BB′*, respectively, in Figure 16.2. Note that these curves are not, in fact, their demand curves in usual sense of the terms: these curves reflect only the marginal benefit which individuals are likely to derive from the use of the road.

The problem that public authorities confront is 'how to determine *the optimum provision for the road* so that social benefit is maximized at a given cost. In other words, the question before the government is *how to determine the most efficient level of output*—the length of the road. In case of private goods,

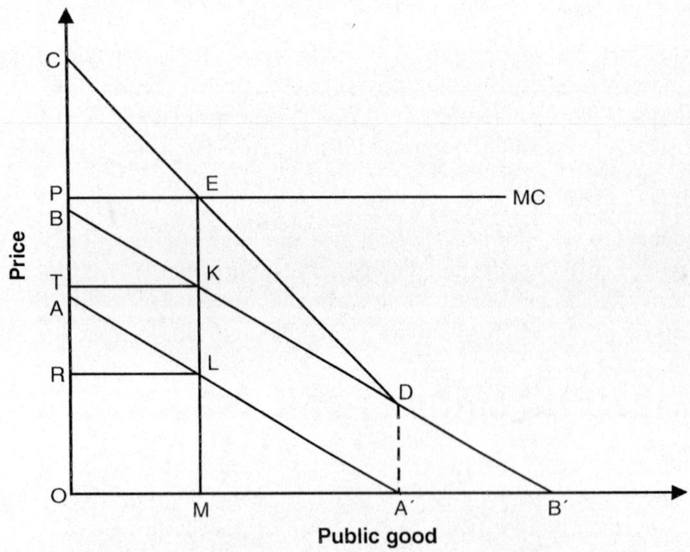

Figure 16.2 *Efficient Provision of a Public Good*

efficient level of output is determined where marginal cost equals marginal benefits. The same principle applies to public goods also but analysis is different, especially with respect to marginal social benefit.

As regards the *marginal cost* (*MC*), since total cost remains constant, is zero for additional consumers. For example, total cost of road construction does not increase with increase in population in the area. Therefore, marginal cost for additional consumer is zero. The fixed marginal cost is shown by the horizontal line marked *MC* in Figure 16.2.

However, there is a difference in the method of working out the *marginal benefits* and to draw *marginal benefit curve.* The need for a different analysis arises because of non-rival nature of the public good. Because of non-rivalry in consumption, social benefit increases when the number of user increases, even if supply of the public good is given. Therefore, total social benefit is obtained by *vertical summation* of benefits revealed by the users, represented by their demand curves. The *vertical summation* of the individual demand curves *AA′* and *BB′* gives the *marginal social benefit curve* or the *aggregate demand curve*, as shown by the curve *CDB′*.

As shown in Figure 16.2. *MC* line and marginal social benefit curve (*CDB′*) intersect at point *E* determining the efficient level of output of the public good at *OM*. At this level of output, *A's* benefit equals *LM* and *B's* benefit equals *KM*. The *marginal social benefit equals LM* + *KM* = *EM*. Note that in vertical summation *LK* = *EK*. At equilibrium point *E*, the output of the public good equals *OM* at which marginal social benefit *EM equals* marginal cost *EM* = *OP*. Therefore, *OM* is the most *efficient level of the public good provision.* However, whether this analysis can be applied in practice is a doubtful case because of *free rider problem*.

EXTERNALITIES AND THEIR CORRECTION

In this section, we discuss how public policy measures—tax and subsidy—can be used to correct externalities and to bring about efficiency in private production. Let us first consider the case of *external costs* and how they can be treated to make production efficient.

Treatment of External Costs

Let us suppose that constant-cost firms of an industry located inside or on the outskirts of the city cause environment pollution, causing health problems for the people. This is a *negative externality*. Suppose also that firms' demand and supply curves are given by *DD′* and *PS*, respectively, as shown in Figure 16.3. A profit-maximizing firm is in equilibrium at point *E*, the point where demand and supply curves intersect. Firm's equilibrium output is OQ_2 and price *OP*. Pollution is a function of production—increase in production causes increasing pollution. The pollution caused by the successive units of industrial production is called *marginal external cost* (*MEC*) to the society. The *MEC* increases with increase in production as shown by the *MEC* curve in Figure 16.3. Note that at equilibrium output OQ_2, each firm causes an external cost to the extent of AQ_2. This cost is not accounted for by the producers and losers are not compensated.

However, when *MEC* is added to private cost indicated by line *PS*, it gives the *social marginal cost* (*MSC*) curve as shown by the curve labelled MS_S. The MS_S curve intersects with the demand curve a point *B*. This point may be called the point of *social equilibrium*. Efficiency requires that production is limited to OQ_1 determined by the social equilibrium point *B* and losers are duly compensated. The market system, however, does not work on this principle. Therefore, firms continue to produce OQ_2 without compensating the losers. Entire profit goes to the producers. One possible way is to impose an excise tax on the producers to the extent of *PT*. With imposition of tax, supply curves shifts to *TS'* which intersects the demand curve at point *B*. Thus, after tax is imposed, equilibrium shifts from point *E* to point *B* and production falls to OQ_1 which is socially efficient level of output. Price equals $OT = BQ_1$ which includes private cost (*OP*) *plus* social cost (*PT*). Total tax collection equals $PT \times OQ_1$. Since $PT = OH$, total tax collection equals $OH \times OQ_1 = OHFQ_1$. This tax revenue may be used to compensate the residents for their external cost. This may be done by providing medical facilities to the people free of cost. However, it is *important* to note here that this measure does not eliminate pollution: it only offers a method of compensating the losers.

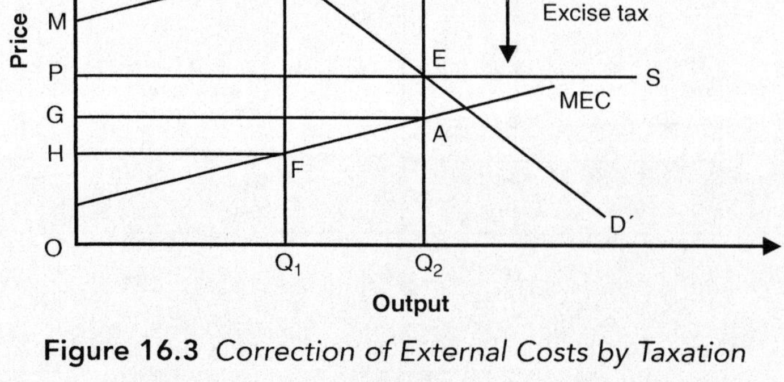

Figure 16.3 *Correction of External Costs by Taxation*

Treatment of External Benefits

Let us now examine how external benefits may be treated to make the output socially efficient. The effects of external benefit and its treatment can be analysed in the manner external cost is treated. The analysis is illustrated in Figure 16.4. Let us suppose that consumption (or production) of certain goods that generate external benefit to the people. The normal demand curve for the commodity generating external benefits is given by the curve *DD′*. Assuming again the constant-cost industry, supply curve is given by the curve *PS*. Marginal benefits accruing to the people is shown by the curve labelled *MEB*. The *MEB* curve is derived by vertically summing up the individual benefits.

Ignoring external benefit, firms would be in equilibrium at point *C* producing output OQ_1 at price *OP*. With the existence of external benefits, the competitive output OQ_1 is not efficient or socially optimum output. For, at output OQ_1, social benefit of *OM* (per unit of output) is not accounted for in the competitive pricing system. Therefore, social marginal cost is not equal to the marginal social benefit: marginal social benefit (marginal utility) is greater than marginal social cost. This violates the rule of efficient output. When *MEB* is vertically summed up with *DD′* curve, demand curve or the margin social benefit curve, shifts to D_SD'. The new demand curve intersects the supply curve *PS* at point *E* determining a socially efficient output at OQ_2. In a competitive system, however, since firms have no way to charge the consumers for their external benefits, they will continue to produce OQ_1. If firms produce OQ_2, given the demand curve *DD′*, they can sell it only at price $OS = BQ_2$ which is much lower than their marginal cost $OP = EQ_2$. They will incur a loss of $EB = PS$ per unit of output. The firms will, therefore, produce only OQ_1.

One of the possible ways to increase the production to its efficient level OQ_2 is that public authorities intervene with excise subsidy to the producers to the extent of $EB = PS$ per unit of output. A big disadvantage of subsidy measure is the financial burden on the government. To balance its budget the

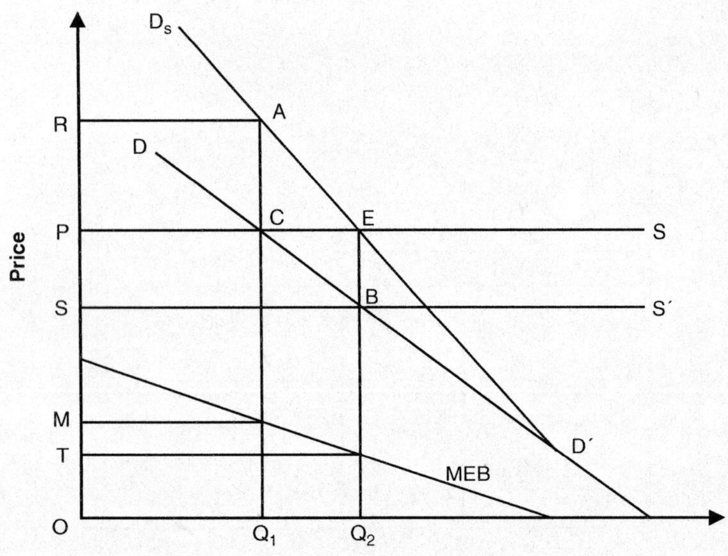

Figure 16.4 *Correcting External Benefits by Subsidies*

government may use sales tax on the consumers to the extent of their external benefit which equals *EB* at output OQ_2. These are all, however, only theoretical possibilities.

With this discussion, we reach the end of our discussion on the welfare economies and use of public polices to make production as efficient as required for maximization of social welfare.

REVIEW QUESTIONS AND EXERCISES

1. What are the conditions for market to work efficiently? What is meant by market failure? What are the factors that cause market failure?
2. When market is perfectly competitive, why do private firms not produce public parks and pollution-free environment?
3. How does growth of monopolies affect the efficient working of the market system? Illustrate how monopolies cause inefficient combination of output?
4. What is the role of perfect information in efficient working of product and input markets? How does imperfect, inadequate and incomplete information cause market failures?
5. Define a public good. What are the characteristics of a public good? Explain with examples how these characteristics affect efficient working of the market system?
6. What is meant by non-rivalry and non-excludability in consumption? Suppose there are two goods: (i) construction of a national highway and (ii) cleaning of Yamuna River. Which of these goods are both non-rival and non-excludable and why?
7. What is meant by 'public good'? How is a public good different from private goods? Which of the following are public goods?
   (a) Rocket launchers,
   (b) Cricket match,
   (c) Public school,
   (d) Police services.
8. What is the efficiency condition for the production of a commodity? Illustrate and explain efficient production of a public good.
9. Suppose Jolly's marginal benefit from night patrolling by police is worth Rs 50. Dolly's marginal benefit is worth Rs 60 and zero benefit for Loly. What is the market demand for night-police patrolling worth of?
10. What is meant by externalities? Explain the external costs and external benefits with appropriate examples. How does the existence of externalities affect efficient allocation of resources?

ENDNOTES

1. In his classic papers 'The Pure Theory of Public Expenditure', *Review of Economics and Statistics*, November 1954 and 'Diagrammatic Exposition of the Theory of Public Expenditure', *Review of Economics and Statistics*, November 1955.
2. Hyman, D.N. (1983), *Public Finance: A Contemporary Application of Theory to Policy* (Chicago: Dryden Press), p. 127.
3. The 'exclusion principle of market' means that those who are not willing to pay or do not pay for a good can be excluded from the benefit of is consumption.

FURTHER READINGS

Baumol, W.J. and Blinder, A.S. (1988), *Economics: Principles and Policy* (Chicago, IL: Harcourt Brace Jovanovich Publishers), 4th Edn. Chapter 29.

Browning, E.K. and Browning, J.M. (1994), *Microeconomic Theory and Applications* (New Delhi: Kalyani Publishers, Reprint), 2nd Edn., Chapters 18 and 19.

Case, K.E. and Fair, R.C. (2002), *Principles of Economics* (New Delhi: Pearson Education Asia), 6th Edn., Chapter 14.

Lipsey, R.G. and Chrystal, K.A. (1999), *Principles of Economics* (London: Oxford University Press), 9th Edn., Chapter 18.

Pindyck, R.S. and Rubinfeld, D.L. (2001), *Microeconomics*, (London: Prentice Hall International), 5th Edn., Chapter 18.

University Question Papers

B.Com. (Hons) II Year
Paper X – 2008
MICROECONOMIC THEORY AND APPLICATIONS – II
(New Course: Admission of 2004 and onwards)

Time : 3 hours *Maximum marks : 75*

Note—*The maximum marks printed on the question paper are applicable for the candidates registered with the School of Open Learning for B.A. (Hons)/B.Com. (Hons). These marks will, however, be scaled down proportionately in respect of the students of regular colleges, at the time of posting of awards for compilation of result.*

*Attempt **all** questions. The marks carried by each part of every question are indicated against the same.*

Q. 1. (*a*) What do you mean by monopoly power? What are the social costs of such a power?

Or

Explain third degree price discrimination. How is a monopolist able to maximise his profit by practising this form of price discrimination? 8

(*b*) What is a multiplant firm? How is it able to maximise its profit?

Or

Derive the Rule of Thumb for pricing under monopoly. Using this concept explain how a zero cost firm will determine its profit maximising output and price. Show it diagrammatically also. 7

Q. 2. (*a*) Explain the short-run equilibrium under monopolistic competition with the help of the perceived and proportionate demand curves.

Or

How do the reaction curves of the duopolists help in determining the Cournot equilibrium? 8

(*b*) How does excess capacity arise in case of monopolistic competition? Is it different from ideal capacity?

Or

What is price leadership? Explain the model of a dominant price leader. 7

Q. 3. (*a*) What is economic rent? Explain the relation between economic rent and reservation price with the help of relevant diagrams.

Or

Explain the relation between the marginal expense of an input and its supply. 7

(*b*) Differentiate between monopolistic and monopsonistic exploitation of labour. Can trade unions help in removing these forms of exploitation?

Or

How can the demand curve of labour be derived when labour is not the only variable factor of production in case of perfect competition in both product and input markets? 8

Q. 4. (*a*) How can we distinguish between risk lovers and risk avertors? With the help of total utility of money curve explain that marginal utility of money will diminish for risk avertors and will increase for risk lovers.

Or

What do you mean by loanable funds? How do their demand and supply help in determining interest rates? 8

(*b*) "Since implicit collusion tends to be fragile, oligopolistic firms often have a strong desire for price stability."
Explain this statement with reference to the kinked demand curve model. 7

Or

What are cartels? Explain why the OPEC cartel was successful in raising oil prices.

Q. 5. (*a*) With the help of the Edgeworth Production Box diagram, explain the general equilibrium of production. What does the production contract curve indicate?

Or

Show how a perfectly competitive market automatically leads to Pareto optimality in exchange, production and product mix? 8

(*b*) What is market signalling? How can it be used to solve the problem of adverse selection resulting from asymmetric information? 7

Or

What is a Public Good? Explain why private markets will fail to provide public goods efficiently?

B.Com. (Hons) II Year

Paper X – 2009

MICROECONOMIC THEORY AND APPLICATIONS – II

(New Course: Admissions of 2004 and onwards)

Time: 3 hours *Maximum marks: 75*

Note—*The maximum marks printed on the Question Paper are applicable for the candidates registered with the School of Open Learning for B.Com. (Hons). These marks will, however, be scaled down proportionately in respect of the students of regular colleges, at the time of posting of awards for compilation of result.*

*Attempt **all** questions. The marks carried by each part of every question are indicated against the same.*

Q. 1. (*a*) Why is there no market supply curve under conditions of monopoly? 7½

Or

What do you mean by peak load pricing? Show how peak load pricing can be a better policy than uniform pricing in case of a public utility company producing electricity? 7½

(*b*) How do you measure the degree of monopoly power? What is the rule of thumb for pricing? Explain Learner's measure of monopoly power.

Or

Explain and distinguish between 1st degree and and 2nd degree price discrimination. What additional profit will the firm get while practising perfect 1st degree price discrimination. 7½

Q. 2. (*a*) Duopolists face the following market demand curve:
$P = 30 - Q$. Q is total production of both firms
$Q = Q_1 + Q_2$. Both firms have zero marginal cost
$MC_1 = MC_2 = 0$.
Calculate Cournot equilibrium with the help of reaction curves and compare it with competitive equilibrium and also compare it if the firms collude. 7½

Or

Why has the OPEC oil cartel succeeded in raising price substantially while the CIPEC copper cartel has not? 7½

(*b*) What is Prisoner's Dilemma? Why do oligopolistic firms find themselves in a Prisoner's Dilemma? 7½

Or

In the Stackelberg model, the firm that sets output first has an advantage. Explain, why? 7½

Q. 3. (*a*) Explain the concept of Transfer Earnings. How is it related to Economic Rent? Explain with suitable diagrams and examples. Also show when the factor earns:

(*i*) Rent

(*ii*) No rent;

(*iii*) Part of income as rent and part as transfer earnings.

Or

"Trade unions can eliminate the portion of total monopsonistic exploitation that is uniquely attributable to monopsony in the labour market; however the portion attributable to monopoly can in no way be eliminated by trade union activity." Explain the statement with the help of a diagram. 7½

(*b*) Why is the market demand curve for a variable productive service not the simple horizontal summation of individual demand curve for a variable productive service? 7½

Or

Give the indifference curve analysis of labour supply curve. Why is it backward bending? 7½

Q. 4. (*a*) Why does an investor need to discount when he gets cash flows in future? Suppose an investment A entitles an investor perpetual income stream of Rs. 1,000 per annum, it costs him Rs. 10,000 now. Another investment B costs him Rs. 3,500 now and entitles him to an income stream of Rs. 1,100 after one year, Rs. 2,420 after two years and Rs. 1,331 after three years. Which of these two would you advise him to go for? Assume that the rate of interest is 10% per annum for the period. 7½

Or

How do investors calculate the present value of a bond? What do you mean by effective yield on bond? If the interest rate is 5% per annum, what is the present value of a perpetuity that pays Rs. 1,000 per year for ever? 7½

(*b*) What does a risk-return indifference curve show? How are risks and return balanced in choosing one's portfolio? 7½

Or

What is the meaning of diminishing, constant and increasing marginal utility of money? Show with the help of total utility of money curve and explain what are

(*i*) risk loving person,

(*ii*) risk neutral person,

(*iii*) risk averse person. 7½

Q. 5. (*a*) "For an economy composed of many consumers and many commodities, the general equilibrium of exchange occurs where the marginal rate of substitution between every pair of commodities is the same for all consumers consuming both the commodities." Explain this statement with the help of Edgeworth Box Diagram.

Or

If there is only one individual in society, how is economic efficiency in production and exchange (and maximum social welfare) achieved? Explain with the help of diagram. 7½ (*b*) Adverse selection is the direct result of asymmetric information—True or False. Explain. How can the problem of adverse selection be overcome? 7½

Or

Why are externalities likely to lead to an inefficient allocation of resources just as public goods do? Can the effect of externality (external cost) be corrected with the help of taxation? 7½

B.Com. (Hons) II Year

Paper X – 2010

MICROECONOMIC THEORY AND APPLICATIONS – II

(New Course: Admissions of 2004 and onwards)

Time: 3 hours *Maximum marks: 75*

Note—*The maximum marks printed on the Question Paper are applicable for the candidates registered with the School of Open Learning for B.Com. (Hons). These marks will, however, be scaled down proportionately in respect of the students of regular colleges, at the time of posting of awards for compilation of result.*

*Attempt **all** questions. The marks carried by each part of every question are indicated against the same.*

Q. 1. (*a*) How do you measure the degree of monopoly power? What is the Rule of Thumb for pricing? Explain Lerner's measure of monopoly power. 7½

Or

Why is there no supply curve under conditions of monopoly? 7½

(*b*) Explain and distinguish between first degree and second degree price discrimination. What additional profit will the firm get while practising perfect first degree price discrimination? 7½

Or

What is a multiplant firm? How is it able to maximize its profit? 7½

Q. 2. (*a*) In a monopolistically competitive market proportional demand curve and long run average cost curve are given below:

$P = 36 - 2Q$ and

$LAC = Q^2 - 18Q + 100$

What is long run equilibrium price and quantity? What is firm's profit? 7½

Or

Why has the OPEC Oil Cartel succeeded in raising prices substantially while the CIPEC Copper Cartel has not? 7½

(*b*) What assumptions underline the Cournot's duopoly model? Explain Cournot's equilibrium with the help of action-reaction curves. 7½

Or

How does excess capacity arise in case of monopolistic competition? Is it different from ideal capacity? 7½

Q. 3. (*a*) Differentiate between monopolistic and monopsonistic exploitation of labour. Can trade unions help in removing these forms of exploitation? 7½

Or

Explain the concept of Transfer Earnings. How is it related to Economic Rent? Explain with suitable diagrams. 7½

(*b*) How can the demand curve of labour be derived when there are many variable factors of production in case of perfect competition in both product and input markets? 7½

Or

For a monopsonist, what is the relationship between the supply curve of labour and marginal wage curve? Show how equilibrium wage rate and employment are determined? 7½

Q. 4. (*a*) How can we distinguish between risk lovers and risk averters? With the help of total utility of money curve, explain that marginal utility of money will diminish for risk averters and will increase for risk lovers. 7½

Or

Use the Prisoner's dilemma model to show why firms attempt to form cartels and yet cheat. 7½

(*b*) If individuals behaved as if they maximize expected utility, explain whether in the following market situation a risk-averter individual will make an investment:

Expected utility from the investment

State of nature	Probability	Monetary outcome	Associated utility
Success	0.40	200	3
Failure	0.60	–100	–4

What is the expected monetary return? 7½

Or

What does a risk-return indifference curve show? How can such indifference curve be used to determine the choice of the best investment portfolio for an individual? 7½

Q. 5. (*a*) 'Adverse selection is the direct result of asymmetric information'. Comment. Explain how this problem of adverse selection can be overcome. 7½

Or

What do you mean by general equilibrium of 'production and exchange'? Show that goods will not be distributed efficiently if MRS ≠ MRT. 7½

(*b*) What is a public good? Explain why private markets will fail to provide public goods efficiently. 7½

Or

Show how Pareto optimality in exchange, production and product mix can be attained in case of a perfectly competitive market. 7½

B.Com. (Hons) II Year

Paper X – 2011

MICROECONOMIC THEORY AND APPLICATIONS – II

(New Course: Admissions of 2004 and onwards)

Time: 3 hours *Maximum marks: 75*

Note—*The maximum marks printed on the Question Paper are applicable for the candidates registered with the School of Open Learning for B.Com. (Hons). These marks will, however, be scaled down proportionately in respect of the students of regular colleges, at the time of posting of awards for compilation of result.*

*Attempt **all** questions. The marks carried by each part of every question are indicated against the same.*

Q. 1. (*a*) How does presence of monopoly lead to deadweight loss as compared to competitive conditions? 7½

Or

Explain the absence of supply curve under monopoly with the help of relevant diagrams. 7½

(*b*) What is peak load pricing? How can a public utility company producing electricity be better off by following a policy of peak load pricing than one of uniform pricing. 7½

Or

What do you mean by third degree discrimination? When is it profitable for a monopolist to discriminate? How will he allocate his output in two markets and charge different price? 7½

Q. 2. (*a*) Explain how excess capacity arises in monopolistic competition? How is Chamberlin's concept of excess capacity different from traditional concept? Is this necessarily undesirable? 7½

Or

Why do price rigidities arise in an oligopolistic market? Explain price rigidity with the help of 'kinked-demand curve' model. 7½

(*b*) In Baumol's sales maximization model, compare the effect of (*i*) an imposition of a lump sum tax and (*ii*) an imposition of a specific tax (per unit of output) on equilibrium position of sales maximiser verses profit maximiser. 7½

Or

Why has OPEC oil cartel succeeded in raising price substantially while the CIPEC copper cartel has not? What conditions are necessary for success of a cartel? 7½

Q. 3. (*a*) Derive firm's demand curve of a factor when several variable factors are used under conditions of perfect competition in both factor and product markets. 7½

Or

Prove that labour supply curve of an individual is backward bending with the help of indifference curve. Can we still have positively sloping market supply curve? 7½

(*b*) Differentiate between monopolistic and monopsonistic exploitation of labour. How can government intervention eliminate monopsonistic exploitation? 7½

Or

Explain economic rent. Explain with suitable diagrams and examples what happens when: 7½
(*i*) Supply is perfectly elastic;
(*ii*) Supply is perfectly inelastic;
(*iii*) Supply is elastic.

Q. 4. (*a*) With the help of Edgeworth consumption box diagram, explain efficiency in exchange of two goods between two consumers. What does contract curve of exchange indicate? 7½

Or

Derive Production possibility curve through production contract curve. What is its shape? 7½

(*b*) Explain the role of externalities in the failure of competitive market. Can the effects of externality be corrected with the help of taxation and subsidies? (Use suitable diagrams) 7½

Or

Show how conditions of perfect competition automatically lead to Pareto optimality in product mix. Use diagrams and state the underlying assumptions. 7½

Q. 5. (*a*) Write short notes on:
(*i*) Difference between the nominal rate of interest and the real rate of interest;
(*ii*) Internal rate of return;
(*iii*) Consumer decision on buying or leasing a car. 7½

Or

An individual is considering two investment projects. Project A will return a loss of \$ 5 if conditions are poor, a profit of \$ 35 if conditions are good and a profit of \$ 95 if conditions are excellent. Project B will return a loss of \$ 15 if conditions are poor, a profit of \$ 45 if conditions are good, and a profit of \$ 135 if conditions are excellent. The probability distribution of conditions are as follows:

Conditions:	Poor	Good	Excellent
Probability:	40%	50%	10%

(*i*) Calculate the expected value of each project and identify the preferred project according to this criterion.
(*ii*) Calculate the standard deviation of the expected value of each project and identify the project with the highest risk.
(*iii*) Which of the two projects should a risk-averse individual prefer? 7½

(*b*) In Duopolists' market, two firms can produce at a constant average and marginal cost of AC = MC = 5. They face a market demand curve given by Q = 53 – P
(*i*) In Cournot's model if they are profit maximizing, find two reaction functions and calculate Cournot's equilibrium (price and output). What are the profits of each firm?
(*ii*) If we follow Stackelberg's model and firm one is price leader then find the equilibrium price and output under this model. What will be their profits? 7½

Or

Explain how risk can be measured by standard deviation of expected income. Draw return-risk indifference curves for two-risk averse individuals A and B, where A is extremely risk averse and B is moderately risk averse. (Indicate standard deviation of expected income on X-axis and expected income on Y-axis). How does the diversification of an investor's portfolio reduce risk? 7½

Index